Lecture Notes in Computer Science 11185

Commenced Publication in 1973
Founding and Former Series Editors:
Gerhard Goos, Juris Hartmanis, and Jan van Leeuwen

Editorial Board

More information about this series at http://www.springer.com/series/7409

Steffen Staab · Olessia Koltsova
Dmitry I. Ignatov (Eds.)

Social Informatics

10th International Conference, SocInfo 2018
St. Petersburg, Russia, September 25–28, 2018
Proceedings, Part I

 Springer

Editors
Steffen Staab (ID)
University of Koblenz
Koblenz
Germany

Olessia Koltsova (ID)
National Research University Higher School
   of Economics
St. Petersburg
Russia

Dmitry I. Ignatov (ID)
National Research University Higher School
   of Economics
Moscow
Russia

ISSN 0302-9743   ISSN 1611-3349 (electronic)
Lecture Notes in Computer Science
ISBN 978-3-030-01128-4   ISBN 978-3-030-01129-1 (eBook)
https://doi.org/10.1007/978-3-030-01129-1

Library of Congress Control Number: 2018955276

LNCS Sublibrary: SL3 – Information Systems and Applications, incl. Internet/Web, and HCI

This Springer imprint is published by the registered company Springer Nature Switzerland AG
The registered company address is: Gewerbestrasse 11, 6330 Cham, Switzerland

Preface

This volume contains the proceedings of the 10th Conference on Social Informatics (SocInfo 2018), held in Saint Petersburg, Russia during September 25–28, 2018. Continuing the tradition of this conference series, SocInfo 2018 brought together researchers from the computational and the social sciences with the intent of closing the gap that has traditionally separated the two communities. The goal of the conference was in fact to provide a forum for academics from many disciplines across social and computational sciences to define common research objectives and explore new methodological advances in their fields. The organizers welcomed a broad range of contributions, ranging from those that apply the methods of the social sciences in the study of socio-technical systems, to those that employ computer science methods to analyze complex social processes, as well as those that make use of social concepts in the design of information systems. The most welcomed were the papers that belonged to more than one discipline.

This year SocInfo received 110 submitted papers from a total of 306 distinct authors, located in 38 different countries. We were glad to have a broad and diverse Program Committee of 138 experts with a strong interdisciplinary background from all over the world. The Program Committee reviewed all submissions and provided the authors with in-depth feedback on how to improve their work. As a novelty, this year SocInfo employed a double-blind peer review process. Papers received at least three reviews by the Program Committee.

The Program Committee selected 34 submissions for oral presentation (30.9% acceptance rate) and 36 submissions to be presented as posters (32.7% acceptance rate). In line with the goal of fostering participation from fields with different publication practices than those of computer science, authors were given the chance to present their work without having it included in the proceedings. Eight submissions opted out from the proceedings, taking the total number of contributions included in these volumes to 62.

In addition to posters and paper presentations, SocInfo 2018 hosted six great keynotes delivered by Ingmar Weber (Qatar Computing Research Institute), Jonathan J. H. Zhu (City University of Hong Kong), Harith Alani (The Open University), Bettina Berendt (KU Leuven), Alexander Boukhanovsky (ITMO University), and Olga Megorskaya (Yandex).

We would like to congratulate and thank all the authors and attendees for selecting this venue to present and discuss their research. We would like to thank everybody involved in the conference organization that helped us in making this event successful.

We owe special thanks to the Steering Committee of this conference for their input and support, particularly the chair of the Steering Committee, Adam Wierzbicki, and Luca Maria Aiello, who is another active member of the committee.

The organizers are extremely grateful to all the reviewers and the members of the Program Committee for their tireless efforts in making sure that the contributions adhered to the highest standards of scientific rigor and originality. We thank our two hardworking program co-chairs, Steffen Staab and Olessia Koltsova, who oversaw the process and put together a great program for this event. We are also grateful to our Organizing Committee chair, Sergei Koltcov and our proceedings chair, Dmitry Ignatov. This event would not have been possible without the generous support of the staff and the faculty of the Laboratory for Internet Studies at Higher School of Economics: Yadviga Sinyavskaya, Oleg Nagorny, Vera Ignatenko, and Daria Yudenkova.

We are extremely grateful to the National Research University Higher School of Economics that kindly provided us with the venue and amazing logistic support.

We are very thankful to our sponsors, particularly the Association for Computing Machinery, Springer, National Research University Higher School of Economics, The Centre for German and European Studies (St. Petersburg State University, Bielefeld University, and German Academic Exchange Service (DAAD) with funds from the German Foreign Office), and the Russian Foundation for Basic Research.

September 2018   Olessia Koltsova
                                                    Steffen Staab

Organization

Program Committee Chairs

Olessia Koltsova (Co-chair)	National Research University Higher School of Economics, Russia
Steffen Staab	University of Koblenz-Landau, Germany

Proceedings Chair

Dmitry I. Ignatov	National Research University Higher School of Economics, Russia

Workshop Chairs

Luca Maria Aiello	Bell Labs, UK
Sergei Koltsov	National Research University Higher School of Economics, Russia

Steering Committee

Chairs

Adam Wierzbicki	Polish-Japanese Academy of Information Technology, Poland
Karl Aberer	École polytechnique fédérale de Lausanne, Switzerland
Katsumi Tanaka	Kyoto University, Japan
Anwitaman Datta	Nanyang Technological University, Singapore
Ee-Peng Lim	Singapore Management University, Singapore
Noshir Contractor	Northwestern University, USA
Michael Macy	Cornell University, USA
Hsinchun Chen	University of Arizona, USA
Sue B. Moon	Korea Advanced Institute of Science and Technology, South Korea
Andreas Ernst	University of Kassel, Germany
Andreas Flach	University of Groningen, The Netherlands
Dirk Helbing	ETH Zurich, Switzerland

Program Committee

Palakorn Achananuparp	Singapore Management University, Singapore
Robert Ackland	Australian National University, Australia
Luca Maria Aiello	Nokia Bell Labs, UK

Vera Ignatenko	National Research University Higher School of Economics, Russia
Dmitry Ignatov	National Research University Higher School of Economics, Russia
Adam Jatowt	Kyoto University, Japan
Marco Alberto Javarone	University of Kent, UK
Mark Jelasity	University of Szeged, Hungary
Pablo Jensen	ENS de Lyon and CNRS, France
Hang-Hyun Jo	Asia Pacific Center for Theoretical Physics, South Korea
Andreas Kaltenbrunner	NTENT, Spain
Kazuhiro Kazama	Wakayama University, Japan
Andreas Koch	University of Salzburg, Austria
Sergei Koltsov	National Research University Higher School of Economics, Russia
Olessia Koltsova (Co-chair)	National Research University Higher School of Economics, Russia
Salla-Maaria Laaksonen	University of Helsinki, Finland
Renaud Lambiotte	University of Oxford, UK
Walter Lamendola	University of Denver, USA
David Laniado	Eurecat – Technology Centre of Catalonia, Spain
Georgios Lappas	Technological Educational Institute of Western Macedonia, Greece
Yanina Ledovaya	St. Petersburg State University, Russia
Deok-Sun Lee	Inha University, South Korea
Juyong Lee	National Heart, Lung, and Blood Institute/National Institutes of Health, USA
Sang Hoon Lee	Korea Institute for Advanced Study, South Korea
Sune Lehmann	Technical University of Denmark, Denmark
Zoran Levnajic	Faculty of Information Studies in Novo Mesto, Slovenia
Elisabeth Lex	Graz University of Technology, Austria
Yu-Ru Lin	University of Pittsburgh, USA
Matteo Magnani	Uppsala University, Sweden
Rosario Mantegna	Università di Palermo, Italy
Gianluca Manzo	CNRS (GEMASS), France
Afra Mashhadi	University of Washington, USA
Emanuele Massaro	Ecole Polytechnique Fédérale de Lausanne, Switzerland
Naoki Masuda	University of Bristol, UK
Peter McMahan	McGill University, Canada
Yelena Mejova	Qatar Computing Research Institute, Qatar
Hisashi Miyamori	Kyoto Sangyo University, Japan
Jose Moreno	Institut de Recherche en Informatique de Toulouse, France
Tsuyoshi Murata	Tokyo Institute of Technology, Japan

Lyle Ungar	University of Pennsylvania, USA
Onur Varol	Northeastern University, USA
Dani Villatoro	Openbank (Grupo Santander), Spain
Wenbo Wang	Wright State University, USA
Ingmar Weber	Qatar Computing Research Institute, Qatar
Joss Wright	University of Oxford, UK
Kevin S. Xu	University of Toledo, USA
Elena Yagunova	St. Petersburg State University, Russia
Taha Yasseri	University of Oxford, UK
Dasha Yudenkova	National Research University Higher School of Economics, Russia
Igor Zakhlebin	Northwestern University, USA
Arkaitz Zubiaga	University of Warwick, UK
Thomas Ågotnes	University of Bergen, Norway

Organizing Committee

Sergei Koltosov (Chair)	National Research University Higher School of Economics, Russia
Vera Ignatenko (Proceedings Management)	National Research University Higher School of Economics, Russia
Oleg Nagornyy (Website)	National Research University Higher School of Economics, Russia
Yadviga Sinyavskaya (EasyChair, Correspondence, and News)	National Research University Higher School of Economics, Russia
Daria Yudenkova (Finance and Documentation)	National Research University Higher School of Economics, Russia

Additional Reviewers

Alexander Beloborodov	Yuri Rykov
Timofey Bryksin	Simon Schweighofer
Arthur Thomas Edward Capozzi	Alfonso Semeraro
Jessie Chin	Panote Siriaraya
Ly Dinh	Salvatore Vilella
Sofia Dokuka	Xiaoyu Wang
Yury Kabanov	Nurudín Álvarez

Sponsors

Association for Computing Machinery
Centre for German and European Studies
National Research University Higher School of Economics
Russian Foundation for Basic Research
Springer

Contents – Part I

Contents – Part II

Full Papers

Process Workflow in Crowdsourced Digital Disaster Responses

Najeeb G. Abdulhamid(✉) , Mark Perry , and Armin Kashefi

Department of Computer Science, Brunel University London, London, UK
{Najeeb.Abdulhamid,Mark.Perry,Armin.Kashefi}@brunel.ac.uk

Abstract. This paper examines the workflow and sense-making activities of digital volunteers, showing how they acquire, assess, process and scrutinise crowdsourced information to warrant confidence that the data satisfies the standard of engagement, production and analysis. We do so by studying a digital disaster response organisation - Humanity Road - through fifteen response operations across thirteen countries using digital ethnography over a period of sixteen months. This paper reports on the findings of this study, using a range of sources such as Skype chat logs, field notes, social media postings, and official documents. Our paper introduces a framework that offers a consistent and structured workflow for the communities of practice related to social media and data aggregation communities within the domain of Digital Humanitarian Networks. Our findings suggest practical implications for both the digital humanitarian organisations and government of the disaster-prone countries.

Keywords: Computer supported cooperative work (CSCW) · Crisis informatics
Crowdsourcing · Digital volunteerism · Disasters · Humanitarian emergencies

1 Introduction

We are living in a world of emergencies and disasters in which even countries favoured by geography or advanced technologies are not entirely insulated. Historically, disasters are characterised with the episodic mass influx of goods, services and volunteers that converge to provide relief using collective behaviour and role enactment [1–3]. With the advent of mobile technologies along with the development, adoption and increasing accessibility of web 2.0 technologies, the convergence phenomenon that was hitherto observed on-site are now found online by remote digital volunteers [4]. Likewise, past studies revealed that disaster affected communities relied on official and unofficial information sourced from social media. The news sourced from social media often act as a source for supporting community resilience when the disaster strikes to enable them to sustain, survive and reunite [5]. Using this information, volunteers can harness collective intelligence using crowdsourcing to provide situational awareness information for decision making as a form of aid [6, 7]. However, their emergence has disrupted the old response playbook of standard operating procedures of emergency response organisations [8]. The rise of such communities, therefore, triggers a renewed academic interest and debates across disciplines.

© Springer Nature Switzerland AG 2018
S. Staab et al. (Eds.): SocInfo 2018, LNCS 11185, pp. 3–22, 2018.
https://doi.org/10.1007/978-3-030-01129-1_1

The focus of this paper is on the established volunteers, unlike most of the existing literature which addresses the activity of spontaneous and unaffiliated volunteers. Specifically, our paper examines the disaster response workflow and crowdsourcing activities of volunteers working under a US-based digital disaster response organisation called Humanity Road (HR). HR is chosen as a case study organisation because of its potentials in adding to our knowledge a peculiar case of how groups are organised, socialised and work together in a virtual space. Furthermore, its work practice also has the potential to highlight how people, organisational culture, and process, as well as technological tools and platforms, are entangled with one another. This paper therefore seeks to answer the following research question: *What activities are being undertaken in processing crowdsourced information?*

Thus far, the existing literature concerning the internet-enabled volunteer groups have tended to address the socio-technical challenges associated with Humanitarian emergencies on three broad themes. First, the studies that explore the verification and information processing activities of unaffiliated and spontaneous groups [9–13]. Second, works that approach this phenomenon from a more technical perspective related to the development of platforms/tools, and models and framework for extracting disaster information [14–16]. Finally, studies that seek to understand the work practice of the established groups [17]. The latter studies focusing on social media and data aggregation communities as an established group have delimited their scope to concentrate mostly on one case study or investigating one disaster type or articulate the usage of a tool/application over a short period. While insightful, these studies have not comprehensively touched on the activities involved in processing crowdsourced information. This was the motivation behind this study to take a step further and investigate this vital yet underscored aspect of information processing within the social media and data aggregation communities.

As a result, this paper contributes to the existing research by introducing a new framework derived from empirical data developed explicitly for the social media and data aggregation community within the domain of established Digital Volunteer Communities (DVCs). This framework emerged from analysis of data gathered from eight types of disaster covering 13 countries within 16 months. The proposed framework provides a structured, scalable and coherent information workflow on the use of crowdsourcing in humanitarian response operation which forms the theoretical contribution of our paper. By taking a holistic approach to studying different disaster types of various scales, across continents over a more extended period, we differentiate ourselves from prior studies regarding methodology by analysing different data sources. These data sources included field notes from participant observation, digital records of the case study organisation, Skype chat logs and interviews. Employing different data sources allowed us to offer a thick description of how volunteers acquire, process, vet and share actionable information. Consequently, this approach provides a unique contribution to the methodological advancement of disaster research within the Computer Supported Cooperative Work (CSCW) and crisis informatics fields.

The remainder of the paper is organised as follows: Sect. 2 provides a review of the related studies. Section 3 discusses background and case study context. Section 4 presents data gathering approach, and in Sect. 5 and 6 we present and discuss our findings and its implications. In Sect. 7, we conclude our work.

2 Digital Volunteer Communities

The Literature on digital disaster response is broad-ranging and cuts across disciplines and fields. Our review suggests lack of consensus in naming these Internet-enabled communities from practitioners and academics. For example, terms such as digital volunteer [communities] [17–19] digital humanitarians [actor networks] [20, 21], volunteer and technical [technological] communities [22, 23] have all been used in various studies and across disciplines. This lack of consensus became visible following the publication of Disaster Relief 2.0 where members of digital humanitarian organisations openly disagreed with the authors of the report for giving their various communities a catch-all label as 'volunteer and technical communities' [24]. For clarity, we refer to these communities as Digital Volunteer Communities (DVCs).

As mentioned in the introduction, our focus is on the established digital volunteer communities. Gorp [22], delineates established digital volunteer communities into software platform development communities, mapping communities, expert network communities and social media and data aggregation communities. We situated our work within the social media and data aggregation communities by studying the collaborative and social computing aspect of HR volunteers and their crowdsourcing activities.

2.1 Related Studies

Previous studies in digital disaster responses have tended to focus on three distinct categories of responders. The first category explores the coordination between digital volunteers and formal/traditional humanitarian relief organisations [25]. The second segment examines their relationship with emergency management agencies [26]. The third category deals with the virtual operation support team (VOST) on one hand, and digital volunteers on the other [17, 27, 28]. Although VOST offers support remotely like any other digital volunteer communities, it is regarded as a distinct entity from the spectrum of the digital volunteers because unlike digital volunteers; its membership came from retired and serving professional emergency management staff who have an internal connection to the response operation [29].

As digital volunteer communities began to mature, scholars have also examined their trajectories and offer insight on how they are changing the landscape of disaster response. For example, Palen et al. [28] explore the path of Humanitarian OpenStreetMap through the lens of two major disasters and provide a glimpse of how it organises its activities. Similarly, Starbird [10] has explored the information processing activities of HR volunteers by examining the management of information using a specific case study of Sacré Coeur hospital following Haiti 2010 earthquake. On the other hand, Starbird and Palen [17] provide an insight into the organisational development and work practice of HR where they traced its origin, identity negotiation, membership and the nature of its work. Nonetheless, these studies have limited scope with regards to the contexts, the use of tools and the duration upon which the response lasted. For instance, in the case of the Peru Earthquake, the entire response operation lasted for 3 hours and involved eight volunteers. As such, our paper, builds on such contributions by observing 17 response operations across 13 countries over a period of 16 months, to provide a holistic understanding of how volunteers acquire, assess, process and scrutinise crowdsourced information. The exploration of such activities will, therefore, contribute to the better understanding of the behind-the-scenes information processing activities of DVCs. Such findings will thus serve as a benchmark for evaluating whether the kind of information services these communities are providing satisfied standards of engagement, production and analysis.

3 Background and Case Study Context

HR uses Skype as its core platform for coordinating its activities. In detail, these activities are organised mainly in 4 different Skype 'windows' named as HR Café, HR Urgent Events, HR Useful Links, and HR Work Diary. HR Café is a window in which volunteers are using as a resort for socialising and exchange pleasantries. HR Urgent Events window is the central hub where volunteers coordinate and monitor the ongoing event around the world. The HR Useful Links window is another resort where volunteers post exciting life hacks, tips, notes, and links while HR Work Diary is serving as a platform for volunteers to stop in and drop a note on what they have been working on so that other team members can stay informed. In addition to these 4 main windows, HR has separate Skype windows for committee meetings, special projects, internal drills and training. Again, HR creates an event specific window whenever it is responding to the significant catastrophe.

4 Methodology

Our approach to understanding this collaborative and social computing phenomenon is through virtual ethnography. Recent studies in CSCW and Crisis informatics have promoted the use of such methods [17, 30, 31].

We used field notes from participant observation, digital records of the case study organisation, Skype chat logs and interviews as our primary source of data for this research. The first author participated in thirty meetings in which twelve related to strategic and operational aspects of the organisation, while the remaining eighteen were associated with volunteer training. Drawing from the theory of role and self [32], the first author took the role of participant-as-observer where he spent the time to take part in the real disaster response activities.

HR also allowed us to use Skype chat log with the condition that all personally identifiable information will be anonymised unless a volunteer expressly agreed to be made public. As such, our review of the Urgent Event Window chatter involves only the response operations that our first author participated or observed. Specifically, the review coverage spans from 15th February 2016 to 22nd May 2017.

We also used Skype to conduct semi-structured interviews with 7 volunteers to find out detailed information about the work process, standards, collaboration, trust, use of

ICT tools and protocols associated with the response operation which lasted between 60 to 120 minutes.

This paper uses 17 selected digital disaster response operations undertaken by HR as its primary unit of analysis. To choose those responses, we consider Fritz [33], cited in Kreps, [34] core properties of disasters – events, social units, response – as our basis for case identification and selection. Accordingly, we attempted to cover a broad range of disasters (events) – dam spillage, earthquakes, explosions, flooding/landslide, hospital project, severe weather, tornado, wildfires – to encompass a comprehensive set of workflow activities from different emergency response operations. Also, our case selection covers 13 countries (social units) drawn across 6 continents – Africa, Asia, Europe, North America, South America, Oceania – with a different type of activation (response) as shown in Appendix 1. Our basis for selecting these events is to have insight into whether there is a difference of approach or procedures across disaster types or countries in digital disaster response work.

Our approach to data analysis is qualitative. As such, we draw from Corbin and Strauss' [35] procedures, and previous examples in CSCW papers [36, 37]. Following that, we review and analyse field notes, chats log, interview transcripts, and digital records iteratively and inductively to find recurrent themes. At the first instance, we began our analysis by making sense of the entire Skype chatter covering the 17 major response operations, thereby extracting themes and subthemes based on our research objectives. Later, we compared notes from our field notes, and other sources mentioned earlier to understand the organisational approach to response coordination.

5   Findings

The purpose of this study was to find out the type of activities involved in processing crowdsourced information. We begin by discussing the process workflow that emerged based on the repeated occurrence across a range of disasters during our sixteen months' observation.

Our observations, along with a careful review of Skype chatter across a range of disasters, revealed an implicitly structured workflow. This workflow starts with Monitoring and continues with Activation, Listing, Listening & Verification, Amplification and ends with Reporting. We categorised these activities into six segments in which each phase is distinct, with a related set of tightly constrained interdependent activities that are repeatedly present in every response operation we observed.

In what follows is the explanation of our findings on the nature of the cooperative work of the HR digital response partly drawn from the Skype chatter during a response operation. The portion of the Skype chatter we illustrate here usually starts with a date and time stamp ([12/03/2016, 20:17:29]) followed by the name of the volunteer that mostly begins with a prefix HR. The Skype chatter portion also includes emoticons that volunteers usually inserts in between the message they want to pass across.

5.1 Monitoring

The foundation upon which digital disaster response is built lies in receiving credible information about the sudden onset or arrival of slow-moving disaster. Obtaining such information entails the beginning of digital disaster response. The HR initiation stage for the response, therefore, begins at the point of watching for disasters to unfold: we refer to this as the Monitoring phase. Our finding reveals HR volunteers employ a different range of applications and platforms for receiving an instant push notification. As such, websites like the Global Disaster Alert and Coordination System (GDAC), U.S. Geological Survey (USGS), the National Hurricane Centre (NHC) and Pacific Disaster Centre (PDC) remained the most preferred source of news for HR volunteers. Furthermore, breaking news websites and media outlets is considered as secondary sources. This is because HR volunteers have learned over the years that "some of these media sources have the history of publishing information very fast, but often get their facts wrong" (Interview, President HR). HR volunteers, therefore, prefer to subscribe to electronic notification systems (ENS) of GDAC, USGS, NHC and PDC among others. By their subscription, these volunteers receive an SMS or email every time a disaster happens or is about to happen. Notification received via these websites sometimes offer a snippet of the disaster impact that helps volunteers to start preparing for a response. The following piece from the Skype logs illustrates how this volunteer received an instant alert and was announcing to the Urgent Event window about the sudden onset of Earthquake in Alaska (Fig. 1):

[12/03/2016, 20:17:29] HR Nicholas Lawson: I just got a phone notification of a magnitude 6.4 EQ near Atka, Alaska - alert doesn't give depths - will look for that - EQ occurred at 18:06 UTC **

Fig. 1. Snapshot of Skype logs extracts 1. - Illustration of notification alert.

As soon as information of such nature is posted in the Urgent Event Window, available volunteers that are hanging around in the Café will report to the window where a series of discussion will begin. The outcome of such meeting will determine whether to keep monitoring the situation or activate the Disaster Desk in which active and inactive volunteers will be invited. Activating Disaster Desk for disaster response signifies the end of the first phase and the beginning of the second phase.

5.2 Activation

In disaster response parlance, activation levels define the kind of response emergency workers will offer during any catastrophe. For instance, Stage 1 (Green) activation is designated for local events that are smaller in proportion in which information is limited or events whose level of impacts is yet to be ascertained. In that instance, volunteers will data mine social media for urgent needs and route it to those offering help and vice versa. Stage 2 (Yellow) activation is when the event is severe and humanitarian emergency organisations are overwhelmed and could not be able to respond to urgent needs promptly. In these circumstances, HR volunteers undertake 'general monitoring' and collaborative authoring of a 'situation report' (SitRep). During stage 2 (Yellow) activation, all regularly scheduled meetings and training sessions of HR may be temporarily disrupted. Stage 3 (Code Red) is designated for massive catastrophe with mass fatalities usually needing international aid.

For HR, Code Red activation needs a collective effort of both active and inactive volunteers. Active volunteers are HR members who are active in all the four main HR Skype windows while inactive members have access to all the windows but resurface to give help when HR social media incident commander sends an activation invitation.

Immediately after activating to Stage 3, the HR Incident Commander will send text messages and formal (email) invitation to both active and inactive volunteers requesting for their help. The email will typically have a brief overview of the catastrophe, the nature of response HR will offer, and a call to report to Urgent Event Window or a choice for amplifying HR work through social media platforms (if the volunteer may not have time to take part in the response operation). Moreover, the Incident Commander will also post the same announcement in the Urgent Event window and will create an event-specific window for managing the response. The following excerpt illustrates how an Incident Commander posted a statement to the Urgent Event Window (Fig. 2):

> [03/10/2016, 17:50:01] HR Javon Malone: (star) Attention team, we anticipate activation this afternoon for Hurricane Matthew. This is a very large storm that will likely impact multiple countries. The DDWG is preparing for our response now. This will likely be a Yellow and quite possibly Red event. We ask that if you are able to sta rt clearing some time in your schedule the next 3-4 days to support our activation. We have a window set up and gave designated this event as Operation Atlantis. Thank you. (f) (f) (f)

Fig. 2. Snapshot of Skype logs extracts 2. - Activation announcement.

In the above extract, the Incident Commander started his post with the star (star) emoticons signifying the start of the new event and ended it with three flower emoticons [(f) (f) (f)] which denote an end of the message. We can deduct from the statement that HR has been watching the forecast. The Incident Commander also mentioned DDWG (the Disaster Desk Working Group) readiness to support the event. The DDGW is a sub-team of active volunteers that have separate windows in which they meet and decide on matters related to disaster response.

From the preceding, we can see that activation phase began as soon as monitoring phase ends and the phase entails the decision-making process and the nature of the response HR will be providing.

5.3   Listing

Following the activation of disaster by the social media incident commander, volunteers will typically start announcing their availability. At this stage, available volunteers will be asked to perform Listing activities. Listing in this context refers to crowdsourcing the most valuable information on the internet that will guide the response and coordination of the disaster. Such activities include researching keywords and event hashtags that will be used for data mining Scanigo – a social media analytic toolkit for extracting disaster information. This toolkit organises tweets into categories, helps in reducing Twitter noise, and identifies likely relevant tweets.

Some volunteers will also be asked to find a country's emergency numbers for dispatch, fire, ambulance, and police while others will be working on listing websites that are responsible for providing official updates. For example, HR co-ordinators will be interested in finding sites, social media handles, location, phone numbers, and emails of country's emergency management agencies. Volunteers will also be asked to offer information related to regional and local organisations of the disaster-affected region.

Listing activities also entail finding social media handles of traditional relief organisations like Save the Children, Doctors without Borders, and Red Cross. HR also encourages its volunteers to provide social media handles and contacts of critical infrastructure companies associated with communication, road, and airport among others. Additionally, volunteers will be expected to provide information on websites, contact address, location, social media handles of organisations dealing with disability, accessibility and functional needs (DAFN) and a host of other interest groups depending on the nature of the catastrophe and the country.

Unlike the 'Monitoring' and 'Activation' phases in which the activities are in sequence, the Listing phase often connects to the next phase (Listening & Verification) in a back and forth manner depending on the nature of the catastrophe. If the situation is not complex and does not need major response effort, the workflow is a straightforward activity. As such, the sequence will be from 'Listing' to 'Listening & Verification' phase. However, if the response initially pertains only to one area, but later the situation keeps magnifying, and various regions are added to the emergency declaration list, then the activity will continuously be in a cyclical iteration between the two phases as illustrated Fig. 3 in Appendix 2. Moreover, our observation reveals another phase called 'Reporting' (see Sect. 5.6) also connects directly to 'Listing' phase during major events. The two dotted arrows in Appendix 2, Fig. 3 becomes active whenever the event is declared to be a major one, and as such there is a need for updating the 'Listing' resources whenever the emergency declaration covers new areas as the event keeps unfolding.

In summary, 'Listing' phase involves the use of manual and automated tools to data mine actionable information that helps people survive, sustain, and reunite. Specifically, during this phase, the volunteers will be looking for information such as emergency numbers for ambulance, fire service, and police that will help people and animals survive, sustain and reunite. Volunteers will also search for contacts including website links, social media handles, telephone numbers, location for organisations, aid agencies, and local support groups among others.

5.4 Listening and Verification

Unlike the previous activities that occur in sequence, our observation across disasters reveal 'Listing' and 'Listening & Verification' are iterative, interrelated and distinct activities that sometimes happen simultaneously. In the context of HR, listening entails data mining social media for finding damage reports and urgent needs such as a request for help, evacuation, medical supplies, missing person or information about reunification centres among other things. In addition, listening includes monitoring the Scanigo platform, searching for isolated and disadvantaged communities as well as tracking the activities of other digital volunteers and aid agencies. It also involves listening to online Emergency Telecommunications groups such as Ham Radio and First Response Radio Team (FRRT).

As soon as a volunteer uncovers information arising from the listening activities, the next action is to post the information to the Urgent Event window for verification. Volunteers will then begin to triangulate the information, in some instances to revert to the original source or contact partners for further clarification or affirmation. If the exercise did not yield any positive outcome, the issue would be put on hold, and other volunteers will continue to monitor the situation. However, if something positive came out of it, a decision may be taken to amplify the information and record the activity on the SitRep. This act of collective effort and decision making is what we refer to as Verification.

Previously, we have shown 'Listing' and 'Listening & verification' workflow move either in sequence or in back and forth manner; however, in this phase, the workflow sequence moves in the forward direction to the next phase called 'Amplification'. In addition to that, during major events, our observation reveals a linkage between the 'Reporting' phase and 'Listening & Verification' phase. This activity evolves when the situation warrants writing a series of SitReps. As such, volunteers' co-authoring reports will be transferring vetted information from the Skype response window and keep adding them to the Google Docs for authoring the SitRep. An illustration of the workflow is in Appendix 2 – Fig. 4.

The figure shows the process workflow at 'Listening & Verification phase' with the 'Listing' as a preceding activity and 'Amplification' as the next stage in the process. The figure also shows a dotted arrow from 'Reporting' phase linking to the 'Listening & Verification' phase. Listening & Verification are ongoing activities until when the disaster desk Incident Commander announce volunteers to stand down.

5.5 Amplification

Amplification comes into effect as soon as volunteers verify or track critical information which needs to be routed to emergency management organisations or disaster-affected communities. The act of sharing such information is what is called amplification. More precisely, amplification involves sharing verified official information sourced from emergency management organisation in charge of response operation and other traditional humanitarian relief agencies to the public. It also involves routeing urgent needs to the emergency management agencies and humanitarian aid organisations. Amplification also includes posting survival tips and reassurance messages by HR volunteers through official and individual volunteers' social media accounts. It also involves urging the public to be cautious of sharing photos and location of the emergency responders while working at the public safety event.

From the context of response workflow, the sequence that leads to 'Amplification' phase starts from 'Listening & Verification', and the workflow continues to the Reporting phase from Amplification phase.

In summary, amplification comes into effect whenever volunteers vetted and approved the information to be shared with the public. This vetting and approval are undertaken at the 'Listening & Verification' phase. As such, the nature of the workflow starts with 'Listening & Verification' phase and is a one-way continuous activity until the disaster response is over. The rate at which HR volunteers amplify information depends on nature, impact, and the affected area(s). It is worthy to note HR amplifies the information across its social media platforms and to encourage volunteers to also amplify the same information through their social media handles.

5.6 Reporting

The Reporting phase comes into effect depending on the nature of the disaster. If the catastrophe needs long hours of response, then HR volunteers will start co-authoring SitRep at the same time amplifying and this will be going on until the response is over. Sometimes as the situation keeps evolving, volunteers will keep updating the resource list. For example, it is possible in the first instance, a state of emergency declared earlier covers only one county, but as the situation unfolds, the declaration will also include nearby counties or regions. As such, some volunteers will update the listing resource while others are working on the main SitRep. Also, as the situation keeps evolving, Listening & Verification will also be going on simultaneously with the Reporting as illustrated in Appendix 2 - Fig. 5. On the other hand, if the event does not require SitRep, reporting will only be in the Urgent Event Window which will later culminate into standing down from the response operation. The Fig. 5 depicts the workflow where volunteers working on the Reporting phase can go back either to the Listing or Listening & Verification Phase. For example, the situation might warrant the need for the original lists to be updated when the disaster covers more regions.

Our observations also reveal the use of four primary tools/platforms in mediating the cooperative work of producing a report popularly called SitRep. First, the use of Skype as a central platform where all the chatter for mediation, verification, and sense-making takes place. Second, the use of Google Sheet where all the event status such as instructions, guides and tip sheet, are filed and archived. Third, the use of Google Docs in which volunteers cooperatively work to develop the SitRep which mainly assembles information and updates that will help people and animals in disaster to survive, sustain and reunite. Fourth, the use of Scanigo; a social media analytic tools for filtering, categorising and ranking torrents of tweets to reduce the time taken for data mining Twitter noise. Additionally, volunteers using the Firefox browser can appropriate HR's plugin while responding to the catastrophe. The custom-made plugin provides a handy dashboard where volunteers could easily find pre-written searches, guides, tips, a list of embassies, twitter lists, emergency numbers and loads of useful information.

From our findings, partners such as the United Nation Office for the Coordination of Humanitarian Affairs (UNOCHA), FEMA, Americares, and Cisco TacOps uses HR SitRep for situational awareness and decision making associated with communication, funding and cooperation. SitRep also guides partners to know who is doing what and where among other aid workers and relief agencies.

In brief, HR digital disaster response workflow starts with a sequence of activities evolving into six distinct phases. The first three phases – monitoring, activation and listing -, developed in series while there is a continuous looping of actions between the listing and listening & verification phase and the sequence will continue from listening & verification phase through amplification to the reporting phase. Next is a back and forth iteration at reporting stage that came into effect from amplification. At the reporting phase, a series of this back and forth iteration centres around listing and listening & verification phases depending on the nature of the catastrophe.

6   Discussion and Implications

Throughout this paper we tried to provide insights into how volunteers acquire, organise, validate and share crowdsourced information as a form aid. In what follows, is the discussion arising from such findings.

6.1   Digital Disaster Response Process Workflow

Regarding our research question that sought to answer the type of the activities involved in processing crowdsourced information, our findings uncover 6 distinct, repeatable patterns associated with every disaster response cycle we studied. This pattern evolves in phases as follows: (1) Monitoring, (2) Activation, (3) Listing, (4) Listening & Verification, (5) Amplification, and (6) Reporting. As seen in Appendix 2, the response pattern shows a combination of linear as well as reciprocal workflow based on the magnitude of the disaster.

Accordingly, based on the results of the study in the investigated contexts, this paper proposes an analytical framework that offers a fresh perspective and deeper insight into the activities of the digital humanitarian response process workflow (Appendix 2 - Fig. 6).

As it is seen in Appendix 2 – Fig. 6, the proposed analytical framework holds the essential steps to understanding digital disaster response crowdsourcing activities. These steps were carefully analysed and cross-checked across 8 disaster types in 13 countries during 17 response operations as explained in the finding section. The conceptualisation of these phases gives an exciting insight into the activities of HR. As such, while our model is high-level enough to allow academics, practitioners and system designers to make sense of the process workflow in HR, at the same time, it provides detailed interpretations of each step in the process and how they are dynamically and reciprocally related to one another. This makes our model flexible in its scalability that can be followed as a roadmap and applied in different contexts across diverse disaster types with different impacts and scales.

This scalability covers the disaster type, impact, affected region and the country. By disaster impact we refer to the number of causalities, property and infrastructural damages. The affected region could be isolated communities or in urban areas. Countries could take the form of developed or developing nations since the HR response lies entirely on the information available online and the emergency response system of the country in question. Keeping this explanation in mind, the workflow moves in sequence from monitoring to reporting phase when the activation is in Green or Purple – an activation designated for special projects. However, once the activation is Yellow or Red, Listing, Listening & Verification, as well as Reporting (as shown in Appendix 2 – Fig. 6), will be in the continuous iteration until the operation ends. The dotted arrows along with numbers (1, 2, 3) illustrate the back and forth processual iteration of the workflow.

By proposing the analytical framework, we generalise from empirical statements (as inputs to generalising) to theoretical statements (as outputs of generalising) [38]. Furthermore, structuring, evaluating and verifying this model upon various heterogeneous cases and contexts across both developed and developing countries generalise our model to provide insight into the domain of social media and data aggregation communities within the digital volunteer communities. It is worth noting that until now, past research within the realm of the use of ICTs in humanitarian emergencies that examined workflow related studies tended to cluster around Volunteered Geographic Information (VGI) and management information systems [39–44]. Unlike this study, some of these studies are technical and deals mostly with studying decision support systems alongside their development and deployment. Interestingly, our workflow shares some commonalities and differences with regards to task initiation and completion with most of these earlier studies mentioned above. In our workflow, we highlight that volunteers crowdsourcing activities began with monitoring and culminated in the activation of the disaster desk. Later, the activity will move to the listing phase. From the listing phase, the activity will keep moving in back and forth manner to the listening & verification as well as amplification and reporting phase. By juxtaposing our workflow with that of Ostermann and Spinsanti [39] in which the authors evaluated the credibility of Volunteered Geographic Information (VGI), one can observe some similarities and differences with regards to the flow. For example, Ostermann and Spinsanti [39] conceptual workflow includes four steps that begin with 'retrieval' and move through 'processing', 'integration' and ended at the 'dissemination' phase. At the retrieval phase, the system retrieves relevant social media and other disaster information using keywords. Next, when the data is retrieved, the workflow will continue with the processing phase where the location and source profile data will be picked and later use to determine relevance, credibility and analysis of the information. The workflow will then continue to the next phase (integration) in which the output generated from the processing phase will be combined with the information from official and authoritative spatial data infrastructures. Last, the result of the integration will then be shared (disseminated) across the stakeholders. In essence, both the workflows have initiation and completion phases. The phases also share some commonalities. For example, in our model, our fourth phase (listening & verification) can be likened to their second and third phases, and their final phase also can be likened to our reporting phase. Both studies also aspire to evaluate the credibility of the information produced using crowdsourcing. However, the parting point is our central concern is offering insight into the activities of social media and data aggregation communities while their studies focus was on the Volunteered Geographic Information (VGI).

Following on from this, we now turn to examine the collaborative and social computing activities performed by volunteers during each response operation. These areas include: tools manipulation, task organisation, communication style, and the group shared awareness:

Tool manipulation: The response workflow mentioned earlier also reveals how HR volunteers are manipulating tools to produce contents. While the use of such devices is common knowledge, but how HR team is shaping the tools in the context of disaster response is what makes this interesting. For example, during a typical response, the HR team uses Skype for coordination, Google Docs for collaborative authoring, Google Sheets as information and project management/reference manual, and Scanigo for listening to social media postings. In other instances where the response dictates the need for more training to volunteers or briefing (like the Burundi Hospital response), HR will use a Google slide deck to visually present ideas for volunteers. As such, the ability to combine automation alongside manual work such as the use of Scanigo or switching from one platform as well as searching or posting information using a mobile phone or desktop computer to another platform suggests a combination of creativity, experience and skills.

Task Organisation: Observing HR workflow also enabled us to understand how they organise activities by dividing the task among themselves. For example, in the Listing phase, the work involves finding health facilities, embassies, telecommunication companies, emergency management organisations and relief agencies among others. At Listening & Verification, some volunteers' role will be listening to isolated communities, others on reunification information and another team will be charged with data mining urgent needs. When it comes to Amplification, some volunteers will take the role of posting information to HR tweeter account, while others will work on Facebook or Instagram. But how they work out what to do and who to do what while responding depends on the available volunteers, their skills, knowledge of contexts, and the nature of the response – slow moving or sudden.

Communication Approach: Another insight associated with our findings involves the nature of information exchange where the communication is characterised using abbreviations, emoticons, typing errors, hedging, emphasis and terminologies. Use of acronyms such as BRB for 'be right back', EQ for an earthquake, SitRep for situation reports and TC for tropical cyclone among others is replete in all their communication. Likewise, HR standardises the use of some selected emoticons for shared awareness among volunteers. In some circumstances, information exchange in the Urgent Event window is characterised by spelling mistakes which can be likened to the altruistic urge and pressure to help. Our observation also reveals the manifestation of caution such as 'heads off' or 'unverified' while posting information to prepare the mind of fellow volunteers.

Group Shared Awareness: The concept of shared awareness within a group is well established in the CSCW literature [45]. Our observation notes how 'Reporting' in the form of 'morning summary', 'evening summary' and 'end of the day summary', among others, plays a significant role in a response operation. During response operations, the HR team will assign a member to take the role of giving a summary and posting it to the Urgent Event window. The reason for this is to make everyone involved aware of the ongoing response, since volunteers' work based on their availability.

6.2 Practical Implications

The main contribution of this paper is that it has generated essential and valuable insights into the phenomenon of digital volunteers about the social media and data aggregation communities. As a result, its findings suggest implications for practice for digital humanitarian organisations, emergency management agencies, governments of disaster-prone countries as well as directions for future research. This paper has sketched out how the crisis information data is monitored, processed, managed, verified and reported. Based on the empirical findings we proposed a new framework to show the order of activities being undertaken in preparing the crowdsourced information. While this framework is the first of its kind to represent the big picture, it provides practitioners, policymakers and system developers with a roadmap currently being followed so they can more seriously consider their contributions to this workflow to improve this process further and more efficient.

Moreover, our findings have important implications for the governments of disaster-prone countries. For example, our inclusion of the different type of disasters and emergencies across countries has revealed the dearth of information that HR makes use of to monitor the official response from the governments of the affected countries, especially from the developing nations. Our experience in Sri Lanka, Burundi, Peru and Fiji have revealed the scarcity of information about websites, social media handles, and emergency numbers of the emergency management organisations where volunteers can find verified official information to route that information to the people. As such, if countries will make information available online by creating websites and having official social media handles, it will enable volunteers to follow and relay official details to those in needs. Likewise, digital disaster response organisations such as HR could also develop a pre-made compendium of information resource list of disaster-prone countries before the sudden onset of disasters. Information resource list is a directory that holds information such as emergency numbers, websites, locations, maps, social media handles of fire, ambulance, police, airports, transportations and emergency response organisations. Developing such compendium will enable organisations such as HR to cut time in crowdsourcing the list at the 'listing' stage while responding to disasters as illustrated in Sect. 5.3. By so doing, the HR process workflow could be reduced to monitoring, activation, listening & verification, amplification as well as reporting.

7   Conclusion

This study contributes to the Computer Supported Cooperative Work (CSCW), Crisis Informatics, Information Systems for Crisis Response and Management (ISCRAM), and Disaster field in two ways: theoretically and methodologically.

As to the theoretical contribution, this study proposes a new analytical framework outlining the various stages/activities involved in the digital disaster response information workflow in the social media and data aggregation communities. Comprehensively derived from the empirical data, this framework contains the critical components that could potentially signal the emergence of new models for DVCs with regards to the social media and data aggregation Community. Our model evolved from diverse types of disasters with different scales and is flexible enough to support multiple scenarios of similar kinds and to be adapted to various disaster types and used by Social Media and Data Aggregation Communities with comparable characteristics in different countries and settings.

Regarding the methodological contribution, this study is among the few that attempts to empirically and comprehensively understand and shed light on the information processing workflow. As mentioned previously, this study employed various data collection methods from 8 disaster types in 13 countries, across 6 continents, covering both developing and developed nations using virtual ethnography over the period of 16 months. To the best of our knowledge, this methodological approach is the first of its kind in this area with regards to the DVCs focusing on social media and data aggregation communities. Taking this approach has provided a holistic understanding of the behind the scene processes and measures in digital disaster response.

Appendices

Appendix 1

See Table 1.

Table 1. Summary of the disasters used in the study

| EVENTS (TYPE) | ANALYSIS PHASE | SOCIAL UNITS | | RESPONSE |
		COUNTRY	CONTINENT	
Dam Spillage	Phase 1	USA (Oroville)	North America	Red
	Phase 1	Japan (Kumamoto)	Asia	Red
Earthquake	Phase 1	Ecuador	South America	Red
	Phase 1	Italy	Europe	Yellow
	Phase 1	Belgium (Brussel)	Europe	Green
	Phase 1	Turkey (Istanbul)	Asia	Green
Explosion	Phase 1	Manchester (UK)	Europe	Green
	Phase 2	Westminster (UK)	Europe	Green
	Phase 1	Sri Lanka	Asia	Green
Flood/Landslide	Phase 1	Peru	South America	Yellow
	Phase 1	USA (Louisiana)	North America	Red
Special project	Phase 1	Burundi	Africa	Purple
	Phase 1	Fiji Tropical Cyclone	Oceania	Green
Severe weather	Phase 1	USA (Oklahoma)	North America	Green
	Phase 2	Hurricane Irma (USA)	North America	Red
	Phase 1	Canada	North America	Yellow
Wild fire	Phase 1	Chile	South America	Green
Legend		Combined participation with the observation		Observation only

Appendix 2

See Figs. 3, 4, 5 and 6.

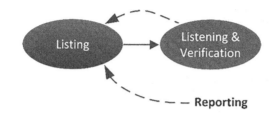

Fig. 3. Illustration of the 'Listing' phase.

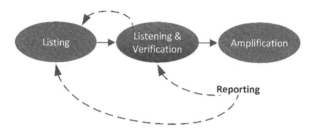

Fig. 4. Illustration of the 'Listening & Verification' phase.

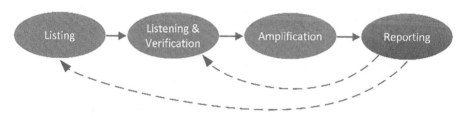

Fig. 5. Illustration of the 'Reporting' phase.

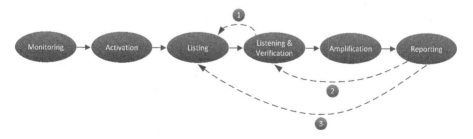

Fig. 6. Process workflow.

References

1. Quarantelli, E.L., Dynes, R.R.: Response to social crisis and disaster. Annu. Rev. Sociol. **3**, 23–49 (1977). https://doi.org/10.1146/annurev.so.03.080177.000323
2. Britton, N.R.: Permanent Disaster Volunteers: Where Do They Fit? Nonprofit Volunt. Sect. Q. **20**, 395–414 (1991). https://doi.org/10.1177/089976409102000404
3. Britton, N.R.: Organised Behaviour in Disaster: A Review. Int. J. Mass Emerg. Disasters. **6**, 363–395 (1988)
4. Hughes, A., Palen, L., Peterson, S.: Social media in emergency management: academic perspective. Critical issues in Disaster Science and Management: A dialogue between researchers and emergency managers (2008)
5. Taylor, M., Wells, G., Howell, G., Raphael, B., et al.: The role of social media as psychological first aid as a support to community resilience building. Aust. J. Emerg. Manag. **27**, 20 (2012)
6. Dufty, N.: Using social media to build community disaster resilience. Aust. J. Emerg. Manag. **27**, 40 (2012)
7. McEntire, D.A.: The status of emergency management theory: issues, barriers, and recommendations for improved scholarship. University of North Texas. Department of Public Administration. Emergency Administration and Planning (2004)
8. Tapia, A.H., Moore, K.A, Johnson, N.J.N.: Beyond the trustworthy tweet: a deeper understanding of microblogged data use by disaster response and humanitarian relief organizations. In: Proceedings of the 10th International ISCRAM Conference, pp. 770–779 (2013)
9. Starbird, K., Muzny, G., Palen, L.: Learning from the crowd: collaborative filtering techniques for identifying on-the-ground twitterers during mass disruptions. In: Proceedings of the 9th International Conference on Information Systems for Crisis Response and Management. ISCRAM 2011, pp. 1–10 (2012)
10. Starbird, K.: Delivering patients to sacré coeur: collective intelligence in digital volunteer communities. In: Proceedings of the Conference on Human Factors in Computing Systems, pp. 801–810 (2013). https://doi.org/10.1145/2470654.2470769
11. Tapia, A.H., LaLone, N.J., Kim, H.-W.H.-W.: Run amok: group crowd participation in identifying the bomb and bomber from the Boston marathon bombing. In: ISCRAM, pp. 265–274 (2014)
12. Dailey, D., Starbird, K.: Visible skepticism: community vetting after Hurricane Irene. In: ISCRAM 2014 Proceedings - 11th International Conference on Information Systems for Crisis Response and Management, pp. 777–781 (2014)
13. Nhan, J., Huey, L., Broll, R.: Digilantism: an analysis of crowdsourcing and the Boston marathon bombings. Br. J. Criminol. **57**, 341–361 (2017). https://doi.org/10.1093/bjc/azv118
14. Imran, M., Elbassuoni, S., Castillo, C., Diaz, F., Meier, P.: Extracting Information Nuggets from Disaster- Related Messages in Social Media (2013)
15. Popoola, A., Krasnoshtan, D.: Information verification during natural disasters. In: Proceedings of the 22nd International Conference on World Wide Web, pp. 1029–1032 (2013). https://doi.org/10.1145/2487788.2488111
16. Gralla, E., Goentzel, J., de Walle, B.V: Understanding the information needs of field-based decision-makers in humanitarian response to sudden onset disasters. In: Proceedings of the 12th International Conference on Information Systems for Crisis Response and Management, pp. 1–7 (2015)

17. Starbird, K., Palen, L.: Working and sustaining the virtual "Disaster Desk." In: Proceedings of the 2013 conference on Computer Supported Cooperative Work - CSCW 2013, pp. 491–502. ACM Press, New York (2013)
18. Hughes, A.L., Tapia, A.H.: Social media in crisis: when professional responders meet digital volunteers. J. Homel. Secur. Emerg. Manag. **12**, 679–706 (2015). https://doi.org/10.1515/jhsem-2014-0080
19. Reuter, C., Ludwig, T., Kaufhold, M.-A., Spielhofer, T.: Emergency services' attitudes towards social media: a quantitative and qualitative survey across Europe. Int. J. Hum Comput Stud. **95**, 96–111 (2016). https://doi.org/10.1016/j.ijhcs.2016.03.005
20. Meier, P.: New information technologies and their impact on the humanitarian sector. Int. Rev. Red Cross. **93**, 1239–1263 (2011). https://doi.org/10.1017/S1816383112000318
21. Sabou, J., Videlov, S.: An analysis on the role of trust in digital humanitarian actor networks. In: Information Systems for Crisis Response and (2016)
22. Van Gorp, A.F.: Integration of volunteer and technical communities into the humanitarian aid sector: barriers to collaboration. In: Proceedings of the Information Systems for Crisis Response and Management, pp. 620–629 (2014)
23. Weinandy, T.: Volunteer and Technical Communities in Humanitarian Response: Lessons in Digital Humanitarianism from Typhoon Haiyan (2016)
24. Standby Task Force: Why We Need a Disaster 2.1 Report. http://www.standbytaskforce.org/2011/04/06/why-we-need-a-disaster-2-1-report/
25. Sabou, J., Klein, S.: How virtual and technical communities can contribute to U.N. led humanitarian relief operations – boundary spanning and the exploration of collaborative information practices. In: PACIS 2016 Proceedings, p. 17 (2016)
26. St. Denis, L.A., Anderson, K.M., Palen, L.: Mastering Social Media: An Analysis of Jefferson County's Communications during the 2013 Colorado Floods, pp. 737–746. Iscram (2014)
27. St. Denis, L.A., Hughes, A.L., Palen, L.: Trial by fire: the deployment of trusted digital volunteers in the 2011 shadow lake fire. In: 9th International ISCRAM Conference, pp. 1–10 (2012)
28. Palen, L., Soden, R., Anderson, T.J., Barrenechea, M.: Success & scale in a data-producing organization: the socio-technical evolution of OpenStreetMap in response to humanitarian events. In: Proceedings of thr ACM CHI 2015 Conference on Human Factors in Computing Systems, vol. 1, pp. 4113–4122 (2015). https://doi.org/10.1145/2702123.2702294
29. Cobb, C., et al.: Designing for the deluge: understanding & supporting the distributed, collaborative work of crisis volunteers. In: Proceedings of the Conference on Computer-Supported Cooperative Work, pp. 888–899 (2014). https://doi.org/10.1145/2531602.2531712
30. Ducheneaut, N., Moore, R.J.: The social side of gaming. In: Proceedings of the 2004 ACM Conference on Computer Supported Cooperative Work - CSCW 2004. p. 360. ACM Press, New York (2004)
31. Irani, L., Hayes, G.: ACM, P.D.-Proceedings of the 2008, 2008, undefined: Situated practices of looking: visual practice in an online world (2008). dl.acm.org
32. Gold, R.L.: Roles in sociological fieldwork gold. Soc. Forces **36**, 217–223 (1958)
33. Fritz, C.E.: Disasters. In: Social Problems, pp. 651–694. Harcourt, Brace & World, New York (1961)
34. Kreps, G.A.: Sociological inquiry and disaster research. Annu. Rev. Sociol. **10**, 309–330 (1984)
35. Corbin, J., Strauss, A.: Grounded theory research: procedures, canons, and evaluative criteria. Qual. Sociol. **13**, 3–21 (1990)

36. Procter, R., Wherton, J., Greenhalgh, T., Sugarhood, P., Rouncefield, M., Hinder, S.: Telecare call centre work and ageing in place. Comput. Support. Coop. Work **25**, 9242–9245 (2016). https://doi.org/10.1007/s10606-015-9242-5
37. Farshchian, B.A., Vilarinho, T., Mikalsen, M.: From Episodes to Continuity of Care: a Study of a Call Center for Supporting Independent Living. Comput. Support. Coop. 309–343 (2017). https://doi.org/10.1007/s10606-017-9262-4
38. Lee, A.A.S., Baskerville, R.R.L.: Gerneralizing generalizability in information systems research. Inf. Syst. Res. **14**, 221–243 (2003). https://doi.org/10.1287/isre.14.3.221.16560
39. Ostermann, F.O., Spinsanti, L.: A conceptual workflow for automatically assessing the quality of volunteered geographic information for crisis management. In: Proceedings of AGILE. pp. 1–6 (2011)
40. Schade, S., Luraschi, G., De Longueville, B., Cox, S., Díaz, L.: Citizens as sensors for crisis events: Sensor web enablement for volunteered geographic information (2010)
41. Bui, T.X., Sankaran, S.R.: Design considerations for a virtual information center for humanitarian assistance/disaster relief using workflow modeling. Decis. Support Syst. **31**, 165–179 (2001)
42. Sebastian, I.M., Bui, T.X.: Emergent groups for emergency response-theoretical foundations and information design implications. In: Proceeding of the AMCIS 2009, p 638 (2009)
43. Sell, C., Braun, I.: Using a workflow management system to manage emergency plans. In: Proceedings of the 6th International ISCRAM Conference. p. 43 (2009)
44. Bui, T., Tan, A.: A template-based methodology for large-scale HA/DR involving ephemeral groups-A workflow perspective. In: 40th Annual Hawaii International Conference on System Sciences, 2007. HICSS 2007. p. 34 (2007)
45. Borghoff, U.M., Schlichter, J.H.: Computer-Supported Cooperative Work (2000)

Transitory and Resilient Salient Issues in Party Manifestos, Finland, 1880s to 2010s

Content Analysis by Means of Topic Modeling

Pertti Ahonen[✉] [iD] and Juha Koljonen

University of Helsinki, Helsinki, Finland
{pertti.ahonen,juha.koljonen}@helsinki.fi

Abstract. The performance of computational methods has been proven many times over. However, special efforts may be needed to ensure access to the research results achieved by means of these methods within specialized social science disciplines. This study joins previous efforts towards the mainstreaming of a specific computational method in the political science field of salience research. Rather than joining previous studies on the influence of the salience of issues to parties upon their electoral results or their propensity to form or join governments, this study represents the part of salience research that examines salience and its changes in their own right. Adapting ideas of digital historical humanities given the long study period, this study inserts salience theory within the frames of critical junctures theory to examine issues discontinuity, and path dependence theory to account for issue resilience. Using Latent Dirichlet Allocation topic modeling with 734 Finnish party manifestos from the 1880s to the 2010s as the research material, testing two hypotheses gave the following results. First, although many issues in the manifestos have been transitory, there have also been issues with resilience over critical junctures. Second, although there are resilient issues whose meanings have stayed the same by and large during longer periods, the meanings of some other resilient issues have pronouncedly changed, either suddenly at critical junctures or gradually during periods of path dependence. The implications for future studies are also discussed.

Keywords: Computational methods · Digital humanities · Critical junctures
Path dependence

1 Introduction

Despite the proven performance of computational methods, special efforts may be needed to make the research results achieved by means of these methods accessible within specialized social science disciplines. This study continues steps taken by others towards mainstreaming computational methods in the political science field of salience research while using a specific computational method.

In salience research, the 'salience' of issues means that these issues are central, important or pivotal to political parties according to their party manifestos or their other explicit statements. Some of salience research has probed the consequences of the

© Springer Nature Switzerland AG 2018
S. Staab et al. (Eds.): SocInfo 2018, LNCS 11185, pp. 23–37, 2018.
https://doi.org/10.1007/978-3-030-01129-1_2

salience that parties give to issues such as their electoral success or failure or their propensity to form or join governments [3, 9, 15, 42, 48]. Salience research with a methodological emphasis also exists, such as elaborating new computational methods to examine salience or comparing results obtained by means of computational methods to results achieved using other methods [33, 34, 37]. However, this article joins two further common types of salience research: one that examines salience in its own right as an indicator of political and policy contents [21], and another that is comprised of longitudinal studies on trajectories of salience [12, 46]. More specifically, this article seeks to contribute to filling an empirical research gap that was identified in the predominance of short- or medium-term rather than longer-term studies on salience and its changes [12, 21, 51]. This article covers the entire period from the 1880s to the 2010s, during which party manifestos have been written and published in Finland.

In short- and medium-term studies on salience it is not relevant to consider profound societal and political historical changes as such changes hardly have occurred [12, 21, 51]. However, both in research using traditional methods and computational methods [25, pp. 88–116] the situation is different if the study period is long. Given the 130-year study period of this paper, salience theory is inserted within the frames of path dependence theory to consider historical continuity [39], and critical junctures theory to consider historical discontinuity [11, 55]. The long study period also calls for distinguishing resilient and transitory issues. A first research question can be formulated:

1. Have there been resilient issues persisting over critical junctures of societal and political transformation in party manifestos, and have there also been transitory issues without path dependence over these junctures, and if there have been either or both types of issues, what are they more exactly?

Referring to previous studies [16, 28], this article also focuses on possible changes in the meanings of politically salient issues despite the empirical resilience of their constituent words insofar as the societal and political context of the issues and the words has experienced profound changes. The second research question becomes:

2. Have meanings of resilient issues transformed while the context of these issues and their constituent words has changed with special reference to critical junctures of societal and political historical transformation, and if so, how have these meanings changed?

Four sections follow. They deal with theory and hypotheses, the method and the research material, the empirical results, and the significance and implications of this study.

2 Theory

2.1 Salience Theory

Budge [8, p. 861] offers a summary of political science research on salience, often alternatively spelled 'saliency': 'Saliency approaches derive from the basic idea that political parties define their policies by emphasizing certain topics more than others, particularly in public documents and debates.' According to salience theory, parties are expected to emphasize issues differently, such as doing so with a different frequency or with different value emphases, rather than taking up different issues than other parties do [9, 42]. Above we have indicated studies that represent three types of salience research [3, 9, 12, 15, 21, 42, 46, 48].

We also indicated above that in short- or medium-term salience research [12, 21, 46] historical continuity and discontinuity may rightfully be of little or no concern. However, we can expect that during the study period of 130 years in this study historical continuity and fundamental societal and political historical transformation have alternated. Taking this into account, we insert salience theory within the frames of a theory of persistence, meaning path dependence theory, and a theory of discontinuous change, meaning critical junctures theory.

2.2   Path Dependence Theory and Critical Junctures Theory

In their treatise on historical digital humanities research, Guldi and Armitage [25, pp. 88–116] argue that computational methods provide novel opportunities for long-term research with a historical orientation. As indicated, in this study efforts are taken to get a hold of the long study period with the help of two theories, path dependence theory and critical junctures theory.

Path dependence approaches have been used in many research fields, from the natural sciences to technology studies, economics, and other social science domains. In this study, we understand path dependence to be comprised of continuity with few or no actor incentives to seek or accept fundamental change [49]. In their turn, critical junctures comprise moments or episodes of historical contingency, during which alternatives for institutional and other change stay open unlike before [11, 55]. Towards the end of a critical juncture opportunities dwindle and path dependence sets in [39].

Country-level examples of path dependence include periods of war or other unrest, periods of peace and stability or stagnation and decline, and periods of institutional resilience and stability. Country-level examples of critical junctures include the gain or loss of independence, changes in international political alignment, the introduction of democracy or autocracy, critical elections that fundamentally mold relationships between political parties, and moments or episodes of discontinuous fundamental institutional change.

2.3   Hypotheses

In this study evidence to specify critical junctures and path dependence is sought from previous historically oriented empirical research. Within historical research it is solidly established that periodization comprises a most important theoretical step to take [35]. Further contextual evidence is brought into this study from comparative studies between countries categorized into groups with resembling members [45]. The first hypothesis can be formulated with special emphasis upon examining historical continuity:

Hypothesis 1: Among the politically salient issues in party manifestos there are issues that are resilient, path-dependent, and transcending critical junctures.

Hypothesis 1 is worded in a general way. However, it is based on the theoretical concepts of critical junctures and path dependence, whose specific timing or duration has to be specified using evidence from previous empirical research. In this study, resilient issues mean those that persist in the longer term, including that these issues may transcend one or more critical junctures. Transitory issues are understood to be composed of issues that lack the characteristics of the resilient issues. Referring to results of previous empirical research, this study also seeks for resilient core issues present in party manifestos, including core issues that have transcended critical junctures, although parties may have made minor or major adaptations to their interpretation of these issues in their manifestos.

Read as if backwards, Hypothesis 1 suggests that issues that are not resilient, path dependent and transcending critical junctures are transitory and inclined to disappear at critical junctures. However, we must consider the possibility that certain issues may reappear after an interval punctuated by one or more critical junctures.

In cross-sectional or short-term studies, the duration of the study period may not make it necessary to consider the possibility that smaller or larger changes may have occurred in the meanings of salient political issues and the meanings of the constituent words of these issues. However, in longer-term studies it may be well-advisable to take possible smaller or bigger changes of meanings into account [16, 28]. The second hypothesis becomes:

Hypothesis 2: While the entire study period is divided into sub-periods at critical junctures, moving from sub-period to sub-period modifications appear in the meanings of salient issues and their constituent words in historically changing societal and political contexts.

Resembling Hypothesis 1, Hypothesis 2 is general in its wording. However, Hypothesis 2 does have a theoretical basis in research on political conceptual history [27], according to which meanings of words are context-bound and may change as the context changes. Hypothesis 2 also shares a part of its theoretical grounding with Hypothesis 1 in that the sub-period division derives from the specification of critical junctures with the support of evidence brought from previous empirical research.

3   Research Material and Research Method

The primary research material includes 734 party manifestos from the 1880s to the 2010s that were available in the Finnish language in the POHTIVA party manifesto database of the Finnish National Data Archive in Spring 2016 [50]. The number of the manifestos to examine can be seen as promisingly many to generate interesting results. Moreover, more differentiation is present in Finland in manifesto types than in some countries. There are general manifestos (alternatively called 'manifestos on principles' or 'manifestos on objectives', for example), electoral manifestos (for parliament elections, for local government elections, and more lately also for the European elections), and special manifestos for individual policy sectors.

As indicated, secondary material from academic research on Finnish social and political history is used for contextualizing the salient issues in the manifestos with evidence on societal and political transformations and for distinguishing critical junctures and periods of path dependence. The study period is divided into sub-periods at critical junctures that are seen as the foremost.

This study uses topic modeling, which is a common method of unsupervised computational content analysis. Words in text documents comprise the observables. In this study, the configurations of words representing political issue areas are examined as topics estimated by means of topic modeling. Issues and topics have also been incidentally equated in the issue salience theory [8, p. 861]. The topics are substantively and contextually interpreted with the support of the secondary historical research material.

Computational topic modeling belongs to 'bag-of-words' methods, in which words are examined irrespective of their roles in sentences but certainly considering the co-location of these words with other words, meaning their 'co-words' [13, 22]. Many words may be important in more than one topic, used in more than one context of utilization, and possibly having more than one meaning, either cross-sectionally or at least over time. Following good practices of computational examination, 'stop-words' were eliminated from the textual data [13, 19, 23, 37]. However, even after this elimination, topics may include common words with substantive contents that are too weak to enable interpretation. To avoid loss of information from truncation, a special computer program of the Finnish government research-supporting company CSC, Ltd., was used to return words to their noun, adjective, or verb roots. However, perfect stop word elimination and lemmatization programs do not exist, the remaining errors have to be corrected manually, and the ultimately remaining low number of errors has to be tolerated.

This study applies Latent Dirichlet Allocation (LDA) topic modeling [1, 6, 7, 24], which is intended for revealing latent configurations in texts. It is for the researcher to interpret these configurations semantically. In LDA, documents comprise mixtures of topics that regulate the probability that words find their way into these documents. In LDA, the topics and their probability distributions in the documents comprise hidden random variables that are built into a hierarchical probability model and estimated by means of approximating the conditional distribution of these variables in the documents examined.

LDA gives that number of topics that the researcher has decided to estimate in a decreasing order or probability, and a list of words in each topic, also in a decreasing order of probability. The technical criteria of LDA allow estimating tens of topics from research material such as the one in this study. However, "[w]hen topic modeling is used to identify themes and assist in interpretation, rather than to predict a knowable state or quantity, there is no statistical test for the optimal number of topics or for the quality of a solution" [14, pp. 582–83]. The criteria to decide upon the number of topics to estimate must be sought from the theoretical background, previous empirical research, the research material, and even the cognitive manageability of smaller rather than larger numbers of topics. Proposing hypotheses and testing them rather than carrying out exploratory analysis provides the auxiliary benefit of better control over topic model robustness [57].

Evidence can be utilized for the approximate number of aggregates of political opinion in a Nordic country with a proportional electoral system, the parliamentary representation of numerous parties, and coalitions of parties when majority governments are formed. Berglund and Lindström [5] proposed a Nordic-Scandinavian five-party system model (see also Knutson [32]), which does not incidentally correspond with Gallagher's [20] estimates of the number of effective parties in the countries of the group. Taking all grounds to decide upon the number of topics to estimate into account we decided to keep the number of topics in all our examinations at the low figure of five.

4 Results

The theoretical background of this study required discerning periods of path dependence in Finnish history from the 1880s to the 2010s, punctuated by critical junctures. Evidence from research on Finland's societal and political history suggests that this country's declaration of independence in December 1917 comprises the first critical juncture during the study period [26]. Finland's withdrawal from World War II in September 1944 defines the second juncture [30, 41, 56]. The 1966 formation of a popular front government that included the Democratic League for the Finnish People (DLFP, SKDL in Finnish; with the Finnish Communist Party as its foremost member) for the first time since 1948 suggests a third critical juncture. The dissolution of the Soviet Union at the end of 1991 opened the opportunity for Finland to join the European Union three years later [44], suggesting 1995 to be a fourth critical juncture.

We used as a starting point a previous study, in which party manifestos written and published in Finland from the 1880s to the 2010 had been examined en bloc using topic modeling [2]. Presented in the order of probability from the highest to the lowest, the five topics estimated were substantially interpreted on the basis of their highest probability words (Fig. 1). The examination indicated the changing probabilities of these five topics during the study period, and connections were drawn between critical junctures of societal and political transformation on the one hand, and on the other the changing proportions of each topic from the total of 1.00 calculated over all topics.

Starting from an examination of the entire research period of 130 years offered two benefits. First, it provided a substantive and technical baseline, and second, it comprised a robustness check as its results can be compared with the results of the topic model estimations carried out separately for each of the five sub-periods separated by critical junctures. Both as a further robustness check and as a check of replicability, each of the topic model estimations for the five sub-periods were run five times. The trial runs suggested that the topical structures presented for the sub-periods were solid enough to present and interpret[1].

4.1 Probing Hypothesis 1 on Resilient Issues in Party Manifestos

As indicated above, five sets of five topics were separately estimated, meaning one set for each of the five sub-periods of the entire study period. Ten highest-probability words in each topic were selected as the basis of the interpretation. The number of manifestos

---

[1] The results of the trial runs are available on request from juha.koljonen@helsinki.fi.

in which each one from among the five topics estimated during each sub-period was the strongest was specially pinpointed (Table 1).

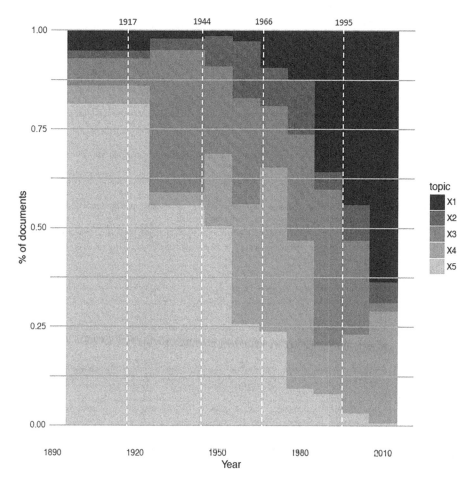

Fig. 1. Five topics in Finnish party manifestos, all parties. (Explanation: In [2], the topics had been given the following names: Topic 1, Municipal Welfare Services, Topic 2, Production Infrastructures, Topic 3, National Development in the International and European Context, Topic 4, Educational and Related Opportunities, and Topic 5 Nation-building and Societal Inclusion. The dashed vertical lines in the figure indicate the critical junctures that previous empirical research on societal and political transformations in Finland suggest.)

Table 1. Estimation of five topics for each of the sub-periods of the study period.

1880–1917 (n = 15)		
Topic 1	n = 5	Country/land, the state, law/justice, law/act, to get/to make, the people, Finland, work, to be able, common
Topic 2	n = 2	Language, municipality, office/position, school, amount/quantity, population, [an evident remaining lemmatization error], typical of, of population, Sweden/Swedish
Topic 3	n = 3	Farm, rent, union, rural dweller, of soil/of land, farming, country/land, to organize, municipality, resource
Topic 4	n = 2	Language, political party, to keep/to maintain, question, office/position, of the state/political, civilization/culture/education, Sweden/Swedish, good, one
Topic 5	n = 3	Municipality, everything, work/labor, workers, time, field/domain, interval, to help/to support, political party, the people
1918–1944 (n = 51)		
Topic 1	n = 14	Country/land, to get/to receive/to acquire, issue, political party, the state, all, great, the people, to be able, government
Topic 2	n = 16	Economy, the people, country/land, action, the state, law/justice, political party, economic, to develop, of law/of act
Topic 3	n = 6	Country/land, to get/to receive/to acquire, farm/space, municipality, rural dweller, work/labor, economy, farm/the act of cultivating, to cultivate, the state
Topic 4	n = 10	The people, work, common, Finland, the state, citizen, country/land, law/justice, to be able, organ
Topic 5	n = 5	Power, the working people, movement, class, time, great, [an evident lemmatization error], shortage, society, high
1945–1966 (n = 51)		
Topic 1	n = 24	Country/land, work/labor, economy, the people, common, action, society, power, municipality, organ
Topic 2	n = 5	Movement, share, action, political party, trade/commerce, member, government, interest/benefit, all, country/land
Topic 3	n = 3	Country/land, production, year, industry, large, to be able, amount, material/substance, raw, economic
Topic 4	n = 15	Municipality, municipal, work/labor, action, to get/to receive/to acquire, task/function, dwelling, all, to aim/to strive, attention
Topic 5	n = 4	The state, same, tax, society, to get/to receive/to acquire, area/region, system, size/whole, taxation, field/domain
1967–1995 (n = 332)		
Topic 1	n = 72	Country/land, energy, production, use, environment, traffic, area/region, forest, nature, to be able
Topic 2	n = 97	Municipality, work/labor, to get/to receive/to acquire, child, dwelling, service, all, the state, to be able, to develop
Topic 3	n = 33	Finland, country/land, to be able, political party, the people, development, work/labor, common, all
Topic 4	n = 52	Activity, education, opportunity, research, culture, development, society, to develop, task/function
Topic 5	n = 78	Work/labor, common, economy, country/land, the people, society, power, to make, the human being, to develop
1996–2012 (n = 285)		
Topic 1	n = 41	To be able, area/region, country/land, environment, Finland, Europe, union, countryside, politics/policy, development
Topic 2	n = 65	Common, the people, society, country/land, economy, the human being, work, right/justice, power, politics/policy
Topic 3	n = 26	Work/labor, tax, income/revenue, Finland, to get/to receive/to acquire, country/land, Finnish, basic, municipality, taxation
Topic 4	n = 104	Municipality, work/labor, to serve, service, good, common, security, [evident lemmatization error], country/land, health
Topic 5	n = 49	Child, municipality, service, family, work/labor, youth, education, to be able, opportunity, culture

Explanation: The words in the word lists are English translations of Finnish words. More than one possible translation is indicated where necessary. Each n for each sub-period indicates the number of manifestos during this period. Each n for each topic during each period indicates the number of manifestos in which the topic is the highest-probability topic. The low number of two for evident lemmatization errors was deemed to be bearable. In the few additional cases in which lemmatization had not been able to return the word in its basic form, this basic form was anyway used as the basis of the interpretation.

Probing Hypothesis 1 on resilient issues does not require more than the selective interpretation and labeling of the twenty-five topics. It is indeed seen as enough to give examples of such issues, and if necessary support the examples with evidence on societal and political transformations in Finland during the study period. Caution is advisable concerning the results where n, the number of manifestos in which a topic indicated, is less than 5.

Questions of Swedishness comprised issues only in the first sub-period from 1880 to 1917 (Topic 2, Topic 4). Soon after Finland's independence, the predominance of the Finnish language was solidly established, and the rights of the Swedish-speakers were given constitutional and other legal guarantees [40]. Issue-raising from the viewpoint of class-conscious organized labor is strongly visible only in Topic 5 and only in three manifestos in the sub-period from 1918 to 1944. Industrial policies comprised a leading issue in a topic only in the 1945 to 1966 period (Topic 3; [43]) although only in three manifestos. Finally, European issues have received emphasis only in the last sub-period, from 1996 to 2012, which has happened in quite a number of manifestos (the highest-probability Topic 1; [44]).

There has been no dearth of resilient issues in the manifestos transcending one or more of the critical junctures of 1917, 1944, 1966, and 1995. Issues of rural development, land reform and farming were present during the first two sub-periods (Topic 3 in both sub-periods; [10, 29]). Issues of law/justice were present in the first sub-period (Topic 1), the 1918 to 1944 sub-period (Topic 1 and Topic 4), and in the 1995 to 2012 sub-period (Topic 2). Issues of services can be found during the 1967 to 1995 period (Topic 2) and the 1996 to 2012 period (Topic 4 and Topic 5). Issues emphasizing work and labor extend through all sub-periods (Topic 5 in the first sub-period, Topic 3 in the second, Topic 1 and Topic 4 in the third, Topics 2, 3, and 5 in the fourth, and Topics 3, 4, and 5 in the fifth sub-period). Issues of municipalities have also been resilient throughout all sub-periods (Topics 2, 3, and 4 in the first, Topic 3 in the second, Topics 1 and 4 in the third, Topic 2 in the fourth, and Topics 3 to 5 in the fifth sub-period [53]).

Evidence thus indicates that resilient issues have been amply present in party manifestos in Finland. Hypothesis 1 can be sustained.

4.2 Probing Hypothesis 2 on Changes in Meanings of Words Constituting Issues in Party Manifestos

The resilient issues in the party manifestos form the empirical basis for probing Hypothesis 2. In the sub-period 1880 to 1917, constituent co-words of a salient issue included both words referring to tenant farmers cultivating land against rents paid to landowners, and words referring to the substantive landless rural population without permanent dwellings of those days (Topic 3, see Table 1). In the sub-period from 1918 to 1944 and in another topic, words referring to farming coexisted with words referring to the acquisition of land by the previous tenant farmers and other previously landless rural dwellers in the course of land reform policies, policies of rural settlement, and development policies aiming towards higher agricultural productivity (Topic 3; [29]).

In the first sub-period from 1880 to 1917, the word meaning 'law/justice' co-existed with other words such as 'the state and law/act', first and foremost indicating a salient issue of concerns with law and order (Topic 1, see Table 1). In the sub-period from 1918 to 1944, law/justice co-existed with words of the economic vocabulary, indicating an issue concerned with the distribution of income and wealth (Topic 2), and with words such as 'the people', 'the state', and 'the citizen', indicating an issue of justice and civil freedoms (Topic 4). After an interval of two sub-periods, in the 1996 to 2012 sub-period law/justice appears again, but now co-existing with words such as 'common', 'society', and 'the human being', indicating an issue of social justice in a welfare state guaranteeing social and economic rights to the citizens (Topic 2; [36]).

The Finnish word for 'service' has received particular emphasis in the two latest sub-periods in the party manifestos. From 1967 to 1995, this word co-existed with such words as 'the municipality', 'work/labor' and the 'child', together indicating a salient issue of municipal welfare service provision to enable the gainful employment of both male and female adults including those with children (Topic 2, see Table 1). From 1996 to 2012, besides words found in the preceding period, the co-words of 'service' included such words as 'family', 'education', 'youth' and 'culture' (Topic 5), indicating an issue of an ever-extending provision of welfare state services by the municipalities [4, 5, 38, 47, 54].

The trajectory of the word for 'work/labor' includes its co-existence with words referring to the municipalities, workers, and help and support activities from 1880 to 1917, indicating a specific salient issue of those days (Topic 5, see Table 1). From 1918 to 1944, 'work/labor' co-exists in two foremost co-word contexts of specific salient issues, namely with words referring to land reform, rural settlement policies and farming on the other hand (Topic 3, see Table 1), and on the other with the word law/justice (Topic 4; [30, 41]). From 1945 to 1966, newly arisen co-words for work/labor include the word for economy during a period during which collective bargaining arose step by step into a major salient political issue in Finland (Topic 1; [17]). During the same period, work/labor also coexisted with such words as 'the municipality', 'municipal', and 'action', indicating an issue of another kind (Topic 4). From 1967 to 1995, co-words of work/labor came to include 'the child', 'dwelling', and 'service', indicating a salient issue of the coordination of collective bargaining and the municipal provision of welfare state services (Topic 2; [18]). From 1996 to 2012, work/labor was present in no fewer than three co-word contexts of salient issues, meaning an economic policy context (Topic 3), a municipal welfare services context with an emphasis on basic social security and health (Topic 4), and another municipal welfare services context with focus on the family, education, the youth, and culture (Topic 5; [31, 38]).

The co-word contexts of the noun 'municipality' and the adjective 'municipal' have changed profoundly during the study period. 1880 to 1917 salient issues included introducing democracy in a local government dominated by the largest taxpayers and landowners until the final year of this period (Topic 2, see Table 1), and municipal roles in relieving problems of tenant farmers, the landless population (Topic 4), and the working class (Topic 5; [29]). In the next sub-period extending to 1944, the second from among the above issues was present in a moderated form after a land reform and other related policies had taken affect (Topic 3). From 1945 to 1966, an issue that stood out included the word for dwelling as one of its constituent words, referring to measures towards aspiring home-builders and home-buyers and towards providing for rental housing

(Topic 4; [52]). The sub-period from 1967 to 1995 added relatively little to the picture of the previous sub-period (Topic 2), whereas the 1996 to 2012 sub-period included the issue of completing the welfare state by means of the municipal provision for basic social security and health (Topic 4) and for child care and other services for families, education services, services for the youth, and cultural services (Topic 5).

Even after major societal and political transformations in Finland, there are words that preserve their original meaning by and large. Moreover, words that used to have a specific historical meaning should be allowed to preserve this meaning in research. However, there are also words whose empirical referents have been pronouncedly modified. Let us take for example the Finnish word for 'landowner'. Early, this word predominantly referred to large and medium landowners with tenants although also to the other independent landowners. Since the 1920s the word no more could refer land-owners holdings tenants as such landowners ceased to exist. Moreover, the word referred to the substantially grown numbers of small landowners. Phenomena themselves have also been modified. For a well-representative example, the municipality became an institution of evolved local democracy in Finland in 1917, and since the 1960s it turned into the foremost provider institution of welfare services.

Resilient words whose meanings have changed because of their diffusion to new co-word contexts are many in the Finnish party manifestos. In conclusion, Hypothesis 2 can be sustained.

5   Discussion

The empirical results enable answering the first research question on whether there have been both resilient issues persisting over critical junctures of societal and political trans-formation and more transitory issues without path dependence over these junctures in the Finnish party manifestos. Both kinds of issues could be amply identified.

The results also make it possible to answer the second research question on changes in meanings of constituent words of resilient salient issues in Finnish party manifestos, while the context of these issues has been changing in connection to critical junctures of societal and political historical transformation. Changes could indeed be discerned in the context-influenced meanings of constituent words of salient issues such as those with rural, land, and farming emphases, emphases of law/justice, services, emphases of work/labor, and emphases of the municipalities and the public services.

This study has combined the computational examination of salient issues and issue areas in Finnish party manifestos, and the longitudinal examination of critical junctures and path dependence of salient political issues in Finnish party manifestos during Finland's societal and political history from the 1880s to the 2010s. The interpretatively augmented computational content analysis that was carried out had both a computational component and a historical interpretative component.

The results obtained could hardly have been achieved otherwise, let alone within the available timeframe and without a major historical archival research project. As was indicated at the beginning, this article joins two from among the types of salience studies, meaning the examination of salience in its own right as an indicator of political and policy contents [21], and examining trajectories of salience in a longitudinal way [12, 46]. This study has first and foremost intended to contribute to these two types rather than other types of salience research.

The two theories used for framing and contextualizing the computational content analysis of Finnish party manifestos do not require the downright explanation of the manifesto contents with reference to critical junctures and path dependence. This is because critical junctures and path dependence contextualize rather than determine the textual contents of party manifestos. Moreover, party manifestos and other political party statements comprise a derivative phenomenon of the flux of political and societal historical transformation, which means that these statements are not equal to the actual or expected phenomena themselves that these statements are about. Being political and societal superstructures, party manifestos may have a relative independence in respect to what they are about, including politics, society and their changes that political parties wish to impose. This means that the coupling of these manifestos to what they are about can be expected to be loose or of an intermediate strength rather than tight. A good deal of the relevance of this study to the empirical research field in which it is positioned can be sought from conclusions such as those above.

This study has also more technical implications. Pruning textual data such as the one used in this study before its examination is laborious and error-prone. Even after the manual elimination of lemmatization errors left after processing with a computer program, a minimum of incomplete lemmatizations remaining has to be tolerated. The study process also emphasizes the technical importance of robustness safeguards and replicability checks.

This study has navigated between two extremes. In one direction we find research that is technically too trivial and substantially too specialized to interest an expert in social informatics. In the other direction lies research that is not technically accessible for common researchers in entrenched social science disciplines, or is not experienced to contribute sufficiently to empirical research within such a discipline.

References

1. Ahonen, P.: Institutionalizing big data methods in political and social research. Big Data Soc. **2**(2), 1–12 (2015). https://doi.org/10.1177/2053951715591224
2. Ahonen, P., Nelimarkka, M.: Political issues and issue areas in party manifestos in Finland, 1880s–2010s: a historically contextualized computational content analysis, in finalization (2018)
3. Armingeon, K., Guthmann, K., Weissstanner, D.: Choosing the path of austerity: how policy coalitions influence welfare state retrenchment in periods of fiscal consolidation. West Eur. Polit. **39**(4), 628–647 (2015). https://doi.org/10.1080/01402382.2015.1111072
4. Arnesen, A.-L., Lundahl, L.: Still social and democratic? inclusive education policies in the Nordic welfare states. Scand. J. Educ. Res. **50**(3), 285–300 (2006). https://doi.org/10.1080/00313830600743316
5. Berglund, S., Lindström, U.: The Scandinavian Party System(s). Studentlitteratur, Lund (1978)

6. Blei, D.M., Ng, A.Y., Jordan, M.I.: Latent dirichlet allocation. J. Mach. Learn. Res. **3**, 993–1022 (2003). http://www.jmlr.org/papers/volume3/blei03a/blei03a.pdf. Accessed 27 Apr 2018

7. Blei, D.M.: Probabilistic topic models. Commun. ACM **55**(4), 77–84 (2012). https://doi.org/10.1145/2107736.2107741

8. Budge, I.: Issue emphases, saliency theory and issue ownership: a historical and conceptual analysis. West Eur. Politics. **38**(4), 761–777 (2015). https://doi.org/10.1080/01402382.2015.1039374

9. Budge, I., Fairlie, D.: Explaining and Predicting Elections. George Allen & Unwin, London (1983)

10. Capoccia, G.: Defending democracy: reactions to political extremism in inter-war Europe. Eur. J. Polit. Res. **39**(4), 431–460 (2001)

11. Capoccia, G., Kelemen, R.D.: The study of critical junctures: theory, narrative, and counterfactuals in historical institutionalism. World Polit. **59**(3), 341–369 (2007). https://doi.org/10.1017/S0043887100020852

12. Cowell-Meyers, K.: The contagion effects of the feminist initiative in Sweden: agenda-setting, niche parties and mainstream parties. Scand. Polit. Stud. **40**, 481–493 (2017). https://doi.org/10.1111/1467-9477.12097

13. DiMaggio, P.: Adapting computational text analysis to social science (and vice versa). Big Data Soc. **2**(2), 1–5 (2015). https://doi.org/10.1177/2053951715602908

14. DiMaggio, P., Nag, M., Blei, D.: Exploiting affinities between topic modeling and the sociological perspective on culture: application to newspaper coverage of U.S. government arts funding. Poetics **41**(6), 570–606 (2013). https://doi.org/10.1016/j.poetic.2013.08.004

15. Dolezal, M., Ennser-Jedenastik, L., Müller, W.C., Winkler, A.K.: How parties compete for votes: a test of saliency theory. Eur. J. Polit. Res. **53**(1), 57–76 (2014). https://doi.org/10.1111/1475-6765.12017

16. Dolezal, M., Ennser-Jedenastik, L., Müller, W.C.: Beyond salience and position taking: how political parties communicate through their manifestos. Party Polit. **23**, 240–252 (2016). https://doi.org/10.1177/1354068816678893

17. Elvander, N.: Collective bargaining and incomes policy in the nordic countries: a comparative analysis. Br. J. Ind. Relations **12**(3), 417–437 (1974). https://doi.org/10.1111/j.1467-8543.1974.tb00015.x

18. Esping-Andersen, G.: The Three Worlds of Welfare Capitalism. Polity Press, Oxford (1990)

19. Feinerer, I.: tm – Text Mining (2013). http://tm.r-forge.r-project.org. Accessed 27 Apr 2018

20. Gallagher, M.: Election Indices (2018). https://www.tcd.ie/Political_Science/people/michael_gallagher/ElSystems/Docts/ElectionIndices.pdf. Accessed 27 Apr 2018

21. Garritzmann, J.L., Seng, K.: Party politics and education spending: challenging some common wisdom. J. Eur. Public Policy **23**(4), 510–530 (2016). https://doi.org/10.1080/13501763.2015.1048703

22. Gill, J.: Bayesian Methods: A Social and Behavioral Sciences Approach, 3rd edn. CRC Press, Boca Raton (2015)

23. Grimmer, J., Stewart, B.M.: Text as data: the promise and pitfalls of automatic content analysis methods for political texts. Polit. Anal. **21**(3), 267–297 (2013). https://doi.org/10.1093/pan/mps028

24. Grün, B., Hornik, K.: Topicmodel: Topic Models (2013). https://cran.r-project.org/web/packages/topicmodels/index.html. Accessed 27 Apr 2018

25. Guldi, J., Armitage, D.: The History Manifesto. Cambridge University Press, Cambridge (2015)

26. Hroch, M.: Social Preconditions of National Revival in Europe: A Comparative Analysis of the Social Composition of Patriotic Groups Among the Smaller European Nations. Cambridge University Press, Cambridge (1985)
27. Ihalainen, P.: Between historical semantics and pragmatics: reconstructing past political thought through conceptual history. J. Hist. Pragmatics 7(1), 115–143 (2006). https://doi.org/10.1075/jhp.7.1.06iha
28. Jahn, D.: Conceptualizing left and right in comparative politics: towards a deductive approach. Party Polit. 17(6), 745–765 (2010). https://doi.org/10.1177/1354068810380091
29. Jörgensen, H.: The inter-war land reforms in Estonia, Finland and Bulgaria: a comparative study. Scand. Econ. Hist. Rev. 54(1), 64–97 (2006). https://doi.org/10.1080/03585520600594596
30. Jussila, O., Hentilä, S., Nevakivi, J.: From Grand Duchy to a Modern State: A Political History of Finland Since 1809. Hurst & Co, London (1999)
31. Kivinen, O., Hedman, J., Kaipainen, P.: From elite university to mass higher education: educational expansion, equality of opportunity and returns to university education. Acta Sociol. 50(3), 231–247 (2007). https://doi.org/10.1177/0001699307080929
32. Knutsen, O.: Political Parties and Party Systems. In: Knutsen, O. (ed.) The Nordic Models in Political Science: Challenged, but Still Viable?. Fagbokforlaget, Bergen (2017)
33. König, T., Marbach, M., Osnabrügge, M.: Estimating party positions across countries and time: a dynamic latent variable model for manifesto data. Polit. Anal. 21, 468–491 (2013)
34. Laver, M., Benoit, K., Garry, J.: Extracting policy positions from political texts using words as data. Am. Polit. Sci. Rev. 97(2), 311–332 (2002). https://doi.org/10.1017/S0003055403000698
35. Lieberman, E.S.: Causal inference in historical institutional analysis: a specification of periodization strategies. Comp. Polit. Stud. 34(9), 1011–1035 (2001). https://doi.org/10.1177/0010414001034009003
36. Lister, R.: A Nordic nirvana? gender, citizenship, and social justice in the nordic welfare states. Soc. Polit. Int. Stud. Gender State Soc. 16(2), 242–278 (2009). https://doi.org/10.1093/sp/jxp007
37. Lowe, W., Benoit, K.: Validating estimates of latent traits from textual data using human judgment as a benchmark. Polit. Anal. 21(3), 298–313 (2013). https://doi.org/10.1093/pan/mpt002
38. Määttä, K., Uusiautti, S.: How do the Finnish family policy and early education system support the well-being, happiness, and success of families and children? Early Child Develop. Care. 182(3–4), 291–298 (2012). https://doi.org/10.1080/03004430.2011.646718
39. Mahoney, J.: Path dependence in historical sociology. Theor. Soc. 29(4), 507–548 (2000). https://doi.org/10.1023/A:1007113830879
40. McRae, K.M.: Conflict and Compromise in Multilingual Societies. Wilfred Laurier University Press, Waterloo (1997)
41. Meinander, H.: A History of Finland. Hurst & Co, London (2011)
42. Meyer, T.M., Wagner, M.: Mainstream or niche? vote-seeking incentives and the programmatic strategies of political parties. Comp. Polit. Stud. 46(10), 1246–1272 (2013). https://doi.org/10.1177/0010414013489080
43. Michelsen, K., Kuisma, M.: Nationalism and industrial development in Finland. Bus. Econ. His. 21, 343–353 (1992)
44. Miles, L. (ed.): The European Union and the Nordic Countries. Routl edge, New York (1996)
45. Møller, J.: When one might not see the wood for the trees: the 'historical turn' in democratization studies, critical junctures, and cross-case comparisons. Democratization 20(4), 693–715 (2013). https://doi.org/10.1080/13510347.2012.659023

46. Pennings, P.: An empirical analysis of the europeanization of national party manifestos, 1960–2003. Eur. Union Polit. **7**(2), 257–270 (2006). https://doi.org/10.1177/1465116506063716

47. Pesonen, P., Riihinen, O.: Dynamic Finland: The Political System and the Welfare State. Finnish Literature Society, Helsinki (2004)

48. Petrocik, J.R.: Issue ownership in presidential elections, with a 1980 case study. Am. J. Polit. Sci. **40**(3), 825–850 (1996)

49. Pierson, P.: Increasing returns, path dependence, and the study of politics. Am. Polit. Sci. Rev. **94**(2), 251–267 (2000). https://doi.org/10.2307/2586011

50. POHTIVA: Database of party manifestos published in Finland. Finnish Social Science Data Archive. http://www.fsd.uta.fi/pohtiva. Accessed 15 May 2016

51. Rauh, C.: Communicating supranational governance? The salience of EU affairs in the German Bundestag, 1991–2013. Eur. Union Polit. **16**(1), 116–138 (2015)

52. Ruonavaara, H.: How divergent housing institutions evolve: a comparison of Swedish tenant co-operatives and Finnish shareholders' housing companies. Hous. Theor. Soc. **22**(4), 212–236 (2006). https://doi.org/10.1080/14036090500375373

53. Sellers, J.M., Lidström, A.: Decentralization, local government, and the welfare state. Governance **20**(4), 609–632 (2007). https://doi.org/10.1111/j.1468-0491.2007.00374.x

54. Simola, H.: The Finnish miracle of PISA: historical and sociological remarks on teaching and teacher education. Comp. Educ. **41**(4), 455–470 (2005). https://doi.org/10.1080/03050060500317810

55. Soifer, H.D.: The causal logic of critical junctures. Comp. Polit. Stud. **45**(12), 1572–1597 (2012). https://doi.org/10.1177/0010414012463902

56. Vehviläinen, O.: Finland in the Second World War: Between Germany and Russia. Palgrave Macmillan, Houndmills (2002)

57. Wilkerson, J., Casas, A.: Large-scale computerized text analysis in political science: opportunities and challenges. Ann. Rev. Polit. Sci. **20**, 1–18 (2017). https://doi.org/10.1146/annurev-polisci-052615-025542

Diversity in Online Advertising: A Case Study of 69 Brands on Social Media

Jisun An[(✉)] and Ingmar Weber

Qatar Computing Research Institute, Hamad Bin Khalifa University,
Doha, Qatar
jisun.an@acm.org, iweber@hbku.edu.qa

Abstract. Lack of diversity in advertising is a long-standing problem. Despite growing cultural awareness and missed business opportunities, many minorities remain under- or inappropriately represented in advertising. Previous research has studied how people react to culturally embedded ads, but such work focused mostly on print media or television using lab experiments. In this work, we look at diversity in content posted by 69 U.S. brands on two social media platforms, Instagram and Facebook. Using face detection technology, we infer the gender, race, and age of both the faces in the ads and of the users engaging with ads. Using this dataset, we investigate the following: (1) What type of content brands put out – Is there a lack of diversity?; (2) How does a brand's content diversity compare to its audience diversity – Is any lack of diversity simply a reflection of the audience?; and (3) How does brand diversity relate to user engagement – Do users of a particular demographic engage more if their demographics are represented in a post?

Keywords: Diversity · Gender · Race · Demographics · Advertising
Brand · User engagement · Social media · Instagram · Facebook

1 Introduction

In the early 1960s, the ad world in the US still had a one-size-fits-all strategy: everyone saw the same advertisement, and the advertisement typically represented White people. Since Tom Burrell [20] started working at Wade Advertising Agency in Chicago as the first African American, most companies have realized that, in his words, "If you don't target, you cannot sell.", leading to an increase in diversity of the people depicted in ads. These changes were, however, slow [7], mainly because many businessmen were afraid to lose sales by including African-American models in promotional materials [5]. Even as recent as 2016, Lloyds reported that in the UK, just 19% of people in ads are from minority groups [17].

Due to the continuing under-representation of minority groups, researchers have studied how different ethnic groups perceive culturally embedded ads, i.e., ads with African-American or Asian actors, and whether they are in favor of it or

© Springer Nature Switzerland AG 2018
S. Staab et al. (Eds.): SocInfo 2018, LNCS 11185, pp. 38–53, 2018.
https://doi.org/10.1007/978-3-030-01129-1_3

not. Somewhat surprisingly, the results are mixed. A few studies showed Whites responded similarly or more favorably to ads with non-White models [5,18]; in contrast, other studies showed integrated or all-Black casts in ads may or may not elicit a backlash among some White college students and adults [6]. Several studies showed that, relative to Whites, non-Whites seem to be more aware of and responded more favorably to ethnically resonant ads [8,18]. However, it has been reported that high-income Asians and Hispanics are known to prefer to see Whites in ads [16], and when choosing a doctor, Kenyans prefer to meet European-looking doctors when a condition is a serious matter [19]. These previous studies have mostly been conducted in a lab-experiment settings, and they have focused on ads on TV or in magazines, which are both forms of media with one-way interaction. Since a brand can see the users' responses on social media directly, social media has an advantage when it comes to understanding what role diversity can play in ads.

In this study, we characterize the diversity among ads of top US brands on social media. To this end, after filtering, we analyze 14,303 posts and 850,109 comments relating to 69 U.S. brands on two popular social media platforms: Instagram (IG) and Facebook (FB). We use computer vision to automatically infer the gender, race, and age of faces depicted in ads, and we apply the same technology to the profile pictures of users engaging with the ads.

With this large-scale data set, we answer the following research questions:

1. How much demographic diversity is there in online advertising in the content put out by major brands on social media?
2. How does the demographic diversity in a brand's posts compare to the diversity of their engaging audience?
3. Is there resonance between the demographics depicted in a particular post and the audience engaging with the post?

We observe that most brands over-represent White faces, compared to their users, and that there is a resonance between a post's demographics and the engaging audience.

2   Related Work

Since ads can reinforce or introduce stereotypes, how particular demographic groups are depicted in ads has long been studied. Until the late 90s, the prime-time ads clearly showed distinct racial segregation with Whites appearing in ads for upscale products, beauty products, and home products while people of color appeared in ads for low-cost, low-nutrition products and athletic and sports equipment ads [10]. In another example, Asian Americans are frequently depicted as highly educated, proficient with technology, and affluent [23].

Studies on how viewers react to ethnically resonant ads, i.e., ads including non-White actors, have shown mixed results. One theory, *in-group preference theory*, posits that in-group members on the basis of race will evaluate other in-group members more favorably than out-group members [24]. Indeed, some researches have shown that people identify more with and respond more favorably to ads with same-race models/actors [24,26]. However, a second theory, *polarized appraisal theory*, predicts that out-group members will be evaluated more extremely (positively or negatively) than in-group members [24]. Some studies showed Whites responded similarly or more favorably to ads with non-White models [5,18]. However, other studies showed that ads with non-White models may or may not elicit a backlash among some White [6]. For other races, Appiah *et al.* reports that, compared to ads with White actors, ads with Black actors are more favored by members of all races [2]. Lastly, relative to Whites, non-Whites often were more aware of and responded more favorably to ethnically resonant ads [8,18]. In this work, we extend these theories on how viewers react to ethnically resonant ads to gender and age and examine whether users engage more with ads showing same-gender, same-race, or same-age group actors (i.e., in-group preference theory).

(a) An example brand's post on Instagram (Nike)   (b) An example brand's post on Facebook (Adidas)

Fig. 1. Example posts by brands on Instagram and Facebook with user comments. Personal profile pictures and names are blackened for privacy concerns.

3   Data and Methodology

For this study, we first select a set of brands. Then, we identify their official accounts on both Instagram and Facebook. For those brands with official accounts, we collect all posts (statuses and posts – jointly referred to as posts) published and the comments they received. We then use an existing computer vision tool to analyze the pictures with faces in the brands' posts and the profile pictures of the users engaging with brands and determine their age, gender, and race.

Brands on Social Media. We use two lists of brands on the Web including BrandFinance's Global 500 2016[1] and Interbrand's Best Global Brands 2016[2].

---

[1] http://brandirectory.com/league_tables/table/global-500-2016.

[2] http://interbrand.com/best-brands/best-global-brands/2016.

We choose to use these two lists due to their availability at the time of data collection. We find that at the end of 2017, the list of global brands has not changed significantly compared to the earlier one. We employed the industry classification method used by BrandFinance to keep the sectors that follow a business-to-consumer model, under the assumption that these brands would be more active in using social media for user engagement. We also limit our focus to U.S. based brands that officially appear in at least one of the following two social media: Instagram and Facebook. This results in a list of 132 brands which further could be categorized into 14 sectors. Furthermore, we only select brands with official brand accounts created by the companies, that use the English language for communication.

Instagram. Among the 132 brands, we find 82 brands with official Instagram accounts. We crawl 107,678 posts published by the brands from the creation of the account to November 28, 2017. Figure 1(a) shows an example post by Nike on Instagram with user comments. Then, we collect all 15.84M public comments made on the posts, which include the URLs of the profile pictures of users.

Facebook. We find 98 brands with official Facebook pages. Using Facebook Graph API, we collect 255,935 posts published from the creation of the page to November 15, 2017. Figure 1(b) shows an example post by Adidas on Facebook with user comments. We collect 1.68M comments of the posts together with the author name and ID. Using the author ID, we were able to access their profile images on Facebook. Due to timeout issues with the Graph API, we only obtained a random subset of the comments left on the 256K posts.

Data Cleaning. We focus our analysis on users who comment on posts by these brands and for whom Face++[3] detects a single human face in the profile image. Furthermore, we limit our analysis to (i) brand posts that show a single, human face, (ii) valid demographics, (iii) brands that have a sufficient number of posts showing faces and receiving comments, and (iv) brands where the act of commenting is generally an expression of positive emotion or implicit "liking". Next, we elaborate on these filtering steps.

Single Faces Only. As a first filter, we use Face++ to detect if a post contains a single, human face. Figure 2(a) shows an example of face detection by Face++ based on a post by Nike. For this, only posts with non-video images are considered. Posts where Face++ detects no or multiple faces are discarded. This leaves us with 14,852 posts for Instagram and 17,196 posts for Facebook. As we observed a false positive rate of around 27% for brand posts, e.g., due to cartoon images, such as the face in the Starbucks logo and other face-like patterns, we then manually filter all of the 32,048 posts, leaving us with 11,944 and 14,068 posts with single, human faces for Instagram and Facebook respectively. Note that for the profile pictures of users commenting on the posts, Face++ performs better as profile pictures tend to have a clean headshot, making manual post-filtering unnecessary.

---

[3] https://www.faceplusplus.com/.

(a) Face detection by Face++

(b) Demographic inferring by Face++

Fig. 2. An example of face detection and demographic inference by Face++ with a post by Nike on Instagram. We note that personal profile pictures and names are blackened for privacy concerns; however, we use unobfuscated images for Face++ when inferring the demographics of users.

Valid Demographics. Experiments on the accuracy of Face++ race inference, reported further down, show that the "Asian" category has many false positives. Hence, we limit our analysis to brand posts and user profiles detected as either White or African-American (AF-AM).

Sufficient Posts and Comments. To be able to perform meaningful statistical analysis, we ignore brands that do not have at least 50 posts with single faces, as well as a total of at least 100 distinct users with single face profile pictures commenting on these posts. This filter is applied separately to Instagram and Facebook.

Positive Engagement. By and large, we observe that the act of commenting on a brand's post is an expression of positive emotion toward the brand. However, for airlines and telecommunication providers, a large fraction of comments are negative or complaints. In our manual inspection, we observed that positive comments were often directly connected to the content of the brand's post (e.g., "I love this pumpkin latte!"), whereas negative comments were posted regardless of what the brand's post is about (e.g., "I tried to call the service center several times, but no one answered."). Hence, we exclude airline and telecommunication provider brands from our analysis as we expect different engagement dynamics in these cases.

At the end of this final filtering step, we are left with a total of 69 distinct brands, 40 on Instagram and 46 on Facebook with their 4,877 and 7,426 posts, respectively.

Demographic Inference. To automatically infer the demographics of the faces in the images posted by brands or in the profile pictures by users, we again use Face++, a deep learning-based image analysis tool, to detect faces given an image and to infer demographics of the faces in the image. When a face is detected, the Face++ API returns information, including a gender, an age estimate, and a race (White, African American (AF-AM) and Asian). Figure 2(b) shows an example of demographic inferring by Face++. Face++ returns other facial features such as whether the face is smiling or not and the emotion shown in the face, which could be relating to user engagement. In this study, we focus on the demographics of the faces in the brands' posts. Face++ has been validated and previously used in several lines of research looking at the demographics of Twitter users [1,3,25,30] and of Instagram Users[4]. In a recent comparative analysis, Face++ performed as good as other state-of-the-art tools such as Microsoft Azure Face API [12]. Moreover, Face++ showed more than 90% accuracy in gender and race detection with high-quality images [12].

Accuracy of Face Detection. To examine the accuracy of the demographic inference by Face++ in our setting, we create a crowdsourcing task on Figure Eight, formerly known as CrowdFlower. For each of the images, three workers first tag whether the image includes a single person's face. If a real face appears, they were asked to infer the gender (Female or Male), race (White, AF-AM, or

---

[4] http://selfiecity.net.

Asian), and age group (Minor [<= 17], Middle, Elders [>= 60] of the face. We
limit access to our task to workers living in the US to reduce the cultural differences in inferring the race of a face in the image as a recent study has reported
that the concepts and definitions of race are not uniform between countries [28].
We find that 29% of the images have either no real person's face or multiple faces.
Among the images with a single face, the accuracy of inferring gender and age
group by Face++ is 86.7% and 87.3%, respectively, while for race detection, the
accuracy is lower at 71.5%. 84.22% (77.78%) of the posts with White (AF-AM)
faces are correctly inferred by Face++. However, we find that the accuracy of
the posts with Asian faces is only 21.77% — 60.48% were classified as White by
Face++. Given the results, we decide to consider only the posts with White and
AF-AM faces for this study. We note that only 2.0% (1.4%) of white (AF-AM)
are misclassified as Asian.

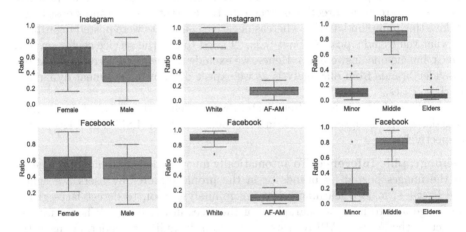

Fig. 3. Demographic distributions by gender, race, and age groups on Instagram and
Facebook. Each box and whisker element summarizes the values across different brands.
Most brands produce roughly gender balanced content, with White (~80%) and 18–60
(~80%) demographics representing the majority of ad images with individual faces.

Users with Faces. We use Face++ to infer the demographics of the faces in
the profile pictures of the users. For this work, we only consider users with a
single, not Asian, face in their profile picture. Furthermore, we focus on users
who leave comments on those 14,303 validated posts, which are 171,179 and
8,841 users for Instagram and Facebook, respectively. Since Face++ performs
well for user profile pictures, which tend to be clean, head-shot, we use the
results by Face++ [12]. On Facebook, we find 48% males and 52% females in
our user dataset. 86.8% of the users are detected as "White" and 13.2% as
"African American (AF-AM)." We group users by their age in three categories:
those with an inferred age below or equal to 17 (denoted as "Minor"), 18 to 60
("Middle"), and over or equal to 60 ("Elders"). The majority group is Middle
which entails 78.4% of users, then Minors with 16%, and Elders with 5.6%.

Compared to FB, Instagram has more female users (60.1%), less white users (85%), more AF-AM (15%), less minors (3.6%), more middle-age users (92.3%), and less elders (4.1%).

Data Ethics. All the data collected comes from publicly accessible data sources. The collected data is securely stored and processed on a password-protected machine. Results are reported for anonymous, aggregate results. All examples of individual-level data, such as comments, are obfuscated, with the exception of posts from brands, featuring professional models.

4   Diversity in Online Ads

We begin by characterizing what faces brands are putting out on their social media. Figure 3 shows gender, race, and age distributions for Instagram and Facebook as boxplots. For Facebook, across all posts with faces, the detected gender is fairly balanced, with 50.6% females. Notably, 89.6% of the users are

Table 1. Top 3 brands for the fraction of each demographic in their posts on Instagram and Facebook. Examples: 81% (79%) of the faces in Under Armour Instagram (Facebook) posts with a single face are males.

Group	Rank	Instagram		Facebook	
		Brand	Ratio	Brand	Ratio
Female	1	Clinique	0.96	Victoria's Secret	0.95
Female	2	Walgreens	0.93	Kohl's	0.84
Female	3	Neutrogena	0.92	Tiffany & Co	0.82
Male	1	Gatorade	0.84	Under Armour	0.79
Male	2	Sprite	0.82	Oracle	0.79
Male	3	Under Armour	0.81	Gillette	0.77
White	1	Ford	1.00	Target	0.99
White	2	Domino	1.00	Victoria's Secret	0.98
White	3	Cisco	0.97	Lowe's	0.98
AF-AM	1	Sprite	0.61	Allstate	0.32
AF-AM	2	Gatorade	0.42	JP Morgan	0.23
AF-AM	3	Google	0.27	McDonald's	0.19
Minor	1	Kroger	0.57	Pampers	0.81
Minor	2	Costco	0.45	Dollar Tree	0.46
Minor	3	Amazon.com	0.35	The Home Depot	0.41
Middle	1	Neutrogena	0.96	Oracle	0.95
Middle	2	Nordstrom	0.95	Uber	0.93
Middle	3	Tiffany & Co	0.94	Xbox	0.93
Elders	1	KFC	0.32	Lowe's	0.09
Elders	2	Whole Foods	0.28	Costco	0.08
Elders	3	Ford	0.28	Kroger	0.07

detected as "White", with 10.4% "African American". The majority age group is middle age (76.8%), followed by minors at 20.5%, and elders at 2.7%. Compared with FB, Instagram has more females (55.3%), less White users (85.6%), more AF-AM users (14.4%), less minors (12.1%), more middle-age users (81.5%), and more elders (6.4%).

Table 1 lists the top three brands ranked by the fraction of faces of a particular demographic attribute in their posts on Instagram and Facebook. Those brands with skewed fraction of a demographic group are ones with a particular target group. For example, cosmetics and sports brands tend to have the highest male or female ratio as they are the one who would consume their product. Ford, for example, has the highest number of White elders models in their posts, revealing their target group. We note that our analysis is based on single-face brand posts.

5   Gap Between Demographics of Ads and Users

Observing predominantly White faces in online advertising could simply be a reflection of the brand's user demographics. Here, we compare the alignment of the demographic distribution in a brand's posts to that of their user base. To this end, we compute the difference between the ratio of a certain demographic group in the ads and that of the engaging users for each brand. A positive value indicates that the corresponding group is over-represented in the ads.

Figure 4 shows the gap between demographics of ads and users for different demographic attributes and by platform. On both Instagram and Facebook, males are over-represented in the brands' ads as the users skew female. Generally, the gender gap is small with a few exceptions, such as Victoria's Secret, which, compared to the many men engaging with the brand, surprisingly over-represents women in their models. On Facebook, AF-AM are under-represented – on average, 10.4% of the posts include AF-AM models, while 13.2% of the FB users are AF-AM. On Instagram, minors and elders are slightly over-represented as Instagram is skewed toward middle-age users. The overall differences across all demographic groups are small.

To look into deeper into the diversity gap of each brand, Table 2 lists the top five brands for the difference of a fraction of each demographic between ads and users. Here, we present a few noteworthy examples.

Several tech companies such as Intel (FB) over-represent female faces. Or, rather, the content they put out is gender balanced but their audience skews toward male. Victoria's Secret (IG), on the other hand, depicts mostly women but attracts many comments from men. Uber (FB) and Paypal (FB, IG) over-represent White faces in their single-face posts, compared to users engaging with the brands. In fact, they do present diverse actors on their social media page. However, White faces are more common in the their images with *single* faces. Sprite and Gatorade (IG) over-represent AF-AM in their posts and many Whites engage.

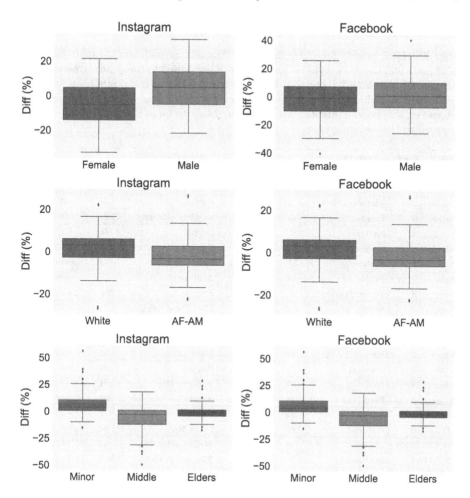

Fig. 4. Difference between the distribution of the demographics of content produced by a brand compared to the users engaging with the brand. Each box and whisker element summarizes the values across different brands. On both Instagram and Facebook, men are over-represented (+1.4% and +5.6%, respectively) compared to a (more female-skewed) user base. AF-AM are under-represented (−2.8% on FB) and the youngest demographics (+4.6% on FB and +8.5% on IG) are over-represented compared to users engaging with the brands.

There are, however, brand-specific outliers with Pampers (IG) most strongly over-representing infants in its posts. Pampers mostly uses infants wearing its products as models for its posts while the engaging users are the Middle group. Another entertaining outlier is KFC (IG), which over-represents the older and White (IG) demographics compared to its user base. The reason is the actor representing a white-haired, white-bearded Colonel Sanders, KFC's figurehead.

Table 2. Top 5 brands for the difference of fraction of each demographic between Brand posts and Users. N(posts) is the number of posts used to compute the percentage difference for each brand. Examples: faces in Victoria's Secret Instagram posts are 18% more female than the (more male) users engaging with the brand. The models used by Pampers on Facebook – infants – are 37% more likely to be in the youngest age group compared to the engaging users.

Group	Rank	Instagram			Facebook		
		Brand	N(posts)	Diff(%)	Brand	N(posts)	Diff(%)
Female	1	Walgreens	101	+21%	Intel	106	+26%
Female	2	Victoria's Secret	532	+18%	Purina	34	+25%
Female	3	Progressive	41	+15%	Victoria's Secret	1443	+21%
Female	4	Pantene	131	+11%	Paypal	71	+19%
Female	5	Google	33	+8%	Domino	55	+16%
Male	1	Starbucks	31	+33%	Sysco	72	+40%
Male	2	Netflix	74	+33%	Allstate	77	+30%
Male	3	Whole Foods	50	+32%	Netflix	216	+24%
Male	4	Sprite	62	+24%	The Home Depot	44	+23%
Male	5	UPS	47	+21%	Subway	67	+20%
White	1	Progressive	41	+22%	Kroger	71	+22%
White	2	Paypal	66	+16%	Uber	60	+17%
White	3	Domino	28	+11%	Paypal	71	+13%
White	4	KFC	37	+11%	Western Digital	91	+11%
White	5	Ford	40	+10%	Target	68	+11%
AF-AM	1	Sprite	62	+27%	Allstate	77	+14%
AF-AM	2	Gatorade	120	+26%	Pizza Hut	63	+12%
AF-AM	3	Costco	38	+11%	McDonald's	31	+8%
AF-AM	4	Starbucks	31	+9%	The North Face	103	+6%
AF-AM	5	Google	33	+8%	The Home Depot	44	+6%
Minor	1	Kroger	84	+56%	Pampers	154	+37%
Minor	2	Costco	38	+39%	Dollar Tree	37	+26%
Minor	3	Amazon.com	23	+30%	Domino	55	+21%
Minor	4	Walmart	93	+30%	Aflac	56	+17%
Minor	5	Target	48	+26%	CVS	68	+17%
Middle	1	Neutrogena	24	+3%	Uber	60	+18%
Middle	2	Electronic Arts	29	+3%	Purina	34	+15%
Middle	3	Nordstrom	212	+1%	Cisco	165	+12%
Middle	4	Victoria's Secret	532	+0%	Intel	106	+11%
Middle	5	Tiffany & Co.	234	−0%	Oracle	210	+10%
Elders	1	KFC	37	+29%	Pizza Hut	63	+5%
Elders	2	Whole Foods	50	+24%	JP Morgan	57	+4%
Elders	3	Ford	40	+21%	Sysco	72	+4%
Elders	4	Netflix	74	+13%	Thermo Fisher Sci.	48	+4%
Elders	5	Starbucks	31	+10%	Lowe's	46	+3%

6   Impact of Gender, Race, and Age on Users' Engagements with Ads

We now turn our focus to how users are *reacting* to the demographics represented in online ads. In particular, we examine whether the users' reactions provide evidence for in-group or out-group preference. We bucket each post by the demographic group it shows, say, a woman. We then compute the fraction of women among the users commenting on the post. This fraction is then compared to the fraction of women commenting on posts that do *not* show a woman (i.e., those that show a man). If showing a woman is linked to observing a higher fraction of women among the engaged users, then we take that as evidence for in-group preference. We then run a two-sided *t*-test on the two sets of values, (a) fractions of the engaged "female" users on posts showing a female model and (b) fractions of the engaged "female" users on posts showing a non-female (e.g., male) to test whether the differences of those fractions are statistically significant. For the age, we use the following two sets of values, (a) fractions of the engaged "minor" users on posts showing a minor and (b) fractions of the engaged "minor" users on posts showing a non-minor (e.g., middle or elders) to run a two-sided *t*-test.

Table 3 shows the mean of (absolute) percentage differences between the two fractions. For all cases shown, group X is linked to a larger fraction of users of group X engaging with the post. For this analysis, we use brands with more than 20 posts having at least 20 face-detected users, resulting in examining 17 brands on Instagram. When using 10 and 15 as a threshold, we find the trends are consistent.

Table 3. In-group Preference Theory test result. Values indicate the mean absolute difference between the engaging user demographics when a post does or does not have the corresponding demographic attribute. For example, for Instagram posts showing a female face, the fraction of female users commenting on this post is 13.3% higher compared to posts not showing a female face (i.e., those showing a male face). For most demographic groups we observe a statistically significant "demographic resonance".

Hypothesis	Female	Male	White	AF-AM	Minor	Middle	Elders
Instagram	+13.3%***	+13.3%***	+4.2%***	+4.2%***	+1.0%***	0.5%	+1.4%***

Significance code: <0.001 ***, <0.01 **, <0.05 *

Our results provide evidence for in-group preference for gender – when the image shows a female/male, female/male users engage more. However, this might be an artifact as this analysis was done *across* brands, and a brand with more female models generally also has a more female user base. Thus, we repeat the analysis *within* each brand, i.e., we look at whether the same brand sees variance in the composition of the engaging users, depending on the demographics of the model in their post.

For four brands, we find statistically significant in-group preferences for gender among the engaging users ($p < 0.05$). For Electronic Arts, Harley Davidson, Polo Ralph Lauren, and Under Armour, female users comment more when posts show a female face (+3.1%, +6.7%, +10.3%, and +6.7%, respectively). Furthermore, we find in-group preference for racial group for the five brands: Michael Kors, Netflix, Polo Ralph Lauren, Victoria's Secret, and YouTube (+2.7%, +5.3%, +14%, +3%, and +2.1%, respectively). We only applied this analysis to binary groups and not to the tertiary age categories. We also note that we do not find any significant cases for out-group preferences (or polarized appraisal theory).

7   Limitations and Discussions

As with any machine inference method, Face++ does occasionally misclassify users. This noise does not, however, generally affect the qualitative conclusions drawn for the following reasons. First, we focus on comparing *relative* differences between distributions, e.g., between the inferred demographics in ad images and in user profiles. Most biases would not affect conclusions of the type "there are more male-looking faces in ads compared to user profiles on Instagram", even if individual faces are misclassified. Second, noisy inference actually *weakens* the results for in-group preference. In the most extreme case of noise, if all demographic labels were assigned independently and at random, it would be impossible to observe, as we do, a systematic link between the demographics in ad images and in the profile images of engaging users. In the future, we plan to correct for this attenuation by modifying the existing methods [27].

For a more focused analysis, we deliberately decided only to consider images with a *single* face. However, it would be interesting to study the engagement with ad images showing several faces, particularly mixed race couples. Occasionally, such images spark an outcry from far-right user groups [21]. We also observed that Uber and Paypal, two brands that over-represent White faces in their single-face posts, have higher levels of diversity in posts with several faces.

All of our analyses only considered the biggest U.S.-based business-to-consumer brands. Such brands are likely to have professional staff highly attuned to potential sensitivities surrounding the representation of minorities. Hence, broadening the scope to include smaller brands might yield different results. Similarly, broadening the scope to include other countries would create a less U.S.-centric view on the topic.

We use the number of comments as a signal for engagement. However, the number of comments is not the same as the number of likes. "Likes" signify how interesting the content is to users, whereas "Comments" quantify the level of discussion on the social media [3]. Thus, our results should not be generalized to the user engagement based on the number of likes. We did, however, remove brands where we observed that commenting was often a sign of *dislike*.

Our current work looks at three important demographic attributes: age, gender, and race. However, the problem of lack of diversity in advertising extends well beyond these three attributes. A case in point is that members of the LGBTQ community are both under- and misrepresented in mainstream advertising [29]. The same holds true for people with disabilities[5]. It might be possible to study some of these issues using similar methods to those used in this work. For example, computer vision could be used to detect wheelchairs or crutches. Similarly, computer vision could detect both a model's and a commenting user's weight status [14] to study if, say, the body shapes of advertising models are representative of the distribution of body shapes in the general population. Prior work looking at the social network structure found evidence for weight-based homophily [15], and one might expect a similar in-group preference for the models used in advertising, where users might be more inclined to engage with an ad that depicts a person with a similar weight status. Computational methods previously developed for the Bechdel Test [9] could potentially also be applied to study the importance members of a particular minority group are given in advertising videos.

Another application of our work beyond traditional advertising is political campaigning. In politics, researchers have studied how the physical appearance of candidates is related to the vote choice and found that attractiveness, familiarity, babyfacedness and age are predictors of vote choice, but after controlling for competence, the effects remained marginal [22]. Our computational approach could expand such studies to understand better how much candidates' physical appearance determines the engagement from the potential voters they attract.

As online advertising is becoming more and more targeted and more and more personalized, it is worth contemplating how recent advances in using computers to generate fake but realistic looking faces will change this industry [13]. For example, would users be more likely to buy a certain product if the model in the ad was a virtual digital twin of themselves? In studies on delayed gratification and how to increase saving behavior, Hershfield et al. observed that people were more likely to accept later monetary rewards when they interact with realistic computer renderings of their future selves [11]. Similarly, showing people a picture of their own aged face under continued exposure to sunlight without adequate protection can increase the use of sunscreen and, potentially, help lower skin cancer rates [4].

8 Conclusion

This paper gives a summary of demographic diversity in online advertising on Instagram and Facebook. Using computer vision to infer the demographics of faces in posts by major brands and in the profile images of users engaging with

---

[5] See https://www.indy100.com/article/disability-adverts-tv-uncomfortable-study-maltesers-wheelchair-8253546 or https://www.campaignlive.co.uk/article/invisibles-why-portrayals-disability-so-rare-advertising/1407945 for two opinion articles on the topic.

these posts, we observe the following. Most brands come close to gender parity in terms of the faces in their posts. However, the majority of faces are White, and only a few older faces are found. Comparing what the brands put out with the demographics of the engaging users, we observe that (i) on both Instagram and Facebook, women are underrepresented in the brands' posts; (ii) on Facebook, White faces are slightly over-represented; and (iii) on both Instagram and Facebook, young faces are slightly over-represented, and middle-age faces are slightly under-represented. There are, however, brand-specific outliers with Pampers most strongly over-representing infants in its posts, whereas KFC over-represents a particular older face – that of Colonel Sanders, the brand's figure-head. Importantly, we provide evidence for resonance between the demographics depicted in a particular post and that of the engaging users. For example, brand posts with an African-American face have, on average, a 4.2% higher percentage of African-Americans among the users engaging with these posts compared to posts without an African-American face.

We believe that our methodology of computationally studying diversity in online advertising could lead to more in-depth analyses, such as sector-specific break-downs or taking the actual content of the comments made by the engaging users into account. It would also be interesting to go beyond single-face images and, in particular, look at the reactions to mixed race images in advertising.

References

1. An, J., Weber, I.: #greysanatomy vs. #yankees: demographics and hashtag use on Twitter. In: ICWSM (2016)
2. Appiah, O.: Black, White, Hispanic, and Asian American adolescents' responses to culturally embedded ads. Howard J. Commun. **12**(1), 29–48 (2001)
3. Bakhshi, S., Shamma, D.A., Gilbert, E.: Faces engage us: photos with faces attract more likes and comments on instagram. In: CHI (2014)
4. Brinker, J.T., Schadendorf, D., Klode, J., Cosgarea, I., Rösch, A., Jansen, P., Stoffels, I., Izar, B.: Photoaging mobile apps as a novel opportunity for melanoma prevention: pilot study. JMIR Mhealth Uhealth **5**(7), e101 (2017)
5. Bush, R.F.: White consumer sales response to black models. J. Mark. **38**(2), 25–29 (1974)
6. Cagley, J.W., Cardozo, R.N.: White response to integrated advertising. J. Advert. Res. **10**(2), 35–39 (1970)
7. Estes, A.C.: Brief History Racist Soft Drinks (2013). https://goo.gl/XvYGD7
8. Forehand, M.R., Deshpandé, R., Reed II, A.: Identity salience and the influence of differential activation of the social self-schema on advertising response. J. Appl. Psychol. **87**(6), 1086–1099 (2002)
9. Garcia, D., Weber, I., Garimella, V.R.K.: Gender asymmetries in reality and fiction: the Bechdel test of social media. In: ICWSM (2014)
10. Henderson, J.J., Baldasty, G.J.: Race, advertising, and prime-time television. Howard J. Commun. **14**(2), 97–112 (2003)
11. Hershfield, H.E., et al.: Increasing saving behavior through age-progressed renderings of the future self. J. Mark. Res. **48**, S23–S37 (2011)

12. Jung, S., An, J., Kwak, H., Salminen, J., Jansen, B.: Assessing the accuracy of four popular face recognition tools for inferring gender, age, and race. In: ICWSM (2018)
13. Karras, T., Aila, T., Laine, S., Lehtinen, J.: Progressive growing of GANs for improved quality, stability, and variation. In: ICLR (2018)
14. Kocabey, E., et al.: Face-to-BMI: using computer vision to infer body mass index on social media. In: ICWSM (2017)
15. Kocabey, E., Ofli, F., Marin, J., Torralba, A., Weber, I.: Using computer vision to study the effects of BMI on online popularity and weight-based homophily. In: SocInfo (2018)
16. Lee, Y.J., Kim, S.: How do racial minority consumers process a model race cue in CSR advertising? A comparison of Asian and White Americans. J. Mark. Commun. 1–21 (2017)
17. Lloyds: Lloyds Diversity Report (2016). https://goo.gl/ehck2D
18. Martin, B.: The influence of ad model ethnicity and self-referencing on attitudes: evidence from New Zealand. J. Advert. **33**(4), 27–37 (2004)
19. Miller, A.N., Kinya, J., Booker, N., Kizito, M., wa Ngula, K.: Kenyan patients attitudes regarding doctor ethnicity and doctor-patient ethnic discordance. Patient Educ. Couns. **82**(2), 201–206 (2011)
20. NPR: This Ad's For You (2015). https://goo.gl/z8jQTB
21. NYTimes: Upbeat Interracial Ad for Old Navy Leads to Backlash. Twice (2016). https://goo.gl/RHkjsS
22. Olivola, C.Y., Todorov, A.: Elected in 100 milliseconds: appearance-based trait inferences and voting. J. Nonverbal Behav. **34**(2), 83–110 (2010)
23. Paek, H., Shah, H.: Racial ideology, model minorities, and the "not-so-silent partner:" stereotyping of Asian Americans in U.S. magazine advertising. Howard J. Commun. **14**(4), 225–243 (2003)
24. Qualls, W.J., Moore, D.J.: Stereotyping effects on consumers' evaluation of advertising: Impact of racial differences between actors and viewers. Psychol. Mark. **7**(2), 135–151 (1990)
25. Reis, J., Kwak, H., An, J., Messias, J., Benevenuto, F.: Demographics of news sharing in the U.S. Twittersphere. In: HT (2017)
26. Sierra, J.J., Hyman, M.R., Torres, I.M.: Using a model's apparent ethnicity to influence viewer responses to print ads: a social identity theory perspective. J. Curr. Issues Res. Advert. **31**(2), 41–66 (2009)
27. Spearman, C.: The proof and measurement of association between two things. Am. J. Psychol. **15**(1), 72–101 (1904)
28. Travassos, C., Williams, D.R.: The concept and measurement of race and their relationship to public health: a review focused on Brazil and the United States. Cadernos de Saúde Pública **20**, 660–678 (2004)
29. Tsai, W.H.S.: Assimilating the queers: representations of lesbians, gay men, bisexual, and transgender people in mainstream advertising. Advert. Soc. Rev. **11**(1) (2010)
30. Zagheni, E., Garimella, V.R.K., Weber, I.: Inferring international and internal migration patterns from twitter data. In: WWW (2014)

Communication Based on Unilateral Preference on Twitter: Internet Luring in Japan

Kimitaka Asatani[1]([✉])(ID), Yasuko Kawahata[2], Fujio Toriumi[1](ID), and Ichiro Sakata[1]

[1] Graduate School of Information Science and Technology,
The University of Tokyo, Hongo, Tokyo 113-8654, Japan
asatani@gmail.com
[2] Gunma University, Aramaki-machi, Maebashi, Gunma 371-8510, Japan
kawahata@si.gunma-u.ac.jp

Abstract. In this paper, we focus on unilateral preference for a group of specific kind of persons as a factor of network formation. Homophily and preferential attachment explain a large part of the formation of online social networks (OSN). Unilateral preference is also assumed to have important roles in OSNs, where high searchability exists with no geographical restriction. To observe unilateral preferences in a social network, we analyzed a user network constructed through interaction between those who make Japanese tweet(s) about "runaway" and those who react to them. In this case, a large proportion of the tweets are assumed to be made by young girls and most of the latter are adult men. By observing the user network, the network is found to have unsurprisingly bipartite structure composed of a thousand former users and several thousand latter users. In spite of a few friendship links among these users, about 19% of users in the latter group take one-to-many communication with users in the former group. Therefore, communications that assumed to be based on unilateral preference exist on a considerable scale. The proportion of reply message between users that regarded to have an intention of luring is surprisingly high (61%). Furthermore, we extract the core of communication by applying k-core network analysis. As a result, the proportion of luring in the core of the network is significantly higher than outside of the k-core network.

Keywords: Internet luring · Social network · Twitter

1 Introduction

Online social networks (OSNs) have no geometrical or temporal restriction and most OSN services also provide search and recommendation functions. Consequently, minority users can mutually connect [1]. Important information and

S. Staab et al. (Eds.): SocInfo 2018, LNCS 11185, pp. 54–66, 2018.
https://doi.org/10.1007/978-3-030-01129-1_4

memes [2] spread in OSNs. However, new risks arise in OSNs, including child pornography [3]. Some people use OSNs as a tool for luring [4] and such criminal activity has been reported worldwide. Last year (August–October 2017), the murderer kidnapped eight young women and one male in only two months using Twitter, 9 of them died in an apartment in Japan turned out [5]. In this case, the suspect found a girl who wants to commit suicide on Twitter. This incident had not been identified until the victim's family investigate her activity on Twitter. This suggests that there will be many risks that have not been apparent in the communication on Twitter. After this crime, tweets about "suicide (in Japanese)" have been officially prohibited by the system. However, other terms used for seeking target persons are not prohibited. Consequently, a lot of luring risks remain on Twitter. We need to explore how such severe communications are addressed on OSNs for preventing risks and for educating young people.

During the past decade, researchers specifically examined structure, growth mechanism [6] and dynamics including information diffusion [7,8] of complex networks. Based on the results of this research, one can predict future links [9], detect communities [10] and identify important persons [11,12] on OSNs. Preferential attachment [6] and homophily [13] are extremely important assumptions underpinning these theories. Preferential attachment is a property by which the number of links attached to a node corresponds to the number of existing links to the node. This property explains the mechanism that some famous people such as Justin Bieber becomes more famous and it results in numerous followers on Twitter. Homophily is a concept by which people who have the same attributes are likely to become friends. This mechanism explains the non-directional highly clustered network structure of a social network. In addition, some local homophily structures exist in the local area of the network. It can be measured by assortative mixing indicator [13,14]. The recent research investigates the information dissemination function and social interaction function of OSN from network structure [15]. Other researchers reveal that people interact about a specific topic in OSN [16] and user interaction in specific interest communities [17]. Some studies reveal that the role of preference in online dating sites [18,19]. However, unilateral preference is not as well researched as the mechanism of network formation.

In OSNs such as Twitter [2], people who have a unilateral preference for a specific kind of person can readily find targets because of the search functions and can approach them without geographical or temporal restrictions. Accordingly, a considerable amount of communication is regarded as based on unilateral preferences. For instance, a person who wants to find a researcher in some field can find and contact them easily. In this case, the Internet enhances the efficiency of our communication. However, in other cases including communication by which men lure young girls, communication efficiency is not always valuable for us. To elucidate and prevent risks on OSNs, many researchers survey risks for minors on OSNs [20–22]. Furthermore, researchers categorize crimes for children [23–25] and investigate the characteristics of criminal [26]. Child abuse is a globally recognized problem against which governments and companies have undertaken many deterrent efforts [27]. Through these studies and activities, individual cases and total risks of OSN are known from the microscopic and macroscopic viewpoints. However, how children and offenders mutually interact and the degree to which risk exists in OSN are still incompletely understood.

In this paper, we analyze the network structure and content of the communication between people who tweet "\#家出(runaway)" and people who react to them and confirm the existence of unilateral preference in the communication. In Japan, "runaway" is used in more serious situations than the English "runaway." People, especially young students, who identify themselves as a runaway must leave their home because of the severe family matter or delinquency. Collected data show that most people who tweet "runaway" are apparently young girls. Most people who react to them are adult men. Using the collected data, we analyze the structure of a user–user networks of communications from aspects of whether the network is formed by unilateral preference. In addition, we investigate the proportion of luring risk existence in the communication. We define risky communications that include messages about inducing an opponent to communicate in private or in the real world. Moreover, we try to detect groups in which risky communications are likely to take a high probability using network analysis.

As a result, the existence of unilateral preference is inferred from the communication network on Twitter. The communication network is bipartite: about 19% of users in the latter group use one-to-many communication with the users in the former group, in spite of the few relationships among users. Accordingly, we assume that unidirectional preferences exist for them. By observing the communication contents, more than half of the tweets are related to luring in the collected data. Results demonstrate that highly active users are more likely to send luring message than others. Additionally, we propose a more efficient method to detect luring tweets that extract the communication core of a communication network extracted using k-core network analysis.

2   Methods

To observe unilateral preferences from the Twitter network, we collect tweets from hashtags related to "\#家出(runaway)" and Replies, Mentions, and Likes of them. "家出" is a Japanese word that means to "runaway from home". The meaning of "家出" does not mean merely to take an excursion from the home but to stop residing there because of a serious family matter or delinquency.

2.1   Network Analysis Between Users

We produce a user–user network from Reply, Like, and Mention reactions to the seed tweets, which contain one or more hashtags as defined in Sect. 3. We also analyze the existence of friendships among network users. Before analysis, we consider what kinds of network structures are presumed to be observed. The network is presumed to have the structure resembling a bipartite graph between the users who make seed tweets and users who react to them, except for cases in which collected user networks are small communities associated with the hashtags. Actually, a bipartite graph structure of a user network does not necessarily indicate the existence of unilateral preferences. For example, considering the hashtag #happy, some people tweet this individually and their friends react to them. In such cases, the detected user network has a bipartite structure, but no unilateral preference to specific kind of person exists.

By contrast, people who have a unilateral preference for a specific kind of person do not react only to their friends: they react to unfamiliar users who appear to have specific attributes. These people can use the Twitter search function to find targets by searching for words indicating a mental condition or some other characteristic. In such cases, people who find a target would be regarded as reacting to more than one target. Accordingly, networks having the three following criteria are created through unilateral preferences.

- The majority consists of two groups of sparse internal communication links. Directed links are drawn unilaterally from one set to the other
- Few mutual friendships (follow–following) exist in the period of communication between users. This point cannot be observed completely because it is difficult to infer a friendship link creation date from the data. Through some links between reaction and target users that are created or deleted after the communication, we can observe the current link by assuming that the friendships are not changed greatly.
- Not a few users have 2 or more out-degrees (linking to the latter multiple users).

To confirm the unilateral preference from the communication network structure based on the hypothesis presented above, we defined three indicators to assess the inter-user communication network. We can infer the existence of unilateral preference when the first indicator (asymmetry of the link A) takes a high value of almost 1, the second indicator density of mutual friendship D_{g_1,g_2} is around zero, and the third indicator (the average number of edges from user R) takes a certain large value.

[asymmetry of the link A]. Users are grouped into a target user set $T = \{u \mid k_u^{in} > 0, k_u^{out} = 0\}$, reaction users $R = \{u \mid k_u^{in} = 0, k_u^{out} > 0\}$, and other users O. Here, k^{in} is the in-degree, and k^{out} represents the out-degree. The asymmetry index of the link is expressed below.

$$A = \frac{N(R) + N(T)}{N(R) + N(T) + N(O)} \tag{1}$$

Density of mutual friendship D_{g_1,g_2}. The density of mutual friendship (follow and following) between group g_1 and g_2.

$$D(g_1, g_2) = \frac{\sum_{x \in g_1, y \in g_2} P(x, y)}{n(g_1) * n(g_2)} \tag{2}$$

The average number of edges from user. R $\bar{k}_R$ is the average number of edges from user R to other users. If $\bar{k}_R$ is higher than 1, some users react to multiple users.

$$\bar{k}_R = N(E_{ij}\{i \in R\})/N(R) \tag{3}$$

2.2 Labeling Luring Reply

In Twitter, reactions of three types can be made to a tweet: Reply, Like, and Mention. A Like reaction is made without text and Mention does not likely to include a message to the person of the original tweet. Therefore, we recognize whether the reaction is luring or not for replies.

People who lure a target use many kinds of words for communication. Distinguishing dangerous communications and others is not easy. Consequently, we only consider whether a communication includes a message about inducing a person to communicate in private or in the real world for judging a message as luring or not. Furthermore, we did not weight the preferences by expression of words. For example, "give me a private message" or "tell me a LINE account (LINE is a widely used private communication tool in Japan)" is regarded as a message inducing someone to visit some private location. In addition to this, "come to my home located in Tokyo" or "Let's meet now" is regarded as being a message inducing someone to do something in the real world.

Based on the rules presented above, three human annotators judge the tweet as luring or not. Tweets judged by more than two annotators as luring tweets are identified as luring tweets. Because of the large size of the dataset, we sampled 300 tweets randomly for each subset of the dataset and judged them as a luring tweet or not.

2.3 Detecting a Subset of Communications Which Includes Luring Reply with a High Probability

For extracting a group of replies in which a high proportion of communication is luring, we propose two simple methods for detecting luring replies.

Tweets from Highly Active Users. We simply assume that tweets from a frequently reacted user R are more likely to be luring tweets than those of other users. Specifically, we collect replies from users who make k or more replies.

Tweets in the Core of Network. In this case, we extract a group of dangerous tweets by observing communication networks. We assume that a typical communication is regarded as made in the core of the network. The core of the communication network is simply extracted using k-core [28] method. The k-core network is the largest sub-graph composed of nodes having k or more degrees. Specifically, tweets between users who belong to k-core (k) of the communication network are extracted.

3   Data

We gather tweets related to each hash (listed in Table 1) tag and all responses (Reply, Mention, Like) made from August 1, 2017, through February 20, 2018. The acquired data consist of 24,773 "runaway"-related tweets from 2,614 people. Hashtags shown in Table 1 are often used together in a tweet. The responses comprise 11,245 Likes, 5,306 Replies, and 894 Mentions from 5,307 people.

Table 1. Hashtags for collecting tweets

Hash tag	Description	Number of tweets collected	Number of unique users
家出	Runaway from home	13,521	1,654
神待ち	"Waiting for supporter" - supporter means person who provides financial or life support	16,279	847
泊めて	Please stay at your home	7,569	992

The characteristics of the people making the collected tweets and responses differ greatly. We estimate that about 74% of the tweets about "runaway" are made by women (apparently young girls) from the gender estimation of sampled 100 users who made tweet(s) about "runaway" by the human annotators. In contrast, most people (94%) of reaction tweets were apparently made by adult men from the estimation of the human annotators. Although those who hide their personage on the net and people who use multiple accounts can be assumed, we assume for this study that such people are few.

4   Results

4.1   Structure of User–User Communication Networks

To elucidate communications between people who tweet related to "runaway" and users who react to them, we analyze the user–user network based on communication. The communication network comprises nodes (users) and edges (reactions). The two-dimensional histogram of out-degree and in-degree is presented in the Left figure of Fig. 1. In this figure, not many users (428 people) have one out-degree or more and one in-degree equal or more. These people are classified into the O (Other) group. Also, 913 users are classified into the T (target) group; 6,780 users are classified into the R (reaction) group. Consequently, the indicator asymmetry of the link is calculated as $A = 0.947$. Accordingly, the network has a structure resembling a bipartite graph.

To investigate how people mutually interact, we observed the degree distribution of T and R groups. The upper right of Fig. 1 shows the in-degree distribution

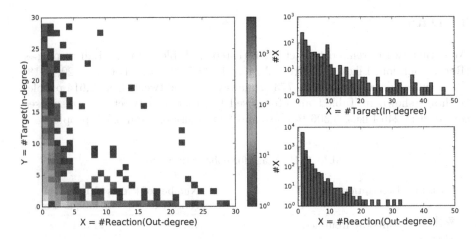

Fig. 1. Left Histogram of out-degrees (horizontal axis) and in-degrees (vertical axis) of the network. **Upper right** distribution of in-degrees in the set T of users. **Lower right** Distribution of out-degrees in the set R of users.

of 913 T users. As this graph shows, many users (659 people) tweeting about "runaway" often receive approaches from multiple people. A plot of the distribution of the out-degrees of 6,780 users of the group R is presented in Fig. 1. We can observe several people (1,324 people) approaching two or more users. The proportion of people who approach multiple targets is 19%. Furthermore, $\bar{k}_R$ (the average number of edges from user R) takes a value of 1.62.

The existence of mutual friendship between users is a possible explanation for several people reacting to multiple targets. To test this hypothesis, we explore the mutual friendship between interested users by examining 3.4% of user pairs because of limitations imposed by restricted access. In Twitter, a mutual friendship is signified by mutual following. We found 106 mutual friendships from the 3.4% sampling and estimate about 3,100 mutual friendships in the total 8,121 users. The mutual friendship density D takes very low values between each community. In addition, the certain amount of unilateral following was found from R group to T groups. However, the opposite relations and mutual friendship are extremely rare between these groups. This result is obtained on the assumption that people extracted from "runaway" tweets have few mutual friendships. R users are presumed to follow T users unilaterally.

Based on analysis of the communication structure and friendship network, we can infer a unilateral preference from R users to T users because several R users react to multiple T users in spite of weak mutual friendship between them. The 19% probability that R users who react to multiple T is apparently not so large, but it seems considerably large if we consider the data collection method: collected data do not cover "runaway" communication. Moreover, the data collection period is limited. The number of T users is almost a thousand. The number of the R user is greater than a thousand if we limit them to those who react to multiple T users, which indicates that communications by unilateral preference are taken between some people. They should not be ignored. In actuality, R users search for targets in Twitter and send messages indiscriminately. They are regarded as a search for a target by the Twitter search function. From the perspective of T users, if a user tweets about "runaway," they receive messages from users who send messages to other users who tweet "runaway."

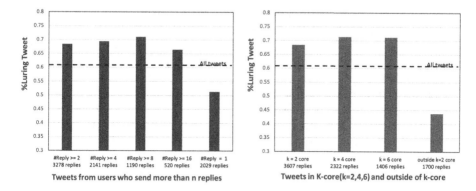

Fig. 2. Left: The proportion of luring tweets by the number of replies. The proportion of luring tweets from people who send x or more (far right bar) replies. The proportion in all tweets (0.610) is shown as a dotted line in this graph. **Right: The proportion of luring tweets from k-core network.** The proportion of luring tweets between people of k-core ($k = 2,4,6$) network and our side of k-core ($k = 2$) network (far right bar).

4.2 Detecting High-Risk Communications

In the detected data, we examined the proportion of luring replies (defined in Sect. 2.2) that can engender luring to a private chat or real–world location. Here, we analyze what kinds of people are likely to lure a person who makes "runaway" tweets or whether the core of the communication network structure represents a danger of luring.

The proportion of luring tweets in all collected replies is almost 61%. This proportion is surprisingly very high. For example, the adult man replies "come to my home in Tokyo" to a girl's tweet "I'm 17 and a high school student. I want to run away from home." Other adult men reply simply "Please message me directly." Non-luring Tweets are usually banter or expressions of concern from the person who tweets. However, some of these tweets might be sent in the pursuit of luring. Results show that surprisingly a large proportion of tweets about "runaway" are triggers for luring.

Highly Active Users. To investigate what kind of person makes luring replies, we simply observe the relationship between the number of replies and the proportion of luring tweets. We first investigate the relationships between a person's number of replies and the ratio of luring tweets. The left panel of Fig. 3 shows that the proportion of luring from people who send many replies is higher than others, which indicates that the person who is very active in this field represents a danger for luring.

Central Core of the User Network. The communication network of all tweets is complex, as shown in the left panel in Fig. 3. Some local clusters created by many-to-one communication exist in the network. Almost all user on K-core networks have K incoming/outgoing links because few users have both incoming/outgoing links as shown in Fig. 1. Therefore, we use K-core detection for extracting users who lure or are lured. The k-core part is yellow ($k = 2$) and red ($k = 6$) in Fig. 3. The network of K–6 is presented in Fig. 3. In this figure, the user has high in-degree in the center (they receive multiple reactions to the tweet). The user has a zero in-degree in the peripheral part. Consequently, the k-core ($k = 6$) of the communication network is almost a bipartite structure. The user located in the peripheral part sends messages to multiple users in the central part. By reading the profile or tweet of each user, most of the former users are assumed to be men and most of the latter are young girls.

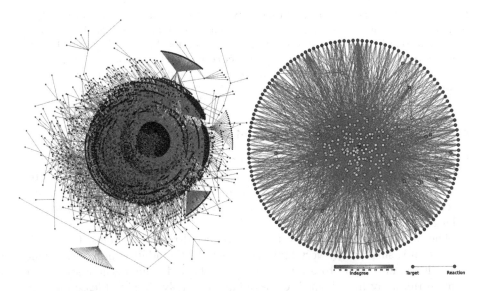

Fig. 3. Left: The largest connected component of user network The k-core part is yellow ($k = 2$) and red ($k = 6$). **Right: k-core ($k = 6$) network of communication** A user-to-user network is based on the "runaway" tweets. Only the k-core part of $k = 6$ is drawn. The edge on the target node side is thick: the higher the in-degree of the node, the brighter its color. (Color figure online)

We investigate whether the danger communication likely to exist in the core of the network. We show the ratio of luring tweets of the k-core network ($k = 2.6$) and outside the k-core ($k = 2$) in the right panel of Fig. 2. The proportions of luring tweets in the k-core network ($k = 2, 4, 6$) are equal to or higher than that of the high active user's (left panel of Fig. 2). The difference of proportion of luring between k-core network ($k = 2$) and outside of the core is significantly high. This indicates that the k-core analysis is very for detecting dangerous communications rather than detecting users who frequently send replies. It is interesting that the proportion of luring tweets in the condition of $k = 4, 6$ is not different much. Contents of some replies from $k = 4, 6$, which is not regarded as luring, are very kind asking about the status of a girl (i.e. "are you OK?"). More detailed analysis of the contents of tweets must be conducted by reading the contents of tweets between target and reaction users. A human annotator or some NLP method must probably be applied for such analyses.

5   Discussion

By observing the conversation network related to "runaway," we confirmed the unilateral preference from a group that consists of girls (inferred from contents and profiles) to a group that of adult men (inferred from contents and profiles) on Twitter. Friendship links and conversations inside the group were rare: there were many one-to-many links to the former group from latter group. Consequently, a person of the latter group is assumed to have unilateral preferences to the former group. Furthermore, the number of users of each set was 1,000 or more. Therefore, communications based on unilateral preference probably exist on a scale that cannot be ignored when discussing communications on a social network.

In addition to the communication structure, we observed the communication contents and asked annotators to ascertain whether communications are luring. Almost half of the communications in the extracted communications were judged to have an intention of luring. That probability is surprisingly high considering the simple method of data collection. The communication becomes even more dangerous as the user sends many replies. Moreover, the network approach, which detects the core of a communication network, more efficiently detects luring tweets than simply observing communication frequency. Almost 71% of tweets are presumed to have the intention of luring. We infer that this network approach is efficient for detecting risky communications based on other sets of hashtags.

Additionally, the existence of thousands of people who want to run away and thousands who want to invite them underscores the magnitude of invitation risk on Twitter. Among the invitations, many factors induced communication with the direct message (DM) at a frequency close to that of a person being directly called to a specific place. It is possible to set DM as OFF with the user's authority or prohibit only DMs from people other than followers. If the invited user permits DMs from any user, then it is considered that DMs can be exchanged beyond public view. Although this DM discussion is beyond the scope of this analysis, exchanges done in that mode must be analyzed. For the present study, we detected dangerous interactions visible on Twitter, but Twitter use presents additional dangers. After the Zama incident [5] in Japan described earlier, tweets related to "suicide" have been officially prohibited by the system. However, a trend similar to that examined in this study is being observed by changing the expressions of words suggesting "suicide (in Japanese)," thereby circumventing the restrictions.

In this study, communications based on unilateral preferences were detected using a "runaway"-related hashtag as a seed. Aside from "runaway" tweets, the network contracted using "suicide" tweet is presumed to have a similar structure. However, we do not know the dangerous keywords comprehensively. Therefore, finding such unilateral preferences from the network structure is important to detect risky communications. Future studies must develop a method to discover a subset in which communications based on unilateral preference exist only from the network structure.

6 Conclusions

In this paper, we confirm the existence of unilateral preference from adult men to people who tweets about "runaway" by analysis of communication network. About 60% of tweets between them have the intention of luring. This result is important for considering and teaching risks in OSN. In the aspect of network science, we consider that unilateral preference should be taken into account as a motive of a member of the network. Further studies are needed to confirm the existence of a local structure based on unilateral preference and to analyze the impact of unilateral preferences on the global structure of the network.

References

1. Hampton, K.N.: Internet use and the concentration of disadvantage: glocalization and the urban underclass. Am. Behav. Sci. **53**(8), 1111–1132 (2010)
2. Kwak, H., Lee, C., Park, H., Moon, S.: What is Twitter, a social network or a news media? In: Proceedings of the 19th International Conference on World Wide Web, pp. 591–600. ACM (2010)
3. O'Keeffe, G.S., Clarke-Pearson, K.: The impact of social media on children, adolescents, and families. Pediatrics **127**(4), 800–804 (2011)
4. Cheng, J., Danescu-Niculescu-Mizil, C., Leskovec, J.: Antisocial behavior in online discussion communities. In: ICWSM, pp. 61–70 (2015)
5. Griffiths, C.K.J.: Japanese man arrested after body parts found in cooler. CNN (2017)
6. Albert, R., Barabási, A.L.: Statistical mechanics of complex networks. Rev. Mod. Phys. **74**(1), 47 (2002)
7. Pastor-Satorras, R., Castellano, C., Van Mieghem, P., Vespignani, A.: Epidemic processes in complex networks. Rev. Mod. Phys. **87**(3), 925 (2015)

8. Guille, A., Hacid, H., Favre, C., Zighed, D.A.: Information diffusion in online social networks: a survey. ACM SIGMOD Rec. **42**(2), 17–28 (2013)
9. Wang, P., Xu, B., Wu, Y., Zhou, X.: Link prediction in social networks: the state-of-the-art. Sci. China Inf. Sci. **58**(1), 1–38 (2015)
10. Xie, J., Kelley, S., Szymanski, B.K.: Overlapping community detection in networks: the state-of-the-art and comparative study. ACM Comput. Surv. (CSUR) **45**(4), 43 (2013)
11. Kempe, D., Kleinberg, J., Tardos, É.: Maximizing the spread of influence through a social network. In: Proceedings of the Ninth ACM SIGKDD International Conference on Knowledge Discovery and Data Mining, pp. 137–146. ACM (2003)
12. Liu, Y., Tang, M., Zhou, T., Do, Y.: Core-like groups result in invalidation of identifying super-spreader by k-shell decomposition. Sci. Rep. **5**, 9602 (2015)
13. Newman, M.E.: Assortative mixing in networks. Phys. Rev. Lett. **89**(20), 208701 (2002)
14. Lee, S.: Effect of online dating on assortative mating: evidence from south korea. J. Appl. Econ. **31**(6), 1120–1139 (2016)
15. Myers, S.A., Sharma, A., Gupta, P., Lin, J.: Information network or social network?: the structure of the twitter follow graph. In: Proceedings of the 23rd International Conference on World Wide Web, pp. 493–498. ACM (2014)
16. Doughty, M., Rowland, D., Lawson, S.: Who is on your sofa?: TV audience communities and second screening social networks. In: Proceedings of the 10th European Conference on Interactive TV and Video, pp. 79–86. ACM (2012)
17. Beguerisse-Díaz, M., Garduno-Hernández, G., Vangelov, B., Yaliraki, S.N., Barahona, M.: Interest communities and flow roles in directed networks: the Twitter network of the UK riots. J. Royal Soc. Interface **11**(101), 20140940 (2014)
18. Hitsch, G.J., Hortaçsu, A., Ariely, D.: Matching and sorting in online dating. Am. Econ. Rev. **100**(1), 130–63 (2010)
19. Curington, C.V., Lin, K.H., Lundquist, J.H.: Positioning multiraciality in cyberspace: treatment of multiracial daters in an online dating website. Am. Sociol. Rev. **80**(4), 764–788 (2015)
20. Mascheroni, G., Ólafsson, K.: Net Children Go Mobile: Risks and Opportunities. Educatt, Milano (2014)
21. Livingstone, S., Haddon, L., Görzig, A., Ólafsson, K.: Risks and safety on the internet: the perspective of European children: full findings and policy implications from the EU kids online survey of 9–16 year olds and their parents in 25 countries. EU Kids Online (2011)
22. DeHart, D., et al.: Internet sexual solicitation of children: a proposed typology of offenders based on their chats, e-mails, and social network posts. J. Sex. Aggression **23**(1), 77–89 (2017)
23. Ortega, E.G., Baz, B.O.: Minors' exposure to online pornography: prevalence, motivations, contents and effects. (la exposición de los menores a la pornografía en internet: prevalencia, motivaciones, contenidos y efectos). Anales de Psicología/Annals of Psychol. **29**(2), 319–327 (2013)
24. Tener, D., Wolak, J., Finkelhor, D.: A typology of offenders who use online communications to commit sex crimes against minors. J. Aggression Maltreatment Trauma **24**(3), 319–337 (2015)
25. Babchishin, K.M., Hanson, R.K., VanZuylen, H.: Online child pornography offenders are different: a meta-analysis of the characteristics of online and offline sex offenders against children. Arch. Sex. Behav. **44**(1), 45–66 (2015)

26. Magaletta, P.R., Faust, E., Bickart, W., McLearen, A.M.: Exploring clinical and personality characteristics of adult male internet-only child pornography offenders. Int. J. Offender Therapy Comp. Criminol. **58**(2), 137–153 (2014)
27. Steel, C.M.: Web-based child pornography: the global impact of deterrence efforts and its consumption on mobile platforms. Child Abuse Negl. **44**, 150–158 (2015)
28. Seidman, S.B.: Network structure and minimum degree. Soc. Netw. **5**(3), 269–287 (1983)

Estimating Group Properties in Online Social Networks with a Classifier

George Berry[1]([✉]) [ID], Antonio Sirianni[1] [ID], Nathan High[1], Agrippa Kellum[1],
Ingmar Weber[2] [ID], and Michael Macy[1]

[1] Cornell University, Ithaca, NY, USA
{geb97,ads334,nmh53,ask252,mwm14}@cornell.edu
[2] Qatar Computing Research Institute, Doha, Qatar
iweber@hbku.edu.qa

Abstract. We consider the problem of obtaining unbiased estimates of group properties in social networks when using a classifier for node labels. Inference for this problem is complicated by two factors: the network is not known and must be crawled, and even high-performance classifiers provide biased estimates of group proportions. We propose and evaluate AdjustedWalk for addressing this problem. This is a three step procedure which entails: (1) walking the graph starting from an arbitrary node; (2) learning a classifier on the nodes in the walk; and (3) applying a post-hoc adjustment to classification labels. The walk step provides the information necessary to make inferences over the nodes and edges, while the adjustment step corrects for classifier bias in estimating group proportions. This process provides de-biased estimates at the cost of additional variance. We evaluate AdjustedWalk on four tasks: the proportion of nodes belonging to a minority group, the proportion of the minority group among high degree nodes, the proportion of within-group edges, and Coleman's homophily index. Simulated and empirical graphs show that this procedure performs well compared to optimal baselines in a variety of circumstances, while indicating that variance increases can be large for low-recall classifiers.

Keywords: Classification error · Quantification learning
Network sampling · Digital demography

1 Introduction

When seeking to understand social interaction online, researchers are commonly faced with a paradox: online data is behaviorally rich but lacks even basic demo-

The authors thank members of the Social Dynamics Laboratory and anonymous reviewers for their helpful suggestions. The authors were supported while this research was conducted by grants from the U.S. National Science Foundation (SES 1357488), the National Research Foundation of Korea (NRF-2016S1A3A2925033), the Minerva Initiative (FA9550-15-1-0162), and DARPA (NGS2). The funders had no role in study design, data collection and analysis, decision to publish or preparation of the manuscript.

S. Staab et al. (Eds.): SocInfo 2018, LNCS 11185, pp. 67–85, 2018.
https://doi.org/10.1007/978-3-030-01129-1_5

graphic annotation. The lack of demographic information frustrates seemingly straightforward questions: for instance, what is the gender breakdown on an online platform? Since many important social science questions require demographic data, classifiers are commonly used to predict node-level attributes such as gender [3,8,24,31], education [7], age [29], race [27,28], income [5,25], or political affiliation [1,2]. However, classifiers introduce error which can bias estimates of group properties, from demographic distributions to cultural homophily.

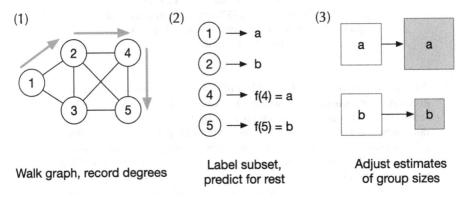

Fig. 1. A demonstration of the steps in the AdjustedWalk process. First, the graph is randomly walked and node degrees are recorded. Second, a subset of the walked nodes are given ground-truth labels (nodes 1 and 2) and a machine learning model is used to predict for the remaining nodes in the sample (nodes 4 and 5). Third, the mean of the relevant quantity (e.g. proportion in b) is estimated using the RWRW estimator and then adjusted to remove bias.

Adding to the challenge posed by limited demographic information, studies often rely on convenience samples of the underlying social network. The combination of classification error and non-representative sampling poses substantial challenges for obtaining valid estimates of group properties.

We propose a framework, which we term AdjustedWalk, to address these dual problems in order to obtain unbiased estimates of group properties in networks. The idea is to combine re-weighted random walk sampling (also called respondent driven sampling) [13,35] with quantification learning [9,10]. The sampling method provides the information necessary for inference over nodes and edges. A subset of the nodes is labeled and classified, and a post-hoc correction is applied to correct for classification bias at the group level.

We assume that the sampling procedure starts with an arbitrary node in an undirected graph, and that node labels are predicted by a possibly biased classifier with a known error rate. We show that the framework proposed performs well relative to baselines in four estimation tasks: group proportions, within-group edge proportions, group visibility (the proportion of the minority group in the top 20% of the degree distribution) [20], and Coleman's homophily index [4].

The problem we study has three parts: drawing a representative sample from a network, building a classifier to predict node attributes, and correcting classification error to obtain unbiased estimates of group proportions. Many previous studies have examined each of these parts individually. Research on applications of respondent driven sampling (RDS) to online social networks has provided a robust toolkit for sampling online social networks when demographics are freely available from the site itself [13–16,35]. On the other hand, many studies have addressed the task of predicting demographics with high observation-level accuracy, with less attention paid to the representativeness of the sample or group-level estimates [1–3,5–8,17,24,25,27,29,37,40]. Finally, a literature on quantification learning [9–11] has addressed the problem of using a classifier to make population inferences. We demonstrate that combining these separate literatures allows social scientists to make better inferences about social groups in online social networks. This has applications for digital demography and can be useful for online-offline comparisons of social interaction, homophily, and representation [20].

1.1   Summary of Contributions

- This paper proposes AdjustedWalk, a framework for estimating group properties in online networks when neither the network nor group labels are known in advance. It contains the following steps: (1) a re-weighted random walk (RWRW) of the graph; (2) training a classifier by labeling a subset of the nodes walked; (3) adjusting group-level error introduced by the classifier to remove bias. The process is visualized in Fig. 1. Importantly, walking the graph before labeling and classification makes it more likely that population-level inferences will be valid.
- The performance of RWRW sampling is compared to three other plausible sampling procedures: node sampling, edge sampling, and snowball sampling [39]. RWRW performs well relative to the optimal sampling method for each task, and performs only slightly worse than node sampling overall despite the absence of a sampling frame.
- An analytical expression for the increased variance of the adjusted estimate is provided, which can be expressed as a function of classifier recall.
- AdjustedWalk is evaluated in a variety of conditions. We examine both simulated and empirical graphs, across a range of sampling fractions and classification accuracies. These analyses demonstrate that relatively small samples perform quite well. When considering classification accuracy, recall scores greater than 0.8 produce reasonable estimates, while recall scores lower than 0.8 quickly increase variance.
- We discuss the conditions under which the results presented here apply to directed graphs in addition to undirected ones.

2 Problem Setup

2.1 Graph and Groups

We sample from a graph $G = (V, E)$, where V indicates vertices and E indicates edges. N is the number of nodes in G. Call a node i and an edge from i to j e_{ij}. Let d_i be the degree of i, $D = \sum_i d_i$ the total degree of the graph, and $\bar{d} = D/N$ the average degree of the graph. We assume G is undirected, so that $e_{ij} \in E \implies e_{ji} \in E$. We also assume there are no self links or multi-edges, that the graph has at least one triangle, that G is connected, and that all edges have weight 1.

Nodes belong to one of two *social groups*, denoted a and b. By convention, b is the minority group. These groups represent characteristics of individuals such as age, race, ethnicity, gender, or wealth status. p_a is the proportion of nodes belonging to group a, and $\mathbf{p} = (p_a, p_b)$ is the vector of *population proportions*. Since $p_a + p_b = 1$, we will frequently reason about one group with the implication that the same analysis holds for the other one. s_{ab} is the proportion of edges from group a to group b, with $\mathbf{s} = (s_{aa}, s_{ab}, s_{bb})$ the vector of *edge proportions*. Since the graph is undirected, s_{ab} represents all edges with one end in a and the other in b.

When a classifier is used to categorize nodes, we do not observe $\mathbf{p}$ or $\mathbf{s}$ directly. We instead obtain estimates of these quantities after classification error. $\mathbf{m} = (m_a, m_b)$ is $\mathbf{p}$ after classification error, and $\mathbf{t} = (t_{aa}, t_{ab}, t_{bb})$ is $\mathbf{s}$ after classification error. We use hat notation (e.g. $\hat{\mathbf{m}}$) for estimates resulting from sampling part of the graph and then classifying the sampled nodes.

2.2 Classification for Quantification

Assume we have a relationship between a set of features x_i and an outcome $y_i \in \{a, b\}, y_i = f(x_i)$. A classifier approximates f, $y_i = \hat{f}(x_i) + \epsilon_i$. The model $\hat{f}$ makes classification errors, which are counted and stored in a confusion matrix

$$F = \begin{bmatrix} \text{count}(\hat{a} \mid a) & \text{count}(\hat{a} \mid b) \\ \text{count}(\hat{b} \mid a) & \text{count}(\hat{b} \mid b) \end{bmatrix}.$$

We use the notation $(\hat{b} \mid a)$ to represent "a true member of a classified as a member b". We will work with the column-stochastic *misclassification matrix*, which we get by column-normalizing $\hat{f}$,

$$C = \begin{bmatrix} c_{\hat{a}|a} & c_{\hat{a}|b} \\ c_{\hat{b}|a} & c_{\hat{b}|b} \end{bmatrix},$$

where $c_{\hat{b}|a} = \text{count}(\hat{b} \mid a)/\text{count}(\hat{a} \mid a) + \text{count}(\hat{b} \mid a))$ represents the probability of a true member of a being classified as b. In practice $\hat{f}$ and C are constructed via cross-validation and holdout sets.

The matrix C is important for removing bias from estimates. We refer to the off-diagonal elements of C as the "misclassification rate", and note that the diagonals are equivalent to both recall and accuracy. Precision depends on the relative sizes of groups. The misclassification rate represents the probability that a true member of group a is classified as b, and vice versa.

If C is known and only $\mathbf{m}$ is observed, $\mathbf{p}$ can be recovered. C maps $\mathbf{p}$ to $\mathbf{m}$,

$$\begin{bmatrix} c_{\hat{a}|a} & c_{\hat{a}|b} \\ c_{\hat{b}|a} & c_{\hat{b}|b} \end{bmatrix} \begin{bmatrix} p_a \\ p_b \end{bmatrix} = \begin{bmatrix} m_a \\ m_b \end{bmatrix},$$

which can be written compactly as

$$C\mathbf{p} = \mathbf{m}. \tag{1}$$

This implies that inverting C provides a way to recover the true population proportions $\mathbf{p}$,

$$\mathbf{p} = C^{-1}\mathbf{m}. \tag{2}$$

This procedure is referred to as "adjusted classify and count" in the machine learning literature on *quantification* [9,10], or recovering population proportions. In general, even high performance classifiers produce biased estimates of group proportions [11], particularly for small groups. While group proportions may be both over- and under-estimated, classifiers tend to favor larger groups since loss functions are optimized at the observation level. This means that the size of large groups is often overstated by classifier predictions. Models which directly try to estimate group proportions [11] usually under-perform models trained at the observation level and then corrected as in Eq. 2.

For quantification, an important assumption is required for inference to be valid from the individual to group level [10].

Assumption 1. *Stable conditional feature distribution*

$$P_{train}(X = x_i | Y = y_i) = P_{population}(X = x_i | Y = y_i) \tag{3}$$

Assumption 1 states that the feature distribution within each class is the same in training set and population. This can fail for some (but not all) types of sample selection bias [23,41]. For instance, Assumption 1 would fail to hold in a case where one group (e.g. men) tended to be sampled only if they had a certain feature (e.g. owned a car), and this feature was used in the model $\hat{f}$. In this case, car owners would be overrepresented in the training set relative to the population. Assumption 1 allows sampling different groups at different rates, as long as the samples drawn from within each group preserve the within-group feature distribution.

If these assumptions hold, then $C_{\text{train}} = C_{\text{population}}$. This implies that bias can be corrected in the entire sample. If the sample is drawn from the population, this provides an inference about the population quantity.

We propose conducting the network walk *before* labeling and classifying cases so that Assumption 1 is more likely to be satisfied. In this case, if the walk draws a valid sample from the population, then Assumption 1 holds. In cases where a classifier is trained on cases not from the sample, Assumption 1 cannot be tested since y_i is unknown in the sample. We also assume that the misclassification matrix C_{train} learned from the labeled set is known exactly. In practice, there is some uncertainty around the confusion matrix, although this can be addressed both through cross validation and the use of holdout set.

2.3   Matrix Adjustment vs. Calibration

We work with the class labels, but an alternative to the matrix method discussed here is to train a second model which calibrates $\hat{f}$. A calibration model takes predicted scores $\hat{s}_i \in [0, 1]$ from $\hat{f}$ and fits a model so that $\hat{s}_i \approx P(y_i = a)$. Gao and Sebastiani [11] examine a variety of quantification methods on many natural language processing tasks and find that the "adjusted classify and count" method used in this paper is statistically indistinguishable from using a calibrated model. However, the calibrated model has somewhat better average performance.

When considering the increased variance of adjustment methods, a closed-form can be derived for the matrix method (shown in the Appendix). A calibration method has the potential to provide lower variance estimates because it incorporates more information. However, it can also be more difficult to assess the increased variance because of correlated errors between observations which enter into the variance. For simplicity, we study the matrix method and note that variance may be reduced by instead fitting a calibration model.

2.4   Graph Walking

Re-weighted random walking (RWRW) is a Markov Chain Monte Carlo (MCMC) sampling procedure [16]. It is also commonly referred to as Respondent Driven Sampling (RDS) [35], which is a process for applying RWRW to offline social networks such as those of jazz musicians [18] or injection drug users [30].

RWRW allows randomly walking a connected, undirected graph and obtaining a valid estimate of node properties through reweighting by node degree. The basic intuition is to conduct a random walk of the undirected graph G, recording node degrees along the walk. The walk itself provides a random sample of edges, while degree information can be used to approximate a random sample of the nodes.

We present only the RWRW estimator here. A derivation may be found in [16]. A more general introduction to the method may be found in [35,38]. For extensions to online network applications, see [21,32].

Assume we wish to take a mean of a function g over the nodes i of graph G, where g is an indicator function for i being a member of minority group b. Choose a seed node with probability $\pi(i) = d_i/D$, or proportional to the node's degree. Then randomly walk the graph starting from the seed for n steps. Each jump samples node i with probability $\pi(i) = d_i/D$. For each node j along the walk, we record the node's degree d_j and $g(X_j)$, where X_j represents the jth node encountered while walking. The RWRW estimator for estimating the proportion of nodes belonging to b (assume no classification error) is given by

$$\hat{p}_b = \frac{1}{\sum_{j=0}^{n-1} 1/d_j} \sum_{j=0}^{n-1} \frac{g(X_j)}{d_j}. \tag{4}$$

Since the random walk naturally samples nodes proportional to degree, we correct for this through the weighting procedure in Eq. 4. This estimator provides an asymptotically unbiased estimate of p_b.

Note that g may be a continuous valued function as well, allowing estimates of mean degree and the degree distribution (see [32] for an example).

In addition to a mean of g over the nodes of the graph, the RWRW process records information which may be used to estimate the distribution of g. We discuss the details in the Appendix, and use this fact to estimate quantiles of the degree distribution for estimating node visibility.

2.5   Walking in a Directed Graph

The RWRW procedure relies on an important property of walks in undirected graphs: the probability of being at a given node at any time is proportional to that node's degree. However, many online networks are directed, such as Twitter follow relationships. If the directed graph can be redefined as an undirected one, than a walk can still be conducted. For instance, if both inlinks and outlinks can be accessed when a node is visited, then the combined inlink-outlink graph can be walked as if it were undirected. If this is not possible, additional approaches are possible but beyond the scope of this paper (see [15] for suggestions).

3   Results

We study four outcomes: proportion of nodes in the minority group, the fraction of in-group edges in the minority group, the percentage of minority group members in the top 20% of the degree distribution (visibility), and Coleman's homophily index.

Node and edge proportions are straightforward measures. Visibility has been studied in recent work [20,39]. It can indicate lack of status among minority group members. For instance, if the minority group comprises 20% of the population but only 10% of the top quintile of the degree distribution, minority group members are systematically underrepresented in the highest status positions.

Coleman's homophily index [4] has long been employed by social scientists. It treats random mixing as a baseline, with a value of 1 indicating perfect homophily and -1 indicating perfect heterophily. For group a, this measure is defined as

$$H_a = \left\{ \begin{array}{l} \frac{s_a - p_a}{1 - p_a} \text{ for } s_a - p_a \geq 0 \\ \frac{s_a - p_a}{p_a} \text{ for } s_a - p_a < 0 \end{array} \right\}. \tag{5}$$

3.1   Simulation Parameters

We follow the procedure in [39] to generate homophilous power-law graphs for the simple case of two groups, a and b. Graphs have 10,000 nodes, mean degree of 8, minority group fraction of 0.2, ingroup preference parameter of 0.8 (strong ingroup preference). The graph generation procedure balances ingroup preference with preference for links to high degree nodes. Note that the preference parameter is not the Coleman homophily index, but is correlated with the homophily index.

These graph parameters present a challenge for the technique presented in this paper, since RWRW is known to have higher variance in homophilous networks.[1]

Misclassification rates (off-diagonals of C) considered are 0%, 10%, 20% and 30%. We discuss the 20% case most frequently because it is high enough to present a challenge for our method and low enough to correspond to much published research. We draw samples of size 1000 to 3000, in increments of 500.

We compare the proposed RWRW method with three other sampling methods that have been used in recent literature: random node sampling, random edge sampling, and snowball sampling [39]. These methods provide reasonable comparisons: we expect node sampling to outperform RWRW for node-level tasks and edge sampling to outperform RWRW for edge-level tasks. Snowball sampling is included since it is a convenience sampling method that was commonly used before RWRW was developed.

3.2   Group Proportions and Visibility

Figure 2 shows node proportion and visibility estimates across the four sampling methods for a 20% misclassification rate and a sample size of 3000[2]. Performance for each sampling method is presented for three cases: no classification error, classification error with no correction, and classification error with correction. We present error distributions rather than the standard normalized root mean squared error [21, 32] in order to assess bias.

For group proportions, node sampling and RWRW are both unbiased, and node sampling has a lower variance as expected. Edge and snowball sampling perform poorly. For visibility, RWRW performs the best since it does not have bias in the corrected case, while applying the correction to node sampling does not remove bias.

A 20% misclassification rate without correction introduces a large magnitude error. While p_b is 20% in the population, misclassification causes this to rise to

---

[1] We also conducted simulations with minority group sizes of 0.35 and 0.5, and ingroup preferences of 0.2 (heterophily) and 0.5. The case we present is on balance the most challenging, although heterophilous graphs can present difficulties as well. We omit these additional cases for brevity, and because homophilous graphs are the case we are most often faced with empirically.

[2] The process for estimating the degree distribution for visibility is described in the Appendix.

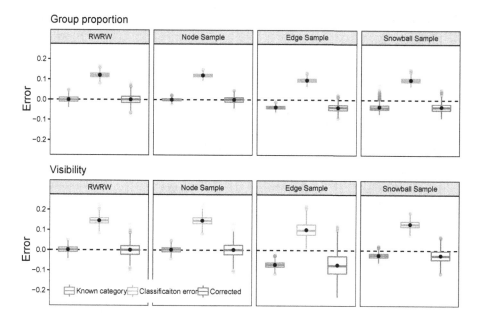

Fig. 2. Estimates of group proportions and minority group visibility across sampling methods for 20% classification error and sample size of 3000. For each plot, estimates are presented for three cases: no classification error, classification error, and corrected classification error. The dashed line at 0 indicates no error, and the black dot for each estimate indicates the mean. Whiskers represent 95% of the distribution. RWRW performs well in both cases, while node sampling has the lowest variance as expected. Correcting for classification error removes bias only for RWRW and node sampling, while edge sampling and snowball sampling demonstrate bias even after correction.

around 30% in all cases, an inflation of 50%. Since uncorrected estimates are low variance, a draw from an uncorrected distribution is likely to produce a poor estimate of the true value. In cases where assessing the size of a minority group is of importance, the upwardly biased estimates can lead to conclusions that understate the differences between groups. Smaller groups are likely to incur larger relative upward biases, since classifier loss functions penalize errors at the observation level and therefore tend to make errors at greater rates on smaller groups.

3.3   Edge Proportions and Homophily

Figure 3 shows error for estimates for edge proportions and homophily. The variance for these measures is larger than for the node-level measures (note the rescaled axes compared to Fig. 2).

Homophily in particular is a difficult inference task since it combines estimates of both group sizes and interaction rates. The error magnitude for uncorrected homophily estimates is large, averaging −0.35 on a −1 to 1 scale. Crossing

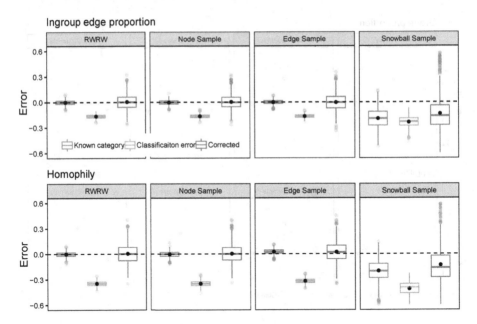

Fig. 3. Estimates of ingroup edge proportions and group homophily across sampling methods for 20% classification error and sample size of 3000. For each plot, estimates are presented for three cases: no classification error, classification error, and corrected classification error. The dashed line at 0 indicates the true value, and the black dot for each estimate indicates the mean. Whiskers represent 95% of the distribution. Ingroup edge proportions are sampled well by RWRW, node sampling, and edge sampling. Homophily is more difficult but is well captured by both RWRW and node sampling.

0 for the homophily score causes a qualitative difference in interpretation. This error can easily turn an insular minority into a gregarious plurality. In the graphs studied here, the true average homophily value is 0.42, meaning that the average error introduced by misclassification is about 83% of the true value.

The corrected estimates remove bias in exchange for an increase in estimate variance. For this level of misclassification (20%), we argue researchers should take the variance in exchange for bias reduction. After correcting for classification error, RWRW produces estimates with error drawn from $\mathcal{N}(0.005, 0.136)$ while the 95th percentile of the uncorrected error distribution is -0.282 (this is the "top" closest to the no-error line). This indicates that nearly all draws (about 98%) from the corrected distribution are lower-error than even the best draws from the uncorrected one.

3.4 Sample Size and Misclassification Rates

Both increasing sample size and building better classifiers have costs. Figure 4 reports the sensitivity of RWRW estimates to sample sizes and classification error rates. Corrected RWRW estimates are unbiased, and are compared to

Performance as a function of misclassification rate and sampling fraction

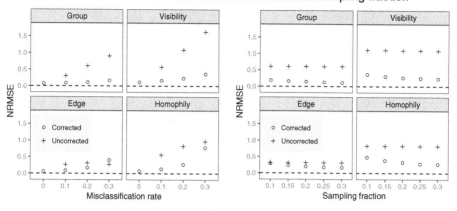

Fig. 4. Performance of RWRW as a function of misclassification rate and sampling fraction. For misclassification rate, a fixed walk size of 3000 is chosen. for a sample size of 3000. Circles indicate that bias correction has been applied, while plus signs indicate no correction. For group proportions and visibility, bias correction reduces NRMSE by a large amount. For edge proportions, the NRMSE reduction is smaller and disappears completely for misclassification rates of 0.3. Homophily shows large gains at misclassification rates of 0.1 and 0.2, and smaller gains at 0.3. In all cases, increasing sample size produces better after-correction estimates while barely changing before-correction estimates.

uncorrected estimates, which are biased but have lower variance. The metric of performance used is the normalized root mean squared error (NRMSE), given by

$$NRMSE = \frac{\sqrt{E[(\hat{\theta} - \theta)^2]}}{\theta}.$$

When increasing classification error (Fig. 4, first panel), two patterns emerge. For group proportions and visibility, bias correction substantially reduces NRMSE at all misclassification rates. On the other hand, the NRMSE reduction is modest for edge proportions at misclassification rates of 0.1 and 0.2, while the uncorrected estimate has lower NRMSE at a misclassification rate of 0.3. For homophily, there is substantial reduction in NRMSE at misclassification rates of 0.1 and 0.2, with a more modest correction at misclassification rate of 0.3.

When examining NRMSE response to sample size (Fig. 4, second panel) while holding misclassification at 20%, we find an interesting pattern: increasing sampling fraction has little effect on the NRMSE of the uncorrected estimate for all measures, but reduces NRMSE for the corrected estimates. This indicates that increasing sampling fraction without correcting for classifier error may not bring estimates closer to the truth. In the simulated graphs here, tripling the sample size hardly changes the error without correction.

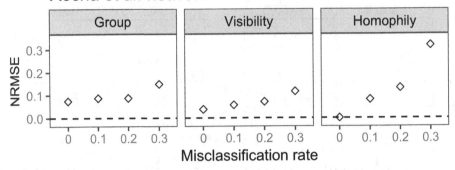

Fig. 5. Performance of RWRW after bias correction on the sexual contact network in [33] as misclassification rate is increased, with sample size given in Table 1. The denominator of the NRMSE is 0 for edge proportions, so we omit that measure. Akin to other studied graphs, this network shows reasonable performance at low misclassification rates, although group proportion NRMSE is somewhat higher than expected. This is potentially caused by the perfectly heterophilous nature of the graph. At high misclassification rates, NRMSE becomes quite large for homophily and begins to rapidly increase for other measures.

4   Empirical Graphs

We study two empirical graphs, the social network Pokec [36] and the sexual contact network studied in [33]. The Pokec graph [36] was crawled from an online social network in Slovakia and comes labeled with gender and age attributes. Age was binarized into "over 28 years old" or not, corresponding roughly to the top quintile of the distribution. The sexual contact network [33] was collected in Brazil and represents links between high end escorts and their clients. We study gender as our category of interest, and note that this network is perfectly heterophilous (all ties are between men and women). Summary statistics for both networks can be found in Table 1. These graphs were preprocessed by limiting the graph to mutual ties in the largest connected component, and then deleting nodes which had missing values for the relevant demographic. In the case of the Pokec graph, where two different demographics are examined, we created separate graphs for each demographic.

Figures 5 and 6 present results for these empirical graphs using RWRW and bias correction as misclassification rate is increased. Performance is comparable to the simulated graphs. For the low-homophily graph (Pokec gender), sampling is quite easy at all misclassification levels. The sexual contact network presents a possible challenge since it is perfectly heterophilous, but performance is in line with the other graphs considered. The Pokec age graph has a moderate amount of homophily, although sampling a relatively small proportion of the network (25,000 out of 764,000 nodes) produces reasonable results.

Table 1. Summary statistics for empirical graphs

	Pokec gender	Pokec age	Sexual contact
Number of nodes	1,198,235	764,845	15,810
Number of edges	8,312,749	4,172,385	38,540
Group studied	Female	>28 years old	Female
Group proportion	51.3%	22.2%	39%
Group homophily	0.034	0.344	−1
Sample size	25,000	25,000	3,000

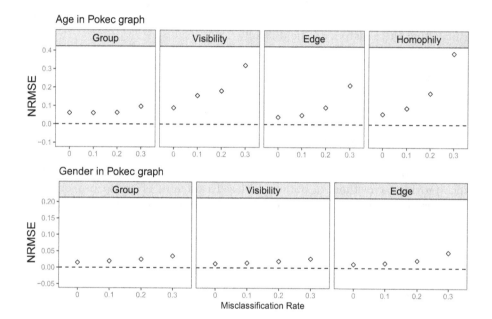

Fig. 6. RWRW performance after bias correction on two graphs derived from the Pokec network [22,36], with sample size given in Table 1. The top panel presents results for age, which is moderately homophilous. The pattern of quickly accelerating error at misclassification rates of 0.3 appears again. The bottom panel shows performance on gender in the Pokec graph, where we omit the homophily measure since its true value is very close to 0 which inflates NRMSE. This is the homophily value closest to 0 that we study in the paper, and as expected performance is quite good (note the y-axis on the bottom panel). Ingroup edge proportion is typically difficult to sample, but even with a misclassification rate of 0.3, performance is strong. This suggests that when graphs do not display large amounts of homophily, less accurate classifiers can be used or smaller samples drawn.

5 Limitations

There are several limitations to the work presented here, which researchers should consider carefully. Most importantly, we have assumed that the classifier error rate is known. Cross validation and holdout sets can be used to estimate this quantity, but empirically some uncertainty will still exist. An alternate route may be to train a calibrated model, although then the challenge becomes estimating the calibration accuracy. In some cases, either with small training sets or difficult classification problems, there may be substantial uncertainty about classifier performance.

Beyond this issue, online networks present data quality issues which may impact the validity of estimates. For instance, bots or inactive accounts which appear to belong to a certain demographic group can bias estimates. Accounting for bias from these factors can be difficult.

6 Conclusion

Classifiers offer an opportunity for social scientists to study demographics and other attributes online, in combination with rich behavioral data often absent from offline surveys. However, care must be taken in order for classification to yield accurate population-level estimates, particularly in networked online settings where the sampling frame is unknown. The framework we study in this paper provides a method to obtain unbiased estimates of group proportions in this setting. Additionally, it can be applied in many domains and requires relatively small adjustments to existing practice. This offers new opportunities for digital demography and comparisons of online settings with offline survey data.

7 Appendix

7.1 Variance of Corrected Estimates

Consider the simple case of classifying group proportions with two groups. We obtain a sample from the population with true proportions $\hat{p}$ and estimated proportions $\hat{m}$. Multiplying out Eq. 2 gives expressions for for the estimated $\hat{p}_a$ and $\hat{p}_b$,

$$\hat{p}_a = \frac{\hat{m}_a c_{\hat{b}|b} - \hat{m}_b c_{\hat{a}|b}}{\det(C)}, \quad \hat{p}_b = \frac{\hat{m}_b c_{\hat{a}|a} - \hat{m}_a c_{\hat{b}|a}}{\det(C)}. \tag{6}$$

The variance of the mean is given by,

$$\mathrm{Var}(E[\hat{p}_a]) = \mathrm{Var}(\frac{E[\hat{m}_a] - c_{\hat{a}|b}}{\det(C)}) \tag{7}$$

$$= \frac{1}{\det(C)^2} \mathrm{Var}(E[\hat{m}_a]), \tag{8}$$

where we use the assumption that C is constant to pull it out of the variance expression.

When there is no classification error, $\det(C) = 1$, and when the classifier guesses randomly (.5 in every cell), $\det(C) = 0$ and the variance is undefined. $\det^2(C)$ provides a clear quantification of the variance increase we expect for group proportions. For instance, if $C = [0.8, 0.2; 0.2, 0.8]$ with $\det^2(C) = 0.6$, we expect a variance increase of $1/0.6^2 = 2.78$. If classifier performance improves to $C = [0.9, 0.1; 0.1, 0.9]$, the variance increase is $1/0.8^2 = 1.56$.

$\text{Var}(E[\hat{m}_a])$ comes from the random walking procedure itself and is generally not known in closed form. Two methods for closed-form variance have been proposed [16,38]. The Volz-Heckathorn [38] estimator is biased but provides reasonable estimates in practice. The Goel and Salganik [16] variance estimator relies on knowing the homophily of the network. Bootstrap resampling methods based on creating "synthetic chains" from the estimated transition matrix between groups have also often been used [19].

Simulations of various RWRW estimators [12] show that factors such as a non-equilibrium seed selection, group homophily, and number of waves from each seed affect both the bias and variance of RWRW estimates. Generally, one long chain provides the best results, rather than many shorter chains. It is easier to sample from lower homophily networks, and equilibrium seed selection (proportional to degree) is useful if one must use relatively short chains. Otherwise, if chains may be long, a burn-in period can be used to simulate equilibrium seed selection.

7.2   Correcting Visibility

While RWRW gives the mean of g over the population of nodes, the distribution of g is often an object of interest. For instance, if we wish to estimate the proportion of minority group members in the top 20% of the degree distribution, we need to estimate the joint distribution of $(g(i), d_i)$ and take nodes in the top 20% of the distribution of d_i.

Fortunately, importance resampling [26,34] based on the data obtained during an RWRW walk provides a method to do this. If we know node i with degree d_i is sampled with probability $\pi(i)$ and we want to sample it with probability $1/N$ (a uniform distribution over the nodes), then we construct an importance weight using the ratio of desired over actual distributions

$$\frac{1/N}{\pi(i)} = \frac{D}{Nd_i} = \frac{\bar{d}}{d_i} = w_i. \tag{9}$$

w_i provides a resampling weight for node i. We then normalize $w_i / \sum_j w_j$ and resample data $(f(i), d_i)$ according to this probability to approximate draws from the desired distribution $1/N$.

An importance resample produces a distribution of $(d_i, g(i))$ which mirrors the distribution in the population. We then sort the resampled nodes by degree d_i and take the proportion in the top 20% of degree where $g(i) = b$, or where i is a member of the minority group. In the case with no classification error, this procedure produces an unbiased estimate of the fraction of minority group members in the top 20% of the degree distribution.

With classification error, we need to add an additional step to correct the importance resample. Call $\hat{m}_b^{\mathcal{I}}(20)$ the measured proportion of group b in the top 20% of the degree distribution in importance resample $\mathcal{I}$. Likewise, there is a vector that contains measures for all groups $\hat{\mathbf{m}}^{\mathcal{I}}(20)$. Then we can use a procedure similar to Eq. 2 to correct the importance resample proportions:

$$\hat{\mathbf{p}}^{\mathcal{I}}(20) = C^{-1}\hat{\mathbf{m}}^{\mathcal{I}}(20). \tag{10}$$

To see when $\hat{\mathbf{p}}^{\mathcal{I}}(20)$ is unbiased, repeat the reasoning for estimating the population proportion $\hat{\mathbf{p}}$ above. This shows that $\hat{\mathbf{p}}^{\mathcal{I}}(20)$ is unbiased when the importance resample provides an unbiased estimate of $\mathbf{m}^{\mathcal{I}}(20)$. A similar argument applies for the variance, and the determinant of C may be used to estimate the increase in variance.

7.3   Correcting Edge Proportions

Correcting estimates of ties between groups presents a more substantial challenge than correcting group proportions. Akin to C, there is a dyadic misclassification matrix M which maps $\mathbf{s}$ to $\mathbf{t}$,

$$M\mathbf{s} = \mathbf{t}, \tag{11}$$

where

$$M = \begin{bmatrix} c_{\hat{a}|a}^2 & c_{\hat{a}|a}c_{\hat{a}|b} & c_{\hat{a}|b}^2 \\ 2 * c_{\hat{a}|a}c_{\hat{b}|a} & c_{\hat{a}|a}c_{\hat{b}|b} + c_{\hat{a}|b}c_{\hat{b}|a} & 2 * c_{\hat{a}|b}c_{\hat{b}|b} \\ c_{\hat{b}|a}^2 & c_{\hat{b}|a}c_{\hat{b}|b} & c_{\hat{b}|b}^2 \end{bmatrix},$$

which implies that we can use a technique similar to Eq. 2 at the dyad level

$$\mathbf{s} = M^{-1}\mathbf{t}. \tag{12}$$

In practice, we obtain a sample $\hat{\mathbf{t}}$ rather than $\mathbf{t}$ for the entire graph, which is then used to estimate true edge proportions $\hat{\mathbf{s}}$. $\hat{\mathbf{s}}$ is unbiased when the sampling method employed produces unbiased estimates of $\mathbf{t}$. If $B = M^{-1}$, the expectation for $\hat{s}_a$ is given by

$$E[\hat{s}_{aa}] = b_{00}E[\hat{t}_{aa}] + b_{01}E[\hat{t}_{ab}] + b_{02}E[\hat{t}_{bb}]. \tag{13}$$

As in the node case, we can expect the variance of $E[\hat{s}_{aa}]$ and $E[\hat{s}_a]$ to increase when applying classification bias correction. Simulations below indicate that variance inflation for $E[\hat{s}_a]$ is larger than for $E[\hat{p}_a]$. Note that $\hat{s}_a = 2\hat{s}_{aa}/(2\hat{s}_{aa} + \hat{s}_{ab})$ is unbiased under the same conditions as $\hat{s}_{aa}$.

If $B = M^{-1}$, then the variance for $\hat{s}_{aa}$ is

$$\text{Var}(E[\hat{s}_{aa}]) = b_{00}^2 \, \text{Var}(E[\hat{t}_{aa}]) + b_{01}^2 \, \text{Var}(E[\hat{t}_{ab}]) + b_{02}^2 \, \text{Var}(E[\hat{t}_{bb}]). \tag{14}$$

References

1. Al Zamal, F., Liu, W., Ruths, D.: Homophily and latent attribute inference: inferring latent attributes of Twitter users from neighbors. In: ICWSM, vol. 270 (2012)
2. Barberá, P.: Less is more? How demographic sample weights can improve public opinion estimates based on Twitter data. Working Paper for NYU (2016)
3. Ciot, M., Sonderegger, M., Ruths, D.: Gender inference of Twitter users in non-English contexts. In: EMNLP, pp. 1136–1145 (2013)
4. Coleman, J.S.: Relational analysis: the study of social organizations with survey methods. Hum. Organ. **17**(4), 28–36 (1958). https://doi.org/10.17730/humo.17.4. q5604m676260q8n7
5. Culotta, A., Cutler, J.: Predicting Twitter user demographics using distant supervision from website traffic data. J. Artif. Intell. Res. **55**, 389–408 (2016)
6. Culotta, A., Kumar, N.R., Cutler, J.: Predicting the demographics of Twitter users from website traffic data. In: AAAI, pp. 72–78 (2015)
7. Ding, Y., Yan, S., Zhang, Y., Dai, W., Dong, L.: Predicting the attributes of social network users using a graph-based machine learning method. Comput. Commun. **73**, 3–11 (2016). https://doi.org/10.1016/j.comcom.2015.07.007. http://linkinghub.elsevier.com/retrieve/pii/S0140366415002455
8. Fang, Q., Sang, J., Xu, C., Hossain, M.: Relational user attribute inference in social media. **17** (2015). https://doi.org/10.1109/TMM.2015.2430819
9. Forman, G.: Counting positives accurately despite inaccurate classification. In: Gama, J., Camacho, R., Brazdil, P.B., Jorge, A.M., Torgo, L. (eds.) ECML 2005. LNCS, vol. 3720, pp. 564–575. Springer, Heidelberg (2005). https://doi.org/10. 1007/11564096_55
10. Forman, G.: Quantifying counts and costs via classification. Data Min. Knowl. Discov. **17**(2), 164–206 (2008). https://doi.org/10.1007/s10618-008-0097-y
11. Gao, W., Sebastiani, F.: From classification to quantification in tweet sentiment analysis. Soc. Netw. Anal. Min. **6**(1) (2016). https://doi.org/10.1007/s13278-016-0327-z
12. Gile, K.J., Handcock, M.S.: Respondent-driven sampling: an assessment of current methodology. Sociol. Methodol. **40**(1), 285–327 (2010). https://doi.org/10.1111/j. 1467-9531.2010.01223.x
13. Gjoka, M., Kurant, M., Butts, C.T., Markopoulou, A.: A walk in Facebook: uniform sampling of users in online social networks. arXiv:0906.0060 [physics, stat], May 2009
14. Gjoka, M., Kurant, M., Butts, C.T., Markopoulou, A.: Walking in Facebook: a case study of unbiased sampling of OSNs. In: Proceedings of - IEEE INFOCOM (2010). https://doi.org/10.1109/INFCOM.2010.5462078
15. Gjoka, M., Kurant, M., Butts, C.T., Markopoulou, A.: Practical recommendations on crawling online social networks. IEEE J. Sel. Areas Commun. **29**(9), 1872–1892 (2011). https://doi.org/10.1109/JSAC.2011.111011. http://ieeexplore. ieee.org/document/6027868/
16. Goel, S., Salganik, M.J.: Respondent-driven sampling as Markov chain Monte Carlo. Stat. Med. **28**(17), 2202–2229 (2009). https://doi.org/10.1002/sim.3613. http://www.ncbi.nlm.nih.gov/pubmed/19572381
17. Gong, N.Z., et al.: Joint link prediction and attribute inference using a social-attribute network. ACM Trans. Intell. Syst. Technol. **5**(2), 1–20 (2014). https:// doi.org/10.1145/2594455

18. Heckathorn, D., Jeffri, J.: Finding the beat: using respondent-driven sampling to study jazz musicians. Poetics **28**, 307–329 (2001). http://www.respondentdrivensampling.org/reports/Heckathorn.pdf
19. Heckathorn, D.D.: Respondent-driven sampling II: deriving valid population estimates from chain-referral samples of hidden populations. Soc. Probl. **49**(1), 11–34 (2002). https://doi.org/10.1525/sp.2002.49.1.11
20. Karimi, F., Gnois, M., Wagner, C., Singer, P., Strohmaier, M.: Visibility of minorities in social networks. arXiv preprint arXiv:1702.00150 (2017)
21. Kurant, M., Gjoka, M., Butts, C.T., Markopoulou, A.: Walking on a graph with a magnifying glass: stratified sampling via weighted random walks. In: Proceedings of the ACM SIGMETRICS Joint International Conference on Measurement and Modeling of Computer Systems, SIGMETRICS 2011, pp. 281–292. ACM, New York (2011). https://doi.org/10.1145/1993744.1993773
22. Leskovec, J., Krevl, A.: SNAP Datasets: Stanford Large Network Dataset Collection, June 2014. http://snap.stanford.edu/data
23. Liu, A., Ziebart, B.: Robust classification under sample selection bias. In: Advances in Neural Information Processing Systems. pp. 37–45 (2014)
24. Liu, W., Ruths, D.: What's in a name? Using first names as features for gender inference in Twitter. In: AAAI Spring Symposium: Analyzing Microtext, vol. 13, p. 01 (2013)
25. Malmi, E., Weber, I.: You are what apps you use: demographic prediction based on user's apps. In: ICWSM, pp. 635–638 (2016)
26. McAllister, M.K., Ianelli, J.N.: Bayesian stock assessment using catch-age data and the sampling-importance resampling algorithm. Candian J. Fish. Aquat. Sci. **54**(2), 284–300 (1997)
27. Messias, J., Vikatos, P., Benevenuto, F.: White, man, and highly followed: gender and race inequalities in Twitter. arXiv preprint arXiv:1706.08619 (2017)
28. Mohammady, E., Culotta, A.: Using county demographics to infer attributes of Twitter users. In: ACL 2014, p. 7 (2014)
29. Nguyen, D.P., Gravel, R., Trieschnigg, R.B., Meder, T.: How old do you think I am? A study of language and age in Twitter (2013)
30. Ramirez-Valles, J., Heckathorn, D.D., Vzquez, R., Diaz, R.M., Campbell, R.T.: From networks to populations: the development and application of respondent-driven sampling among IDUs and Latino gay men. AIDS Behav. **9**(4), 387–402 (2005). https://doi.org/10.1007/s10461-005-9012-3
31. Rao, D., Yarowsky, D., Shreevats, A., Gupta, M.: Classifying latent user attributes in Twitter, pp. 37–44 (2009)
32. Ribeiro, B., Towsley, D.: Estimating and sampling graphs with multidimensional random walks. In: Proceedings of the 10th ACM SIGCOMM Conference on Internet Measurement, IMC 2010, pp. 390–403. ACM, New York (2010). https://doi.org/10.1145/1879141.1879192
33. Rocha, L.E.C., Liljeros, F., Holme, P.: Simulated epidemics in an empirical spatiotemporal network of 50,185 sexual contacts. PLOS Comput. Biol. **7**(3), e1001109 (2011). http://journals.plos.org/ploscompbiol/article?id=10.1371/journal.pcbi.1001109.
34. Rubin, D.B.: The calculation of posterior distributions by data augmentation: comment: a noniterative sampling/importance resampling alternative to the data augmentation algorithm for creating a few imputations when fractions of missing information are modest: the SIR algorithm. J. Am. Stat. Assoc. **82**(398), 543–546 (1987). https://doi.org/10.2307/2289460

35. Salganik, M.J., Heckathorn, D.D.: Sampling and estimation in hidden populations using respondent-driven sampling. Sociol. Methodol. **34**(1), 193–240 (2004). https://doi.org/10.1017/CBO9781107415324.004
36. Takac, L.: Zabovsky: data analysis in public social networks, Lomza, Poland (2012)
37. Volkova, S., Bachrach, Y., Armstrong, M., Sharma, V.: Inferring latent user properties from texts published in social media. In: AAAI, pp. 4296–4297 (2015)
38. Volz, E., Heckathorn, D.D.: Probability based estimation theory for respondent driven sampling. J. Off. Stat. **24**(1), 79 (2008)
39. Wagner, C., Singer, P., Karimi, F., Pfeffer, J., Strohmaier, M.: Sampling from social networks with attributes. In: WWW, pp. 1181–1190 (2017). https://doi.org/10.1145/3038912.3052665
40. Wang, P., Guo, J., Lan, Y., Xu, J., Cheng, X.: Your cart tells you: inferring demographic attributes from purchase data, pp. 173–182. ACM Press (2016). https://doi.org/10.1145/2835776.2835783
41. Zadrozny, B.: Learning and evaluating classifiers under sample selection bias. In: Proceedings of the Twenty-first International Conference on Machine Learning, p. 114. ACM (2004)

Computational Analysis of Social Contagion and Homophily Based on an Adaptive Social Network Model

Guusje Boomgaard, Falko Lavitt, and Jan Treur[✉]

Behavioural Informatics Group, Vrije Universiteit Amsterdam, Amsterdam,
Netherlands
guusjeboomgaard@hotmail.com, falkolavitt@gmail.com,
j.treur@vu.nl

Abstract. This study combined the Social Science principles of homophily and social contagion within an approach to adaptive network modeling. The introduced adaptive temporal-causal network model incorporates both principles. This model was used to analyse an empirical data set concerning delinquency behaviour data among secondary school students. A mathematical analysis provided more in depth insight in the behavior of the model.

Keywords: Social network · Social contagion · Homophily

1 Introduction

In a world where globalization is increasing even more rapidly each year individuals come in contact with many individuals all over the world, and their opinions and behavior are influenced by an increasing number of different people, and are therefore best viewed from a network-oriented perspective. Network-Oriented Modelling can be used to describe opinions and behaviors of people in relation to the connections between them. Graphical representations of social networks consist of nodes that depict (the states of) different persons in a network, which are connected by uni- or bidirectional links.

A often studied type of behavior in relation to social networks is delinquent behavior. Typically, persons who show delinquent behavior have a higher chance to initiate a relationships with other persons showing delinquent behavior. This will often result in more delinquent behavior since their relationship exposes both of them to a social context stimulating delinquency. Because of this cyclic relationship between connecting and showing the behaviour, it is difficult to ascertain a direction of causality. Many studies found a correlation between delinquent behavior and exposure to delinquent peers [5, 9]. Furthermore, being affiliated with delinquent peers is one of the most important predictors of future delinquent behaviour [6], cited in [8]. A theory called 'Social Learning' posed by Akers *et al.* [1] suggests that social behaviour is shaped through operant conditioning. Especially groups that encourage delinquent behaviour are a major force of reinforcement for delinquency. Relationships within

S. Staab et al. (Eds.): SocInfo 2018, LNCS 11185, pp. 86–101, 2018.
https://doi.org/10.1007/978-3-030-01129-1_6

social networks thus have to be taken into account when studying delinquent behaviour.

Network-Oriented Modeling based on temporal-causal networks [15] makes use of a temporal component added to networks of causal relations. This offers the possibility to model processes that make social networks dynamic and adaptive over time. One of those processes is described by the social contagion principle. When two persons are connected, their opinions become more alike. This principle thus has an influence of the states of two connected persons. Another process that takes place over time is adaptation of a social network by the homophily principle. When two persons are connected and they share similar opinions and/or behaviors, their connection tends to strengthen. Note that these two principles indeed have a cyclic interaction implying a tendency to reinforce one another.

In this paper, an adaptive temporal-causal network model will be introduced that incorporates both the social contagion principle and the homophily principle. The model was used to analyse a dataset by Knecht [10], about delinquency behaviour and friendships among secondary school students. First, the social contagion principle and the homophily principle are discussed in relation to a modelling approach based on temporal-causal networks. After this, example simulations performed with the model in order to explore the effect of different parameters on the model will be discussed. Then, it is shown how the model was verified using mathematical analysis and validated using the empirical dataset [10].

2   The Adaptive Social Network Model

This section describes how an adaptive temporal-causal network model was developed based on the principles of social contagion and homophily. This temporal-causal network model is based on the Network-Oriented Modelling approach described in [15]. Causal modelling, causal reasoning and causal simulation have a long tradition in AI; e.g., [11, 12, 14]. The Network-Oriented Modelling approach based on temporal-causal networks described in [16] can be viewed as part of this causal modelling tradition. It distinguishes itself by incorporating a dynamic and adaptive temporal perspective, both on states and on causal relations. This dynamic perspective enables modelling of cyclic and adaptive networks, and also of timing of causal effects. According to this Network-Oriented Modelling approach a model can be represented conceptually in two ways: as a (labeled) graphical conceptual representation (e.g., Figure 1), and in the form of a matrix (e.g., Tables 1, 2 and 3). The conceptual representation of the temporal-causal network model was translated into to its numerical representation, by the following systematic method [15]:

- At each time point t each state Y in the model has a real number value in the interval [0,1], denoted by $Y(t)$.
- At each time point t each state X connected to state Y has an impact on Y defined as **impact**$_{X,Y}(t) = \omega_{X,Y} X(t)$ where $\omega_{X,Y}$ is the weight of the connection from X to Y
- The aggregated impact of multiple states X_i on Y at t is determined using a combination function $c_Y(..)$:

$$\textbf{aggimpact}_Y(t) = \textbf{c}_Y(\textbf{impact}_{X_1,Y}(t), \ldots, \textbf{impact}_{X_k,Y}(t))$$
$$= \textbf{c}_Y(\omega_{X_1,Y}X_1(t), \ldots, \omega_{X_k,Y}X_k(t))$$

where X_i are the states with connections to state Y

- The effect of $\textbf{aggimpact}_Y(t)$ on Y is exerted over time gradually, depending on speed factor η_Y:

$$Y(t+\Delta t) = Y(t) + \eta_Y[\textbf{aggimpact}_Y(t) - Y(t)]\Delta t, \text{ or}$$
$$dY(t)/dt = \eta_Y[\textbf{aggimpact}_Y(t) - Y(t)]$$

- Thus the following difference and differential equation for Y are obtained:

$$Y(t+\Delta t) = Y(t) + \eta_Y\left[\textbf{c}_Y(\omega_{X_1,Y}X_1(t), \ldots, \omega_{X_k,Y}X_k(t)) - Y(t)\right]\Delta t$$
$$dY(t)/dt - \eta_Y\left[\textbf{c}_Y(\omega_{X_1,Y}X_1(t), \ldots, \omega_{X_k,Y}X_k(t)) - Y(t)\right]$$

Examples of combination functions are the identity function $\textbf{id}(.)$, the sum combination function, the scaled sum combination function $\textbf{ssum}_\lambda(\ldots)$ and the advanced logistic sum combination function $\textbf{alogistic}_{\sigma,t}(\ldots)$:

(a) $\textbf{c}_Y(V) = \textbf{id}(V) = V$
(b) $\textbf{c}_Y(V_1, \ldots, V_k) = \textbf{sum}(V_1, \ldots, V_k) = V_1 + \ldots + V_k$
(c) $\textbf{c}_Y(V_1, \ldots, V_k) = \textbf{ssum}_\lambda(V_1, \ldots, V_k) = (V_1 + \ldots + V_k)/\lambda$
     where λ is the scaling factor usually defined as the sum of the incoming weights for state Y
(d) $\textbf{c}_Y(V_1, \ldots, V_k) = \textbf{alogistic}_{\sigma,\tau}(V_1, \ldots, V_k) = [(1/(1+e^{-\sigma(V_1 + \ldots + V_k - \tau)}))$
     $-1/(1+e^{\sigma\tau})](1+e^{-\sigma\tau})$
     where σ is a steepness parameter and τ a threshold parameter.

State dynamics: social contagion
The social contagion principle describes causal effects of states on states through the connections. Due to this effect when two states are connected their state values will become more alike. Here, X_B describes a state X for a certain person B. This principle is modelled as [15]:

$$dX_B/dt = \eta_B[\textbf{c}_B(\omega_{A_1,B}X_{A_1}, \ldots, \omega_{A_k,B}X_{A_k}) - X_B]$$
$$X_B(t+\Delta t) = X_B(t) + \eta_B[\textbf{c}_B(\omega_{A_1,B}X_{A_1}(t), \ldots, \omega_{A_k,B}X_{A_k}(t)) - X_B(t)]\Delta t$$

where $X_{A_1}, \ldots, X_{A_k}$ are the nodes with outgoing connections to X_B. The combination function that will be used for the states X_B is the advanced logistic combination function.

Connection dynamics: homophily
The homophily principle is used to update the connection weights of the model based on the state values of the connected states. For a conceptual representation, see

the bending arrows in Fig. 1. When the activation levels of two connected states are similar, this has an increasing effect on the weight of the connection between those states. Conversely, when the activation levels of two states are more different, this will weaken their connection (see also [13]). For the Network-Oriented Modeling approach used here, the following equations, based on a combination function $c_{\omega A,B}(..)$ that still can be chosen, are the general numerical representation for homophily:

$$\omega_{A,B}(t+\Delta t) = \omega_{A,B}(t) + \eta_{\omega_{A,B}}[c_{\omega_{A,B}}(X_A(t), X_B(t), \omega_{A,B}(t)) - \omega_{A,B}(t)]\Delta t$$

$$d\omega_{A,B}/dt = \eta_{\omega_{A,B}}[c_{\omega_{A,B}}(X_A, X_B, \omega_{A,B}) - \omega_{A,B}]$$

For the combination function the following logistic function (called aloghom(..)) was used; (Treur, 2016, p. 309):

$$c_{\omega_{A,B}}(V_1, V_2, W) = W + \text{Pos}(\alpha(0.5 - 1/(1+e^{-\sigma(|V_1-V_2|-\tau)})))\,(1-W)$$
$$- \text{Pos}(-\alpha(0.5 - 1/(1+e^{-\sigma(|V_1-V_2|-\tau)})))W$$

Here Pos(x) = (|x| + x)/2 = x when x is positive, 0 otherwise. This function takes into account a threshold parameter τ such that when $|V_1 - V_2| < \tau$ the connection weight increases, when $|V_1 - V_2| > \tau$ it decreases, and when it happens that $|V_1 - V_2| = \tau$, it is stationary.

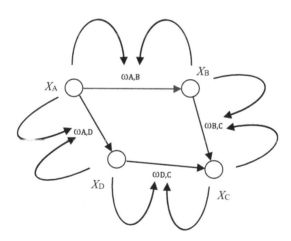

Fig. 1. Conceptual representation of the Homophily principle

3   Example Network and Network Analysis

To illustrate the temporal-causal network model, example network consisting of 20 nodes and 92 edges is used. These nodes form 4 distinct communities, and are bridged from one another only through one node per community. Each of these bridge nodes is only connected to their own community and to the other three bridge nodes, which actually makes them together a fifth community. Figure 2 illustrates this example network. The bridge nodes are nodes X_1, X_6, X_{11}, and X_{16}, and all have the highest number of in-degrees: 7. The average degree of all nodes in the network is 4.6. As was expected, the analysis also shows that nodes X_1–X_5 form one community, X_6–X_{10} form another community, and so on. The modularity is 0.62. This measure indicates the strength of dividing this network into 4 or communities. The betweenness and the closeness centrality measures can be used to say something about the importance of particular nodes. The betweenness centrality measures describe how often a node appears when calculating the shortest route between nodes in the network and, perhaps unsurprisingly, has the highest value for the 4 bridge nodes: 120. Similarly, the closeness centrality is also the highest for the bridge nodes, with a value of 0.61. This indicates that the bridge nodes have the lowest average distance from that node to any other node in the network.

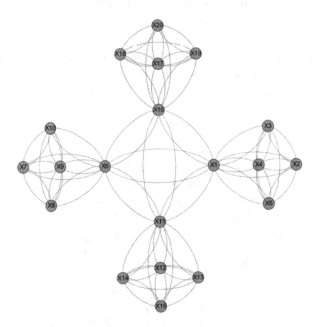

Fig. 2. Example social network

Table 1 illustrates the initial weights of the connections between the nodes. The blue cells in Table 1 represent the nodes that form bridges between the communities, and the different coloured cells illustrate the different communities in the network. The network parameter values are illustrated in Table 3. Here, the speed factor for the connection weights is set to 0.1, and the speed factor for the changing state values is set to 0.01. The steepness value σ for the social contagion principle is set at 1, and the σ for the homophily principle is set at 35. The thresholds τ for these principles are set at 0.05 and 0.01 for social contagion and homophily respectively. As can be seen in Table 2, the initial values of the states are distributed over [0–1], with an interval of

0.1. The initial values were chosen such that communities could have an average high initial value [0.6 – 10] or an average low initial value [0.1 – 0.5]. In this way, the effects the communities have on each other will show more clearly than when the different communities would have the same average initial values.

Table 1. Initial connection weights

	X_1	X_2	X_3	X_4	X_5	X_6	X_7	X_8	X_9	X_{10}	X_{11}	X_{12}	X_{13}	X_{14}	X_{15}	X_{16}	X_{17}	X_{18}	X_{19}	X_{20}
X_1		0.5	0.5	0.5	0.5	0.9	0	0	0	0	0.9	0	0	0	0	0.9	0	0	0	0
X_2	0.5		0.5	0.5	0.5	0	0	0	0	0	0	0	0	0	0	0	0	0	0	0
X_3	0.5	0.5		0.5	0.5	0	0	0	0	0	0	0	0	0	0	0	0	0	0	0
X_4	0.5	0.5	0.5		0.5	0	0	0	0	0	0	0	0	0	0	0	0	0	0	0
X_5	0.5	0.5	0.5	0.5		0	0	0	0	0	0	0	0	0	0	0	0	0	0	0
X_6	0.9	0	0	0	0		0.5	0.5	0.5	0.5	0.9	0	0	0	0	0.9	0	0	0	0
X_7	0	0	0	0	0	0.5		0.5	0.5	0.5	0	0	0	0	0	0	0	0	0	0
X_8	0	0	0	0	0	0.5	0.5		0.5	0.5	0	0	0	0	0	0	0	0	0	0
X_9	0	0	0	0	0	0.5	0.5	0.5		0.5	0	0	0	0	0	0	0	0	0	0
X_{10}	0	0	0	0	0	0.5	0.5	0.5	0.5		0	0	0	0	0	0	0	0	0	0
X_{11}	0.9	0	0	0	0	0.9	0	0	0	0		0.5	0.5	0.5	0.5	0.9	0	0	0	0
X_{12}	0	0	0	0	0	0	0	0	0	0	0.5		0.5	0.5	0.5	0	0	0	0	0
X_{13}	0	0	0	0	0	0	0	0	0	0	0.5	0.5		0.5	0.5	0	0	0	0	0
X_{14}	0	0	0	0	0	0	0	0	0	0	0.5	0.5	0.5		0.5	0	0	0	0	0
X_{15}	0	0	0	0	0	0	0	0	0	0	0.5	0.5	0.5	0.5		0	0	0	0	0
X_{16}	0.9	0	0	0	0	0.9	0	0	0	0	0.9	0	0	0	0		0.5	0.5	0.5	0.5
X_{17}	0	0	0	0	0	0	0	0	0	0	0	0	0	0	0	0.5		0.5	0.5	0.5
X_{18}	0	0	0	0	0	0	0	0	0	0	0	0	0	0	0	0.5	0.5		0.5	0.5
X_{19}	0	0	0	0	0	0	0	0	0	0	0	0	0	0	0	0.5	0.5	0.5		0.5
X_{20}	0	0	0	0	0	0	0	0	0	0	0	0	0	0	0	0.5	0.5	0.5	0.5	

Table 2. Initial state values

X_1	X_2	X_3	X_4	X_5	X_6	X_7	X_8	X_9	X_{10}	X_{11}	X_{12}	X_{13}	X_{14}	X_{15}	X_{16}	X_{17}	X_{18}	X_{19}	X_{20}
0.1	0.2	0.3	0.4	0.5	0.6	0.7	0.8	0.9	1	0.1	0.2	0.3	0.4	0.5	0.6	0.7	0.8	0.9	1

Table 3. Network parameter values

η weights	η states	σ contagion	τ contagion	σ homophily	τ homophily
0.1	0.01	1	0.05	35	0.01

4 Simulation Examples

A number of simulation experiments were conducted on the example network described above to investigate the effects of homophily and social contagion, changing bridge connection weights, changing initial values, and changing homophily threshold values. It was expected that the effect of the social contagion and the homophily principle will first cause the individual nodes within communities to converge towards a single point, and afterwards the communities as a whole converge. It was also expected that with high bridge connection weights, the communities as a whole will be drawn together more rapidly than with low bridge connection weights. In other simulations it was investigated what the effect is if the initial values within the communities are close together, and when they are spread out. Through the homophily principle it is expected that the states with similar initial values will converge more than if their initial values are further apart. All these expectations were met in general, but sometimes may depend on the settings.

In the first simulation example discussed here the initial values of the nodes are distributed equally over the interval [0, 1] with a step size of 0.1. This means that there are two communities with initial values between 0.1 and 0.5: communities [X1 – X5; X11 – X 15], and two communities with initial values between 0.6 and 1: communities [X6 – 10; X16 – X20]. The nodes X1, X6, X11, and X16 are the nodes that bridge the communities to each other. In Fig. 3 we can see that even relatively low bridge connection weights cause the different communities to converge to a single point, but not as quickly, as when compared to higher bridge connection weights. The point of convergence occurs at approximately $t = 800$ and the accompanying value of the states is around 0. All connection weights go to 1. Note that the communities with initial values between 0.1 and 0.5 are drawn less strongly towards this point, whereas the communities with initial values between 0.6 and 1 are more strongly pulled towards this point of convergence. Also note that the final state values are lower than any of the initial state value. This shows that the logistic combination function has the capability of amplifying the state values. This is not the case for a scaled sum combination which is also often used for social contagion.

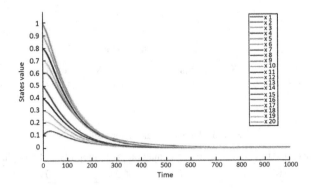

Fig. 3. Bridge connection weights at 0.1

The second simulation presented shows a more chaotic behaviour, at least at first sight. Here the homophily threshold has been set higher, at 0.075. The results are plotted below in Fig. 4. Whereas previously all nodes values converge to a state value of 0, this is not the case here. Some nodes go in the direction of state values 0.6 and 0.7, and other go in the direction of state values 0, 0.1, and 0.2. This may look quite chaotic at first sight, but actually is not really, as is shown below. Continuing the pattern for a longer time shows that in this case the state values do not converge but end up in a (non-chaotic) limit cycle, while the connection weights do converge to 0 or 1; see Fig. 5. Such patterns do not occur when the scaled sum combination function is used for the states.

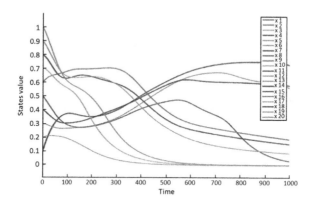

Fig. 4. Threshold τ set at 0.075: chaotic behaviour at first sight

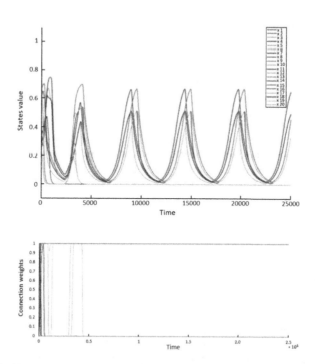

Fig. 5. Threshold τ set at 0.075; pattern ending up in a limit cycle for the states (upper graph) and stationary values 0 and 1 for the connection weights (lower graph)

When the threshold for the homophily principle was set to 0.2, the results are as shown in Fig. 6. All state values now converge into two groups with state values close to 1. This can be explained by the higher threshold which makes more states more attracted to each other.

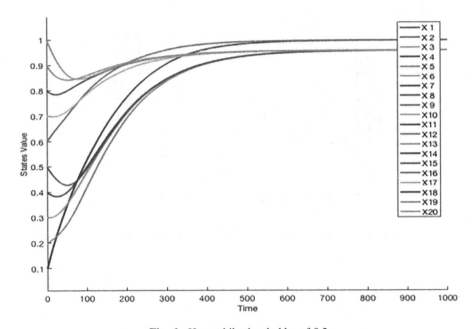

Fig. 6. Homophily threshold τ of 0.2

5   Verification by Mathematical Analysis

In order to verify the behaviour of the model a mathematical analysis was performed. For this mathematical analysis stationary points were identified from an example simulation. Given a state Y, a *stationary point* of Y at t occurs when $dY(t)/dt = 0$. Using the temporal causal network model, stationary points at t can be described by the specific criterion: **aggimpact**$_Y(t) = Y(t)$, called stationary point equation, also written as

$$\mathbf{c}_Y\left(\omega_{X_1,Y}X_1(t), \ldots, \omega_{X_k,Y}X_k(t)\right) = Y(t)$$

with $X_1, \ldots, X_k$ the states with outgoing connections to Y.

The model is in *equilibrium* at t when the above criterion holds for every state Y of the model.

For the verification of the model a simulation with bridge connection values of 0.9 was used. A long duration was used in order for the model to be able to reach an equilibrium state. The model seems to be in equilibrium around $t = 4500$. In Table 4 the results of the mathematical analysis are shown. As can be seen in Table 4, the stationary point equation holds for all the analyzed states with a good accuracy.

Table 4. Results the mathematical analysis of stationary points

State	X_2	X_{11}	X_{16}	X_{12}
Time point	4500	70	30	15
State value	0.85310	0.3051	0.6350	0.2080
Aggregated impact	0.85325	0.3133	0.6409	0.2114
Deviation	−0.00015	−0.0082	−0.0059	−0.0034

Also the equilibria for the connections were addressed. Recall the following combination function used for connections:

$$\mathbf{c}_{\omega_{A,B}}(V_1,\ V_2,\ W) = W + \text{Pos}(E)\,(1 - W) - \text{Pos}(-E)W$$

with $E = \alpha(0.5 - 1/(1 + e^{-\sigma(|V_1 - V_2| - \tau)}))$.
The stationary point criterion $\mathbf{c}_{\omega A,B}(V_1,\ V_2,\ W) = W$ provides the equation

$$\text{Pos}(E)\,(1 - W) - \text{Pos}(-E)W = 0$$

where $\text{Pos}(x) = x$ when $x > 0$ and 0 otherwise. This equation can be solved by considering three cases: $E > 0$, $E < 0$, $E = 0$.

$$
\begin{aligned}
E > 0 &: E(1 - W) = 0 &\Leftrightarrow&\quad E = 0 \text{ or } W = 1\\
E < 0 &: EW = 0 &\Leftrightarrow&\quad E = 0 \text{ or } W = 0\\
E = 0 &: E = 0
\end{aligned}
$$

Therefore, there are three solutions: $W = 0$ or $W = 1$ or $E = 0$. In simulations it turns out that $E = 0$ is non-attracting, so that does not occur naturally. That leaves us with the following two solutions for the equilibrium values of the connection weights: $\omega_{X,Y} = 0$ or $\omega_{X,Y} = 1$. This is indeed what is observed in all simulation experiments. The connections that become 1 define the emerging clusters: they connect states within one emerging cluster (not necessarily the initial communities). For the sake of completeness, also the equation $E = 0$ can be solved more explicitly, resulting in $E = 0 \Leftrightarrow |V_1 - V_2| = \tau$. As mentioned, this turns out to be a non-attracting equilibrium. Below, a more detailed Mathematical Analysis of the network model is addressed, also taking into account the state dynamics. Note that the combination functions used here for both states and connections are logistic. Therefore theory relatively easy achievable for scaled sum functions does not apply here. The following addresses these logistic functions, thereby generalizing some of its properties in Definitions 2 and 3.

Definition 1 (Cluster). In an equilibrium state a cluster **C** is a maximal subnetwork in which all connections are 1.

Definition 2 (Threshold τ). The function $c(V_1, V_2, W)$ uses a *threshold* τ for $|V_1-V_2|$ if for all W with $0 < W < 1$ and all V_1, V_2 it holds

(i) $c(V_1, V_2, W) > W \Leftrightarrow |V_1-V_2| < τ$
(ii) $c(V_1, V_2, W) = W \Leftrightarrow |V_1-V_2| = τ$
(iii) $c(V_1, V_2, W) < W \Leftrightarrow |V_1-V_2| > τ$

Definition 3 (Strict, symmetric)

(a) The function $c(V_1, V_2, W)$ is called *strict* if it holds:
     (i) If $|V_1-V_2| < τ$ then $c(V_1, V_2, 0) > 0$
     (ii) If $|V_1 - V_2| > τ$ then $c(V_1, V_2, 1) < 1$
(b) $c(V_1, V_2, W)$ is called *symmetric* if
    $c(V_1, V_2, W) = c(V_2, V_1, W)$.

Definition 4 (Symmetric network). A network is called *weakly symmetric* if for all nodes X_A and X_B it holds $\omega_{A,B} = 0 \Leftrightarrow \omega_{B,A} = 0$ or, equivalently: $\omega_{A,B} > 0 \Leftrightarrow \omega_{B,A} > 0$. The network is called *fully symmetric* if $\omega_{A,B} = \omega_{B,A}$ for all nodes X_A and X_B. An adaptive network is called *continually (weakly/fully) symmetric* if at all time points it is (weakly/fully) symmetric.

Proposition 1

(a) When the combination function $c(V_1, V_2, W)$ is symmetric, and initially the network is fully symmetric, then it is continually fully symmetric.
(b) **aloghom**$_{τ,α}(V_1, V_2, W)$ uses threshold τ, and is strict and symmetric.

Proof

(a) This follows from the fact that in this case the difference equation for $\omega_{A,B}$ is symmetric in X_A and X_B
(b) When $0 < W < 1$, the conditions in Definition 1 follow from:

$$|V_1-V_2| < τ \Leftrightarrow α(0.5 - 1/(1+e^{-σ(|V_1-V_2|-τ)})) > 0 \Leftrightarrow \textbf{aloghom}_{τ,α}(V_1, V_2, W) > W$$

$$|V_1-V_2| = τ \Leftrightarrow α(0.5 - 1/(1+e^{-σ(|V_1-V_2|-τ)})) = 0 \Leftrightarrow \textbf{aloghom}_{τ,α}(V_1, V_2, W) = W$$

$$|V_1-V_2| > τ \Leftrightarrow α(0.5 - 1/(1+e^{-σ(|V_1-V_2|-τ)})) < 0 \Leftrightarrow \textbf{aloghom}_{τ,α}(V_1, V_2, W) < W$$

Therefore **aloghom**$_{τ,α}(V_1, V_2, W)$ satisfies Definition 2.
The conditions (i) and (ii) of Definition 3a) can be verified as follows. If $|V_1 - V_2| < τ$, then $α$ $(0.5 - 1/(1+e^{-σ(|V_1-V_2|-τ)})) > 0$, and therefore, for $W = 0$ it holds **aloghom**$_{τ,α}(V_1, V_2, W) = W + α$ $(0.5 - 1/(1+e^{-σ(|V_1-V_2|-τ)})) (1-W) > 0$. If $|V_1 - V_2| > τ$, then $α$ $(0.5 - 1/(1+e^{-σ(|V_1-V_2|-τ)})) < 0$, and therefore for $W = 1$ it holds **aloghom**$_{τ,α}(V_1, V_2, W) = W + α$ $(0.5 - 1/(1+e^{-σ(|V_1-V_2|-τ)})) W < 0$. It can immediately be verified from the formula that **aloghom**$_{τ,α}(V_1, V_2, W)$ is symmetric. ∎

Theorem 1. Suppose the combination function $c(V_1, V_2, W)$ uses threshold τ for $|V_1 - V_2|$ and is strict, and the network reaches an equilibrium state with values $\underline{X}_A$ for the nodes X_A and $\omega_{A,B}$ for the connection weights $\omega_{A,B}$. Then:

(a) (i) For every two nodes X_A and X_B if their equilibrium values $\underline{X}_A$ and $\underline{X}_B$ have distance less than τ, then $\omega_{A,B} = 1$ and $\omega_{B,A} = 1$, and they are therefore in the same cluster. In particular, if $\underline{X}_A = \underline{X}_B$, then $\omega_{A,B} = 1$ and $\omega_{B,A} = 1$ and X_A and X_B are in the same cluster:

    (ii) Conversely, if $\omega_{A,B} > 0$ or $\omega_{B,A} > 0$, then $|\underline{X}_A - \underline{X}_B| \leq \tau$.

(b) (i) For any nodes X_A and X_B if their equilibrium values $\underline{X}_A$ and $\underline{X}_B$ have distance more than τ, then their mutual connections have weight 0: $\omega_{A,B} = 0$ and $\omega_{B,A} = 0$.

    (ii) Conversely, if $\omega_{A,B} < 1$ or $\omega_{B,A} < 1$, then $|\underline{X}_A - \underline{X}_B| \geq \tau$.

Therefore, if X_A and X_B are in different clusters, then $|\underline{X}_A - \underline{X}_B| \geq \tau$, and in particular, $\underline{X}_A \neq \underline{X}_B$.

Proof

(a) (i) Suppose two nodes are given with equilibrium values $\underline{X}_A$ and $\underline{X}_B$ with distance less than τ: $|\underline{X}_A - \underline{X}_B| < \tau$. By Definition 2(ii) it follows from the equilibrium equation $c_{\omega A,B}(\underline{X}_A, \underline{X}_B, \omega_{A,B}) = \omega_{A,B}$ that $0 < \omega_{A,B} < 1$ cannot be true, therefore $\omega_{A,B} = 0$ or $\omega_{A,B} = 1$. By from strictness Definition 3a)(i) it follows that 0 is not an equilibrium value. Therefore $\omega_{A,B} = 1$, and in the same way $\omega_{B,A} = 1$.

(b) (i) This is similar, using Definition 2(iii) and Definition 3a)(ii).

    a)(ii) This converse of a)(i) follows from the logical contraposition of b)(i).

    b)(ii) This converse of b)(i) follows from the logical contraposition of a)(i).   ∎

6 Validation Through an Empirical Data Set

To validate this model, a data set was used from Knecht [10] containing data from a friendship network in a Dutch school class. Data was collected at four time points, every three months during the first year of secondary school (age 11–13 years) and contained for each person their delinquency behavior during this period. In total, the class consisted of 26 students, however, for only 21 students the data was complete for all four measurements. In order to obtain a relationship network, students were asked to indicate up to 12 classmates which they considered good friends. For the model, relationships were indicated as shown in Table 5.

The delinquency behavior was measured as a rounded average over four types of minor delinquencies (stealing, vandalism, graffiti, and fighting). More specifically, this was measured in terms of frequency of delinquent behavior over the last three months ranging from 1 (never) to 5 (more than 10 times). For the indication of state levels in the model, the delinquency behavior was transformed as [0.1, 0.3, 0.7]. Note that there are only three categories, since 1 (never) and 5 (more than 10 times) did not occur in

Table 5. Coding the relationships

Connection weight [0, 1]	Description
0.9	A and B mutually consider each other 'good friends'
0.6	A indicates B as a 'good friend', but B does not indicate A as a 'good friend'
0.1	A and B do not indicate the other as 'good friend'

the measured data. The data was simulated for $t \in [0, 270]$ using a step size of $\Delta t = 1$, to simulate over a period of 270 days (3 months). At $t = 0$ the initial values for states and connections were taken from the first time point of the empirical data. The simulated values for states and connections at time point 90, 180 and 270 were compared to the second, third and fourth time point of the empirical data respectively. In order to compare the simulated data to the empirical data, the parameters of the simulated data were tuned to the empirical data using the fast Simulated Annealing algorithm in Matlab. For the optimization of the parameters the Sum of Squared Residuals (SSR) error function was used. The found optimized parameters are shown in Table 6. The pattern of the error between the empirical and the simulated data is shown in Fig. 7.

Table 6. Results of the parameter tuning

Parameter	Interval	Value
η states	[0,1]	0.015490
η connections	[0,1]	0
τ social contagion	[0,1]	0.079053
σ social contagion	[0,25]	0.648528
τ homophily	[0,1]	0.015945
σ homophily	[0,25]	0

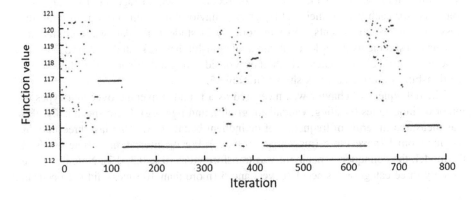

Fig. 7. SSR value during parameter tuning over 700 iterations

The lowest SSR value is 120.6342, which leads to the average squared deviation of 0.0857. The square root of this is 0.2928, which can be considered the average linear deviation. Given that the numbers expressing the empirical data for connections and states already have themselves inherent deviations of 0.1 to 0.3, as they were expressed on scales with gaps of 0.2, 0.3, 0.4 or even 0.5, an average linear deviation below 0.3 for the model may be reasonably close to the best result theoretically possible. The speed factor found for the connection dynamics was very low, which indicates that not much changed in the connections in the considered period of 9 months. That is indeed the case in the empirical data. For example, many students that initially were no friends (value 0.1) were also no friends after 9 months (again value 0.1). Perhaps a 9 months period is a bit short to expect more substantial changes in the friendships.

7   Discussion

This study combined the principles of homophily and social contagion as a basis for an adaptive temporal-causal network model. Both for the dynamics of contagion and of homophily logistic combination functions were used, which is new, as such models usually use a linear function (scaled sum) for social contagion and a linear or quadratic function for homophily. It has been found that the use of logistic combination functions provides a positive contribution in that they enable to generate patterns beyond what linear functions for contagion can do (e.g., the emotion absorption contagion model in [4]). For example, patterns are possible with states that converge to values higher or lower than all initial state values. In the empirical literature on contagion different types of such processes are described, in particular for emotion contagion spirals; e.g., [7]. In such spiraling cases the levels can drive each other upward beyond all initial levels until they eventually reach a maximal or optimal value (or downward to a minimal value). In this paper we found it an interesting addition to the available literature to explore the possibilities of a logistic function; it indeed shows this type of spiraling effects. Therefore logistic functions may suit certain domains better. Such a pattern can be considered an amplification process, comparable to the emotion amplification contagion model based on a quadratic function for contagion discussed in [4]. Note that the models in [4] are non-adaptive (they work with static connections), which is another importance difference with the model presented here.

On the other hand, using a linear function for contagion makes mathematical analysis relatively easy, which is not the case for logistic functions as used here, as they complicate mathematical analysis. Nevertheless, with some effort still some results were achieved about the emerging clusters and equilibrium values for states and connection weights, which explained many of the patterns that were observed in simulations.

For the validation, as discussed, the error (average linear deviation) of the simulated model was found at 0.29. This is not bad considering that the network consisted of 21 persons and only a small number of time points were available (only three time points were used to compare both data; the first time point was used for the initial values of the simulated model). Furthermore, it can be noted that the numbers expressing the empirical data only use very distant discrete values, whereas the simulated data take on a wider range of numbers: any real number. The empirical values were expressed on scales with gaps of 0.2, 0.3, 0.4 or even 0.5; therefore, an average linear deviation below 0.3 for the model may be reasonably close to the best result theoretically possible.

Unfortunately, there are only a limited amount of longitudinal datasets available at this moment. In the future, when more data sets might be available, this model could be validated for data sets with bigger sample sizes and more measured time points.

The discussed model shows similarities to the model described in Blankendaal *et al.* [3], who also used a temporal network model to simulate data. However, they used a scaled sum function to integrate the homophily principle in the model, and also a linear function for the contagion process. We chose to implement the logistic function since to our opinion this function fits the idea of the homophily better. The scaled sum function does not take into account the number of connections that have an impact on a certain state, whereas the logistic combination function does take that aspect into account. Furthermore, van Beukel *et al.* [2] also used a logistic combination function for the homophily principle to simulate data. In their case connections of weight 0 or 1 cannot change. Because that is not a desirable property, the logistic function used in the current paper was a different, more advanced variant of the logistic function, which makes it possible that connections of weight 0 or 1 still can change.

References

1. Akers, R.L., Krohn, M.D., Lanza-Kaduce, L., Radosevich, M.: Social learning and deviant behavior: a specific test of a general theory. Am. Sociol. Rev. **44**(4), 636–655 (1979)
2. van den Beukel, S., Goos, Simon H., Treur, J.: Understanding homophily and more-becomes-more through adaptive temporal-causal network models. In: De la Prieta, F., et al. (eds.) PAAMS 2017. AISC, vol. 619, pp. 16–29. Springer, Cham (2018). https://doi.org/10.1007/978-3-319-61578-3_2
3. Blankendaal, R., Parinussa, S., Treur, J.: A temporal-causal modelling approach to integrated contagion and network change in social networks. In: Proceedings of the 22nd European Conference on Artificial Intelligence, ECAI 2016, vol. 285, pp. 1388–1396. IOS Press Frontiers in Artificial Intelligence and Applications (2016)
4. Bosse, T., Duell, R., Memon, Z.A., Treur, J., van der Wal, C.N.: Agent-based modeling of emotion contagion in groups. Cogn. Comput. **7**, 111–136 (2015)
5. Cairns, R.B., Cairns, B.D., Neckerman, H.J., Gest, S.D., Gariépy, J.L.: Social networks and aggressive behavior: peer support or peer rejection. Dev. Psychol. **24**, 815–823 (1988)
6. Elliott, D.S., Menard, S.: Delinquent friends and delinquent behavior: temporal and developmental patterns. In: Hawkins, J.D. (ed.) Delinquency and Crime: Current Theories. Cambridge Criminology Series, pp. 28–67. Cambridge University Press, New York (1996)
7. Frederickson, B.L., Joiner, T.: Positive emotions trigger upward spirals toward emotional well-being. Psychol. Sci. **13**, 172–175 (2002)
8. Gifford-Smith, M., Dodge, K.A., Dishion, T.J., McCord, J.: Peer influence in children and adolescents: crossing the bridge from developmental to intervention science. J. Abnorm. Child Psychol. **33**(3), 255–265 (2005)
9. Haynie, D.L.: Friendship networks and delinquency: the relative nature of peer delinquency. J. Quant. Criminol. **18**(2), 99–134 (2002)

10. Knecht, A.: Empirical data: collected by Andrea Knecht (2008). https://www.stats.ox.ac.uk/~snijders/siena/tutorial2010_data.htm
11. Kuipers, B.J.: Commonsense reasoning about causality: deriving behavior from structure. Artif. Intell. **24**, 169–203 (1984)
12. Kuipers, B.J., Kassirer, J.P.: How to discover a knowledge representation for causal reasoning by studying an expert physician. In: Proceedings of the 8th International Joint Conference on Artificial Intelligence, IJCAI 1983, William Kaufman, Los Altos, CA, pp. 49–56 (1983)
13. Parunak, H.V.D., Downs, E., Yinger, A.: Socially-constrained exogenously-driven opinion dynamics. In: Fifth International IEEE Conference Self-Adaptive and Self-Organizing Systems (SASO 2011) (2011)
14. Pearl, J.: Causality. Cambridge University Press (2000)
15. Treur, J.: Network-Oriented Modeling: Addressing Complexity of Cognitive, Affective and Social Interactions. Springer, Cham (2016)

An Agent-Based Modelling Approach to Analyse the Public Opinion on Politicians

Thijs M. A. Brouwers ⓘ, John P. T. Onneweer ⓘ, and Jan Treur(✉) ⓘ

Behavioural Informatics Group, Vrije Universiteit Amsterdam,
Amsterdam, Netherlands
tbrouwers95@gmail.com, johnonneweer@gmail.com,
j.treur@vu.nl

Abstract. A politician's popularity can be measured by polls or by measuring the amount of times a politician is mentioned on the Internet in a positive or negative manner. This paper introduces an approach to an agent-based computational model to model a politician's popularity within a population that participates on the Internet over time. A particle swarm optimization algorithm is used for parameter tuning to identify the characteristics of all agents based on the analysis of public opinions on a politician found on the Internet. The properties of the network are verified by applying a social network analysis. A mathematical analysis is used to get more in depth understanding on the model and to verify its correctness.

Keywords: Opinion dynamics · Network model · Politician

1 Introduction

The process of opinion formation cannot be separated from the specific social network in which an individual is situated. An individual observes the behavior of and receives information from a small subset of society, consisting of friends, family, coworkers and peers, and a certain group of (opinion) leaders that he or she listens to and respects; all of them can have a substantial influence on the individual's opinion [9, 11]. Interactions will lead to dynamics in opinion formation [1]. The opinion dynamics in a network may lead to consensus among or polarization between the agents or, more general, to a certain fragmentation of the opinion patterns [5].

Information obtained within a social context can be interpreted differently among individuals. Some information will be more trusted than others and conjectures are formed about members and their intentions in the social network [1]. In a population or group, it seems that multiple groups, specifically groups of easily influenced individuals influence the opinion of an entire network more than powerful individuals alone [17].

Thierry Baudet is a much discussed politician in the Netherlands in 2017. He is the founder and leader of the political party Forum for Democracy. With this newly, right-wing and national conservative party, he managed to win two seats in the House of Representatives in the general election of 2017. After being elected, he made a number of striking statements and acts, causing a lot of fuss in the media. With these, sometimes controversial, statements and acts, he has made himself very popular with some,

© Springer Nature Switzerland AG 2018
S. Staab et al. (Eds.): SocInfo 2018, LNCS 11185, pp. 102–116, 2018.
https://doi.org/10.1007/978-3-030-01129-1_7

while others became fiercely against him. According to the polls of Maurice de Hond, the party would win fifteen seats at the end of 2017. It can be argued that the popularity in a network influences the popularity in the polls.

Within a social network, which is exposed to information as described above, a process of opinion formation takes place. In general, agents will, to a certain extent, take into account the opinions of other agents when forming their own opinion. They will neither simply share nor firmly disregard the opinions of others, which can be modelled by different weights on the opinions of others. There also may be a difference in how easily agents change their opinion, which can be modelled as well.

The goal of this paper is to present an agent-based computational model to simulate the overall opinion on Baudet over time. It takes into account agents representing persons who have access to and post on web pages. The computational model was designed by a Network-Oriented Modelling approach based on temporal-causal networks, which in previous work has turned out a useful and easy to use means to model social networks and their dynamics [16]. Manual sentiment analysis was performed to determine whether the contents of the web pages had a positive or negative tone on Baudet.

2   The Temporal-Causal Network Model

In this section, first the Network-Oriented Modeling approach used [16] is briefly explained. This Network-Oriented Modeling approach is based on temporal-causal networks. Causal modeling, causal reasoning and causal simulation have a long tradition in AI; e.g., [7, 8, 12]. The Network-Oriented Modeling approach based on temporal-causal networks described in [16] can be viewed on the one hand as part of this causal modeling tradition, and on the other hand from the perspective on mental states and their causal relations in Philosophy of Mind (e.g., [6]), and from the perspective of social networks where nodes affect each other. It is a widely usable generic dynamic AI modeling approach that distinguishes itself by incorporating a dynamic and adaptive temporal perspective, both on states and on causal relations. This dynamic perspective enables modeling of cyclic and adaptive networks, and also of timing of causal effects.

Temporal-causal network models can be represented at two levels: by a conceptual representation and by a numerical representation. These representations can be used to display the network graphically and for numerical simulations. The model usually includes a number of parameters for domain, person or social context-specific characteristics. Parameter tuning methods are available to estimate the values for such parameters.

A conceptual representation of a temporal-causal network model represents, in a declarative manner, states and connections between those states that represent impacts of states on each other, as assumed to hold for the addressed application domain. The states have activation levels that vary over time. Connections can have different strengths, and states can be affected by more than one other state. Moreover, states can have a different extent of flexibility; some states may be able to change fast, while other states are a more rigid and change more slowly. These three notions are covered by elements in the Network-Oriented Modeling approach based on temporal-causal net-works, and are reflected in the conceptual representation of a temporal-causal network model [15, 16]:

- **Connection weight** $\omega_{X,Y}$: Each connection from a state X to a state Y has a con-nection weight value $\omega_{X,Y}$ representing the strength of the connection.
- **Combination function** $c_Y(..)$: For each state a combination function $c_Y(..)$ is used to combine the causal impacts of other states on state Y.
- **Speed factor** η_Y: For each state Y a speed factor η_Y is used to represent how fast a state is changing upon causal impact.

A simple conceptual representation of the designed model is shown in Fig. 1. A single agent of the population represents a part of the Dutch population who think alike. To get a manageable network model it was decided to limit the number of agents which each are considered in some way to represent the different types of persons in the real world. Since there are 150 seats in the Dutch House of Representatives and one seat should represent a part of the Dutch population with the same political preference, a total of 150 agents is used in the proposed network. The connections represent how they affect each other's opinions. The opinion state represents the overall opinion of the network as a whole. Because it can be discussed that voting behaviour of a population relates to but may not be exactly equal to their overall opinion about the politician or party, another state is included that represents the voting behavior of the population. The state values represent the opinion on the Dutch politician called Baudet. A state value of 1 means that the agent has only positive opinions on Baudet, whereas a state value of 0 means there are no positive opinions on Baudet within that agent, only neutral or negative opinions. An arrow between two agents means that there is a connection from one agent to the other agent by which the former agent influences the latter agent.

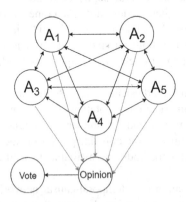

Fig. 1. A conceptual representation of the temporal-causal network model

A scale-free network is a network with a degree distribution that follows a power law. It has nodes with a degree that by far exceed the average degree of the network [2]. These highest-degree nodes are often called hubs, and are closely followed by other nodes with a smaller degree and so on. An important characteristic of a scale-free network is the clustering coefficient distribution, which decreases as the node degree increases. This distribution also follows a power law, which implies that low-degree nodes belong to dense subgroups [2]. Subgroups are connected to each other through hubs. In a social network, of the type used in this study, the subgroups are communities in which everyone knows everyone, and everybody has a few relationships to people outside the community. In such network, there are some people who are connected to a large number of communities within the network (e.g. celebrities, politicians).

However, in the proposed network the nodes have a high degree. The number of communities within the network thus will be small. The degrees are based on the activity of the members on the Internet. Some are online a lot, being influenced by others often. Others may be less online, resulting in fewer degrees. Because nowadays in life it is easy to propagate opinions on the Internet, with a high reach, we assumed that every member of the network has a high degree. Within the proposed scale-free network connections between agents are defined by their weight. A connection weight of 0 means there is no connection from one agent to another. Connection weights are numbers in the [0, 1] interval stand for a connection from one agent to another. This method implements that it is possible that agent X has a connection towards agent Y, while agent Y has no connection towards agent X. The connections are a basis for contagion between agents. All agents have an initial value which represents their initial opinion on Baudet. Over time agents will be influenced by other agents, by accessing the Internet. Here they will be influenced by the opinions of others, and influence others with their own opinion.

According to the Network-Oriented Modeling approach based on temporal-causal networks used, combination functions can have different forms. They specify for each state a way how multiple impacts on this state are aggregated. For this aggregation a variety of standard combination functions are available, among which sum and scaled sum combination functions as discussed below.

A conceptual representation of a model can be transformed systematically or even automatically into a numerical representation of the model as follows [15, 16]:

- at each time point t each state Y has a real number value $Y(t)$ in [0, 1]
  at each time point t each state X connected to state Y has an impact on Y defined as

$$\mathbf{impact}_{X,Y}(t) = \omega_{X,Y}X(t)$$

where $\omega_{X,Y}$ is the connection weight

- The *aggregated impact* of multiple states X_i on Y at t is determined by:

$$\mathbf{aggimpact}_Y(t) = \mathbf{c}_Y(\mathbf{impact}_{X_1,Y}(t), \ldots, \mathbf{impact}_{X_k,Y}(t))$$
$$= \mathbf{c}_Y(\omega_{X_1,Y}X_1(t), \ldots, \omega_{X_k,Y}X_k(t))$$

where X_i are the states with connections to state Y

- The effect of **aggimpact$_Y$(t)** on Y is exerted *over time gradually*:

$$Y(t + \Delta t) = Y(t) + \eta_Y[\mathbf{aggimpact}_Y(t) - Y(t)]\Delta t$$
$$\text{or } dY(t)/dt = \eta_Y[\mathbf{aggimpact}_Y(t) - Y(t)]$$

- Thus, the following *difference* and *differential equation* for Y are obtained:

$$Y(t + \Delta t) = Y(t) + \eta_Y[\mathbf{c}_Y(\omega_{X_1,Y}X_1(t), \ldots, \omega_{X_k,Y}X_k(t)) - Y(t)]\Delta t$$
$$dY(t)/dt = \eta_Y[\mathbf{c}_Y(\omega_{X_1,Y}X_1(t), \ldots, \omega_{X_k,Y}X_k(t)) - Y(t)]$$

Software environments are available in Matlab and Python that do this transformation and enable to run simulation experiments. For any set of values for the connection weights, speed factors and any choice for combination functions, each node gets a difference or differential equation assigned. For the model considered here, this makes a set of 152 coupled equations, that together, in mutual interaction, describe the model's behavior. Note that the parameters and in particular the speed factors enable to obtain realistic differences between individual agents in the model to tune the model to the characteristics of people in the real world.

For all agents a scaled sum function **ssum$_\lambda$(.,.)** is used as combination function. The opinion state is defined by a sum function **sum(.,.)** [16]:

$$\mathbf{c}_Y(V_1, \ldots, V_k) = \mathbf{sum}(V_1, \ldots, V_k) = V_1 + \ldots + V_k$$
$$\mathbf{c}_Y(V_1, \ldots, V_k) = \mathbf{ssum}_\lambda(V_1, \ldots, V_n) = (V_1 + \ldots + V_k)/\lambda$$

where λ is the scaling factor. The voting state uses the identity function **id(.)**, defined as **id(V) = V**. In our network, where all connection weights are assumed ≥ 0, the scaling factor λ is defined as the sum of the incoming weights for any agent. For example, the scaling factor of agent 1 $\lambda = \omega_{A_1}$ is defined as the sum of the incoming weights of all other agents: $\omega_{A_1} = \omega_{B_1,A_1} + \ldots + \omega_{B_k,A_1}$. The combination function for agent 1 is

$$c_{A_1}(V_1, \ldots, V_k) = \mathbf{ssum}_{\omega_{A_1}}(V_1, \ldots, V_k) = (V_1 + \ldots + V_k)/\omega_{A_1}$$

The difference and differential equation are as follows:

$$A_1(t + \Delta t) = A_1(t) + \eta_{A_1}[\mathbf{ssum}_{\omega_{A_1}}(\omega_{B_1,A_1}B_1(t), \ldots, \omega_{B_k,A_1}B_k(t)) - A_1(t)]\Delta t$$
$$dA_1(t)/dt = \eta_{A1}\left[\mathbf{ssum}_{\omega_{A_1}}(\omega_{B_1,A_1}B_1(t), \ldots, \omega_{B_k,A_1}B_k(t)) - A_1(t)\right]$$

The **sum(.,.)** combination function is used for the opinion state. For example, the difference and differential equation for state A_{opinion} are as follows:

$$A_{\text{opinion}}(t + \Delta t) = A_{\text{opinion}}(t) +$$
$$\eta_{A_{\text{opinion}}}[\mathbf{sum}(\omega_{A_1,A_{\text{opinion}}}A_1(t), \ldots, \omega_{A_{150},A_{\text{opinion}}}A_1(t)) - A_{\text{opinion}}(t)]\Delta t$$
$$dA_{\text{opinion}}(t)/dt = \eta_{A_{\text{opinion}}}[\mathbf{sum}(\omega_{A_1,A_{\text{opinion}}}A_1(t), \ldots, \omega_{A_{150},A_{\text{opinion}}}A_{150}(t)) - A_{\text{opinion}}(t)]$$

For the voting state they are

$$A_{voting}(t+\Delta t) = A_{voting}(t) + \eta_{A_{voting}}[\omega_{A_{opinion},A_{voting}}A_{opinion}(t) - A_{voting}(t)]\Delta t$$
$$dA_{voting}(t)/dt = \eta_{A_{voting}}[\omega_{A_{opinion},A_{voting}}A_{opinion}(t) - A_{voting}(t)]$$

3 Social Network Analysis

Gephi version 0.9.2. [3] has been used to analyse the social network, which is shown in Fig. 2. The network consists of 152 nodes and 7059 edges. The average degree is 46.441, with a highest in-degree of 150 for the Opinion node. Within the agents, node 36 has the highest in-degree of 108. This means this agent has 108 incoming connections. Using the notion of centrality of nodes within a network, the relative importance of a node in the network can be determined. In this social network the centrality of the node would represent the popularity of the agent on the web. Node 5 has the highest betweenness centrality of 2152.369, after which node 141 follows with 1998.363, node 14 with 1832.571 and node 78 with 1224.405. High values for betweenness centrality are most likely popular agents who influence the other connecting agents the most. The number of communities in this network is 7 and the modularity is 0.83. The Opinion and Vote node are communities on itself. There are also 4 nodes which have very few to zero in-degrees, each forming a separate community. All other nodes are part of the remaining community.

For gathering *real world data* on the popularity of Baudet on the web, all search results on google.com with 'thierry baudet' as search term were analyzed and classified manually. The web pages analyzed were of all types. The majority concerned web pages of news agencies and blogs where people could give their opinion.

Based on the content of the web page an overall sentiment of that particular page was given: positive, neutral or negative. Evaluation of sentiment was based on signal words and the positive or negative connection that was given to those words. For example in the sentence: "He was brave to say such words in such a public." gives a positive sentiment based on the word 'brave'. In total, 920 web pages dating from January 2017 to December 2017 were analyzed for positive, neutral or negative sentiment. Potential classification errors could have had influence on the sentiment analysis, but as the analysis was done by two persons in accordance with each other, this risk was minimised. Therefore, potential errors are expected not to affect the overall course of the sentiment. Furthermore, poll outcomes from the monthly political poll of Maurice de Hond in 2017 were gathered to analyze voting behaviour.

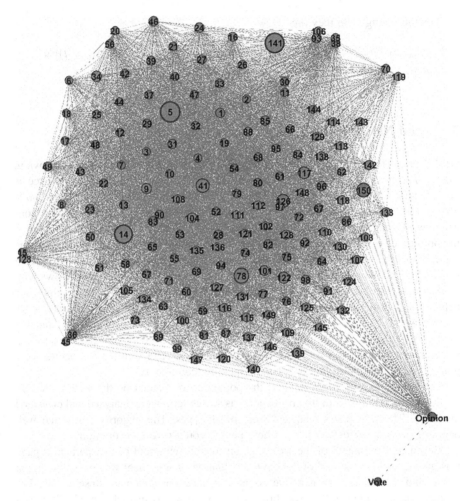

Fig. 2. Nodes size according to their betweenness centrality. The bigger the node, the higher their betweenness centrality value.

4   Validation Based on Real World Data

Matlab v2017 was used to simulate the numerical representation of the model. As the model uses continuous state values between 0 and 1, the empirical opinion data was aggregated by the percentage of positive mentions relative to total amount of mentions in each month. As the maximum amount of seats in the House of Representatives in The Netherlands is 150, the empirical vote data was aggregated by dividing it by 150. The initial value of the Opinion state was 0.22 and of the Vote state 0.01, derived from the month of January 2017 of the empirical data. For the assignment of the initial values of the agents, the initial value of the opinion state is taken into account. It is assumed that, initially, 22 percent of all agents had a positive opinion on Baudet. Therefore a random value above the average opinion is assigned to these agents. The remaining 78 percent of the agents were assigned a random value below the average opinion. A step size Δt of 0.1 was used, with a maximum t of 12. To compare the empirical data against the model data, 11 time points were chosen. The opinion and vote values at time point 2 to 12 of the empirical data are compared with time points 11, 21, 31, 41, 51, 61, 71, 81, 91, 101 and 111 of the Opinion and Vote state of the model.

To make the model fitting with the real world data, a large number of parameters has been tuned by Particle Swarm Optimization (PSO) [13]. The speed factors of all agents, the initial values of the Opinion state and Vote state, the connection weights between all agents and the assignment of initial values to the agents were tuned; see Table 1.

Table 1. Parameters tuned by optimization algorithm

Parameter	Notation	Interval
Connections between all agents	$\omega_{i,j}$	[0, 1]
Speed factors for all agents	η_i	[0, 1]
Speed factor for opinion state	$\eta_{opinion}$	[0, 1]
Speed factor for vote state	η_{vote}	[0, 1]
Assignment of initial values	150*	[0, 1]*

* the 150 initial values for the agents were first
selected and during the tuning process allocated to the
150 agents

This makes a total of 22802 parameters that were tuned by the Particle Swarm Optimization algorithm.

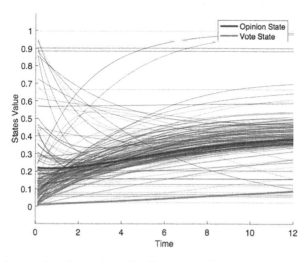

Fig. 3. Simulation results after tuning. The lines not indicated in the legend represent the opinion towards Thierry Baudet of the 150 agents in the model.

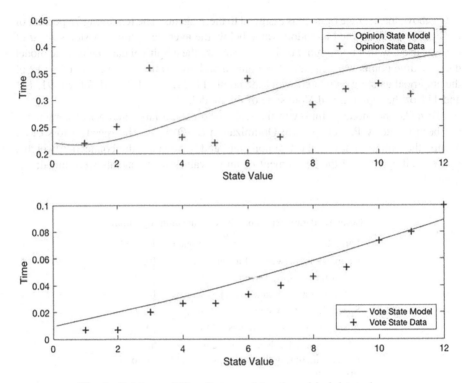

Fig. 4. Opinion and Vote State: model and empirical data values.

As fitness function for the Particle Swarm Optimization algorithm the sum of squares SSR of the differences between empirical and model data was used. The goal of the algorithm was to minimize this difference by tuning the parameters. After tuning, the sum of squares SSR was 7.257×10^{-5}. This gives an average deviation of $\sqrt{(SSR/11)} = 0.0026$. The simulation after tuning is shown in Fig. 3. Figure 4 shows the values of the Opinion and Vote state of the model and empirical data.

5   Verification by Mathematical Analysis

In this section, it is discussed how a Mathematical Analysis of the behavior of the model was performed. Doing this, the model was verified by comparing simulation outcomes to analysis results. Moreover, more in depth understanding of the outcomes was obtained. A formula has been derived for the trend of the sum of all agent state values, in the form of the derivative of that sum; see Theorem 1. The following Lemma 1 can easily be verified.

Lemma 1. For a scaled sum combination function $\mathbf{ssum}_\lambda(..)$ with scaling factor $\lambda = \omega_A = \omega_{B_1,A} + \ldots + \omega_{B_k,A}$ the outcome of the function is a weighted average of the incoming state values:

$$\mathbf{ssum}_{\omega_A}\big(\omega_{B_1,A}B_1(t), \ldots, \omega_{B_k,A}B_k(t)\big) = \big(\omega_{B_1,A}/\omega_A\big)B_1(t) + \ldots + \big(\omega_{B_k,A}/\omega_A\big)B_k(t)$$

where the sum of the weights $\omega_{Bi,A}/\omega_A$ for the state values is 1.

Theorem 1. In a network based on the scaled sum combination function with scaling factor $\lambda = \omega_X$ the following holds:

$$\mathbf{d}\sum_A A(t)/\mathbf{d}t = \sum_B \left[\sum_{A,A\neq B}(\eta_A\omega_{B,A}/\omega_A - \eta_B\omega_{A,B}/\omega_B\right]B(t)$$

and

$$\mathbf{d}\sum_A A(t)/\mathbf{d}t = \sum_B \left[\sum_{A,A\neq B}(\eta_A\omega_{B,A}/\omega_A) - \eta_B\right]B(t)$$

with ω_X the sum of all $\omega_{C,X}$ for C not equal to X.

Proof. This requires some algebraic rewriting. First replace each connection weight $\omega_{B,A}$ by $\omega_{B,A}/\omega_A$ so that it results in $\sum_{B\neq A}\omega_{B,A} = 1$. Then rewrite as follows:

$$\mathbf{d}\sum_A A(t)/\mathbf{d}t = \sum_A \mathbf{d}A(t)/\mathbf{d}t$$
$$= \sum_A \eta_A\left[\sum_{B\neq A}\omega_{B,A}B(t) - A(t)\right]$$
$$= \sum_A \eta_A\left[\sum_{B\neq A}\omega_{B,A}B(t) - \sum_{B\neq A}\omega_{B,A}A(t)\right]$$
$$= \sum_A \eta_A\sum_{B\neq A}\omega_{B,A}[B(t) - A(t)]$$
$$= \sum_{A,B\neq A}\eta_A\omega_{B,A}[B(t) - A(t)]$$

Thus it is obtained

$$\mathbf{d}\sum_A A(t)/\mathbf{d}t = \sum_{A,B,B\neq A}\eta_A\omega_{B,A}[B(t) - A(t)]$$
$$\mathbf{d}\sum_B B(t)/\mathbf{d}t = \sum_{A,B,B\neq A}\eta_B\omega_{A,B}[A(t) - B(t)]$$

Add these two to obtain

$$\mathbf{2d}\sum_A A(t)/\mathbf{d}t = \sum_{A,B,B\neq A}\eta_A\omega_{B,A}[B(t) - A(t)] + \sum_{A,B,B\neq A}\eta_B\omega_{A,B}[A(t) - B(t)]$$
$$= \sum_{A,B,B\neq A}\eta_A\omega_{B,A}[B(t) - A(t)] + \eta_B\omega_{A,B}[A(t) - B(t)]$$
$$= \sum_{A,B,B\neq A}\left[\eta_A\omega_{B,A}B(t) - \eta_A\omega_{B,A}A(t) + \eta_B\omega_{A,B}A(t) - \eta_B\omega_{A,B}B(t)\right]$$
$$= \sum_{A,B,B\neq A}\left[(\eta_A\omega_{B,A} - \eta_B\omega_{A,B})B(t) - (\eta_A\omega_{B,A} - \eta_B\omega_{A,B})A(t)\right]$$
$$= \sum_{A,B,B\neq A}\left[(\eta_A\omega_{B,A} - \eta_B\omega_{A,B})B(t)\right] - \sum_{A,B,B\neq A}\left[(\eta_A\omega_{B,A} - \eta_B\omega_{A,B})A(t)\right]$$
$$= \sum_{A,B,B\neq A}\left[(\eta_A\omega_{B,A} - \eta_B\omega_{A,B})B(t)\right] - \sum_{A,B,B\neq A}\left[(\eta_B\omega_{A,B} - \eta_A\omega_{B,A})B(t)\right]$$
$$= \sum_{A,B,B\neq A}(\eta_A\omega_{B,A} - \eta_B\omega_{A,B})B(t) - (\eta_B\omega_{A,B} - \eta_A\omega_{B,A})B(t)$$
$$= \sum_{A,B,B\neq A}\left[(\eta_A\omega_{B,A} - \eta_B\omega_{A,B}) - (\eta_B\omega_{A,B} - \eta_A\omega_{B,A})\right]B(t)$$
$$= \sum_{A,B,B\neq A}2(\eta_A\omega_{B,A} - \eta_B\omega_{A,B})\,B(t)$$

Therefore it is found

$$\mathbf{d}\sum\nolimits_{A} A(t)/\mathbf{d}t = \sum\nolimits_{A,B,B\neq A} \left(\eta_A \omega_{B,A} - \eta_B \omega_{A,B}\right) B(t)$$

This can be rewritten into

$$\mathbf{d}\sum\nolimits_{A} A(t)/\mathbf{d}t = \sum\nolimits_{B} \sum\nolimits_{A,A\neq B} \left(\eta_A \omega_{B,A} - \eta_B \omega_{A,B}\right) B(t)$$
$$= \sum\nolimits_{B} \left[\sum\nolimits_{A,A\neq B} \left(\eta_A \omega_{B,A} - \eta_B \omega_{A,B}\right)\right] B(t)$$
$$= \sum\nolimits_{B} \left[\sum\nolimits_{A,A\neq B} \eta_A \omega_{B,A} - \eta_B \sum\nolimits_{A,A\neq B} \omega_{A,B}\right] B(t)$$
$$= \sum\nolimits_{B} \left[\sum\nolimits_{A,A\neq B} \eta_A \omega_{B,A} - \eta_B\right] B(t)$$

In terms of the original connection weights this is

$$\mathbf{d}\sum\nolimits_{A} A(t)/\mathbf{d}t = \sum\nolimits_{B} \left[\sum\nolimits_{A,A\neq B} \left(\eta_A \omega_{B,A}/\omega_A - \eta_B \omega_{A,B}/\omega_B\right)\right] B(t)$$

or

$$\mathbf{d}\sum\nolimits_{A} A(t)/\mathbf{d}t = \sum\nolimits_{B} \left[\sum\nolimits_{A,A\neq B} \left(\eta_A \omega_{B,A}/\omega_A\right) - \eta_B\right] B(t) \quad\blacksquare$$

The latter formula explains that the sum increases when the speed factor is low for states with a high state value:

[$B(t)$ high $\Rightarrow \eta_B$ low] $\Rightarrow$ the terms in the sum with high $B(t)$ have a higher coefficient

$$\Rightarrow \mathbf{d}\sum\nolimits_{A} A(t)/\mathbf{d}t > 0$$

Indeed, the outcome of the tuning process shows a tendency of relatively lower speed factors for states with high initial value; see Fig. 5. The general idea behind this is that due to slower changing of nodes with higher values, their impact over time on the whole population will be stronger than the impact of nodes that change relatively fast due to which they soon adapt to the other nodes and then lose their influence.

Based on the connection weights, and speed factors generated by the optimization algorithm, and the simulated state values of the model, the equation

$$\mathbf{d}\sum\nolimits_{A} A(t)/\mathbf{d}t = \sum\nolimits_{B} \left[\sum\nolimits_{A,A\neq B} \left(\eta_A \omega_{B,A}/\omega_A\right) - \eta_B\right] B(t)$$

from Theorem 1 has been checked. In Fig. 5 the outcome is shown. It turns out that the standard error of the estimate $\sqrt{(SSR/N)}$ is 0.0140, which is good; this is such a small difference that it is hardly visible in Fig. 6. This contributes verification outcomes for both the formula and the implementation of the model and provides reliable evidence for the implemented model to do what is expected.

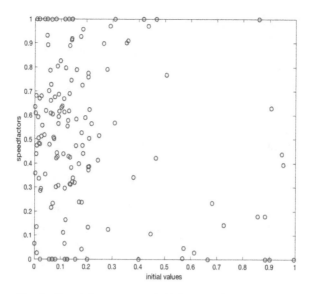

Fig. 5. Speed factors versus initial state values after tuning

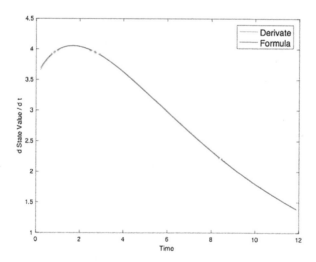

Fig. 6. The outcome of $\mathbf{d} \sum_A A(t) / \mathbf{d}t$ in red and $\sum_B [\sum_{A,A \neq B} (\eta_A \, \omega_{B,A}/\omega_A) - \eta_B] \, B(t)$ in blue (Color figure online)

6 Mathematical Analysis of Equilibria

When simulated for longer time periods, the model reaches an equilibrium state. In such an equilibrium state, the state values usually turn out equal. This has been analysed mathematically as well.

Definition

(a) The network model is in *equilibrium* at t if $dY(t)/dt = 0$ for all states.
(b) The network is called *weakly symmetric* if for all nodes A and B it holds $\omega_{A,B} = 0$
    $\Leftrightarrow \omega_{B,A} = 0$ or, equivalently: $\omega_{A,B} > 0 \Leftrightarrow \omega_{B,A} > 0$.
(c) The network is called *fully symmetric* if $\omega_{A,B} = \omega_{B,A}$ for all nodes A and B.

Lemma 2. Let a network be given based on the scaled sum combination function with scaling factor $\lambda = \omega_A = \omega_{B1,A} + \dots + \omega_{Bk,A}$, then the following hold:

a) If for some node A at time t for all nodes B with $B(t) > A(t)$ it holds $\omega_{B,A} = 0$, then $A(t)$ is decreasing at t: $dA(t) / dt \leq 0$.
b) If, moreover, a node B exists with $B(t) < A(t)$ and $\omega_{B,A} > 0$, then $A(t)$ is strictly decreasing at t: $dA(t)(t) / dt < 0$.

Proof: (a) Using Lemma 1, from the expressions for $c_A(\dots)$ it follows that $c_A(\dots) \leq A(t)$, and therefore $dA(t)/dt \leq 0$, so $A(t)$ is decreasing at t. b) In this case $c_A(\dots) < A(t)$ and therefore $dA(t)/dt < 0$, so $A(t)$ is strictly decreasing. ∎

Theorem 2. Suppose a weakly symmetric network is based on the scaled sum combination function with scaling factor $\lambda = \omega_X$. Then in an equilibrium state all connected states have the same value.

Proof: Suppose in an equilibrium state at t some nodes A and B exist such that $A(t) \neq B(t)$ and $\omega_{B,A} > 0$ and $\omega_{A,B} > 0$. Take a node A with this property with highest value A. Then for all nodes C with $C(t) > A(t)$ it holds $\omega_{C,A} = 0$, and there exists a B with $B(t) < A(t)$ and $\omega_{B,A} > 0$. Now apply Lemma 2b) to this node A. It follows that $dA(t)/dt < 0$, so A is not in equilibrium at t. This contradicts the assumption. Therefore all nodes that are connected have the same state value in this equilibrium. ∎

This Theorem 2 explains what is observed in the simulations. Connected states converge to the same value, but isolated states can keep their original value.

7 Discussion

Persons within a social network, for example, family or co-workers, influence each other [11]. Also, some persons within a network tend to influence others more then other persons, those so-called 'opinion leaders' can have a strong influence on the opinions within those network [9]. This paper presented a computational network model to analyse the popularity of a politician within a population that participates on the Internet. The approach enabled to identify the characteristics of agents in the network based on the analysis of public opinions on that politician found on the Internet. The model was designed as a scale-free agent network [2], according to the Network-Oriented Modeling approach presented in [16]. The model was tuned to the aggregated public opinion, using a Particle Swarm Optimization algorithm [13]. The model was verified by social network analysis and by mathematical analysis.

There are studies that model the outcome of elections based on behavior of people on social media [4, 10, 14], but as far as the authors know not how in a social network an opinion towards a specific politician changes over time. Therefore there is no comparison available for the proposed model that does this based on the sentiment on the web.

Often in a model for the social contagion principle, all the state values converge without showing an upward or downward general trend. However, it was found that by using low speed factors for states with a high value, the mean of all states first show an upward trend and after a longer time converge to a value substantially above an expected mean of all initialization state values. This phenomenon was also verified and explained by the mathematical analysis. Apparently, as in most of the literature the speed factors for all agents are set equal (or there even is not such a concept in the model able to make differences in speed), this phenomenon is not often showing up. But from an agent-based modeling perspective it is quite natural to consider personalized agent characteristics, in particular for the speed factors.

Connecting the probability to vote to the overall public opinion by a sum function may be a bit too simplistic view on voting behavior, for example, when a certain politician is popular in a group, this does not mean other politicians would not be even more popular. In future research variations of the model should include more in-depth modelling on voting behavior based on the overall public opinion dynamics.

This paper showed that dynamics of an overall opinion of a network can be modelled, and that in a population where the overall opinion is negative, positive agents may be less influenced or are less likely to change their opinion than negative agents.

References

1. Acemoglu, D., Ozdaglar, A.: Opinion dynamics and learning in social networks. Dyn. Games Appl. **1**(1), 3–49 (2011)
2. Barabási, A.L., Albert, R.: Emergence of scaling in random networks. Science **286**(5439), 509–512 (1999)
3. Bastian, M., Heymann, S., Jacomy, M.: Gephi: an open source software for exploring and manipulating networks. In: ICWSM, vol. 8, pp. 361–362 (2009)
4. DiGrazia, J., McKelvey, K., Bollen, J., Rojas, F.: More tweets, more votes: Social media as a quantitative indicator of political behavior. PLoS ONE **8**(11), e79449 (2013)
5. Hegselmann, R., Krause, U.: Opinion dynamics and bounded confidence models, analysis, and simulation. J. Artif. Soc. Soc. Simul. **5**(3) (2002)
6. Kim, J.: Philosophy of Mind. Westview Press, Boulder (1996)
7. Kuipers, B.J.: Commonsense reasoning about causality: deriving behavior from structure. Artif. Intell. **24**, 169–203 (1984)

8. Kuipers, B.J., Kassirer, J.P.: How to discover a knowledge representation for causal reasoning by studying an expert physician. In: Proceedings of the 8th International Joint Conference on Artificial Intelligence, IJCAI 1983, William Kaufman, Los Altos, CA, pp. 49–56 (1983)

9. Lazarsfeld, P.F., Gaudet, H., Berelson, B.: The People's Choice: How the Voter Makes Up His Mind in a Presidential Campaign. Columbia University Press, New York (1965)

10. Metaxas, P.T., Mustafaraj, E., Gayo-Avello, D.: How (not) to predict elections. In: Proceedings of the Third International Conference on Social Computing, SocialCom 2011, pp. 165–171. IEEE (2011)

11. Nickerson, D.W.: Is voting contagious? evidence from two field experiments. Am. Polit. Sci. Rev. 102(01), 49–57 (2008)

12. Pearl, J.: Causality. Cambridge University Press, New York (2000)

13. Poli, R., Kennedy, J., Blackwell, T.: Particle swarm optimization. An overview. Swarm Intell. 1, 33–57 (2007)

14. Sang, E.T.K., Bos, J.: Predicting the 2011 Dutch senate election results with twitter. In: Proceedings of the workshop on semantic analysis in social media, pp. 53–60. Association for Computational Linguistics (2012)

15. Treur, J.: Dynamic modeling based on a temporal–causal network modeling approach. Biologically Inspired Cogn. Architectures 16, 131–168 (2016)

16. Treur, J.: Network-Oriented Modelling: Addressing Complexity of Cognitive, Affective and Social Interactions. Springer, Cham (2016). https://doi.org/10.1007/978-3-319-45213-5

17. Watts, D.J., Dodds, P.S.: Influentials, Networks, and Public Opinion Formation. J. Consum. Res. 34(4), 441–458 (2007)

A Comparison of Classical Versus Deep Learning Techniques for Abusive Content Detection on Social Media Sites

Hao Chen[(⊠)], Susan McKeever, and Sarah Jane Delany

Dublin Institute of Technology, Dublin, Ireland
hao.chen@mydit.ie, {susan.mckeever,sarahjane.delany}@dit.ie

Abstract. The automated detection of abusive content on social media websites faces a variety of challenges including imbalanced training sets, the identification of an appropriate feature representation and the selection of optimal classifiers. Classifiers such as support vector machines (SVM), combined with bag of words or ngram feature representation, have traditionally dominated in text classification for decades. With the recent emergence of deep learning and word embeddings, an increasing number of researchers have started to focus on deep neural networks. In this paper, our aim is to explore cutting-edge techniques in automated abusive content detection. We use two deep learning approaches: convolutional neural networks (CNNs) and recurrent neural networks (RNNs). We apply these to 9 public datasets derived from various social media websites. Firstly, we show that word embeddings pre-trained on the same data source as the subsequent classification task improves the prediction accuracy of deep learning models. Secondly, we investigate the impact of different levels of training set imbalances on classifier types. In comparison to the traditional SVM classifier, we identify that although deep learning models can outperform the classification results of the traditional SVM classifier when the associated training dataset is seriously imbalanced, the performance of the SVM classifier can be dramatically improved through the use of oversampling, surpassing the deep learning models. Our work can inform researchers in selecting appropriate text classification strategies in the detection of abusive content, including scenarios where the training datasets suffer from class imbalance.

Keywords: Text classification · Abuse detection · Deep learning

1 Introduction

An increasing number of social media platforms facilitate users in posting their personal opinions online, resulting in rapid growth in the volume of user-generated content (UGC) over the past decade. This UGC inevitably carries the risk of containing inappropriate, potentially abusive content which aims to deliberately insult other online users through profane or hurtful language. Social

© Springer Nature Switzerland AG 2018
S. Staab et al. (Eds.): SocInfo 2018, LNCS 11185, pp. 117–133, 2018.
https://doi.org/10.1007/978-3-030-01129-1_8

media companies have a responsibility to combat abusive content by assessing or moderating posted content. The moderation strategies used in most websites can be categorised as either pre-published or post-published, depending on whether the moderation process is carried out before or after publication. In pre-published moderation, content posted by users will be checked before it is made available online. Usually, pre-published moderation relies on human moderators (e.g. BBC online news) or simple word filters (e.g. Both YouTube and Facebook provide functionality to allow users to make a list of blocked words). Human moderation of all content is expensive and lacks scalability, while word filters lack the ability to detect more subtle semantic abuse. In post-published moderation, the content is posted directly online, with abusive content detection reliant on crowdsourcing mechanisms, such as user reporting systems (e.g. Twitter) or moderators' determination (e.g. Reddit). In this case, the abusive content may have already resulted in negative consequences as it has been made available to an online audience. Given the huge volume of UGC, reliance on manual moderation of all content is impractical. The development of moderation tools to automatically review abusive content on social media websites is a priority.

Published research initially focused on the use of models based on traditional supervised classifiers in order to tackle abusive content detection. The text content was represented by a set of occurrence-based features such as bag of words or ngrams, and then fed into typical classifiers such as SVM or Naive Bayes. These feature representations count the frequency of words in text content but largely ignore word order and do not capture syntactic information. Adding hand-crafted features that are generated by experts can alleviate the shortcoming of traditional features. Nevertheless, this requires human effort and introduces domain specific dependencies into the model. In recent years, deep learning, as one of the solutions that can extract features automatically, has achieved state-of-the-art performance in many natural language processing (NLP) tasks such as sentiment analysis [13]. Likewise, recent studies of abusive content detection have focused on the use of deep learning based models. However, comparisons of traditional and deep learning approaches are difficult, due to the variety of datasets used across different researchers' work. Most researchers in this domain use their own private datasets, resulting in models that are dependent on their data and that cannot be compared to other work. In this paper, we address this issue by conducting an empirical comparison of traditional classification models and deep learning based models for abusive text detection. We use 9 datasets in order to generate results across a wide spectrum of data sources.

In addition, abusive datasets typically have an imbalance in class distribution, with a very small proportion of abusive instances. This is similar to the online reality (e.g. under 1% of abusive tweets are identified in Twitter [17,38]). In our work, we examine the impact of class imbalance by using multiple imbalanced datasets including both public sources and our own collected dataset. Our contributions are as follows: (1) We demonstrate the improvement on detection results using word embeddings that are pre-trained on a data source that is consistent with the classification data source; (2) Using an empirical comparison, we show that deep learning models have higher detection accuracy than the traditional SVM classifier when trained with extremely imbalanced datasets. However, when oversampling is used to address class imbalance, the performance of the SVM classifier increases far more rapidly than deep learning models; (3) Unlike most previous research efforts which typically use one dataset, we carried out our experiments on 9 datasets, thus generating results that are not tied to a single data source.

The reminder of this paper is structured as follows. Section 2 reviews the literature in the field; Sect. 3 describes the experimental datasets used for our work; Sect. 4 explains the methodologies that we have used to tackle the classification task; Sect. 5 presents the experiments and results; and Sect. 6 concludes the present work and discusses the future work.

2   Related Work

Automatically identifying abusive user-generated content on social media sites has attracted increasing attention from machine learning researchers over recent years. Existing strategies for abuse detection rely primarily on the use of supervised classification. In this section, we focus the literature review on two aspects, traditional machine learning techniques and deep learning neural networks.

2.1   Traditional Machine Learning

Much of the previous research uses traditional supervised classification algorithms to tackle abusive content detection. One of the key steps in generating a successful classification model is the use of appropriate features. The shallow approach to tackle the abuse detection task is to rely on the concept of lexical matching. Reynolds et al. [32] engineered features based on matching content words against a pre-defined profane words list. In order to avoid misspelling and abbreviation, Sood et al. [36] improved on the static keyword-based approach by using the Levenshtein Distance. However, a high percentage of profane words do not in fact constitute abusive content [20]. The typical content-based feature representations in abusive content detection are bag of words (BoW), and ngrams [41]. In addition, Mehdad et al. [24] have shown that using ngrams at the character level is more effective than using ngrams at the word level due to the out-of-vocabulary issue where the words are in the training data and not in the testing data. Apart from these simple surface features, abuse detection can also benefit from other knowledge based features. Xu et al. [38] included part of speech (POS) tagging to improve the classifier accuracy; Dadvar et al. [9] incorporated expert domain knowledge into feature engineering. They proposed a model where the feature space was designed by twelve experts who have a strong background in psychology, communication science and social studies; Yin et al. [39] demonstrated that the baseline result of simply using ngrams features was significantly improved by adding the other information such as contextual features and semantic features; Likewise, Chatzakou et al. [4] used features including user profile information and user network-based information.

In additional to feature representation investigation, many studies have concentrated on the classification algorithms. The widely used traditional classifiers in this domain include Naive Bayes (NB) [7,11], Logistic Regression (LR) [26,37], Support Vector Machines (SVM) [7,8,23,38,39], and Decision Tree (DT) [11]. However, there is no single classifier that generally achieves the best classification performance. Dinakar et al. [11] showed that NB outperformed DT in their experiment; Davidson et al. [10] found that LR and SVM tended to perform significantly better than other classifiers while Dadvar et al. [8] have shown the NB is slightly better than SVM. To avoid overfitting with a single classifier, Burnap [3] proposed an ensemble model which leveraged strengths of different types of classifiers and noted better performance than using a single classifier.

2.2 Deep Learning

Recent research has focused on the use of deep learning to tackle the task of abuse detection. In particular, this trend is sparked by the emergence of embedding techniques such as word2vec [25] and paragraph2vec [22] where each word or paragraph is represented by a vector in a low-dimension vector space. Both word and paragraph vectors are learned using a neural network that predicts context words given the current word, which preserves the syntactic and semantic information. One of the earliest research works on applying this embedding technique in the abuse detection domain is Djuric et al. [12]. They used paragraph2vec [22] to learn the distributed low-dimensional representation for comments that are then used as input to a logistic regression classifier. Serra et al. [35] also proposed a language model to generate a comment vector before inputting to a neural network based classifier. Given that using word2vec/paragraph2vec to represent the input text requires a huge amount of textual content, a lot of research uses pre-trained word embeddings such as W2V [25] by Google and Glove [29] by Stanford for the abuse detection task. Simple approaches to using pre-trained word embeddings for comment representation inlcude averaging [33] and concatenating [42] the word vectors of all words in the comment. Both of these approaches when combined with traditional classifiers resulted in poorer prediction performance to the more complex approaches such as using deep learning classifiers. Currently, convolutional neural network (CNN) and recurrent neural network (RNN) are widely used deep learning neural networks. Incorporating these with pre-trained word embedding representations for the input text, both Gamback [15] and Park et al. [27] have achieved success on the task of abuse detection by applying the CNN model. Gao et al. [16] used Bi-directional Long Short Term Memory (Bi-LSTM), a type of RNN model, to identify abusive comments. They found that this model had better classification results in comparison to logistic regression. Badjatiya et al. [1] carried out extensive experiments using different classifiers for the task of hate speech detection on a Twitter dataset. They found that deep learning models comment embedding generation, with those comments vectors then fed into a decision tree classifier delivered the best results. In addition, Zhang et al. [41] had good classification results with a combination model that extended the basic CNN by adding a RNN layer using gated recurrent unit.

Metadata is also of benefit to deep learning models. Pavlopoulos et al. [28] improved the performance of RNN model by adding the user-based embedding which is a dense vector that represents user profile information; Founta et al. [14] provided a unified deep learning architecture capable of leveraging extra information including sentiment polarity, hashtags existence, and emoticons usage, which increased area under the curve (AUC) by 5%. In addition, Pitsilis et al. [30] proposed an ensemble LSTM classifier that incorporated various features associated with user history information.

3   Datasets

A major barrier to the use of machine learning for identifying abusive user-generated content is the lack of recognised gold-standard labelled research datasets in the domain [34]. Most existing studies are carried out on datasets that are privately collected by the associated researchers. As a result, studies in detection of abusive content suffer from a lack of comparable empirical results against common datasets [34]. To alleviate this issue and generalise our results, we used nine datasets in this paper.

We gathered eight publically available labelled datasets from a variety of social media sites including Twitter [23,38], YouTube [8], MySpace [2,39], Formspring [32], Kongregate [39], and SlashDot [39]. In addition to these eight datasets, we collected our own user-generated abusive content dataset, using comments from a general news platform. We used crowd-sourcing to label the comments. We refer to our total 9 datasets as D1, D2 through to D9 for the rest of paper. The detail of these datasets are presented in our previous research [5,6]. Table 1 summarises the basic properties including the number of instances, average number of words across instances, the class distribution of positive (abusive) instances to negative (non-abusive) instances. We also include information about the approach and results published by the authors of each dataset publication, including the overall results achieved, the measurements used to evaluate, whether oversampling was used to improve the balance of classes in the dataset, the feature representation used and the classifier used.

With the exception of D1 which has a balance of classes, most datasets display class imbalance, with a very small proportion of abusive instances. In particular, the proportion of positive, abusive instances of D5, D6 and D7 is less than 5%. For these datasets, the original authors use oversampling of the positive (abusive) class instances in order to re-balance the class distribution, and thus improve the effectiveness of their classification models.

The previous work associated with these datasets focused on classic machine learning methods. As shown in Table 1, two researchers (D3, D4) used a lexicon matching approach where the text content was predicted as abusive based on whether it contained one of the pre-defined profane words. For D2, knowledge-based features such as users' profile information were manually engineered using domain expertise. The majority of researchers used word ngrams for feature representation and SVM as the classifier. In addition, logistic regression (LR) and rule-based classifiers have also been applied in some cases. In terms of evaluation, there is no standard performance measurement used across these datasets. Overall accuracy (D3, D4) is one of the measurements used for the classification task, which is a drawback when the dataset is imbalanced. Most of the work assessed the classifier using recall (D1, D8, D9), in particular positive recall (D5, D6, D7). AUC is also used in this domain (D2).

Table 1. Summary of dataset

	# of Instances	Avg. Length	Class Dist. (Pos./Neg.)	Oversample	Feature	Classifier	Results by Author	Metrics
D1	3110	15	42/58	No	Ngrams	SVM	0.79	Recall
D2	3466	211	12/88	No	Knowledge	SVM	0.57	AUC
D3	1710	337	23/77	No	Lexical	Rule-Based	0.64	Overall Acc
D4	13153	26	6/94	No	Lexical	Rule-Based	0.82	Overall Acc
D5	4802	5	1/99	Yes	Ngrams	SVM	0.14	Pos. Recall
D6	4303	94	1/99	Yes	Ngrams	SVM	0.12	Pos. Recall
D7	1946	56	3/97	Yes	Ngrams	SVM	0.35	Pos. Recall
D8	1340	13	13/87	No	Ngrams	LR	0.58	Recall
D9	2000	59	21/79	Yes	Ngrams	SVM	0.62	Recall

4 Methodology

In this section, we describe in detail the methods that we used in this work. We start with briefly explaining the data pre-processing. We then discuss the feature representations used, followed by the explanation of two types of classifiers, SVM and two off-the-shelf deep neural networks. We explain our use of oversampling for dataset re-balancing. Finally, we discuss the metrics used to evaluate and compare the classifiers' performance.

Pre-processing. Our first step was to pre-process the data in order to normalize text content. All capital letters in text were replaced by lowercase. The URL links were extracted and replaced by the generic term *url_links*. User names (name followed by the symbol '@') were also replaced by the anonymous term *@username*. Given that user-generated content is typically short, we did not implement dimensionality reduction techniques such as removing stop-words and stemming.

Feature Representation. We used two types of feature representation in this work: traditional text representations and word vectors. A typical traditional representation, ngrams are created by splitting the comment text into n continuous sequential word (or character) occurrences. In our previous work [5], we identified that word ngrams (1–4 word level) was the best performing feature representation. In addition, we applied document frequency reduction, removing the features that occur most and least often.

As an alternative to traditional feature representation, we used word vectors based on pre-trained word embeddings. From individual word vectors, we generated comment vectors, representing a user post. We perform comment embedding in two ways: In our first method, we simply averaged the word vectors for the words that appeared in the comment. We use this approach for comment vectors to input into the SVM classifier. The second method for comment embedding is used when combining word vector input with a deep learning classifier, whereby we feed word vectors into the deep learning model which automatically generates the comment embedding as part of layer determination.

Classifier. We used a support vector machine as a baseline classifier, given that it is a commonly used classifier that is shown to work well for the task of text classification. For our deep learning model comparison, we implemented two popular architectures, convolutional neural networks (CNNs) and recurrent neural networks (RNNs). We adopted the CNN model based on Kim's paper [21] and Bi-LSTM (Bi-directional Long Short Term Memory) structure [18,19] for the RNN model. We used word vectors as input for both models, and a softmax layer as output for predicting the probabilities of two classes (positive and negative). We used categorical cross entropy as the loss function and Adam optimiser to train the model. In addition, the two deep learning neural networks are performed as mini-batch gradient descent where the batch size is 50. As our datasets are not large enough to include a validation set split, we excluded the early stopping technique and set the number of epochs at 50 based on a pilot experiment. As our text content (user posts/comments) varies in length across instances, we used zero-padding in order to make each input the same size, setting this size to be length of the longest comment in the corresponding dataset. In addition, we used fine-tuning in order to update pre-trained word embeddings while modeling the classifier.

The choice of hyper-parameters plays an important role in the accuracy of deep learning models and optimising these parameters is always data-dependent. However, as we are performing our experiments on nine different datasets, we kept the same hyper-parameter settings for all datasets in order to make our results comparable across datasets. We attempted to apply optimal hyper-parameters based on the guidelines by Zhang et al. [40] for CNN and Reimers et al. [31] for RNN respectively. For the CNN model, we used rectified linear unit (ReLU) as the activation function, and multiple filters (the window sizes were 2,3,4) where each filter has 100 feature maps. In addition, we applied dropout during training process (rate is 0.5), and $l2$ regularization for avoiding over-fitting. For the RNN model, we implemented one-layer Bi-LSTM and set the size of the hidden layer to 100. The other hyper-parameters are the same as those used with CNN. Finally, Table 2 lists our four end-to-end experimental configurations that we wish to compare: Configuration 1 is the classic feature representation and SVM classifier; Configuration 2 is a hybrid approach using a word vector representation with an SVM classifier. Configurations 3 and 4 are our two deep-learning approaches, using CNN and RNN classifiers with word vectors as input.

Table 2. The proposed learning configurations for the detection of abusive content

Configuration	Feature	Classifier
1	Ngrams	SVM
2	Average word vector	SVM
3	Word vector	CNN
4	Word vector	Bi-LSTM

Oversampling. According to the class distribution in Table 1, most datasets are imbalanced, containing a low proportion of abusive (positive) instances. To address this, we used resampling of positive instances in the training set before training the classifiers. To be specific, we randomly oversampled the minority class instances (abusive instances) in order to increase the class distribution to an appropriate balanced level. The balanced level was decided based on our previous work [5]. To allow for random selection, we oversampled twice and then averaged the results. In addition, given that the parameters of the neural networks were initialized randomly, we also trained our deep learning model twice and averaged the results. Oversampling was performed on the training set only, with test data untouched.

Measurement. We used stratified 10-fold cross validation for our model training. All results are reported using class accuracy metric, also known as recall. This is a standard text classification metric which indicates the ability of the classifier to find all instances of a specific class. We are particularly interested in accuracy over the positive class (abusive instance recall), as we assume that the consequence of failing to identify an abusive comment is more serious than neutral content being classified as abusive. Due to the imbalanced class distributions across the datasets, we also used average class accuracy (average recall) to avoid the scenario that the classifier is skewed by a single class.

5   Experiments and Results

In this section, we explain our experiments and results. As a precursor to comparing classical versus deep learning based approaches, we carried out an experiment to analyse the impact of different word embeddings on deep learning models. Secondly, we present the classification performance of the proposed four configurations from Table 2 on our datasets. Thirdly, we further investigate the capability of these four configurations in tackling the issue of class imbalance. We perform experiments on five extracted datasets with varying levels of class balance with and without using oversampling.

5.1   Word Embedding Experiment

The choice of word embedding to represent text input is a factor to be considered when evaluating the performance of deep learning classifiers. We assume that a word embedding model trained on the same source body of text as the downstream classification dataset will perform better. To validate this assumption, we compared three different word embedding strategies using our own D9 dataset. We use this dataset because we have a large corpora of news comments from the same source as D9 to use to learn the word vectors. Our corpus contains nearly 138 million tokens, as shown in Table 3. Firstly, we trained using the word2vec approach [25]. Once we have finished the training process, each word is represented by a 100 dimension vector, and the size of the word vocabulary is approximately 145,000. We then used our word vectors as input to two deep learning classifiers (CNN and RNN). We repeated the process using two popular pre-trained word embeddings, namely W2V [25] and Glove [29]. Both of these two pre-trained word embeddings are trained on corpora larger than ours, so in theory, giving a richer word vector representation. However, the percentage of overlap words between D9 and the training corpora used for learning the word embeddings is higher for the news corpus where 97% of words in D9 can be identified.

Table 3. Pre-trained word embeddings

	Source	# of Tokens	# of Vocabulary	Dimension	Overlap percentage
Glove	Wikipedia	6B	400K	100	94%
W2V	Google news	100B	3M	300	92%
News comments	News site	138M	145K	100	97%

Although our own word embedding training corpus is the smallest, the subsequent word vectors from this corpus achieve the best abusive recall using both CNN and RNN models as shown in Fig. 1. Compared to the results of using W2V and Glove, the abusive recall of using our own news comment word embeddings is an improvement of more than 20% for the CNN model and nearly 15% for RNN model respectively. Therefore, we suggest that word embeddings created from the same data source as the dataset used to train (and evaluate) the classifier is a practical strategy. For the remainder of our experiments, however, we use published word embedding as we do not have access to the various corpora from which our remaining eight datasets are derived. We apply Glove in the subsequent experiments as Glove achieves slightly better results than the W2V for D9 as noted from in Fig. 1.

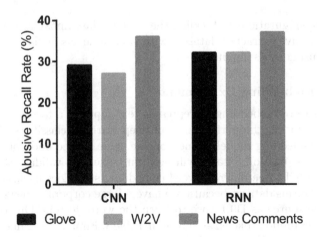

Fig. 1. The performance of deep learning models on the different word embeddings

5.2 Baseline Classification

The aim of this experiment is to assess the performance of the two deep learning models for the detection of abusive user posts and compared them to SVM with ngrams and word vector inputs. Table 4 shows abusive recall (%) and average recall (%) of our four configurations (Table 2) on nine datasets (Table 1). We highlighted the best result per dataset in bold. Generally, the performance of two SVM classifier configurations exceeded the two deep learning models for most datasets (7 out of 9). In particular, SVM with average word vectors achieved the highest abusive recall on 5 datasets. This is surprising given the shallow approach to generating comment vectors through averaging the words vectors for the words in the input. Configuration 1, SVM with ngrams, also has comparative performance, achieving 3 best results. For the deep learning models, CNN performs the best for D1 and D3. However, it performs the worst on the other 6 datasets. The performance of RNN is average in comparison to the SVM and CNN approaches, achieving neither best nor worst results for any dataset.

Table 4. Abusive recall and average recall (in brackets) of 4 classification configurations on 9 datasets. WV is short for word vectors.

	D1	D2	D3	D4	D5	D6	D7	D8	D9
Ngrams+SVM	70(75)	**35(62)**	91(93)	**62(77)**	58(78)	12(56)	18(58)	65(78)	33(60)
Avg. WV+SVM	65(71)	30(59)	66(76)	59(74)	**58(76)**	**51(71)**	**48(68)**	**77(85)**	**48(66)**
WV+CNN	**73(73)**	4(51)	**93(95)**	34(66)	57(78)	11(55)	14(57)	59(78)	29(61)
WV+RNN	68(73)	6(51)	81(89)	45(71)	50(75)	14(57)	18(58)	60(77)	32(60)

Overall, deep learning models proved to be less accurate classifiers than the classic SVM classifier. For example in D6, the abusive recall of the CNN model decreased nearly 40% compared to the SVM model with average word vector input. In D2, recall is approximately 30% lower for the RNN model as against the SVM using ngrams. Given that most datasets in this experiment have been oversampled to a relatively balanced level [5], we investigated whether over-sampling boosts the performance of the various classifiers to different degrees. According to the summary of datasets in Table 1, we found that deep learning models usually perform worse on the scenario where the class distribution of the original dataset is very imbalanced. For example, the recall rates of the CNN model are 11% and 14% in D6 and D7 respectively where there were less than 3% abusive instances in the datasets. On the other hand, SVM performs worse on the dataset where the original class distribution is more balanced (e.g. D1 and D3). We suggest that these results reveal that the oversampling technique boosts the SVM performance more than the performance of the deep learning models. To investigate this we conducted more experimentation described below.

5.3   Experiments of Balancing and Oversampling

The aim of these experiments were to investigate the impact of class imbalance on deep learning classifiers. The approach taken was as follows: We adjusted the datasets so that their class distribution was close to balanced. We used the class distribution of D1 (42%/58%) in Table 1 as the baseline. We then randomly removed negative instances (under-sampled) on other datasets to reach this baseline class distribution. We had to exclude datasets D5, D6, D7 and D8 as the number of abusive instances in the resulting datasets was too low to conduct 10-fold cross validation. Therefore, five of the datasets were suitable for use in this experiment. A summary of the number of posts per class in the five datasets after undersampling is shown in Table 5.

Table 5. Dataset sizes after undersampling to get to 42%/58% class distribution

	D1	D2	D3	D4	D9
#of Pos.	1303	417	390	836	424
#of Neg.	1807	576	539	1154	586
#of Total	3110	993	929	1990	1010

We wanted to examine the impact of varying levels of class balance on perfor-mance of the models. For each dataset, using all non-abusive instances, we added abusive instances in order to measure performance at different levels of class imbalance. To do this, we created 10 different positive percentages per dataset, ranging from 1% to 42% (the whole dataset) in intervals of 5%. We then mea-sured classification accuracy using our previous four configurations (Table 2) for each level of class distribution. In addition, we performed oversampling on each level of class distribution in order to investigate the impact of oversampling on performance. To be specific, at each level of class distribution, we randomly over-sampled the abusive instances to reach the positive percentage of the baseline distribution 42%/58%. The results are shown in Fig. 2.

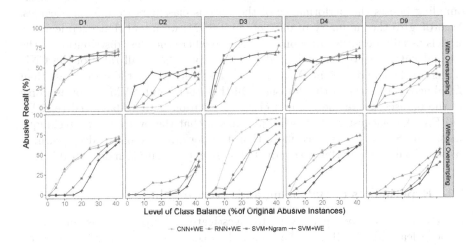

Fig. 2. Abusive Recall for all classifiers across datasets with varying levels of class balance, with and without oversampling. The x-axis represents the original positive percentage in the dataset before oversampling was applied.

Overall, balancing the dataset improves the classifiers' performance due to the increased levels of the positive class in the training data, which is to be expected. However, it is difficult to distinguish the best classifier configuration.

In general, using the original datasets without oversampling, both of the deep learning models outperform the SVM model when the dataset is extremely imbalanced. The SVM classifier with ngrams input cannot detect any abusive comment on D3 when the positive percentage is below 20%. It shows even worse abuse detection ability in D2 where abusive recall remains at zero until the positive class proportion in the dataset is increased above 30%. On the contrary, deep learning models achieve superior results when the dataset is highly skewed by the negative instances.

For example, at 5% positive proportion in D1 and D3, abusive recall is raised in both CNN and RNN models but two SVM model configurations have no ability to detect abusive comments. However, once oversampling is used, the results are quite different. The performance of both SVM configurations is rapidly boosted and outperforms both deep learning models at the low level of class balance. In addition, we note that the SVM configurations tend to saturate earlier than the deep learning models when re-balancing the dataset. For example, there is hardly any improvement after 20% for SVM (ngrams) for all datasets. However, the performance of deep learning models is increased at a close to linear rate as levels of class balance increase.

Depending solely on abusive recall to evaluate the performance of a classifier provides an incomplete picture. Increases in the proportion of the instances that are positive may sacrifice the negative class recall (i.e. the proportion of non-abusive instances correctly predicted as non-abusive). Therefore, we also investigated the average recall as shown in Fig. 3. Average recall starts approximately at 50% where the positive recall is around 0% and negative recall is close to 100% when the dataset is extremely imbalanced. Similar to the abusive recall, average recall increases as class balance increases, both with and without oversampling.

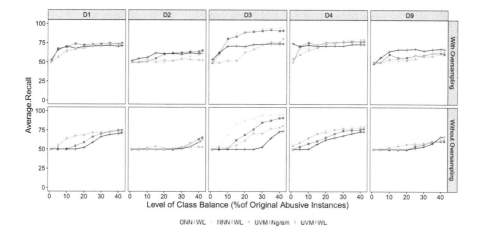

Fig. 3. Average Recall for all classifiers across datasets with varying levels of class balance, with and without oversampling. The x-axis represents the original positive percentage in the dataset before oversampling was applied.

To analyse the impact of oversampling on different classifier configurations, we re-organized our results and displayed it as Fig. 4 which compares with and without oversampling for each classifier across each dataset. It is interesting to note that the influence of oversampling for both deep learning models is limited, as shown in the top two rows in Fig. 4. In particular for the RNN model, there is barely any difference between two results with and without oversampling. Although the ability of the CNN model to detect abuse is boosted by oversampling, the gain is not comparable to the benefit that oversampling brings to the SVM models. Among the four classification configurations, the abusive recall of using SVM with average word embeddings is increased dramatically when oversampling is performed.

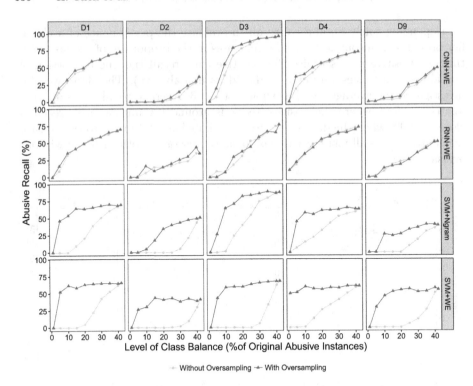

Fig. 4. Abusive Recall with and without oversampling for each classifier on each dataset across varying levels of class balance. The x-axis represents the original positive percentage in the dataset before oversampling was applied.

6   Conclusion

The purpose of our work was to explore the automatic detection of abusive content using a variety of supervised machine learning techniques. In particular we aimed to compare the more traditional approaches against the more recent neural network based approaches. We compared the following classification models, SVM classifier and two deep neural based classifiers: CNN and RNN. We also compared ngrams versus word embeddings for feature representation. We highlight the following points from this work: (1) Using word embeddings which were pre-trained on the same data source as the subsequent task is a benefit to the abuse detection task; (2) Based on results across nine datasets, we showed the SVM classifiers achieved the best results on balanced datasets, with balance achieved through oversampling; (3) We conducted a comprehensive analysis of the ability of the different classifiers to deal with class imbalance. The results show that deep learning models performed well on extremely imbalanced datasets while SVM had no ability to identify the minority abusive content class; (4) Once we applied oversampling techniques to re-balance the dataset, we revealed that oversampling is an effective approach to improve SVM performance while the improvement for deep learning based models is limited.

In future, we would like to investigate in-depth whether the classification results would be influenced by the intrinsic characteristics of individual datasets and sources such as the size of dataset, the average word length etc. Moreover, given the imbalanced nature of the data in the task of detecting abusive content, our future work will aim to modify the current deep learning models in order to improve abusive text detection when the training dataset is imbalanced.

References

1. Badjatiya, P., Gupta, S., Gupta, M., Varma, V.: Deep learning for hate speech detection in tweets. In: Proceedings of the 26th International Conference on World Wide Web Companion, pp. 759–760. International World Wide Web Conferences Steering Committee (2017)
2. Bayzick, J., Kontostathis, A., Edwards, L.: Detecting the presence of cyberbullying using computer software. In: 3rd Annual ACM Web Science Conference (WebSci 11), pp. 1–2 (2011)
3. Burnap, P., Williams, M.L: Cyber hate speech on Twitter: an application of machine classification and statistical modeling for policy and decision making. Policy Internet **7**(2), 223–242 (2015)
4. Chatzakou, D., Kourtellis, N., Blackburn, J., De Cristofaro, E., Stringhini, G., Vakali, A.: Mean birds: detecting aggression and bullying on Twitter. In: Proceedings of the 2017 ACM on Web Science Conference, pp. 13–22. ACM (2017)
5. Chen, H., Mckeever, S., Delany, S.J.: Harnessing the power of text mining for the detection of abusive content in social media. In: Angelov, P., Gegov, A., Jayne, C., Shen, Q. (eds.) Advances in Computational Intelligence Systems. AISC, vol. 513, pp. 187–205. Springer, Cham (2017). https://doi.org/10.1007/978-3-319-46562-3_12
6. Chen, H., Mckeever, S., Delany, S.J.: Presenting a labelled dataset for real-time detection of abusive user posts. In: Proceedings of the International Conference on Web Intelligence, pp. 884–890. ACM (2017)
7. Chen, Y., Zhou, Y., Zhu, S., Xu, H.: Detecting offensive language in social media to protect adolescent online safety. In: Privacy, Security, Risk and Trust (PASSAT), 2012 International Conference on and 2012 International Confernece on Social Computing (SocialCom), pp. 71–80. IEEE (2012)
8. Dadvar, M., Trieschnigg, D., de Jong, F.: Experts and machines against bullies: a hybrid approach to detect cyberbullies. In: Sokolova, M., van Beek, P. (eds.) AI 2014. LNCS, vol. 8436, pp. 275–281. Springer, Cham (2014). https://doi.org/10.1007/978-3-319-06483-3_25
9. Dadvar, M., Trieschnigg, R.B., de Jong, F.M.G.: Expert knowledge for automatic detection of bullies in social networks. In: 25th Benelux Conference on Artificial Intelligence, BNAIC 2013, TU Delft (2013)
10. Davidson, T., Warmsley, D., Macy, M., Weber, I.: Automated hate speech detection and the problem of offensive language. arXiv preprint arXiv:1703.04009 (2017)
11. Dinakar, K., Reichart, R., Lieberman, H.: Modeling the detection of textual cyberbullying. Soc. Mob. Web **11**(02), 11–17 (2011)

12. Djuric, N., Zhou, J., Morris, R., Grbovic, M., Radosavljevic, V., Bhamidipati, N.: Hate speech detection with comment embeddings. In: Proceedings of the 24th International Conference on World Wide Web, pp. 29–30. ACM (2015)
13. dos Santos, C., Gatti, M.: Deep convolutional neural networks for sentiment analysis of short texts. In: Proceedings of COLING 2014, the 25th International Conference on Computational Linguistics: Technical Papers, pp. 69–78 (2014)
14. Founta, A.-M., Chatzakou, D., Kourtellis, N., Blackburn, J., Vakali, A., Leontiadis, I.: A unified deep learning architecture for abuse detection. arXiv preprint arXiv:1802.00385 (2018)
15. Gambäck, B., Sikdar, U.K.: Using convolutional neural networks to classify hatespeech. In: Proceedings of the First Workshop on Abusive Language Online, pp. 85–90 (2017)
16. Gao, L., Huang, R.: Detecting online hate speech using context aware models. arXiv preprint arXiv:1710.07395 (2017)
17. Gao, L., Kuppersmith, A., Huang, R.: Recognizing explicit and implicit hate speech using a weakly supervised two-path bootstrapping approach. arXiv preprint arXiv:1710.07394 (2017)
18. Graves, A., Schmidhuber, J.: Framewise phoneme classification with bidirectional lstm and other neural network architectures. Neural Netw. **18**(5–6), 602–610 (2005)
19. Hochreiter, S., Schmidhuber, J.: Long short-term memory. Neural Comput. **9**(8), 1735–1780 (1997)
20. Hosseinmardi, H., Mattson, S.A., Rafiq, R.I., Han, R., Lv, Q., Mishra, S.: Detection of cyberbullying incidents on the instagram social network. arXiv preprint arXiv:1503.03909 (2015)
21. Kim, Y.: Convolutional neural networks for sentence classification. arXiv preprint arXiv:1408.5882 (2014)
22. Le, Q., Mikolov, T.: Distributed representations of sentences and documents. In: International Conference on Machine Learning, pp. 1188–1196 (2014)
23. Mangaonkar, A., Hayrapetian, A., Raje, R.: Collaborative detection of cyberbullying behavior in Twitter data. In: 2015 IEEE International Conference on Electro/Information Technology (EIT), pp. 611–616. IEEE (2015)
24. Mehdad, Y., Tetreault, J.: Do characters abuse more than words? In: Proceedings of the 17th Annual Meeting of the Special Interest Group on Discourse and Dialogue, pp. 299–303 (2016)
25. Mikolov, T., Chen, K., Corrado, G., Dean, J.: Efficient estimation of word representations in vector space. arXiv preprint arXiv:1301.3781 (2013)
26. Nobata, C., Tetreault, J., Thomas, A., Mehdad, Y., Chang, Y.: Abusive language detection in online user content. In: Proceedings of the 25th International Conference on World Wide Web, pp. 145–153. International World Wide Web Conferences Steering Committee (2016)
27. Park, J.H., Fung, P.: One-step and two-step classification for abusive language detection on Twitter. arXiv preprint arXiv:1706.01206 (2017)
28. Pavlopoulos, J., Malakasiotis, P., Bakagianni, J., Androutsopoulos, I.: Improved abusive comment moderation with user embeddings. arXiv preprint arXiv:1708.03699 (2017)
29. Pennington, J., Socher, R., Manning, C.D., Glove: global vectors for word representation. In: Empirical Methods in Natural Language Processing (EMNLP), pp. 1532–1543 (2014)
30. Pitsilis, G.K., Ramampiaro, H., Langseth, H.: Detecting offensive language in tweets using deep learning. arXiv preprint arXiv:1801.04433 (2018)

31. Reimers, N., Gurevych, I.: Optimal hyperparameters for deep LSTM-networks for sequence labeling tasks. arXiv preprint arXiv:1707.06799 (2017)
32. Reynolds, K., Kontostathis, A., Edwards, L.: Using machine learning to detect cyberbullying. In: 2011 10th International Conference on Machine Learning and Applications and Workshops (ICMLA), vol. 2, pp. 241–244. IEEE (2011)
33. Sax, S.: Flame wars: automatic insult detection (2016)
34. Schmidt, A., Wiegand, M.: A survey on hate speech detection using natural language processing. In: Proceedings of the Fifth International Workshop on Natural Language Processing for Social Media, pp. 1–10 (2017)
35. Serra, J., Leontiadis, I., Spathis, D., Blackburn, J., Stringhini, G., Vakali, A.: Class-based prediction errors to detect hate speech with out-of-vocabulary words. In: Abusive Language Workshop, vol. 1. Abusive Language Workshop (2017)
36. Sood, S., Antin, J., Churchill, E.: Profanity use in online communities. In: Proceedings of the SIGCHI Conference on Human Factors in Computing Systems, pp. 1481–1490. ACM (2012)
37. Xiang, G., Fan, B., Wang, L., Hong, J., Rose, C.: Detecting offensive tweets via topical feature discovery over a large scale Twitter corpus. In: Proceedings of the 21st ACM International Conference on Information and Knowledge Management, pp. 1980–1984. ACM (2012)
38. Xu, J.-M., Jun, K.-S., Zhu, X., Bellmore, A.: Learning from bullying traces in social media. In: Proceedings of the 2012 Conference of the North American Chapter of the Association for Computational Linguistics: Human Language Technologies, pp. 656–666. Association for Computational Linguistics (2012)
39. Yin, D., Xue, Z., Hong, L., Davison, B.D., Kontostathis, A., Edwards, L.: Detection of harassment on web 2.0. In: Proceedings of the Content Analysis in the WEB, vol. 2, pp. 1–7 (2009)
40. Zhang, Y., Wallace, B.: A sensitivity analysis of (and practitioners' guide to) convolutional neural networks for sentence classification. arXiv preprint arXiv:1510.03820 (2015)
41. Zhang, Z., Luo, L.: Hate speech detection: a solved problem? The challenging case of long tail on Twitter. arXiv preprint arXiv:1803.03662 (2018)
42. Zhong, H., et al.: Content-driven detection of cyberbullying on the instagram social network. In: IJCAI, pp. 3952–3958 (2016)

March with and Without Feet:
The Talking About Protests and Beyond

Wen-Ting Chung[1], Yu-Ru Lin[1(✉)], Ang Li[1], Ali Mert Ertugrul[1,2],
and Muheng Yan[1]

[1] University of Pittsburgh, Pittsburgh, PA 15260, USA
yurulin@pitt.edu
[2] Middle East Technical University, Ankara, Turkey

Abstract. *By what means* do social media contribute to social movements? This question has been studied for decades, but rarely from
the collective sense-making perspective. When a particular crying out
for social change is taking place, people nowadays begin to talk on
social media platforms. We examined the focuses of people's talking
in a protesting context where multiple protesting tactics were involved
including both online and offline activism. By analyzing Twitter messages during Ferguson unrest in August 2014, we revealed two distinct
types of online conversations: one discusses offline protests concerning
more immediate happenings; the other goes beyond involving *meaning-
making* to diagnose and digest the disorienting thoughts and feelings.
To characterize the discussions, we developed two coding schemes, first
to differentiate the discussion of offline protests from others, and second
to differentiate ways of meaning-making. This study is the first attempt
to identify the challenges of differentiating tweets consisting of street
protest information, and the developed coding scheme, together with
machine classification, can be applied to identifying tweets consisting
of street protest information. We observed that while mainstream media
often focused on what happened on street, during Ferguson protests, only
one out of every 4.5 tweets focused on offline activities. Our study offers
evidence for considering social media's significance from an alternative
perspective – the media are not simply the witness or facilitator of offline
protests, but leave traces that afford to study collective mind activities
and changes such as meaning contesting and perspective shifting that
are essential for social change.

Keywords: Collective sensemaking · Online activism
Social movement · Mixed methods · Black Lives Matter

1 Introduction

People throughout history, by leveraging various forms of protesting, have continued acting to speak out indignation intending to alter existing realities. Walking
on streets has been an impactful means. Recently, the nature of protesting and

© Springer Nature Switzerland AG 2018
S. Staab et al. (Eds.): SocInfo 2018, LNCS 11185, pp. 134–150, 2018.
https://doi.org/10.1007/978-3-030-01129-1_9

its tactics started to be influenced and diversified by the rise of the Internet and especially by social media. Social media has shown its potential of creating original, powerful ideas and new ways of crying out, assembly, and demonstration such as hashtage activism (e.g., "#MeToo," "#BlackLivesMatter," and "#OccupyWallStreet") and offered new channel to coordinate with other forms of protesting, e.g., to mobilize the revolution of Arab Spring.

Prior works that studied the role of social media in relation to social protesting often fall into two categories. The first line of research studied online activism, i.e., the activism that primarily takes place online, such as hashtag activism [3,9,25], in contrast to traditional activism happening offline. The second concerned the online activities as a facilitator that helps to mobilize offline protests or predict the happenings of offline protests [2,7,8,12,23]. In this work, we take an alternative perspective to investigate the social significances of social media, from which we leverage the unique affordance of social media that allows people to engage in real-time collective sense-making and meaning-making during a protesting context. Today, when a particular crying out for social change is taking place, people come to social media to not only get and disseminate information, initiate and organize mobilization, but to talk.

Understanding what ordinary people, not limited to activists, have been talking in the protesting context is crucial to fathom social change. First, being situated in protesting context, people face a peculiar circumstance in which their used form of life is questioned. This often brings disorienting feelings and thoughts, and a new possibility for people to reshape identity and reality. Second, while successful activism may bring about concrete outcomes such as the change of laws, policies, and material existence of institutions, a society's transformation will not achieve without people's change of minds. For example, prejudice toward African-Americans continues through generations despite of the critical legislation and policies made following the Civil Rights Movement since the 1950s in the US. Moreover, the success of activism does not necessarily lead to the favorable change in people's behaviors and minds. Therefore, it is necessary to look beyond the online- or offline-activism perspectives.

We focus on people's talking about event happenings in the context of Black Lives Matter (BLM) movement that campaigns against systemic racism and violence towards black people. The activists first used social media to reach people and form networks. The hashtag "#BlackLivesMatter" was created in 2013 by Patrisse Cullors, Alicia Garza, and Opal Tometi, followed by a set of tactics offered online. Social media platforms, especially Twitter, have facilitated and witnessed this movement especially in several cases of police killing such as in Ferguson and New York City. Hashtag activisms were initiated by Twitter users, including "#MikeBrown," "#HandsUpDontShoot,","#ICantBreath", "#JusticeForEricGarner". A series of offline protests took places locally or nationally across cities, including marches, rallies, vigils, art performing, public demonstrations, etc. The diversity of protest tactics offers a rich study resource. We particularly situated our investigation on Ferguson unrest in August 2014 after the police killing of Michael Brown.

Our study is guided by the following research questions. First, while mainstream media mostly focused on reporting what happened on the street, we ask whether such a focus remains in social media discussion.

Q1: Were all social media discussions during Ferguson unrest about offline pretests? If not, how much was centered on offline protests? What did people talk about offline protests?

Q2: What else did people talk about, when the discussion was not about offline protests?

Q3: What type of discussion received more attention?

Second, answering the aforementioned questions requires a taxonomy for what discussion was about. However, such a taxonomy does not exist and creating a new one is challenging because even discerning whether a tweet is specifically talking about an offline protest activity or not is not trivial. So, we proposed such a question.

Q4: Can we distinguish online discussion specifically relevant to offline protests from the discussion? To what extent can this task be done by human and by machine?

In this work, we present an open human coding methodology to code themes emerged regarding what people were talking about during the Ferguson unrest. To characterize the discussions, we developed two coding schemes, first to differentiate the discussion of offline protests from others, and second to identify ways of meaning-making. Our study is the first attempt to identify the challenges of differentiating online discussions that are directly relevant to offline protests. Our coding schemes, refined through an iterative coding process, are capable of obtaining informative and reliable signals to distinguish various activities relevant to BLM movement. Together with machine classification, we show that the coding results can be applied to identify tweets that consist of street protest information. Further, we observed the unique means social media provide in exploring the collective mind changes in relation to social change.

2 Related Work

2.1 The Affordance of Social Media for Social Movement and Change

Prior works concerning social media as a means for social movement often contrast the use of online platform with those traditional forms of protest offline. [2,3,9,23,25]. Less have moved beyond the online-versus-offline dichotomy and considered that multiple channels may contribute together, with distinct or complementary affordances. There are, however, few discussions beginning to break the dichotomy, by proposing a synthesis perspective, highlighting the change of the nature of activism and movement tactics in general.

Tufekci argued that online platforms enable building distinctive capacities to facilitate social change [22]. Casciani discussed how social media changed protest [4]. He compared, with and without social media, how a protest can reach and change, and by what means, throughout the different phases of social movement. For example, it is much less likely that the police would respond to the social pressure in a timely manner when confronted with the crowd on street, compared with the public questioning from social media. More, social media could reach and call out people with speed and scale that traditionally pamphlets cannot. However, there have been discussions as to whether online demonstration lacks long-term effects [16,21]. Castells [5] considered the *affordances* of activism both online and offline: the cyberspaces enable autonomy, co-creating of meaning, and power negotiation; meanwhile, offline activism and activities are essential, as the solidarity formed through real-world networking that allow people to resist and change the physical coercion cannot be replaced by online communication and networking.

2.2   What Activity Counts an Protest Event Offline

The hashtag, #BlackLivesMatter has been widely used on social media as a slogan when referring to the social movement concerning systemic disparity against black people [9]. Also, together with #BlackLivesMatter, other hashtags such as #Ferguson, #MikeBrown, #JusticeForEricGarner were populated during the Ferguson and other related protests [3,10]. The online conversations with these hashtags relevant to those social events and protest activities have often been considered as critical means to study the recent movements. Nevertheless, the activities and information captured through these hashtags were not necessarily about the protest activities that took place offline. In order to differentiate tweets specifically relevant to offline protests, we first discuss conceptual and operational definitions of protest in both social theories and empirical social studies, examine their limitations, and finally present more suitable criteria.

A general conceptual definition of *protest* is *"the act of challenging, resisting, or making demands upon* authorities, powerholders, and/or actual beliefs and practices" [13]. While protest takes the form of social movement, the criteria of a social movement entail that protest is a "collective, organized, sustained, and noninstitutional" [13] effort, in which the *collective action* speaks for dignity, humanity, request to address *injustice*, and seek for *empowering oppressed population* [5,11].

In social movement literature, a variety of working definitions have been developed and adopted [15]. However, most of the studies used news articles as data sources and their event-unit approach and criteria were inapplicable to social media data, due to the distinct nature of these two media in discussing or referring to protests. For example, in newspaper report, when an article covers a protest event, usually, it is supposed to consist of the 5 W's and H information – Who, What, When, Where, Why, and How (e.g., who is protesting, who the protesters are targeting, what claims are made, at what time, in what location, with what methods) [18]. On social media, how users communicate or mention about a protest event is quite different from the news reporters. For example, there is a word limit on Twitter. Even if a Twitter user intended to "report" an event as a newspaper reporter usually does, with the word limit, conceiving the content with 5 W's and H would be challenging. Usually, there are three types of information a Twitter users can flexibly utilize – text, image/video, and hyperlinks – to inform or call the public's attention on an event and offer information. More, a unique feature prevailed in relevant conversations is the use of hashtags. In the context of social movement, a new hashtag may be created to declare a claim that may initiate a series of protest activities, or be popularized when social media users resonated the goal and started using it to offer an interpretive signifier for their posted conversations. In brief, it is no longer appropriate to identify offline protest by looking for an event with traditional variables identified in social movement literature.

Our classification scheme was informed by and refined from the criteria given in the Collective Action (DoCA) dataset [18]. DoCA is current the largest protest event dataset that includes the protests occurred in the US. In this dataset, a protest event is defined based on the following criteria: (1) protest actions, (2) public actions, (3) collective acts, and (4) a specific claim or grievance about the desirability to change society. The variables of each event include source index, nature of the event (e.g., violence, arrestment, police involved), etc.

2.3   Criteria of Recognizing Offline Protest Event

We incorporated these theory-grounded criteria while making an adjustment to account for the characteristics of social media conversations. Instead of considering criteria to identify protest events, our inclusion criteria are for identifying *offline protest activities* relevant to BLM.

1. **Claim:** The protest activity has a specific claim or grievance expression. In many cases, the claims were revealed by the users' use of hashtags. For example, the hashtags, "#Justice," "#JusticeForEricGarner," and "MikeBrown" were often used to grieve the dead, or demand justice for these cases.
2. **Offline and public:** The protest activity has to be public and offline action; the protesters have to show up with their physical body in public spheres for demonstrating their claims. It *cannot* be online protests, e.g., by modifying Twitter account photos in a similar manner for grief or protest reasons. This may be determined based on various types of information in a tweet: (i) words signaling activities that are usually public, taking place in streets, squares, or other public spheres, e.g. "protest," "rally," "march," "(peaceful) gathering," "demonstration," "(unarmed) assembly," or "riot; (ii) words signaling public locations where the activity takes place (e.g., Times Square).
3. **Individual vs. collective:** Conventionally, a protest was defined as taking place in a collective form, meaning that more than one person has to participate. Here, we decided to apply a less restricted definition because the information in a tweet is usually insufficient to tell whether there is more than one protester. For example, a tweet with a photo showing an individual

protester was likely to be part of a public collective protest activity. Therefore, in this work, we include all the tweets relevant to offline BLM protests regardless whether we know it is a collective form or not.

3 Data

We first collected a BLM-relevant tweet dataset by scraping data with hashtags suggested by [9], using Twitter REST API. With an attempt to identify both online and offline BLM activism, including the tweets posted around the intense period of offline protests is critical. Thus, we deliberately chose the period of Ferguson protests occurring in August, 2014. Our dataset consists of the tweets posted between Aug. 8th, 2014 (one day before the shooting) and Aug. 26th (17 days after the shooting), 2014. As shown in Fig. 1, 12,115,997 tweets in total were requested through the API, and 7,996,238 of

Date	Request	Valid	Geo
2014-08-08	3,711	3,029	31
2014-08-09	87,782	63,584	325
2014-08-10	305,146	202,857	1,487
2014-08-11	492,976	393,563	3,272
2014-08-12	429,320	326,471	2,436
2014-08-13	1,127,521	823,746	6,514
2014-08-14	1,853,331	440,713	3,722
2014-08-15	842,786	669,860	6,602
2014-08-16	626,698	502,380	4,591
2014-08-17	1,180,365	932,131	8,114
2014-08-18	1,553,868	982,938	8,881
2014-08-19	1,247,489	961,216	8,700
2014-08-20	790,842	629,971	5,699
2014-08-21	471,526	381,125	3,367
2014-08-22	280,160	80,591	693
2014-08-23	155,031	130,969	1,339
2014-08-24	196,849	81,148	739
2014-08-25	320,899	266,514	2,362
2014-08-26	149,697	123,432	1,072

Fig. 1. The daily volume of tweets in our collection.

them were still valid (not deleted, and open to the public) at the time of scraping. Among those valid tweets, 69,946 tweets were geotagged.

To answer the research questions, we develop two human coding tasks: (a) *differentiating coding* – to differentiate whether a tweet talked specifically about BLM offline protests or not, and (b) *characterizing coding* – to characterize twitter users' collective meaning-making. For (a), two subsets of tweets were sampled from all the data collected. Through our preliminary inspection of the dataset, we observed that tweets with geotags were more likely to be relevant to offline activities comparing to those without, and tweets about offline activities were much fewer than those not. Since our goal was to sample as much and diverse of both online and offline tweets, we determined to focus on geotagged tweets when developing the coding scheme. We first created a randomly sampled 1200 tweets extracted from the whole dataset – 200 tweets per day, from the six days, August 9, 10, 14, 16, 18 and 23, which are the first two and the peak days of tweet volume along the Ferguson protest timeline. This subset of data, referred to as the *pilot set*, was used in the pilot stages of developing our classification scheme. We then created another subset randomly sampled from tweets posted on each day, referred to as the *final set*, that did not overlap with the pilot set. Specifically, 200 tweets per day (3600 in total) were randomly sampled (except for the day of Aug. 8th, since it is before the shooting and no protest is expected on that day). Next, all of the sampled tweets were shuffled and randomly assigned to create 18 batches with 200 tweets each, in order to eliminated possible bias of the human coders. For (b), we selected the most popular and disseminated tweets. A sample of 104 tweets, each receiving retweets over 3000 times and together a total of 626,310 retweets were selected.

4   Method

We describe our method in human coding and machine classification.

4.1   Human Coding

To answer the research questions (Q1–Q3), we created taxonomies by developing two coding schemes: (a) differentiating and (b) characterizing coding.

4.1.1   Differentiating Coding

This coding scheme guided such a task: *What information we should look for, in order to discern whether the tweet is referring specifically to an offline BLM protest?*. We developed a codebook and tested its reliability. We discuss our classification taxonomy and coding procedure.

Classification Taxonomy. The final classification scheme includes three sets of codes: (1) *Relevancy*: Four codes; (2) *Theme*: Four codes; and (3) *Confidence*: the coder rated their confidence level of their rated relevancy and theme codes.

Relevancy Coding. First, the coder determines the relevancy of a tweet – whether the tweet content refers to a protest activity relevant to BLM movement (denoted as *p-act*). Four codes (Y, N, I, and O) can be applied:

- Yes (Y): The tweet is talking about a *p-act*, a protest activity relevant to BLM.
- Non-P-Activity (N): The tweet subject is relevant to BLM, but the tweet subject is *not* on protest activity.
- Insufficient (I): The tweet is possibly talking about a *p-act*. The content seems to refer to a protest activity relevant to BLM, but the information is not sufficient. Example cases are showing the "conflicting" situation between police and the public, but not specifically mentioning this is a *p-act*.
- Off-topic (O): The topic is NOT relevant to BLM or their related activities, such as a spam tweet.

Theme Coding Second, the coder determines the theme(s) for those tweets coded as either Y or I– meaning that they are or possibly are on the subject of a protest activity relevant to BLM. There are four theme categories, and a tweet can be coded with *multiple* categories:

- Thm1: **Describing happenings in a protest activity.** The tweet has information about the happenings of a protest activity that may be described as "protest," "rally," "march," "gathering," "demonstration," "assembly", or "riot." The crowd may be described as "crowd," "folks," "people," "protesters," "demonstrators," or "mobs." The tweets may include images/videos of a gathered crowd. Some activities may involve the confrontation/fight between the crowd and police (also, its force equipment: gas tear, gear, dog, weapon, etc.).

- Thm2: **Calling for joining a protest activity.** The tweet content is to call people for joining the protest, either including the information of a specific time/location or not; both count.
- Thm3: **Commenting on a protest activity.** The tweet content is about commenting on the protest, expressing and communicating a personal feeling, emotion, as well as opinion, thought, view, reflection, etc.
- Thm4: **Live Streaming a protest activity.** Live reporting of the protests.

Confidence Level Coding. The coders are asked to assign their confidence level to their decisions on both *Relevancy* and *Theme* codes. Three codes (H– High, M– Medium, and L– Low) can be applied.

Coding Process. The classification scheme discussed earlier was derived through an iterative coding process that incorporates (1) an open-coding phase, (2) a pilot coding phase, and (3) a final coding phase.

Open-Coding Phase. Two coders (two of the authors, later referred as code developers) worked in an iterative procedure to identify emerging categories and themes, created codes, tested and revised the codes. At this phase, a subset of 1200 tweets (pilot set) were used and the results reached the agreement rate of 98% for Relevancy Code, and 99% for Theme Code. The first version of codebook, codebook-beta, was created. The agreed coding results served as beta version of gold standard, later referred as golden-beta. The codebook has not included the Confidence Code; only had Relevancy Code and Theme Code.

Pilot Coding Phase. Next, we conducted a pilot study to (1) test whether our coding scheme was clear and sufficient to deliver reliable outcomes, (2) identify the issues of inapplicability, and (3) revise the coding schemes accordingly. Seven external coders, who had not involved in the development of coding scheme, were recruited; we provided training sessions with more than 10 hours of coding tutorial and exercise. Each of them was first assigned to code a subset of 200 tweets from the 1200 tweets that the code-developers had coded (denoted as *Subset A*), following codebook-beta. The external coding results were compared with the golden-beta. For the inconsistent results, the two code-developers held an open discussion with the external coders as a group in order to refine the codebook. The inter-rater reliability, indicated by Cohen's kappa, for the coding results of Relevancy coding (between each coder's results and the golden-beta) ranged from .53 to .72, considered as moderate to substantial. For Thm1, the values of Cohen's kappa ranged from .26 to .47; for Thm2, 31 to .74; for Thm3, .22 to .68; for Thm4, .11 to .58.

One major issue identified was that the coding results influenced much by the coders' prior personal experiences and knowledge particularly relevant to the history of the development of civil rights in the US, Ferguson protests, and BLM in general. The influence on Theme coding was observed to greater than Relevancy coding; specifically, those who showed more knowledge about what had happened in Ferguson protests were more certain about the mentioning of certain things in a tweet referred to the offline protests. To address this issue, we created a new code category to indicate the coders' confidence level of their decisions. The external coders then continued working on a second 200 tweets (denoted as *Subset B*) from the 1200 tweets, but do not overlap with the first 200 tweets), in which they asked to report confidence levels to test whether reporting confidence levels helped. The inter-rater reliability, indicated by Cohen's kappa, for the coding results of Relevancy coding (between each coder's results and the golden-beta) ranged from .42 to .64, indicating moderate to substantial. For Themes, the overall reliability increased. For Thm1, the values of Cohen's kappa ranged from .66 to .74; Thm2, from .28 to .67; Thm3, from .34 to .65. No tweets include information of Thm4 in *Subset B*. Based on these results, the codebook was finalized (denoted as codebook-final). Finally, a subset of 1000 tweets (*Subset C*, i.e., the whole 1200 tweets excluding *Subset B*) was given to seven external coders; the results were compared with the golden-beta. At this final stage, the Cohen's kappa for Relevancy ranged from .55 to .56; for Thm1, from .58 to .62; Thm2, .33 to .40; Thm3, .49 to .55; Thm4, .40 to .42.

Final Coding Phase. Our final coding was based on the final codebook, using the final set of a randomly sampled 3600 tweets (200 tweets from each day, from Aug 9 to 26); these 3600 tweets are a subset disjoint from the previously mentioned 1200 tweets used to develop coding schemes. All coders (two code-developers and seven external coders) participated in this coding process in pairs, and each tweet was coded by two coders. Coders coded the tweets independently first, and then paired coders discussed the conflicting results to seek an agreement in codes. For the results coded independently, the inter-rater reliability, indicated by pairwise Cohen's kappa, is .58. For themes, the values of Cohen's kappa are .60, .46, .44, and .10 for Thm1, Thm2, Thm3, Thm4, respectively. After discussion, paired coders reached consensus with agreement rates of 99%. The low reliability of Thm4 resulted from some coders' misidentifying the information sources other than live-streaming (such as news articles). The conflicting results were resolved after clarification and the paired coders reached agreement on most cases.

4.1.2 Characterizing Coding

To uncover how Twitter users made sense of Michael Brown's death and the protest activities, we coded the 104 most re-tweeted tweets. We focused on the most retweeted tweets because the significant number of retweets suggested these are the most resonated communication in the collective sense- and meaning-making processes. Our open-coding identified the major *themes*. The themes were identified in part by applying Park's meaning-making model [20], which includes a set of essential tenets of meaning-making commonly recognized across theoretical perspectives in literature. In particular, the model considers that people hold orienting systems that provide cognitive frameworks by which they interpret experiences and being motivated to take actions, and while encountering situations that challenge these orienting systems, people appraise the situations and designate meanings to them. In other words, the discrepancy between the prior held mental models and strange happenings leads to meaning-making. The process forms new connections between the *selves* and the *disorienting informa-tion*, in specific contextualized happenings. For example, people may *reaffirm*, *disapprove, associate the self in a new way with, replace, revise*, or *question* the elements in prior mental models and construct new ones through the meaning-making process. Grounded in this theoretical framework, our analysis focused on how the tweet content revealed such meaning-making processes and identified ten themes out of the most retweeted contents, which will be detailed in the result section.

4.2 Machine Classification

We investigated whether simple tools can be developed to differentiate tweets directly relevant to offline protests from others. If protest-related discussions can be detected algorithmically, it will provide a useful lens into the kinds of social discourses centered around offline and online activism. To answer this question (as part of Q4), we conducted experiments on various machine classification techniques. With the tweet labels obtained from the human coding process, the goal is to automatically detect the category (*p-act* or not) for a given tweet.

Experiment Setup. We used the final coded tweets (3600 in total) in our exper-iments, with approximately 16% tweets were labeled as protest-related messages. To classify whether a given tweet was labeled as *p-act* or not, we applied Sup-port Vector Machines (SVM), Artificial Neural Networks (ANNs), and Logistic Regression (LR). The prediction performance was evaluated based on a 10-fold cross-validation (CV) on the labeled data. To evaluate different classification techniques, *precision, recall, F-score* and *AUC* values were calculated.

Features. In this work, we combined domain-specific features and content rep-resentations (using word embedding (Word2Vec) [19] features to classify protest-related tweets.

Domain-specific features were extracted based on the social movement litera-ture [17,24]. We considered four factors related to why people protest, namely *grievance* (a felt sense of illegitimate injustice), *identity* (identification of groups/ communities that bring about a shared sense of future destiny and social respon-sibility), *emotions* (affective responses to the focal issues/happenings) and *social embeddedness* (interaction in communities that shapes shared concerns). To cap-ture the features that reveal the *emotions, grievance*, and *identity*, we used three dictionaries: LIWC [6], SentiSense [1], and Moral-Laden [14]. For each set of fea-tures, we considered its occurrence in the given tweet and represented it as a binary variable. Furthermore, we used three Twitter-centric engagement fea-tures, *number of words, number of retweets* (log-transformed) and *mention of URL*, to represent the *social embeddedness*. In total, we extracted 50 features to indicate the aforementioned factors.

Word embedding features were extracted based on the continuous vector representation of tweets – specifically, the Skip-gram technique of the Word2Vec [19] to obtain the vector representation. This word embedding technique is able to discover semantic relation among terms in the corpus. We first performed a pre-processing step to remove hashtags, mentions, links and the "RT" keyword, a number of emoticons, punctuation marks and stop words from the tweets' content. For training, the window size was set to 10 and the number of negative words was selected as 5, empirically. The length of the continuous vectors was set to 200. Our Word2Vec training corpus consists of 2M tweets where all of them are relevant to the application domain. In order to obtain vector representation of a tweet, vector representations of its all words are summed and normalized. As a result, a tweet was represented as 250-dimensional vector together with the domain-specific features.

Table 1. *Relevancy* code distribution.

		Y	I	N	O	Not agree	Invalid	Total
Pilot	# of tweets	184	62	902	21	26	5	1200
	%	15.33%	5.17%	75.17%	1.75%	2.17%	0.42%	
Final	# of tweets	570	260	2597	43	19	111	3600
	%	15.83%	7.22%	72.14%	1.19%	0.53%	2.28%	
Total	# of tweets	754	322	3499	64	45	116	4800
	%	15.71%	6.71%	72.90%	1.33%	0.94%	2.42%	

Table 2. *Theme* code distribution. A tweet can be coded with multiple categories. The first four cases are tweets coded with any of the category, and the last five cases are tweets coded with two of the categories. Proportions were given in relation to the total number of *Relevancy* tweets (1076 tweets that coded with either Y or I).

	Thm1	Thm2	Thm3	Thm4	Thm1,Thm2	Thm1,Thm3	Thm1,Thm4	Thm2,Thm3	Thm3,Thm4
# of tweets	597	18	464	29	5	254	18	4	3
%	55.48%	1.67%	43.12%	2.70%	0.46%	23.61%	1.67%	0.37%	0.28%

5   Results

We present our results: (1) differentiating coding that distinguishes what was talked in the original posted tweets – whether relevant or irrelevant to offline protests and how, (2) characterizing coding that identifies the types of specific meaning-making in the most retweeted tweets, (3) machine classification that shows how likely machine could differentiate *p-act* from *non-p-act* tweets, and finally, we (4) summarize findings corresponding to the four research questions.

5.1   What Did People Come to Talk About During Ferguson Protests?

Table 1 shows the distribution of the annotated results by human coders. The classification taxonomies derived from the differentiating coding was detailed in 4.1.1. Among the coded tweets, 15.71% (754) were annotated as relevant to offline BLM protests; 6.71% (322) of the tweets likely to be relevant;

Table 3. *Confidence* code distribution.

	H* (HH/HM/MH)	M* (MM/HL/LH)	L* (LL/LM/ML)	Total
YY	367	123	38	528
II	15	24	26	65
NN	2217	123	38	2378
OO	19	2	0	21
I*	173	99	69	341
O*	35	7	0	42
Divergent	129	43	22	194

and 72.90% (3499) not directly relevant. Combining these two categories (Y and I), we found one out of every 4.5 tweets (22.42%, 1076 tweets) consists of information pertinent to offline BLM protests. The category, O (off-topic) can be regarded as noise – only 1.33% (64 tweets) fall into this category that did not concern BLM movement at all. Table 2 further shows the distribution of what specific information was referred to in those tweets coded as relevant to offline protests (either Y or I). We found 55.48% (597) of the tweets were coded with Thm1, suggesting the majority of *p-act* tweets contained information about describing happenings in a protest activity. There are 42.47% (457) of the tweets coded with Thm3– commenting on the protests. While a tweet may both describe and comment on the protest, such tweets account for 23.33% (251 tweets) of the relevant tweets. The numbers of tweets coded with Thm2 and Thm4 are much lower than Thm1 and Thm3. There are 29 tweets that live-streamed the protests (Thm4), accounted for less than 3% of the relevant tweets. While during the Ferguson unrest, the public attention was greatly paid to live-streaming tweets, our result suggests such firsthand, live reporting remained sparse in the original tweets but was replied/retweeted considerably once being published.

5.2   What Was the Most Retweeted Tweets Talking About?

Among the most retweeted 104 tweets, 39 tweets are *non-p-act* (37.5%), and 65 tweets are *p-act* (62.5%). Such combination is very different from that of the differentiating coding results, in which *non-p-act* tweets accounted for about 72.9% of the randomly sampled tweets. Such difference indicates that among the most retweeted tweets, there are higher percentages of *p-act* tweets.

Table 4 shows the results of our characterizing coding: a total of 10 emerging codes of meaning-making. Table 5 indicated that though the most retweeted *p-act* tweets involves in 8 ways of meaning-making, the emphasis was put more on the immediate happenings relevant to solidarity (code 7) and the police's militarized action and violation of the First Amendment (code 8); these two accounted for 63.8% of the original tweets and 63.0% of the retweet *p-act* discussion. The most retweeted *non-p-act* tweets involved more diverse ways of meaning makings concerning truth and meaning contesting (codes 3 and 4), penetrating biased views (code 6), critical information gathering and disseminating (code 5), associating current happenings to the past and future (code 1), and reaffirming grievance relevant to systemic racism (code 2).

Some types of meaning-making were found in both the *non-p-act* and *p-act*, but two types (codes 5 and 6) only found in *non-p-act*, and four types (codes 7–10) only in *p-act*. More, for meaning-making found in both *non-p-act* and *p-act* tweets (codes 1–4), *p-act* received more retweets.

Table 4. Discursive codes of meaning-making

Code	Discursive Themes of Meaning-Making	non-p	p
1	**Question "history has ever changed?"** e.g., ponder the social progress of addressing discrimination towards African-Americans or racism in general	✓	✓
2	**Reaffirm the grief and grievance** e.g., highlight that a life was dead, which is not just a case but another case, and the systemic racism is still reality	✓	✓
3	**Wrestle with "what is the truth?"** e.g., question mainstream media, suggest alternative evidences and truths	✓	✓
4	**Reframe the mainstream's framing** e.g., use sarcasm to ridicule the happenings perceived unbelievable, penetrating problematic framings	✓	✓
5	**Critically attend to and disseminate the new released information** e.g., attend and disseminate the evidences of the killing not reported by mainstream media	✓	
6	**Penetrate the biased views on the black** e.g., craete visual presentation to contrast the black's life and being with the white's	✓	
7	**Reaffirm sense of solidarity and togetherness** e.g., report people - local, national, or international - coming to support the protests in Ferguson		✓
8	**Negotiate and transfer disoriented perception and emotion for happenings against the First Amendment** e.g., associate police's response to protests with whether it indicates US is a democracy or tyranny, being shocked by the police's militarized response and interaction with protesters, report protesters and journalists being arrested		✓
9	**Disapprove the messiness in the protests** e.g., disapprove protesters' violent behaviors		✓
10	**Contest the mainstream media with live Streaming** e.g., live report what is going on by uploaded photos, videos and descriptions		✓

Table 5. (a,b) Percentages relevant to the total numbers of tweets (retweets) within each *non-p* or *p* category. (c,d) Percentages relevant to the total numbers of tweets (retweets) within each theme.

Theme	(a) # of tweets		(b) # of retweets		(c) # of tweets		(d) # of retweets	
	non-p	p	non-p	p	non-p	p	non-p	p
1	33.3%	11.3%	31.3%	9.5%	64.0%	36.0%	76.6%	23.4%
2	20.8%	6.3%	23.5%	4.9%	66.7%	33.3%	82.5%	17.5%
3	4.2%	5.0%	15.5%	5.5%	33.3%	66.7%	73.9%	26.1%
4	12.5%	5.0%	9.9%	8.5%	60.0%	40.0%	53.7%	46.3%
5	18.8%	0.0%	13.7%	0.0%	100.0%	0.0%	100.0%	0.0%
6	10.4%	0.0%	6.1%	0.0%	100.0%	0.0%	100.0%	0.0%
7	0.0%	42.5%	0.0%	34.7%	0.0%	100.0%	0.0%	100.0%
8	0.0%	21.3%	0.0%	28.3%	0.0%	100.0%	0.0%	100.0%
9	0.0%	5.0%	0.0%	5.3%	0.0%	100.0%	0.0%	100.0%
10	0.0%	3.8%	0.0%	3.4%	0.0%	100.0%	0.0%	100.0%

5.3 To What Extent Can Protest-Related Messages Be Detected Automatically?

We conducted experiments on various machine classification techniques, where the objective is to classify whether a given tweet was labeled as *p-act* or not. The classification methods, feature engineering, and the experiment setup are given in Sect. 4.2. Table 6 shows the results of the classification for each method that achieved the best performances on the dataset. We report the results of two variants of each method in which we used the domain-specific features alone and the combined features including both domain-specific and word embedding features. The results indicate that, while the domain-specific features can be extracted without relying on a given corpus or pre-training step, the results suffered from low precision (in the cases of ANN and LR) or very low recall (in the case of SVM). Using the combined features achieved significantly better performance than using the domain-specific features alone. With the combined set of features, the best *AUC* value (0.837) was obtained with ANN and LR methods whereas the highest *F-score* value (0.616) was achieved by LR. Moreover, the results of ANN reported in Table 6 were obtained using an architecture having two hidden layers containing 64 and 32 hidden units in its first and second layers, respectively. We also conducted experiments with ANNs with more hidden layers yet, but observed no significant improvement.

We further examined the cases for which machine misclassified. These include tweets that were labeled as *p-act* but misclassified as *non-p-act* (false *non-p-act*), and vice verse (false *p-act*). In the former case, we found many of these tweets

Table 6. Classification results

	Domain features			Combined features		
	SVM	ANN	LR	SVM	ANN	LR
Precision	0.718	0.343	0.366	0.740	0.541	0.545
Recall	0.101	0.588	0.592	0.449	0.700	0.707
F-score	0.177	0.433	0.453	0.559	0.611	**0.616**
AUC	0.647	0.661	0.684	0.836	**0.837**	**0.837**

(talking about what happened in protest) tend to have photos and videos, but our classifiers relied solely on a tweet's textual content, suggesting the importance of incorporating multimedia information in the classification. In the later case, some misclassifications occur when the tweets contain words signaling offline protest activities (e.g., stand or join) but in fact, these words were used in a metaphorical or hypothetical statement. For example, *"I think people in #Ferguson will just standing outside in the street tonight scratching their heads and chin checking. #HowDidWeGetHere"* was misclassified as *p-act*. This suggests more sophisticated NLP techniques (e.g., metaphor detection) may be used to distinguish these situations.

Overall, our experiment results indicate it is possible to use machine classifiers to distinguish the protest-related messages. However, a better performance may be achieved with multimedia information, more sophisticated NLP techniques, and larger set of labeled data.

5.4 Summary of Key Findings

For Q1, not all but only about 22.43 % Twitter discussion during Ferguson unrest talked about offline protests. The most reported what happened on sites

(Thm1); the second commented on the protests (Thm3)– these two consisted of the most communication, for example, *"Protestors were marching hours before curfew - peaceful & completely legal. Multiple reports of children hit with gas. #Ferguson," "I'm really upset with what's going on in #Ferguon right now...my heart goes out to EVERYONE involved and I hope this violence ends soon."* These tweets focused primarily on immediate happenings of protests. For Q2 and Q3, we focused on the most retweeted tweets and discovered 10 ways by which Twitter users engaged in meaning-making of events happenings. Among *p-act*, people engaged mostly to reaffirm solidarity and interpret the First Amendment, while *non-p-act* linked the disorienting events to historical happenings, questioned the status quo, wondered the future, and invented creative ways to penetrating and contest with mainstream framing. For Q4, our human coding schemes, together with a developed codebook, delivered reliable results. The experiments of machine classification suggested the possibility of differentiating offline protests by machine; we identified the issues that can be further improved.

6   Discussion, Conclusions, and Future Work

This study offers insights as to what collective sense-making processes took place in the context of BLM protesting. We highlight several observations. First, while the online talking consisted of more original *non-p-act* tweets, *p-act* tweets were retweeted more. This suggests that the collective attention was caught largely by offline happenings. However, collective communications engaging in meaning negotiation that went beyond the immediate events took place too, which may challenge individuals' habitual orienting systems and facilitate the mindset shifts for social change. People questioned whether the history has ever changed, being shocked by and then reaffirming the grievance toward the systemic racism against the black. The single mostly retweeted tweet was a *non-p-act*, which received 45,410 retweets that questioned the history ever changed by contrasting two photos; one historical, the other of the present time.

Our study is, to our knowledge, the first attempt at developing a classification scheme that can determine whether the online conversation on social media platforms has to do with offline BLM protests. We constructed a codebook that offers the coding guidance, which has been tested to deliver reliable coding results. Our criteria for identifying relevant tweets are theory-driven, and our coding approach to constructing the classification scheme presents a new coding methodology and gives piratical suggestions.

Through the process, we also identify a major issue for human coding that the information posted may not explicitly indicate the relevancy. Hence, the coders may rely on their prior knowledge and experiences when making an annotation decision, leading to less reliable coding outcomes. To overcome such challenge, we invented the confidence coding allowing coders to reflect their hesitation or confusion resulting from such nature of online discussions of offline protests/activism. The result suggests an increased reliability and a high degree of the validity of coders' annotation. This strategy would be useful for developing coding scheme relevant to activism or other social movement contexts.

Our future plans include expanding our analysis to a highly relevant protesting context (e.g., the protests happened in Nov. 2014). Such analysis would allow us to compare whether people's meaning-making may change and how as they followed the development of the case. As for machine classification, we found our machine classifiers can distinguish the protest-related messages with reasonable performance. To further improve the classification performance, we plan to incorporate multimedia information and more sophisticated language features.

Acknowledgement. The authors thank Joshua Bloom for his insight in the early stage of this research. The authors would like to acknowledge the support from NSF #1634944. Any opinions, findings, and conclusions or recommendations expressed in this material do not necessarily reflect the views of the funding sources.

References

1. de Albornoz, J.C., Plaza, L., Gervás, P.: Sentisense: an easily scalable concept-based affective lexicon for sentiment analysis. In: LREC, pp. 3562–3567 (2012)
2. Bastos, M.T., Mercea, D., Charpentier, A.: Tents, tweets, and events: the interplay between ongoing protests and social media. J. Commun. **65**(2), 320–350 (2015)
3. Bonilla, Y., Rosa, J.: # ferguson: digital protest, hashtag ethnography, and the racial politics of social media in the united states. Am. Ethnol. **42**(1), 4–17 (2015)
4. Casciani, D.: How social media changed protest. http://www.bbc.com/news/magazine-11953186. Accessed 10 May 2018
5. Castells, M.: Networks of Outrage and Hope: Social Movements in the Internet Age. Wiley, Chichester (2015)
6. Chung, C., Pennebaker, J.W.: The Psychological Functions of Function Words. Social Communication, pp. 343–359 (2007)
7. Conover, M.D., Davis, C., Ferrara, E., McKelvey, K., Menczer, F., Flammini, A.: The geospatial characteristics of a social movement communication network. PloS one **8**(3), e55957 (2013)
8. De Choudhury, M., Jhaver, S., Sugar, B., Weber, I.: Social media participation in an activist movement for racial equality. In: ICWSM (2016)
9. Freelon, D., McIlwain, C.D., Clark, M.D.: Beyond the hashtags:# ferguson,# blacklivesmatter, and the online struggle for offline justice (2016)
10. Gallagher, R.J., Reagan, A.J., Danforth, C.M., Dodds, P.S.: Divergent discourse between protests and counter-protests:# blacklivesmatter and# alllivesmatter. arXiv preprint arXiv:1606.06820 (2016)
11. Glasberg, D.S., Shannon, D.: Political Sociology: Oppression, Resistance, and the State. SAGE Publications, London (2010)
12. González-Bailón, S.: The dynamics of protest recruitment through an online network. Sci. Rep. **1**, 197 (2011)
13. Goodwin, J., Jasper, J.M.: The Social Movements Reader: Cases and Concepts. Wiley, New York (2014)
14. Graham, J., Haidt, J., Nosek, B.A.: Liberals and conservatives rely on different sets of moral foundations. J. Pers. Soc. Psychol. **96**(5), 1029 (2009)
15. Hanna, A.: MPEDS: automating the generation of protest event data (2017)
16. Heller, N.: Is there any point to protesting? https://www.newyorker.com/magazine/2017/08/21/is-there-any-point-to-protesting. Accessed 10 May 2018

17. Klandermans, B., van Stekelenburg, J.: The political psychology of protest. Eur. Psychol. **18**(4), 224–234 (2013)
18. McAdam, D., McCarthy, J.D., Olzak, S., Soule, S.A.: Dynamics of collective action (2009)
19. Mikolov, T., Sutskever, I., Chen, K., Corrado, G.S., Dean, J.: Distributed representations of words and phrases and their compositionality. In: Advances in Neural Information Processing Systems, pp. 3111–3119 (2013)
20. Park, C.L.: Making sense of the meaning literature: an integrative review of meaning making and its effects on adjustment to stressful life events. Psychol. Bull. **136**(2), 257 (2010)
21. Thorpe, J.: Do political protests actually change anything? https://www.bustle.com/p/do-political-protests-actually-change-anything-29952. Accessed 10 May 2018
22. Tufekci, Z.: Twitter and Tear Gas: The Power and Fragility of Networked Protest. Yale University Press, New Haven (2017)
23. Valenzuela, S.: Unpacking the use of social media for protest behavior: the roles of information, opinion expression, and activism. Am. Behav. Sci. **57**(7), 920–942 (2013)
24. Van Stekelenburg, J., Klandermans, B.: The social psychology of protest. Curr. Sociol. **61**(5–6), 886–905 (2013)
25. Yang, G.: Narrative agency in hashtag activism: the case of #blacklivesmatter. Media Commun. **4**(4), 13 (2016)

Fake News as We Feel It: Perception and Conceptualization of the Term "Fake News" in the Media

Evandro Cunha[1,2(✉)], Gabriel Magno[1], Josemar Caetano[1], Douglas Teixeira[1], and Virgilio Almeida[1,3]

[1] Department of Computer Science, Universidade Federal de Minas Gerais (UFMG), Belo Horizonte, Brazil
{evandrocunha,magno,josemarcaetano,douglas,virgilio}@dcc.ufmg.br
[2] Leiden University Centre for Linguistics (LUCL), Leiden, The Netherlands
[3] Berkman Klein Center for Internet and Society, Harvard University, Cambridge, USA

Abstract. In this article, we quantitatively analyze how the term "fake news" is being shaped in news media in recent years. We study the perception and the conceptualization of this term in the traditional media using eight years of data collected from news outlets based in 20 countries. Our results not only corroborate previous indications of a high increase in the usage of the expression "fake news", but also show contextual changes around this expression after the United States presidential election of 2016. Among other results, we found changes in the related vocabulary, in the mentioned entities, in the surrounding topics and in the contextual polarity around the term "fake news", suggesting that this expression underwent a change in perception and conceptualization after 2016. These outcomes expand the understandings on the usage of the term "fake news", helping to comprehend and more accurately characterize this relevant social phenomenon linked to misinformation and manipulation.

Keywords: Social computing · Digital humanities
Corpus linguistics · Misinformation · Fake news

1 Introduction

The term "fake news", defined as "false, often sensational, information disseminated under the guise of news reporting" [6], gained so much attention that it was named the Collins Word of the Year 2017 due to its unprecedented usage increase of 365% in the Collins Corpus [6]. Even though the concept of news articles aimed to mislead readers is by no means new [24], it seems to exist a relationship between the very expression "fake news" with the 2016 presidential election in the United States of America: Davies [8], using data from the NOW Corpus, shows that "there is almost no mention of 'fake news' until the first week

© Springer Nature Switzerland AG 2018
S. Staab et al. (Eds.): SocInfo 2018, LNCS 11185, pp. 151–166, 2018.
https://doi.org/10.1007/978-3-030-01129-1_10

of November [2016] (...) and then it explodes in Nov 11–20, and has stayed very high since then". The author adds that the reason "why people all of the sudden started talking about something that had really not been mentioned much at all until that time" was "the US elections, which were held on November 9, 2016".

The sudden popularization of an already existing term (that is, not a neologism) in a language poses interesting questions regarding how concepts around this term are perceived by the speakers of that language. We might ask, for instance: what changed (if anything) in terms of conceptualization of this expression after its boom? Was there any kind of shift in the meaning of this expression when it became widely employed? If so, was this shift uniform across different varieties of the language? These are some of the issues of interest in *lexicology*, the area of linguistics focused in the study of the lexicon, that has been fostered thanks to advances in *corpus linguistics*, concerned with the use of big real-world corpora to the study of language.

The goal of this article is to provide a closer look at how newspapers and magazines across the world shape the term "fake news" – which is a relevant social phenomenon linked to misinformation and manipulation, and that has been facilitated by the rise of the Internet and online social media in recent years. We investigate the perception and the conceptualization of this expression through the quantitative analysis of a large corpus of news published in 20 countries from 2010 to 2018, thus making it possible to examine not only the diachronic development of this term, but also its synchronic usage in different parts of the English-speaking world. We complement our investigation with data collected from online search queries that help to measure how the public interest in the expression "fake news" and in the concepts around it changed over time in different places.

1.1 Related Work

In 2010, Michel et al. [17] coined the term *culturomics* meaning a method to study human behavior, cultural trends and language change through the quantitative diachronic analysis of texts, including of digitized books provided by the project Google Books. Several studies explore this method to investigate topics such as the dynamics of birth and death of words [20], semantic change [12], emotions in literary texts [1] and general characteristics of modern societies [22]. However, many criticisms arose regarding limitations of inferences derived from the analysis of Google Books due to factors that range from optical character recognition errors and overabundance of scientific literature [19] to the lack of metadata in the corpus [13].

Leetaru [15] proposes a somewhat complementary approach that he calls *culturomics 2.0*, which uses historical news data instead of books and can, according to the author, "yield intriguing new understandings of human society". In the same vein, Flaounas et al. analyze the European mediasphere [11] and the writing style, gender bias and the popularity of particular topics [10] in large corpora of news articles. Landsall-Welfare et al. [14], also using a large dataset of media reports, observe a change of framing and sentiment associated with nuclear power after the Fukushima nuclear disaster. They detected effects on attention, sentiment, conceptual associations and in the network of actors and actions linked to nuclear power following the accident.

In this investigation, we combine many of the methods employed in the related works mentioned above. However, as far as we are concerned, this is the first paper that uses these methods to examine in details how the relevant term "fake news" is being reported by news media in different parts of the world and in two distinct periods in the history of this expression.

1.2   Research Question

Our main research question is: *was the rise of the public interest in the term "fake news" accompanied by changes in its conceptualization and in the perception about it?* Based on sociolexicological theories, that defend the existence of a considerable relationship between linguistic and extralinguistic factors with regards to the vocabulary of a language [5,16], our hypothesis is that the change of interest in the phenomenon *fake news* might have altered the general usage of the expression referring to it. Indeed, the results obtained in our investigations indicate, in general, a positive answer for our research question. Among other findings, we show modifications in the related vocabulary and in the mentioned entities accompanying the term "fake news", in addition to changes in the topics associated to this concept and in the overall contextual polarity of the pieces of text around this expression in media articles after 2016.

This article is structured as follows: in the next section, we present the process of acquisition and preparation of the main data source used in our investigations; in Sect. 3, we describe our analyses, present the found results and discuss their implications; finally, in Sect. 4, we summarize the outcomes of our study and conclude this paper by discussing possible future outlooks.

2   Data Source

The main dataset used in this study comes from the Corpus of News on the Web (NOW Corpus), which contains articles from online newspapers and magazines written in English and based in 20 different countries from 2010 to the present time [7]. This corpus is available for download and online exploration at https://corpus.byu.edu/now/ and, according to its authors, "is [as of April 2018] by far the largest corpus (of any language) that is available in full-text format". Our analyses are relative to a version of the corpus available in the month of April 2018, containing around six billion words of data.

In this dataset, we searched for all the occurrences of the term "fake news". For each occurrence, the online version of the corpus provides a concordance line, or *context* – that is, a piece of text of approximately 20–30 words around (before and after) the searched term. For example, for a certain news article published in July 25 2017 in the Kenyan newspaper Daily Nation, the context around the term "fake news" is: *(...) of social media and a study that said 90* *per cent of Kenyans had encountered **fake news**. WhatsApp and Facebook are the two leading sources of misinformation, often (...).* All of our analyses were performed in these contexts, since words immediately surrounding a key term are more relevant to the conceptualization of this term than words further away from it, though in the same text. Wynne [27] adds that the main reason for using keywords in context (KWICs) in corpus linguistics is that "interesting insights into the structure and usage of a language can be obtained by looking at words in real texts and seeing what patterns of lexis, grammar and meaning surround them".

The total number of occurrences of "fake news" extracted from the NOW Corpus in April 30 2018 is 41,124. These occurrences encompass news articles published in all the 20 countries represented in the corpus, that were grouped in six regions based on their geographical locations (Africa, British Isles, Indian subcontinent, Oceania, Southeast Asia and The Americas), since it has been observed that offline and online news outlets tend to give preference to local and national news, to domesticate news about other countries and to reflect imbalanced information flows between the developed and the developing worlds [2].

These occurrences also cover each year in the corpus (from 2010 to 2018). Due to the previously observed increase in the usage of the term "fake news" during and after the 2016 presidential election in the United States of America (mentioned in Sect. 1), we categorized the occurrences in two periods: before and after the 2016 US election. The election was held in November, but we set the delimitation date between these periods in the end of the first semester of 2016 (June 30) in order to include the political campaign in the period *after US election*. Table 1 shows the number of contexts containing the term "fake news" in our dataset according to the geographical origin of the corresponding news media and the year and period of publication of the news article.

3   Analyses and Results

In this section, we display and examine the outcomes of our investigations. Each analysis is introduced by a description of how it is able to contribute answering to our research question, followed by the methodology employed and finally by a presentation and discussion of the results found.

3.1   Web Search Behavior

Before analyzing the data obtained from the NOW Corpus, we investigate whether it is possible to observe a change in Web search behavior regarding the expression "fake news" corresponding to the high increase in its use during and after the 2016 presidential election in the United States of America mentioned in Sect. 1.

Data obtained from Google Trends[1], an online tool that indicates the frequency of particular terms in the total volume of searches in the Google Search

---

[1] https://trends.google.com/trends/.

Table 1. Number of contexts containing the term "fake news" in our dataset according to (a) the geographical origin of the corresponding news media and (b) the year and period (before or after the 2016 presidential election in the United States of America) of publication of the news article.

(a) Geographical origin of news media

Region	Country	Occurrences
Southeast Asia	Singapore	3,722
	Malaysia	3,455
	Philippines	3,058
	Hong Kong	171
	Total: 25,3% / 10,406	
The Americas	United States	6,775
	Canada	2,960
	Jamaica	124
	Total: 24,0% / 9,859	
British Isles	Great Britain	4,213
	Ireland	2,035
	Total: 15,2% / 6,248	

Region	Country	Occurrences
Africa	South Africa	2,493
	Nigeria	1,974
	Kenya	1,368
	Ghana	300
	Tanzania	1
	Total: 14,9% / 6,136	
Oceania	Australia	3,052
	New Zealand	1,446
	Total: 10,9% / 4,498	
Indian subcontinent	India	2,961
	Pakistan	772
	Sri Lanka	147
	Bangladesh	97
	Total: 9,7% / 3,977	

(b) Year and period of publication of news article

Year	2010	2011	2012	2013	2014	2015	2016	2017	2018
Occurrences	24	43	57	64	89	95	4,766	25,293	10,693

Period	before US election	after US election
Occurrences	494	40,630

engine, displays that public interest in the term "fake news" was approximately constant from 2010 until 2016, when it greatly and suddenly increased, as indicated by Fig. 1. This data also shows that, in the period before the 2016 US presidential elections, most of the countries with the highest proportions of searches for the term "fake news" were from the Eastern world. However, after the US election, the proportion of searches for this expression in Western countries increased considerably, especially in Europe. The 10 countries with the highest proportion of searches for the term "fake news" in both periods are listed in Table 2.

A closer look at the data from Google Trends also reveals that the great increase in the public interest for the expression "fake news" coincided with a change in the focus of Web searches. Table 3 shows the five most frequent search terms employed by users who also searched for "fake news" in the periods before and after the US election. We observe that, before the US election, searches for "fake news" were generic and regarded topics related to the media industry

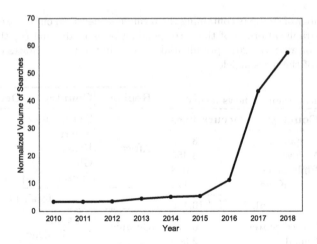

Fig. 1. Normalized volume of searches for the expression "fake news" on Google Search from 2010 to 2018.

Table 2. Countries with the highest proportion of searches for "fake news" on Google Search before and after US election.

Period	Countries
Before US election	India, United Arab Emirates, Singapore, United States, Macedonia, Qatar, New Zealand, Canada, Pakistan, Australia
After US election	Singapore, Philippines, United States, Canada, South Africa, Norway, Denmark, Ireland, United Kingdom, Switzerland

itself, like "article", "stories" and "report"; after the US election, however, these searches started to be more focused on political affairs and in the spread of fake news, mentioning entities like the elected president of the United States of America in 2016 (Donald Trump), the television news channel CNN (that devotes large amounts of its coverage to US politics) and the social media Facebook (considered a major source of fake news on the Internet).

Table 3. Most frequent search terms related to "fake news" on Google Search before and after US election.

Period	Search terms
Before US election	fake news generator, fake news article, fake news stories, make fake news, fake news report
After US election	trump news, the fake news, fake news trump, cnn news, fake news facebook

In this section, we used data obtained from the Google Trends tool. From the next section on, however, all of our analyses use the data described in Sect. 2, obtained from the NOW Corpus.

3.2   Co-occurring Named Entities

The analysis of *named entities* – that is, real-world entities such as persons, organizations and locations that can be denoted with proper names [26] – co-occurring with certain terms is an interesting way to contextualize these concepts. In our case, by identifying which entities are linked to the expression "fake news" in different periods of time and in different parts of the world, we are able to observe relationships of "who and where" in the recent history of our key-term.

In our dataset of news articles, we employed a simple method to identify named entities: we made use of the fact that newspapers and magazines consistently capitalize nouns representing named entities and counted all the words that appear capitalized in the contexts; then, we manually analyzed the most frequent capitalized words in each subdivision of the corpus (i.e. representing each region and period) to remove words not relative to named entities (such as "I", "SMS", "March" and words capitalized for other reasons) and to merge duplicated entities represented more than once (e.g. "Donald" and "Trump").

Table 4 shows the five most mentioned named entities in the periods before and after the 2016 US presidential election, regardless of geographical origin of the corresponding news media. Before the US election, it is possible to observe a strong connection between humor and fake news: with exception of Facebook, all the other most mentioned named entities are related to satirical TV shows and hosts based in the United States of America. On the other side, in the period after the US election, there is a movement towards politically related entities (Donald Trump), traditional media sources (CNN) and social networking services (Facebook and Twitter). It is interesting to notice that this shift matches the already mentioned (in Table 3) shift of interest towards political affairs and the spread of fake news observed in Web searches.

Table 4. Most mentioned entities in the periods before and after US election.

Period	Entities
Before US election	The Daily Show, Jon Stewart, Onion News Network, Facebook, Stephen Colbert
After US election	Donald Trump, Facebook, US, CNN, Twitter

When we make this same diachronic comparison, but now considering the geographical origin of the corresponding news media, we observe a noteworthy phenomenon: the global standardization of the named entities related to *fake news*. Table 5 indicates that local entities are more relevant in the period before the US election, when names of geographical regions (Ekiti), countries (Nigeria, China), local political parties (PDP – People's Democratic Party of Nigeria, BJP – Bharatiya Janata Party of India) and local personalities (Shahid Afridi, King Salman, Korina Sanchez) appear frequently among the most mentioned entities. In the contexts after the US election, however, Donald Trump, Facebook and US are the three most mentioned entities for nearly all the regions – with the sole exception of The Americas, where CNN replaces US.

Table 5. Most mentioned entities in the periods before and after US election, considering the geographical origin of the corresponding news media.

Region	Period	Entities
Africa	Before	PDP, Ekiti, Nigeria
	After	Donald Trump, Facebook, US
British Isles	Before	Facebook, The Daily Show, Stephen Colbert
	After	Donald Trump, Facebook, US
Indian subcontinent	Before	Shahid Afridi, King Salman of Saudi Arabia, BJP
	After	Facebook, Donald Trump, US
Oceania	Before	Twitter, The Daily Show, NBC
	After	Donald Trump, Facebook, US
Southeast Asia	Before	Korina Sanchez, US, China
	After	Facebook, Donald Trump, US
The Americas	Before	The Daily Show, Jon Stewart, Onion News Network
	After	Donald Trump, Facebook, CNN

3.3 Semantic Fields of the Surrounding Vocabulary

Besides the investigation of the named entities that accompany a given key-term, the analysis of the general vocabulary co-occurring with it is also valuable. In our case, one of the possible methods of performing such analysis is by observing the semantic fields (i.e. groups to which semantically related items belong) of the words co-occurring with the expression "fake news" in our contexts.

For performing this task, we first lemmatized all the words in the contexts by employing the WordNet Lemmatizer function provided by the Natural Language Toolkit [3] and using *verb* as the part-of-speech argument for the lemmatization method. By applying this lemmatization, we grouped together the inflected forms of the words so that they could be analyzed as single items based on their dictionary forms (*lemmas*).

Then, we used Empath [9], "a tool for analyzing text across lexical categories"[2], to classify the lemmatized words according to categories that represent different semantic fields, such as diverse topics and emotions. For every context,

---

[2] https://github.com/Ejhfast/empath-client.

we calculated the percentage of words belonging to each semantic field represented by an Empath category. Due to the high number of categories predefined by Empath (194 in total), we selected eight that showed interesting results and are relevant for our discussion: *government, internet, journalism, leader, negative emotion, politics, social media* and *technology*. By way of example, the category *internet* includes 79 words such as *homepage, download* and *hacker*, while the category *journalism* contains 69 words, including *report, article* and *newspaper*.

Figure 2 displays the average percentage of words in these categories for all the six regions considered here, both before and after the 2016 US election. By analyzing the graphs presented, we observe interesting differences and trends regarding the quantitative utilization of words from the semantic fields considered. We highlight the high increase in the use of words from the related categories *government, leader* and *politics* (and also from the supposedly unrelated category *negative emotion*) and the high decrease in the use of words from the categories *internet, journalism* and *technology* (but not *social media*) in almost all regions after the US election.

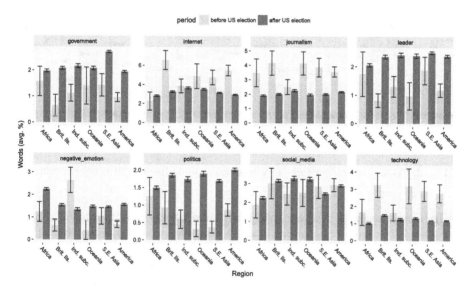

Fig. 2. Percentage of words in each semantic field represented by an Empath category. Error bars indicate standard errors.

We hypothesize that these results indicate a change in the focus of the news considered here: before the 2016 US election, the term "fake news" was probably more mentioned in contexts in which the focus was the *environment* where they occur (Internet, newspapers etc.), sometimes even meta-discussions on the very topic of fake news and its dissemination; during and after the US election, however, the discussion seems to have migrated to themes more close to the *content* of the fake news themselves (politics, elections etc.).

3.4 Co-occurrence Networks

Another possible method of investigating the vocabulary accompanying a key-term in a corpus is through the observation of co-occurrence networks. In our case, this method enables us to visually analyze the words that co-occur with the expression "fake news" in the contexts that we are considering. Here, we compare co-occurrence networks between the periods before and after the 2016 US election, regardless of the geographical origin of the media outlets. These networks are represented here by graphs, in which each node corresponds to a word and each edge corresponds to an association between two given words.

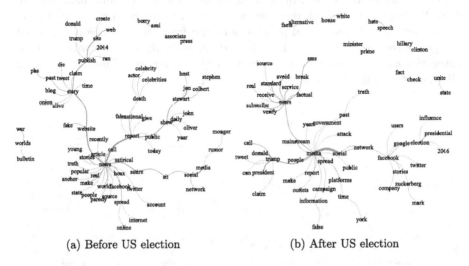

(a) Before US election   (b) After US election

Fig. 3. Co-occurrence networks of words before and after the 2016 US election.

To build our graphs of co-occurring words, we followed the steps below. First, we counted the number of contexts in which two given words co-occur, so that we have the volume of co-occurrences for each pair of words. Then, we normalized these values in order to work with percentages instead of working with the absolute number of co-occurrences. To improve the visualization of the graphs, we filtered out minor relationships and highlighted the strongest ones by removing nodes and edges when the co-occurrence percentage was lower than 0.8% (for the period before the US election) and 0.5% (for the period after the US election), and by plotting the width of the edges proportionally to the strength of association between two given words. Finally, we obtained the *maximum spanning trees* of both graphs, which are presented in Fig. 3.

This method of investigation enables us to make several qualitative observations. Comparing the two graphs, we notice clear changes in the relationships between the words co-occurring with "fake news" in our contexts. For instance, before the US election, the main cluster contains words related to the news industry itself ("article", "stories", "hoax") and to Internet ("website", "twitter", "facebook", "account"). Corroborating previous findings (Sect. 3.2), there is also another cluster containing words referring to satirical TV shows and hosts ("daily", "show", "colbert", "oliver", "stewart"). In the graph representing the period after the 2016 US election, we start to observe terms linked to specific events, mainly the US election itself. Interestingly, some terms that surround meta-discussions about fake news also appear, highlighting relevant related concepts: *fact check, hate speech, post truth* and *alternative facts*.

3.5 Topics Addressed in the Contexts

In addition to studying the vocabulary around a key-term, it is also possible to find the main topics addressed in the pieces of text surrounding the occurrences of the expression "fake news" in our corpus.

For this task, we used latent Dirichlet allocation (LDA) [4], a way of automatically discovering topics discussed in texts. First, we lowercased and tokenized all the words in the dataset. Then, we removed stop words using the list provided by the Natural Language Toolkit – after having added the words "fake" and "news" to this list, since they appear in all contexts. Finally, we ran the LDA algorithm using gensim [21], a Python library for topic modeling. We used topic coherence score [18] to choose the optimum number of topics k to be returned by the algorithm. Thus, for each region, we ran the LDA algorithm starting with $k = 2$ and ending with $k = 20$, and chose the best LDA model, that is, the LDA model with highest topic coherence score. All regions had, respectively, $k = 2$ and $k = 14$ for the periods before and after the US election, except The Americas, that had $k = 8$ and $k = 14$. For each region, the LDA returned these k topics containing words ordered by importance in the corresponding context, filtered both by region and topic. We then selected the most important topic as the representative of each region and period. Table 6 shows the main topic for each region in both periods (before and after the US election) and the top ranked ten words produced by our LDA model.

Unlike in the period before the US election, the words related to each topic inferred by LDA are cohesive among each other in the period after the US election. We observe, for all regions, a relevant frequency of words related to politics and social networks in the period after the US election. More specifically, the words "russian", "russia", "election" and "facebook" rank high in this period. In the period before the US election, most of the top words are related to Internet and to the spread of misinformation, in all regions.

3.6 Polarity

Our final analysis explores a different feature of the contexts in which the expression "fake news" appear in our dataset: their *polarities*, that is, whether the expressed opinion in the texts is mostly positive, negative or neutral. Here, we performed sentiment analysis [23] in each one of the contexts in our dataset

Table 6. Main topic for each region. Inside each topic, ten words are presented in order of importance according to the LDA output.

Region	Period	Main topic words
Africa	Before	become, world, party, south, leave, week, online, state, give, member
	After	trump, people, spread, president, truth, propaganda, thing, look, show, nigerian
British Isles	Before	Story, account, real, daily, website,new, show, use, death, state
	After	propaganda, source, russian, american, russia, lie, mean, popular, politics, allegation
Indian subcontinent	Before	create, spread, report, death, also, lot, say, not, social, do
	After	facebook, also, problem, user, issue,company, russian, state, work, zuckerberg
Oceania	Before	people, story, site, report, website,mortgage, would, fool, year, day
	After	election, influence, media, create, russian,question, policy, discuss, presidential, word
Southeast Asia	Before	article, website, story, report, site, celebrity, death, publish, go, viral
	After	public, government, fact, twitter, proliferation,day, official, however, phenomenon, concern
The Americas	Before	release, chip, firm, flurry, blue, target, date, breadcrumb, irresponsible, last
	After	facebook, problem, network, company, also,believe, publish, work, policy, russian

using SentiStrength[3] [25], a tool able to estimate the strength of positive and negative sentiment in short texts. Given a piece of text, this tool returns a score that varies from -4 (negative sentiment) to $+4$ (positive sentiment).

We are interested in analyzing how polarity changes over time and in different regions when it comes to "fake news" and how this can be perceived in our dataset. Figure 4 depicts the average polarity of the contexts in each region before and after the 2016 US presidential election. We first observe a clear dominance of negative polarities in all periods and regions, indicating that the term "fake news" is often related to negative words [28] and sentiments – which is not surprising, since the concept of fake news seems to be strongly associated with negative concepts, like misinformation, manipulation and the spread of untrue facts.

---

[3] http://sentistrength.wlv.ac.uk/.

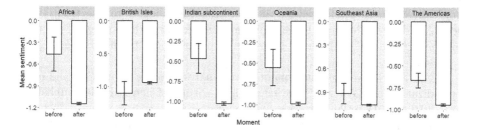

Fig. 4. Average polarity of the contexts in each region before and after US election (bars indicate the standard error of the mean).

In this figure, we also observe that, in general, the polarity expressed in the contexts in the period after the US election is more negative than before. The only exception is in the British Isles, where the difference of polarity between the periods is not statistically relevant. This result seems to corroborate findings presented in previous sections of this article, which demonstrated that, before the 2016 US election, the term "fake news" was often linked to satirical TV shows and more general topics, while in the period during and after the election the topics became more related to the spread of false information in the context of political activity.

3.7   Summary of Results

The most relevant outcomes of the analyses presented in this section can be summarized and integrated as follows:

- the interest for the term "fake news" suddenly increased after the 2016 US election, as indicated by the rise of news about it and of Google Search queries for this expression (Sect. 3.1);
- this growth was accompanied by a change of framing around the term "fake news" – from, for instance, topics regarding the media industry itself to those related to political affairs (Sects. 3.1, 3.3, 3.4 and 3.5);
- the named entities linked to the expression "fake news" not only changed towards political topics, but also suffered from global standardization after the US election (Sect. 3.2);
- the negativity of the news containing the term "fake news" increased after the US election (Sect. 3.6).

All these results suggest that, as hypothesized in Sect. 1, the rise of public interest in the term "fake news" came with changes in its conceptualization and in the perception about it.

4   Concluding Remarks

Due to the increased role of the Internet in modern societies, topics regarding misinformation and manipulation in online environments seem to be subject to progressively more public debate and interest, including from the traditional media. Understanding how these topics are viewed through the eyes of opinion leaders is crucial to comprehend how public opinion about them is being shaped in present day.

In this article, we present a quantitative analysis on the perception and conceptualization of the term "fake news" in a corpus of news articles published from 2010 to 2018 in 20 countries. We investigate how media sources have been reporting topics related to fake news and whether the rise of the public interest in this very expression during and after the 2016 presidential election in the United States of America was accompanied by changes of perception and shifts in sentiment about it. We observed changes in the vocabulary and in the mentioned entities around the term "fake news" in our corpus, in the topics related to this concept and in the polarity of the texts around it after 2016, as well as in Web search behavior of Google Search users interested in this concept.

We are also interested in understanding whether the term "fake news" is framed differently across the globe – and, if so, which are these differences. The existence of such variations may result in different shifts in the meanings and in the sentiments around these concepts in various regions of the world, which justifies this study as a way to more clearly understand how the public opinion is being steered in the current context in different countries of the English-speaking world.

In this paper, we analyzed the usage of the term "fake news" in a diachronic perspective, but only considered two historical moments: before and after a key event in the history of this expression (the 2016 US presidential election). In the future, we plan to consider a larger spectrum of periods, particularly to understand whether (and, if it is the case, when) the conceptualization of "fake news" changed once again. We also intend to add analyses using data from other relevant sources, including Twitter posts and Wikipedia edits.

References

1. Acerbi, A., Lampos, V., Garnett, P., Bentley, R.A.: The expression of emotions in 20th century books. PLOS ONE 8(3), e59030 (2013)
2. Berger, G.: How the Internet impacts on international news: exploring paradoxes of the most global medium in a time of 'hyperlocalism'. Int. Commun. Gaz. 71(5), 355–371 (2009)
3. Bird, S., Loper, E., Klein, E.: Natural Language Processing with Python. O'Reilly Media Inc., Sebastopol (2009)
4. Blei, D.M., Ng, A.Y., Jordan, M.I.: Latent Dirichlet allocation. J. Mach. Learn. Res. 3, 993–1022 (2003)
5. Cambraia, C.N.: Da lexicologia social a uma lexicologia sócio-histórica: caminhos possíveis. Revista de Estudos da Linguagem 21(1), 157–188 (2013)
6. Collins Dictionary: Word of the year 2017 (2017). https://www.collinsdictionary.com/woty. Accessed 4 May 2018
7. Davies, M.: Corpus of News on the Web (NOW): 3+ billion words from 20 countries, updated every day (2013). https://corpus.byu.edu/now/

8. Davies, M.: Fake news (2017). https://corpus.byu.edu/now/help/fake-news.asp. Accessed 4 May 2018
9. Fast, E., Chen, B., Bernstein, M.S.: Empath: understanding topic signals in large-scale text. In: Proceedings of the 2016 CHI Conference on Human Factors in Computing Systems, pp. 4647–4657. ACM (2016)
10. Flaounas, I., et al.: Research methods in the age of digital journalism: massive-scale automated analysis of news-content - topics, style and gender. Digit. Journal. **1**(1), 102–116 (2013). https://doi.org/10.1080/21670811.2012.714928
11. Flaounas, I., Turchi, M., Ali, O., Fyson, N., De Bie, T., Mosdell, N., Lewis, J., Cristianini, N.: The structure of the EU mediasphere. PLOS ONE **5**(12), e14243 (2010)
12. Gulordava, K., Baroni, M.: A distributional similarity approach to the detection of semantic change in the Google Books Ngram corpus. In: Proceedings of the GEMS 2011 Workshop on GEometrical Models of Natural Language Semantics, pp. 67–71. Association for Computational Linguistics (2011)
13. Koplenig, A.: The impact of lacking metadata for the measurement of cultural and linguistic change using the Google Ngram data sets - reconstructing the composition of the German corpus in times of WWII. Digit. Sch. Humanit. **32**(1), 169–188 (2017). https://doi.org/10.1093/llc/fqv037
14. Lansdall-Welfare, T., Sudhahar, S., Veltri, G.A., Cristianini, N.: On the coverage of science in the media: a big data study on the impact of the Fukushima disaster. In: 2014 IEEE International Conference on Big Data, pp. 60–66. IEEE (2014)
15. Leetaru, K.: Culturomics 2.0: Forecasting large-scale human behavior using global news media tone in time and space. First Monday **16**(9) (2011). http://firstmonday.org/article/view/3663/3040
16. Matoré, G.: La méthode en lexicologie: domaine français. Didier, Paris (1953)
17. Michel, J.B., et al.: Quantitative analysis of culture using millions of digitized books. Science **331**(6014), 176–182 (2011)
18. Newman, D., Lau, J.H., Grieser, K., Baldwin, T.: Automatic evaluation of topic coherence. In: Human Language Technologies: The 2010 Annual Conference of the North American Chapter of the Association for Computational Linguistics, HLT 2010, pp. 100–108. Association for Computational Linguistics, Stroudsburg, PA, USA (2010). http://dl.acm.org/citation.cfm?id=1857999.1858011
19. Pechenick, E.A., Danforth, C.M., Dodds, P.S.: Characterizing the Google Books corpus: strong limits to inferences of socio-cultural and linguistic evolution. PLOS ONE **10**(10), e0137041 (2015)
20. Petersen, A.M., Tenenbaum, J., Havlin, S., Stanley, H.E.: Statistical laws governing fluctuations in word use from word birth to word death. Sci. Rep. **2**, Article number 313 (2012)
21. Řehůřek, R., Sojka, P.: Software framework for topic modelling with large corpora. In: Proceedings of the LREC 2010 Workshop on New Challenges for NLP Frameworks, pp. 45–50. ELRA, Valletta, Malta, May 2010. http://is.muni.cz/publication/884893/en
22. Roth, S.: Fashionable functions: a google ngram view of trends in functional differentiation (1800–2000). Int. J. Technol. Hum. Interact. **10**(2), 34–58 (2014)
23. Silva, N.F.F.D., Coletta, L.F.S., Hruschka, E.R.: A survey and comparative study of tweet sentiment analysis via semi-supervised learning. ACM Comput. Surv. **49**(1), 15:1–15:26 (2016). https://doi.org/10.1145/2932708
24. Standage, T.: The true history of fake news. 1843 Magazine (2017). https://bit.ly/2sh9OYQ. Accessed 4 May 2018

25. Thelwall, M., Buckley, K., Paltoglou, G., Cai, D., Kappas, A.: Sentiment in short strength detection informal text. J. Am. Soc. Inf. Sci. Technol. **61**(12), 2544–2558 (2010). https://doi.org/10.1002/asi.v61:12
26. Tjong Kim Sang, E.F., De Meulder, F.: Introduction to the CoNLL-2003 shared task: language-independent named entity recognition. In: Proceedings of the 7th Conference on Natural Language Learning at HLT-NAACL 2003. Association for Computational Linguistics (2003)
27. Wynne, M.: Searching and concordancing. In: Corpus Linguistics. An International Handbook, vol. 1, pp. 706–737 (2008)
28. Zollo, F.: Emotional dynamics in the age of misinformation. PLOS ONE **10**(9), 1–22 (2015). https://doi.org/10.1371/journal.pone.0138740

Inferring Human Traits from Facebook Statuses

Andrew Cutler$^{(\boxtimes)}$ and Brian Kulis

Boston University, Boston, MA, USA
{acut,bkulis}@bu.edu

Abstract. This paper explores the use of language models to predict 20 human traits from users' Facebook status updates. The data was collected by the myPersonality project, and includes user statuses along with their personality, gender, political identification, religion, race, satisfaction with life, IQ, self-disclosure, fair-mindedness, and belief in astrology. A single interpretable model meets state of the art results for well-studied tasks such as predicting gender and personality; and sets the standard on other traits such as IQ, sensational interests, political identity, and satisfaction with life. Additionally, highly weighted words are published for each trait. These lists are valuable for creating hypotheses about human behavior, as well as for understanding what information a model is extracting. Using performance and extracted features we analyze models built on social media. The real world problems we explore include gendered classification bias and Cambridge Analytica's use of psychographic models.

Keywords: Social media · Psychographic prediction · NLP

1 Introduction

Facebook's 2 billion users spend an average of 50 min a day on Facebook, Messenger, or Instagram [1]. Industry seeks to obtain, model and actualize this mountain of data in a variety of ways. For example, social media can be used to establish creditworthiness [2,3], persuade voters [4,5], or seek cognitive behavioral therapy from a chatbot [6]. Many of these tasks depend on knowing something about the personal life of the user. When determining the risk of default, a creditor may be interested in a debtor's impulsiveness or strength of support network. A user's home town could disambiguate a search term. Or—reflecting society's values—a social media company may be less willing to flag inflammatory language when the speaker is criticizing their own [7].

Social media's endlessly logged interactions have also been a boon to understanding human behavior. Researchers have used various social networks to model bullying [8], urban mobility [9], and the interplay of friendship and shared interests [10]. Such studies do not have the benefit of a controlled setting where a single variable can be isolated. However, orders of magnitude more observations in participants' natural habitat offer more fidelity to lived experience [11].

© Springer Nature Switzerland AG 2018
S. Staab et al. (Eds.): SocInfo 2018, LNCS 11185, pp. 167–195, 2018.
https://doi.org/10.1007/978-3-030-01129-1_11

Additionally subjects can be sampled from countries not so singularly Western, Educated, Industrialized, Rich, and Democratic—or WEIRD, in the parlance of Henrick et al. [12].

In this paper we show how readily different personality and demographic information can be extracted from Facebook statuses. Our reported performance is useful to learn how traits are related to online behavior. For example, sensational interests as measured by the Sensational Interest Questionnaire (SIQ) have been studied for internal reliability [13], relationship to physical aggression [14], and role in intrasexual competition [15]. Yet work connecting SIQ with social media use relies on individually labeling sensational interests in statuses and is only predictive among males [16]. Our model performs well for both males and females without hand-labeling statuses. Similarly, other research found no relationship between satisfaction with life (SWL) and status updates [17]; we show modest test set performance. Finally, although Facebook Likes have been shown to be highly predictive of many personal traits [18], language models with good performance on this dataset have been limited to predicting personality, age, and gender [19–21].

The benchmark also helps assess the efficacy of services that explicitly or implicitly rely on inferring these traits. This is valuable to those developing new services as well as to users concerned about privacy. Of particular interest is the role of psychographic models in Cambridge Analytica's (CA) marketing strategy. From leaked internal communications, in 2014 CA amassed a dataset of Facebook profiles and traits almost identical to those in the myPersonality dataset [22]. The week after CA's project became public, Facebook's stock plummeted $75 billion [23]. One factor in that drop was the belief that Facebook had allowed a third party to create a powerful marketing tool that could manipulate elections [22,24]. There are dozens of publications on the myPersonality dataset. However, this is the first to predict SIQ, fair-mindedness, and self-disclosure, which CA discussed in relation to building user models [22].

Besides performance benchmarks, the other major contribution of this paper are the most highly weighted words to predict each trait. The weights also say something about human behavior. The interpretation here is more complex: regression on tens of thousands of features is fraught with over-fitting and colinearity. Despite those problems, in Sect. 3 we argue that the weights can still be treated as a data exploration tool similar to clustering. We provide examples of previously studied relationships that are borne out in the word lists, and believe the lists are a useful tool to develop yet unstudied hypotheses.

Highly weighted features are also an important way to analyze models. We argue in Sect. 4.4 that a militarism predictor CA may have built is accurate, but extracts obvious features. Additionally, by inspecting the features in an Atheist vs. Agnostic classifier we find many gendered words. We demonstrate the bias empirically, then fix the classifier to be more fair. This approach is instructive for interrogating more critical models built on social media data.

This paper includes many contributions that could stand alone. We show that the text of Facebook statuses can predict user SWL and SIQ. We expand the prediction of political identity from a single spectrum (liberal/conservative) to twelve distinct ideologies with varying levels of overlap and popularity. On that task, we establish state of the art performance with a model that also provides informative features for every pairwise political comparison. We recreate models CA may have built, and report their performance and the type of information they extracted. We bring character level deep learning to gender prediction. To our knowledge, we also set the standard for predicting IQ, fair-mindedness, self-disclosure, race, and religion from Facebook statuses. Finally, we propose a novel method to make classification less biased.

Given the broad scope of this paper, some contributions are given less space than they would typically merit. Even so, we believe it is important to report results on many traits in a single paper. This demonstrates the power of a simple model and allows task difficulty and extracted features to be compared across traits without concerns about changing experimental setup.

2   Background

2.1   myPersonality Dataset

From 2008 to 2012, over 7 million Facebook users took the myPersonality quiz produced by the psychologist David Stillwell [11]. After answering at least 20 questions, users were scored on the Big Five personality axes: openness, creativity, extraversion, agreeableness, and neuroticism. Over 3 million of those users agreed to give researchers access to their extant Facebook profile and their personality scores. A much smaller subset of users answered additional questionnaires about their interests, Friends' personality, belief in astrology, and other personal information. The research community has added to the dataset by providing race labels for several hundred thousand users; representing the text of statuses in terms of their Linguistic Inquiry and Word Count (LIWC) statistics [25]; and much more. Labels used in this study are listed in Tables 1 and 2, along with descriptive statistics. To see all available labels, visit myPersonality.org.

myPersonality.org lists 43 publications that use this data. Most work explores the relationship between personality and easily extractable features such as number of Friends or Likes, geographic location, or user-Like pairs. For example, user-Like pairs are shown to be better predictors of a personality than one's spouse [26]. In 2013, Schwartz et al. introduced the open vocabulary approach (or bag of words) to personality, gender, and age prediction [19]. This significantly outperforms closed-vocabulary approaches such as LIWC that rely on domain knowledge to assign each word to one or more of 69 categories. For an excellent overview of related work, we direct readers to that paper's introduction [19].

Table 1. Prediction accuracy on continuous data

Label	N	EV
Personality		
Openness	84451	0.171
Conscientiousness	84451	0.120
Extroversion	84451	0.141
Agreeableness	84451	0.090
Neuroticism	84451	0.100
Sensational interests		
Militarism	4074	0.165
Violent-occult	4074	0.192
Intellectual recreation	4074	0.033
Occult credulousness	4074	0.144
Wholesome activities	4074	0.108
Satisfaction with life	2502	0.034
Self disclosure	2006	0.092
Fair-mindedness	2006	0.064
IQ	1807	0.128

Explained Variance (EV) is $1-\frac{\text{Var}(y-\hat{y})}{\text{Var}(y)}$, where $\hat{y}$ is the predicted label.

Table 2. Prediction accuracy on categorical data

Label	N	Classes	Mode	Homogeneity	F1-score	Acc
Gender	109104	2	0.598	0.519	0.92	0.903
Race	22059	3	0.682	0.52	0.74	0.766
Political identity	19769	12	0.213	0.133	0.33	0.337
Religious identity	8388	5	0.488	0.318	0.54	0.541
Belief in star sign	7115	5	0.331	0.245	0.32	0.334

Mode is the ratio of the dominant class. Homogeneity is the probability two random samples will be of the same class. The F1-Score is the harmonic mean of precision and recall. For non-binary labels, the precision and recall for each class is weighted by its support.

2.2 Language Models

Bag of Words. The majority of our experiments use bag of words (BoW) term frequency-inverse document frequency (tf-idf) preprocessing followed by ℓ_2 regularized regression. First, the vocabulary is limited to the k most common words in a given training set. Then a matrix of word counts, N, is constructed, where N_{ij} refers to how often word j is used by subject i. Each row is normalized to sum to one, moved to a log scale, and divided by d, the ratio of documents in which each word appears. In more formal notation, each element of the tf-idf matrix is defined by

$$W_{ij} = \frac{1 + \log\left(\frac{N_{ij}}{\sum_{i=1}^{k} N_{ij}}\right)}{d_j}.$$

W is then normalized so each row lies on the unit sphere. W can now be used for linear classification or regression with ℓ_2 regularization on the parameters. This is commonly called Ridge Regression. For binary classification problems, labels are assigned values of $\{-1, 1\}$ and a threshold determines predicted label. For categorical data with more than two labels, we train a classifier on each pair of labels. Predicted label is decided by majority vote of the $\frac{c(c-1)}{2}$ classifiers, where c is the number of classes.

Character-Level Convolutional Neural Network. For gender prediction, we also train a 49 layer character level convolutional neural network (char-CNN) described in [27]. Much like successful computer vision architectures [28], each character is embedded in continuous space and combined with neighbors by many layers of convolutional filters. Unlike BoW models, CNNs preserve the temporal dimension, allowing the use of syntactic information. While a great advantage, and theoretically more similar to human cognition, this requires different preprocessing. During training, all inputs must be the same length along the temporal axis despite the wide variation in total length of users' statuses. We chose to split users' concatenated statuses into chunks of no more than 4000 characters, and no less than 1000, as this is enough text for humans to perform gender classification [29]. Each chunk contains roughly 800 words. Chunks from the same user are assigned entirely to either the training or test set. Unfortunately, preprocessing differences do not allow for a direct comparison between methods. However, enforcing the same preprocessing for both models would necessarily limit one.

2.3 Labels

Tables 1 and 2 provide statistics of the continuous and categorical data respectively. What follows is a brief description of each label and how it was collected.

Gender is the binary label users supplied when setting up their Facebook account. Offering this information was common before 2008, and mandatory from 2008–2014. In 2014, (after the collection of this dataset) Facebook added 56 more gender options but still uses a binary representation to monetize users [30].

Race labels provided in the dataset are inferred from profile pictures using the Faceplusplus.com algorithm which can identify races termed White, Black, and Asian. A noisy measure of visual phenotype is not the gold standard for the study of race, however, our results indicate it is related to social media use.

Political Identity is limited to the twelve most common responses: IPA, anarchist, centrist, conservative, democrat, doesn't care, hates politics, independent, liberal, libertarian, republican, and very liberal. These are heterogenous categories from an open-ended question. No work was done to limit labels to political parties (eg. remove "doesn't care"), disambiguate misspelled or similar responses (eg. combine "anarchy" and "anarchist" or "liberal" and "very liberal"), or limit responses to one country. To produce the word list for Liberals and Conservatives in Table 15, we combine "liberal", "very liberal", and "democrat as well as "conservative", "very conservative", and "republican". The most likely meaning of IPA is the Independence Party of America, which was in its nascence during this survey. The party is most popular among young people disaffected by the two party system, a sentiment reflected by the users who report IPA.

Religion categories were limited to the nine most common responses, and similar labels were combined. Three variants of Catholic—"catholic", "christian-catholic", and "romancatholic"—were merged to form Catholic. Likewise, Christian refers to "christian", "christian-baptist" and "christian-evangelical". The entire list includes: Atheist, Agnostic, Catholic, Christian, Hindu, and None.

Belief in Star Sign is the user's response to "Horoscopes provide useful information to help guide my decisions?" Options include: Strongly Agree, Slightly Agree, No Opinion, Slightly Disagree, and Strongly Disagree.

Personality is determined on five axes—Openness, Conscientiousness, Extroversion, Agreeableness, and Neurotocism—by a survey. Users answer 20–300 questions which are used to score each personality component on a scale of 1–5. There is a large body of research showing that five factor analysis is explanatory for behavior [31], and its measurement is reproducible [32]. That work is now adapting to larger datasets collected online [11].

Sensational Interests include Militarism, Violent-Occult, Intellectual Recreation, Occult Credulousness, and Wholesome activities. Users can indicate "Great Dislike", "Slight Dislike", "No Opinion", "Slight Interest", and "Great Interest" for 28 different items including: "Drugs", "Paganism", "Philosophy", "Survivalism", and "Vampires and Wolves". Interest levels are calculated by summing responses from relevant items. The full calculation can be found in [13].

IQ is determined by 20 questions that conform to Raven's Standard Progressive Matrices. The development and validation of these questions is explained in [33] and [34]. Because performance on IQ tests has been rising at roughly 0.3 points a year over the past century and IQ is defined as mean 100, the scoring of a test is properly defined over an age cohort [35]. These scores do not take age into account and the mean is 114.

Satisfaction with Life, Self-disclosure, and Fair-Mindedness are assessed by separate questionnaires. SWL is a measure of global well being somewhat robust to short term mood fluctuations [36].

3 The Interpretation of Feature Weights

A common approach to understand traits in social science is to solve

$$X = UT + \epsilon,$$

where X is observations of subjects, T is the traits of subjects, U is a transition matrix, and ϵ is model error [3,13,37–43]. Traits are preferred to be orthogonal to promote compactness without sacrificing modeling power. The Big 5 personality model is both criticized and defended on grounds of trait independence, explanatory power, and measureability, which conforms to the linear model above [44]. Because the traits are defined by language they will not be completely orthogonal. Additionally, observations are not independent. As such, values in U will have dependencies across both rows and columns. Some traits like personality are used to predict other traits or life events [13,40]. Learning those relationships can be interpreted as informing our beliefs about column dependencies for U when both traits are part of T.

In this paper, X is the tf-idf word matrix, T is defined by our labels, and the model weights are some estimate of U we define as $\hat{U}$. Row dependencies in $\hat{U}$ are based on how words function. For example, 'camp' and 'camping' perform similar roles in a status. Likewise, the relationship between IQ and agreeableness will be embedded in the columns of $\hat{U}$. However, many of the tasks have little training data and the solution is ill-posed. Regularization encourages generalization, but does not provide any guarantees. Further, sometimes ϵ dominates the model when observations are not very explanatory or the relationship to a trait is not linear. Given these challenges, what confidence can be placed in the estimate $\hat{U}$?

These problems mirror those faced when clustering data. Clustering does not come with guarantees it will yield sensible answers in diverse scenarios [45]. However, it is broadly useful when exploring large sets of data [46–48]. Similarly, $\hat{U}$ can be viewed as a way of ranking features for exploration. A highly ranked observation is not proof it is important. But several highly ranked observations with functional coherence may suggest a hypothesis; particularly when coupled with domain knowledge of row and column dependencies in U.

The 55 most highly weighted features for each label are reported in the Appendix. Though the word lists are shown in order of importance, this ranking is not strict. Different regularization, preprocessing, or train/test splits can alter the ordering, especially when there are few examples. Additionally, more common words with lower weights may be used more often in a model's prediction, but may not appear at the top of a list. One may use ℓ_1 regularization to obtain an arbitrary small number of non-zero weights [49]. This encourages weighting common words and provides more stable rankings. We demonstrate that approach with our IQ model in Sect. 4.2.

There are many well-studied phenomena embedded in the $\hat{U}$ produced by our work. For example, Sarah Palin is the only politician indicated in the liberal word list in Table 15. Likewise, Nancy Pelosi ranks just below Ronald Reagan among conservative words. This accords with literature on the memorability of negative ads [50], importance of outgroup prejudice for social identity [51,52], and biases women face in politics [53,54]. We hope the many word lists in the Appendix will be useful to researchers in the development of new hypotheses.

$\hat{U}$ is also useful to understand models built on social media data. Until recently, the models themselves were not very important. However, machine learning can now be used to estimate sensitive traits such criminal recidivism [43]. Given the literalness with which estimates are often interpreted, it is essential to note that model weights are causal for the predicted label. In Sect. 4.5 we use our understanding of the input features to characterize information the model extracts to predict religion. This dataset also includes demographic labels, which show predicted religion labels are more gendered than the ground truth.

We hope the included word lists (a) highlight unstudied relationships about these traits (b) illustrate what kind of information is extracted from social media by machine learning systems.

4   Results and Discussion

4.1   Experimental Setup

All BoW experiments employ the same preprocessing. Users must have over 500 words in the sum of all their statuses. 80% of the data is randomly assigned to the training set; the remaining samples constitute the test set. The vocabulary is limited to the 40,000 most common words in each training set. Words must be used by at least 10 users but no more than 60% of users in the training set. The regularization parameter is tuned via efficient leave one out cross validation [55] when $n < 10,000$, and 3-fold cross validation for larger datasets. All BoW models are implemented using the sklearn library [56]. Table 1 reports the number of samples and explained variance (EV) of the predictions on continuous data. Table 2 reports the number of classes, ratio of samples in the dominant class, homogeneity, and performance on tasks with categorical data.

4.2   Performance

Gender. Table 3 compares our gender predictor to several other methods. The BoW model with a vocabulary of 500,000 yields accuracy of 92.8%, 1.4% more accurate than the tri-gram model reported by Schwartz et al. [19]. Even though the same dataset is used, the comparison is not direct. The tri-gram model seeks to remove the age information from words, has a larger vocabulary, preserves some temporal relationships in the tri-grams, and draws a different train/test split. Moreover, the preprocessing is more restrictive and only includes users with at least 1000 words. Notwithstanding these discrepancies, which may boost or

Table 3. Gender prediction

Model	Accuracy
Human Majority Vote	0.840
LIWC	0.784
Tri-grams	0.914
Tri-grams + LIWC	0.916
BoW (40k Vocab)	0.903
BoW (500k Vocab)	0.928
49 layer char-CNN	0.901

Human baseline is the majority vote ($n = 210$) in gender prediction on Twitter data [29]. LIWC and Tri-grams are reported in [19].

dampen performance, the results are very similar. When the LIWC representation is added to the tri-grams, there is a slight improvement to 91.6% accuracy. Preprocessing is even less similar for the char-CNN described in the Sect. 2.2. The human baseline of 84.0% consists of volunteer judgments based on 20–40 user tweets as reported by Nguyen et al. [29]. This is less text than is available to the other models, and from a different social media platform. But, with 210 volunteer guesses per user, it provides a relevant human baseline.

Personality. After gender, personality is the most studied trait in this paper. Likewise, Schwartz et al. achieve the best results to date [19]. They report the square root of EV to two significant digits: 0.42, 0.35, 0.38, 0.31, 0.31. In that format, we are just 0.01 beneath the state of the art for openness and agreeableness, 0.01 better for neuroticism, and equivalent for the remaining traits. As with gender, we achieve this with a simpler model.

Political Identity. Prediction accuracy of 33.7% is a gain of 11.7% over the baseline strategy of always predicting the mode, 'doesn't care'. As noted in the experiments section, training samples are weighted inversely to their class representation; therefore, ignoring any class will result in an equal loss. This does not provide the highest classification accuracy. However, we believe when some classes are sparsely populated an MSE optimal classifier that is highly biased toward the mode should not be the standard. For reference, equal sample weights and the same training scheme yield classification accuracy of 36.3% and a weighted f1 score of 31.6%. Five classes—IPA, hates politics, independent, libertarian, and very liberal—have no representation in the test set predictions. The weighted classifier predicts each class at least once.

According to Preotiuc-Pietro et al., all previous research on predicting political ideology from social media text has used binary labels such as liberal vs
conservative or Democrat vs Republican. They broaden the classification task
to include seven gradations on the liberal to conservative spectrum [57]. When
predicting ideological tilt from tweets, they achieve a 2.6% boost over baseline
(19.6%) with BoW follow by logistic regression. Word2Vec feature embeddings
[58] and multi-target learning with some hand-crafted labels yield an 8.0% boost.
From classification along grades of a single spectrum, we significantly expand the
task to twelve diverse identities with varying levels of representation and ideological overlap while maintaining classification accuracy.

In Table 6 we report the matrix of highest weighted words for separating users
in each pairwise class comparison. As with race, belief in star sign, and religion,
we plan on making expanded pairwise lists available online. In Table 7 we report
the confusion matrix. Note that many errors are between similar labels, such as
liberal and democrat. Ease of training, strong performance, and representation
of minority classes make a majority vote system of shallow pairwise classifiers a
good approach for this task.

For binary comparison, by pooling {'very liberal','liberal','democrat'} and
{'very conservative','conservative','republican'} we achieve 76.4% accuracy;
12.1% above baseline. Table 15 shows the top 55 liberal and conservative words.

Religion. Religion seems to be more difficult to glean from statuses than political identity. At 54.1%, accuracy is a modest 5.3% above guessing the mode. The
most highly weighted pairwise words are on Tables 8 and 9 shows the confusion
matrix. The most highly weighted word to distinguish someone who is agnostic
from an atheist is 'boyfriend'. This led us to look deeper at that pairwise classifier in Sect. 4.5. Binary labels were constructed by pooling {'catholic', 'christian-
catholic', 'romancatholic', 'christian', 'christian-baptist'} and {'atheist', 'agnostic','none' }. We achieve 78.0% accuracy, 5.2% above baseline. Those words are
on Table 15. To our knowledge, there is no other multi class religion predictor to
which our results can be compared.

IQ. In a genome wide association meta study of 78,308 individuals, 336 single
nucleotide polymorphisms were found to explain 2.1–4.8% of the IQ variance
among the test population [59]. We achieve 12.8% EV with a model trained on
less than 2000 users and their statuses. Using ℓ_1 regularization to limit the vocabulary to the ten most informative words—final, physics; ayaw, family, friend,
heart, lmao, nite, strong, ur—still yields 5.6% EV. The relative accuracy of such
a trivial model that leverages intuitive features is a helpful comparison for any
project predicting this important trait. To our knowledge, this is the only work
to date that infers IQ from social media.

The selected features are also informative. Words suggesting intelligence—
'final' and 'physics'—are parsimonious and singularly academic. Whereas the
university experience is sufficient to find users with high IQ, features inversely
related to IQ are more focused on disposition. From Table 10, agreeableness

is implied by 'family' and 'heart'; conscientiousness is implied by 'family' and 'lmao'; and low openness is implied by 'ur'. Overall, the list can be characterized as prosocial, or at least concerned with social relationships. Predicting low IQ with prosocial features seems to challenge some previous research.

Gottlieb et al. observed that learning disabled children were more likely to engage in solitary play [60]. Play has also been observed to be more aggressive [61]. More directly related to our task, McConaughy and Ritter showed a positive correlation between the IQ of learning disabled boys and social competence scores; and a negative correlation between IQ and behavior problem scores [62]. For further review of the subject see [63].

An MSE optimal classifier seeks to generalize information about samples near the average. This can cause bias when classifying minorities, but is instructive when interpreting features. Features should say something about the majority of our sample, those with IQ near the mean. This explains why antisocial behavior among those with extremely low IQ does not preclude prosocial behavior indicating moderately lower IQ. Reflecting the limitations of this type of study, words like 'family', 'friend', and 'heart' could also be caused by differing norms for social media use or many other factors. Prosocial words predicting lower IQ does however suggest interesting future work.

Sensational Interests. In this study, SIQ is the easiest continuous variable to predict, even with an order of magnitude less training data than personality. The SIQ asks lists 28 discrete interests like 'black magic' and 'the armed forces'. Very similar terms can be recovered from statuses: 'zombie', 'blood', 'vampire'; 'military', 'marines', 'training'. Personality tests, on the other hand, ask more abstract questions like 'I shirk my duties' for conscientiousness. Many of these duties seem to be extracted in Table 10: 'studying', 'busy','obstacles'. But many more training examples are required for similar performance.

This is the first work to demonstrate an automatic system for predicting SIQ. Previous research relied on manually counting the number of sensational interests in statuses. The count was only correlated with militarism among men; the relationship was negative for women [16].

Satisfaction with Life. Previous research cast doubt on the relationship between status updates and SWL [17]. The number of positive words used on Facebook nationwide in a given day, week, or month, is inversely correlated with the SWL of that time period's myPersonality participants. The interpretation of that result is that it "challenges the assumption that linguistic analysis of internet messages is related to underlying psychological states." Here we show that a BoW model accounts for 3.4% of the variance in SWL scores. Moreover, the most important words the model finds are intuitive. Lower SWL is implied by "fucking", "hate", "bored", "interview", "sick", "hospital", "insomnia", "farmville", and "video". The deleterious effects of joblessness, anger, chronic illness, and isolation are well documented. Words positively associated with SWL—"camping", "imagination", "epic", "cleaned", "success"—make similar sense.

Conversational AI on Facebook Messenger is an efficacious and scalable way to administer cognitive behavioral therapy [6]. Our results show linguistic analysis can shed light on underlying psychological states. This is important to find users that could benefit from such treatment.

Belief in Star Sign. Compared to political identity, BSS has seven fewer classes and a far more homogeneous distribution. Even so, the BSS classifier performs slightly worse than the politics classifier and roughly on par to the baseline of predicting the mode. Unlike our race, gender, politics and sensational interests, we don't wear belief in astrology on our sleeve.

4.3 Model Selection

BoW models are somewhat unintuitive. Humans use syntactic information when decoding language, which the model discards. Yet, for many tasks they achieve state of the art performance. We compare our BoW to a character-level CNN on gender prediction, our most data rich problem. A character-level CNN is well suited to large amounts of messy, user generated data. Pooling layers in a CNN allow generalization of words like "gooooooooo" and "goooooo", while BoW must learn distinct weights. Surprisingly, the CNN does not outperform the simple BoW as shown in Table 3.

We found the choice of prediction model is not as important as preprocessing. In initial experiments, Support Vector Machines [64] and logistic regression, and ℓ_2 regularized regression yielded similar performance, depending on choice of n-grams and whether Singular Value Decomposition was used [65]. We implement ridge regression and classification for simplicity.

Inferring human traits from social media is now being done using deep models [57,66]. That may be useful in some cases, but for this project the deep model offered no performance boost or intuition to underlying human behavior. Perhaps a continuous bag of words [58] and recurrent neural network [67] would have done better, but researchers should not consider deep learning essential for this field. Moreover, any performance gains should be weighed against loss of interpretability.

4.4 Cambridge Analytica

With current technology, Facebook statuses are a better predictor of someone's IQ than the totality of their genetic material [59]. When a marketing firm adds such a tool to their arsenal it is natural to be suspicious. Indeed, The Guardian article that broke the CA story was headlined "'I made Steve Bannon's psychological warfare tool': meet the data war whistleblower" [24]. (Steve Bannon is the former chief executive of the Trump presidential campaign.) However, closer inspection of psychographic models casts doubt on their ability to add value to an advertising campaign, even when the predictions are accurate. In this paper we show that militarism is one of the most easily inferred traits. At 16.5% explained variance, it is more predictable than any of the big 5 personality traits except openness, even with just 5% of the training data. SIQ is also a much stronger predictor of aggressive behavior than the Big 5 [14]. If this trait was actionable for the Trump campaign, it is interesting that the two most highly weighted features are 'xbox' and 'man'. Gaming interest and gender are already available via Facebook's advertising platform; reaching that demographic does not require an independent model. Additionally, Steve Bannon's belief in the political power of gamers predates CA's psychographic model by a decade [68].

Readers are encouraged to view the word lists in the Appendix through the lens of task accuracy on Tables 1 and 2. They may come to the same conclusion as the Trump campaign who, according to CBS News, "never used the psychographic data at the heart of a whistleblower who once worked to help acquire the data's reporting – principally because it was relatively new and of suspect quality and value" [69]. Performance results and extracted features allow for more informed discussion; particularly for SIQ, fair-mindedness and self-disclosure on which we report the first accurate prediction model.

There are limitations to this analysis. Our models only use statuses; Likes and network statistics could increase accuracy. Further, other psychographic traits beyond militarism may be politically useful but have no obvious demographic stand-in. Finally, we don't have access to CA's exact dataset and instead built our models on the myPersonality dataset (Table 5).

Table 4. Agnostic vs Atheist confusion matrix

		Predicted (Men)			Predicted (Women)		
		Agnostic	Atheist	Total	Agnostic	Atheist	Total
True	Agnostic	36	33	69	86	21	107
	Atheist	28	58	86	34	16	50
	Total	64	91		120	37	

Table 5. Fair Agnostic vs Atheist confusion matrix

		Predicted (Men)			Predicted (Women)		
		Agnostic	Atheist	Total	Agnostic	Atheist	Total
True	Agnostic	40	29	69	85	22	107
	Atheist	31	55	86	31	19	50
	Total	71	84		116	41	

4.5 Gender Bias in Atheist vs Agnostic Classifier

Highly weighted atheist words include "fucking", "bloody", "maths", "degrees", "disease", "wifey", and "religion". Meanwhile, "beautiful", "santa", "friggin", "thank", "hubby", "miles", and "paperwork" imply the user is agnostic. This paints a picture of academic, male, disagreeable and British atheists. Agnostic words are more positive, female, and related to mundane preparation. A more complete list is shown in Table 15. What follows is an empirical analysis of our estimator's gender bias, a discussion of fairness, and results debiasing the model.

In this dataset, atheists and agnostics are 33.5% and 50.3% female respectively. This is a stronger female preference for agnosticism than random surveys across the United States which report 32% and 38%, respectively [70]. Table 4 shows the confusion matrices for men and women. The ratio of predicted to true agnostics is 0.945 for men and 1.35 for women. Similarly, the ratio of false atheist to false agnostic predictions is 90.8% larger for men than women. The classification of women, the minority in this dataset, is highly distorted.

Models built to generalize information often amplify biases in training data. Cooking videos elicit female pronouns in machine-generated captions 68% more than male pronouns, even though the training shows only 33% more women cooking [71]. Word embeddings used in machine translation [72], information retrieval [73], and student grade prediction [74] produce analogies such as "man is to computer programmer as woman is to homemaker" [75].

There are many notions of fairness defined over an individual [76–78], population [79,80], or information available to the model [81]. Building a fair estimator often requires domain knowledge to define a similarity metric [76], make corpus-level constraints [71], or construct a causal model that separates protected information from other latent variables [78]. In this paper, we will use the notion of Disparate Mistreatment to measure fairness [79]. That is, if protected classes experience disparate rates of false positive, false negative or overall misclassification, the estimator is unfair.

To mitigate Disparate Mistreatment we explicitly encode gender—$\{-1, 0, 1\}$ for {male, unknown, female}—in the feature vector during train time. At test time the gender of all samples is encoded as unknown. The intuition is that latent variables are amplified when they are easy to extract and correlated with the target. As demonstrated by the accuracy of our race and gender predictors, that is often the case for protected information. There often exist more informative, if more subtle, traits than the protected features. For example, atheists and agnostics report a yawning gap in those that don't believe in God, at 92% and 41% [70]. Additionally, religiosity is shown to be correlated with both Agreeableness and Conscientiousness [82]. But gender is much easier to extract then belief in God or personality. By explicitly giving the model gender information, we hope that the model will do more to extract those other features.

Table 6. Pairwise politics words

IPA	anarchist	centrist	conserv.	dem.	doesn't care	hates	pol. indep.	lib.	liber.	repub.	v. lib.
IPA	fuck	wishes	wishes	smh	yay	rain	congrats	wishes	money	church	damn
anarchist	excited		wishes	driving	excited	lol	dont	driving	excited	ready	ready	excited
centrist	xd	fuck		lord	today	tattoo	shit	surgery	shit	government	school	damn
conservative	xd	fuck	damn		fb	anymore	shit	damn	damn	art	school	damn
democrat	xd	fuck	wishes	tonight		stupid	fuck	died	wishes	government	church	wishes
doesn't care	packers	fuck	wishes	lord	smh		shit	definitely	wishes	government	church	damn
hates politics	class	music	dey	loves	fb	tht		movie	wishes	email	camp	damn
independent	xd	fuck	wishes	lord	valentine	sitting	fuck		wishes	beer	parents	damn
liberal	xd	fuck	final	lord	im	xd	im	gonna		government	church	damn
libertarian	xd	fuck	headache	lord	walk	xd	dont	till	packing	government	girls	vacation
republican	xd	fuck	wishes	wishes	smh	mum	fuck	minute	wishes	fucking		damn
very liberal	xd	xd	boy	lord	im	xd	xd	school	missing	im	im	

Table 7. Politics confusion matrix

						Predicted Label							
IPA	IPA	anar.	centrist	conserv.	dem.	doesn't care	hates pol.	indep.	lib.	liber.	repub.	v. lib.	Total
IPA	0	2	3	3	11	18	2	1	3	1	16	1	61
anarchist	0	24	4	3	5	21	1	3	15	5	4	3	88
centrist	2	9	74	40	52	66	3	6	95	7	43	4	401
conservative	2	5	29	113	26	31	0	7	53	5	62	0	333
democrat	5	17	53	36	321	101	4	18	80	9	89	3	736
doesn't care	3	39	51	29	122	373	12	12	105	12	102	9	869
hates politics	0	4	6	1	6	30	5	3	6	0	2	0	63
independent	0	8	16	13	35	22	1	8	29	4	25	1	162
liberal	1	18	51	27	74	51	6	6	223	15	24	13	509
libertarian	0	12	17	9	17	28	0	6	32	11	12	4	148
republican	1	8	19	57	67	64	1	8	29	3	179	3	439
very liberal	0	4	25	2	11	22	2	2	67	1	6	3	145
Total	14	150	348	333	747	827	37	80	737	73	564	44	3954

Table 8. Pairwise religion words

	Athiest	Agnostic	Catholic	Christian	None
Athiest		boyfriend	thank	church	lol
Agnostic	fucking		prayers	church	lol
Catholic	fucking	fucking		lol	lol
Christian	fucking	fucking	mass		xmas
None	fucking	apartment	god	church	

Table 9. Religion confusion matrix

	Predicted label					
	Athiest	Agnostic	Catholic	Christian	None	Total
Atheist	**68**	29	17	16	21	151
Agnostic	54	**69**	27	55	11	216
Catholic	27	37	**172**	130	9	375
Christian	35	48	126	**560**	26	795
None	22	11	19	50	**39**	141
Total	206	194	361	811	106	1678

This approach produces much less Disparate Mistreatment of men and women. The ratio of predicted to true agnostics moves closer to parity at 1.02 for men and 1.22 for women. Additionally, the ratio of false atheist to false agnostic predictions is now only 31.8% larger for men, compared to 90.8% without intervention. The most highly weighted agnostic words for the new fair classifier are also less gendered; "hair", "wifey", and "boyfriend" are no longer in the top 55, as reported in Table 15. We also saw no decay in classification rate.

The gender bias of the atheism classifier is clear by simply inspecting its most heavily weighted features. More opaque models should be subjected to more rigorous inspection for bias (Tables 11, 12, 13, 14 and 16).

Table 10. Personality words

Openness		Conscientious		Extroversion	
-	+	-	+	-	+
bored	art	lost	gym	internet	party
boring	poetry	fucking	ready	quiet	guys
husband	beautiful	xd	weekend	bored	amazing
attitude	universe	phone	excited	listening	audition
shopping	peace	im	success	apparently	baby
dinner	poem	bored	finished	computer	haha
tv	writing	fuck	studying	stupid	dance
game	books	gonna	busy	pc	girls
proud	theatre	sick	vacation	hmm	fabulous
ur	dream	procrastination	arm	anime	blast
dentist	mind	internet	officially	tt	ready
daughter	book	computer	family	dark	im
dont	woman	probably	relax	probably	wine
haha	guitar	cousins	tennis	sims	success
stupid	damn	hates	wonderful	didn	lets
ni	awesome	sims	special	watching	excited
ipod	tea	anybody	win	slow	super
bed	apartment	charger	glad	depressing	text
justin	insomnia	sister	piano	calculus	chill
gift	xd	playing	scholarship	kind	phone
2nd	adventure	grounded	received	anymore	dear
hurt	cali	poker	lmao	repost	parties
ohh	far	tt	degrees	maybe	support
baseball	philosophy	status	state	draw	loves
mum	sigh	momma	tons	yay	pics
pray	nature	ftw	motor	trying	hey
school	maybe	press	obstacles	books	big
repost	music	dead	research	shadow	hit
booked	blues	failed	extremely	bother	met
lord	chill	forgot	circumstances	damned	pirate
ops	fam	depression	workout	suppose	ben
nice	epic	lazy	paid	reading	rocked
tmr	places	youtube	100	cat	gang
dam	rights	420	hit	poor	sex
idol	dragons	school	surgery	depression	sing
snowing	woot	http	law	sigh	btw
pissed	vampire	awsome	university	games	gorgeous
shut	soul	pokemon	anatomy	drawing	musical
maths	eclipse	woke	blessings	odd	cali
msn	drawing	dammit	hmmmm	10th	girlfriend
aldean	strange	hair	husband	pokemon	stoked
vodka	planet	wished	counting	nice	folks
comes	yay	cleaning	calc	essay	ponder
eid	dreams	fine	louis	pointless	wanna
alot	blood	dunno	delhi	managed	hahahaha
waste	sushi	enemy	final	looks	pool
worst	smoking	social	drive	grr	tanning
kiero	contact	yo	lets	darkness	hello
soo	lines	procrastinator	iphone	saw	pumped
mas	deep	black	lunch	crying	chillin
staff	genius	magic	yankees	lonely	theatre
12	novel	wasn	running	laptop	kiss
piss	smh	fans	weather	shouldn	office
transformers	worried	kinda	zone	paranoid	cock
car	folks	trying	smart	walking	lauren

Table 11. Personality words continued

Agreeable		Neurotic		Satisfaction With Life	
-	+	-	+	-	+
fucking	wonderful	loving	sick	bored	family
stupid	amazing	girlfriend	nervous	fuck	loving
kill	awesome	wife	stressed	fucking	hope
shopping	haha	awesome	depression	hates	thankful
shit	smile	parties	depressed	bday	india
burn	happiness	party	anymore	apparently	wonderful
bitch	phone	weekend	lonely	damn	busy
pissed	urself	haha	stress	internet	friend
punch	family	doing	fucking	zero	heart
hates	blessed	game	tired	chem	man
death	status	sunday	trying	wat	yum
hell	music	kansas	depressing	supposed	fb
suck	woop	guy	sims	ma	glad
freak	hands	delicious	anxiety	hating	beautiful
piss	heart	beach	worst	spend	lauren
dead	spirit	definitely	hair	la	lord
xmas	smiles	swag	fed	dumb	wine
karma	guy	started	scream	young	swim
fight	moment	ready	fine	british	energy
blood	beautiful	hunting	nightmare	killed	lunch
awful	movie	power	rip	hmm	locked
deal	theres	funniest	tears	france	woot
misery	car	melody	horrible	chances	sons
fuck	dancing	hawaii	flu	simply	special
enemies	lord	action	worse	exams	trust
fake	guitar	hit	issues	mum	wish
pathetic	sore	chillin	scared	main	weeks
irony	sara	workout	stressful	hate	day
dumb	help	flow	fml	edge	father
cunt	walk	portland	care	dnt	tried
care	excited	seat	shes	party	journey
devil	prayers	smart	stressing	kept	hospital
black	knowing	snowboarding	ugh	dat	email
ich	valentines	knowing	sad	didn	business
russian	borrow	sore	gary	months	santa
idiots	laura	greatest	hates	du	walked
cunts	notifications	success	die	rain	lights
wtf	beard	basketball	actually	pass	kingdom
crap	reli	update	scary	bus	work
truck	snowboarding	gf	boyfriend	okay	lol
deleted	sorry	women	pills	australia	mommy
anger	chillin	gotta	crying	shooting	turkey
die	hill	followed	kitty	england	nap
tu	whats	jumping	awful	africa	revenge
nightmare	hearts	fool	hurt	rachel	truly
annoyed	kindness	dancing	bored	fml	son
rip	study	greatness	fair	metal	final
bloody	worry	blast	screaming	uk	reached
drama	clients	woke	dreading	school	survived
bitches	smells	ass	friggin	wtf	dont
stupidity	troops	hitting	suicide	matt	0
hair	sing	cock	miserable	freakin	god
wifi	goood	wise	quiet	15	kitchen
fat	holy	kiss	xd	200	normal
rage	faster	toes	sadness	free	blessing

Table 12. Sensational interest words

Militaristic		Violent-Occult		Intellectual	Recreation
-	+	-	+	-	+
sleeping	man	lord	hell	im	life
ugh	xbox	pray	zombie	course	jon
sad	gets	cousins	damn	boring	beautiful
excited	gotta	church	fuck	painful	dancing
lovely	good	michael	bitch	decision	yoga
oh	training	allah	ass	hurts	thankful
hair	headed	jesus	drink	bus	peace
shopping	truck	game	blood	game	kinda
husband	guitar	0	lmao	stupid	truly
sick	guys	summer	xd	bak	la
cares	bro	gosh	woot	hero	ich
mum	gun	praise	halloween	problem	miss
boyfriend	boom	sunday	play	yeah	likes
lady	epic	dad	guys	christ	comfort
concert	work	loving	drunk	gona	lol
today	weight	mum	thanx	id	wtf
gaga	gym	team	animal	sittin	insomnia
okay	bike	hospital	sanity	die	chicken
pic	dang	10	fucking	horse	children
adorable	game	tv	dragons	yell	tired
sunday	blast	christ	burn	chuck	lovely
ordered	lol	heal	vampires	2day	ap
birth	war	usa	blah	tommorrow	funny
lots	black	personal	man	ow	things
poor	fish	best	loved	bored	man
ben	military	ray	pissed	fukin	simple
fine	woot	nervous	lil	inbox	thank
settings	12	thing	bday	race	period
birthday	till	look	send	basketball	countdown
cousins	ppl	week	body	word	baby
shoes	brave	2morrow	metal	rhys	beach
art	17	quite	head	tell	hey
omg	fight	poor	piss	step	depression
stop	success	brazil	blast	wats	jobs
wear	marines	cup	theyre	coke	cure
prince	hrs	zumba	cause	football	manage
round	sword	account	gun	penguins	sugar
come	make	website	death	won	aware
neighbours	ko	tryna	vampire	facebookers	singing
basement	friend	study	bleh	letters	egg
music	hit	haha	tattoo	awsome	taste
speak	play	soccer	ppl	dont	rains
thoughts	pics	feeling	dead	blah	log
story	hahaha	christmas	woman	till	taught
weird	troops	round	purple	playing	coolest
awful	army	youth	peaceful	dead	yellow
quite	running	story	message	fact	cheers
rachel	mag	bible	shit	learned	small
hear	strong	woah	angel	visit	society
alice	knw	grace	kinda	address	fly
tea	beer	prayers	tongue	14	social
promised	hehehe	plan	sushi	chilling	boo
jesus	comwatch	feat	wolf	win	beauty
actually	xoxo	anybody	poke	pokemon	world
counting	run	stressed	kick	sees	sunshine

Table 13. Sensational interest words continued

Occult	Credulousness	Wholesome	Activities	Belief in	Star Sign
-	+	-	+	No	Yes
church	zombie	coke	woot	minutes	omg
praise	ass	michigan	camping	didn	im
jesus	bitch	stupid	fish	church	ready
lord	halloween	pathetic	life	praise	friend
bible	animal	ops	yesterday	jesus	mind
christ	sign	husband	beautiful	probably	ass
team	omg	didn	rain	physics	butt
quite	xd	hurts	man	jess	stay
loving	job	kurwa	mexico	white	tom
pray	woot	evil	wish	religion	tomarrow
paper	wish	afternoon	river	iv	october
game	cure	problem	love	officially	promise
blessed	street	taylor	path	imagine	lol
salvation	vampire	idea	moon	christ	searching
ops	guys	jess	haha	germany	bitch
summer	send	glee	snow	giants	bleh
michael	lol	mum	bike	saw	eye
spent	thanx	mental	hahaha	wants	cute
youth	luck	meg	ghost	north	family
cousins	wtf	mad	baking	decided	halloween
word	nature	360	grandma	discovered	hanging
god	cancer	pissed	live	11th	haunted
homework	woohoo	club	goin	ouch	japanese
alarm	miss	uni	sky	skin	mother
0	barely	lyrics	cat	doesn	dinner
haha	moment	head	animal	bacon	card
player	bar	recently	netflix	train	help
sunday	safe	internet	birds	hahaha	bored
college	proud	min	smile	lasts	luv
wedding	woman	lesson	happiness	america	luck
prayer	mom	bus	mom	haven	neighbors
glory	away	rly	yum	burning	yum
forgiveness	dare	debate	fishing	pray	fireworks
ann	inches	kevin	truly	thursday	lmao
mm	boyfriend	inbox	fell	jessica	tt
political	il	jeez	make	prince	tired
fact	nd	official	clean	knew	person
greatest	pls	nite	portland	umm	nd
confused	aware	ms	smells	quiero	watch
appreciated	xmas	lack	lake	deserves	ya
algebra	hell	saw	create	heres	prom
brazil	solstice	troy	making	finds	crazy
travel	date	sims	2010	kim	upload
daughter	vampires	school	josh	heard	elf
bacon	copy	thinks	children	punch	hehe
laura	purple	thanking	laughing	groups	crack
personal	haunted	die	sa	car	bell
week	theyre	hates	law	amazing	human
greater	lmao	stuff	jobs	sick	finish
statement	later	band	earth	tape	lnk
messed	interview	thieves	gets	drink	june
tv	peeps	feels	hehehe	morn	change
em	peaceful	elm	swimming	dallas	costume
poor	drunk	germany	wa	cops	shit
trust	dunno	sat	monkeys	waters	decorating

Table 14. Psychographic words

Self-Disclosure		Fair-Mindedness		IQ	
-	+	-	+	-	+
bored	family	bored	excited	nite	exam
fuck	loving	wat	business	ur	hours
fucking	hope	soon	says	lmao	sigh
hates	thankful	dad	apartment	alot	camping
bday	india	xd	great	family	finish
apparently	wonderful	stage	delicious	omg	paper
damn	busy	pass	sure	2011	wtf
internet	friend	moon	needed	city	il
zero	heart	haha	seattle	lol	finds
chem	man	kitty	uni	help	important
wat	yum	tired	airport	wew	read
supposed	fb	mum	thankful	boy	physics
ma	glad	farmville	dallas	heart	google
hating	beautiful	face	learn	com	ra
spend	lauren	drank	weekend	angie	xd
la	lord	fuk	definitely	www	wifi
dumb	wine	fuck	dinner	ha	text
young	swim	ma	card	333	weeks
british	energy	sun	amazing	tom	studying
killed	lunch	crap	tonight	goodnight	training
hmm	locked	bday	exciting	history	course
france	woot	shit	degrees	xxx	student
chances	sons	hopefully	classes	xdd	magic
simply	special	feel	support	friend	kinda
exams	trust	fails	priceless	morning	everytime
mum	wish	va	oh	mum	raining
main	weeks	big	certainly	christmas	yea
hate	day	nd	government	eid	maths
edge	father	smoke	ticket	kay	semester
dnt	tried	yay	food	gives	maybe
party	journey	watchin	january	din	exciting
kept	hospital	sick	couple	beautiful	point
dat	email	wedding	php	folks	kno
didn	business	regret	journey	luv	excited
months	santa	seconds	universe	0	imma
du	walked	im	21	hacked	months
rain	lights	ignore	grateful	secrets	flying
pass	kingdom	tt	pay	iam	final
bus	work	lose	size	forgiveness	nah
okay	lol	marriage	class	strong	library
australia	mommy	lolz	situation	busy	used
shooting	turkey	fukin	duke	jo	chem
england	nap	picture	honesty	hate	brain
africa	revenge	blessing	austin	ti	everybody
rachel	truly	slow	tires	nightmare	awesome
fml	son	anxiety	29	ayaw	groups
metal	final	cy3	sisters	prayer	progress
uk	reached	library	mother	fought	champion
school	survived	tmr	heading	ow	calculus
wtf	dont	fucking	bc	sana	behave
matt	0	epic	piece	tired	den
freakin	god	il	summer	afraid	badly
15	kitchen	marie	breakfast	para	times
200	normal	bunch	answer	sum	mobil
free	blessing	loaded	surgery	movie	fun

Table 15. Religion and politics words

Agnostic vs Atheist		A. vs A. (Fair)		Religious vs Not		Conservative vs Liberal	
extra	physics	miles	fucking	church	fucking	church	damn
miles	fucking	working	physics	pray	fuck	truck	happy
turn	snowing	extra	wat	prayers	xmas	government	fb
hair	shit	awhile	fuck	god	damn	america	smh
packing	wat	packing	bloody	easter	shit	pray	marriage
awhile	write	turn	shit	lord	bloody	haha	xmas
insane	bloody	super	write	blessed	hell	prayers	chicago
working	enter	**hubby**	maths	christmas	ass	deer	sex
hubby	fuck	chill	xx	ugh	india	christmas	hell
points	sigh	free	snowing	praying	zombie	country	fam
friggin	thinks	sleepy	enter	hw	fuckin	tonight	lovely
santa	talk	santa	thinks	ppl	halloween	17	halloween
heck	weeks	heck	talk	prayer	car	lord	health
wishes	town	ready	science	game	yay	awesome	saw
child	science	friggin	sigh	believe	social	god	yoga
free	maths	vacation	hai	family	xx	military	celebrate
boyfriend	degrees	work	cancer	ready	quite	texas	gay
lady	lolz	thursday	person	fb	religion	freedom	apartment
learn	record	late	coursework	bless	drink	savior	wtf
super	xmas	points	town	im	oh	dad	thoughts
houston	tom	pack	xd	calling	using	bible	shit
service	hai	houston	weeks	dang	shitty	jesus	glee
pack	person	insane	tom	paper	internet	supper	gaga
late	dat	ya	film	jesus	fucked	girls	da
wanting	tyler	relax	dat	school	damned	huge	palin
hasn	cod	join	kill	camp	omfg	praying	2010
mai	afraid	busy	lolz	gosh	meh	camp	help
sleepy	untill	learn	msn	heart	indian	soldiers	mexico
worked	present	child	english	success	post	byu	mother
fly	**wifey**	headed	xmas	mary	head	christ	indian
chill	movie	favorite	chemistry	strength	cricket	disney	lady
join	xx	beautiful	afraid	butt	any1	risen	studies
kyle	cancer	season	na	fishing	dragon	beach	social
dun	boring	san	pierced	brother	lovely	tournament	art
thursday	rape	fly	dick	military	body	troops	holiday
taken	month	worked	anatomy	sad	new	schools	shitty
childhood	kill	service	bbc	uncle	boyfriend	leave	ve
mother	welcome	spring	tell	senior	teeth	ill	free
thank	clinton	wanting	untill	fair	nice	blonde	earthquake
headed	nicht	halloween	memory	mom	fml	armed	street
ya	ay	lady	bothered	tan	warped	xbox	phone
london	brother	thank	horse	watching	woke	reagan	lakers
beautiful	tell	childhood	record	em	bleh	utah	ur
jail	hadn	mai	cod	president	wednesday	served	fine
hates	pierced	hair	ki	smh	gods	tide	relationship
paperwork	wild	paperwork	nicht	love	afford	gators	asshole
wanna	use	4th	sheep	haha	japanese	pelosi	worried
clear	perfect	hopefully	chem	future	tongue	husband	purple
san	return	missed	brother	best	robert	stinks	putting
til	needed	peace	fancy	emails	sophie	trial	omg
halloween	paid	hasn	degrees	goin	holy	picked	nature
bring	half	trip	disease	football	eye	beep	prop
kindle	horse	mother	realised	latest	tattoo	gun	black
vida	disease	sunshine	room	thank	decent	trailer	live
powers	chuck	kyle	religion	matthew	odd	ready	eid

Table 16. Race words

White vs. Black		White vs. Asian		Black vs. Asian	
tonight	smh	tonight	asian	smh	korea
dad	fb	blonde	tt	fb	sa
stupid	lord	town	tmr	lord	na
exited	fam	fuckin	korea	wit	asian
thinks	nigeria	ass	chinese	aint	gay
ends	yall	college	ng	da	chinese
journey	black	gas	na	yall	internet
meet	fathers	dope	korean	lol	korean
hahahahahaha	mj	worse	china	say	monday
fun	yuh	night	ang	fam	xd
awesome	gon	men	aq	jackson	tmr
ability	birthday	sons	asians	cos	shooting
night	mad	adult	chen	michael	philippines
mas	lol	pretty	guys	finals	3d
wouldnt	finish	theres	thailand	ass	babe
chargers	dey	idea	taiwan	yuh	heaven
bein	asap	hope	karaoke	black	important
aftr	tryna	ability	sa	ny	tan
pretty	jackson	melissa	chan	sooooo	thailand
eh	came	state	dream	mad	yummy
tom	degrassi	unique	company	mind	completely
exhausted	wat	weekend	craving	season	woot
tough	iz	screaming	zzz	wat	smell
great	hw	mamaya	holiday	birthday	bought
running	pple	tune	wanna	degrassi	fly
exciting	jus	figure	ms	hell	tt
yankees	braids	inside	nguyen	chelsea	worry
politics	haters	exited	singapore	woman	ruin
mirror	females	wine	yang	figure	passed
pepsi	misfits	5th	hu	african	skating
roll	god	superman	fat	nigeria	english
animal	man	emotionally	ftw	episode	belong
grr	omg	sell	gg	iz	shot
gay	african	sitting	rice	smart	mas
tattoo	desires	february	tttt	saying	grandpa
2nite	chelsea	easter	damnit	asap	lazy
spend	female	months	555	attention	sacrifice
monday	cousin	saying	wong	knowing	grr
sorrow	holla	expecting	achieve	ki	broken
ed	smart	rollin	pa	meeting	yang
healthy	laker	wheres	mode	hw	beer
enjoyable	favour	eminem	lmao	sings	chatting
actually	dis	apparently	pride	india	meet
charity	money	does	bbq	gas	shoulder
delete	happy	status	super	self	ang
iron	mii	legit	1st	ready	funn
blonde	aye	30	long	college	shoes
comforted	hard	wen	skating	mj	wood
standards	wuz	eric	mean	search	dad
shot	ready	yelled	heart	years	apart
chose	nigga	mis	dx	misfits	aj
chatting	jamaica	breaking	faith	blessed	line
damage	bus	homework	expectation	advice	jack
innocent	facebook	actually	research	boys	totally
thnx	cos	wishes	hard	fathers	tomorrow

5   Conclusion and Future Work

We match or set the state of the art for the 20 traits in this paper. Additionally, we provide the top words for many pairwise classification problems, and top 55 words for regression or binary classification problems. We hope researchers from many fields find the benchmarks and word lists useful. Our analysis of psychographic models in marketing as well as gender bias in a religion classifier are examples of how these performance measures and extracted features can be used together.

In future work we hope to explore what types of unfairness can be solved by our approach in Sect. 4.5. Further, models built on traits with few examples are well suited to be augmented by transfer learning. This is especially pressing for detecting states like low satisfaction with life, which can be somewhat ameliorated at low cost.

References

1. Stewart, J.B.: Facebook has 50 minutes of your time each day. It wants more. The New York Times, vol. 5 (2016)
2. SunCorp, Digitising reputation pays off in the rental market (2017)
3. Khandani, A.E., Kim, A.J., Lo, A.W.: Consumer credit-risk models via machine-learning algorithms. J. Bank. Financ. **34**(11), 2767–2787 (2010)
4. Cogburn, D.L., Espinoza-Vasquez, F.K.: From networked nominee to networked nation: examining the impact of web 2.0 and social media on political participation and civic engagement in the 2008 Obama campaign. J. Polit. Mark. **10**(1–2), 189–213 (2011)
5. González, R.J.: Hacking the citizenry? Personality profiling, big data and the election of Donald Trump. Anthropol. Today **33**(3), 9–12 (2017)
6. Fitzpatrick, K.K., Darcy, A., Vierhile, M.: Delivering cognitive behavior therapy to young adults with symptoms of depression and anxiety using a fully automated conversational agent (woebot): a randomized controlled trial. JMIR Mental Health **4**(2), e19 (2017). https://doi.org/10.2196/mental.7785. PMID: 28588005, PMCID: 5478797
7. Allan, R.: Hard questions: who should decide what is hate speech in an online global community? (2017)
8. Cheng, J., Danescu-Niculescu-Mizil, C., Leskovec, J.: Antisocial behavior in online discussion communities. In: ICWSM, pp. 61–70 (2015)
9. Noulas, A., Scellato, S., Lambiotte, R., Pontil, M., Mascolo, C.: A tale of many cities: universal patterns in human urban mobility. PloS one **7**(5), e37027 (2012)
10. Yang, S.-H., Long, B., Smola, A., Sadagopan, N., Zheng, Z., Zha, H.: Like like alike: joint friendship and interest propagation in social networks. In: Proceedings of the 20th International Conference on World Wide Web, pp. 537–546. ACM (2011)
11. Kosinski, M., Matz, S.C., Gosling, S.D., Popov, V., Stillwell, D.: Facebook as a research tool for the social sciences: opportunities, challenges, ethical considerations, and practical guidelines. Am. Psychol. **70**(6), 543 (2015)
12. Henrich, J., Heine, S.J., Norenzayan, A.: The weirdest people in the world? Behav. Brain Sci. **33**(2–3), 61–83 (2010)

13. Egan, V., Auty, J., Miller, R., Ahmadi, S., Richardson, C., Gargan, I.: Sensational interests and general personality traits. J. Forensic Psychiatry **10**(3), 567–582 (1999)
14. Egan, V., Campbell, V.: Sensational interests, sustaining fantasies and personality predict physical aggression. Pers. Individ. Differ. **47**(5), 464–469 (2009)
15. Weiss, A., Egan, V., Figueredo, A.J.: Sensational interests as a form of intrasexual competition. Pers. Individ. Differ. **36**(3), 563–573 (2004)
16. Hagger-Johnson, G., Egan, V., Stillwell, D.: Are social networking profiles reliable indicators of sensational interests? J. Res. Pers. **45**(1), 71–76 (2011)
17. Wang, N., Kosinski, M., Stillwell, D., Rust, J.: Can well-being be measured using facebook status updates? Validation of facebook's gross national happiness index. Soc. Indic. Res. **115**(1), 483–491 (2014)
18. Kosinski, M., Stillwell, D., Graepel, T.: Private traits and attributes are predictable from digital records of human behavior. Proc. Natl. Acad. Sci. **110**(15), 5802–5805 (2013)
19. Schwartz, H.A., et al.: Personality, gender, and age in the language of social media: the open-vocabulary approach. PloS One **8**(9), e73791 (2013)
20. Farnadi, G., et al.: Computational personality recognition in social media. User Model. User Adapt. Interact. **26**(2–3), 109–142 (2016)
21. Sap, M., et al.: Developing age and gender predictive lexica over social media. In: Proceedings of the 2014 Conference on Empirical Methods in Natural Language Processing (EMNLP), pp. 1146–1151 (2014)
22. The New York Times, How trump consultants exploited the data of millions (2018)
23. Watch, M.: Facebook valuation drops $75 billion in week after cambridge analytica scandal (2018)
24. The Guardian, I made Steve Bannons psychological warfare tool: meet the data war whistleblower (2018)
25. Pennebaker, J.W., Francis, M.E., Booth, R.J.: Linguistic inquiry and word count. In: LIWC 2001, vol. 71, no. 2001, p. 2001. Lawrence Erlbaum Associates, Mahway (2001)
26. Youyou, W., Kosinski, M., Stillwell, D.: Computer-based personality judgments are more accurate than those made by humans. Proc. Natl. Acad. Sci. **112**(4), 1036–1040 (2015)
27. Conneau, A., Schwenk, H., Barrault, L., Lecun, Y.: Very deep convolutional networks for text classification. In: Proceedings of the 15th Conference of the European Chapter of the Association for Computational Linguistics: Volume 1, Long Papers, vol. 1, pp. 1107–1116 (2017)
28. Krizhevsky, A., Sutskever, I., Hinton, G.E.: Imagenet classification with deep convolutional neural networks. In: Advances in Neural Information Processing Systems, pp. 1097–1105 (2012)
29. Nguyen, D., et al.: Why gender and age prediction from tweets is hard: lessons from a crowdsourcing experiment. In: Proceedings of COLING 2014, The 25th International Conference on Computational Linguistics: Technical Papers, pp. 1950–1961 (2014)
30. Bivens, R.: The gender binary will not be deprogrammed: ten years of coding gender on facebook. New Media Soc. **19**(6), 880–898 (2017)
31. Digman, J.M.: Personality structure: emergence of the five-factor model. Ann. Rev. Psychol. **41**(1), 417–440 (1990)
32. McCrae, R.R., Costa, P.T.: Validation of the five-factor model of personality across instruments and observers. J. Personality Soc. Psychol. **52**(1), 81 (1987)

33. M. LLC, The development and piloting of an online IQ test (2014)
34. Kosinski, M.: Measurement and prediction of individual and group differences in the digital environment. Department of Psychology, University of Cambridge (2014)
35. Flynn, J.R.: Massive IQ gains in 14 nations: what IQ tests really measure. Psychol. Bull. **101**(2), 171 (1987)
36. Diener, E., Emmons, R.A., Larsen, R.J., Griffin, S.: The satisfaction with life scale. J. Pers. Assess. **49**(1), 71–75 (1985)
37. Cooke, L., Wardle, J., Gibson, E., Sapochnik, M., Sheiham, A., Lawson, M.: Demographic, familial and trait predictors of fruit and vegetable consumption by preschool children. Public Health Nutr. **7**(2), 295–302 (2004)
38. Peciña, M., et al.: Personality trait predictors of placebo analgesia and neurobiological correlates. Neuropsychopharmacology **38**(4), 639 (2013)
39. Quilty, L.C., Sellbom, M., Tackett, J.L., Bagby, R.M.: Personality trait predictors of bipolar disorder symptoms. Psychiatry Res. **169**(2), 159–163 (2009)
40. Tett, R.P., Jackson, D.N., Rothstein, M.: Personality measures as predictors of job performance: a meta-analytic review. Pers. Psychol. **44**(4), 703–742 (1991)
41. Park, G., et al.: Automatic personality assessment through social media language. J. Pers. Soc. Psychol. **108**(6), 934 (2015)
42. Cesare, N., Grant, C., Nsoesie, E.O.: Detection of user demographics on social media: a review of methods and recommendations for best practices. arXiv preprint arXiv:1702.01807 (2017)
43. Kleinberg, J., Mullainathan, S., Raghavan, M.: Inherent trade-offs in the fair determination of risk scores. arXiv preprint arXiv:1609.05807 (2016)
44. John, O.P., Srivastava, S.: The big five trait taxonomy: history, measurement, and theoretical perspectives. In: Handbook of Personality: Theory and Research, vol. 2, pp. 102–138 (1999)
45. Kleinberg, J.M.: An impossibility theorem for clustering. In: Advances in Neural Information Processing Systems, pp. 463–470 (2003)
46. Jain, A.K., Murty, M.N., Flynn, P.J.: Data clustering: a review. ACM Comput. Surv. (CSUR) **31**(3), 264–323 (1999)
47. Shamir, R., Sharan, R.: 1 1 algorithmic approaches to clustering gene expression data. In: Current Topics in Computational Molecular Biology, p. 269 (2002)
48. Dixon, S., Pampalk, E., Widmer, G.: Classification of dance music by periodicity patterns (2003)
49. Meinshausen, N., Yu, B.: Lasso-type recovery of sparse representations for high-dimensional data. Ann. Stat. **46**, 246–270 (2009)
50. Lau, R.R., Sigelman, L., Rovner, I.B.: The effects of negative political campaigns: a meta-analytic reassessment. J. Polit. **69**(4), 1176–1209 (2007)
51. Huddy, L.: Group identity and political cohesion. In: Emerging Trends in the Social and Behavioral Sciences: An Interdisciplinary, Searchable, and Linkable Resource (2003)
52. Branscombe, N.R., Wann, D.L.: Collective self-esteem consequences of outgroup derogation when a valued social identity is on trial. Eur. J. Soc. Psychol. **24**(6), 641–657 (1994)
53. Schneider, M.C., Bos, A.L.: Measuring stereotypes of female politicians. Polit. Psychol. **35**(2), 245–266 (2014)
54. Dolan, K.: The impact of gender stereotyped evaluations on support for women candidates. Polit. Behav. **32**(1), 69–88 (2010)

55. Vehtari, A., Gelman, A., Gabry, J.: Efficient implementation of leave-one-out cross-validation and WAIC for evaluating fitted bayesian models. arXiv preprint arXiv:1507.04544 (2015)
56. Pedregosa, F., et al.: Scikit-learn: machine learning in Python. J. Mach. Learn. Res. **12**, 2825–2830 (2011)
57. Preoţiuc-Pietro, D., Liu, Y., Hopkins, D., Ungar, L.: Beyond binary labels: political ideology prediction of twitter users. In: Proceedings of the 55th Annual Meeting of the Association for Computational Linguistics (Volume 1: Long Papers), vol. 1, pp. 729–740 (2017)
58. Mikolov, T., Sutskever, I., Chen, K., Corrado, G.S., Dean, J.: Distributed representations of words and phrases and their compositionality. In: Advances in Neural Information Processing Systems, pp. 3111–3119 (2013)
59. Sniekers, S., et al.: Genome-wide association meta-analysis of 78,308 individuals identifies new loci and genes influencing human intelligence. Nature Genet. **49**(7), 1107 (2017)
60. Gottlieb, B.W., Gottlieb, J., Berkell, D., Levy, L.: Sociometric status and solitary play of LD boys and girls. J. Learn. Disabil. **19**(10), 619–622 (1986)
61. Bryan, T., Wheeler, R., Felcan, J., Henek, T.: come on, dummy an observational study of children's communications. J. Learn. Disabil. **9**(10), 661–669 (1976)
62. McConaughy, S.H., Ritter, D.R.: Social competence and behavioral problems of learning disabled boys aged 6–11. J. Learn. Disabil. **19**(1), 39–45 (1986)
63. Bellanti, C.J., Bierman, K.L.: Disentangling the impact of low cognitive ability and inattention on social behavior and peer relationships. J. Clin. Child Psychol. **29**(1), 66–75 (2000)
64. Suykens, J.A., Vandewalle, J.: Least squares support vector machine classifiers. Neural Process. Lett. **9**(3), 293–300 (1999)
65. Golub, G.H., Reinsch, C.: Singular value decomposition and least squares solutions. Numerische mathematik **14**(5), 403–420 (1970)
66. Iyyer, M., Enns, P., Boyd-Graber, J., Resnik, P.: Political ideology detection using recursive neural networks. In: Proceedings of the 52nd Annual Meeting of the Association for Computational Linguistics (Volume 1: Long Papers), vol. 1, pp. 1113–1122 (2014)
67. Felbo, B., Mislove, A., Søgaard, A., Rahwan, I., Lehmann, S.: Using millions of emoji occurrences to learn any-domain representations for detecting sentiment, emotion and sarcasm. arXiv preprint arXiv:1708.00524 (2017)
68. Wired, The decline and fall of an ultra rich online gaming empire (2008)
69. CBS News: Trump campaign phased out use of Cambridge analytica data before election (2018)
70. Pew, Religious landscape study (2014)
71. Zhao, J., Wang, T., Yatskar, M., Ordonez, V., Chang, K.-W.: Men also like shopping: reducing gender bias amplification using corpus-level constraints. arXiv preprint arXiv:1707.09457 (2017)
72. Zou, W.Y., Socher, R., Cer, D., Manning, C.D.: Bilingual word embeddings for phrase-based machine translation. In: Proceedings of the 2013 Conference on Empirical Methods in Natural Language Processing, pp. 1393–1398 (2013)
73. Clinchant, S., Perronnin, F.: Aggregating continuous word embeddings for information retrieval. In: Proceedings of the Workshop on Continuous Vector Space Models and Their Compositionality, pp. 100–109 (2013)
74. Luo, J., Sorour, S.E., Goda, K., Mine, T.: Predicting student grade based on free-style comments using word2vec and ann by considering prediction results obtained in consecutive lessons. International Educational Data Mining Society (2015)

75. Bolukbasi, T., Chang, K.-W., Zou, J.Y., Saligrama, V., Kalai, A.T.: Man is to computer programmer as woman is to homemaker? Debiasing word embeddings. In: Advances in Neural Information Processing Systems, pp. 4349–4357 (2016)
76. Dwork, C., Hardt, M., Pitassi, T., Reingold, O., Zemel, R.: Fairness through awareness. In: Proceedings of the 3rd Innovations in Theoretical Computer Science Conference, pp. 214–226. ACM (2012)
77. Joseph, M., Kearns, M., Morgenstern, J., Neel, S., Roth, A.: Rawlsian fairness for machine learning. arXiv preprint arXiv:1610.09559 (2016)
78. Kusner, M.J., Loftus, J., Russell, C., Silva, R.: Counterfactual fairness. In: Advances in Neural Information Processing Systems, pp. 4069–4079 (2017)
79. Zafar, M.B., Valera, I., Gomez Rodriguez, M., Gummadi, K.P.: Fairness beyond disparate treatment & disparate impact: learning classification without disparate mistreatment. In: Proceedings of the 26th International Conference on World Wide Web, pp. 1171–1180. International World Wide Web Conferences Steering Committee (2017)
80. Hardt, M., Price, E., Srebro, N., et al.: Equality of opportunity in supervised learning. In: Advances in Neural Information Processing Systems, pp. 3315–3323 (2016)
81. Grgic-Hlaca, N., Zafar, M.B., Gummadi, K.P., Weller, A.: The case for process fairness in learning: Feature selection for fair decision making. In: NIPS Symposium on Machine Learning and the Law, vol. 1, p. 2 (2016)
82. Saroglou, V.: Religiousness as a cultural adaptation of basic traits: a five-factor model perspective. Personality Soc. Psychol. Rev. **14**(1), 108–125 (2010)

Assessing Competition for Social Media Attention Among Non-profits

Rosta Farzan[1(✉)] and Claudia López[2]

[1] University of Pittsburgh, 135 North Bellefield, Pittsburgh, PA 15213, USA
rfarzan@pitt.edu
[2] Universidad Técnica Federico Santa María, Av. España 1680, Valparaíso, Chile

Abstract. Most non-profits maintain a social media presence with the hope to increase their popularity and achieve goals, such as to collect donations or recruit volunteers. While there is a strong vibe about the popularity of social media, there is very little empirical evidence on whether and how nonprofits can benefit from social media participation. We propose a method to quantify and assess the relationship between public social media attention and the amount of donations non-profits receive as a measure of success. We aim to address an essential limitation of prior research which has focused on studying the impact of social media on non-profits in isolation. To do so, we conducted a study of the Facebook participation of 76 non-profit organizations in Chile. Our results highlight factors that contribute to competition for public attention and show at what level social media attention relates to donation support.

Keywords: Local non-profits · Facebook · Donations
Attention competition

1 Introduction

Many non-profits have turned to social media to take advantage of its potential for citizen participation [2,3,10]. Given that social media platforms are among the most visited websites in the world (with Facebook and Twitter ranked 3rd and 13th, respectively, as of May 2018[1]), it might seem inevitable for these organizations to use them to reach their audiences, disseminate relevant information, recruit volunteers, or attract donors.

Nevertheless, several studies argue that non-profits are missing the opportunity to use social media to strengthen relationships with the public [2,5,11–13]. Content analysis of samples of non-profit's social media posts reveal that most non-profit's post social media content to disseminate *information* rather than to create a sense of *community* among their connections or request that they take an *action* [2,3,5,9,13]. This pattern was also found in earlier studies that compared

---

[1] http://www.alexa.com/topsites Last retrieved on May 17th, 2018.

© Springer Nature Switzerland AG 2018
S. Staab et al. (Eds.): SocInfo 2018, LNCS 11185, pp. 196–211, 2018.
https://doi.org/10.1007/978-3-030-01129-1_12

the prevalence of one-way vs. two-way communication [11,12]. This may be a missed opportunity for non-profits as most studies have argued that a two-way dialogue is more beneficial than one-way information dissemination. Nevertheless, there has been limited empirical evaluation of whether and how non-profits can truly benefit from participation in social media [9]. Even though social media platforms allow to measure responsiveness (e.g., likes, comments, retweets), only a few studies have taken a behavioral approach to assessing the public response of alternative kinds of social media posts [9]. Besides, while non-profits' social media activity might have cumulative effects on their audience responses over time, the long-term evolution of social media activity and their response have remained understudied. Most importantly, prior research has frequently studied non-profits as independent entities without considering that they generally aim to reach a common audience: a local community. This overlooks the complexities of competing for a community's attention and their implications for the online audiences that non-profits can reach.

This work presents an observational study of the Facebook activity of 76 non-profits in Chile over a period of seven years. We propose a method to quantify variation on Facebook attention within and between groups of non-profits targeting similar goals. Then, we study the relationship between these variations on social media attention and the level of donations the non-profits had collected. Our results indicate that competition for attention varies among groups of non-profits with a different focus; while groups such as those focusing on health support have less inequality among themselves, groups focusing on social inclusion experience a higher level of inequality. Moreover, while the amount of attention on social media significantly relates to how many donations the organizations receive, the stability of social media attention also can play an important role. The research questions that guide this work are: (1) How do different kinds of non-profits that co-exist in a geographical community share (or compete for) social media attention? (2) How do non-profits' share of social media attention relate to the achievement of their strategic goals, such as collection of donations?

2   Related Work

Inspired by social media's potential to support collective action, several books for non-profits professionals aim to persuade them to adopt and more effectively use social media [4,6,7]. Based on lessons learned from practice, these books offer guidelines about how to set an account on different social media platforms, what can be done in each of them, and how some non-profits have obtained benefits from their social media presence. However, when discussing how to obtain such benefits, non-profits tend to report on anecdotal evidence and successful cases. It remains unclear whether other non-profits can apply the same guidelines and whether the same practices would work for them.

More systematic studies in the field of public relations and social computing have found that non-profits have adopted social media to a great extent, especially Facebook and Twitter. A worldwide study of human rights non-profits reports that Facebook has the highest adoption rate (above 80%) and Twitter follows it closely (above 70%) [10]. These figures are even higher among large American organizations (86.7% and 79.9% for Facebook and Twitter, respectively) [2]. The relevance of social media for non-profits has encouraged Facebook to create a special website[2] to help non-profits manage their Facebook presence and a offers tool for fund-raising.

An influential study of the 100 largest American non-profits concluded that their social media posts can be categorized into three main categories of communicative functions, namely *information, community* and *action* [5]. *Information* characterizes posts that aim to transfer information from the organization to the public, such as news about the non-profits' activities. These posts also have been described as one-way communication in prior work [11,12]. *Community* represents interactive conversations posts between non-profits and the public (called two-way communication in [11,12]), as well as posts that aim to strengthen the relationship with the nonprofits' audience, such as to thank or to give recognition to someone. *Action* includes posts that ask the public to "do something" for the non-profit. This category includes event promotion, donation appeals, lobbying or advocacy requests, and calls for volunteers [5].

Adopting this taxonomy, research has found that most non-profits' posts have *information* purposes rather than *community* or *action* goals [2,3,5,9,13]. This pattern also had been found in earlier studies that compare the prevalence of one-way vs. two-way communication [11,12]. Although most studies argue that these results reveal that non-profits are missing the opportunity to use social media to strengthen relationships with the public [2,5,11–13], there is limited evidence about the consequences of different kinds of social media use among non-profits. Most studies have assumed that dialogic (or two-way) communication is better for non-profit public relations [9]. However, this relationship has been supported only by self-reported attitudinal data from studies on websites. Even though social media platforms measure responsiveness (e.g., through likes, comments, retweets), few studies have taken a behavioral approach to assessing the online public response of alternative ways to use social media [9].

Moreover, actions on social media might have cumulative effects on readers' reactions that would not be revealed by the previously mentioned cross-sectional studies. For example, adding many *community* posts every day might lead to information overload, and readers can grow tired and stop reacting positively to the posts. On the other hand, posting very few posts (of any kind) might not be enough to be visible and to reach all people that the organization aims to reach online. The consequences of non-profit social media activity over long periods of time remains understudied. One prior study [5] categorized non-profits according to the kinds of posts they create over four weeks; however, it did not report on the impact of each kind on user engagement. It is possible that their observation period was too short to observe the impact. Overall, the long-term consequences of a series of social media actions taken by a non-profit are still unknown [9].

---

[2] https://non-profits.fb.com/ Last retrieved on Jul 15th, 2016.

Non-profits do not live in a vacuum on social media. They often compete for the attention of the same community members. For example, non-profits located in an area share an audience formed by residents of that area [8]. These residents are most likely the only people who can be recruited as volunteers; therefore, local non-profits often compete with each other to attract the share of volunteers they need. Local proximity is also associated with favorable attitudes regarding donations [1] and adds to the competition factor among non-profits in close proximity. Many non-profits are based in similar causes, which means they compete for a limited number of local individuals who care about the same cause. In addition, there can be positive inter-dependencies among local non-profits that work for the same or similar causes, such as increasing visibility or legitimacy of their causes within the local community. The potential competition or inter-dependency among non-profits have been largely ignored in the most previous literature. An exception is a study of human-rights non-profits worldwide and its competition for online attention [10]. This study found that more affluent and well-known profits attract more online attention than less prosperous organizations. Further, it revealed that online attention is more unequally distributed than traditional media attention among all sampled non-profits [10].

3 Methods

3.1 Data Collection

We first sampled all of the non-profits that are located in the three most populated regions in Chile and belong to the four most popular categories of non-profits in the country. We focused on non-profits located in three regions: *Metropolitana*, *Valparaíso* and *Bío Bío*. Together, these areas are home to more than 11 million people (62% of the country's population). Due to a Chilean Law on Transparency and Access to Public Information, information such as registered NGOs and donations information are available to citizens and thus, enabled us to make a request on the Ministry's website. Though all non-profits can register in the Ministry, registered organizations tend to be large with more resources. This is due to the significant amount of effort and resources needed for organizations to enroll and propose donation-funded projects. As of November 2015, there were 317 non-profits legally registered in Chile, which were classified into nine categories. We chose to sample the four most popular categories because they seem to attract more attention from the Chilean civil society: Quality of Life and Integration, Education, Disability, and Infancy. The resulting sample had 247 non-profits. Sixteen non-profits had offices in more than a single region in our sample, and 46 were categorized into multiple categories. Most non-profits have offices in the *Metropolitana* region where the country's capital is located. About half of the organizations focus on Quality of Life and Integration.

We collected information from Ministry's website to characterize their adoption of social media sites. We found that 226 (91.5%) of the sampled non-profits had an active web page, 189 (76.5%) had an account on Facebook and 174 (70.5%) were on Twitter. Fewer non-profits had accounts on YouTube (33.6%),

Instagram (18.6%), and other social media platforms (less than 6%). Given that Facebook was widely adopted, we collected data generated related to the sampled non-profits from 2008 to May 2016 on their public Facebook accounts. We built python scripts to query the Graph API 2.5[3] automatically to get such data.

We complemented the Facebook data with public information about the donations received by non-profits in Chile from 2008 to 2015 as registered by the country's Social Development Ministry. These donations are regulated by the Law of Social Donations (#19,885) which allows a tax deduction for citizens and companies who donate to organizations of the civil society. Donors can direct their money to a specific non-profit as long as the non-profit is included in a registry of non-profits with projects previously approved. Alternatively, donations can be directed to a shared fund that will be later re-distributed among projects presented by all non-profits in the country, included those that are not part of the registry. We will focus on the donations directed to specific non-profits only as they reflect the donors' intention to support a specific cause.

Merging social media data and donations data led us to a final dataset of Facebook activity of a sample of 76 local non-profits in Chile from 2009 to 2015. It includes 41,672 posts on Facebook that received 1,715,478 likes and 95,466 comments. Together, these 76 organizations received $95,038,659,886 Chilean pesos (CLP), which is equivalent to approximately $150,855,016 US dollars.

3.2 Quantifying Competition for Social Media Attention

Our first goal was to compute measurements that would allow us to quantify competition among the non-profits. In deciding on such measurement, it is critical to use measures that are based on more than the amount of activity capturing the "rich gets richer" phenomena. Instead, measures should take into account the dynamics of social media interactions for late adopters and smaller non-profits. Using an aggregate measure of likes such as mean or median will not adequately capture the potential inequality of social media attention resulting from the competition for limited resources. Therefore, we adopted both a centrality measure and a standardized dispersion measure.

To capture dispersion and variation over time, we utilized Coefficient of Variance (CV) which is a standardized dispersion measure of a frequency distribution. We computed CV of Facebook likes and comments as the Standard Deviation over Mean number of likes and comments in one year period. In our case, CV represents whether the non-profit's social media posts receive a similar level of attention over time or skewed attention on a specific number of posts. An overall negative slope of CV over time represents a more stable level of attention. To capture centrality, we used the percentage of FB likes and comments that each non-profit received over each year of our data collection.

To better understand how non-profits compete with those who are focused on similar interests versus those targeting different goals, we classified the non-profits based on their mission. As our sample of non-profits was reduced when

---

[3] https://developers.facebook.com/ Last retrieved on January 27th, 2016.

we merged the donations data and to take into account the self-defined missions of the non-profits in our sample, we dropped the previously mentioned categorization provided by the Ministry. Instead, we manually coded each non-profit based on their mission statements on their web pages with a set of keywords best explaining their mission. Overall, we identified 36 keywords explaining the goals of all 76 non-profits in our dataset. Examples of such keywords include "sustainable development", "social inclusion", "child and adolescent protection", and "mental health." We assumed the major mission of the non-profits stayed consistent over the years. We then conducted a two-step clustering analysis to classify all 76 non-profits based on their keywords, using Bayesian Criterion (BIC) and Akaike's Information Criterion (AIC) to optimize the number of clusters. As a result, our set of 76 non-profits were clustered into five groups. The set of keywords associated with each cluster is presented in Appendix 1. Based on the associated keywords, we conceptualized five clusters as follows: C1: Health support, C2: Social inclusion, C3: Community development, C4: Informal training, and C5: Formal education.

Table 1 shows the total number of non-profits in each cluster who have any active participation on Facebook as well as the number of active non-profits in each cluster in every year of our data collection. It should be noted that there is an overlap between the years; i.e., organizations active every year of our data collection were included in the total data seven times.

Table 1. Total # of non-profits in each cluster and over time

	2009	2010	2011	2012	2013	2014	2015
Health support	2	3	8	8	10	12	12
Social inclusion	1	2	5	6	9	11	11
Community development	2	5	8	9	14	17	20
Informal training	2	2	4	7	9	10	10
Formal training	0	2	4	5	4	4	4

4   Results

4.1   Assessing Competition Among Non-profits

To assess the level of competition among the non-profit organization for social media attention, we used Mixture models to estimate the mean CV of likes and comments and mean percentage of likes and comments for each cluster of non-profits over time. Our model controls for the overall activity level of a non-profit by including the total number of posts by each non-profit in each year. It also accounts for the non-independence of observations among the same organizations and cluster of organizations by using a multi-level model considering each observation as embedded in year and cluster.

Facebook Likes. Overall, CV of likes is significantly associated with time, the cluster of non-profits, number of posts, and an interaction of time and clusters, as presented in Table 2. As shown in Fig. 1, over time the variance in attention to posts by non-profits increases. The distribution of attention becomes more unequal as time goes by from 2009 to 2015. Among different clusters of non-profits, the Health Support cluster (C1) has the lowest dispersion in the number of likes they received, and the Informal Training cluster (C4) has the highest dispersion of the number of likes.

Table 2. Mixture model of Coefficient of Variance of attention on facebook

	CV of likes			CV of comments		
	Wald χ^2	df	Sig	Wald χ^2	df	Sig
Year	24.64	6	<.0001	17.47	6	.008
Cluster	19.33	4	.001	7.02	4	.14
Number of posts	9.301	1	.002	.450	1	.50
Year*Cluster	251.40	23	<.000	207.694	22	<.0001

Moreover, the trend of change over time varies significantly across different clusters (as shown in Fig. 2) and is confirmed by the significant interaction effect. For clusters Health Support (C1) and Community Development (C3), the pattern of growth is very stable with little change over time. The Health Support cluster (C1) also exhibits a very small variation among the non-profits within the cluster as presented by the small error bars. This result suggests that health support non-profits are more likely to face competition with other clusters as opposed to within their own clusters. On the other hand, non-profits in Community Development (C3) face a higher level of competition within their cluster, as revealed by larger error bars.

The clusters Informal Training (C4) and Formal Education (C5) share a similar pattern of significant increase in 2012 and then a drop in 2013. In both cases, the increase in 2012 also is accompanied by a higher level of variation among the non-profits in their cluster as shown by the larger error bars. This peak of attention inequality could be related to large-scale social protests led by students demanding better quality, less-segregated, and free education, which took place between 2011 and 2013 in Chile. The high inequality is revealing that while both formal and informal education attracted attention from the public in social media, attention was not equally shared by all organizations in these clusters. The Social Inclusion cluster (C2) has a less stable pattern of variability with higher inequality of attention over time as compared to other clusters.

We then studied the centrality of likes by estimating the average percentage of likes in each cluster over time. First, it can be noted that the competition grew from 2009 until 2015. Over time, more organizations were active in almost every cluster (see Table 1) and the mean share of likes per cluster has shrunk (as presented in Fig. 3). In particular, while in 2009 one single Informal Training non-profit dominated over 90% of likes, over the years other organizations have been

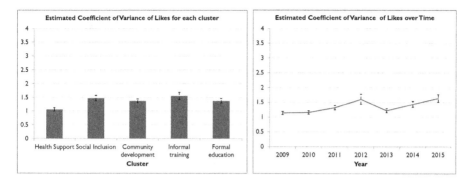

Fig. 1. Overall trend of Coefficient of Variance of FB likes

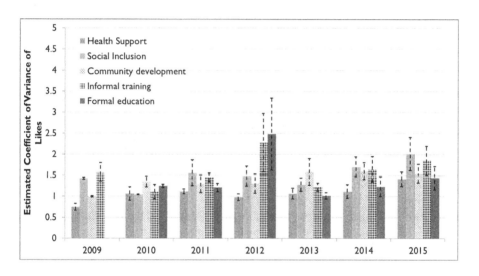

Fig. 2. Trend of Coefficient of Variance of FB likes over time across all clusters

able to claim a significant share of likes. In every cluster, there was a substantial increase in the number of non-profits that had a presence on Facebook in 2011. Consequently, we see a decrease in the average proportion of likes gathered by each cluster in that year. The number of organizations in the Community Development cluster has grown consistently and more than other clusters during the observation period (especially since 2013). At the same time, their mean share of attention has declined. This reveals that organizations who joined Facebook later were able to catch up and attract part of the attention already available to Community Development. Nevertheless, the estimated overall attention for Community Development has been smaller than for Social Inclusion, Informal Training, and Health Support since 2013.

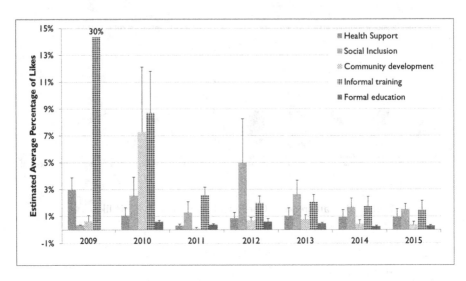

Fig. 3. Average percentage of FB likes in each cluster over time

Analyzing the patterns of centrality and dispersion together provides insights into understanding the dynamics of social media attention across clusters of non-profits over time. For example, there was a similar number of organizations in the clusters Social Inclusion, Informal Training and Formal Education in 2012; however, the average number of likes of the Social Inclusion group was higher. This reveals that Social Inclusion organizations captured a larger share of attention in that year. As we discussed earlier, there were higher levels of inequality of attention within the Informal Training and Formal Education clusters in the same year. This might indicate that the social movement for better quality, less-segregated, and free education attracted a larger share of attention to initiatives related to social inclusion, informal training, and formal education, but there was more inequality of attention within the last two clusters. Competition in these two clusters resulted in some organizations attracting most of the attention to the topic.

On the other hand, the non-profits in the Community Development group seem to have been the first to notice the importance of Facebook and were a majority in 2010. This was accompanied by a significant increase in their average share of likes, thus revealing that they were capturing a considerable part of the social media attention by then. Nevertheless, this pattern was not sustainable over time. More organizations joined, their share of likes decreased, and the measures of dispersion changed only slightly. Together, this unveils that they lost part of their share of attention to other clusters and had concentrated on a mild competition within their cluster. Note that this is not necessarily an adverse outcome. It is possible that Community Development non-profits do not require substantial levels attention and instead prefer to focus on targeting specific audiences within the particular communities that they aim to support.

Health support non-profits seem to face more competition with other groups of non-profits as opposed to within their cluster. While a majority of them joined Facebook in 2011, that year was particularly negative regarding the share of attention they received. Nevertheless, since then, they have attracted a slightly larger share of likes on average, and every time that new organizations joined Facebook, the cluster's dispersion measures grow more compared to other clusters than within their cluster. This reveals that while Health Support non-profits might have been losing the competition to other clusters in 2011, they have been able to take back some of the shared attention in the following years.

Facebook Comments. As opposed to likes, as presented in Table 2, CV of comments is not significantly different among clusters. The number of posts is not a significant predictor of change of CV. The number of posts is associated with changes in attention expressed through likes, but it does not relate to the commenting behavior. As presented in Fig. 4, similar to likes, over time the inequality of attention regarding comments also increases; i.e., over time a specific group of non-profits or a particular group of posts are more likely to draw comments than the average.

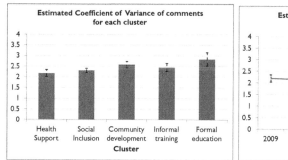
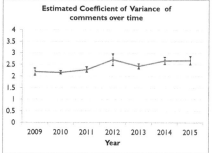

Fig. 4. Overall trend of Coefficient of Variance of FB comments

Similar to FB likes, there is a significant interaction between clusters and time. Competition increases significantly over time mainly for the Information Training (C4) group, while it is very unstable (increasing and decreasing) for the Formal Education (C5) group. The Community Development (C3) group exhibits a somewhat stable pattern within the cluster and over time changes in the number of comments they receive. Figure 5 presents the trend of CV of comments across different clusters over time.

Patterns of the centrality of comments closely follow the patterns of the centrality of likes as presented in Fig. 6. Similarly, over time, domination of a specific group of non-profits has been reduced, and there is a more equal share of comments claimed by different non-profits. Besides, the pattern of a larger share of attention devoted to Social Inclusion, Informal Training and Formal

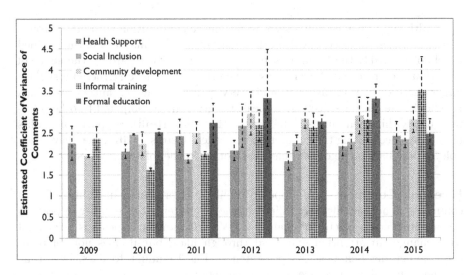

Fig. 5. Trend of Coefficient of Variance of FB comments over time across all clusters

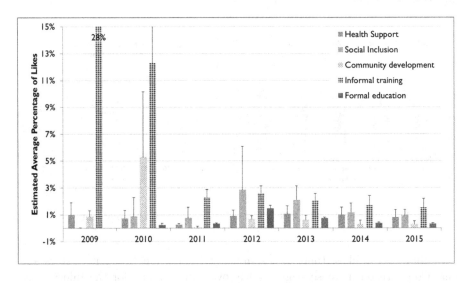

Fig. 6. Average percentage of FB comments in each cluster over time

Education in 2012 also is observed in this data. However, non-profits belonging to the Social Inclusion cluster attracted a smaller share of comments compared to likes, especially after 2012. In turn, non-profits of Informal Education captured, on average, a more substantial proportion of the comments. Other patterns are similar to those observed using likes as a basis to measure social media attention.

Overall, using the CV and average percentage as measures of dispersion and centrality of social media attention, we have been able to study inequality of attention within and between clusters of organizations over time. Our results suggest that particular groups of non-profits are more likely to compete with others with similar topics of interest while others face more competition with non-profits with a different focus.

4.2   Social Media Attention and Public Donation

Our dataset includes the donations reported for each of these 76 non-profits for years 2009 to 2015. Therefore, we can analyze the relationship between the social media attention and donations non-profits received longitudinally. We conducted a two-step regression analysis first to assess which factors contribute to a non-profit receiving a donation or not and then for those who had received any donations; we assessed the factors associated with the volume of donations. In each case, our model included the cluster, year, total number of posts (logged transformed to avoid skewness), and coefficient of variation for comments and likes as the independent variables. Ideally, it may be important to include characteristics of organizations such as size of organization, tenure and characteristics of the users such as demographics, and donation behavior in the model. However, this information was not available to us; we plan to collect such information in the future. We used logistic regression in the first model with the binary variable of donation made or not as the dependent variable. For the second model, we used negative binomial with the amount of donation as the dependent variable. The model is a hierarchical model considering each observation to be associated with a non-profit repeated every year and within the topic cluster. The independent variables included in the model are not correlated with each other.[4]

The first regression shows that none of the factors except the year is a significant predictor of the outcome of whether a non-profit received a donation or not (year: $\chi^2 = 20.1, df = 5, Sig. = .001$). Not surprisingly over time, non-profits are more likely to receive donations, ranging from 40% in 2010 to 85% in 2015.

Table 3. Relationship between donations, social media activity and attention

	χ^2	Exp(B)	df	Sig
Topic cluster	12.361	Categorical	4	.015
Year	6.148	Not Significant	5	.292
Log number of posts	5.313	1.37	1	.021
Coefficient of variance of likes	.015	Not Significant	1	.901
Coefficient of variance of comments	11.315	.66	1	.001

The results of the second model, shown in (Table 3), reveal the following:

---

[4] The proportion of likes and comments were both highly correlated to the number of posts; therefore, we decided to keep only the number of posts in our analysis.

- There is a significant difference among clusters. The estimated average of donations for each cluster is presented in Table 4. Non-profits focusing on Formal Education receive smaller donations, and the Community Development cluster receives the largest donations. However, not all the differences are significant as there is a very high variation within the clusters. The Formal Education cluster receives significantly less than all except the Social Inclusion group.
- There is no significant impact of the year; i.e., while over time there are more non-profits that receive donations, the average amount of donation per non-profit does not change significantly over time.
- The number of posts significantly relate to the amount of donation; i.e., a unit increase in number of posts is related to an increase of 1.37 CLP increase in donation.
- There is no significant relationship between CV of likes and donations while there is a significant relationship between CV of comments and donations. Stability of receiving a similar level of likes over time does not correlate with amount of donations. However, the ability to receive a steady number of comments over time relates to a higher amount of donations; i.e. a unit increase in CV, which means higher variation in number of comments, leads to 34% CLP (factor of .66) decrease in donation.

Table 4. Estimated averages of donations by cluster, keeping other variables constant. The values are in Chilean Peso (CLP)

Cluster	Mean (CLP)	Std. error (CLP)
Health support	198,576,201.40	72,929,004.83
Social inclusion	102,342,577.00	53,254,363.32
Community development	230,336,775.80	64,088,905.83
Informal training	156,518,935.90	63,944,084.30
Formal education	32,515,298.97	17,061,150.60

CV of likes and CV of comments could allow us to assess the relationship between changes in social media attention and donation. Therefore, we repeated the same regression models with the percentages of likes and percentage comments in each cluster to assess the relationship between the amount of attention as opposed to the variation of attention. The models were the same except replacing CV of likes with Percentage of Likes and CV of Comments with Percentage of Comments. Besides, we had to drop the number of posts as it is highly correlated with the average number of likes and comments (Spearman's ρ of .821 and .834 respectively). Moreover, the average number of comments and likes are also highly correlated; therefore, we included each separately in the models. The results show that the average number of likes and comments are both positively correlated with the amount of donation as presented in Table 5; one unit increase

in average percentage of likes is associated with a factor of 15,835 CLP increase
in donation and one unit increase in average percentage of comments is associated with a factor of 57.97 CLP increase in donation. While these numbers
can seem very high increase, it should be noted that one unit increase in average percentage of likes and comments is a very challenging goal, as it involves
increasing the attention share among all other similar non-profits.

Table 5. Relationship between donations and average percentage of likes and comments

	χ^2	Exp(B)	Std.error	df	Sig
Ave % of likes	29.89	15,835.35	1.77	1	.0001
Ave % of comments	10.352	57.97	1.26	1	.001

5 Discussion

As non-profits increasingly pursue a presence in social media, it is crucial to
better understand the implications of such a decision for the achievement of their
strategic goals. Is it useful to join Facebook when almost every other non-profit
is already there? How does the effort involved in generating social media activity
relate to the important goals such as attracting donations? This work offers a
method to study the dynamics of competition for social media attention within
an ecosystem of non-profits over a period of seven years. By combining the use of
centrality and dispersion measures of the frequency distribution of Facebook likes
and comments that non-profits receive, we revealed the patterns of competition
within and between clusters of non-profits sharing similar missions. We then
used these measures to study the association of social media attention with the
volume of donations collected by the organizations annually.

We applied the method to a sample of non-profits located in the three most
populated regions of Chile. The dataset included Facebook posts and donations
data over a period of seven years. Clustering non-profits according to their similarity of goals allowed us to characterize competition within and between groups
of non-profits. The results show that Health Support non-profits face more competition with other clusters than among themselves. Social media attention also
reflects the occurrence of significant events in the country such as the educational
reform protests in 2012, which has been related to the increase of attention for
non-profits with a focus on Social Inclusion, Informal Training and Formal Education. Across clusters, late adopters have been able to gather some attention
and reconfigure the distribution of social media attention. Finally, while the
number of posts created by non-profits only influenced the number of donations,
the share of attention they gather, and their stability of attention regarding comments are positively related to donations. Future work will explore competition
among non-profits across other dimensions such as geographical distance and

foundation time. In addition, studies will include a more diverse set of outcome measures beyond donations such as success in campaigns and public mobilization, or recruitment of volunteers.

Acknowledgments. This work was partially funded by CONICYT Chile, under grant Conicyt-Fondecyt Iniciación 11161026.

A   Appendix

See Fig. 7.

		Health support	Social inclusion	Community development	Informal training	Formal education
Apoyo a la Vida Intrahospitalaria	Support for in-hospital life	2				
Apoyo a Organizaciones Sociales	Support to Social Organizations				1	
Capacitaciones	Trainings				1	
Comunidades Indígenas	Indigenous Communities				1	
Deportes	Sports				1	
Desarrollo Sustentable	Sustainable development				1	
Educación	Education				14	8
Educación Ambiental	Environmental education				2	
Educación Cultural	Cultural Education				1	1
Educación Escolar	School Education			2		3
Educación Formal	Formal Education					1
Educación Inclusiva	Inclusive Education				4	
Educación no Formal	Informal Education				6	
Educación para Adultos	Adult Education		1			
Educación Pre-escolar	Preschool Education			2	4	1
Educación Superior	Higher Education				1	1
Educación Tecnológica	Education in Technology			1		
Emprendimiento	Entrepreneurship			1		
Enfoque Religioso	Religious Approach		1		1	2
Esducación Escolar	School Education				1	
Fortalecimiento de la Familia	Strengthening the Family			2		
Gestión de Proyectos	Project Management			1		
Inclusión Laboral	Labor Inclusion			2	3	1
Inclusión Social	Social Inclusion		12			
Medicina Alternativa	Alternative Medicine			1		
Pre-escolar	Preschool					1
Programa de Adopción	Adoption Program			1		
Programa específico de intervención	Specific intervention program	1			5	1
Protección infanto-juvenil	Child and adolescent protection	2	1		5	
Rehabilitación del consumo de drogas	Rehabilitation of drug use		1			
Rehabilitación Física	Physical rehabilitation	2	1			
Salud	Health	13	3			2
Salud infanto-juvenil	Child and adolescent health	5				
Salud Mental	Mental health	2			1	
Seguridad Social	Social Security			1		
Transformación de espacios públicos	Transformation of public spaces				3	

Fig. 7. List of keywords associated with each cluster of non-profit organization, in Spanish and English. The numbers in each cell indicate the distribution of the keyword for that cluster

References

1. Grau, S.L., Folse, J.A.G.: Cause-related marketing (CRM): the influence of donation proximity and message-framing cues on the less-involved consumer. J. Advert. **36**(4), 19–33 (2007)
2. Guo, C., Saxton, G.D.: Tweeting social change: how social media are changing nonprofit advocacy. Nonprofit Volunt. Sect. Q. **43**, 57–79 (2013). https://doi.org/10.1177/0899764012471585
3. Hou, Y., Lampe, C.: Social media effectiveness for public engagement: example of small nonprofits. In: Proceedings of the 33rd Annual ACM Conference on Human Factors in Computing Systems, pp. 3107–3116. ACM (2015)
4. Kanter, B., Fine, A.: The Networked Nonprofit: Connecting with Social Media to Drive Change. Wiley, Hoboken (2010)
5. Lovejoy, K., Saxton, G.D.: Information, community, and action: how nonprofit organizations use social media. J. Comput. Mediat. Commun. **17**(3), 337–353 (2012)
6. Mansfield, H.: Social Media for Social Good: A How-to Guide for Nonprofits. McGraw Hill Professional, New York (2011)
7. Mathos, M., Norman, C.: 101 Social Media Tactics for Nonprofits: A Field Guide. Wiley, Hoboken (2012)
8. McPherson, J.M., Rotolo, T.: Testing a dynamic model of social composition: diversity and change in voluntary groups. Am. Sociol. Rev. **61**, 179–202 (1996)
9. Saxton, G.D., Waters, R.D.: What do stakeholders like on facebook? Examining public reactions to nonprofit organizations' informational, promotional, and community-building messages. J. Public Relat. Res. **26**(3), 280–299 (2014)
10. Thrall, A.T., Stecula, D., Sweet, D.: May we have your attention please? Human-rights NGOs and the problem of global communication. Int. J. Press Polit. **19**, 160–180 (2014). https://doi.org/10.1177/1940161213519132
11. Waters, R.D., Burnett, E., Lamm, A., Lucas, J.: Engaging stakeholders through social networking: how nonprofit organizations are using facebook. Public Relat. Rev. **35**(2), 102–106 (2009)
12. Waters, R.D., Jamal, J.Y.: Tweet, tweet, tweet: a content analysis of nonprofit organizations' twitter updates. Public Relat. Rev. **37**(3), 321–324 (2011)
13. Xu, W.W., Chiu, I.H., Chen, Y., Mukherjee, T.: Twitter hashtags for health: applying network and content analyses to understand the health knowledge sharing in a twitter-based community of practice. Qual. Quant. **49**(4), 1361–1380 (2015)

A Generalized Force-Directed Layout for Multiplex Sociograms

Zahra Fatemi[1], Mostafa Salehi[1], and Matteo Magnani[2]([✉])

[1] Faculty of New Sciences and Technologies, University of Tehran, Tehran, Iran
{fatemi.z,mostafa_salehi}@ut.ac.ir
[2] InfoLab, Department of Information Technology, Uppsala University,
Uppsala, Sweden
matteo.magnani@it.uu.se

Abstract. Multiplex networks are defined by the presence of multiple edge types. As a consequence, it is hard to produce a single visualization of a network revealing both the structure of each edge type and their mutual relationships: multiple visualization strategies are possible, depending on how each edge type should influence the position of the nodes in the sociogram. In this paper we introduce *multiforce*, a force-directed layout for multiplex networks where both intra-layer and inter-layer relationships among nodes are used to compute node coordinates. Despite its simplicity, our algorithm can reproduce the main existing approaches to draw multiplex sociograms, and also supports a new intermediate type of layout. Our experiments on real data show that multiforce enables layered visualizations where each layer represents an edge type, nodes are well aligned across layers and the internal layout of each layer highlights the structure of the corresponding edge type.

Keywords: Visualization · Multiplex network · Layout
Force-directed

1 Introduction

Sociograms, that is, visual representations of the relationships between individuals, have been used since the origins of social network analysis, a notable example being Moreno's seminal work introducing this concept [22]. In the same book we also find a sociogram representing a multiplex network, where multiple types of relationships between the same group of individuals coexist. However, while several layout algorithms for simple graphs have been developed since then, developments in visualization methods for multiplex networks have been limited.

One natural way to visualize a multiplex network is to treat it as an edge-typed multi-graph using different colors and line styles to distinguish between the different edge types, as in Fig. 1(a) and as done by Moreno himself. However, this option can quickly lead to a very dense representation hiding relevant network structures even for very small networks [26]. Alternatively, different types of

© Springer Nature Switzerland AG 2018
S. Staab et al. (Eds.): SocInfo 2018, LNCS 11185, pp. 212–227, 2018.
https://doi.org/10.1007/978-3-030-01129-1_13

connections can be sliced into different layers, with the same node replicated on multiple layers, as in Fig. 1(b-d). This approach has been used in the literature to represent social/historical [21,23] networks, but also several other types of multiplex networks, from traffic [4,19] to biological [4] and financial [7] networks, sometimes visualized in a 2.5-dimensional space.

However, replicating the same node on multiple layers introduces a new question: how should the positions of multiple occurrences of the same node relate to each other? Two main approaches for visualizing multiplex networks sliced into layers have been used: visualizing each layer independently of the others, as in Fig. 1(b), or keeping the same layout in all layers, so that all occurrences of the same node will result aligned on a straight line if the layers are visualized one besides the other, as in Figs. 1(c) and (d).

Using the first approach we can appreciate the structure of each layer. For example, in Fig. 1(b) we can see clear communities in the first (left-most) layer, representing the relationship *eating lunch together*, but less evident groups in the last layer about *working* relations. However, we get no information about the relationships between layers, e.g., whether the communities in the first layer correspond to tight groups also in the last.

Using the second approach it is easier to find the same nodes across different layers, but this does not necessarily help in understanding relationships between whole layers, and can also be misleading. As an example, in Fig. 1(c) all the nodes are aligned on the layout computed on the first layer, and this creates the illusion of the presence of similar communities in the fourth and fifth layers. Computing the layout on a combination of all edges in all layers or on one of the other layers, as in Fig. 1(d), has instead the effect of hiding the communities found in the first layer.

In this paper we claim that (1) the aforementioned approaches are just specific cases of a more general method, and can thus be produced by the same (simple) algorithm, and that (2) this algorithm can also produce new intermediate layouts between the ones mentioned above. These ideas are not new, as they were already explored in the context of dynamic graph drawing [8]. We call the general layout and algorithm described in this paper and tested on multiplex social networks *multiforce*.

Multiforce is based on a force-directed algorithm (in this paper we extend the popular Fruchterman-Reingold method) and uses two main types of forces: *intra-layer* and *inter-layer*, that can be tuned to impact specific layers more or less than others. Intra-layer forces attract neighbors inside the same layer, making them closer, as in traditional layouts for monoplex networks. Inter-layer forces try to align instances of the same node on different layers[1]. Figure 2 gives an intuition of how these forces operate. In addition, we use repulsive forces as in the original algorithm, and also gravity for the cases where no inter-layer forces are active and the network contains more than one component.

---

[1] In theory inter-layer forces can also be used to visualize more general networks, where edges can cross layers, but in this work we focus on multiplex networks.

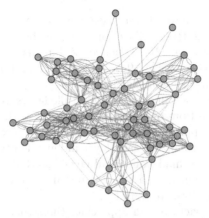

(a) Multi-graph (color figure). Communities
are visible, edge types are mixed together

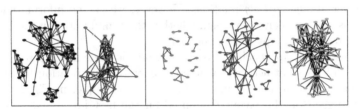

(b) Sliced, independent. Edge-type-specific communities are visible

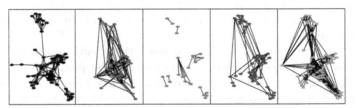

(c) Sliced, aligned on first layer. Visible node correspondence across layers,
phantom communities appear in other layers

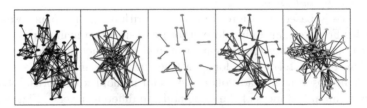

(d) Sliced, aligned on last layer

Fig. 1. Four visualizations of the AUCS multiplex network

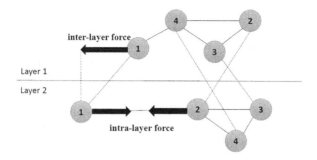

Fig. 2. The effect of intra-layer and inter-layer forces on node positions

To perform an objective comparison between our approach and a traditional non-multiplex force-based layout algorithm we have defined two quality metrics called respectively *external fit* and *internal fit*. These are naturally defined as the forces which would be active on the nodes if we were only trying to respectively align them across layers or draw them according to the internal structure of each layer. We have then used these metrics to characterize different settings of our general algorithm when applied to real social networks. In addition to this evaluation, we have also executed our algorithm on a simple dataset to qualitatively characterize the resulting diagrams.

2 The Multiforce Layout

Multiforce belongs to the slicing class of multiplex layouts, and is different from existing approaches, because it allows a balancing of the effects of intra-layer and inter-layer relationships. Multiforce extends the Fruchterman-Reingold algorithm [10]. This is one of the most popular options available in graph analysis software packages, although it is not a state-of-the-art method; several variations of this approach have been developed, but its simplicity allows us to focus on the simple variation of the way in which forces are defined, which can then be adapted to more complex algorithms. As mentioned in the introduction, multiforce is based on two types of attractive forces. The nodes are positioned on a set of planes, one for each layer or type of relationship – this setting is sometimes called 2.5-dimensional, because it looks 3-dimensional but the z-coordinates of the nodes are fixed and limited to the number of planes/layers. In this paper we visualize all layers on the same plane as in Fig. 1, because a 3-dimensional graph is visually intriguing but not easy to understand without the option of interactively rotating the diagram. Intra-layer forces, that can be weighted differently in each layer, attract pairs of nodes connected on the same layer. Inter-layer forces influence the position of nodes in different layers connected by inter-layer edges, or corresponding to the same node in the case of multiplex networks.

The same idea behind multiforce was already proposed and tested in the context of dynamic graphs [8], where layers are not unordered as in the case of multiplex networks but are organized in a sequence.

The pseudo-code of multiforce is presented in Algorithm 1, and the algorithm is implemented in the *multinet* library[2]. The algorithm takes a multiplex network $G = (N, L, V, E)$ as input, where N is a set of nodes, L is a set of layers, (V, E) is a graph and the elements of V are pairs ⟨node, layer⟩. We notate v.layer the layer of an element $v \in V$ and v.node the node corresponding to an element $v \in V$.

Lines 13–29 are the same as in the original algorithm, and compute the displacement of each node based on its neighbors (attractive forces) and other nodes (repulsive forces), with the addition of weights that can be used to specify on which layers the layout should be computed according to the original algorithm (27–28). Lines 30–37 extend the original algorithm and compute the displacement caused by the position of the node on other layers, to control node alignment. This is also weighted, to allow the user to turn this feature on and off for all or some layers (34–35). In our tests the function *cool* (45) reduces t linearly, so that it becomes 0 at the last iteration.

Some details of our algorithm can also be changed without affecting its underlying idea. First, we can modify lines 6–12 to assign the same initial random coordinates to the same node across different layers, anticipating line 8 before the for loop. A weighting factor INLA[v] can also be added at line 20, so that both attractive and repulsive forces are reduced or reinforced together. Finally, lines 41 and 42 have been retained from the original algorithm and ensure that the nodes do not exit the frame specified by the user, but are not necessary if the final coordinates are re-scaled to fit it or a gravity force is added to control the spreading of the nodes so that all slices retain similar extreme coordinates. In this paper gravity is only used in the examples with no inter-layer forces and multiple components on the same layer.

2.1 Main Settings

The multiforce algorithm can produce both existing and new layouts using the following settings:

1. **Multi-graph:** this layout, where each node has a specific position that does not depend on the layer and all edge types are considered when computing the node coordinates, is obtained by setting the same positive value for intra-layer weight in each layer and infinite (or, in practice, very high) inter-layer weights. The intra-layer weights will then keep nodes aligned across layers, and intra-layer forces will produce the layout by moving these "node pillars" around.

2. **Sliced, independent:** this layout corresponds to the application of the force-based algorithm on each layer, and is obtained by using positive intra-layer weights and setting inter-layer weights to 0.

3. **Sliced, aligned on layer** x: this layout is computed based on one of the layers, and nodes are kept aligned on the other layers. It is obtained by

---

[2] https://cran.r-project.org/package=multinet.

Algorithm 1. Multiforce

Require: $G = (N, L, V, E)$: a multiplex network
Require: W: width of the frame
Require: L: length of the frame
Require: #iterations
Require: INLA, INTERLA: intra- and inter-layer weights
 1: $f_r = \text{function}(z, k)\{ \text{ return } k^2/z; \}$
 2: $f_a = \text{function}(z, k)\{ \text{ return } z^2/k; \}$
 3: $\text{area} := W \cdot L$
 4: $k := \sqrt{\frac{\text{area}}{|N|}};$
 5: $t := \sqrt{|N|};$
 6: **for** $(n \in N)$ **do**
 7:    **for** $(v \in V \text{ s.t. } v.\text{node} = n)$ **do**
 8:       $(x, y) = \text{random coordinates};$
 9:       $\text{pos}[v] = (x, y)$
10:       $z[v] := \text{index}(v.\text{layer});$
11:    **end for**
12: **end for**
13: **for** $(i = 1 \text{ to } \#\text{iterations})$ **do**
14:    // calculate repulsive forces
15:    **for** $(v \in V)$ **do**
16:       $\text{disp}[v] := \mathbf{0};$
17:       **for** $(u \in V)$ **do**
18:          **if** $(u \neq v \text{ and } u.\text{layer} = v.\text{layer})$ **then**
19:             $\triangle := \text{pos}[v] - \text{pos}[u];$
20:             $\text{disp}[v] := \text{disp}[v] + (\triangle/|\triangle|) * f_r(|\triangle|);$
21:          **end if**
22:       **end for**
23:    **end for**
24:    // calculate attractive forces inside each layer
25:    **for** $((u, v) \in E)$ **do**
26:       $\triangle := \text{pos}[v] - \text{pos}[u];$
27:       $\text{disp}[v] := \text{disp}[v] - (\triangle/|\triangle|) * f_a(|\triangle|, k) * \text{INLA}[v];$
28:       $\text{disp}[u] := \text{disp}[u] + (\triangle/|\triangle|) * f_a(|\triangle|, k) * \text{INLA}[u];$
29:    **end for**
30:    // calculate attractive forces across layers
31:    **for** $(n \in N)$ **do**
32:       **for** $(\{u, v\} \text{ with } u, v \in V, u.\text{node} = v.\text{node} = n)$ **do**
33:          $\triangle := \text{pos}[v] - \text{pos}[u];$
34:          $\text{disp}[v] := \text{disp}[v] - (\triangle/|\triangle|) * f_a(|\triangle|, k) * \text{INTERLA}[v, u];$
35:          $\text{disp}[u] := \text{disp}[u] + (\triangle/|\triangle|) * f_a(|\triangle|, k) * \text{INTERLA}[u, v];$
36:       **end for**
37:    **end for**
38:    // assign new positions
39:    **for** $(v \in V)$ **do**
40:       $\text{pos}[v] := \text{pos}[v] + (\text{disp}[v]/|\text{disp}[v]|) * \min(\text{disp}[v], t);$
41:       $\text{pos}[v].x := \min(W/2, \max(-W/2, \text{pos}[v].x));$
42:       $\text{pos}[v].y := \min(L/2, \max(-L/2, \text{pos}[v].y));$
43:    **end for**
44:    // reduce the temperature
45:    $t := \text{cool}(t);$
46: **end for**

specifying a positive intra-layer weight for layer x and setting the other intra-layer weights and the inter-layer weights to 0.

4. **Balanced:** this intermediate layout is obtained by setting a positive weight (for example, 1) for all inter- and intra-layer forces.

In Sect. 3 we experimentally study the stability of the layouts depending on the chosen weights, showing that they are very stable and largely independent of the specific values we use for the positive weights.

2.2   Time Complexity

When the number of layers is constant, the asymptotic time complexity of multiforce is the same as for simple networks, with a larger constant. Separating nodes based on repulsive forces requires to compare each of the $|N|$ nodes on each layer with all the other nodes on the same layer, for a total time complexity of $O(|N|^2|L|)$ if no spatial indexes are used. Computing inter-layer forces on a node requires access to all its replicas, one on each other layer, for a total complexity of $O(|L|^2|N|)$. For a complete network with $|N|$ nodes and $|L|$ layers, there are at most $(|L|\frac{|N|(|N|-1)}{2})$ intra-layer edges contributing to attractive forces. In the typical case when $|L|$ is small or significantly smaller than $|N|$ the time complexity of drawing a multiplex network with the multiforce layout is thus $O(|N|^2)$ assuming a constant number of iterations. In general, the complexity is $O(|N|^2|L| + |L|^2|N|)$.

3   Experimental Evaluation

In this section we present an experimental evaluation of the new type of layout (balanced) enabled by multiforce, divided into two parts. First, we provide a quantitative evaluation where we show how the algorithm can produce layouts that are close to an ideal case when executed on a number of real datasets. Then, we execute the algorithm on the real dataset shown at the beginning of the article, to provide an additional qualitative analysis.

Please notice that we are not claiming that a balanced layout is the best possible: each of the layouts we can obtain using multiforce, including the ones already existing in the literature, highlights some aspects of the network. Therefore, it is important to be able to produce many of them during an exploratory analysis, and to be able to choose among them when presenting an analysis depending on what aspect we want to emphasize. The additional focus we put on the balanced layout in this section is only due to the fact that the other layouts that can be produced by multiforce have already been used and described in previous works.

3.1   Quantitative Evaluation

In this section we compare different layouts against an ideal case where each layer is drawn independently of the others, to optimize its internal readability, and at the same time all occurrences of the same node across different layers are kept perfectly aligned. Notice that such an ideal visualization is impossible to obtain in general, except when the two layers are (almost) identical. To compute the distance between the ideal case and our tests we can define two measures representing these two criteria: the sum of the forces still active on the nodes inside each layer (called internal fit) and the displacement between nodes in different layers (called external fit), also computed as the sum of the inter-layer forces still active at the end of the algorithm. Notice that an optimal diagram as defined above would contain both internally stable and aligned nodes, so both measures would be close to 0, indicating the best possible layout (assuming that a force-based approach is used).

In this context, we perform two experiments. The first tests the effect of the parameters (intra- and inter-layer forces) on the external and internal fit when applied to our working example. Figure 3 shows that the results are very stable with respect to the input parameters. We remind the reader that the objective is to achieve low values for both internal and external fit.

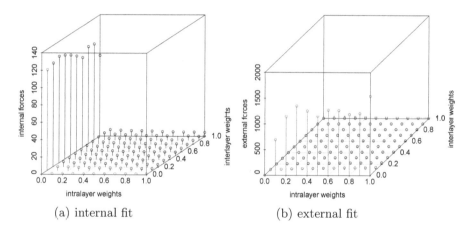

(a) internal fit   (b) external fit

Fig. 3. Effect of parameters on internal and external fit. Low internal and external forces (vertical axis) correspond to an ideal layout. For most combinations of inter- and intra-layer weights both forces are low.

In addition to the indication of the stability of the parameters, Fig. 3 suggests that a balanced layout can obtain good scores on both internal and external fit at the same time when using both intra-layer and inter-layer forces. We compare the results of the various approaches on the real datasets summarized in Table 1:

- A hybrid online/offline social network with five types of relationships among the employees of a CS department [26], also used as our working example.
- Traditional multiplex networks from the Social Network Analysis literature.
- A dataset showing the relationship among physicians in four different cities, collected to investigate information diffusion about drugs [13].

– Two transport networks, one with flight connections in Europe [3] and one
about the London underground [5].

Table 1. Properties of real-world networks

Network	# Layers	# Nodes	# Edges
Social/Hybrid – AUCS	5	61	1240
Social/Historical – Padgett	2	15	35
Social – Krackhardt High Tech	3	16	166
Social – Lazega Law Firm	3	212	1663
Social – Physicians	3	241	1370
Transport – EU airlines	37	417	3588
Transport – London	3	369	441

Table 2. Results of experiments on real data

Network	Balanced		Independent		Aligned (avg)		Multi-graph	
	Inter	Ext	Inter	Ext	Inter	Ext	Inter	Ext
AUCS	4.78	9.17	1.03	1489.21	149.72	0.15	112.713	0.02
Padgett-Florentine-Families	2.02	3.71	0.27	67.19	26.53	0.07	10.899	0.00
Krackhardt High Tech	4.92	9.79	0.40	84.86	117.02	0.06	19.766	0.00
Lazega Law Firm	4.61	8.40	1.96	40.26	55.73	0.05	551.532	0.02
Physicians	5.06	6.36	2.93	1342.36	66.83	0.46	1451.43	0.10
EU Air	3.66	6.12	1.58	3142.33	217.67	0.30	851.04	0.98
London	2.73	1.52	2.10	138.84	95.46	0.04	131.88	0.03

For each network, Table 2 shows how different layouts behave with respect to
the two aforementioned measures (internal fit and external fit) in the plots. We
remind the reader that high values of the former means that some layers have
not been correctly visualized according to their internal structure, for example,
the nodes in a community may have been spread around instead of being close
to each other. A high value of the latter means that nodes are not aligned across
layers, for example, a node may have been visualized in the top left corner in
one layer and in the top right in the other. The ideal case would be to have 0
for both metrics. For each network, several settings have been tested.

As expected, for each network the independent visualization generates nodes
that are not well aligned, represented by high external forces active on the nodes.
On the contrary, computing the layout based on one layer prevents other layers
from having good internal layouts, as shown by the high internal forces active

on the nodes when the aligned strategy is used. The balanced option (first case) presents internal layouts that are less good than the ideal case, and node alignments that are also less good than the best possible option, but both are significantly better than the aspect not optimized using other strategies. In practice, this corresponds to layouts similar to the one shown in Fig. 4. The multi-graph approach presents results that in many cases may seem similar to the average of the results obtained using the aligned approach. However, consider that the results for the aligned approach are an average, where for each test the layout is computed on a different layer. Therefore, with the aligned approach there is always one layer with nearly optimal internal fit (that is, with a very low value).

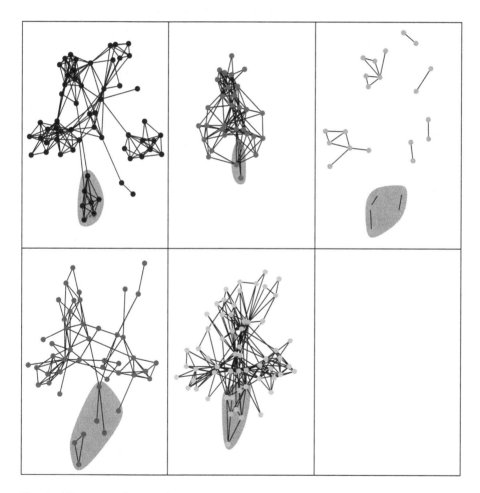

Fig. 4. Alignment of network structures across layers using a balanced visualization, with both intra-layer and inter-layer forces active. One community in the first layer has been highlighted, and the same nodes are also highlighted on the other layers (when present)

3.2 Qualitative Evaluation of the New Balanced Layout

In Fig. 4 we have visualized the 5-layer social network already shown in the introduction using both inter- and intra-layer forces, following the intuition discussed in the previous section about the ability of this setting to keep nodes reasonably aligned while preserving intra-layer structures. Each layer has been drawn according to their internal organization, showing peculiar structures: for example, the nodes in the community marked in the top-left diagram are not present in all the other layers, and where present they are not so well connected to each other. However, we can also see how the nodes belonging to this community have been visualized at similar locations in the other layers, providing information about inter-layer relationships. We can see, for example, that the community is split into two sub-communities in the third (top-right) layer, that it is not present in the fourth layer, where the same nodes are connected to different parts of the graph but a core subset of them is still forming a triangle, and that they form a similar but less dense community in the fifth layer. Notice that in the fourth layer the nodes are still more or less in the same position as in the first layer, despite the fact that they do not form a community. In this way it becomes easier to locate them – in an interactive plot we can also use a 2.5-dimensional visualization as in the previous section, making the task straightforward as long as the nodes are more or less aligned.

4 Related Work

In this section we describe existing approaches to compute network layouts with a single type of edges, also known as monoplex networks, and for multiplex networks.

4.1 Monoplex Network Visualization

Many layouts have been designed to visualize monoplex networks. Here we briefly review the ones that are more relevant for our approach. For an extensive review, the reader may consult [29].

Multi-scale layouts first create some core sub graphs, then they add other nodes until all nodes and edges have been processed [17,29]. *Random layouts* [6] and *circular layouts* [20] are two categories of layouts which are appropriate for small graphs with few nodes and edges, because they do not consider aesthetic criteria: many edge crossings and node overlappings can appear.

Among the most used visualization methods, *force-directed* algorithms consider a graph as a physical system where forces change the position of nodes. The two best known force-directed layouts are *Fruchterman-Reingold* [10] and *Kamada-Kawai* [14,15]. In the Fruchterman-Reingold layout nodes have repulsive power and push other nodes away, while edges attract neighboring nodes. In this layout nodes are considered as steel rings having similar loads and edges are like springs attracting neighbouring rings. This algorithm consists of three main steps. First, all nodes are distributed randomly. Second, repulsive forces separate nodes. The value of repulsive force depends on the positions of the nodes. Third, for each edge and based on the position of nodes after repulsion, attractive forces are calculated [10]. In the Kamada-Kawai layout an energy function is defined for the whole graph based on shortest paths between nodes, and positions are iteratively updated until the graph's energy is minimized [15].

Bannister et al. [1] proposed a force-directed layout to change the position of nodes so that more graph-theoretically central nodes are pushed towards the centre of the diagram. In this algorithm, an additional force called gravity is used to change the position of more central nodes. For each node v in a graph G the position of the node is influenced by the following force:

$$I[v] = \sum_{u,v \in V} f_r(u,v) + \sum_{(u,v) \in E} f_a(u,v) + \sum_{v \in V} f_g(v) \tag{1}$$

where f_r and f_a are respectively repulsive and attractive forces, and f_g is the gravity force, measured as:

$$f_g(v) = \gamma_t M[v](\xi - P[v]) \tag{2}$$

In this equation $M[v]$ is the mass of node v, which can be set according to node degree, $P[v]$ is the position of v, γ_t is the gravitational parameter and $\xi = \Sigma_v P[v]/|V|$ is the centroid of all nodes. Notice that forces in the equations above are vectors.

Other extensions of force-directed layouts have considered the inclusion of additional domain-specific information in the definition of the forces. An example is [34], where the definitions of attractive and repulsive forces include terms representing trust in social networks.

Traditional force-directed methods are suitable only for small networks, but they are very popular because they often practically succeed in highlighting communities (that is, groups of well connected nodes) and increasing graph readability. To address their shortcomings, force-based layout algorithms are sometimes split into multiple phases, with an initial preprocessing of the data to generate good starting node dispositions or to reduce data complexity. As an example, Gajer et al.'s method first partitions the graph into subgraphs [31]. The smallest subgraph is then processed independently and thus more efficiently. Afterwards, a force-directed refinement round changes the values of initial node positions and the next smallest subgraph is added to the previous one, with these steps being repeated untill all nodes have been processed. [35] follows the same steps, setting initial node positions in a different way. Similarly, Peng et al. proposed the Social Network Analysis Layout (SNAL) by also separating a network into subgroups, analyzing relationships between them and positioning nodes based on their relative centralities [32]. Recent works have shown how to use force-based approaches on relatively large graphs [33].

Another family of layouts, that can also be combined with force-directed algorithms, are *constraint-based* layouts [9]. These layouts force nodes to appear at specific positions. For example, nodes are placed on a frame in a way that they do not overlap, or are horizontally and vertically aligned, as in the *orthogonal* layout [9,29]. In these layouts it is more difficult to isolate special structures such as communities and time complexity is noticeably high.

One important assumption in graph drawing is a correspondence between some aesthetic features of the diagrams and their readability. Therefore, some visualization algorithms explicitly target these features. One such criterion is that too many edge crossings make a graph more difficult to interpret. The crossing number $cr(G)$ of a graph G is the smallest number of crossings appearing in any drawing of G [27]. Several algorithms have been proposed to reduce edge crossing in monoplex networks. For example, Shabbeer et al. [28] developed a stress majorization algorithm, as initial proposed in [11]. In [27] and [2] the concept of edge crossing is elaborated and equations for measuring the number of edge crossings in different graphs are reviewed. Another aesthetic feature impacting graph readability is node overlapping. Two popular methods to reduce node overlapping were proposed in [12,18].

4.2   Multiplex Network Visualization

Different methods have been discussed for visualizing multiplex networks. We categorize these methods into four main classes: slicing, flattening, simplification-based, and indirect.

One way of visualizing multiplex networks is to consider each layer or relationship type as a monoplex network and to connect these monoplex networks using inter-layer edges [4]. The layers can have aligned layouts or independent layouts, as shown in our initial example. Aligned layouts help users find similar nodes in different layers by forcing the same node to have the same coordinates on all layers, but structures existing only on one layer (for example communities) may not be clearly visualized. Independent layouts can show specific structures of each layer, but may hide inter-layer patterns [26].

In flattening-based methods all nodes and edges are placed on the same plane. In a *node-colored* network, nodes from different layers are shown with different colors [16], while for multiplex networks colors can be used to distinguish edges of different types. Apart from suffering from the same problems of aligned slicing, the disadvantage of this method is that for networks with high edge density relationships among nodes can be hidden by edges from non-relevant layers and readability quickly decreases due to the network's clutter.

Given the information overload associated to the presence of multiple types of edges, a third approach consists in adding a so called *simplification* step before using one of the two approaches above [26]. The simplification step removes edges or layers that are not considered relevant for the visualization task. In general, this can also be used as a pre-processing step before computing our multiforce layout.

The last approach tries to visualize information derived from the network instead of directly visualizing the original layers, which are again considered to be too complex to allow a simple visual representation. Renoust et al. [25] proposed a system for visual analysis of group cohesion in flattened multiplex networks. This system, called *Detangler*, creates a so-called substrate network from unique nodes of the multiplex network and a so-called catalyst network from edges of different types. Erten et al. [30] proposed three modified force-directed approaches for creating slicing, flattened and split views of multilayer networks by considering edge weights and node weights. The weights of nodes and edges are based on the number of times they appear in different layers. In this approach interlayer relationships between nodes are ignored and node weights are the same for all nodes when multiplex networks are visualized, so this approach does not consider the specific features of the networks targeted in our work.

An extreme case of indirect methods, that we mention for completeness, consists in not visualizing nodes and edges at all but only indirect network properties, such as the degree of the nodes in the different layers or other summary measures [4,24,26]. These approaches are complementary to graph drawing, and can also be used in combination with our proposal.

5 Conclusion

A theoretically optimal force-based layout for multiplex networks would be able to reveal the structure of each layer and the relationships between different layers at the same time. Unfortunately, this is not possible in general, because these two aspects may not be aligned in real data, with some layers not being similar to the others.

To address this problem, we proposed multiforce, a force-directed algorithm in which both intra-layer and inter-layer forces can affect the position of nodes. Intra-layer forces keep connected nodes together and improve the identification of communities, while inter-layer forces help users finding the same nodes in different layers.

In the evaluation of the method we showed that while the algorithm supports more traditional layouts it can also generate what we call *balanced visualizations* where both internal properties and node alignments are handled. This has been presented on a real dataset, to give a qualitative idea of how the layouts produced by this approach look like, and quantitatively, introducing two quality metrics and showing how a balanced approach can satisfactorily address both at the same time on several real datasets from different domains. At the same time, traditional approaches are better at optimizing either one or the other quality metric. We thus believe that the main value of multiforce is its ability to represent all the strategies mentioned in the article, so that an analyst can switch from one to the other depending on which aspects s/he wants to focus on.

Acknowledgements. We thank Prof. Ken Wakita for his comments on an early version of this manuscript, and Prof. Mats Lind for insightful discussions. The work by Matteo Magnani has been funded by the European Union's Horizon 2020 research and innovation programme under grant agreement No 732027.

References

1. Bannister, M.J., Eppstein, D., Goodrich, M.T., Trott, L.: Force-directed graph drawing using social gravity and scaling. In: Didimo, W., Patrignani, M. (eds.) GD 2012. LNCS, vol. 7704, pp. 414–425. Springer, Heidelberg (2013). https://doi.org/10.1007/978-3-642-36763-2_37
2. Buchheim, C., Chimani, M., Gutwenger, C., Jnger, M., Mutzel, P.: Crossings and Planarization. CRC Press, Hoboken (2013)
3. Cardillo, A., Gómez-Gardeñes, J., Zanin, M., Romance, M., Papo, D., del Pozo, F., Boccaletti, S.: Emergence of network features from multiplexity. Sci. Rep. **3**, 1344 (2013)
4. De Domenico, M., Porter, M.A., Arenas, A.: MuxViz: a tool for multilayer analysis and visualization of networks. J. Complex Netw. **3**, 159–176 (2014)
5. De Domenico, M., Solé-Ribalta, A., Gòmez, S., Arenas, A.: Navigability of interconnected networks under random failures. PNAS **111**, 8351–8356 (2014)
6. Díaz, J., Petit, J., Serna, M.: A survey of graph layout problems. ACM Comput. Surv. **34**(3), 313–356 (2002)
7. Dwyer, T., Gallagher, D.R.: Visualising changes in fund manager holdings in two and a half-dimensions. Inf. Vis. **4**(3), 227–244 (2004)
8. Brandes, U., Mader, M.: A quantitative comparison of stress-minimization approaches for offline dynamic graph drawing. In: van Kreveld, M., Speckmann, B. (eds.) GD 2011. LNCS, vol. 7034, pp. 99–110. Springer, Heidelberg (2012). https://doi.org/10.1007/978-3-642-25878-7_11
9. Dwyer, T., Marriott, K., Schreiber, F., Stuckey, P., Woodward, M., Wybrow, M.: Exploration of networks using overview+detail with constraint-based cooperative layout. IEEE Trans. Vis. Comput. Graph. **14**(6), 1293–300 (2008)
10. Fruchterman, T.M.J., Reingold, E.M.: Graph drawing by force-directed placement. Softw. Pract. Exp. **21**(11), 1129–1164 (1991)
11. Gansner, E.R., Koren, Y., North, S.: Graph drawing by stress majorization. In: Pach, J. (ed.) GD 2004. LNCS, vol. 3383, pp. 239–250. Springer, Heidelberg (2005). https://doi.org/10.1007/978-3-540-31843-9_25
12. Huang, X., Lai, W., Sajeev, A.S.M., Gao, J.: A new algorithm for removing node overlapping in graph visualization. Inf. Sci. **177**(14), 2821–2844 (2007)
13. Coleman, H.M.J., Katz, E.: The diffusion of an innovation among physicians. Sociometry **20**(4), 253–270 (1957)
14. Moody, J., McFarland, D., Bender deMoll, S.: Dynamic network visualization. Am. J. Sociol. **110**(4), 1206–1241 (2005)
15. Kamada, T., Kawai, S.: An algorithm for drawing general undirected graphs. Inf. Process. Lett. **31**(1), 7–15 (1989)
16. Kivelä, M., Arenas, A., Barthelemy, M., Gleeson, J.P., Moreno, Y., Porter, M.A.: Multilayer networks. J. Complex Netw. **2**(3), 203–271 (2014)
17. Koren, Y., Carmel, L., Harel, D.: ACE: a fast multiscale eigenvectors computation for drawing huge graphs. In: IEEE Symposium on Information Visualization, INFOVIS 2002, pp. 137–144 (2002)
18. Kumar, P., Zhang, K.: Visualization of clustered directed acyclic graphs with node interleaving. In: Proceedings of the 2009 ACM Symposium on Applied Computing, SAC 2009, New York, NY, USA, pp. 1800–1805. ACM (2009)
19. Kurant, M., Thiran, P.: Layered complex networks. Phys. Rev. Lett. **96**(13), 138701 (2006)

20. Ma, D.: Visualization of social media data: mapping changing social networks. Master's thesis, the Faculty of Geo-Information Science and Earth Observation of the University of Twent (2012)

21. Magnani, M., Rossi, L.: The ML-model for multi-layer social networks. In: Proceedings of the International Conference on Social Network Analysis and Mining (ASONAM), pp. 5–12. IEEE Computer Society (2011)

22. Moreno, J.: Who Shall Survive?: A New Approach to the Problem of Human Inter-relations. Nervous and Mental Disease Publishing Co., Washington, D.C. (1934)

23. Padgett, J.F., McLean, P.D.: Organizational invention and elite transformation: the birth of partnership systems in renaissance florence. Am. J. Sociol. **111**(5), 1463–1568 (2006)

24. Redondo, D., Sallaberry, A., Ienco, D., Zaidi, F., Poncelet, P.: Layer-centered approach for multigraphs visualization. In: Proceedings of the International Conference on Information Visualisation (iV), pp. 50–55 (2015)

25. Renoust, B., Melanon, G., Munzner, T.: Detangler: visual analytics for multiplex networks. Comput. Graph. Forum **34**(3), 321–330 (2015)

26. Rossi, L., Magnani, M.: Towards effective visual analytics on multiplex and multi-layer networks. Chaos Solitons Fractals **72**, 68–76 (2015)

27. Schaefer, M.: The graph crossing number and its variants: a survey. Electron. J. Comb. **1000**, DS21 (2013)

28. Shabbeer, A., Ozcaglar, C., Gonzalez, M., Bennett, KP.: Optimal embedding of heterogeneous graph data with edge crossing constraints. In: Presented at NIPS Workshop on Challenges of Data Visualization, p. 1 (2010)

29. von Landesberger, T., et al.: Visual analysis of large graphs: state-of-the-art and future research challenges. Comput. Graph. Forum **30**(6), 1719–1749 (2011)

30. Erten, C., Kobourov, S.G., Le, V., Navabi, A.: Simultaneous graph drawing: layout algorithms and visualization schemes. In: Liotta, G. (ed.) GD 2003. LNCS, vol 2912, pp. 437–449. Springer, Heidelberg (2004). https://doi.org/10.1007/978-3-540-24595-7_41

31. Gajer, P., Goodrich, M.T., Kobourov, S.G.: A multi-dimensional approach to force-directed layouts of large graphs. Comput. Geom. **29**(1), 3–18 (2004)

32. Peng, W., SiKun, L.: Social network analysis layout algorithm under ontology model. SOFTWARE **6**(7), 3–18 (2011)

33. Ortmann, M., Klimenta, M., Brandes, U.: A sparse stress model. J. Graph Algorithms Appl. **21**(5), 791–821 (2017)

34. Ma, N., Lu, Y., Gan, H., Li, Z.: 2013 10th Web Information System and Application Conference - Trust Network Visualization Based on Force-Directed Layout, (wisa), yangzhou, china, 10 November 2013–15 November 2013 (2013)

35. Baur, M., Brandes, U., Gaertler, M., Wagner, D.: Drawing the AS graph in 2.5 dimensions. In: Pach, J. (ed.) GD 2004. LNCS, vol. 3383, pp. 43–48. Springer, Heidelberg (2005). https://doi.org/10.1007/978-3-540-31843-9_6

The Anatomy of a Web of Trust:
The Bitcoin-OTC Market

Bertazzi Ilaria[1], Huet Sylvie[1], Deffuant Guillaume[1], and Gargiulo Floriana[2(✉)]

[1] IRSTEA, 9 Avenue Blaise Pascal, 63170 Aubiere, France
ilaria.bertazzi@irstea.fr
[2] CNRS, GEMASS, 20 rue du Berbier du Mets, 57013 Paris, France
floriana.gargiulo@gmail.com

Abstract. Bitcoin-otc is a peer to peer, over-the-counter marketplace for trading with bitcoin crypto-currency. To mitigate the risks of the unsupervised exchanges, the establishment of a reliable reputation systems is needed: for this reason, a web of trust is implemented on the website. The availability of all the historic of the users interaction data makes this dataset a unique playground for studying reputation dynamics through others evaluations. We analyze the structure and the dynamics of this web of trust with a multilayer network approach distinguishing the rewarding and the punitive behaviors. We show that the rewarding and the punitive behavior have similar emergent topological properties (apart from the clustering coefficient being higher for the rewarding layer) and that the resultant reputation originates from the complex interaction of the more regular behaviors on the layers. We show which are the behaviors that correlate (i.e. the rewarding activity) or not (i.e. the punitive activity) with reputation. We show that the network activity presents bursty behaviors on both the layers and that the inequality reaches a steady value (higher for the rewarding layer) with the network evolution. Finally, we characterize the reputation trajectories and we identify prototypical behaviors associated to three classes of users: trustworthy, untrusted and controversial.

Keywords: Reputation · Webs of trust · Multilayer networks · Bitcoin

1 Introduction

Bitcoin, perhaps the most hip cripto-currency currently available, consists in a purely peer-to-peer version of electronic cash; it is used for on line payments to be sent directly from one trading party to the other without going through a financial institution [2]. In such an anonymous, decentralized exchange system, mutual trust plays a crucial role in determining the feasibility of a vivid marketplace. Digital signatures and peer-to-peer network of data sharing over transactions provide part of the solution, in which the second one is specifically

Supported by CNRS-INFINITI.

thought as a tool to prevent any double spending behavior. However in over-the-count markets, where alongside with bitcoin, other crypto and real currencies and other types of goods are exchanged peer to peer, without a central control, a user-generated system to establish the credibility of individuals, as buyer and sellers, is needed. It is not only to guarantee the actual transaction of value, but also to monitor the goodness of the global exchange, and the correct behavior of anonymous users.

The case of the platform considered here, the Bitcoin-OTC market [3], goes beyond the well known user-reputation mechanisms. These classical mechanisms are implemented in many system of on line platforms (ratings, gradings, reviews, etc.) that are now ubiquitous for any form of exchange, both virtual and physical, and sometimes even human interactions, from restaurant [5] to hosting [4] and carpooling services, and so on. In our case, a recently rising system of user reputation is implemented: the Web of Trust.

Web of Trust is originated in cryptography, where it defined a structure of public and private key exchange, to establish the authenticity of the binding between a public key and its owner. It consists in a decentralized trust model (alternative to the ones which relies on a certificate authority). The idea is that, as time goes on, users accumulate keys from other people that they may want to designate as trusted introducers. Users gradually accumulate and distribute with their key a collection of certifying signatures from others. This will create a decentralized fault-tolerant web of confidence for all public keys. The scheme is flexible and leaves trust decisions in the hands of individual users [1]. In web 2.0 applications, the idea beyond the Web of Trust is to provide a way to grant mutual trust between buyers and sellers that have no direct interactions, but it is based on the experience other users: the peculiarity lies in the fact that the "intermediary" is already in the proximity of both users. The Web of Trust is created by the complex interactions between users, and the emergent structure it assumes is the resultant of the collective intelligence the virtual community can put in place. Understanding the structure and the dynamics of this kind of objects is therefore crucial both for analyzing the robustness of the OTC markets and, more in general, as a controlled playground to understand the reputation formation mechanisms. Different simulation models exist to explain the formation of reputation hierarchies [7,8] and several experimental studies [9], online and offline have been realized in the last years. But data-driven studies in this field remain rares [10], because of the difficulties to find available data on p2p interactions. While the recent literature on user-item evaluation system is enormous, due to the amount of available data in commercial and Q&A platforms, the Bitcoin-OTC database is one of the extremely few cases allowing us to study, from the beginning to the end, the evolution of reputation in a community as the direct effect of others' evaluations.

The specific features of the Bitcoin-OTC dataset that require careful attention are mainly two: firstly, the fact that reputation here is not seen as direct effect of the entire interaction history of a user, but actors perceive another user's trust relying only on the ratings of people she trusts in the first place. The *get-*

trust command on which this mechanism is based shows the cumulative trust for a person coming from people that users trust directly, capped by how much they are trusted. The second feature is given by the website guidelines on what ratings to hand out: +1 is the first rate to be given to a new person with which a user had a good transaction, as the number of well gone interactions between the same couple of users increases, the rate may be updated upwards, where +10 is to be reserved for *"close friends and associates you know in person"*, whereas negative rates are given after a not so good, or really bad transaction. Other considerations like the size of transactions, relationship nature and interaction, length of history, etc., may impact. Because of the specificities of the dataset and the relative importance of such feature also for other similar datasets, we approached them via a multilayer network approach [11], as we will justify in the next section.

The paper continues as follows: Sect. 2 presents the data structure and the analytical method used, Sect. 3 presents the results in terms of static properties of the ratings network, temporal activity of the interactions over 6-years observations, and network dynamical properties. Conclusions follows with some behavioral hypothesis that may explain the presented results.

2   Data and Methods

Bitcoin-otc is a peer to peer (over-the-counter) marketplace for trading with bitcoin. To mitigate the risks of the p2p unsupervised exchanges, a Web of Trust is implemented to have access to the counterpart's reputation before transactions, as presented above. In this Web of Trust an user i can rate another user j with an integer score s_{ij} varying between –10 to 10. The dataset has been directly mined by the web page [3]. The dataset contains 5,878 users and 35,795 ratings exchanged between 2011 and 2017.

The website proposes a behavioral rule concerning the scores: it is suggested to assign the score 1 to a positive rating if the rater met the rated only once and to reinforce using higher scores in case of repeated meetings. This rule generates a high prevalence of $s_{ij} = 1$ but, at the same time, it is frequently broken: repeated interactions among the users remain extremely rare and high scores are assigned also at the first interaction. We assume that the socio-psychological micro-mechanisms governing rewarding and punitive ratings could be a priori different. Due to this reason we study the web of trust as a multiplex weighted directed network with two different layers: the rewarding layer, L^+, containing only the positive scores and the punitive layer, L^-, containing the negative scores.

Each user is therefore identified with a node both on the rewarding and the punitive layer. On both the layers the weighted edges are labelled with the time of the interaction and with the absolute value of the score associated ($w_{ij} = s_{ij}$ for the rewarding layer and $w_{ij} = -s_{ij}$ for the punitive).

As predictable [15, 16], the number of edges on the rewarding layer ($N_e^+ = 32305$) is much higher than in the punitive one ($N_e^- = 3490$). As we can observe in Fig. 1, also the distribution of the scores is different between the two layers: in L^+, due to the norm suggested by the website, the score $s = 1$ is dominant, while in L^- in order to emphasize the punitive gesture the score $s = -10$ is the most frequent.

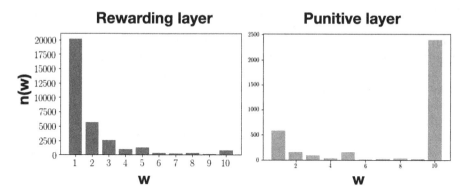

Fig. 1. Weight distribution for the rewarding (left plot) and the punitive (right plot) layer

To each node i we associate the following of values:

– **In-degrees = number of received scores on the two layers**

$$k_{in}(i) = (k_{in}^+(i), k_{in}^-(i)) \tag{1}$$

– **Out-degrees = number of given scores (activity) on the two layers**

$$k_{out}(i) = (k_{out}^+(i), k_{out}^-(i)) \tag{2}$$

– **Positive and Negative reputation**

$$\rho^+(i) = \sum_j w_{ji}^+, \rho^-(i) = \sum_j w_{ji}^- \tag{3}$$

Finally, for each user we define the global reputation, as it is reported and visible for all the users on the website:

$$\rho(i) = \rho^+(i) - \rho^-(i) \tag{4}$$

3   Results

3.1   Static Properties

We start analyzing the aggregate properties of the network, where the time label of the network edges is not considered. In Fig. 2A we analyze the probability distributions of the positive and negative reputation. We notice that, notwithstanding the significant differences between the score distributions and the number of edges of the two layers, the two reputations follow the same power law distribution. In the inset, we displayed the distribution of users' global reputation ρ. The global reputation is definitely not symmetric, showing non-trivial interactions between the two layers. Clustering coefficient measures the tendency to form triangles in a network: for a node i, a clustering coefficient $c(i) = 1$ signifies that in its neighborhood are all connected as a triangle; $c(i) = 0$, on the contrary, implies a star topology (without triangles). The clustering coefficient of nodes as function of the total degree (for the undirected and unweighted version of the network) is displayed in Fig. 2B. We can observe that, for the rewarding layer, the clustering is in general higher than for the punitive layer, above all for high degree nodes. Comparing each layer with a randomized reshuffling of the network that maintains the degree distribution (configuration model), we observe that the clustering coefficient is higher than the null case for the rewarding layer and lower for the punitive. This is coherent with balance theory suggesting that, in a triadic structure, three negative interactions are not balanced ([6,12]). For investigating the role of the norm proposed concerning the score 1, we further divided the L^+ in a layer with $w_{ij} > 1$ and another one with $w_{ij} = 1$. The average value of the clustering for the first case is $\langle c_{(>1)} \rangle = 0.063$, while for the second case it is lower $\langle c_{(=1)} \rangle = 0.022$. This suggests that breaking of the norm could be due to triangular structures: users trust someone not only because of interaction they directly had but also because of the trust friends address her.

In Fig. 2C we study the average degree of neighbors as a function of the node degree. For both layers this indicator decreases with the degree, indicating a typical disassortative mixing (low degree users are preferentially connected to high degree ones and vice-versa), extremely diffused in social networks.

After the statistical properties, we concentrated on the nodes' ranking according to the different attributes. In particular, $k_{in}^+, k_{in}^-, k_{out}^+, k_{out}^-$ and ρ. In Fig. 2F we represented these quantities according to the ranking for k_{in}^+, the number of positive ratings received. The nodes with a high in-degree in the rewarding layer usually are the most active (high out-degree both on the rewarding and the punitive layer), and clearly have high reputation. Notice however that the nodes higher in the k_{in}^+ ranking also receive several negative scores (k_{in}^-). In Fig. 2G we compare nodes' ranking according to these measures, using the Kendall-Tau index. We observe that reputation is clearly correlated with the number of received scores in the rewarding layer (k_{in}^+) and with the rewarding activity (k_{out}^+). On the contrary the punitive activity (k_{out}^-), and the number of incoming negative scores (k_{in}^-) are scarcely correlated with all the other measures.

To reinforce such findings we represent the mean and standard deviation of ρ of each k_{in} level in Figs. 2D and E for both layers. It is even more clear that users' reputation is positively related to incoming interactions of the rewarding layer, whereas it is not so clearly correlated on the punishing one (it grows then becomes stable).

Users' Categorization. We analyze now the users' properties between the two layers, and in particular we analyze the position of the users in the space (ρ^+, ρ^-).

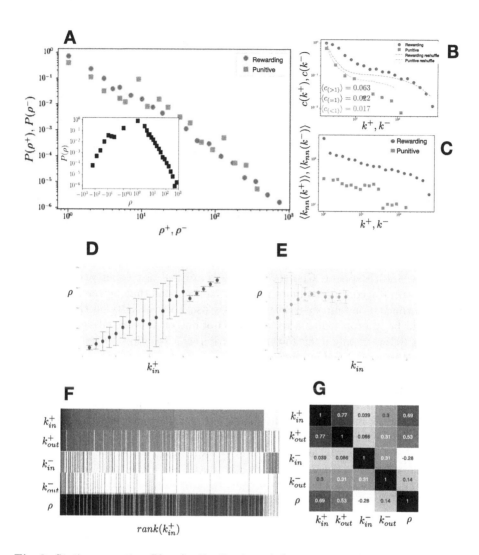

Fig. 2. Static properties. Plot A: distribution of the positive and the negative reputation. Inset: Global distribution of the reputation. Plot B: Clustering coefficient spectrum for the rewarding and the punitive layer, compared with the spectrum for a randomized version of the network. Plot C: Average neighbors degree spectrum for the two layers. Plot D: mean and standard deviation of the reputation as a function of the in-degrees of the rewarding layer. Plot E: mean and standard deviation of the reputation as a function of the in-degrees of the punitive layer. Plot F: In and out degrees of the nodes on the two layers and reputation, with the nodes sorted according to the in-degree ranking. Plot G: Kendall–Tau index between the node rankings for in and out degrees on the two layers and for reputation.

We divide the plane in three areas, as described in Fig. 3A: $A1 = [\rho^+ < 0.25\rho^-]$, $A2 = [0.25\rho^- < \rho^+ < 0.75\rho^-]$, $A3 = [\rho^+ > 0.75\rho^-]$.

The users in the first area, $A1$, have an high positive reputation and a low negative, therefore, in this area we can place *trustworthy* users. On the contrary the users in the third area, $A3$, are *untrusted*, having low positive and high negative reputation. Finally, the users in the second area, $A2$, are *controversial* having similar values for positive and negative reputation. The largest part of the users are trustworthy. In the plot of Fig. 3B we can observe the distribution of the global reputations in the three different areas. Not surprisingly the untrusted users have a negative reputation and the trustworthy ones a positive one. Reputations associated to the controversial are lower. More interestingly, we can observe that the untrusted users have in general a lower activity (k_{out}) on both layers. Controversial users have a similar activity on the two layers and in general have the highest activity on the punitive layer. Finally the trustworthy users are extremely active for rewarding and much less for punishing. We can argue that the untrusted users are like "trolls" appearing and cheating one or more users just once. In such a way they quickly construct their negative reputation and disappear. Controversial users are real users that gain and give negative scores according to more complex mechanisms that better mimic reputation formation in human society. In this sense, their activity on the punitive layer could be interpreted as a reciprocation of one or more negative scores.

In Fig. 3C we finally analyze the reputation as a function of the aggregated in-degree (the sum of the number of ratings received on each layer). In an ideal case, if at each interaction the score $s = 1$ is received, as it should be if the users were following the rule proposed by the website, the points should be placed on the line $\rho(t) = k_{in}(t)$. On the contrary, if the maximum or minimum scores would be always given, the points should be placed respectively on the lines $\rho(t) = 10k_{in}(t)$ and $\rho(t) = -10k_{in}(t)$. We can observe that the trustworthy users are located slightly above the $\rho(t) = k_{in}(t)$ line, while the controversial ones slightly beyond. On the contrary, the untrusted users are mostly located on the $\rho(t) = -10k_{in}(t)$ line. We will come back to this point in the last section when analyzing the reputation trajectories.

3.2   Temporal Activity

In this section we analyze the temporal patterns of the network activity. Aggregating events on a daily time window, in Fig. 4 we show the number of edges, namely rating, over time. The rewarding layer shows evident activity peaks. The shadowed areas in the figure represent the three major Bitcoin bubbles and we can observe that the number of events in the web of trust, reasonably corresponding to an increase of the trading activity on the web site, is a growing function in the bubble periods. The punitive layer, on the contrary has generally a very low activity, but important activity burst, not related to the bubbles, appear. In particular an extremely large punitive activity can be identified between the small bubble of 2013 and the big bubble of 2013.

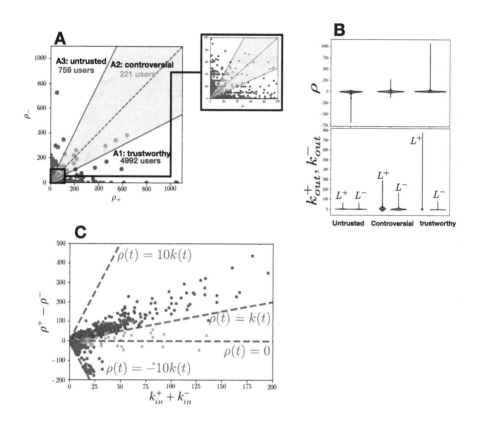

Fig. 3. Plot A: Identification of trustworthy (green), untrusted (blue) and controversial users (orange) with a zoom on the lower values. Plot B: Violin plot of the normed distributions of the reputation (upper plot) and of the activities (lower plot) for the three categories of users. Plot C: reputations of each user as a function of the sum of the in-degrees on the two layers. The colors of the points represent the users' categories (trustworthy, untrusted, controversial). The red lines represent limit reputation growth scenarios: $\rho(t) = 10k_{in}(t)$ is the case when, at each interaction, the maximum score $s = 10$ is received. $\rho(t) = k_{in}(t)$ is the case when, at each interaction, the score $s = 1$ is received, $\rho(t) = -10k_{in}(t)$ is the case when, at each interaction, the minimum score $s = -10$ is received (Color figure online)

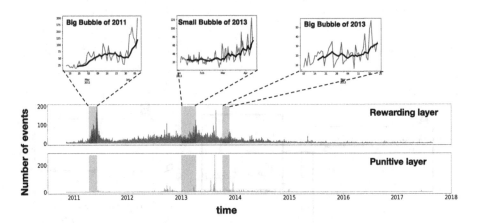

Fig. 4. Number of rating events time series for the rewarding (in blue) and the punitive (in orange) layer. The shadowed areas represent the three major bitcoin bubbles and the upper subplots the zoom of the time series behavior in the bubble periods. (Color figure online)

In Fig. 5A we show the event plot of the two layers: a colored trait represents the days where some activity has been present. The rewarding layer has been active almost continuously between 2012 and 2015. The event plots suggest the presence of burstiness in the system activity: a typical behavior observed in different complex systems, implying activity peaks concentrated on short periods alternated to long inactivity periods [14].

In Fig. 5B we study the inter-event distribution, where the inter-event time Δt is defined as the time elapsed between two subsequent rating events reaching a certain user. The power law behavior of the inter-events is a fingerprint of burstiness, contrarily to the exponential distribution that would be originated by a Poisson process. The measure in the lower plot of Fig. 5A is an indicator of bursty behavior, defined in [14]: B = 1 corresponds to a bursty behavior, B = 0 is neutral, and B = 1 to a regular behavior. We analyze this indicator, separately, for all the years of the data collection. Confirming the observation from the power law inter-events distribution, a bursty behavior is present, above all during the period of major activity of the website. The behavior on the two layers is similar if we look at the inter-event times. However, from the measure of B, we can see the bursty behavior is slightly more pronounced for the punitive layer.

The rating activity follows circadian patterns (Fig. 5C): since most of the Bitcoin-OTC users are located in the US (GTM-6), and that timings are relative to Greenwich time, we can observe that the activity is more intense during the day than during the night. In particular punitive behaviors are more frequent around lunch time, between 11am and 2pm. Also week cycles are present (Fig. 5D), characterized by a lower activity in the week-end. In particular negative behaviors are extremely rare during the week-end.

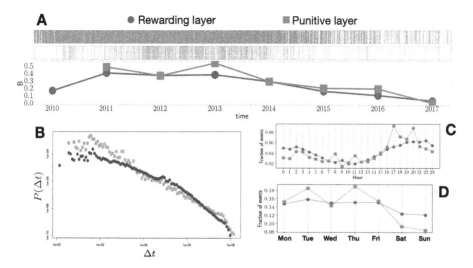

Fig. 5. Plot A: Event plot for the two layers and burstiness coefficient for all the years in the data collection. Plot B: interevent distribution. Plot C: fraction of events as a function of the hour of the day (Greenwich time). Plot D: Fraction of events as a function of the day of the week.

3.3   Network Dynamical Properties

We first perform global measures to understand how positive and negative reputation are distributed. We computed the Gini index for positive and negative reputation. Gini index is an indicator of inequality and it ranges between $Gini = 0$, when an uniform distribution is present, to $Gini = 1$ when all the analyzed quantity is owned by a single individual. Measuring the Gini index for each day of the evolution (Fig. 6A), we observe that both for positive and negative reputations, it increases fast and after it reaches a stable value. The inequality, at the stable point, is in general quite high and larger for the rewarding layer ($G_{eq}^{+} = 0.75$, $G_{eq}^{-} = 0.6$).

Secondly we focus on the reputation ranking, for positive, negative and global reputation. In Fig. 6B we compare the top 10 of the rankings at time t, $top10_t$, with the top 10 of the ranking at time $t + 1$, $top10_{t+1}$, using the extended Jaccard index, introduced in [13]. As for the original Jaccard index the modified version is such that $J(rank1, rank2) = 1$ when the rankings rank1 and rank2 are completely equivalent, and gives a value 0 when these latter are not correlated at all. After a transient period the top 10 lists become quite stable, even if showing continuous fluctuations. Surprisingly the fluctuations of the global reputation do not follow the fluctuation of the positive reputation, meaning the interplay with the punitive layer plays a central role in the reputation dynamics. Moreover reputation top 10 shows a certain regular periodicity, for the period of maximum use of the Bitcoin-OTC site (2012–2015).

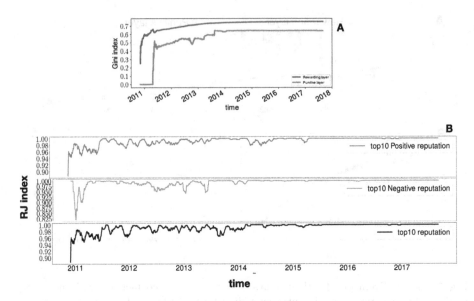

Fig. 6. Plot A: Gini index for positive and negative reputations. Plot B: Extended Jaccard index for the comparison between the top 10 lists at time t and time $t + 1$ for positive, negative and global reputation.

Finally we focus on individual trajectories. For doing this we analyze, for each user, the time flattened trajectories, namely, the sequence of reputation changes (dropping the times when reputation does not change). In the left plot of Fig. 7 we show the trajectories for the users that, at a certain point of the system evolution, entered the top 10 of positive or negative reputations. Notice that while the users in the top 10 of positive reputation have a linear growth, with a slope usually higher than one, users in the top 10 of negative reputations, can in general have high global reputations since they alternate phases of growing positive reputation and phases of growing negative reputation. In the right plot of Fig. 7 we show the trajectories for trustworthy, untrusted and controversial users, as defined previously. Untrusted users have fast linear reputation decreasing trajectories while trustworthy users have slow linear increasing trajectories. Controversial users experience phases of reputation growth following the slow linear trend of trusted users alternated to fast reputation crashes, following the fast linear trend of untrusted users.

4   Conclusions

This paper aims to analyze an interesting database of an online p2p exchange community, over the mutual evaluation of users in respect to trading behaviors. We choose a Network analysis approach, with a multilayer representation, because it allows to distinguish the specific features of rewarding and punitive behaviors.

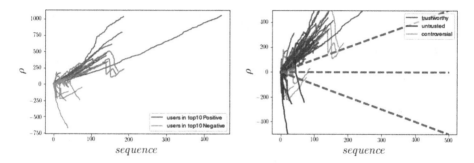

Fig. 7. Left plot: Flattened reputation trajectories for users in the top 10 list of positive and negative reputations. Right plot: Flattened reputation trajectories for trustworthy, untrusted and controversial users.

The dataset is characterized by a great majority of positive rates, where in most cases interactions happens only once. This leads, given the suggested rule in attributing the rates presented in the second paragraph, to a great abundance of rates = 1, but the clustering coefficient for ratings higher than 1, presented in Sect. 3.1 also underlines another aspect: the Web of Trust idea reinforces rewards even in the first encounter, when a mutual trustee is present, despite of the suggested guidelines. Looking at the ranking on in/out degree on the two layers, we can make the hypothesis that there exists a virtuous circle of activity on the rewarding layer (having a series of good rate is correlated to giving good grades), but the fact of having several negative incoming votes is not uniquely coming from retaliation behavior, as underlined by the fact that people with high k_{in}^+ may also have many k_{in}^-. In terms of accumulation of positive and negative ratings as interactions increase, we can see that, from Fig. 2, that where the rewarding layer behaves intuitively, the punishing one is slightly more complex to explain: this is possible to make the hypothesis that there is a strategic behaviour on the side of some users, that increases their reputation on the negative side of the network, but also have to increase the positive reputation in order to remain active in the system and find possible new interactions.

If we look at the specific users' trajectories, we can subdivide the reputaion (a proxy of the goodness/viciousness of a user's trading behavior) in three categories: *trustworthy, untrusted* and *controversial.* Where the growth of the first group is steady and linear, the second group exhibits a non symmetric, steeper degrowth, leading to the idea that punishing rates are more firmly and quickly given than trust is granted. *Controversial* behaviour on the other hand displays a mix of both trajectories. Dynamically, it is to expect that the reputation distribution gets more and more unequal because of the persistence of some users, that are active since the beginning, and the newcomers who still have to accumulate credibility. This is reinforced also if we look at the top-10, which become more and more stable.

Going beyond the analysis of the Bitcoin-OTC market, several other noticeable results, concerning human reputation studies, can be pointed out from our analysis and deserve discussions. Firstly, our results show that reputation is gained slowly while it is lost sharply. This result has been already proven in psychological experiments like [19,23]; in particular, this studies prove that good reputation is more easily lost than gained, and authors have argued about some complementary explanations for this phenomenon, like the idea of asymmetry of trust [21], or the heuristics used for an impression judgment: judgments are inordinately influenced by an actor's more negative attributes. This is probably related to the fact a negative information is perceived as more diagnostic of an actor's true character than positive information [17].

Secondly, we noticed that despite the rule given by the platform, some users, relying on intermediary users, rate higher than 1 at their first transaction. This is a real peculiarity of social systems, which can't be easily governed by an a priori institution: social norms emerge from the interaction between users and are hardly predictable. This is particularly true when the behaviour to adopt is advised by trusted users as shown by the Theory of Reasoned Action [18]. This theory points out how important is the subjective norm, the norm recommended by the important others, in the decision-making regarding the behaviour to adopt.

A final comment about *controversial* users: it is possible to argue that they maintain themselves in the system through a particular strategy. But this would imply that they have the capacity to control the rate they receive, which is not really in accordance with our second noticeable result. Differently we may argue that *controversial* users emerge from different strategies over the next rate to give. The anchoring bias, exhibited by [22], is known as impacting the value given by a user, based on the value proposed by the adviser, i.e. the anchor. Then, when users base their choice of an adviser on his global reputation, this can be very different from when they use their trusted users's trust as an anchor. This particular anchor can vary from the global reputation, but also from a user to another since the set of trusted users is not the same. When users have two types of information, global reputation, and trust from their trusted users, we know that the global reputation, that we can assimilate to the descriptive norm, is not very strong in behavior determination [20]. When a user receives a negative rating, event becoming more and more probable due to the fact it has to satisfy the increasing expectations [24], she can enter in a negative loop, and perhaps being saved by few people. Overall, despite the fact our work show the existence of controversial users, we don't know much about the conditions of their emergence and maintenance. This is certainly an issue for next studies.

References

1. Caronni, G.: Walking the web of trust. In: Proceedings IEEE 9th International Workshops on Enabling Technologies: Infrastructure for Collaborative Enterprises, pp. 153–158, Gaithersburg, MD (2000)
2. Nakamoto, S.: Bitcoin: a peer-to-peer electronic cash system (2008). https://bitcoin.org/bitcoin.pdf
3. https://bitcoin-otc.com . Accessed 13 May 2018

4. Lauterbach, D., et al.: Surfing a web of trust: reputation and reciprocity on couch-surfing.com. In: International Conference on Computational Science and Engineering, vol. 4. IEEE (2009)

5. Scellato, S., et al.: Socio-spatial properties of online location-based social networks. ICWSM **11**, 329–336 (2011)

6. Heider, F.: Social perception and phenomenal causality. Psychol. Rev. **51**(6), 358 (1944)

7. Deffuant, G.: The leviathan model: absolute dominance generalised distrust, small worlds and other patterns emerging from combining vanity with opinion propagation. JASSS **16**(1), 5 (2013)

8. Manzo, G.: Heuristics, interactions, and status hierarchies: an agent-based model of deference exchange. Soc. Methods Res. **44**(2), 329–387 (2015)

9. Vincenz, F.V., et al.: Arbitrary inequality in reputation systems. Sci. Rep. **6**, 38304 (2016)

10. Richardson, M., Agrawal, R., Domingos, P.: Trust management for the semantic web. In: Fensel, D., Sycara, K., Mylopoulos, J. (eds.) ISWC 2003. LNCS, vol. 2870, pp. 351–368. Springer, Heidelberg (2003). https://doi.org/10.1007/978-3-540-39718-2_23

11. Battiston, F.: Structural measures for multiplex networks. Phys. Rev. E **89**(3), 032804 (2014)

12. Antal, T.: Social balance on networks: the dynamics of friendship and enmity. Physica D **224**(1–2), 130–136 (2006)

13. Gargiulo, F.: The classical origin of modern mathematics. EPJ Data Sci. **5**(1), 26 (2016)

14. Goh, K.-I.: Burstiness and memory in complex systems. EPL (Europhys. Lett.) **81**(4), 48002 (2008)

15. Guha, R., et al.: Propagation of trust and distrust. In: Proceedings of the 13th International Conference on World Wide Web. ACM (2004)

16. Leskovec, J., et al.: Signed networks in social media. In: Proceedings of the SIGCHI Conference on Human Factors in Computing Systems. ACM (2010)

17. Skowronski, J.J.: Negativity and extremity biases in impression formation: a review of explanations. Psychol. Bull. **105**(1), 131–142 (1989)

18. Ajzen, I.: Nature and operation of attitudes. Ann. Rev. Psychol. **52**(1), 27–58 (2001)

19. Bonaccio, S.: Advice taking and decision-making: an integrative literature review, and implications for the organizational sciences. Organ. Behav. Hum. Decis. Processes **101**(2), 127–151 (2006)

20. Rivis, A.: Descriptive norms as an additional predictor in the theory of planned behaviour: a meta-analysis. Curr. Psychol. **22**(3), 218–233 (2003)

21. Slovic, P.: Perceived risk, trust, and democracy. Risk Anal. **13**(6), 675–682 (1993)

22. Tversky, A.: Judgment under uncertainty: heuristics and biases. Sci. Am. Assoc. Adv. Sci. **185**(4157), 1124–1131 (1974)

23. Yaniv, I.: Advice taking in decision making: egocentric discounting and reputation formation. Organ. Behav. Hum. Decis. Processes **83**(2), 260–281 (2000)

24. Yau-fai Ho, D.: On the concept of face. Am. J. Sociol. **81**(4), 867–883 (1976)

Gender Wage Gap in the University Sector: A Case Study of All Universities in Ontario, Canada

Laura Gatto[1], Dar'ya Heyko[1], Miana Plesca[2], and Luiza Antonie[1]([✉])

[1] School of Computer Science, University of Guelph, Guelph, Canada
{gattol,dheyko,lantonie}@uoguelph.ca
[2] Department of Economics and Finance, University of Guelph, Guelph, Canada
miplesca@uoguelph.ca

Abstract. By analyzing salary data from the Ontario Sunshine List for the University Sector and combining it with productivity characteristics for research and teaching, we extend our understanding of the variables that contribute to the gender wage gap in Academia. Longitudinal analysis confirms that employees labelled as female are less represented in administration roles and full faculty positions. While the gender imbalance on the list is getting less extreme, with the proportion of women on the Sunshine List increasing from 11% in 1997 to about 40% nowadays, this increase in female representation is more likely to occur at incomes close to the access threshold of $100,000. While women do not achieve wage parity even when sorted by faculty position, within each academic rank the gender wage gap is smaller than the overall wage gap, which further confirms that, even in the ivory tower, men select into more lucrative positions than women. Controlling for productivity measures for research with h-index and for teaching with overall Rate My Professors (RMP) shows a modest effect of these productivity measures on wage formation and no effect on the wage gaps.

Keywords: Gender wage gap · University sector
Productivity characteristics

1 Introduction

In Canada, the gender wage gap has had renewed interest in public discourse with regular media reports confirming women are not paid the same as men for equal work. Despite increased levels of labour market participation and educational attainment, the gender wage gap is projected to continue [25]. When comparing full-time full-year workers annual wages in Canada, women currently earn 74 cents for every dollar men earn. Even when accounting for the number of hours worked, which are higher for men, women still only earn 88 cents for every dollar men earn [21]. The Pay Equity Commission of the Government of Ontario also reports a gender wage gap of 26% in favour of men [3]. There is also evidence that

© Springer Nature Switzerland AG 2018
S. Staab et al. (Eds.): SocInfo 2018, LNCS 11185, pp. 242–256, 2018.
https://doi.org/10.1007/978-3-030-01129-1_15

the gender wage gap may be increasing in certain public sectors in Ontario. In [5], the authors analyzed Ontario's public sector salary data, reporting that only one third of the records on the list are female. They also find evidence that the gender wage gap is increasing in the university sector. The Canadian Association of University Teachers (CAUT), in a 2011 Equity report, confirms that the average salary for male faculty is $101,113 compared to an average salary of $90,165 for female faculty across all ranks [4]. Provincially, the Ontario Confederation of University Faculty Associations (OCUFA) also find salary anomalies by gender in favour of men in Ontario universities, with the gap persisting even after some institutions provided monetary pay-outs to female faculty to reduce the gap [2]. Considering university's generally have four standard faculty ranks with incremental steps to tenure and promotion, a persisting gender wage gap is rather problematic.

Research on wage generally includes the method of adding human capital conditions (those characteristics related to salary gains) to determine what variables directly relate to an increase in salary. In gender wage gap analysis, researchers often include an additional layer of analysis to measure if gender bias exists for returns on investment for the same productivity characteristics. For example, female faculty receive 16% increase in salary for their investment in obtaining an advanced degree compared to a 20% salary return for male faculty [8]. Since 1997, the Ontario Government's Public Sector Disclosure Act, publishes annually a list of employees who earn a salary of $100,000 or more, referred to as the Sunshine List [1]. Considered the highest earners in the public sector, this list includes employee's first and last name, their sector, their employer, and taxable benefits earned in addition to their base salary. What is not included is gender[1]. We intentionally assign gender by first name to Sunshine List records in the university sector and link metrics associated with research and teaching, the two main determinants used in tenure and promotion. With a dataset of 124,265 records from the Sunshine List university sector reported from 1997 to 2015, we track salary and promotional trends over time linking measures of research productivity with h-index values and teaching ability from Rate My Professors[2] overall quality scores.

1.1   Contributions

This research contributes a more complete picture of gender wage gap trends over a period of 18 years for the highest earners in Ontario Universities by: (1) analyzing women's representation on the list; (2) segmenting data by faculty rank and administrative roles to show representation by gender; (3) measuring the gender wage gap over time by position; (4) quantifying the relationships that exist between research output and teaching excellence; and, (5) determining if

---

[1] For purposes of this paper, and in congruence with past research, we use the term gender in reference to being male and female. The term also recognizes socially constructed attributes we assign biological sex which is relevant to this research.

[2] www.ratemyprofessors.com.

men and women receive the same returns for higher scores for research and teaching.

2   Related Work

Canadian universities are generally publicly funded, which necessitates a certain level of reporting and transparency regarding employment characteristics. Furthermore, the salary data inherently controls for occupation, sector and standard naming conventions for faculty rank. Over forty years of research regarding Canadian faculty salaries finds some evidence of a salary differential in favour of men, even when controlling for human capital characteristics [10,12,13,22,23,27]. In academia, research output and student teaching ratings are generally considered the two main evaluators in tenure and promotion.

Research productivity, generally accepted as the main indicator of academic success, is associated with the amount a researcher publishes and the impact their research has in their field. The Hirsch-index (h-index), introduced by Hirsch in 2005, is the calculuation of the number of publications (h) with citation numbers less than or equal to h. The value factors in both quantity (number of published works) and quality (number of citations) for unbiased comparisons of scientific output and impact [15]. For example, a researcher who published 10 articles receiving one citation each and a researcher who has one publication with 30 citations would both have the same h-index score of 1. In order to have a high h-value, a researcher has to regularly publish and be cited by other researchers. This measure has been widely adopted and applied at the individual, department, university and even at the journal level [9,11,20]. The Higher Education Quality Council of Ontario Canada applies h-index at the faculty and university level to rank research productivity [28]. Using h-index does have limitations. The value can be skewed in the following situations: papers with substantial citation rates, publications with large numbers of co-authors, self-citations, and what is considered a high score can vary across disciplines [16]. The value can change depending on source of data [19]. Gender may also impact the h-index as women tend to publish less and have less tenure [14,17,26]. As the Sunshine List reports salaries for high earners, the assumption is that the people on the list have had reasonable tenure, thus somewhat reducing concerns of career length for this data. The other variable considered in the tenure and promotion process is teaching ability. Even though most universities use student teaching evaluations as performance indicators, generally researchers do not have access to these evaluations. It is no surprise that there is increased literature analyzing data collected from ratemyprofessors.com (RMP) [7]. Recognizing that teaching evaluations can be influenced by gender [6,18], regardless if offered by university staff in the classroom or on-line, the student driven site provides large datasets of evaluations that are not readily accessible in any other medium.

In addition to analyzing the gender wage gap in the university sector over time, we link salary data, h-index values and overall RMP ratings. A study that follows a similar approach analyzes Economics faculty on the Sunshine List from 1996 to 2015, reporting a strong correlation between salary increase and publication rates in top peer reviewed Economic journals, but weaker correlation regarding overall teaching quality ratings on ratemyprofessors.com [24]. Our research differs in that we primarily focus on gender analysis and we include all faculty on the Sunshine List, not only for Economics professors.

3   Data Sources and Data Integration

3.1   Sunshine List

The Ontario Ministry of Finance, Public Sector Salary Disclosure Act (passed in 1996, amended in 2004) requires public sector organizations that receive substantial provincial funding to annually disclose the names, job titles and salaries including taxable benefits for all employees with a salary of $100,000 or above before taxes. This report is referred to as the Ontario' Sunshine List, thus we'll refer to this dataset as the Sunshine List. The data collected spans from 1997 to 2015 inclusive with the following fields: sunshine I.D.; sector; employer; position; surname; given name; salary; taxable benefits. There is no field for gender on the SL. While the Sunshine List has 652,804 records from 12 sectors, in this paper we focus on the University Sector. A gender predication model developed by Antonie et al. [5] assigns gender by first name and gender frequency from data available by the US Social Security Bureau (1,825,433 records from 1880 to 2014). The total number of records over the 1997 to 2015 time period for the University Sector is 146,243. To reduce the potential for error with the gender prediction model, records with first names not located on the US database are removed resulting in 131,787 records. If the gender probability for a name was 95% or greater for one gender, that gender is assigned. Names below that frequency threshold are removed resulting in 124,415 records. We also found and removed 150 instances of individuals having two records on the list in the same year, leaving us with a final dataset of 124,265.

3.2   Productivity Characteristics of H-Index and Rate My Professors (RMP)

H-index scores are predominately found using Publish or Perish (1) software or directly from Google Scholar (2) and extrapolated to account for all years of the salary data. We collected h-index data for a third of the records on the Sunshine List. Data related to teaching performance is accessed from the site www.ratemyprofessors.com. Data fields consisted of course code, faculty name, and University. Average quantitative scores from 1 (low) to 5 (high) for *Overall Rating* and *Level of difficulty* from 1 (easy) to 5 (hard) were scraped and compiled. Integrating data from multiple sources makes available more characteristics to be used in the data analysis phase. In our research, we are interested to analyze how productivity characteristics affect the gender wage gap. In order to be able to perform this detailed analysis, we have linked the records on the Sunshine

List with the records of the RMP dataset and h-index scores based on the person's full name and their employer. We integrated these records based on exact matches of a person's full name and employer.

4 Gender Wage Gap Analysis

4.1 Gender Gap in Representation in the University Sector

The data is cleaned to manage incongruent naming of institutions resulting in records for 35 Institutions in Ontario, Canada in the university sector on the Sunshine List. What is noteworthy is the number of records for university sector is substantially increasing. For example, in 1997 there were 1031 records on the Sunshine List to which we assigned gender for this sector; by 2015, the number of records jumped to 13,707, an increase or more than tenfold from 1997. One catalyst of this growth may be the increase in student population. Until recently, the substantial funding provided by the Province of Ontario to post-secondary institutions incentivized universities to increase student enrolment, and while faculty complement increased by less than the student population, it increased nevertheless. Another reason for the increase in the number of records on the Sunshine List in all sectors is accounting-related. While incomes in the economy continue to grow faster than inflation, the threshold for the Sunshine List has remained at $100,000 nominal dollars. If this threshold were allowed to increase at the pace of inflation, in 2015 the corresponding amount would be $142,744. We provide some experiments where we allow for the Sunshine List threshold to change at the annual pace of inflation, using the Consumer Price Index series provided by the Bank of Canada. Even in this scenario there would be a substantive increase in the number of records on the Sunshine List in all sectors including the University one, where there would be 6153 individuals by 2015.

Out of the 124,265 records with gender predicted from first names in the US Social Security data with 95% or greater probability, 31.8% (39,493) of these records were identified as female. Figure 1 shows the increase in the number of records separately by gender. The number of records increased for both men and women. Given how few women were on the Sunshine List to begin with, the gender gap in participation on the Sunshine list has narrowed as a result of more women entering the list, as shown in Fig. 2. A somewhat similar narrowing of the representation gap can be observed when we impose the real dollar threshold (adjusted for inflation) in Fig. 3, except the narrowing of the gender gap in representation is less pronounced. This suggests that there are more women entering the Sunshine List at the lower income distribution − between the nominal threshold of $100,000 and the threshold adjusted for inflation − and this is why the gender gap narrows faster on the actual list which does not account for inflation in the threshold.

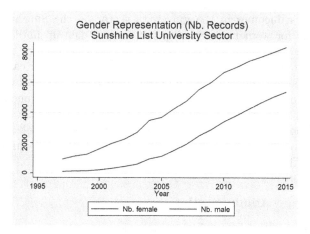

Fig. 1.

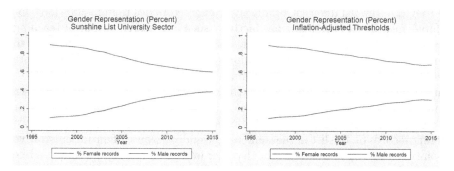

Fig. 2.   Fig. 3.

4.2   Average Gender Gap in Salaries in the University Sector

The Sunshine List reports labour income from two sources, salaries and taxable benefits. We perform our analysis on the sum of the two, salary and benefits, which we refer to as "income". The gender wage gap results are qualitatively the same whether we use income or we only focus on salaries, because benefits are small. The mean salary for the university sector across all years is $134,453 and the mean benefits are $760 over this period. When comparing income (or salary) by gender, we find no gender wage gap in the late nineties, when women even outperform men in terms of earnings; in fact, in 1997, women earn a mean salary that is $4,372 greater than men's that year, as evidence that the very small group of women at that time on the Sunshine List was a very selected group. Figure 4 shows how the income advantage of women over men disappears after 2000, and it constantly increases. If we report instead income in real 1997 dollars as in Fig. 5 we see the same pattern for the gender wage gap, which becomes increasingly larger, especially around 2008. We can also see that in real dollar terms, incomes in the university sector on the Sunshine List have been decreasing for women across all years and for men up until early 2000 s. If we repeat the same analysis using income in real 1997 dollars, as well as the threshold in real 1997 dollars, Fig. 6 shows that for these higher earners there is no drop in incomes, except for women in the few earlier years, and we see a large increase in the gender gap following the 2008 recession. We can conclude that the increase in the gender wage gap was driven by two phenomena: a stagnation of the income of top women earners starting in the late 2000 s, as well as an increase in the share of women with earnings near the nominal $100,000 threshold in the later Sunshine List years.

4.3 Faculty and Administration

To better understand what drives the gender wage gap in the university sector, we analyze separately records for workers in administrative roles, such as Deans or Presidents, and regular faculty appointments. Administrative jobs pay more, and they also reward different productivity characteristics than faculty jobs; for example, measures of academic productivity such as research output or teaching success are valued less, if at all, in the salaries of administrators compared to regular faculty. We also note that administration appointments for faculty are often term-limited, so it is not uncommon for faculty to move from faculty to administration roles and vice versa in their academic careers, and we assign an "administrator" indicator only for those years when an individual holds a senior administrative duty. We also find 150 instances of the same person having two different records on the list in the same year, usually because of an administrative appointment on top of a regular faculty one; in those instances we only use one record for the individual with the sum of their income, and we assign it an administrative designation.

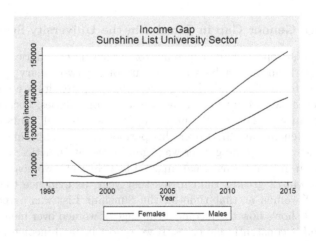

Fig. 4.

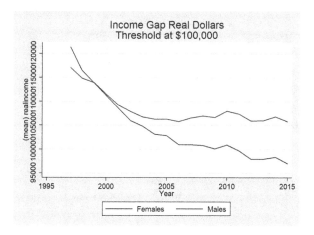

Fig. 5.

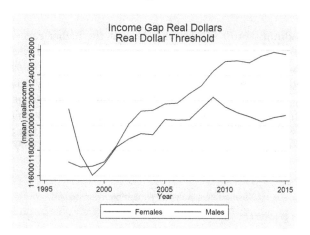

Fig. 6.

To assign the administrative position indicator, we used the following key-words or abbreviations: *dean, direct, manager, analyst, service, plan, resource, president, vp, vice, libra, advis, execut, chair, secret, legal, physician, staff, admin, service, registrar, head, officer, provost, architect, develop, supervisor, counsel, special, senior, graduate, coordinat, lead, hand, engineer, psychol, coach, clerk, control, principal, cio, ceo, operat, project, tech, comptroller, research, cao, systems, programmer, veterinarian, treasurer,* and *bursar.*

Figure 7 confirms that administration salaries are higher than regular fac-ulty ones. Furthermore, the gender wage gap persists within each category: both administrative staff and regular faculty records show a gender wage gap, larger for administrators in the earlier years but increasing more for faculty in the later years. Moreover, since the mid 2010 s, male faculty's salaries have caught

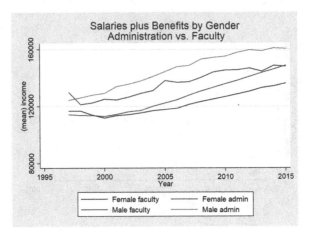

Fig. 7.

up with female administrator salaries. Looking at the higher earners on the list, who would have made the Sunshine List even if the threshold was adjusted for inflation, we can see from Fig. 8 that their incomes increased in real terms and the gender gap did not increase for any group. This seems to indicate that the decrease in real incomes, as well as the deteriorating relative performance of females, comes from newly entrants on the list. It is likely that middle management on campuses, as well as sessional lectures, who come on the Sunshine List at incomes close to the nominal $100,000 threshold, are more likely to be female.

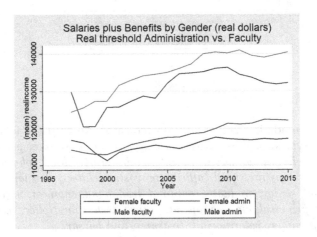

Fig. 8.

4.4   Faculty Position by Rank

We investigate the gender wage gap across one more dimension: rank of faculty. Similarly as in the case of administrative positions, in order to assign faculty ranks: Sessional, Assistant, Associate or Full Professor, we search through position titles using keywords and assign to *lecture, instruct or sessional* the Sessional rank; to *assist, assistant* we assign Assistant Professor, to *associate, associer* we assign Associate rank, and to *prof, professeur, tenure, full* we assign Full Professor rank. We are left with about one third of observations to which we could not assign rank conclusively, and we exclude those from this part of the analysis.

Because of the $100,000 earnings threshold to make it on the list, we end up with a distribution of faculty by rank which is different from the faculty population. In particular, Sessional and Assistant groups are under-represented on the Sunshine List, because their earnings tend to be lower, while Full Professors are overrepresented. In our Sunshine List data, Associate Professors are a little over a third of the records, and Full Professors make up more than half of the records with assigned rank status. Figure 9 reveals a striking observation: within each academic rank, there is almost no gender wage gap! The aggregate gender wage gap comes from the fact that in the high earner group of Full Professors, males are overrepresented in proportion of 74% compared to 26% women (approximately 30,000 records for men versus 10,500 for women). In the other rank categories, the gender distribution is respectively 60% men versus 40% women as Associate Professor, 55% men versus 45% women as Assistant Professor, and 60% men versus 40% women as Sessional.

5   Gender Wage Gap Analysis - Productivity Characteristics

5.1   Regression Analysis

To quantify the joint effect of rank and administrative status on the gender wage gap, we run regression analysis. Other than rank and administrative indicator, we can account for the variation in the gender wage gap due to employer − some universities may have in place policies to reduce the gender wage gap or encourage promotion of women −, field of study − women in fields where they are underrepresented, such as STEM, tend to have a lower wage gap if employed in that field, because they are strongly positively selected in that field. We can also add year indicators to account for the time variation in the gender wage gap.

The basic model we run is a regression

$$Y = \beta_0 + \beta_1 \cdot Male + beta \cdot X$$

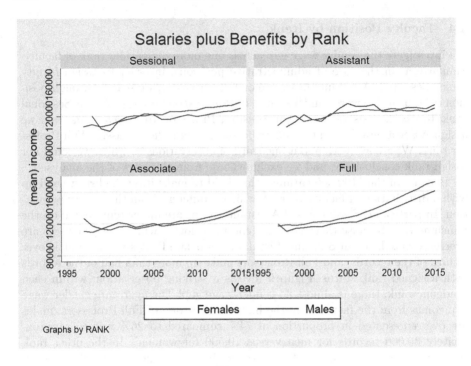

Fig. 9.

where Y is the outcome of interest, which is salaries in our case, β_0 is the intercept, *Male* is a gender indicator equal to 1 for men and 0 for women, and X are the other characteristics we control for, such as university, field, year, rank (sessional, assistant, associate, or full professor, relative to rank not known), and an indicator whether in administration. The Y outcome considered here is log real income, mostly for convenience because then the coefficients lend themselves right away to percentage interpretation.

There are seven specifications reported in Table 1, listing coefficients and standard errors (in parentheses) clustered at the individual level. The first specification is a simple regression of log income on a gender indicator. The coefficient on the *Male* variable represents the percentage gap between men and women; put differently, from specification (1) we see that men earn on average 6.8% more than women do. Moreover, the constant represents log earnings for women, so the average earnings for women from this specification would be $exp(11.488) = 97,538$, while men earn 6% on top of that. Specification (2) adds year controls and university fixed effects, and not much changes.

Specification (3) accounts for heterogeneity in the gender wage gap by rank, in the following way. The linear prediction from this estimation is $log(income) = \beta \cdot X + \beta_1 \cdot Male + \beta_2 \cdot Male \cdot sessional + \beta_3 \cdot Male \cdot assistant + \beta_4 \cdot associate + \beta_5 \cdot full$. Since $Male = 1$ for men and $Male = 0$ for women, we obtain that the impact of one rank, say *associate*, on the gender wage gap is $\beta_1 + \beta_4$. Specification (3) therefore indicates that, *ceteris paribus*, the gender wage gap for assistants and for associates is smaller than the mean gap of 6.5% by about 3.9% points for assistants and 3.7% points for associates, consistent with what we have documented in Sect. 4.

To further confirm that the gender gap within ranks is smaller than the overall wage gap, we run separate wage regressions for each of the rank categories. Column (5) then reports results similar to those from the model run in column (2), except it does it separately for each rank category. The results in column (5) confirm that the gender wage gap is about 5.5% for sessionals, 2.6% for assistant professors, 2.7% for associated professors, and 6.1% for full professors. This demonstrates once again that within rank the gender wage gap is smaller, and we obtain a larger aggregate gender wage gap because of the differential selection into rank by gender. Put differently, across rank, most males are full professors, and most females are associate professors, so taking two random individuals from each group, the likelihood is the woman will be from a lower-paying rank, and will have a higher wage gap when compared to a random male than when compared to a male within her own rank.

5.2   Adding Research and Teaching Productivity

We measure research productivity by the publicly available h-index, and the teaching productivity by the evaluation score from the website Rate My Professor. This is not a random sample, and we were limited in the availability of records on both h-index and teaching evaluation. Nevertheless, we can still investigate the role of research and teaching productivity characteristics on the gender wage gap. Because we are only left with 17,711 records with non-missing h index and teaching score, we first replicate the gender wage gap analysis on this subsample. The gender gap is about 3.3%, smaller than the overall gap for the entire Sunshine List and not statistically significant.

Adding controls for research and productivity does not affect this gender wage gap. The effect of the h index on income is not very large, a unit increase in the h index leading to 0.1% points increase in income. Nevertheless, a unit increase in the h index is on a different scale of magnitude, and we could perhaps discuss the effect of increasing the h index by 10 points not one. The effect of teaching productivity is slightly larger than that of research in this sample, with a unit increase in the teaching score resulting in a 1.1% increase in income, or around $1,500 dollars per year.

Table 1. Determinants of the gender wage gap in Ontario's Sunshine List university sector

	(1)	(2)	(3)	(4)	(5)	(6)	(7)
Male	0.068	0.063	0.065	0.061		0.033	0.032
	(0.003)	(0.003)	(0.010)	(0.024)		(0.034)	(0.033)
Sessional			−0.072	−0.042	0.055	−0.215	−0.183
			(0.015)	(0.030)	(0.015)	(0.070)	(0.066)
Assistant			−0.017	0.039	0.026	0.161	0.167
			(0.015)	(0.036)	(0.013)	(0.096)	(0.090)
Associate			0.032	0.079	0.027	−0.039	−0.027
			(0.009)	(0.022)	(0.005)	(0.040)	(0.040)
Full			0.151	0.197	0.061	−0.003	0.002
			(0.009)	(0.025)	(0.006)	(0.039)	(0.038)
Male*Sessional			−0.002	−0.014		0.173	0.163
			(0.021)	(0.040)		(0.085)	(0.081)
Male*Assistant			−0.039	−0.058		−0.220	−0.214
			(0.019)	(0.045)		(0.107)	(0.100)
Male*Associate			−0.037	−0.046		−0.027	−0.030
			(0.012)	(0.029)		(0.039)	(0.039)
Male*Full			−0.006	0.000		−0.016	−0.019
			(0.012)	(0.030)		(0.036)	(0.035)
h index							0.001
							(0.000)
RMP							0.011
							(0.004)
Admin			0.114				
			(0.005)				
Intercept	11.488	11.583	11.011	11.028		11.621	11.557
	(0.003)	(0.042)	(0.069)	(0.103)		(0.119)	(0.121)
Year controls	NO	YES	YES	YES	YES	YES	YES
University controls	NO	YES	YES	YES	YES	YES	YES
Field controls	NO	NO	YES	YES	YES	YES	YES
R squared	0.022	0.068	0.216	0.248		0.309	0.321

6   Conclusions

We have documented that women have not achieved gender parity in administrative roles, even among Ontario's top earners in the University Sector. Women's representation decreases as we move up faculty ranks; since a higher rank is associated with higher pay, this selection of women into lower paying ranks is responsible for most of the gender wage imbalance since within each faculty rank the gender wage gap is smaller than the overall gap. We have illustrated the effect of productivity related measures, such as the h-index and teaching ratings from ratemyprofessors.com, on wages and on the gender wage gap.

References

1. Ontario Ministry of Finance, Public sector salary disclosure. http://www.ontario. ca/government/public-sector-salary-disclosure
2. Pay equity among faculty at Ontarios universities OCUFAs submission to the Ontario gender wage gap steering committee. https://ocufa.on.ca/assets/OCUFA-Submission-on-the-Gender-Wage-Gap-FINAL.pdf
3. Pay Equity Commision, Government of Ontario. http://www.payequity.gov.on.ca/ en/about/pubs/genderwage/wagegap.php
4. The persistent gap: understanding male-female salary differentials amongst Canadian academic staff. https://www.caut.ca/sites/default/files/the-persistent-gap-mdash-understanding-male-female-salary-differentials-amongst-canadian-academic-staff-mar-2011.pdf
5. Antonie, L., D'Angelo, A., Grewal, G., Plesca, M.: Analyzing the gender wage gap in Ontario's public sector. In: 2015 IEEE 14th International Conference on Machine Learning and Applications (ICMLA), pp. 465–470. IEEE (2015)
6. Arbuckle, J., Williams, B.D.: Students' perceptions of expressiveness: age and gender effects on teacher evaluations **49** (2003)
7. Azab, M., Mihalcea, R., Abernethy, J.: Analysing RateMyProfessors evaluations across institutions, disciplines, and cultures: the tell-tale signs of a good professor. In: Spiro, E., Ahn, Y.-Y. (eds.) SocInfo 2016. LNCS, vol. 10046, pp. 438–453. Springer, Cham (2016). https://doi.org/10.1007/978-3-319-47880-7_27
8. Barbezat, D.A., Hughes, J.W.: Salary structure effects and the gender pay gap in academia. Res. High. Educ. **46**(6), 621–640 (2005)
9. Bornmann, L., Daniel, H.D.: Does the h-index for ranking of scientists really work? Scientometrics **65**(3), 391–392 (2005)
10. Brown, L.K., Troutt, E., Prentice, S.: Ten years after: sex and salaries at a Canadian university. Can. Public Policy **37**(2), 239–255 (2011)
11. Costas, R., Bordons, M.: The h-index: advantages, limitations and its relation with other bibliometric indicators at the micro level. J. Inf. **1**(3), 193–203 (2007)
12. Doucet, C., Smith, M., Durand, C.: Pay structure, female representation and the gender pay gap among university professors. Relat. Ind./Ind. Relat. **67**(1), 51–75 (2012)
13. Guppy, N.: Pay equity in Canadian universities, 1972–73 and 1985–86. Can. Rev. Sociol. Anthropol. **26**(5), 743–759 (1989)
14. Harzing, A.W., Alakangas, S., Adams, D.: hia: an individual annual h-index to accommodate disciplinary and career length differences. Scientometrics **99**(3), 811–821 (2014)
15. Hirsch, J.E.: An index to quantify an individual's scientific research output. Proc. Nat. Acad. Sci. U.S.A. **102**(46), 16569 (2005)
16. Hirsch, J.E.: Does the h index have predictive power? Proc. Nat. Acad. Sci. **104**(49), 19193–19198 (2007)
17. Kelly, C.D., Jennions, M.D.: The h index and career assessment by numbers. Trends Ecol. Evol. **21**(4), 167–170 (2006)

18. MacNell, L., Driscoll, A., Hunt, A.N.: Whats in a name: exposing gender bias in student ratings of teaching. Innovative High. Educ. **40**(4), 291–303 (2015)

19. Meho, L.I., Rogers, Y.: Citation counting, citation ranking, and h-index of human-computer interaction researchers: a comparison of scopus and web of science. J. Assoc. Inf. Sci. Technol. **59**(11), 1711–1726 (2008)

20. Mingers, J., Yang, L.: Evaluating journal quality: a review of journal citation indicators and ranking in business and management. Eur. J. Oper. Res. **257**(1), 323–337 (2017)

21. Moyser, M.: Women and Paid Work. Statistics Canada (2017)

22. Ornstein, M., Stewart, P.: Gender and faculty pay in Canada. Can. J. Sociol./Cah. Canadiens de sociologie, 461–481 (1996)

23. Ornstein, M., Stewart, P., Drakich, J.: Promotion at Canadian universities: the intersection of gender, discipline, and institution. Can. J. High. Education **37**(3), 1 (2007)

24. Sen, A., Ariizumi, H., DeSousa, N.: Evaluating the relationship between pay and research productivity: panel data evidence from Ontario universities. Can. Public Policy **40**(1), 1–14 (2014)

25. Shannon, M., Kidd, M.P.: Projecting the trend in the Canadian gender wage gap 2001–2031: will an increase in female education acquisition and commitment be enough? Can. Public Policy/Analyse de Politiques, pp. 447–467 (2001)

26. Symonds, M.R., Gemmell, N.J., Braisher, T.L., Gorringe, K.L., Elgar, M.A.: Gender differences in publication output: towards an unbiased metric of research performance. PLoS One **1**(1), e127 (2006)

27. Warman, C., Woolley, F., Worswick, C.: The evolution of male-female earnings differentials in Canadian universities, 1970–2001. Can. J. Econ./Rev. Can. d'économique **43**(1), 347–372 (2010)

28. Weingarten, H.P., Hicks, M., Jonker, L., Liu, S.: The diversity of Ontarios Universities: a data set to inform the differentiation. Higher Education Quality Council of Ontario, Toronto, ON (2013)

Analyzing Dynamic Ideological Communities in Congressional Voting Networks

Carlos Henrique Gomes Ferreira[(⊠)] [iD], Breno de Sousa Matos, and Jussara M. Almeira

Department of Computer Science, Universidade Federal de Minas Minas Gerais, Belo Horizonte, Brazil
{chgferreira,brenomatos,jussara}@dcc.ufmg.br

Abstract. We here study the behavior of political party members aiming at identifying how ideological communities are created and evolve over time in diverse (fragmented and non-fragmented) party systems. Using public voting data of both Brazil and the US, we propose a methodology to identify and characterize ideological communities, their member polarization, and how such communities evolve over time, covering a 15-year period. Our results reveal very distinct patterns across the two case studies, in terms of both structural and dynamic properties.

Keywords: Political party systems · Community detection
Complex networks · Temporal analysis

1 Introduction

Party systems can be characterized based on their fragmentation and polarization [30]. Party fragmentation corresponds to the number of parties existing in a political system (e.g., a country) while polarization is related to the multiple opinions that lead to the division of members into groups with distinct political ideologies [14,30]. In countries where the party system has a low fragmentation, the polarization of political parties can be seen more clearly since one party tends to occupy more seats supporting the government and the other opposes it [21]. On the other hand, in fragmented systems the multiple political parties often make use of coalitions, a type of inter-party alliance, to raise their relevance in the political system and reach a common end [2,8]. Thus, a great amount of ideological similarity, as expressed by their voting decisions, is often observed across different parties.

Previous work has analyzed the behavior of political party members through the modeling of voting data in signed and weighted networks [3,4,10,11,19,24, 25,28]. These prior efforts tackled topics such as community detection, party cohesion and loyalty analysis, governance of a political party and member influence in such networks. However, the identification and characterization of ideological communities, particularly in fragmented party systems, require observing

© Springer Nature Switzerland AG 2018
S. Staab et al. (Eds.): SocInfo 2018, LNCS 11185, pp. 257–273, 2018.
https://doi.org/10.1007/978-3-030-01129-1_16

some issues, such as: (i) presidents define coalitions throughout government in order to strengthen the implementation of desired public policies, which may be ruptured after a period of time [8,20]; (ii) political members have different levels of partisanship and loyalty, and their political preferences may change over time [3,5]; and (iii) different political parties may have the same political ideology, being redundant under a party system [23].

In such context, we here study the behavior of political party members aiming at identifying how ideological communities are created and evolve over time. To that end, we consider two case studies, Brazil and US, which are representatives of distinct party systems: whereas the former is highly fragmented and redundant [23], the latter is not fragmented but rather polarized with two major parties, although some party members can be considered less polarized [11,25]. Using public datasets of the voting records in the House of Representatives of both countries during a 15-year period, we characterize the emergence and evolution of communities of House members with similar political ideology (captured by their voting behavior) by using complex network concepts. Specifically, we tackle three research questions (RQs):

- **RQ1: How do ideological communities are characterized in governments with different (i.e., fragmented and non-fragmented) party systems?** We model the voting behavior of each House of Representatives during a given time period using a network, where nodes represent House members, and weighted edges are added if two members voted similarly. We use the Louvain algorithm [7] to detect communities in each network and characterize structural properties of such communities. Unlike prior community analysis in the political context, we compare the properties of these communities in fragmented and in non-fragmented party systems.
- **RQ2: How can we identify polarization in the ideological communities?** We use neighborhood overlap [13] to estimate the tie strength associated to each network edge, characterizing it as either strong or weak. This approach to estimate tie strength has been employed in several contexts [16,18,22,37] and also in the political context [35]. However, these prior studies were not interested in analyzing and comparing distinct political systems, as we do here. We use strong ties to identify polarized communities in each analyzed network.
- **RQ3: How do polarized communities evolve over time?** We analyze how polarized communities evolve over the years of a government, characterizing how the membership of such communities change over time.

In sum, the key contributions of our work are: (i) a methodology to identify and analyze dynamic ideological communities and their polarization in party systems based on complex network concepts; and (ii) two case studies covering strikingly different party systems over a quite broad time period. Our study shows that in fragmented party systems, such as Brazil, although party redundancy exists, some ideological communities exist and may, indeed, be polarized. However, such polarized communities are highly dynamic, greatly changing their membership over consecutive years. In the US, on the other hand, despite the strong and temporally stable party polarization, there are members, within each party, that exhibit different levels of polarization.

The rest of this paper is organized as follows. Section 2 briefly discusses related work, whereas Sect. 3 describes our modeling methodology and case studies. We then present our main results, tackling RQ1-RQ3 in Sects. 4–6. Conclusions and future work are offered in Sect. 7.

2 Related Work

Complex networks constitute a set of theoretical and analytical tools to describe and analyze phenomena related to interactions occurring in the real world [29]. Among the many properties of a network, the interactions between pairs of nodes can be used to define the strength of these links (or *tie strength*) [13]. Indeed, tie strength is a property that has been widely studied in several domains. For example, the tie strength between pairs of people was studied in the phone call and Short Message System (SMS) networks, where a higher frequency of SMS and longer call duration characterize stronger ties [37]. The different types of interactions between Facebook users have also been used to define tie strength on that system [18]. Similarly, tie strength was used to build geolocation models based on Twitter data and exploited in the prediction of user location [22].

In the political context, the study of political ideologies has been largely accomplished through the analysis of roll call votes networks. In a roll call votes network, the nodes represent people (e.g., congressmen), and two nodes are connected if they have voted similarly in one (or more) voting sessions. In [3], the authors studied the committee's formation in the US House of Representatives using roll call votes networks, finding that there is a cooperation between the Democratic and Republican parties. Although the polarization in recent decades has been increasing, there are moderate members in both parties, who cooperate with each other. In the same direction, authors in [28] studied the committees and subcommittees of US House of Representatives exploiting the network connections that are built according to common membership. Analogously, the polarization in the US Senate was evaluated using a network defined by the similarity of Senators' votes [25].

In [11], the authors studied the relations between members of the Italian parliament according to their voting behavior, analyzing the community structure with respect to political coalitions and government alliances over time. Similarly, the cohesiveness of members of the European Parliament was investigated through the analysis of network models combining roll call votes and Twitter data [10]. Other approaches study the behavior of political members modeling roll call votes using signed networks. However, this type of analysis is appropriate for modeling only polarized systems [4]. Signed networks have also been used to evaluate aspects related to political governance and political party behavior [19]. In addition, an algorithm was proposed to evaluate signed networks and a case study was conducted using a European Parliament network capturing voting similarities between members [24]. In [19], the roll call votes of the Brazilian House of Representative was modeled using signed networks. The results revealed inefficient coalitions with the government as parties that make such coalitions have members distributed in different ideological communities over time. Orthogonally, others have investigated the ideology of political members and users through profiles of social networks [1,12,34].

Unlike prior work, our focus here is on the characterization of ideological communities in *diverse*, i.e., both fragmented and non-fragmented, party systems. We also propose to use tie strength, computed based on neighborhood overlap, to identify polarized communities under the party systems diversities, evaluating their evolution over time, on both party systems.

3 Methodology

In this section, we describe the methodology used in our study. We start by presenting basic concepts (Sect. 3.1) followed by our case studies (Sect. 3.2), and then describe our modeling of voting behavior (Sect. 3.3).

3.1 Basic Concepts

The House of Representatives is composed of several members who occupy the seats during each government period. House members participate in a series of voting sessions, when bills, amendments, and propositions are discussed and voted. Thus, attending such sessions is the most direct way for members to express their ideologies and positioning. When these members are associated with a large number of political parties, the party system in question is regarded as fragmented. In this case, during a term of office, coalition governments are established, leading political parties to organize themselves into ideological communities, defending together common interests during voting sessions [20,30].

One can evaluate the behavior of parties and their members in terms of how cohesive they are as an ideological community by analyzing voting data using widely disseminated metrics, such as Rice's Index. However, the use of Rice Index has been shown to be problematic when there are more than two voting options (other than only *yes* and *no*) [17], as is the case, for example, in the European Parliament and in our study, as we will see later.

Instead, we here employ the *Partisan Discipline* and *Party Discipline* metrics [23]. The former captures the ideological alignment of a member to her party (estimated by the behavior of the majority), and the latter expresses the ideological cohesiveness of a party. Given a member m, belonging to party p_m, the *Partisan Discipline* of m, pd_m is given by the fraction of all voting sessions to which m attended and voted similarly to the majority of p_m's members. That is, let n be the number of voting sessions attended by member m and $I(m, p_m, i)$ be 1 if member m voted similarly to the majority of members of p_m in voting session i $(i = 1..n)$ and 0 otherwise. Then:

$$pd_m = \frac{\sum_{i=1}^{n} I(m, p_m, i)}{n} \tag{1}$$

The *Partisan Discipline* can be generalized to assess the discipline and ideological alignment of a member to any community (not only his original party). The *Party Discipline* of a party p is computed as the average *Partisan Discipline* of all of its members, that is, $PD(p) = \frac{\sum_{m=1}^{M} pd_m}{M}$, where M is the number of members of p. *Party Discipline* captures how cohesive a party (or community) is in a set of votes. Both metrics range from 0 to 1, where 1 indicates that a member or party is totally disciplined (or cohesive) and 0 otherwise.

3.2 Case Studies

We consider two case studies: Brazil and US. In Brazil, the House of Representatives consists of 513 seats. A member vote can be either *Yes, No, Obstruction* or *Absence* in each voting session. A *Yes* or *No* vote expresses, respectively, an agreement or disagreement with the given proposition. Both *Absence* and *Obstruction* mean that the member did not participate in the voting, although an *Obstruction* expresses the intention of the member to cause the voting session to be cancelled due to insufficient quorum. Similarly, the US House of Representatives includes 435 seats, and a member vote can be *Yes, No* or *Not Voting*, whereas the last one indicates the member was not present in the voting session. In our study, we disregard *Absence* and *Not Voting* votes, as they do not reflect any particular inclination of the members with respect to the topic under consideration. However, we do include *Obstructions* as they reflect an intentional action of the members and a clear opposition to the topic. Thus, for Brazil, three different voting options were considered.

For both case studies, we collected voting data from public sources. The plenary roll call votes of Brazil's House of Representatives are available through an application programming interface (API) maintained by the government[1]. We collected roll call votes between the 52th and 55th legislatures, from 2003 to 2017. US voting data covering the same 15-year period (i.e., between the 108th and 115th congresses) was collected through the ProPublica API[2]. Each dataset consists of a sequence of the voting session; for each session, the dataset includes date, time and voting option of each participating member.

In a preliminary analysis of the datasets, we noted that some members had little attendance to the voting sessions, especially in Brazil. Thus, we chose to filter our datasets to remove members with low attendance as they introduce noise to our analyses. Specifically, we removed members that had not attended (thus had not associated vote) to more than 33% of the voting sessions during each year[3]. On average, 19% and 1.98% members were removed from the Brazilian and US datasets for each year, respectively.

---

[1] http://www2.camara.leg.br/transparencia/dados-abertos/dados-abertos-legislativo (In Portuguese).

[2] https://projects.propublica.org/api-docs/congress-api/.

[3] This threshold was chosen based on Article 55 of the Brazilian Constitution that establishes that a deputy or senator will lose her mandate if she does not attend more than one third of the sessions.

Table 1. Overview of our datasets.

			Brazil					
Leg.	Year	President (Party)	# of Voting Sessions	# of Votes	# of Parties	# of Members	Avg. PD	SD PD
52th	2003	Lula (PT)	150	106755	23	435	88.23%	0.08
	2004	Lula (PT)	118	71576	23	377	87.43%	0.08
	2005	Lula (PT)	81	50616	24	382	88.91%	0.07
	2006	Lula (PT)	87	62358	24	419	91.12%	0.05
53th	2007	Lula (PT)	221	190424	31	478	92.45%	0.07
	2008	Lula (PT)	157	122482	31	452	92.34%	0.07
	2009	Lula (PT)	156	125759	30	465	91.87%	0.06
	2010	Lula (PT)	83	63255	29	452	92.46%	0.05
54th	2011	Dilma (PT)	98	78662	29	481	89.34%	0.08
	2012	Dilma (PT)	79	60219	28	454	89.56%	0.05
	2013	Dilma (PT)	158	115751	29	451	88.70%	0.06
	2014	Dilma (PT)	87	66154	28	451	92.93%	0.04
55th	2015	Dilma (PT)	273	231031	28	502	85.84%	0.06
	2016	Dilma (PT) Temer (PMDB)	218	156006	28	452	90.12%	0.05
	2017	Temer (PMDB)	230	159704	29	435	89.76%	0.08
			United States					
Cong.	Year	President (Party)	# of Voting Sessions	# of Votes	# of Parties	# of Members	Avg. PD	SD PD
108th	2003	George W. Bush (R)	623	258867	3	432	95.76%	0.03
	2004	George W. Bush (R)	502	203557	3	427	95.11%	0.03
109th	2005	George W. Bush (R)	637	264735	3	432	95.02%	0.03
	2006	George W. Bush (R)	511	210592	3	428	94.98%	0.04
110th	2007	George W. Bush (R)	956	297957	2	414	92.23%	0.04
	2008	George W. Bush (R)	605	244734	2	426	92.73%	0.04
111th	2009	Barack Obama (D)	929	385344	3	431	93.78%	0.02
	2010	Barack Obama (D)	631	253296	3	422	95.34%	0.01
112th	2011	Barack Obama (D)	908	377601	2	428	91.98%	0.01
	2012	Barack Obama (D)	621	253812	2	425	91.50%	0.01
113th	2013	Barack Obama (D)	594	245430	2	427	93.04%	0.01
	2014	Barack Obama (D)	531	217822	2	426	93.24%	0.01
114th	2015	Barack Obama (D)	662	277732	2	432	94.87%	0.01
	2016	Barack Obama (D)	588	241263	2	427	95.11%	0.01
115th	2017	Donald Trump (R)	708	292503	2	427	95.99%	0.00

Table 1 shows an overview of both (filtered) datasets, with Brazil on the top part of the table and the US on the bottom. The table presents each year covered, the acting president[4] and his/her party[5], total number of voting sessions, total number of member votes, as well as numbers of parties and members occupying seats in the House of Representatives during the year. The two rightmost columns, *Avg. PD* and *SD PD*, present the average and standard deviation of the *Party Discipline* computed across all parties.

Starting with the Brazilian dataset, we can see that the number of parties occupying seats has somewhat grown in recent years, characterizing an increasingly fragmented party system. However, in general, average *PD* values are very high (ranging from 85% to 92%), with small variation across parties, indicating that, despite the fragmentation, most party members have high partisan

---

[4] Brazilian president Dilma Rousseff was impeached from office and, therefore, Brazil had two Presidents that year.

[5] For Brazil: Worker's Party (PT) and the Brazilian Democratic Movement Party (PMDB). For the US: Democratic (D) and Republican (R).

discipline. Regarding the American dataset, Table 1 shows that the number of voting sessions is much larger than in Brazil. This is because the API of the Brazilian House of Representative provides only data related to votes in plenary, while the US dataset covers all votes. Moreover, although the numbers of members are comparable to those in the Brazilian dataset, the number of parties occupying seats in each year is much smaller. Indeed, only two parties, namely Republican (R) and Democrat (D), fill all seats in the House of Representatives since the 112th Congress. Thus, unlike the Brazilian case, party fragmentation is not an issue in the US. Moreover, just like in Brazil, parties have a high party discipline.

3.3   Network Model

We model the dynamics of ideological communities in voting sessions in each country using graphs as follows. We discretize time into non-overlapping windows of fixed duration. For each time window w analyzed, we create a weighted and undirected graph $G^w(V, A)$ in which $V = \{v_1, v_2, ...v_n\}$ is a set of vertices representing House members and each edge (v_i, v_j) is weighted by the similarity of voting positions of members v_i and v_j. Specifically, the weight of edge (v_i, v_j) is given by the ratio of the number of sessions in which both members voted similarly to the total number of sessions to which both members attended, during window w. Since in Brazil, government coalitions are usually made every year, we choose one year as the time window for analyzing community dynamics.

After building each graph, we noted that all pairs of members voted similarly at least once in all years analyzed and in both countries and, therefore, all graphs built are complete. This reflects the fact that some voting sessions are not discriminative of ideology or opinion, as most members (regardless of party) voted similarly. Thereby, it is necessary to filter out edges that do not contribute to the detection of ideological communities. To that end, we analyzed the distributions of edge similarity for all networks. Representative distributions for specific years, for both Brazil and US, are shown in Figs. 1a and b, respectively. We note that while the distributions for US exhibit clear concentrations around very small (roughly 0.3) and very large (around 0.85) similarity values, the similarity distributions for Brazil exhibit greater variability, which is consistent with the greater fragmentation of the party system.

We argue that, for the sake of removing edges from the graphs, a similarity threshold should not be much smaller than the average partisan discipline of individual members. That is, two members that have similarity much lower than their partisan disciplines should not be considered as part of the same ideological community. On the other hand, the higher the similarity threshold chosen, the larger the number of edges removed and the more sparse the resulting graph is. After experimenting with different thresholds, we chose to remove all edges with weights below the 90th percentile of the similarity distribution for the Brazilian graphs. For the US, we removed edges with weights below the 55th percentile of the similarity distribution. Both percentiles correspond roughly to a similarity value of 80%, which is not much smaller than the average partisan disciplines in both countries (see Table 1). We removed nodes that become isolated after the edge filtering, that is, single-node communities are not included in our analyses.

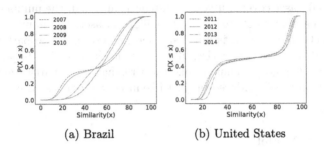

(a) Brazil   (b) United States

Fig. 1. Cumulative distribution function of edge similarity.

In sum, we model the voting sessions in each country using two sets of networks, one network per year. Then, we use the Louvain Method [7] to identify ideological communities in each network. This method has been extensively used to detect network communities in various domains [9,15,27]. It is based on the optimization of *modularity* [26], a metric to evaluate the structure of clusters in a network. *Modularity* is large when the clustering is good and it can reach a maximum value of 1. In this study, we use *modularity* and *party discipline* as main metrics to assess the cohesiveness of the communities found. The former captures the quality of the result with respect to the topological structure of the communities in the network, whereas the latter, computed for the communities (rather than for individual parties), captures quality in terms of context semantics. In the next sections, we discuss the results of our analyses.

4   Identifying Ideological Communities

We start our discussion by tackling our first research question (RQ1) and characterizing the ideological communities discovered in both Brazilian and US networks. Table 2 shows an overview of all networks for both countries, presenting some topological properties [13], i.e., numbers of nodes (*# of nodes*) and edges (*# of edges*), number of connected components (*# of CC*), average shortest path length (*SPL*), average degree, clustering coefficient and density[6]. Note the difference between the number of nodes in this table and the number of members in Table 1, corresponding to nodes that were removed after the edge filtering.

---

[6] The *density* of a network is given by the ratio of the total number of existing edges to the maximum possible number of edges in the graph. The *clustering coefficient*, on the other hand, measures the degree at which the nodes of the graph tend to group together to form triangles, and is defined as the ratio of the number of existing closed triplets to the total number of open and closed triplets. A triplet is three nodes that are connected by either two (open triplet) or three (closed triplet) undirected ties.

Table 2 also summarizes the characteristics of the ideological communities identified using the Louvain algorithm. In the four rightmost columns, it presents the number of communities identified, their *modularity* (*Mod.*) as well as average and standard deviation of the party discipline (*Avg PD* and *SD PD*), computed with respect to the ideological communities.

Starting with the Brazilian networks (top part of Table 2), we can observe great fluctuation in most topological metrics over the years, but, overall, the networks are sparse: the average shortest path length is short, the average clustering coefficient is moderate and the network density is low. Also, the number of communities identified is much smaller than the total number of parties (see Table 1) confirming the fragmentation and ideological overlap of multiple parties. Yet, the *party discipline* of these communities is, on average, very close to, and, in some cases, slightly larger than the values computed for the individual parties, despite a somewhat greater standard deviation observed across communities. Thus, these communities are indeed very cohesive in their voting patterns.

Table 2. Characterization of networks and ideological communities

Brazil											
Year	# of Nodes	# of Edges	# of CC	Avg. SPL	Avg. Degree	Avg. Clustering	Density	# of Comm.	Mod.	Avg. PD	SD PD
2003	342	9329	5	1.83	55.01	0.65	0.16	8	0.11	95.48%	2.22
2004	326	7079	2	1.90	43.43	0.62	0.13	4	0.14	92.68%	3.36
2005	359	7211	1	3.18	40.17	0.59	0.11	5	0.21	88.32%	3.64
2006	419	8613	1	2.47	41.11	0.61	0.09	4	0.36	90.50%	2.36
2007	427	11394	3	1.77	53.37	0.67	0.12	6	0.14	95.97%	1.26
2008	400	10180	2	1.62	50.90	0.70	0.12	5	0.08	95.78%	1.94
2009	434	10784	2	1.92	49.70	0.66	0.11	4	0.18	91.45%	3.49
2010	446	10151	1	2.42	45.52	0.64	0.10	4	0.19	92.01%	1.29
2011	408	11519	2	1.89	56.47	0.60	0.13	6	0.12	93.69%	3.76
2012	345	6527	3	2.47	46.11	0.48	0.11	4	0.33	87.00%	4.25
2013	449	10094	1	2.21	44.96	0.61	0.10	4	0.38	86.51%	4.18
2014	450	10036	1	2.18	44.60	0.58	0.09	3	0.43	91.14%	1.79
2015	490	12563	1	2.90	51.28	0.69	0.10	5	0.60	85.90%	3.11
2016	425	10159	2	1.44	47.81	0.66	0.11	4	0.38	92.62%	1.83
2017	306	9434	4	1.64	47.65	0.72	0.12	6	0.24	90.25%	3.16
United States											
Year	# of Nodes	# of Edges	# of CC	Avg. SPL	Avg. Degree	Avg. Clustering	Density	# of Comm.	Mod.	Avg. PD	SD PD
2003	431	41892	2	1.11	194.39	0.95	0.45	2	0.48	93.60%	1.03
2004	426	40928	2	1.10	192.15	0.95	0.45	2	0.48	92.97%	0.55
2005	431	41892	2	1.10	194.39	0.95	0.45	2	0.48	92.60%	0.79
2006	426	41112	2	1.10	193.01	0.95	0.45	2	0.49	91.45%	0.33
2007	414	38471	2	1.12	185.85	0.94	0.45	2	0.44	91.55%	3.78
2008	424	40729	2	1.11	192.12	0.94	0.45	2	0.46	95.45%	1.97
2009	429	41698	2	1.15	194.40	0.94	0.45	2	0.40	93.86%	2.42
2010	420	39969	1	3.06	190.33	0.95	0.45	3	0.43	94.92%	1.86
2011	426	41119	2	1.18	193.05	0.96	0.45	3	0.44	90.31%	1.91
2012	417	40545	3	1.17	194.46	0.96	0.46	3	0.44	91.63%	1.86
2013	423	40921	2	1.11	193.48	0.96	0.45	2	0.47	93.23%	1.03
2014	418	40735	2	1.08	194.90	0.96	0.46	2	0.48	94.37%	0.34
2015	427	41890	2	1.09	196.21	0.95	0.46	2	0.47	94.40%	1.36
2016	423	40927	2	1.11	193.51	0.95	0.45	2	0.48	94.70%	1.36
2017	423	40928	2	1.09	193.51	0.95	0.45	2	0.46	96.02%	0.44

In contrast, the topological structure of the identified communities, as expressed by the *modularity* metric, is very weak, especially in the former years. That is, there is still a lot of similarity across members of different ideological communities. We note that in the former years the government had greater support from most parties, voting similarly in most sessions. Such approval dropped during a period of political turmoil that started in 2012, when the distinction of ideologies and opinions become more clear [6,33]. This may explain why the *modularity* starts low and increases in the most recent years, when there is greater distinction between different communities. Note that this happens despite the large average party discipline maintained by the communities. That is, these two metrics provide complementary interpretations of the political scenario.

Turning our attention to the US (bottom part of Table 2), we note that, unlike in Brazil, most metrics remain roughly stable throughout the years. The networks are much more dense, with higher average clustering coefficient and density and shortest path length. The number of identified communities coincides with the number of connected components as well as with the number of political parties (see Table 1) in most years. These communities are more strongly structured, despite some ideological overlap, as expressed by moderate-to-large *modularity* value. Moreover, these communities are consistent in their ideologies, as expressed by large party disciplines, comparable to the original (party-level) ones. These metrics reflect the political behavior of a non-fragmented and stronger two-party system, quite unlike the Brazilian scenario.

In sum, in Brazil, the several parties can be grouped into just a few ideological communities, with strong disciplined members, although the separation between communities is not very clear. In the US, on the other hand, ideological communities are more clearly defined, both structurally and ideologically, though some inter-community similarity still remains.

5   Identifying Polarized Communities

As mentioned, the ideological communities identified in the previous section still share some similarity, particularly for the Brazilian case. In this section, we address our second research question (RQ2), with the aim of identifying polarized communities, i.e., communities that have a more clear distinction from the others in terms of voting behavior. To that end, we take a step further and consider that members of the same polarized community should not only be neighbors (i.e., similar to each other) but should also share most of their neighbors. Thus two members that, despite voting similar to each other, have mostly distinct sets of neighbors should *not* be in the same group.

To identify polarized communities, we start with the networks used to identify the ideological communities and compute the *neighborhood overlap* for each edge. The neighborhood overlap of an edge (v_i, v_j) is the ratio of the number of nodes that are neighbors of both v_i and v_j to the number of neighbors of at least one of v_i or v_j [13]. The neighborhood overlap of v_i and v_j is taken as an estimate of the strength of the tie between the two nodes. Edges with tie strength below (above) a given threshold are classified as *weak* (*strong*) ties. We consider that weak ties come from overlapping communities, and strong ties are edges within a polarized community. Thus, edges representing weak ties are removed. As before, all nodes that become isolated after this second filtering are also removed.

Once again the selection of the best neighborhood overlap threshold was not clear as it involves a complex tradeoff: larger thresholds lead to more closely connected communities and higher *modularity*, which is the goal, but also produce more sparse graphs, resulting in a larger number of isolated nodes which are disregarded. Thus, for each network, we selected a threshold that produced a good compromise between the two metrics. Figure 2 shows an example of this trade-off for one specific year (2017) in Brazil, with the selected threshold value shown in green. For Brazil, the selected threshold fell between 0.40 and 0.55, while for the United States this range was from 0.1 to 0.28. We then re-executed the Louvain algorithm to detect (polarized) communities in the new networks.

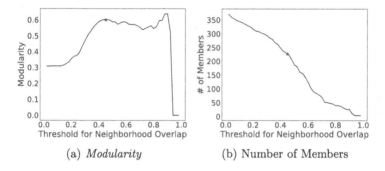

(a) *Modularity*   (b) Number of Members

Fig. 2. Impact of Neighborhood Overlap Threshold for Brazil, 2017 (Selected threshold in green). Color figure online

Table 3 presents the topological properties of the networks as well as the structural and ideological properties of the identified polarized communities, for both Brazil and US. Focusing first on the Brazilian networks (top part of the table), we see that the number of nodes with strong ties decreases drastically (by up to 66%) as compared to the networks analyzed in Sect. 4. This indicates the large presence of House members that, despite great similarity with other members, are not strongly tied (as defined above) to them, and thus do not belong to any polarized community. The number of connected components dropped for some years and increased for others, suggesting that some components in the first set of networks were composed of structurally weaker communities or of multiple smaller communities. Network density, average shortest path length, and clustering coefficient also dropped, indicating more sparse networks, as expected.

The number of polarized communities somewhat differs from the number of communities obtained when all (strong and weak) ties are considered, increasing in most years. This suggests that some ideological communities identified in Sect. 4 may be indeed formed by multiple more closely connected subgroups.

Table 3. Characterization of strongly tied networks and polarized communities

	Brazil										
Year	# of Nodes	# of Edges	# of CC	Avg. SPL	Avg. Degree	Avg. Clustering	Density	# of Comm.	Mod.	Avg. PD	SD PD
2003	186	1436	1	1.48	15.44	0.38	0.08	4	0.35	97.78%	0.86
2004	154	866	1	1.52	11.25	0.33	0.07	5	0.36	97.11%	0.57
2005	119	1210	2	1.19	20.34	0.59	0.17	4	0.37	95.40%	0.93
2006	136	590	10	1.37	8.68	0.52	0.06	12	0.57	96.62%	2.16
2007	175	977	3	1.68	11.17	0.32	0.06	6	0.44	97.31%	1.36
2008	216	1019	2	1.94	9.44	0.23	0.04	5	0.42	97.11%	0.46
2009	209	1217	1	1.30	11.65	0.41	0.05	5	0.56	94.57%	1.67
2010	225	726	6	1.45	6.45	0.22	0.02	11	0.51	94.31%	1.80
2011	250	1891	1	1.78	15.13	0.31	0.06	4	0.40	96.56%	0.86
2012	145	1151	3	1.84	29.82	0.48	0.11	6	0.37	94.42%	1.98
2013	318	4437	5	1.77	27.91	0.58	0.08	9	0.47	91.30%	2.17
2014	287	1672	3	1.37	11.65	0.41	0.04	5	0.63	94.04%	1.28
2015	372	6290	6	1.41	33.82	0.64	0.09	9	0.64	93.93%	1.70
2016	269	1726	3	1.43	12.83	0.44	0.04	8	0.63	95.08%	1.21
2017	227	1631	5	1.58	14.37	0.44	0.06	6	0.60	95.25%	2.01

	United States										
Year	# of Nodes	# of Edges	# of CC	Avg. SPL	Avg. Degree	Avg. Clustering	Density	# of Comm.	Mod.	Avg. PD	SD PD
2003	431	41872	2	1.11	194.30	0.95	0.45	2	0.47	93.60%	1.03
2004	426	40741	2	1.12	191.27	0.95	0.45	2	0.48	92.97%	0.55
2005	431	41886	2	1.11	194.37	0.95	0.45	2	0.47	92.60%	0.79
2006	426	41073	2	1.10	192.83	0.95	0.45	2	0.48	91.45%	0.33
2007	414	38462	2	1.12	185.81	0.94	0.44	2	0.42	91.55%	3.78
2008	423	40708	2	1.11	192.47	0.95	0.45	2	0.43	95.49%	1.93
2009	428	41690	2	1.15	194.81	0.94	0.45	2	0.40	93.89%	2.45
2010	418	39958	2	1.13	191.19	0.95	0.45	3	0.43	94.86%	1.97
2011	422	41112	2	1.15	194.84	0.97	0.46	3	0.45	90.01%	3.16
2012	413	40529	2	1.07	196.27	0.97	0.47	3	0.44	91.70%	2.17
2013	421	40910	2	1.10	194.35	0.96	0.46	2	0.46	93.32%	0.94
2014	417	40717	2	1.08	195.29	0.96	0.46	2	0.48	94.40%	0.38
2015	424	41759	2	1.08	196.98	0.95	0.46	2	0.47	94.53%	1.41
2016	418	40890	2	1.08	195.65	0.96	0.46	3	0.46	95.67%	0.80
2017	421	40923	2	1.08	194.41	0.95	0.46	2	0.48	95.37%	0.11

Yet, those numbers are still smaller than the number of parties in each year
(Table 1). Moreover, compared to the ideological communities first analyzed,
the polarized communities are stronger both structurally and ideologically, as
expressed by larger values of *modularity* and average party discipline.

For the US case, the numbers in Table 3 are very similar to those in Table 2.
Less than 2% of the nodes have only weak ties and were removed from the
networks in all years. Thus, almost all members have strong ties to each other,
building ideological communities that are, in general, very polarized.

In sum, despite the fragmented party system, polarization can be observed in
Brazil, to some degree, in a number of smaller strongly tied communities. In the
US, on the other hand, almost all members and communities are very polarized.

6   Temporal Analysis

We finally turn to RQ3 and investigate how the polarized communities evolve
over time. To that end, we compute two complementary metrics, namely *persistence* and normalized mutual information [32,36], for each pair of consecutive

years. We define the *persistence* from year x to $x + 1$ as the fraction of all members of polarized communities in x who remained in some polarized community in $x + 1$. A *persistence* equal to 100% implies that all members of polarized communities in x remained in some polarized community in $x + 1$. Yet, the membership of individual communities may have changed as members may have moved to different communities. To assess the extent of change in community membership over consecutive years, we compute the normalized mutual information (NMI) over the communities, taking only members who persisted over the two years.

NMI is based on Shannon entropy of information theory [31]. Given two sets of partitions X and Y, defining community assignments for nodes, the mutual information of X and Y can be thought as the informational "overlap" between X and Y, or how much we learn about Y from X (and about X from Y). Let $P(x)$ be the probability that a node picked at random is assigned to community x, $P(x, y)$ be the probability that a node picked at random is assigned to both x in X and y in Y. Also, let $H(X)$ be the Shannon entropy for X defined as $H(X) = -\sum_x P(x) log P(x)$. The NMI of X and Y is defined as:

$$NMI(X, Y) = \frac{\sum_x \sum_y P(x, y) log \frac{P(x,y)}{P(x)P(y)}}{\sqrt{H(X)H(Y)}} \tag{2}$$

NMI ranges from 0 (all members changed their communities) to 1 (all members remained in the same communities).

Table 4 shows *persistence* (*Pers*) and NMI results for all pairs of consecutive years and both countries. For Brazil (BR), the values of *persistence* varied over the years, ranging from 46% to 80%. Thus, a significant number of new nodes join polarized communities every year. Indeed, in most years, roughly half of the members of polarized communities are newcomers. Moreover, the values of NMI are small, especially in the earlier years, reflecting great change also in terms of nodes switching communities. This is consistent with a period of less clear distinction between the communities and weaker polarization, as discussed in the previous sections. Since 2012, the values of NMI fall around 0.6, reflecting greater stability in community membership. For the US, on the other hand, both *persistence* and NMI are very large, approaching the maximum (1). Almost all members persist in their polarized communities over the years.

Table 4. Temporal evolution of polarized ideological communities.

Sequential years	2003	2004	2005	2007	2008	2009	2011	2012	2013	2015	2016
	2004	2005	2006	2008	2009	2010	2012	2013	2014	2016	2017
BR Pers.	58.24%	46.30%	53.04%	68.26%	63.80%	61.38%	80.08%	67.87%	61.23%	57.85%	57.47%
NMI	0.14	0.16	0.20	0.22	0.18	0.26	0.14	0.59	0.56	0.65	0.58
US Pers.	98.13%	90.80%	98.36%	97.57%	86.74%	96.24%	96.18%	96.76%	97.85%	97.63%	86.26%
NMI	0.97	0.97	1.00	1.00	1.00	0.94	0.96	0.80	1.00	0.97	0.98

A visualization of some of these results is shown in Fig. 3 which presents the flow of nodes across polarized communities over the years of 2015 to 2017 in Brazil and in the US. Each vertical line represents a community, and its length represents the number of members belonging to that community who persisted in some polarized community in the following year. Thus, communities for which all members did not persist in any polarized community in the following year are not represented in the figure. Recall that, according to Table 3, the number of polarized communities in Brazil in 2015, 2016 and 2017 was 9, 8 and 6, respectively. A cross-analysis of these results with Fig. 3a indicates that members of only 4 out of 9 polarized communities in 2015 persisted polarized in the following year. Moreover, two polarized communities in 2016 were composed of only newcomers and both communities disappeared in 2017 (as they do not appear in the figure). Similarly, one polarized community in 2017 was composed of only newcomers. The figure also shows a great amount of switching, merging and splitting across communities over the years. Figure 3b, on the other hand, illustrates the greater stability of community membership in the US.

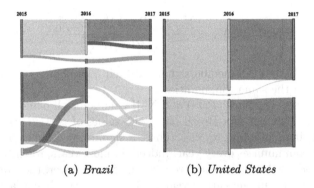

(a) *Brazil*   (b) *United States*

Fig. 3. Dynamics of polarized communities over 2015–2017.

7   Conclusions and Future Work

We have proposed a methodology to analyze the formation and evolution of ideological and polarized communities in party systems, applying it to two strikingly different political contexts, namely Brazil and the US. Our analyses showed that the large number of political parties in Brazil can be reduced to only a few ideological communities, maintaining their original ideological properties, that is well disciplined communities, with a certain degree of redundancy. These communities have distinguished themselves both structurally and ideologically in the recent years, a reflection of the transformation that Brazilian politics has been experiencing since 2012. For the US, the country's strong and non-fragmented party system leads to the identification of ideological communities in the two main parties throughout the analyzed period. However, there are still some highly similar links crossing the community boundaries. Moreover, for some years, a third community emerged, without however affecting the strong discipline, ideology and community structure of the American party system.

We then took a step further and focused on polarized communities by considering only tightly connected groups of nodes. We found that in Brazil, despite the party fragmentation and the existence of some degree of similarity even across the identified ideological communities, it is still possible to find a subset of members that organize themselves into strongly polarized ideological communities. However, these communities are highly dynamic, changing a large portion of their membership over consecutive years. In the US, on the other hand, most ideological communities identified are indeed highly polarized and their membership remain mostly unchanged over the years.

As future work, we intend to further analyze ideological communities in our datasets by characterizing members in terms of their centrality as well as proposing new metrics of tie strength for this particular domain. We also intend to extend our study to other party systems.

Acknowledgments. This work was partially supported by the FAPEMIG-PRONEX-MASWeb project – Models, Algorithms and Systems for the Web, process number APQ-01400-14, as well as by the National Institute of Science and Technology for the Web (INWEB), CNPq and FAPEMIG.

References

1. Agathangelou, P., Katakis, I., Rori, L., Gunopulos, D., Richards, B.: Understanding online political networks: the case of the far-right and far-left in Greece. In: Ciampaglia, G.L., Mashhadi, A., Yasseri, T. (eds.) SocInfo 2017. LNCS, vol. 10539, pp. 162–177. Springer, Cham (2017). https://doi.org/10.1007/978-3-319-67217-5_11
2. Ames, B.: The Deadlock of Democracy in Brazil. University of Michigan Press (2009)
3. Andris, C., Lee, D., Hamilton, M.J., Martino, M., Gunning, C.F., Selden, J.A.: The rise of partisanship and super-cooperators in the U.S. house of representatives. PLOS ONE **10**(4), 1–14 (2015)
4. Arinik, N., Figueiredo, R., Labatut, V.: Signed graph analysis for the interpretation of voting behavior. In: International Workshop on Social Network Analysis and Digital Humanities (2017)
5. Baldassarri, D., Gelman, A.: Partisans without constraint: political polarization and trends in american public opinion. Am. J. Soc. **114**(2), 408–446 (2008)
6. BBC: Brazil profile - timeline (2018). http://www.bbc.com/news/world-latin-america-19359111
7. Blondel, V.D., Guillaume, J.L., Lambiotte, R., Lefebvre, E.: Fast unfolding of communities in large networks. J. Stat. Mech. Theor. Exp. **2008**(10) (2008)
8. Budge, I., Laver, M.J.: Party Policy and Government Coalitions. Springer, London (2016). https://doi.org/10.1007/978-1-349-22368-8
9. Cai, Q., Ma, L., Gong, M., Tian, D.: A survey on network community detection based on evolutionary computation. Int. J. Bio-Inspired Comput. **8**(2), 84–98 (2016)

10. Cherepnalkoski, D., Karpf, A., Mozetič, M.: Cohesion and coalition formation in the european parliament: Roll-call votes and twitter activities. PLOS ONE **11**(11), 1–27 (2016)

11. Dal Maso, C., Pompa, G., Puliga, M., Riotta, G., Chessa, A.: Voting behavior, coalitions and government strength through a complex network analysis. PLOS ONE **9**, 1–13 (2015)

12. Darwish, K., Magdy, W., Zanouda, T.: Trump vs. Hillary: what went viral during the 2016 US presidential election. In: Ciampaglia, G.L., Mashhadi, A., Yasseri, T. (eds.) SocInfo 2017. LNCS, vol. 10539, pp. 143–161. Springer, Cham (2017). https://doi.org/10.1007/978-3-319-67217-5_10

13. Easley, D., Kleinberg, J.: Networks, Crowds, and Markets: Reasoning About a Highly Connected World. Cambridge University Press, New York (2010)

14. Fiorina, M.P., Abrams, S.J.: Political polarization in the american public. Ann. Rev. Polit. Sci. **11**(1), 563–588 (2008)

15. Fortunato, S.: Community detection in graphs. Phys. Rep. **486**(3), 75–174 (2010)

16. Granovetter, M.S.: The strength of weak ties. In: Social Networks, pp. 347–367. Elsevier (1977)

17. Hix, S., Noury, A., Roland, G.: Power to the parties: cohesion and competition in the european parliament, 1979–2001. Br. J. Polit. Sci. **35**(2), 209–234 (2005)

18. Jones, J.J., Settle, J.E., Bond, R.M., Fariss, C.J., Marlow, C., Fowler, J.H.: Inferring tie strength from online directed behavior. PLOS ONE **8**(1), 1–6 (2013)

19. Levorato, M., Frota, Y.: Brazilian Congress structural balance analysis. J. Interdisc. Methodologies Issues Sci. Graphs Soci. Syst. (2017)

20. Mainwaring, S., Shugart, M.S.: Presidentialism and Democracy in Latin America. Cambridge University Press, Cambridge (1997)

21. Mann, T.E., Ornstein, N.J.: It's even worse than it looks: how the American constitutional system collided with the new politics of extremism. In: Basic Books (2016)

22. McGee, J., Caverlee, J., Cheng, Z.: Location prediction in social media based on tie strength. In: Proceedings of the 22Nd ACM International Conference on Information & Knowledge Management, CIKM 2013, pp. 459–468. ACM, New York (2013)

23. Vaz de Melo, P.O.S.: How many political parties should brazil have? a data-driven method to assess and reduce fragmentation in multi-party political systems. PLOS ONE **10**(10), 1–24 (2015)

24. Mendonça, I., Trouve, A., Fukuda, A.: Exploring the importance of negative links through the European parliament social graph. In: Proceedings of the 2017 International Conference on E-Society, E-Education and E-Technology, ICSET 2017, pp. 1–7. ACM, New York (2017)

25. Moody, J., Mucha, P.J.: Portrait of political party polarization. Netw. Sci. **1**(1), 119–121 (2013)

26. Newman, M.E.J.: Modularity and community structure in networks. Proc. Nat. Acad. Sci. **103**(23), 8577–8582 (2006)

27. Plantié, M., Crampes, M.: Survey on social community detection. In: Ramzan, N., van Zwol, R., Lee, J.S., Clüver, K., Hua, X.S. (eds.) Social Media Retrieval, pp. 65–85. Springer, London (2013). https://doi.org/10.1007/978-1-4471-4555-4_4

28. Porter, M.A., Mucha, P.J., Newman, M.E.J., Warmbrand, C.M.: A network analysis of committees in the U.S. house of representatives. Proc. Nat. Acad. Sci. **102**(20), 7057–7062 (2005)

29. Rossetti, G., Cazabet, R.: Community discovery in dynamic networks: a survey. ACM Comput. Surv. **51**(2), 35:1–35:37 (2018)

30. Sartori, G.: Parties and Party Systems: A Framework for Analysis. ECPR Press (2005)
31. Shannon, C.E.: A mathematical theory of communication. ACM SIGMOBILE Mob. Comput. Commun. Rev. **5**(1), 3–55 (2001)
32. Vinh, N.X., Epps, J., Bailey, J.: Information theoretic measures for clusterings comparison: variants, properties, normalization and correction for chance. J. Mach. Learn. Res. **11**, 2837–2854 (2010)
33. Vox: Brazil's political crisis, explained (2016). https://www.vox.com/2016/4/21/11451210/dilma-rousseff-impeachment
34. Wang, Y., Feng, Y., Hong, Z., Berger, R., Luo, J.: How polarized have we become? A multimodal classification of trump followers and clinton followers. In: Ciampaglia, G.L., Mashhadi, A., Yasseri, T. (eds.) SocInfo 2017. LNCS, vol. 10539, pp. 440–456. Springer, Cham (2017). https://doi.org/10.1007/978-3-319-67217-5_27
35. Waugh, A.S., Pei, L., Fowler, J.H., Mucha, P.J., Porter, M.A.: Party polarization in congress: a social networks approach. arXiv preprint arXiv:0907.3509 (2009)
36. Wei, W., Carley, K.M.: Measuring temporal patterns in dynamic social networks. ACM Trans. Knowl. Discov. Data **10**(1), 9:1–9:27 (2015)
37. Wiese, J., Min, J.K., Hong, J.I., Zimmerman, J.: "You never call, you never write": Call and SMS logs do not always indicate tie strength. In: Proceedings of the 18th ACM Conference on Computer Supported Cooperative Work and Social Computing, CSCW 2015, pp. 765–774. ACM, New York (2015)

Quantifying Media Influence and Partisan Attention on Twitter During the UK EU Referendum

Genevieve Gorrell$^{(\boxtimes)}$ ⓘ, Ian Roberts, Mark A. Greenwoodⓘ,
Mehmet E. Bakirⓘ, Benedetta Iavarone, and Kalina Bontchevaⓘ

University of Sheffield, Sheffield, UK
g.gorrell@sheffield.ac.uk

Abstract. User generated media, and their influence on the information individuals are exposed to, have the potential to affect political outcomes. This is increasingly a focus for attention and concern. The British EU membership referendum provided an opportunity for researchers to explore the nature and impact of the new infosphere in a politically charged situation. This work contributes by reviewing websites that were linked in a Brexit Tweet dataset of 13.2 million tweets, by 1.8 million distinct users, collected in the run-up to the referendum. In this dataset, 480,000 users have been classified according to their "Brexit" vote intent. Findings include that linked material on Twitter was mostly posted by those in favour of leaving the EU. Mainstream news media had the greatest impact in terms of number of links tweeted, with alternative media and campaign sites appearing to a much lesser extent. Of the 15 most linked mainstream media, half show a substantially greater appeal to the leave camp, with two of them very much so. No mainstream media had a consistent appeal among remain supporters. Among the sites that were highly favoured by one voter valence or the other, the leave sites had by far the greatest impact in terms of number of appearances in tweets. Remain-preferred sites were less linked, and dominated by explicit campaign sites. Leave-preferred sites were more numerously linked, and dominated by mainstream and alternative media.

1 Introduction

"Post-truth politics" [6] and "weaponized relativism"[1] describe strategies by which misleading information can be used to shape debates, redirect attention and sow confusion in order to influence political outcomes. In recent times, concern has been raised about the opportunities social media may be creating for use of these strategies, and the consequent undermining of democracy.

---

[1] https://www.theguardian.com/commentisfree/2015/mar/02/guardian-view-russian-propaganda-truth-out-there.

© Springer Nature Switzerland AG 2018
S. Staab et al. (Eds.): SocInfo 2018, LNCS 11185, pp. 274–290, 2018.
https://doi.org/10.1007/978-3-030-01129-1_17

Furthermore, social media can create a skewed or biased information environment that may affect voters' perspectives. This has rightly become the focus for research [20], which is starting to yield insights. The British EU membership referendum ("Brexit") provided an opportunity to explore the nature and extent of social media impact in a politically charged situation.

In this work, we explore the informational materials that appeared in tweets about Brexit. With the aim of deepening our understanding of who exerted an influence in the run-up to the referendum, and how their influence played out, the work is organized around the following research questions:

RQ1: Who were the most prominent information sources in the Brexit debate on Twitter? Specifically, what domains were most linked?

RQ2: Is there evidence of differential media sharing patterns between leave and remain supporters? In what ways are leave and remain campaigns responding differently to opportunities afforded by the Twitter medium? How are readers responding to materials?

RQ3: What influence has partisan and misleading material had? Who is supplying biased material? How effective have these materials been?

Key to the work presented here is a foundation of a list of around half a million Twitter users accurately classified according to their Brexit vote intent; "remainers" expressed or indicated their intention to vote for the UK to remain in the EU, and "leavers", their intention to vote "leave". The work explores similar territory to that covered by Faris et al. [4], who analyze mainstream media and asymmetries in the context of the 2016 US general election; we extend this with a contrasting political scenario in a different country, and through our focus on Twitter. Moore and Ramsay [15] analyse mainstream media behaviour in the run-up to the referendum; our work builds on theirs by exploring how the behaviour they discuss relates to a medium's partisan appeal. Previous work has also shared valuable evidence of Twitter partisan activity in the run-up to the referendum [9,16]; our voter classification enables us to bring an additional perspective and rich possibilities for exploration of partisan dynamics.

The aggregate data on which this work is based are available for download.[2]

2   Related Work

The work presented here is set against a backdrop of increasing awareness of the ways in which the internet and social media are changing society. Social media have been widely observed to provide a platform for fringe views. Faris et al. [4]

---

[2] http://www.dcs.shef.ac.uk/~genevieve/publications-materials/brexit-domains-shared-materials.ods.

showed that social media seem to amplify more extreme views, with materials linked on Twitter being more outré than the open web, and on Facebook even more so, a finding echoed by Silverman [19]. Barberá and Rivero [2] and Preotiuc-Pietro et al. [18] both show that Twitter users with more ideologically extreme positions post more content than those with moderate views.

Researchers also report consistent asymmetries in the way these changed conditions play out. Allcott and Gentzkow [1], during the run-up to the 2016 US presidential election, found 115 pro-Trump fake news stories, which were shared a total of 30 million times. They found 41 pro-Clinton fake news stories, which were shared a total of 7.6 million times. This disparity is again echoed in Silverman's [19] work.

There is little evidence of a difference in the way information consumers of different political valences respond to materials that might account for asymmetry [1,4]. Instead, Faris et al. suggest that in the case of the 2016 presidential election it was the cooperative behaviour of pro-Trump media themselves that led to an advantage, in a phenomenon they dub "network propaganda". This raises questions about the reach of such a network or the conditions under which it might arise elsewhere, and its relationship to political views if any.

A body of work [12,13] has begun to explore Brexit opinion and sentiment as expressed on Twitter. Howard and Kollanyi [9] share our interest in propaganda, but their work concerns "bots" and the role of automated activity on Twitter. Their group have also specifically investigated Russian involvement in Brexit [16]. Bastos and Mercea [3] also study the impact of bot activity, and present some observations about the nature of the content linked by the bots. They state that such materials are likely to be user-generated, tabloid-style emotionally orientated materials. Such work highlights the presence of organized attempts to influence. Matsuo and Benoit[3] focus on differences in the dialogue between leave and remain camps. Moore and Ramsay [15] also highlight differences in the tone of the different campaigns.

The role of Twitter misinformation in the context of the 2016 US presidential election has attracted much research attention, as previously discussed. Less research has reviewed similar situations in other countries. Ferrara [5] focuses on the anti-Macron disinformation campaign in the run-up to the 2017 French presidential election. A series of white papers from the Oxford Internet Institute explore junk news and misinformation in a variety of countries' elections [7,8, 10,11,17]. Such work offers the opportunity to find patterns that extend beyond local situations. This work forms a part of that effort.

3   Methodology

The basis of the work is a large collection of tweets collected using the GATE Cloud Twitter Collector[4], a tool that allows tweets to be gathered according

---

[3] http://blogs.lse.ac.uk/brexit/2017/03/16/more-positive-assertive-and-forward-looking-how-leave-won-twitter/.

[4] https://cloud.gate.ac.uk/shopfront/displayItem/twitter-collector.

to search criteria as they appear, and processed using GATE[5] text processing pipelines to enrich the tweets with relevant background information, including the EU membership stance of the author. The method is described more fully by Maynard *et al.* [14]. In the next section we describe collecting the tweets, then after that the user vote intent classification.

Throughout the work we make use of Partisanship Attention Score (PAS), first introduced by Faris *et al.* [4]. This metric is a simple ratio of the number of times a source is linked by one valence of user, for example leavers, versus the other valence. In this work we use "leave-PAS" to describe a PAS in which leave linkers outnumber remain linkers, and "remain-PAS" to describe a PAS in which remain linkers dominate. We have grouped sources into five sets; those in which a PAS is greater than 30:1 (one leave set and one remain set), those in which the PAS is greater than 3:1 (leave and remain) and those with a more balanced PAS of less than 3:1. The 30:1 and 3:1 ratios were selected heuristically–throughout the work we are careful to reflect on how that choice might affect the results.

3.1   Tweet Collection

Around 17.5 million tweets were collected up to and including 23 June 2016 (EU referendum day). The highest volume was 2 million tweets on Jun 23rd (only 3,300 lost due to rate limiting), with just over 1.5 million during poll opening times. Of the 2 million, 57% were retweets and 5% replies. June 22nd was second highest, with 1.3 million tweets. The 17.5 million tweets were authored by just over 2 million distinct Twitter users (2,016,896). The work presented here focuses on a subset of these, covering the month up to and including June 23rd. Within that period, there were just over 13.2 million tweets, from which 4.5 million were original tweets (4,594,948), 7.7 million were retweets (7,767,726) and 850 thousand were replies (858,492). These were sent by just over 1.8 million distinct users. The tweets were collected based on the following keywords and hashtags: *votein, yestoeu, leaveeu, beleave, EU referendum, voteremain, bremain, no2eu, betteroffout, strongerin, euref, betteroffin, eureferendum, yes2eu, voteleave, voteout, notoeu, eureform, ukineu, britainout, brexit, leadnotleave.* These were chosen for being the main hashtags, and are broadly balanced across remain and leave hashtags, though the ultimate test of the balance of the dataset lies in the number of leavers and remainers found in it, which is discussed below.

Most URLs found in tweets have been shortened, either automatically by Twitter or manually by the user, which has the side effect of obfuscating the original domain being linked to. For this work we expanded the URLs in tweets using the following approach. From manual analysis of the URLs we accumulated a list of 18 URL shorteners or redirect services: shr.gs, bit.ly, j.mp, ow.ly, trib.al, tinyurl.com, ift.tt, ln.is, dlvr.it, t.co, feeds.feedburner.com, redirect.viglink.com, feedproxy.google.com, news.google.com, www.bing.com, linkis.com, goo.gl, and adf.ly. All URLs from other domains were considered to already be expanded. (A small number of minor URL shorteners have gone unexpanded due to the long

---

[5] https://gate.ac.uk/.

tail in this large tweet set and the necessity of manually identifying shortening services.) When we saw a shortened URL it was expanded, either by following HTTP redirects or using the API of the shortener, recursively until the resulting URL no longer pointed to a domain in our list of shorteners.

3.2 User Vote Intent Classification

Classification of users according to vote intent was done on the basis of tweets authored by them and identified as being in favour of leaving or remaining in the EU. Such tweets were identified using 59 hashtags indicating allegiance, given in the online experimental materials[6]. Hashtags in the final position more reliably summarise the tweeter's position, so only these were used. Consider, for example. "is Britain really #strongerin? I don't think so! #voteleave".

This approach was evaluated using a set of users that explicitly declared their vote intent. A company called Brndstr[7] ran a campaign offering a topical profile image modification in response to a formulaic vote intent declaration mentioning their brand. This enabled a ground truth sample to be easily and accurately gathered. On these data, we found our method produced a 94% accuracy even on the basis of a single partisan tweet (where three are required, an accuracy of 99% can be obtained, though only 60,000 such users can be found, as opposed to 290,000 with at least one partisan tweet). The Brndstr data itself, consisting of around 100,000 users of each valence, was also used to supplement the set, raising the accuracy further, and resulting in a list of 208,113 leave voters and 270,246 remain voters. Table 1 gives detailed statistics for three conditions; one matching tweet found for that user, two found or three found. "Total" is the total number of users found with that number of matching tweets. "Brndstr found" is the number of those users found in the Brndstr set, and so able to be evaluated. The remaining figures refer to that set, providing an accuracy for the total list of users found using the given minimum number of partisan tweets.

There may be a case for using a threshold of two hashtags in order to produce a more balanced set of leavers and remainers, but this would disproportionately exclude remainers with more moderate feelings (if the number of hashtags can be seen as an indicator of this). The resulting set is somewhat slanted toward remainers, demonstrating the obvious; that Twitter isn't a representative sample of the UK population, who voted to leave the EU to the order of 52%. However, leavers were more vocal and apparent in the data presented below, contrary to what we would expect if the higher number of remainers had affected the result. It is possible that some users changed their mind about how to vote after making their Brndstr declaration, but voters making an online declaration of their vote intent are perhaps those less likely to vacillate, and the work can in either case be seen as an exploration of the behaviour of those who held a particular allegiance during the time period studied.

---

[6] http://www.dcs.shef.ac.uk/~genevieve/publications-materials/brexit-domains-shared-materials.ods.

[7] http://www.brndstr.com/.

Table 1. Brexit classifier accuracy

	Total	Brndstr found	Of found correct	Accuracy	Cohen's kappa
Leavers, 3#	34539	1142	1129	0.987	0.972
Remainers, 3#	26674	603	594		
Leavers, 2#	49080	1368	1350	0.984	0.966
Remainers, 2#	50972	901	882		
Leavers, 1#	114519	1935	1801	0.943	0.885
Remainers, 1#	175042	1744	1667		

4   RQ1: Who Were the Most Prominent Information Sources in the Brexit Debate on Twitter?

Across the whole corpus, the top 100 most posted domains were manually grouped into high level categories, and the number of links in tweets to domains in each category are shown in Fig. 1. The dominant domain to appear was Twitter itself, appearing whenever anyone posts an image, as well as when they link to another tweet. After that, the greater proportion of the links are to items in a wide variety of mainstream news media. "Other content hosts" refers to smaller content platforms such as Instagram; YouTube and Facebook are listed separately. Finally, smaller amounts of material are linked from referendum campaign sites and alternative media. (Alternative media range from publications that are nearly mainstream through to conspiracy sites and fake news.) The "long tail" of a further 17,000 less linked domains that haven't been manually classified are included in the chart to give a quantification of the unknown; note that this unknown section is likely to contain many more small alternative media,

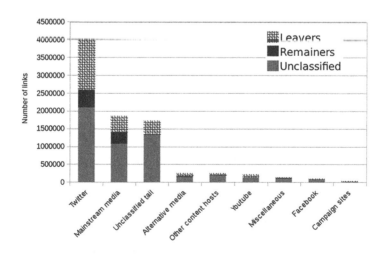

Fig. 1. Types of links posted

blogs etc. than mainstream media. Also only domains that were tweeted at least once by a user that has been classified for vote intent were included. The actual number of domains mentioned in the set is much greater.

The graph broadly agrees with Table 1 of Narayanan *et al.* [16]. We are also able divide each count into three parts, indicating the proportion of tweets in that section by unclassified users, remainers and leavers. It is evident at a glance that remainers were tweeting less linked material, since their representation is smaller. Also there were fewer remainers in the unclassified tail (that is, the column of unclassified sites, not the unclassified users), suggesting perhaps a preference for more popular sites on the part of remainers. It is unknown how many leavers, remainers and undecideds constitute the unclassified users (the grey bottom section of the columns) but there's no particular reason why the classified users wouldn't give a representative impression.

Figure 2 shows the sites that had the most impact, in terms of total number of times they appeared in tweets in the Brexit dataset. These were almost entirely mainstream media, mostly UK media, with the exception of the remain campaign site "ukstronger.in" and the UK government domain. The graph gives total counts of appearances of the most influential domains, colour coded by partisanship attention score (PAS); the ratio of links from leave voters to remain voters or vice versa. Platforms such as Facebook, where the site doesn't author the content, are excluded. Only link appearances in original tweets are used in this graph (not appearances in retweets or replies). Tables 2 and 3 in Appendix A give a longer list of sites. The full set is also available for download[8].

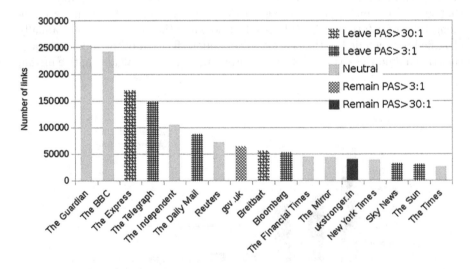

Fig. 2. Number of appearances of high impact sites

---

[8] http://www.dcs.shef.ac.uk/~genevieve/publications-materials/brexit-domains-shared-materials.ods.

On page 13 of Moore and Ramsay [15] a similar graph shows the number of referendum-related articles published by UK media. The number of Brexit articles published by a medium shows a strong correlation to its link presence on Twitter (0.71). In fact, the Express has been somewhat less taken up on Twitter than its engagement with the subject might predict; Fig. 4 and its discussion later in the paper may offer further insights on this point.

RQ1 Discussion. It is evident that mainstream media were the dominant source of linked materials in the Brexit discussion on Twitter, with the six most influential domains all being British mainstream media as shown in Fig. 2. Smaller in influence but nonetheless significant were alternative media, with Breitbart appearing in ninth place in Fig. 2, user-shared content on other content platforms such as Facebook, and campaign sites. This suggests a continuing important role for traditional media, though leaves questions about how social media, and indeed alternative media, may interact to popularize certain materials and influence the focus. It is also apparent that the most popular domains were either neutral in their appeal or appealed to leavers, with only two smaller sources, the government and the "Stronger In" campaign, appealing to remainers. This subject is taken up more fully in the next section.

5   RQ2: Is There Evidence of Differential Media Sharing Patterns Between Leave and Remain Supporters?

Figure 3a shows British mainstream newspapers ranked from left to right in order of their leave PAS ratio (ratio of appearances in leave tweets against appearances in remain tweets). PAS ratio is shown on the graph; however, for those media with negative leave PAS ratios, the remain PAS ratio has been plotted (ratio of appearances in remain tweets against those in leave tweets). In this way, both leave and remain media can be shown commensurately on the same graph. The point at which the PAS ratios switch direction is indicated with a vertical dashed line. The extreme right of the graph, therefore, shows the newspaper with the highest remain PAS ratio (The Guardian/Observer combined). Two horizontal lines indicate PAS ratios of 3:1 and 30:1. PAS ratios for link appearances in all tweets and just original tweets are shown.

Several British newspapers declared their allegiances regarding Brexit, reportedly giving media supporting the UK leaving the EU an audience of around 4.8 million, while those in favour of remaining in the EU reach just over 3 million[9]. Stance information is included in Fig. 3a in the form of coloured marks– a blue diamond for leave and a red circle for remain. Both marks appear for the Mail because the Daily Mail shares its domain with the Mail on Sunday. The Daily Mail were in favour of leaving the EU, and the Mail on Sunday, with a

---

[9] https://www.huffingtonpost.co.uk/entry/which-newspapers-support-brexit_uk_5768fad2e4b0a4f99adc6525.

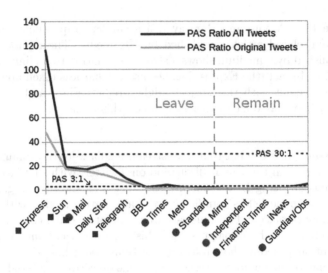

Partisanship Attention Score

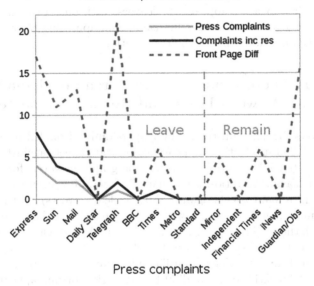

Press complaints

Fig. 3. PAS (a) and Press Complaints (b) for UK Mainstream News Media

slightly lower circulation, were in favour of remaining. Several other domains include the Sunday edition of the newspaper, but only in the case of the Mail do these have different Brexit stances. The Times and the Standard appear with leave PAS scores (to the left of the dashed line) despite a remain allegiance. The PAS scores however are low.

There are various explanations for why remain media materials might have a lower PAS, indicating appeal to both sides of the debate. In order to gather more information about the nature of the materials linked, and the extent of their partisanship, press complaints about stories that could impact on voters' feelings about EU membership in the months preceding the referendum were examined. Figure 3b provides this information, in a graph in which media are ordered according to their PAS, to match the preceding graph. Cases where a story appeared in print and online are counted one time only. The green line indicates the number of upheld press complaints for that medium. The purple line also includes the number of complaints for which a resolution was found. The majority of press complaints regarded articles that were anti-immigration in their focus. The graph also includes an orange dashed line plotting data taken from Moore and Ramsay [15]. They provide data about the number of leave and remain front pages published by media in the weeks leading up to the referendum. The number plotted ("bias") is the magnitude of number of leave front pages minus number of remain front pages, as shown in the equation below. The point at which the number flips from indicating leave bias to remain bias is again indicated with a dashed line on the graph. Zero-scoring media are those for which Moore and Ramsay do not provide statistics.

$$bias = \sqrt{(leave - remain)^2}$$

Figure 4 presents counts of sites according to their PAS status. A threshold of 20 total original tweets by leavers and remainers was applied, in order to exclude sites for which too little evidence was available to classify them. The graph shows peaks to either extreme, despite the stringent 30:1 criterion, reinforcing previous researchers' findings that extreme content tends to proliferate on social media [2, 4, 18, 19]. On the right we see the actual link counts to the sites. Twitter mentions have not been included, since they give a large, uninformative boost to the neutral count. Were other content-neutral platforms to be excluded, this count would be lower still. (Table 2 in Appendix A gives the top 20 sites in each PAS category, in terms of total links; a number of content neutral platforms can be seen there to illustrate the point). This conflation of content-neutral with ideologically neutral does not affect the observation that the extremes no longer

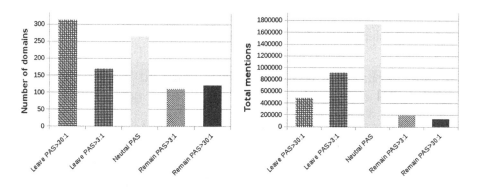

Fig. 4. All domains vs total mentions by PAS of domain

outnumber the moderate sites. It seems most Twitter users prefer less extreme materials of those on offer; a suggestion that would also explain the Express being somewhat less popular than its Brexit engagement would seem to warrant, as discussed above.

RQ2 Discussion. The data have shown that all of the media that declared their support for the remain cause were broadly neutral in their appeal, with the exception of the Guardian/Observer, who, when retweets and replies are counted, has a leave PAS greater than 3:1. The media that declared their official support for leave all to varying extent appealed more to leavers. This brings to mind Faris et al.'s [4] conclusion from their study of the 2016 US presidential election that mainstream media ranging from left to centre right show more investment in principles of neutrality. The Brexit question cut across the political spectrum, although in terms of media stance, the left-leaning papers favoured remain and the right, leave. However, it is also possible that leavers engaged with remain materials for other reasons. In order to gather more data, we reviewed press complaints data, and also compared front page partisanship data from Moore and Ramsay [15]. It is interesting to note that PAS seems to echo upheld press complaints better than it does partisanship as indicated by front pages. There are prominent cases where media published many stories in keeping with their Brexit stance, but without attracting press complaints; namely the Telegraph and the Guardian. Materials supportive of a particular stance don't *per se* seem to draw partisan attention—the PAS of both these media is low.

This is important in correctly interpreting Fig. 2. The medium with the biggest impact is the Guardian, which published many pro-remain articles. So in this sense, there wasn't a lack of attention to pro-remain materials, and if the colour coding of the graph were based on the "front page diff" used above, the impression created would be quite different. PAS captures something different. Manual review of the tweets suggests that Guardian articles tend to be factual in tone, and attract critical engagement from leavers. Express articles tend to use emotive and suggestive language, and seem to attract less discussion. Moore and Ramsay's analysis [15] gives much information about the rhetorical styles employed by the press in the run-up to the referendum. Circulation size does not explain the number of complaints received, with the Express having less than half the readership of any of the four largest media.[10]

6   RQ3: What Influence Has Partisan and Misleading Material Had?

We saw in Sect. 5 that high PAS scores show a potential relationship with upheld press complaints, and that polarity of PAS is a good indicator of the stance of the source, as determined from press front pages. In this section we use PAS

---

[10] http://www.pressgazette.co.uk/nrs-national-press-readership-data-telegraph-overtakes-guardian-as-most-read-quality-title-in-printonline/.

scores of greater than 30:1 to select sources that may be misleading for further examination. Sites of either camp with at least 1000 total mentions in tweets in the dataset and at least 50 tweets, retweets or replies by leavers or remainers were manually analysed. We present the sites divided into 4 categories; mainstream media, alternative media, campaign sites and other sites. "Others" includes for example personal blogs or special interest websites not primarily focused on Brexit.

Figure 5 shows that remain PAS > 30:1 sites are dominated by explicit campaign sites. As we would expect given the data above, among leave influencers we see more mainstream media—note that the only high PAS mainstream media were leave media; namely the Express. We also see a much greater role for alternative media in the leave campaign. The total impact of leave PAS > 30:1 media was 389,000 mentions. For remain it was 70146 mentions, or 18% of the PAS > 30:1 impact. All sites with a PAS higher than 30:1 and more than 5000 mentions are shown in Fig. 6. The Express dominates, with the US alternative medium Breitbart in second place. As indicated above, remain sites are mainly campaign sites. Other leave sites are media ranging from alternative to conspiracy, plus the campaign site "voteleavetakecontrol.org". A longer list can be found in Table 3 in Appendix A.

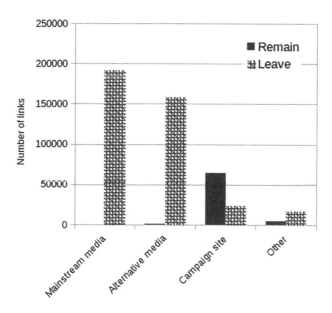

Fig. 5. Who are the PAS > 30:1 influencers?

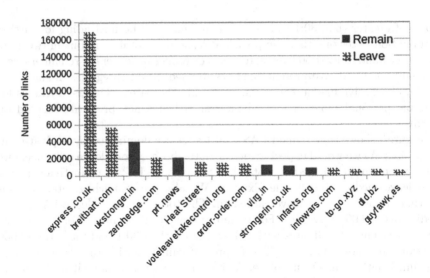

Fig. 6. Who are the PAS > 30:1 sites?

The press complaints data provides another opportunity to review uptake of partisan material. The impact of the misleading articles, at least on Twitter, seems to be relatively minor. By far the most mentioned was the claim that "the Queen backs Brexit", receiving 2969 textual mentions, including 180 retweets of a Russian troll account, despite having run before data began to be collected, making data incomplete. The next most widely mentioned misleading headline was mentioned 199 times only. In contrast, the exonerated article "Far Right in Plot to Hijack Brexit" was the most mentioned remain headline among the press complaints, and was mentioned in text 235 times. Previous research has suggested that false rumours spread faster than true ones [21]. Claims that shaped the referendum debate offer another contrast case. Particularly prominent was leave's claim that the EU costs the UK £350 million each week. A claim was also made by George Osborne, the then Chancellor, in favour of remain; namely that leaving the EU could cost households £4,300 per year by 2030. In our data, the remain claim appeared 9510 times in tweet text. The leave claim appeared 32755 times in text. Moore and Ramsay [15] state that the remain claim was discussed in 365 newspaper articles, whereas the leave claim was discussed in only 147. The greater media interest in the Osborne claim is unsurprising given his position of authority, but this didn't translate into interest on Twitter. The appearance of the leave claim on the side of a bus perhaps proved compelling, appearing in photographs 900 times in our data.

RQ3 Discussion. Key observations from Fig. 5 include that in terms of mentions in tweets, the influence of leave sites dwarfs that of remain sites. It is also notable in that figure that high remain-PAS sites were mostly explicit campaign sites;

in other words, openly partisan, with no suggestion of providing reportage. The range of media providing high leave-PAS materials, plus the presence of Breitbart raises the question of whether these findings demonstrate a similar phenomenon happening in the UK as described by Faris *et al.*, or whether indeed it is simply the same phenomenon - an extension of the same network of propaganda.

7   Conclusion

Websites linked in topically related tweets during the run-up to the 2016 UK EU membership election were most often neutral or bipartisan in their appeal. However, sources with partisan appeal also captured a sizeable portion of the debate, and of those, the leave-partisan materials were much more heavily propagated. Materials with a strong appeal to leavers rather than remainers were plentiful and diverse, and included mainstream media and alternative media including US and other foreign sources. Materials with a strong appeal to remainers were fewer and less influential, and mainly comprised explicit campaign sites.

Mainstream media with a stated remain stance produced materials appealing to both sides of the debate. Some mainstream media with a stated leave stance produced materials predominantly appealing to leavers. Number of upheld press complaints shows a stronger resemblance to a site's partisan appeal than the bias of the source as determined by its number of pro-leave front pages or its stated stance, suggesting that partisan appeal is capturing something other than the extent to which a source provides a voice for a particular opinion, and that misinformation may be a part of it. However, since the sample is small, further work is required to support this. On the other hand, on the remain side, the campaign site "ukstronger.in" also showed a highly partisan appeal. One explanation for differential appeal might lie in the extent to which certain behaviours, for example the suggestion of entrenched opinion, discourage debate. Examination of the tweets shows for example that the pro-remain Guardian attracted interest in the form of critical comment, which the Express did not do to the same extent. Whilst highly partisan materials are of concern in that they may more often be misleading, and are attracting significant attention, information consumers did show a preference for linking more moderate materials, which supports the suggestion that they may be encouraging discussion to a greater extent.

Data show support for Faris *et al.*'s [4] hypothesis of network propaganda, in that a vocal anti-immigration narrative emerged, and it is possible that congruence of message accounted for the greater interest in leave materials of highly partisan appeal. However, further work would be required to support this.

Acknowledgments. This work was partially supported by the European Union under grant agreements No. 687847 "Comrades" and No. 654024 "SoBigData", the UK Engineering and Physical Sciences Research Council grant EP/I004327/1 and the British Academy under call "The Humanities and Social Sciences Tackling the UKs International Challenges".

A   Most Linked Websites

See Tables 2 and 3.

Table 2. PAS > 3:1 Sites and Sites with Neutral Appeal

Remain PAS > 3:1	Total	Neutral	Total	Leave PAS > 3:1	Total
gov.uk	63119	twitter.com	4018371	Youtube	226382
theconversation.com	8495	The Guardian	253474	The Telegraph	148565
internacional.elpais.com	6915	BBC	242131	Daily Mail	86888
blogs.lse.ac.uk	6532	Facebook	109552	Bloomberg	53071
jkrowling.com	5975	The Independent	104572	news.sky.com	32016
economist.com	5220	amp.twimg.com	80727	The Sun	30255
eureferendum.gov.uk	4095	Reuters	71776	snpy.tv	28281
timeshighereducation.com	3738	wp.me	58287	Russia Today	23064
politics.co.uk	3344	Financial Times	44497	cnn.it	22617
politicalscrapbook.net	3266	mirror.co.uk	43467	on.wsj.com	20332
secure.avaaz.org	3159	buff.ly	40646	itv.com	17200
leftfootforward.org	3014	paper.li	39458	on.mktw.net	16838
touchstoneblog.org.uk	2655	New York Times	38441	blogs.spectator.co.uk	13298
zeit.de	2476	Huffington Post	33697	cnb.cx	12946
snp.org	2455	econ.st	29956	forbes.com	11967
tagesschau.de	2396	The Times	25519	yhoo.it	7955
cer.org.uk	2216	cards.twitter.com	21589	Sputnik	7032
greenpeace.org.uk	2078	standard.co.uk	15335	reportuk.org	6712
lavanguardia.com	2049	instagram.com	14671	International Business Times	6577
birminghammail.co.uk	1856	El Economista	13665	marketwatch.com	6090

Table 3. PAS > 30:1 Sites

Remain PAS > 30:1	Total	Leave PAS > 30:1	Total
ukstronger.in	39221	express.co.uk	168846
prt.news	20452	breitbart.com	55493
virg.in	11708	zerohedge.com	20531
strongerin.co.uk	10672	Heat Street	14889
infacts.org	8165	voteleavetakecontrol.org	14235
ebx.sh	4670	order-order.com	12804
voteremain.win	2567	infowars.com	7306
unite4europe.org	1554	to-go.xyz	6107
owl.li	1462	dld.bz	5561
energydesk.greenpeace.org	1169	guyfawk.es	5072
scotlandineurope.eu	1166	specc.ie	4709
weareeurope.org.uk	1151	telegraaf.nl	4659
realnewsuk.com	1070	dailysquib.co.uk	4396
euromove.org.uk	968	davidicke.com	4184
bmj.com	900	twibble.io	4138
neweuropeans.net	788	brexitthemovie.com	3997
greens.scot	741	eureferendum.com	3673
richardcorbett.org.uk	712	au.news.yahoo.com	3447
uktostay.eu	696	indiegogo.com	3369
chokkablog.blogspot.co.uk	691	live.pollstation.com	3269

References

1. Allcott, H., Gentzkow, M.: Social media and fake news in the 2016 election. J. Econ. Perspect. **31**(2), 211–36 (2017)
2. Barberá, P., Rivero, G.: Understanding the political representativeness of Twitter users. Soc. Sci. Comput. Rev. **33**(6), 712–729 (2015)
3. Bastos, M.T., Mercea, D.: The Brexit botnet and user-generated hyperpartisan news. Soc. Sci. Comput. Rev. (2017)
4. Faris, R., Roberts, H., Etling, B., Bourassa, N., Zuckerman, E., Benkler, Y.: Partisanship, propaganda, and disinformation: online media and the 2016 US presidential election. Berkman Klein Center for Internet & Society Research Paper (2017)
5. Ferrara, E.: Disinformation and social bot operations in the run up to the 2017 French presidential election. First Monday **22**(8) (2017)
6. Higgins, K.: Post-truth: a guide for the perplexed. Nature News **540**(7631), 9 (2016)
7. Howard, P.N., Bolsover, G., Kollanyi, B., Bradshaw, S., Neudert, L.M.: Junk news and bots during the US election: what were Michigan voters sharing over Twitter? Technical report, Data Memo 2017.1. Project on Computational Propaganda, Oxford, UK (2017)

8. Howard, P.N., Bradshaw, S., Kollanyi, B., Bolsolver, G.: Junk news and bots during the French presidential election: what are French voters sharing over Twitter in round two? Technical report, Data Memo 2017.4. Project on Computational Propaganda, Oxford, UK (2017)

9. Howard, P.N., Kollanyi, B.: Bots, #strongerin, and #brexit: computational propaganda during the UK-EU referendum. Technical report, Working Paper 2016.1. Project on Computational Propaganda, Oxford, UK (2016)

10. Kaminska, M., Kollanyi, B., Howard, P.N.: Junk news and bots during the 2017 UK general election: what are UK voters sharing over Twitter? Technical report, Data Memo 2017.5. Project on Computational Propaganda, Oxford, UK (2017)

11. Kollanyi, B., Howard, P.N.: Junk news and bots during the German federal presidency election: what were German voters sharing over Twitter? Technical report, Data Memo 2017.2. Project on Computational Propaganda, Oxford, UK (2017)

12. Lansdall-Welfare, T., Dzogang, F., Cristianini, N.: Change-point analysis of the public mood in UK Twitter during the Brexit referendum. In: 2016 IEEE 16th International Conference on Data Mining Workshops (ICDMW), pp. 434–439. IEEE (2016)

13. Mangold, L.: Should I stay or should I go: clash of opinions in the Brexit Twitter debate. Computing **1**(4.1) (2016)

14. Maynard, D., Roberts, I., Greenwood, M.A., Rout, D., Bontcheva, K.: A framework for real-time semantic social media analysis. Web Semant. Sci. Serv. Agents World Wide Web **44**, 75–88 (2017)

15. Moore, M., Ramsay, G.: UK media coverage of the 2016 EU referendum campaign. King's College London (2017)

16. Narayanan, V., Howard, P.N., Kollanyi, B., Elswah, M.: Russian involvement and junk news during Brexit. Technical report, Data Memo 2017.10. Project on Computational Propaganda, Oxford, UK (2017)

17. Neudert, L.M., Kollanyi, B., Howard, P.N.: Junk news and bots during the German parliamentary election: what are German voters sharing over Twitter. Technical report, Data Memo 2017.7. Project on Computational Propaganda, Oxford, UK (2017)

18. Preoţiuc-Pietro, D., Liu, Y., Hopkins, D., Ungar, L.: Beyond binary labels: political ideology prediction of Twitter users. In: Proceedings of the 55th Annual Meeting of the Association for Computational Linguistics (Volume 1: Long Papers). vol. 1, pp. 729–740 (2017)

19. Silverman, C.: Lies, damn lies and viral content. Technical report, Tow Center for Digital Journalism (2015)

20. Skjeseth, H.T.: All the president's lies: media coverage of lies in the US and France. Technical report, Reuters Institute for the Study of Journalism, University of Oxford (2017)

21. Vosoughi, S., Roy, D., Aral, S.: The spread of true and false news online. Science **359**(6380), 1146–1151 (2018)

Ballparking the Urban Placeness: A Case Study of Analyzing Starbucks Posts on Instagram

Gaurav Kalra[1,2]📵, Minsang Yu[2]📵, Dongman Lee[2(✉)]📵, Meeyoung Cha[2]📵, and Daeyoung Kim[1,2]📵

[1] Auto-ID Labs and School of Computing, KAIST, Daejeon, South Korea
[2] School of Computing, KAIST, Daejeon, South Korea
{gvkalra,sunflower_94,dlee,meeyoungcha,kimd}@kaist.ac.kr

Abstract. Placeness or the "sense of a place" plays a vital role in urban design and planning. Research on placeness in the past has been conducted via conventional methods like surveys to reveal essential insights for urban planners and architects. For taking a glimpse into placeness by analyzing common factors across geographies, we choose Instagram posts from Starbucks as a case study, owing to its the-next-door coffee shop psychological construct. We conduct our research by first adopting a flexible ontological framework to organize the concepts governing placeness. Next, we curate a dataset of community generated Instagram posts from Starbucks in three major metropolitan cities of the world: New York, Seoul, and Tokyo. The curated dataset is then automatically enriched with contextual attributes such as activity, visitor demographics, and time via machine learning techniques. We finally analyze and validate the quantitative variations in contextual information with findings from well-accepted cross-cultural case studies. Our results show that placeness mined from Starbucks, a prominent urban third-place, can be reliably utilized to discover surrounding urban placeness.

Keywords: Cultural study · Placeness · Community media

1 Introduction

Urban architects characterize place as a combination of physical, social, and cultural meanings, defining it as "sense of a place" [15] or simply *placeness* [34]. The physical dimension represents space and its bricks-and-mortar setup, whereas, the social and cultural aspects represent activities and events contained within the context under consideration [28]. This subtle yet precise distinction between space and place has proved to be useful in designing a wide array of collaborative environments [15,23]. For instance, the Active and Green Spaces project undertaken by the Government of Japan has tried to improve the mental

---

M. Yu—Co-primary author, order chosen alphabetically.

© Springer Nature Switzerland AG 2018
S. Staab et al. (Eds.): SocInfo 2018, LNCS 11185, pp. 291–307, 2018.
https://doi.org/10.1007/978-3-030-01129-1_18

health of its citizens [26]. However, the constant dynamics surrounding any place means that the associated analysis needs to always be in flux. To this end, social media have been recently exploited for contemporary research in placeness for social implications of a given place in terms of activity, demographics, and time. For instance, social media analysis carried out by the Livehoods Project [6] and Social-Urban neighborhood search [43] have focused on large sets of check-in data gathered from specific geographic areas to capture the dynamics of a city as shown in Fig. 1. Building upon such efforts, in this paper, we experiment the feasibility to *sniff* meaningful placeness concepts from orders of magnitudes smaller data.

Although it is necessary to accurately discover placeness for practical reasons, the potential for exploring placeness from small data is exciting, because it could serve as an economical complementary tool for urban designers and businesses who often do not have access to massive datasets. The first challenge in this journey is to choose a psychologically congruent baseline setting (i.e., the scope over which placeness concept could be drawn and validated). In our quest, we choose Starbucks owing to its the-next-door coffee shop psychological construct, and for a cross-cultural variance, we choose three major metropolitan cities of the world: New York, Seoul, and Tokyo. To curate our dataset, we exploit Instagram [19], a visual-oriented community media platform, containing a rich set of images [18] capable of facilitating a multifaceted and multidimensional placeness research.

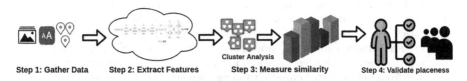

Step 1: Gather Data   **Step 2: Extract Features**   **Step 3: Measure similarity**   **Step 4: Validate placeness**

Fig. 1. Process of mining placeness from social media: (Step 1) Geo-tagged data is collected from predefined geographic areas or places. (Step 2) Feature vectors are constructed to describe the dataset. (Step 3) Similarity map of the gained constructs are analyzed, which is then clustered to identify prominent groups. (Step 4) Validation of the groups is carried out for evaluating mined placeness.

To enrich the image data with contextual information, we extract visual features by utilizing two existing deep-learning service platforms. One is the Microsoft cognitive APIs [32], which infers contextual tags from images such as indoor, wall, and person. The contextual tags are then used by our activity classifier, which classifies an Instagram post into one of the five prevalent activities at Starbucks: *(1) Socializing, (2) Dining, (3) Take-out, (4) Souvenir,* and *(5) Work*. Next is the Face++ platform [10] that has shown reliable results for recognizing people's faces for inferring demographics such as ethnicity, gender, and age [47]. The set of derived contextual information, coupled with the metadata information on Instagram posts (i.e., time of post), form the basis of our placeness ontology.

Our analysis demonstrates that Starbucks can be utilized as a reliable indicator of social and cultural semantics on urban placeness. We validate this hypothesis over the New York area as our test-bed, with three sample areas of 1-km radius each, to obtain an average similarity of 70% compared to previously conducted studies that require several orders of magnitude larger data [6]. We also extend the analysis to New York, Seoul, and Tokyo, from a cross-cultural perspective to *re-discover* well-accepted works from social studies.

While preliminary, this work shows that qualitative aspects of neighborhoods and hot spots can be mined from (relatively light-scale) quantitative analyses on live stream data. The same methodology can be extended to handle other kinds of geographic data and reveal their real-time cultural semantics. Given that a plethora of applications offers place-driven recommendations (e.g., Google Now, Foursquare, Apple Siri), findings in this work could imply that one needs to go beyond the rigid placeness grouping. Our data, although gathered from an identical shop "Starbucks" in three cities, indicated different semantics and contexts depending on geography. Likewise, location recommendations could better consider the dynamic and cultural changes associated with urban placeness by conducting continual and lightweight measurements.

2   Related Works

In the past, researchers have gathered datasets to conduct placeness research for a variety of purposes in different domains and many methodologies have been introduced for extracting semantics of a place. We present these related works classified into two broad categories:

Domain of Placeness Modeling. As multitude of location-based services become increasingly available on personal smart devices for both public users and researchers, there have been a number of recent works to extract place semantics and exploit them for designing HCI (Human-Computer Interaction) systems. While the universal theme of place modeling has been the integration of virtual and real characteristics, both private and public spaces have been examined. For public spaces, place characteristics are mostly exploited by utilizing visitors' attributes [7, 29, 37], activities conducted or visitor opinions [12, 21], or ambiance exhibited by the place [3, 13, 46]. On the other hand, private spaces have retrieved their place characteristics from the IoT (Internet-of-Things) sensors [9, 36, 39].

Methodology of Placeness Modeling. A number of approaches exist in place modeling that consider the heterogeneity of contexts and data sources. For instance, keywords matching methods [8, 16, 30] are commonly used for text-based social media, and temporal analysis is widely applied to sensor data. Previous works that focus on text or time-stamp extract semantics from the text and make temporal relation to the extracted attribute. Other methods utilize vision [1, 3, 17] and audio [5] analysis to generate labels for a placeness model. The plethora of feature extracting and modeling methods showcase the interest of the research community in placeness for designing socially aware systems.

To contribute to this goal, we analyze a contemporary and cross-cultural dataset at a well-known *third place* [11,31,35] between office and home, i.e., Starbucks. We envision that an indirect technique, such as ours via Starbucks, will generate more research interest to study society and infer cultural semantics as more community contributed content becomes available on the web.

3   Methodology

3.1   Placeness Ontology

Conventionally, placeness is studied by observing patterns in extracted features based on induction and probability, providing meaningful contextual information of a location. While our methodology contributes in similar insights, we adopt an ontology-based framework [4], enabling us to recognize and classify polymorphic placeness of a location following guidelines from existing knowledge base so that multiple characteristics of a place do not go unnoticed.

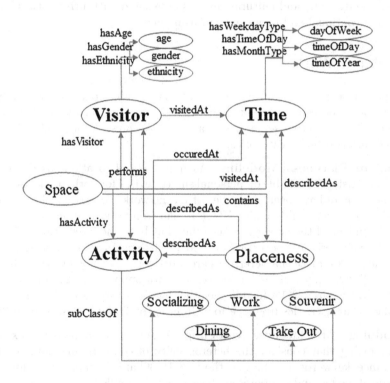

Fig. 2. Placeness Ontology

As shown in the placeness ontology in Fig. 2, physical space *contains* placeness which is described by a visitor's activity and the time when the activity was executed. Visitors are classified by their age, gender, and ethnicity; whereas the time of day, the day of week and time of year are defined as temporal characteristics. Types of activities are divided into five major classes: Socializing, Dining, Work, Take Out, and Souvenir. The choice of our classes is derived from urban area characteristics adapted to the context of coffee shops. In a notable work on crowd analysis [27], the authors identified five classes of activities: Life, Work, Shopping, Entertainment, and Food. In the context of Starbucks, we examined 1,000 random posts and found promising patterns that indicate characteristics drawn from people's behaviors associated with an urban area (often conducted at city or neighborhood level) may be extended to even a smaller indoor space. This observation is also reflected in [35], whose research called a coffee shop as a *third place* that is capable of supporting multiple behavioral characteristics. Consequently, we mapped the five activity classes of a broader urban place to the five activity types that we observed at Starbucks. Life was mapped to Socializing, Work to Work, Shopping to Souvenir, Entertainment to Take-out, and Food to Dining.

3.2 Dataset

Unit of Computation. One post on Instagram is a collection of upto ten photos and videos. In the context of placeness ontology, this implies that an *instance* of the Activity class (i.e., Socializing, Dining, Work, Souvenir, and Take-Out) should be a combination of all the features extracted from the constituent photos and videos. In practice, however, we found that a vast majority of the posts on Instagram (92.94% of our dataset) consists of only a single image. Therefore, to keep our model simple, we decided to choose the unit of computation as an image and in the rest of this paper utilize the terms *post(s)*, *image(s)*, and *photo(s)* interchangeably.

Data Collection. Overall, we gathered a total of 23,577 (New York), 37,137 (Seoul), and 47,248 (Tokyo) geo-tagged Instagram posts from 103 (New York), 219 (Seoul), and 67 (Tokyo) locations of Starbucks as shown in Fig. 3. We found the target locations manually by searching on Google Maps and then obtained the posts explicitly containing GPS tags of the identified Starbucks locations. Such a scale of social media posts can be gathered via the API (Application Programming Interface) easily without setting up any massive data infrastructure.

To augment the dataset with visitor demographics, we utilized an API by Face++ platform [10] which returns the facial features (e.g., age, gender, ethnicity, emotion, and smiling) of all the detected faces. Interestingly, Face++ platform identifies the mermaid in Starbucks logo as a woman in her thirties; to correct this misclassification, we trained a binary classifier using CNN (Convolutional Neural Network) and additionally augmented the detected faces as a Starbucks logo or not.

Next, we filter out the posts which do not contain any visitor demographic information, and that leaves us with a total of 6,493 (New York), 7,425 (Seoul), and 6,773 (Tokyo) posts. This filtration step was necessary for constructing an instance of our ontology, in accordance with the relationship of placeness and visitor information discussed in theory [28]. However, as we shall see shortly,

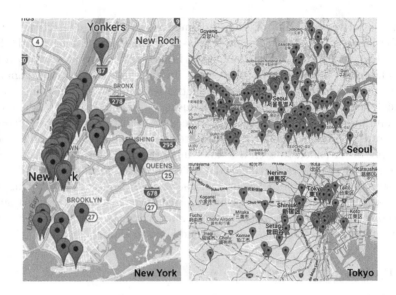

Fig. 3. Location of Starbucks across New York, Seoul, and Tokyo from where we obtained geo-tagged posts on Instagram

this doesn't imply that the final dataset contains images with only faces (such as selfies).

3.3   Feature Extraction

We reduce the dimension of an Instagram post and represent it as a function of three main parameters in placeness research: activity, visitor, and time as shown in Fig. 4. Activity information is represented as a Word2Vec embedding [33] of visual tags obtained from the Microsoft cognitive API [32]. Visitor information is represented as the number of faces detected, along with their respective demographics. The average number of faces per image was similar across the cities, ranging from 1.57 (New York), 1.59 (Seoul) to 1.80 (Tokyo). Time information is represented as the season, i.e., time-of-the-year (Spring, Summer, Fall, and Winter), time-of-the-day (Night, Morning, Afternoon, and Evening; abbreviated as NMAE), and day-of-the-week (Monday to Sunday). Although the time information is drawn from meta-data of each post, which lists the time of image upload rather than the exact time an image was taken, many anecdotal pieces of evidence report that (nearly all) pictures are uploaded within a day, and the majority of photos are uploaded within an hour on Instagram.

All three kinds of information (i.e., Activity, Visitor, and Time) are critical for describing urban placeness based on social theories [28]. In particular, the activity information is essential for characterizing the social and cultural dimensions of a place.

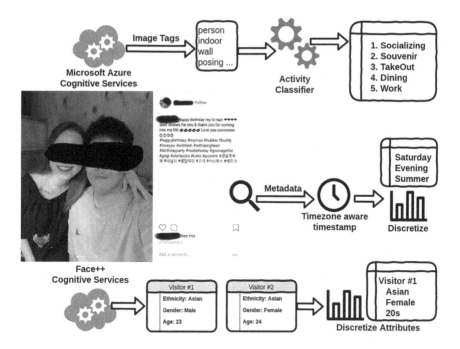

Fig. 4. Feature extraction process for an Instagram post as a function of activity (top), time (middle), and visitor (bottom)

3.4 Activity Classification Model

We utilize 27,109 posts from the unfiltered dataset which contains posts with or without demographics for training, and 2,445 posts for testing. To categorize activities, we built an unsupervised activity classifier, which clusters on a word embedding space. The clusters become activity categories, and then a trained classifier classifies each post into its probabilistic class. To construct our classifier, we first extract visual tags from each image in the training set to build a word-embedding space based on the similarity between tags. We implement a 300-dimensional *Word2vec* model [33] as the similarity model, considering each set of tags from an image as an individual sentence so that the objects within the same image have higher similarity than those in other images.

The model is trained with 27,109 posts and contains 517 different objects where each of them appears at least five times in the dataset. Before going into the clustering stage, we reduce the dimensions of *Word2vec* model into two by using t-SNE analysis, to enable efficient and faster clustering. Finally, we perform k-means clustering with 5 class labels on the feature vector, to categorize a post into Socializing, Dining, Takeout, Souvenir, and Work. Then to convert each post into its activity category, we calculate the probabilistic score of each category by using the Euclidean distance from the cluster's center. For each post in the test set, the activity is represented as the one with the highest score with at least an 80% threshold.

4   Evaluation

In this section, we evaluate our methodology in three ways: At first, we do a manual verification of our classification mechanism to calculate the accuracy from a humans perspective. Next, we compare our results for New York with a big-data based research effort to find if Starbucks can ballpark urban placeness. Finally, we take a qualitative approach and compare our results with well-accepted cross-cultural case studies to discover social dynamics.

4.1   Manual Verification

The first evaluation step involved human coding. We randomly sampled 100 posts from each city from the testing set for manual verification by three human coders (none of the authors participated in this coding step) and ask them a very simple question: "According to your quick judgment, which category does this post best belong to?" and provided the coders with the five activity categories. Based on the responses, we calculated the accuracy of the model by using a commonly utilized metric in Visual-Question-Answering [42] for reducing inter-human variability:

$$\text{Accuracy}(\text{answer}) = min\left\{\frac{\#\ \text{humans that said answer}}{3}, 1\right\}$$

The overall accuracy of the model is calculated by averaging the individual accuracy of respective posts and is reported to be 67.4%. An example set of correctly and incorrectly classified images is shown in Fig. 5. Incorrectly classified images indicate that our algorithm's classification was not co-aligned with the majority judgment of human coders. While the overall accuracy is in an acceptable range (i.e., nearly 70%), we believe automated classification could perform better in the future with more advanced algorithms. We leave this as future work as our primary focus in this paper is to test the feasibility of utilizing small data for extracting urban placeness.

4.2   Comparison Against Big Data Analysis

The main idea of this project is to replicate the efforts taken by big data-based urban research by only utilizing several orders of magnitude smaller data. Here, as a comparison, we compare the similarity and placeness concepts gained from our data against the Livehoods [6] project. The Livehoods project aims to create

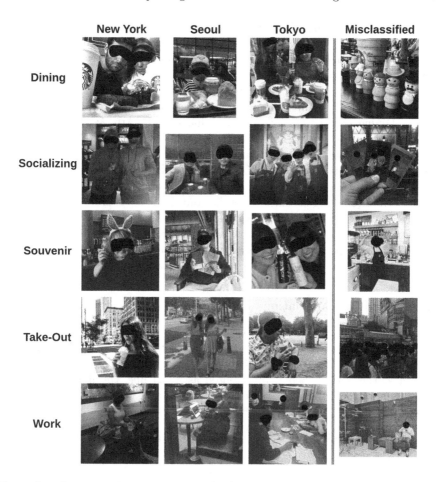

Fig. 5. Sample images classified correctly (left) and incorrectly (right) based on manual coding. Human coders independently judged the activity type of each image and their majority vote was compared against automated classification. The overall accuracy is in the acceptable range (i.e., nearly 70%).

	Region A	Region B	Region C
No. of Starbucks	23	33	28
No. of Instagram posts	892	1644	1280
No. of Livehood venues	7377	11436	5141
AVG(Similarity)	0.72	0.69	0.73
STD-DEV(Similarity)	0.18	0.17	0.15

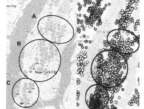

Fig. 6. Similarity values against the Livehoods data for each region **A**, **B**, and **C** of 1-km radius. On the right side, we show the geographic mapping between our dataset and Livehoods dataset (extreme right). Each marker in our dataset represents the location of Starbucks. And each marker in Livehoods dataset represents a venue.

dynamic social boundaries, in contrast to municipal demarcations, of a city by using data gathered from social media. They discover social boundaries in a city by using a spectral clustering algorithm from millions of Foursquare check-in data. For each such social boundary, it provides a *composition*, which is a list of facilities contained in the social boundary and also termed as *Livehood venues*. Since placeness of a facility is supportive of an activity, we map the two as follows—Dining (Food), Socializing (Nightlife spot(s), Arts & Entertainment), Take-out (Great Outdoors, Travel & Transport, Travel spots), Work (Home(s) Work Other(s)), and Souvenir (Shops, Shop(s) & Service(s)). Next, we calculate the cosine similarity of normalized term-frequency across three overlapping regions of a 1-km radius in the two datasets. The similarity values are reported in Fig. 6. An interesting observation is that our data size is orders of magnitude smaller compared to the Livehoods data. In summary, based upon the manual verification and similarity score with Livehoods, we gain nearly 70% confidence in treating Starbucks as a *barometer* for gauging different aspects of Society. In the next section, we will explore our results from a qualitative perspective.

4.3   Qualitative Co-relation

As another way of validation, we calculated the distribution of attributes in our ontology for each city as shown in Fig. 7. In the figure, if the frequency of observed pattern is less than 90% of the maximum number of that city, we have gray-scaled the line. In Seoul, represented as a red line, the most visible pattern is (Female, 20s, Dining, Evening, Saturday, Fall), which indicates that the

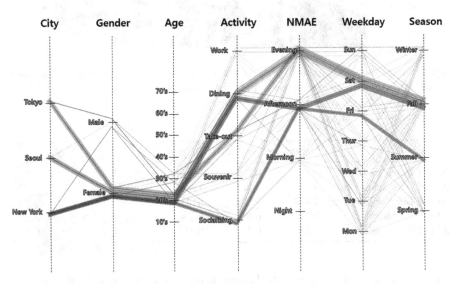

Fig. 7. Quantitative variations in ontology instances across all the Starbucks locations studied in three cities. The line-width between two attributes is proportional to the number of observed patterns.

visitors are mostly Females in their Twenties, visiting Starbucks for Dining on Saturday Evenings during Fall season. In Tokyo, represented as a green line, the noticeable pattern is similar to Seoul, i.e., (Female, 20s, Take-out, Evening, Saturday, Fall), with the principal activity being Take-out. In the case of New York, represented as a blue line, there are two significant driving patterns (Female, 20s, Dining, Afternoon, Saturday, Fall) and (Female, 20s, Socializing, Afternoon, Friday, Summer) indicating that the city shows a mostly social attitude in their usage of Starbucks.

We now compare the detailed findings against existing research by Visitor, Time, and Activity with quantitative analysis in the context of cross-cultural social studies. In our results, we observe that Seoul is mostly driven by a young crowd in their early twenties while New York and Tokyo are in their late twenties and thirties.

Visitor. We calculated three parameters as shown in Table 1 to ascertain that GPS tagged posts of Starbucks are in-fact suitable to gauge placeness of nearby areas. Nearby areas data is collected at random using Instagram from places within seven kilometers of the Starbucks locations in our dataset. The visitor statistics of Starbucks are in-tandem with nearby places, further verifying our claim that a prominent place such as Starbucks can be reliably utilized to discover surrounding urban placeness. An interesting observation is noted in the city of Seoul, where the average age of visitors at Starbucks is almost six years younger to the nearby places. To the best of our knowledge, this is an expected outcome due to a strong influence of Confucianism tradition in Korean society, wherein *age-bands* play a vital role as the deciding factor of "who is allowed to be present where; in a socially acceptable way" [20] (in Korean).

Table 1. Visitor statistics of Starbucks and nearby places

	New York		Seoul		Tokyo	
	Starbucks	Nearby	Starbucks	Nearby	Starbucks	Nearby
Females-to-Males	1.2	1.0	1.9	1.4	1.3	0.95
AVG (Age)	32	35	25	31	31	32
STD-DEV (Age)	11	12	12	12	12	14

Time. We analyzed the variations in the number of posts over the seven days of a week and observed some interesting patterns as shown in Fig. 7, which may be explained by one-person household statistics across the three cities. From Monday to Thursday, the three cities showcase a similar number of posts, however, New York shows a slight increase from Friday to Saturday and then a steep dip on Sunday. On the other hand, Tokyo keeps its momentum high over the weekend and surpasses New York and Seoul, which shows a pattern in-between Tokyo and New York. We believe that these observations may be attributed to one-person households; wherein New York [40], Seoul [24], and Tokyo [38] has 29.9%, 35.7%, and 41% single person household respectively. A lower percentage of single person household signifies that people live with someone and over-the-weekend (especially Sunday) unwind at their homes before the week begins again.

Activity. We analyzed the three cities in accordance with their activity patterns as shown in Figs. 8, 9 and 10 to derive meaningful cultural correlations. The bars are split from bottom to top as follows: Age (0–80; split interval 10), Gender (Females; Orange, Males; Blue), NMAE (Night-Evening), Weekday (Monday-Sunday), and Season (Spring, Summer, Fall, and Winter)

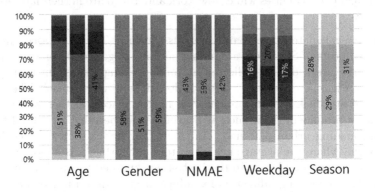

Fig. 8. New York: Variations in Age, Gender, NMAE, Weekday, and Season for top-3 activities; Socializing, Take-Out, Dining (left to right) have most common visitors of age group 20s (51%), 20s (38%), and 30s (41%) respectively. (Color figure online)

New York. People in New York seems to utilize Starbucks for mostly social perspective (at least when they log their activities via posting pictures on Instagram). This pattern can be observed in Fig. 7 by the blue line, majorly spread over Socializing and Dining carried out in the Afternoon. We believe that this is rooted in the dynamic and heterogeneous nature exhibited by the cultural city of the world [45]. However, people in the United States have been found to "background their face-to-face experiences as they focus more on electronic space for work" [22]. We believe that due to the limitations we discuss in Sect. 5, this aspect is not reflected in our analysis.

Seoul. The distribution of social and dining aspect at Starbucks in Seoul is almost similar, and approximately 75% is at the higher spectrum. Moreover, the Take-outs are comparatively less, reflecting that a good majority of visitors like to hang around together in cafés especially during evenings. This pattern can be observed in Fig. 7 by the red line, converging into Evening for the various activities. We believe that this finding is attributed to the availability of high-speed free Internet [44], a sense of safe and cozy environment [25] and easy

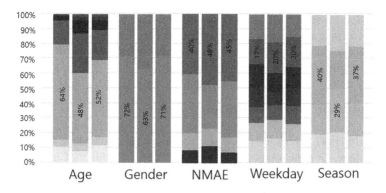

Fig. 9. Seoul: Variations in Age, Gender, NMAE, Weekday, and Season for top-3 activities; Socializing, Take-Out, Dining (left to right) have most common visitors of age group 20s (64%), 20s (48%), and 20s (52%) respectively. (Color figure online)

connectivity offered by public transportation systems [41]. This phenomenon of socializing with their closed ones has also been observed in strategy and international marketing case studies conducted inside Korea [2].

Tokyo. The social aspect of Starbucks in Tokyo is rated consistently low across all the data points. Additionally, Take-Out is concentrated to Evening as shown by the green line in Fig. 7, which otherwise is considered to be a time for socializing. We believe that this finding is attributed to the low socializing characteristic exhibited by the people living in Tokyo and also noticed by urban design and health researchers [26] (i.e., socializing will be associated with other places than coffee shops). The society is considered to be a workaholic, with a tendency of not exposing one's personal life. To quote, "Tokyo does not make much use of its waterfronts, and can learn from other cities on that, especially around socializing and physical activity." Extrapolating this finding to the dining category reflects

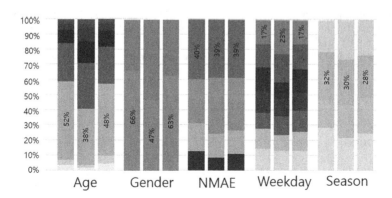

Fig. 10. Tokyo: Variations in Age, Gender, NMAE, Weekday, and Season for top-3 activities; Socializing, Take-Out, Dining (left to right) have most common visitors of age group 20s (52%), 20s (38%), and 20s (48%) respectively. (Color figure online)

that a large number of Starbucks stores exhibit diverse dining activity patterns. To the best of our knowledge, this may be a reflection of a corporate branding strategy for targeting the otherwise non-socializing population, in which case, it is expected to improve the urban mental health.

5   Conclusion and Remarks

Urban architects characterize place as a combination of physical, social and cultural meanings. In this research, we explored the possibility of utilizing small-scale crowd-generated data for extracting placeness of a given public space, i.e., Starbucks, in three metropolitan cities. While we started out this research expecting a high degree of "Work" related posts from our own experience, we found that "Socializing," "Dining," and "Take-out" are three most prominent activity classes in the observed cities. This result may be due to the kind of data that we examined; images logged on Instagram may have specific meanings and also may be due to our filtration criteria of processing only the posts containing visitor demographics. This problem may be alleviated by extracting demographics from user profiles by utilizing other researches, for instance [14].

Nonetheless, we believe our research has well-demonstrated that small data focused on a common public place (i.e., Starbucks) can be utilized cost-effectively to gain placeness concepts. Moreover, the quantitative analysis has deep-rooted qualitative implications. Since it is the first step in quantifying the cross-cultural social and cultural semantics by utilizing a common *third-place*, all aspects could not be ascertained with a very high confidence level. However, our research shed lights on how crowd-generated data could potentially replace cost-intensive surveys conducted by urban designers and architects.

Acknowledgments. Minsang Yu and Dongman Lee were supported by Institute for Information & communications Technology Promotion (IITP) grant funded by the Korea government (MSIP) (No. 2017-0-00537, Development of Autonomous IoT Collaboration Framework for Space Intelligence). Gaurav Kalra and Daeyoung Kim were supported by International Research & Development Program of the National Research Foundation of Korea (NRF) funded by the Ministry of Science, ICT & Future Planning of Korea (2016K1A3A7A03952054). Meeyoung Cha was supported by Basic Science Research Program through the National Research Foundation of Korea (NRF) funded by the Ministry of Science and ICT (No. NRF-2017R1E1A1A01076400). The authors are grateful to Byoungheon Shin, Joowon Yoon, and Zhantore Orynbassarov for their help.

References

1. Akdemir, U., Turaga, P., Chellappa, R.: An ontology based approach for activity recognition from video. In: Proceedings of the 16th ACM International Conference on Multimedia, pp. 709–712. ACM (2008)
2. Alon, I.: Global Franchising Operations Management: Cases in International and Emerging Markets Operations. FT Press, Upper Saddle River (2012)

3. Benkhedda, Y., Santani, D., Gatica-Perez, D.: Venues in social media: examining ambiance perception through scene semantics. In: Proceedings of the 2017 ACM on Multimedia Conference, pp. 1416–1424. ACM (2017)
4. Choi, J.J., Kim, J., Park, H., Lee, W.: Extracting placeness from social media: an ontology-based system. In: Proceedings of the 2017 IEEE/ACM International Conference on Advances in Social Networks Analysis and Mining 2017, pp. 644–651. ACM (2017)
5. Chon, Y., Lane, N.D., Kim, Y., Zhao, F., Cha, H.: Understanding the coverage and scalability of place-centric crowdsensing. In: Proceedings of the 2013 ACM International Joint Conference on Pervasive and Ubiquitous Computing, pp. 3–12. ACM (2013)
6. Cranshaw, J., Schwartz, R., Hong, J., Sadeh, N.: The livehoods project: utilizing social media to understand the dynamics of a city. In: Sixth International AAAI Conference on Weblogs and Social Media (2012)
7. Cranshaw, J., Toch, E., Hong, J., Kittur, A., Sadeh, N.: Bridging the gap between physical location and online social networks. In: Proceedings of the 12th ACM International Conference on Ubiquitous Computing, pp. 119–128. ACM (2010)
8. Dearman, D., Truong, K.N.: Identifying the activities supported by locations with community-authored content. In: Proceedings of the 12th ACM International Conference on Ubiquitous Computing, pp. 23–32. ACM (2010)
9. Despouys, R., Sharrock, R., Demeure, I.: Sensemaking in the autonomic smarthome. In: Proceedings of the 2014 ACM International Joint Conference on Pervasive and Ubiquitous Computing: Adjunct Publication, pp. 887–894. ACM (2014)
10. FacePlusPlus. https://tinyurl.com/y9pk2p6s. Accessed 22 Jan 2018
11. Felton, E.: Eat, drink and be civil: sociability and the cafe. M/C J. **15**(2) (2012). https://tinyurl.com/ybolcvgw
12. Gao, H., Tang, J., Hu, X., Liu, H.: Content-aware point of interest recommendation on location-based social networks. In: AAAI, pp. 1721–1727 (2015)
13. Graham, L.T., Gosling, S.D.: Can the ambiance of a place be determined by the user profiles of the people who visit it? In: ICWSM (2011)
14. Han, K., Lee, S., Jang, J.Y., Jung, Y., Lee, D.: Teens are from mars, adults are from venus: analyzing and predicting age groups with behavioral characteristics in instagram. In: Proceedings of the 8th ACM Conference on Web Science, pp. 35–44. ACM (2016)
15. Harrison, S., Dourish, P.: Re-place-ing space: the roles of place and space in collaborative systems. In: Proceedings of the 1996 ACM Conference on Computer Supported Cooperative Work, pp. 67–76. ACM (1996)
16. Hiruta, S., Yonezawa, T., Jurmu, M., Tokuda, H.: Detection, classification and visualization of place-triggered geotagged tweets. In: Proceedings of the 2012 ACM Conference on Ubiquitous Computing, pp. 956–963. ACM (2012)
17. Hochman, N., Schwartz, R.: Visualizing instagram: tracing cultural visual rhythms. In: Proceedings of the Workshop on Social Media Visualization (SocMedVis) in Conjunction with the Sixth International AAAI Conference on Weblogs and Social Media (ICWSM 2012), pp. 6–9 (2012)
18. Hu, Y., Manikonda, L., Kambhampati, S., et al.: What we instagram: a first analysis of instagram photo content and user types. In: ICWSM (2014)
19. Instagram. https://tinyurl.com/ydaftvgy. Accessed 22 Jan 2018
20. Jee, E.J.: Research on Age Discrimination in Korea (2018). ISBN 979-11-85663-40-1

21. Kim, D.H., Han, K., Estrin, D.: Employing user feedback for semantic location services. In: Proceedings of the 13th International Conference on Ubiquitous Computing, pp. 217–226. ACM (2011)
22. Kleinman, S.S.: Cafe culture in france and the united states: a comparative ethnographic study of the use of mobile information and communication technologies. Atl. J. Commun. **14**(4), 191–210 (2006)
23. Kling, R., McKim, G., Fortuna, J., King, A.: Scientific collaboratories as socio-technical interaction networks: a theoretical approach. arXiv preprint arXiv:cs/0005007 (2000)
24. Korean Statistical Information Service. https://tinyurl.com/y92qomdj. Accessed 22 Jan 2018
25. KoreaTimes: Safety in South Korea. https://tinyurl.com/y8gh4gz4. Accessed 22 Jan 2018
26. Layla McCay, E.S., Chang, A.: Urban design and mental health in Tokyo: a city case study. J. Urban Des. Ment. Health **3** (2017). https://tinyurl.com/yd9fcfud
27. Lee, R., Wakamiya, S., Sumiya, K.: Urban area characterization based on crowd behavioral lifelogs over Twitter. Pers. Ubiquitous Comput. **17**(4), 605–620 (2013)
28. Loukaitou-Sideris, A., Banerjee, T.: Urban Design Downtown: Poetics and Politics of Form. University of California Press, Berkeley (1998)
29. Lv, M., Chen, L., Xu, Z., Li, Y., Chen, G.: The discovery of personally semantic places based on trajectory data mining. Neurocomputing **173**, 1142–1153 (2016)
30. Matassa, A.: Interaction with a personalised smart space to enhance people everyday life. In: DC@ CHItaly, pp. 34–45 (2015)
31. McCosker, A., Wilken, R.: Café space, communication, creativity, and materialism. M/C J. **15**(2) (2012). https://tinyurl.com/ybsbdhu5
32. Microsoft Cognitive Services Computer Vision API - v1.0. https://tinyurl.com/y9owxtj2. Accessed 22 Jan 2018
33. Mikolov, T., Sutskever, I., Chen, K., Corrado, G.S., Dean, J.: Distributed representations of words and phrases and their compositionality. In: Advances in Neural Information Processing Systems, pp. 3111–3119 (2013)
34. Motloch, J.: Placemaking: urban landscape system management. Syst. Res. Behav. Sci. **7**(4), 273–285 (1990)
35. Oldenburg, R.: The Great Good Place: café, Coffee Shops, Community Centers, Beauty Parlors, General Stores, Bars, Hangouts, and How They Get you Through the Day. Paragon House Publishers, New York (1989)
36. Popovici, M., Muraru, M., Agache, A., Negreanu, L., Giumale, C., Dobre, C.: An ontology-based dynamic service composition framework for intelligent houses. In: 2011 10th International Symposium on Autonomous Decentralized Systems (ISADS), pp. 177–184. IEEE (2011)
37. Redi, M., Quercia, D., Graham, L.T., Gosling, S.D.: Like partying? Your face says it all. predicting the ambiance of places with profile pictures. arXiv preprint arXiv:1505.07522 (2015)
38. Savills World Research, Japan. https://tinyurl.com/y8qg5e59. Accessed 22 Jan 2018
39. Schmohl, R., Baumgarten, U.: The contextual map - a context model for detecting affinity between contexts. In: Bonnin, J.-M., Giannelli, C., Magedanz, T. (eds.) MOBILWARE 2009. LNICST, vol. 7, pp. 171–184. Springer, Heidelberg (2009). https://doi.org/10.1007/978-3-642-01802-2_13
40. Statista. https://tinyurl.com/y9djayvx. Accessed 22 Jan 2018
41. TripAdvisor: Traveling in South Korea. https://tinyurl.com/jq6xpgr. Accessed 22 Jan 2018

42. VQA Evaluation Metric. https://tinyurl.com/ybefxfvt. Accessed 22 Jan 2018
43. Wakamiya, S., Lee, R., Sumiya, K.: Social-urban neighborhood search based on crowd footprints network. In: Jatowt, A., Lim, E.-P., Ding, Y., Miura, A., Tezuka, T., Dias, G., Tanaka, K., Flanagin, A., Dai, B.T. (eds.) SocInfo 2013. LNCS, vol. 8238, pp. 429–442. Springer, Cham (2013). https://doi.org/10.1007/978-3-319-03260-3_37
44. Wikipedia: Internet in South Korea. https://tinyurl.com/q7aj4km. Accessed 22 Jan 2018
45. Wikipedia: New York. https://tinyurl.com/yau834xo. Accessed 22 Jan 2018
46. Zambaldi, V.F., Pesce, J.P., Quercia, D., Almeida, V.A.: Lightweight contextual ranking of city pictures: urban sociology to the rescue. In: ICWSM (2014)
47. Zhou, E., Fan, H., Cao, Z., Jiang, Y., Yin, Q.: Extensive facial landmark localization with coarse-to-fine convolutional network cascade. In: Proceedings of the IEEE International Conference on Computer Vision Workshops, pp. 386–391 (2013)

A Full-Cycle Methodology for News Topic Modeling and User Feedback Research

Sergei Koltsov[1]($\boxtimes$) ⓘ, Sergei Pashakhin[1] ⓘ, and Sofia Dokuka[2] ⓘ

[1] National Research University Higher School of Economics,
St. Petersburg 190008, Russia
skoltsov@hse.ru
[2] Institute of Education, National Research University Higher School
of Economics, Moscow 101000, Russia

Abstract. Online social networks (OSNs) play an increasingly important role in news dissemination and consumption, attracting such traditional media outlets as TV channels with growing online audiences. Online news streams require appropriate instruments for analysis. One of such tools is topic modeling (TM). However, TM has a set of limitations (the problem of topic number choice and the algorithm instability, among others) that must be addressed specifically for the task of sociological online news analysis. In this paper, we propose a full-cycle methodology for such study: from choosing the optimal topic number to the extraction of stable topics and analysis of TM results. We illustrate it with an analysis of online news stream of 164,426 messages formed by twelve national TV channels during a one-year period in a leading Russian OSN. We show that our method can easily reveal associations between news topics and user feedback, including sharing behavior. Additionally, we show how uneven distribution of document quantities and lengths over classes (TV channels) could affect TM results.

Keywords: Topic modeling · Text mining · TV news · News consumptions
Online social networks · Social media

1 Introduction

Social media play an increasingly important role in information spread within and across societies. In particular, younger generations of news consumers increasingly access them through social media news streams rather than through traditional media channels. As a result, social media aggregate digital traces of both news content and audience feedback that are matched together. This gives media professionals and social scientists a unique possibility to directly establish relations between content features of news and audience reactions to them in a way never possible before. However, the research community still lacks methodological routines that would allow social scientists to carry out full-cycle studies without inventing and testing new algorithms or data mining techniques.

© Springer Nature Switzerland AG 2018
S. Staab et al. (Eds.): SocInfo 2018, LNCS 11185, pp. 308–321, 2018.
https://doi.org/10.1007/978-3-030-01129-1_19

In this paper, we develop a full-cycle approach for such a research by proposing a system of methodological steps arranged into a sequence. All elements of the system were tested in previous research, but here we show how to unite them, use them thoughtfully with attention to algorithmic limitations and how to interpret the outputs sociologically. We further apply our approach to the task of assessing audience feedback to the topics in a stream of Russian-language news in a Russian social networking site.

The first part of a research aimed at relating news content to audience feedback is to determine the features of the content. As the scope of our work is limited to news texts, further on we address texts only. They may differ in a number of aspects, such as source, time of issuing, length, genre, but above all – topics. The latter, unlike most other news features, are particularly hard to determine when news are too numerous to read. Topic modeling as a group of algorithms has been used for this [1]. However, TM is difficult to understand, its features and behavior are under researched, and its limitations are not widely known and even less resolved. One of the most straightforward problems of TM that researchers face at the very beginning of its use is the problem of the "right" number of topics that has to be somehow set by a user. Due to these problems, despite some progress in the recent years, TM is still not widely adopted by social scientists and media practitioners. Meanwhile, news topic is a most important factor among others that can offer useful explanations of audience feedback. In this work we show how to integrate this method in a social research pipeline.

The second part of such research is to measure audience behavior which, in case of social networking sites, is limited to their technical functionality. News consumption is usually measured through the number of visits (clicks), unique visitors and the time spent on a news item page, however, this information is most often missing from the open access. What is usually present is user feedback embodied in user likes, comments, and sharing actions. Meanings that stand behind these types of actions are different. Likes are most often used to express approval, solidarity, or at least satisfaction with the news item features, such as its newsworthiness or ability to entertain. Comments, on the other hand, are signs of high involvement of a commenter into the issue, which does not necessarily mean agreement but usually indicates issue importance and controversy [2]. Moreover, long threads of comments often conceal heated and even polarized discussions in which commenters oppose each other rather than news authors and which use the news itself just as a starting point for discussing issues that are related to the news topic but are not identical to it. Finally, sharing occurs when users think a news item has a practical utility [3] or demands involvement of other audience members.

While sharing is of ultimate importance for media practitioners as it increases media audiences and advertising revenues, all three types of feedback are meaningful for broader social science. In this paper, we outline how these types of feedback may be interpreted in relation to topics they refer to.

The rest of the paper is organized as follows. In the next section we introduce information needed before the start of the proposed research cycle: we give a brief description of topic modeling as a method and review the entropic approach to the choice of optimal topic number. Then, in the third section, we describe our data set used to illustrate our methodological pipeline. Sections four and five introduce the suggested sequence of data analysis, while describing various problems and some rules of thumb on how to overcome them. In particular, Sect. 4 describes the procedure we used to choose the optimal number of topics, extract stable topics and for topic labeling. Section five describes how information on topics was matched with user feedback and what interpretations were obtained. We conclude with a brief summary of the proposed approach.

2 Before the Start: Thermodynamic and Entropic Approaches to Finding the Optimal Number of Topics

Before describing the suggested research pipeline we give a most general explanation of this method, then paying more attention to its key problem – choice of the number of topics – and the solution that we offer as a part of the proposed research cycle.

As an extended version of cluster analysis, topic modeling (TM) is a family of mathematical algorithms that allows simultaneous fuzzy co-clustering of both objects and features, namely texts (documents, d) and terms (words, n-grams or other text properties, w). Mathematical foundations of topic modeling are described elsewhere [1]. TM input data is the term-document matrix where cells are frequencies of terms in documents, and its output consists of two matrices: term-topic (e.g. word-topic) matrix ϕ_{wt} and document-topic matrix θ_{td}, where cells are probabilities of either terms or documents in topics. The sums of probabilities of all topics in a document and of all words in a topic are equal to one, however, the sums of probabilities of all documents in a topic and of all topics assigned to a word may take any values. The latter two sums can be interpreted as the salience of a topic in the collection and the importance of a word in the collection, respectively.

Topics are viewed as latent variables whose distribution is unknown. Thus, to build a topic model means to solve the reverse task of finding an array of latent topics T or an array of one-dimensional conditional distributions $p(w|t) = \varphi(w, t)$ for each topic t constituting matrix ϕ_{wt} as well as an array of one-dimensional distributions $p(t|d) = \theta(t, d)$ for each document d using observable variables d and w.

One of the convenient methods of distribution restoring is Gibbs sampling employed by Steyvers and Griffiths who based their approach of the Potts model [4, 5]. This version of topic modeling is used here as it has shown better suitability for finding the optimal topic number with the thermodynamic approach that we also adopt in this paper as a part of the suggested research pipeline.

The problem of optimal topic number choice remains largely unsolved. However, topic modeling literature suggests several approaches to the problem. For instance, Cao et al. [6], based on the ideas of cluster analysis, propose to look at a topic as a semantic cluster (a set of terms) which makes it possible to compute its intracluster distance. They propose to use the cosine similarity measure as the function to be minimized. Thus, the optimal topic number would be at the minimum of average cosine similarity measure computed between all pairs of topics in a given solution. Another approach is based on Kullback-Leibler (KL) divergence [7]. The authors propose to look for the minimum KL across solutions for different topic numbers as follows. First, matrices ϕ_{wt} and θ_{td} are decomposed using SVD; then, in a pairwise manner KL divergences for vectors of singular values are computed. The optimal topic number corresponds to the situation when both matrices contain the same number of singular values. The described approaches have several limitations. First, it is unclear how the minimum of the proposed functions is related to the principle of entropy maximization – a standard approach to account for "information usefulness" in information theory. Second, additional SVD transformation or KL computation hinder application of such approaches to big data. For example, in the second approach, the authors compute KL for a document collection of less than 2,500 texts. These approaches do not consider the influence of initial distribution on the results of TM as was shown in [8]. Finally, a well-known approach to automatically finding an optimal number of topics is the hierarchical Dirichlet process (HDP) [9]. It constructs a hierarchy of topics in the form of a tree whose depth must be predefined by a user. The problem of the number of topics is thus transformed into a problem of the levels of the tree, but not truly resolved [10]. Here, we do not consider this algorithm because the thermodynamic approach developed further below demands additional investigation to be adapted for HDP.

In this work, to find the optimal number of topics, we follow an approach based on finding the minimum of free energy or the minimum of the Rényi entropy [11]. This approach assumes that it is possible to view a collection of documents and words as a mesoscopic informational statistical system (a complex system). This allows to formulate and compute Gibbs-Shannon entropy (S), as well as internal energy (E) and the Helmholtz free energy, of such a mesoscopic system:

$$
\begin{aligned}
\Lambda_F = F(T) - F_0 &= (E(T) - E_0) - (S(T) - S_0) \cdot T \\
&= -\ln\left(\frac{\sum_{t=1}^{T}\sum_{n=1}^{N}P_{nt}}{T}\right) - T \cdot \ln\left(\frac{N_{k1}}{N \cdot T}\right)
\end{aligned}
\tag{1}
$$

where $S(T) = -\ln\left(\frac{\sum_{t=1}^{T}\sum_{n=1}^{N}P_{nt}}{T}\right)$ is an internal energy, $\ln\left(\frac{N_{k1}}{N \cdot T}\right)$ is the Gibbs-Shannon entropy and Λ_F is a free energy. Following this, the number of topics (or clusters) is the informational system temperature; this parameter should be set by a user. The principle to guide the user's choice that is proposed in this approach is the search of the minimum of non-extensive entropy of the system.

Since the information measure is the entropy with opposite sign, the maximum entropy corresponds to the minimum of information. Thus, it is possible to reduce the search of the optimal topic number to the search of the minimum of the Rényi entropy expressed through free energy using escort distribution [12]:

$$
S_{q=1/T}^{R} = \frac{F}{T-1}, q = \frac{1}{T}
\tag{2}
$$

Here, the $q = \frac{1}{T}$ value is viewed as a formal parameter (the number of topics/clusters) which is possible to change during a computational experiment. Thus, the search for the optimal topic number is reduced to varying topic/cluster number in TM and the search for the minimum Rényi entropy for each topic solution. It is necessary to note, that the presented approach assumes that the divergence of entropy could be achieved with $q = 1$. This means that the information of topic solution for just one topic is equal to zero. On the other hand, with $T \to \infty$ we have uniformly distributed probabilities of terms over topics which also corresponds to the maximum entropy or the minimum of information.

3 Selecting Data

Following the general goal of the type of studies for which our pipeline is proposed, here we narrow this goal to the task of finding the most liked, most commented and most shared topics in the news stream generated by the leading Russian TV channels in the most popular Russian social networking site – VKontakte (VK). Television, until recently, was the most popular media channel in Russia and hence the object of the major concern for the government. It is through television (especially *Channel 1*) that the government has been used to disseminate most of its messages to the population. With the massive outflow of younger audiences to the Internet, however, the government has made special efforts to channel its controlled content via social media and to direct social media users to TV websites that host video content. Therefore, it is important to understand what content is thus channeled to online audiences and how those audiences react to it.

To account for this, we collected the data from the VK pages of eight leading state TV channels including *Russia Today* (*RT*) in Russian, one government news agency and three media outlets of varying degree of independence: oppositional online TV *Dozhd*, *Echo Moskvy* radio as "permitted opposition" and *RBC* business channel that attempts to be neutral (for full list see Table 4). Other national media did not show any substantial presence in VK.

The data collection proceeded as follows. First, we collected news texts posted by the 12 chosen media channels on social network *VK* during the entire year of 2017. The resulting dataset consists of 164,426 Russian language posts and 185,029 unique words. Then, for each post we collected the following metadata: (1) number of likes for posts; (2) number of shares; (3) number of comments; (4) number of likes for comments; (5) date and time of publishing; (6) post URL. The dataset thus contains the total number of 111,626 comments, 527,147 likes and 121,073 shares. Finally, the news texts were cleared and lemmatized with MyStem lemmatizer, with stop-words being removed.

4 Finding the Optimal Topic Number

To describe the topical structure of the news collection, we began with choosing the optimal number of topics. For this, we ran models with varying number of topics in the range $T = [2; 400]$ in the increments of two. During each iteration, we calculated the Gibbs-Shannon entropy, internal energy, free energy as defined in (1) and the Rényi entropy as defined in (2). Given the known instability problem of TM algorithm [13], at each iteration we performed three runs of our model with identical starting conditions and then averaged the values of all four aforementioned parameters. Figure 1 presents the curve of the Rényi entropy and shows that there are two minima corresponding to the maxima of information. The first minimum lies at 12 topics and the second one is at 146. Thus, we use two topic models, corresponding to the maximum information, for further analysis, and illustrate how to choose between them.

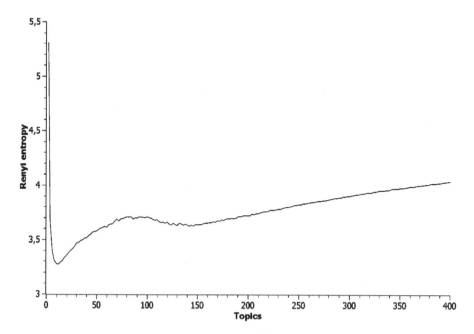

Fig. 1. The Rényi entropy of a topic model as a function of topic number.

4.1   Extracting Stable Topics

In topic modeling, there is a chance that a solution will contain topics impossible to reproduce even with the same data and algorithm parameters. For end users it means that they cannot make reliable judgments about topic composition of collections of their interest. At the moment, for unreproducible topics it is impossible to say whether their instability is explained by the inability of the algorithm to detect them or they are just algorithmic artifacts. It is thus not recommended to make any substantial conclusions based on the analysis of such topics. However, the topics that do get reproduced in each solution, can be analyzed and compared to each other, however, keeping in mind that the set of stable topics may be not a complete list of all the topics occuring in a given collection.

To select stable topics, we suggest to run TM several times with the same parameters, but not less than three, which is what we did here. Then, for each topic, we ranked words by probability and performed a pairwise comparison of each topic from every solution with the normalized Kulbak-Leibler measure [13]. Finally, we selected similar topics at the level of KL $\geq 90\%$. The use of such threshold for TM is justified in [14]. We applied the proposed algorithm to the two topic solutions (12 topics and 146 topics). We found only five stable topics in the first solution, and 86 the second solution. For further analysis, we used only these stable topics.

4.2   Labeling Stable Topics

To interpret topics, it is necessary to label them, and a problem of choosing between the runs of the same solution arises. However, if only stable topics are taken into analysis, this choice can be made at random since topics that get reproduced in three and more runs, are virtually identical. Therefore, in this study we picked a random run, ranked matrices ϕ_{wt} and θ_{td} by probabilities and asked three independent coders to assign a label for each stable topic based on interpretation of its top words and documents. For labeling, we used up to 500 top words and documents (but usually much fewer, around 20). A standard problem with labeling TM results is a difficulty to calculate intercoder agreement since labels are usually open-end expressions. However, in the case of news, and especially in the subset of stable topics, topics are usually well pronounced and therefore labeled unanimously except a few "trash" topics that are hard to interpret. The judgment on whether similar labels are the same or different is easy to made, but it can be made by the consensus between coders, if necessary. Then intercoder agreement can be calculated which is what we did. Namely, we assessed it with Krippendorff's alpha for multiple raters. The coders achieved excellent overall agreement with alpha = 1 for five stable topics (12 topics solution) and 0.88 for 86 stable topics (146 topics solution).

5   Matching Topics with User Feedback Data and Interpreting Results

5.1   Choosing the Best Solution

The global entropy minimum most often occurs at a relatively small number of topics (between 10 and 20), even for large collections with dozens of thousands of texts. It usually corresponds to solutions that yield very general topics. These solutions are suitable for getting a quick and most general understanding of a collection's content if it is completely unknown. Oftentimes, the global minimum may indicate solutions with topics that are not most general, but are most lexically dissimilar thus covering only the most visible "top" of the collection's topical structure (see Table 1). The next best minimum, however, usually points at solutions that are of the highest analytical usefulness for researchers (compare Tables 1 and 2). Subject-area expertise choice based on interpretability and analytic utility is an approach between solutions suggested by the founders of topic modeling Blei and Lafferty [15], however, prior finding of global and local minima helps to reduce the number of alternatives to just two or three. All this suggests that a TM user should not blindly follow the global entropy minimum. Instead, the better practice would be to examine all entropy minima for relevance to the research goals before committing to the analysis. Further on, we use a 146-topic solution.

Table 1. Likes, reposts, comments and comments likes distributions for stable topics of the 12 topics solution (estimated on ∼ 500 most probable documents with no missing metadata).

Stable topic	N likes	N reposts	N comments	N comments likes
Russian sport achievements	106234	3800	16134	23328
Money & Russian markets analysis	61584	9032	17180	22952
Russian culture	71830	5623	6756	14630
Science news	110953	8594	24526	25605
American movie culture	93225	5537	20403	32286

5.2   Assessing Relation of User Feedback to Topics

As each text contains all topics in different proportions, and this proportions decrease rapidly from the top text in a given topic to its bottom text, it is not easy to match topics to user feedback. Users attach their likes or comments to texts, not topics, whose representation in text may be high or low. One way suggested in [16] is to multiply the number of likes by the probability of a given topic in a given text and then to summarize the obtained values across all texts. A limitation of this approach is that the long tail of low probabilities may in the end outweigh the influence of the small number of texts in which a topic is best pronounced. Another approach is to use only top N texts for calculating the "likability" or "sharebility" of a topic. A limitation of this approach is that it ignores the degrees to which each text belongs to a given topic. And a third approach is to combine both. Here, we use the second approach as an example selecting 500 top texts. The average probability of all topics in these texts is 0.27 which is 38 times higher than random (1/146). This allows us to ignore differences in probabilities among those 500 texts.

Table 2 shows top ten stable topics from the 146-topic solution ranked by the numbers of likes, reposts, comments and likes to comments. Top topics shared across all types of feedback are topics of *Mixture of controversial events* as well as coverage of *Russian Orthodox church* and various Christian celebrations. *Mixture of controversial events* unites a number of most resonant scandals that burst out during the year, so it is well understandable why it is the leader in all aspects of feedback.

While most liked topics are related to *Russian sport achievements* (including hockey and figure skating) as well as Russian military campaign in Syria (*Syria & Russia*) and other military advances, the most shared topics are about corruption (*Navalny-Usmanov controversy*), *Rulemaking* and Russian finance news (*Finance, pension fund and the Finance Ministry*). Most commented topics include *Ukraine & separatist proto-states* as well as *Russian athletes doping controversy* and *Street actions and Protests*. It thus can be seen that high "likability" is most likely to be generated by topics that can produce and maintain national pride. High sharing levels are likely to be produced by social problems and some practically useful topics (recipes), and high numbers of comments correspond to the largest number of sharp conflicts. Large numbers of likes to comments, however, are caused by topics other than those that produce the highest likability of news themselves. As said in the introduction, large number of comments usually indicate hot, often polarized discussions (which is confirmed by the nature of the detected topics that generate them), and thus likes born in the course of such discussions indicate solidarity with the parties of the discussion rather than satisfaction with news. From this, it is clear that likes to comments should not be used together with likes to news items as the indicators of audience's satisfaction with news content.

Table 2. Top 10 stable topics from the 146 topics solution ranked by the number of likes, reposts, comments and likes to comments (estimated on $\sim$ 500 most probable documents with no missing metadata).

Rank	By likes	By reposts	By comments	By likes in comments
1	Mixture of controversial events	Mixture of controversial events	Mixture of controversial events	Mixture of controversial events
2	Russian sport achievements	WW2 commemoration	2018 Russian presidential campaign	2018 Russian presidential campaign
3	WW2 commemoration	Navalny-Usmanov controversy	'Matilda' movie controversy	Russian athletes doping controversy
4	Sport: hockey	Rulemaking	Russian opinion polls	Finance, pension fund and the Finance Ministry
5	Sport: figure skating	Russian opinion polls	Street actions & protests (international)	Russian opinion polls
6	Food & recipes	Finance, pension fund and the Finance Ministry	Finance, pension fund and the Finance Ministry	'Matilda' movie controversy
7	Russian Orthodox Church	FSB and counterterrorist activities	WW2 history related events (international)	Street actions & protests (international)
8	FSB and counterterrorist activities	Russian Orthodox Church	Russian Orthodox Church	Putin & his addresses
9	Syria & Russia	Food & recipes	Russian athletes doping controversy	Russian Orthodox Church
10	Russian navy	Astronomy & NASA news	Ukraine & separatist proto-states	FSB and counterterrorist activities

5.3 Assessing Topical Compositions of Collection Subsets and Feedback Received by Them: Topicality of TV Channels

The discussed above results reflect only the cumulative effect of all 12 TV channels combined. However, both topic composition and user feedback related to different topics could significantly vary by channel. For instance, a given topic might be most represented in only two channels, but one of them might still gain more likes than the other. To account for this, we, first, calculated the proportion of texts from each channel among 500 top texts of all stable topics. Second, we calculated the proportion of likes and shares received by the texts of each given channel from among all likes and shares received by 500 top texts of each stable topic, respectively. This approach may also be easily transformed into the approach offered in [16] by multiplying the number of likes and shares by the probability of a given topic in a text.

From Table 3 we can see that the dominant role in topic composition as well as in total topic likability and shareability belongs to just four TV channels. Namely, state-controlled channels *Russia Today*, *RIA News, Russia 24* and *NTV* dominate the landscape and produce thematically similar content that forms a hegemonic discourse [17]. Conventionally neutral *RBC* closely follows the leaders by its presence in the most liked and shared topics. The only oppositional TV channel, *Dozhd* is also present, and it predictably emerges within some of the most conflict topics *Street Actions & Protests* and *Matilda movie controversy*. The movie was heavily criticized by the officials, banned from display and then reinstated.

While difference between the mainstream and the oppositional agendas in quite predictable, the apparent domination of just a few channels in our topic model deserves special consideration. It persists across all stable topics when measured both as the proportion of texts and as salience. This effect can be explained via examination of the document and word distributions in the data. The largest influence on TM results is exerted by sources with (1) relatively large number of messages, and (2) with relatively longer texts. As can be seen from Table 4, each channel on average posts 200–300 word long messages. Because the four dominant sources have more documents and words, they accumulate higher topic probabilities (see Table 4).

This effect thus should be taken into consideration by researchers. One way to deal with it is to obtain more balanced samples. However, as sampling may distort true topical structures, another strategy can be chosen. Topic saliences, as suggested elsewhere [16], may be calculated as the sums of probabilities of each topic over all texts, or, as we would suggest, over N most probable texts in each topic. When aggregated by source (e.g. TV channel), topics, on average, will tend to show higher saliences in overrepresented channels. Therefore, to compare topic saliences across channels, they can be normalized based on the distribution of text quantities and lengths among channels.

Table 3. Contribution of TV channels into topic salience, "likability" and "sharebility"

Stable topic	Channel weight in a topic, %	Channel likes, %	Channel reposts, %
Mixture of controversial events	RIA News – 98%	RIA News – 99.54%	RIA News – 99.80%
Russian sport achievements	Russia Today – 41.29%	Russia Today – 31.90%	Russia Today – 26.75%
	Russia-24 – 17.43%	Russia-24– 8.76%	Russia-24 – 10.96%
	RIA News – 16.6%	RIA News – 47.03%	RIA News – 42.19%
	NTV – 12.45%	NTV – 2.86%	NTV – 4.61%
Syria & Russia	RIA News – 33.68%	RIA News – 54.46%	RIA News – 44.63%
	Russia Today – 30.58%	Russia Today – 33.42%	Russia Today – 36.60%
	Russia-24 – 13.00%	Russia-24– 4.93%	Russia-24– 7.05%
	NTV – 10.95%	NTV – 2.40%	NTV – 4.36%
Russian athletes doping controversy	Russia Today – 30.50%	Russia Today – 24.66%	Russia Today – 23.42%
	RBC – 17.3%	RBC – 17.13%	RBC – 20.15%
		RIA News – 37.75%	RIA News – 30.52%
		NTV – 5.83%	
	RIA News – 15.87%		NTV – 7.10%
	NTV – 15.67%		
Russian Orthodox Church	NTV – 21.49%	NTV – 5.93%	NTV – 8.37%
	RIA News – 20.66%	RIA News – 51.86%	RIA News – 39.25%
	Russia-24 – 16.53%	Russia-24– 7.89%	Russia-24– 8.93%
	Dozhd – 10.95%	Dozhd – 2.03%	Dozhd – 2.61%
'Matilda' movie controversy	Dozhd – 21.44%	Dozhd – 13.88%	Dozhd – 17.02%
	Russia Today – 19.17%	Russia Today – 16.18%	Russia Today – 14.80%
			RBC – 34.26%
	RBC – 18.76%	RBC – 27.73%	RIA News – 23.89%
	RIA News – 15.00%	RIA News – 34.85%	

(*continued*)

Table 3. (*continued*)

Stable topic	Channel weight in a topic, %	Channel likes, %	Channel reposts, %
Street actions & protests (international)	Dozhd – 25.67%	Dozhd – 12.19%	Dozhd – 15.38%
	RBC – 22.77%	RBC – 40.83%	RBC – 47.90%
	RIA News – 20.08%	RIA News – 33.49%	RIA News – 19.33%
	NTV – 13.04%	NTV – 2.08%	NTV – 2.89%
Putin & his addresses	NTV – 21.85%	NTV – 5.66%	NTV – 8.73%
	Russia Today – 21.65%	Russia Today – 22.88%	Russia Today – 19.08%
			RBC – 23.44%
	RBC – 14.64%	RBC – 13.54%	RIA News – 35.62%
	RIA News – 12.57%	RIA News – 48.68%	
FSB and counterterrorist activities	NTV – 23.81%	NTV – 6.78%	NTV – 9.05%
	RIA News – 20.08%	RIA News – 57.47%	RIA News – 40.94%
	Russia-24 – 13.25%	Russia-24– 7.45%	Russia-24 – 10.62%
	Russia Today – 12.42%	Russia Today – 12.33%	Russia Today – 14.10%

Table 4. General distribution of posts, likes, reposts and subscribers in dataset

Chanel	N of messages	N of comments	Posts likes	N of reposts	N of subscribers
Russia Today	96440	7491681	13405188	869569	1083472
RIA News	28947	3562463	13024009	706123	2149674
NTV	28298	466976	1583383	160728	313140
Russia-24	22300	553084	742878	1597518	142129
Dozhd	19300	557997	1214643	108189	425127
Channel 5	18097	137680	500796	53522	90607
Russia-1	17640	127940	820069	113462	78492
RBC	10800	178627	2111679	236643	631525
Channel 1	5700	346299	3758479	322667	1740665
Mir-24	5500	4412	63197	11237	24700
TVC (News)	4400	2994	29811	4053	7895
Russia-Culture	2900	6363	138730	25336	35709

6 Conclusion

In this paper, we presented a full-cycle methodology for news topic modeling and user feedback research. This methodology offers a series of steps to overcome various latent limitations of topic modeling and, above all, mitigates the problem of topic number choice. Our solution to this problem is based on the search for the minimum of the Rényi entropy. Furthermore, we formulated an approach for stable topic extraction based on the normalized Kullback-Leibler divergence. Additionally, we illustrated the proposed research pipeline with an analysis of a one-year online stream formed by 12 national TV channels and broadcasted online via VK social network (12 and 146 topics models). We demonstrated that audience feedback varies depending on news topics and showed how this and other effects can be captured with our approach. Positive topics like athletic achievements receive more likes and are discussed significantly less; more discussed topics, on the other hand, are more related to problems and conflicts and are generally receive less likes. Finally, using metadata of online news items, we showed the overrepresentation effect of the leading TV channels in topic models. This finding opens a new question about data normalization in topic modeling.

Acknowledgement. The reported study was funded by RFBR according to the research project № 18-011-00997 A.

References

1. Daud, A., Li, J., Zhou, L., Muhammad, F.: Knowledge discovery through directed probabilistic topic models: a survey. Front. Comput. Sci. China **4**, 280–301 (2010). https://doi.org/10.1007/s11704-009-0062-y
2. Ziegele, M., Breiner, T., Quiring, O.: An exploratory analysis of discussion factors in user comments on news items: what creates interactivity in online news discussions? J. Commun. **64**, 1111–1138 (2014). https://doi.org/10.1111/jcom.12123
3. Bobkowski, P.S.: Sharing the news: effects of informational utility and opinion leadership on online news sharing. J. Mass Commun. Q. **92**, 320–345 (2015). https://doi.org/10.1177/1077699015573194
4. Landau, D.P., Binder, R.: A guide to Monte Carlo simulations in statistical physics. Cambridge University Press, Cambridge (2009)
5. Griffiths, T.L., Steyvers, M.: Finding scientific topics. PNAS **101**, 5228–5235 (2004). https://doi.org/10.1073/pnas.0307752101
6. Cao, J., Xia, T., Li, J., Zhang, Y., Tang, S.: A density-based method for adaptive LDA model selection. Neurocomputing **72**, 1775–1781 (2009). https://doi.org/10.1016/j.neucom.2008.06.011
7. Arun, R., Suresh, V., Veni Madhavan, C.E., Narasimha Murthy, M.N.: On finding the natural number of topics with latent Dirichlet allocation: some observations. In: Zaki, M.J., Yu, J.X., Ravindran, B., Pudi, V. (eds.) PAKDD 2010. LNCS (LNAI), vol. 6118, pp. 391–402. Springer, Heidelberg (2010). https://doi.org/10.1007/978-3-642-13657-3_43
8. Roberts, M.E., Stewart, B.M., Tingley, D.: Navigating the local modes of big data: the case of topic models. In: Alvarez, R.M. (ed.) Computational Social Science, pp. 51–97. Cambridge University Press, Cambridge (2016)

9. Teh, Y.W., Jordan, M.I., Beal, M.J., Blei, D.M.: Hierarchical Dirichlet processes. J. Am. Stat. Assoc. **101**, 1566–1581 (2006)
10. Blei, D.M., Griffiths, T.L., Jordan, M.I., Tenebaum, J.B.: Hierarchical topic models and the nested Chinese restaurant process. Adv. Neural. Inf. Process. Syst. **16**, 17–24 (2004). https://doi.org/10.1016/0169-023X(89)90004-9
11. Koltcov, S.N.: A thermodynamic approach to selecting a number of clusters based on topic modeling. Tech. Phys. Lett. **43**, 584–586 (2017). https://doi.org/10.1134/S1063785017060207
12. Beck, C., Schlögl, F.: Thermodynamics of Chaotic Systems. Cambridge University Press, Cambridge (1993)
13. Koltcov, S., Nikolenko, Sergey I., Koltsova, O., Filippov, V., Bodrunova, S.: Stable topic modeling with local density regularization. In: Bagnoli, F., Satsiou, A., Stavrakakis, I., Nesi, P., Pacini, G., Welp, Y., Tiropanis, T., DiFranzo, D. (eds.) INSCI 2016. LNCS, vol. 9934, pp. 176–188. Springer, Cham (2016). https://doi.org/10.1007/978-3-319-45982-0_16
14. Koltcov, S., Koltsova, O., Nikolenko, S.: Latent Dirichlet allocation: stability and applications to studies of user-generated content. In: Proceedings of the 2014 ACM Conference on Web Science. ACM, Bloomington, Indiana, USA, pp. 161–165 (2014)
15. Blei, D.M., Lafferty, J.D.: Topic models. In: Text Mining: Classification, Clustering, and Applications, pp. 71–94. CRC Press (2009)
16. Nagornyy, O., Koltsova, O.: Mining media topics perceived as social problems by online audiences: use of a data mining approach in sociology. Higher School of Economics Research Paper No. WP BRP 74/SOC/2017. SSRN (2017). https://ssrn.com/abstract=2968359 or http://dx.doi.org/10.2139/ssrn.2968359
17. Prozorov, S.: Russian conservatism in the Putin presidency: the dispersion of a hegemonic discourse. J. Polit. Ideol. **10**, 121–143 (2005). https://doi.org/10.1080/13569310500097224

Network-Oriented Modeling of Multi-criteria Homophily and Opinion Dynamics in Social Media

Olga Kozyreva, Anna Pechina, and Jan Treur[✉]

Behavioural Informatics Group, Department of Computer Science,
Vrije Universiteit Amsterdam, Amsterdam, The Netherlands
o.d.kozyreva@gmail.com, a.pechina@student.vu.nl, j.treur@vu.nl

Abstract. In this paper we model the opinion dynamics in social groups in combination with adaptation of the connections based on a multicriteria homophily principle. The adaptive network model has been designed according to a Network-Oriented Modeling approach based on temporal-causal networks. The model has been applied to a dataset obtained from a popular social media platform – Instagram, using the official Instagram API. The network model has also been analysed mathematically, which provided evidence that the implemented model does what is expected.

Keywords: Adaptive network · Multicriteria homophily · Opinion dynamics
Social media · Instagram

1 Introduction

In the era of social media platforms, it is an interesting challenge to study people's activity online. As the area of social media is actively developing nowadays, people use it as a platform to earn money, and therefore, the opinion dynamics in social media is in particular an interesting topic to study. Many people are using online social networks, such platforms as Facebook, Twitter or Instagram are very convenient as sources of information. People can use these platforms to be informed about latest news. As these online media are gaining popularity, fake news are spreading with a higher speed over the internet. Misinformation has been listed by the Worlds Economic Forum as one of the main threats to the modern society. Therefore, it is of a big interest, to study the way opinions spread over the internet. In this work, we study the opinion dynamics on the popular social media - Instagram. We study how people show interest in the subjects of finance, international education and photography, by analyzing their activity on Instagram. To study the opinion dynamics we apply the Network-Oriented Modeling approach based on temporal-causal networks described in [1]. This approach is often used to study the dynamics of various processes in terms of networks [2–5]. A series of recent studies shows that the temporal-causal approach can also be used to model the dynamics in social networks in particular [6, 7].

In [8] the authors analyzed the emotion dynamics using the data that they obtained from Twitter. In their work, authors analyse the emotions of users and try to predict it using the temporal-causal network model. They assume that Twitter users can influence each other and therefore by analysing one's online activity, the future emotions can be predicted. Authors show that the model works for Twitter data in terms of analysing negative emotions such as anger and sadness.

In our work we use a similar approach, because also users on Instagram can influence each other if they are subscribed to each other. Instead of emotions, we analyse their opinion dynamics. Users on Instagram can observe what other people who they follow on Instagram like and comment. We assume that if a user is subscribed to some people on Instagram, he or she is influenced by their opinion. By subscribing to someone, a user gets notifications about what that user likes. We test this theory by analysing users activity online basing on the activity of their friends, who they follow.

A similar method is used by [9]. They use the homophily principle [10–12] and the contagion process [13] and describe it as: the more a person interacts with someone else, the more their opinions or beliefs or emotions or other states will converge. They show that the model works for predicting relationships between high school friend groups in terms of choosing a sport in their school.

The homophily principle is used in the same way in our research with one important difference. In all literature mentioned above, homophily was applied to one criterion only. Here the approach is generalised to multicriteria homophily. The more users interact with each other online, the more they influence each other in a broader way, which means that they influence each other's interests in a plural sense. We examine this theory by analysing users activity on bloggers accounts, as it indicates the interests of people. We apply the defined multicriteria homophily principle to the data that describes online activity of various users on Instagram, that we obtained using the official Instagram API.

2 The Network-Oriented Modeling Approach Used

In the Network-Oriented Modeling approach used, the nodes in a network are interpreted as states (or state variables) that vary over time, and the connections are interpreted as causal relations that define how each state can affect other states over time. To acknowledge this perspective of dynamics and causality on networks, this type of network has been called a *temporal-causal network* [1]. A conceptual representation of a temporal-causal network model by a *labeled* graph provides a fundamental basis. More specifically, a conceptual representation of a temporal-causal network model in the first place involves representing in a declarative manner states and connections between them that represent (causal) impacts of states on each other, as assumed to hold for the application domain addressed. This part of a conceptual representation is often depicted in a *conceptual picture* by a graph with nodes and directed connections. However, a full *conceptual representation* of a temporal-causal network model also includes a number of labels for such a graph. First, in reality not all causal relations are equally strong, so some notion of strength of a connection is used as a label for connections. Second, when more than one causal relation affects a state, some way to aggregate multiple causal impacts on a state is used. Third, a notion of speed of change of a state is used for timing of the processes. These three notions, called *connection weight*, *combination function*, and *speed factor*, which make the graph of states and connections a labeled graph, form the defining structure of a temporal-causal network model in the form of a conceptual representation; see Table 1.

Table 1. Conceptual representation of a temporal-causal network model

Concepts	Notation	Explanation
States and connections	$X, Y, X \to Y$	Describes the nodes and links of a network structure (e.g., in graphical or matrix format)
Connection weight	$\omega_{X,Y}$	A *connection weight* $\omega_{X,Y} \in [-1, 1]$ denotes the strength of the causal impact of state X on state Y through connection $X \to Y$
Aggregating multiple impacts on a state	$c_Y(..)$	For each state Y a *combination function* $c_Y(..)$ is chosen to combine the causal impacts of other states on state Y
Timing of the effect of causal impact	η_Y	For each state Y a *speed factor* $\eta_Y \geq 0$ is used to represent how fast a state is changing upon causal impact

Combination functions can have different forms, as there are many different approaches possible to address the issue of combining multiple impacts. To provide sufficient flexibility, the Network-Oriented Modelling approach based on temporal-causal networks incorporates for each state, a way to specify how multiple causal impacts on this state are aggregated by a combination function. For this aggregation a library with a number of standard combination functions are available as options, but also own-defined functions can be added.

Next, the numerical-mathematical foundations of temporal-causal networks are discussed in more detail. This is done by showing how a conceptual representation as discussed above (based on states and connections enriched with labels for connection weights, combination functions and speed factors), define a numerical representation [1], Chap. 2. This is shown in Table 2; here Y is any state in the network and $X_1, ..., X_k$ are the states with outgoing connections to Y.

Table 2. Numerical representation of a temporal-causal network model

Concept	Representation	Explanation
State values over time t	$Y(t)$	At each time point t each state Y in the model has a real number value in $[0, 1]$
Single causal impact	$\textbf{impact}_{X,Y}(t) = \omega_{X,Y} X(t)$	At t state X with connection to state Y has an impact on Y, using connection weight $\omega_{X,Y}$
Aggregating multiple impacts	$\textbf{aggimpact}_Y(t)$ $= c_Y(\textbf{impact}_{X_1,Y}(t), ..., \textbf{impact}_{X_k,Y}(t))$ $= c_Y(\omega_{X_1,Y}X_1(t), ..., \omega_{X_k,Y}X_k(t))$	The aggregated causal impact of multiple states X_i on Y at t, is determind using combination function $c_Y(..)$
Timing of the causal effect	$Y(t + \Delta t)$ $= Y(t) + \eta_Y [\textbf{aggimpact}_Y(t) - Y(t)] \Delta t$ $= Y(t)$ $+ \eta_Y[c_Y(\omega_{X_1,Y}X_1(t), ..., \omega_{X_k,Y}X_k(t)) - Y(t)]\Delta t$	The causal impact on Y is exerted over time gradually, using speed factor η_Y; here the X_i are all states with connections to state Y

The difference equations in the last row in Table 2 form the numerical representation of a temporal-causal network model and can be used for simulation and mathematical analysis, and also be written in differential equation format:

$$Y(t + \Delta t) = Y(t) + \eta_Y[c_Y(\omega_{X_1, Y}X_1(t), \dots, \omega_{X_k, Y}X_k(t)) - Y(t)]\Delta t$$

$$dY(t)/dt = \eta_Y[c_Y(\omega_{X_1, Y}X_1(t), \dots, \omega_{X_k, Y}X_k(t)) - Y(t)]$$

These can be used for simulation and for mathematical analysis.

Often used examples of combination functions are the *identity* **id**(.) for states with impact from only one other state, the *scaled sum* **ssum**$_\lambda$(..) with scaling factor λ, and the *advanced logistic sum* combination function **alogistic**$_{\sigma,\tau}$(..) with steepness σ and threshold τ:

$$\mathbf{id}(V) = V$$

$$\mathbf{ssum}_\lambda(V_1, \dots, V_k) = (V_1, \dots, V_k)/\lambda$$

$$\mathbf{alogistic}_{\sigma,\tau}(V_1, \dots, V_k) = [(1/(1 + e^{-\sigma(V_1 + \dots + V_k - \tau)})) - 1/(1 + e^{\sigma\tau})](1 + e^{-\sigma\tau})$$

For adaptive networks, the connection weights $\omega_{X,Y}$ are not constant, but are considered time dependent states $\omega_{X,Y}(t)$ themselves with difference or differential equations describing how they change over time. Then they can be modeled like states with their own combination functions.

3   The Adaptive Network Model

Assume there are n people and each of them has opinion about m topics. There are directed connections between people. If one person is influenced by another, then his opinion about topics is changing to be similar to the opinion of the influencer. To model such a situation we use the Network-Oriented Modeling approach based on temporal-causal networks described in [1].

3.1   Network Structure and Conceptual Representation of the Model

There are nm states and each state represents a pair of a person and his opinion about a topic. Each person has one opinion value per topic. We denote state corresponding to opinion of person i about topic k by X_{ik}. Values of states are between 0 and 1. Speed factors for opinion values of the same person are the same and they represent how fast this person is influenced. The speed factor of person i is denoted by η_i. All states of opinion values about one topic are connected one another and there are no other connections. Connections are directed and they have weights. Weights are between 0 and 1. The weight of the connection from state X_{ik} to state X_{jk} are denoted by ω_{ijk}. Weights represent strength of influence of one person's opinion on another person's opinion. Strength of influence of one person on another changes over time. To model this we developed the adaptive network in sense that weights of connections change over time.

We want the strength of influence depend only on pair of people, but not on the topic, so the weights satisfy the following expression:

$$\omega_{ijk}(t) = \omega_{ijl}(t) \text{ for all } i, j, k, l, \text{ and } t$$

Figure 1 represents a conceptual representation of the network model for 3 bloggers: F (Finance), P (Photography) and E (Education) and 3 users: i, j, m. As we model social interaction in the online social platform Instagram, we present bloggers and ordinary users in our model. Bloggers represent accounts that are dedicated to one specific topic (finance, education, ...). Each user has a set of states that denote his opinion regarding the topic, every blogger (F-Finance, E-Education, P-Photography) influences user i with a particular weight $\omega_{F,i}, \omega_{E,i}, \omega_{P,i}$. Weights of connections among users i and j are denoted by ω_{ij} and calculated based on the opinion values of the person. The weight of a connection between two users or a user and a blogger changes over time with a speed, that is defined by a speed factor different for every user: η_i, η_j, η_m for users i, j, m respectively, as it is illustrated in Fig. 1. All states of one person change with the same speed over time.

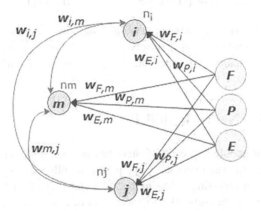

Fig. 1. Conceptual representation of the temporal-causal network model

3.2   Numerical Representation of the Network Model

Next, we are going to describe how values of states change over time numerically. In general the differential equation for state $X_{ik}(t)$ is as follows:

$$dX_{ik}(t)/dt = \eta_{ik}[\mathbf{aggimpact}_{ik}(t) - X_{ik}(t)]$$

To model contagion [13] the scaled sum is chosen as combination function for all states; taking into account topology of the network, we have

$$c_{X_{ik}}(V_1, .., V_k) = (V_1 + .. + V_k)/\lambda$$
$$\text{with } \lambda = \sum\nolimits_{j=1}^{n} \omega_{jik}(t)$$
$$\mathbf{aggimpact}_{ik}(t) = \sum\nolimits_{j=1}^{n} \omega_{jik}(t)X_{jk}(t) / \sum\nolimits_{j=1}^{n} \omega_{jik}(t)$$

Speed factors for opinion values on different topics of the same person are the same ($\eta_{ik} = \eta_i$) so the final differential equation for state $X_{ik}(t)$ is:

$$dX_{ik}(t)/dt = \eta_i[\sum\nolimits_{j=1}^{n} \omega_{jik}(t)X_{jk}(t) / \sum\nolimits_{j=1}^{n} \omega_{jik}(t) - X_{ik}(t)]$$

Finally, we need to describe how weights of connections change over time based on the homophily principle [10–12]. In the introduced model this change is based on a *multicriteria homophily principle*. Usually, the homophily principle is formulated as: if two states have close values, then the connection between them becomes stronger over time. In our model, we want the weight to represent connection between people taking into account not just one but multiple criteria. So we do not compare opinion values of two people on one specific topic, but on all of the topics. We chose the Euclidean distance as a measure of similarity between two persons i and j:

$$\text{similarity}_{ij}(t) = \sqrt{\sum\nolimits_{k=1}^{m} \left(X_{ik}(t) - X_{jk}(t)\right)^2}$$

If the similarity is smaller than some threshold (or tipping point) that we set in our model, then the connection between people becomes stronger. If it is bigger than the threshold the connection becomes weaker over time. We denote this threshold by τ. Using this, as a generalisation of the linear homophily combination function from [1], Chap. 11, p. 307, this time we define the combination function for the connection ω_{ijk} by

$$c_{\omega ijk}(U_1, \ldots, U_m, V_1, \ldots, V_m, W) = W + W(1 - W)(\tau - \sqrt{\sum\nolimits_{k=1}^{m} (U_k - V_k)^2}$$

where U_k stands for $X_{ik}(t)$, V_k stands for $X_{jk}(t)$, and W for $\omega_{ijk}(t)$. Then the final differential equation for weight ω_{ijk} is

$$d\omega_{ijk}(t)/dt = \mu_{ij}[c_{wijk}(X_{i1}(t), \ldots, X_{im}(t), X_{j1}(t), \ldots, X_{jm}(t), \omega_{ijk}(t)) - \omega_{ijk}(t)]$$
$$= \mu_{ij}\omega_{ijk}(t)(1 - \omega_{ijk}(t))(\tau - \sqrt{\sum\nolimits_{k=1}^{m} (X_{ik}(t) - X_{jk}(t))^2})$$

Here μ_{ij} represents the update speed parameter for all connections between opinion values of persons i and j. The term

$$\omega_{ijk}(t)(1 - \omega_{ijk}(t))$$

takes care that the weights stay in the range from 0 to 1. Note that the right part of the equations depends on k only in term $\omega_{ijk}(t)(1 - \omega_{ijk}(t))$, so if at time point 0 it holds $\omega_{ijk}(t) = \omega_{ijl}(t)$ for all k and i, then the same holds at any point of time. So, in our model, we achieve the situation when the way one person's opinion influences on another person's opinion does not depend on the topic but only on relationship between these two persons.

4 Simulation Examples

To discover properties of the model and the impact of different parameters on the result of the simulation we performed the simulations for a small example network. The network consists of 9 states representing the opinions of 3 persons on 3 topics. Person 1 at the beginning has strong positive opinion about all topics. On the opposite, Person 3 at the beginning has strong negative opinions about all topics. These two people have low speed factor equal to 0.001. Person 2 has positive opinion on first two topics and negative opinion on the third topic. His speed factor is relatively high and equal 0.03. Initial values for all states and speed factors can be found in Table 3. Persons 1 and 3 have only a small influence on each other. Initially, both weights between them are equal to 0.01. Persons 1 and 2 are connected with initial weight 0.2 for both directions. Persons 2 and 3 are connected with initial weight 0.8. Initial weights can be found in Table 4. Update speed for all weights is set to 0.8. Threshold τ is equal to 0.3.

Table 3. Initial state values and speed factors for the example network

	Opinion 1	Opinion 2	Opinion 3	Speed factor
Person 1	0.91	0.89	0.9	0.001
Person 2	0.82	0.78	0.2	0.03
Person 3	0.11	0.1	0.09	0.001

Table 4. Initial connection weights between persons for the example network

	Person 1	Person 2	Person 3
Person 1	-	0.2	0.01
Person 2	0.2	-	0.8
Person 3	0.01	0.8	-

With the described configuration of the network model, we expect that the opinion of Persons 1 and 3 on all topics stay constant as well as the weakness of the connection between them. We are mostly interested in dynamics of the opinion of Person 2 and his connection to the other 2 people. Simulation was performed for time values from 0 to 150 with time step equal to 1. The resulting plot for the opinion dynamics of people in a system can be found in Fig. 2(a). Resulting plot for weights can be found in Fig. 2b. It can be seen that the opinion of Person 2 on first and second topics first goes down as it is strongly influenced by Person 2. But then the weights between Persons 2 and 3 become 0, so over time the opinions of Persons 1 and 2 converge for all topics, the connection between them becomes strong and Person 2 becomes isolated.

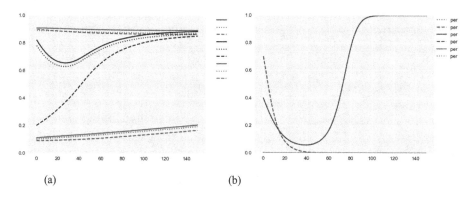

(a)   (b)

Fig. 2. First simulation; threshold value is $\tau = 0.3$, speed factor for weights is $\mu = 0.8$ (a) Opinion state dynamics (b) Connection dynamics

It is interesting to observe that at the beginning all connections tend to become weaker. This can be explained by the relatively small value of the threshold. To discover the effect of the value of the threshold on simulation results, another simulation was performed for threshold value equal to 0.5. All other values described above remained the same. Results for the second simulation can be found on Figs. 3a and b. In this case it is easy for two persons to have a similar opinion, so after 15 time steps both weights start to grow. The final network is symmetric with respect to the 2nd Person. He has strong connections with both Persons 1 and 3, so his opinion about all topics converge to 0.5. Opinions of Persons 1 and 3 also converge to 0.5, but slowly.

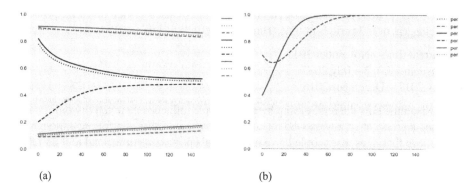

(a)   (b)

Fig. 3. Second simulation: changed threshold value: $\tau = 0.5$

Next, we wanted to investigate influence of the update speed parameters for weights on simulation results. Now, threshold is set again to 0.3 and the speed parameter is changed from 0.8 to 0.4. Results can be found in Fig. 4. In this case weights change too slowly, so opposite to the first situation, weight of connection between Persons 1 and 2 becomes 0 and weight of connection between Persons 2 and 3 becomes 1 at the end. Opinion values of Person 2 converge to opinion values of Person 2 on all topics.

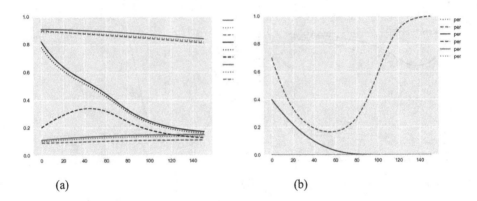

Fig. 4. Third simulation: changed update speed factor for weights $\mu = 0.4$

5 Empirical Data

As an empirical data set, we obtained data from Instagram using the official Instagram API. Instagram is a popular social media platform, where people share their photos and can post on different topics. Popular users who have many subscribers and dedicate their posts to particular subjects such as diets, pets, kids etc. are called bloggers. Users on Instagram follow bloggers if they are interested in a content of their blog and can show interest in one's posts by leaving likes under photos. The Instagram API allows us to obtain the list of people who subscribed to a user and to count the number of likes under one's posts. To monitor the opinion dynamics of people on Instagram, we obtained lists of followers for 4 bloggers who post on different subjects and counted likes that users left under the posts of these bloggers over 3 periods of time. Three time periods that we used:

- Current time – November 2017
- November 2017 – July 2017
- July 2017 – December 2016.

To examine how the relationship between people influence their activity online, we obtained a group of followers who all subscribed to each other and follow 4 bloggers. We believe that likes that people leave under each's posts can correspond to their relations, therefore, we set the weights equal to number of likes that they leave under each other's posts. Weights were normalized, so the max value is 1 and the min is 0. This approach of 'calculating' someone's opinion on a particular subject basing on his/her activity online is described in the literature [14], where authors show that someone's opinion can be performed as a value distributed between 0 and 1: $p(u) \in [0, 1]$. In this case "1" means that person is very much interested in the subject and "0" that he/she is not interested. In our work, an opinion value "1" corresponds to the situation when the user puts the most likes under the blogger's post, and "0" to the situation, when the user does not put any likes under blogger's post.

We chose to crawl the data from accounts of 4 Russian bloggers who post about: finance ("ilevyant", 22.1k followers), education ("ksenianiglas", 10.7k followers) and photography ("maxlistov", 68.1k followers). Overall there are 41 users who are subscribed to these 4 bloggers, among them we chose active users who leaves likes under posts of bloggers and also subscribed to each other. We set the likes that users leave under bloggers posts as a value of the connection weight that corresponds to user's interest in one of the subjects. Part of the dataset that we obtained for the first time period is presented in Table 5 below: the likes. We calculated the number of likes that each user leaves under posts of a blogger in a particular time period. Then we applied the network model to the real data and got the results shown in Fig. 5.

Table 5. Examples of the empirical data: the likes

Users\Bloggers	Blogger finance	Blogger education	Blogger photography	Blogger business
User 1	0	0	0	0
User 2	10	11	3	1
User 3	0	0	0	0
User 4	0	1	0	0
...	...	...	...	...
User 41	1	1	0	0

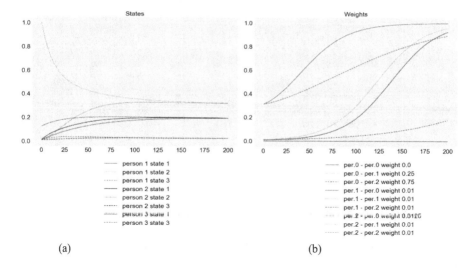

(a)   (b)

Fig. 5. Results of the simulation based on the empirical data set

The graph in Fig. 5 represents changing in states for users that we calculated using the described network model, initial value of states for each user correspond to a weight between user and a blogger, obtained from a real data.

6   Parameter Tuning

Not all users are being active on Instagram and tend to leave likes under someone's posts. We used the parameter tuning based on the modeling results regarding changing of weights between users and bloggers and, we used the data about three most active users, who leave more likes under blogger's posts than others do. In our model, we use: weights between users and bloggers that correspond to the users interests in subjects of finance, education and photography; weights between users that correspond to how they influence each other and speed factor – value that describes how fast state of one user changes over time. Two of these three variables that we use are based on the real data, so we implement the parameter tuning to a value of speed factor. In order to tune parameters we use the method called exhaustive search.

Exhaustive search as a parameter tuning method [1], represents enumerating all possible values of speed factor for the model and checking the accuracy of the model. Values of speed factor that correspond to the highest accuracy of the model would represent a result of exhaustive search. The two graphs below present modeling results before parameter tuning (Fig. 6(a)) and after the parameter tuning (Fig. 6(b)).

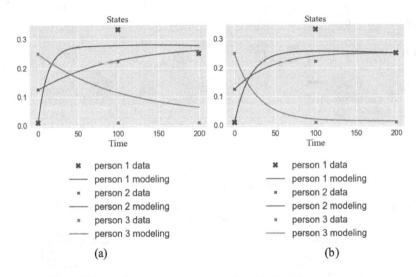

(a)   (b)

Fig. 6. (a) Results before parameter tuning (b) After parameter tuning

As a result of parameter tuning, we obtained three values of speed actors for examined three users: 0.05 for 1 user, 0.02 for the second and 0.09 for the third. The error value for these values was found to be: 0.12, 0.04 and 0.11, respectively. It can be seen that after tuning the speed factors for these three users, the modeling more accurately represents real data. We calculated the error value for the obtained values as the absolute value of the sum of differences between all dataset values and values predicted by modeling.

7   Mathematical Analysis and Verification

In this section we analyse model properties in analytic way. In general, stationary points or equilibria for the temporal-causal network model can be described. A stationary point of a state corresponds to a point in time after which no changes in a state occur. An equilibrium correspond to the same situation but for all states, i.e. if no changes occur for all states. These points can be analysed from the differential equations. Additionally, it can be found when a certain state Y is increasing or decreasing when a state is not in a stationary point or equilibrium:

- Y has a stationary point at t if $dY(t)/dt = 0$
- Y is increasing at t if $dY(t)/dt > 0$
- Y is decreasing at t if $dY(t)/dt < 0$.

Some states and time points have been selected at which no changes occur, which for a temporal-causal network is expressed in this criterion for having a stationary point:

$$\mathbf{c}_Y\left(\boldsymbol{\omega}_{X_1, Y}X_1(t), \dots, \boldsymbol{\omega}_{X_k, Y}X_k(t)\right) = Y(t)$$

where $X_1, \dots, X_k$ are the states connected to Y. We will only show one example of it regarding the state that correspond to "Finance". The time point after which no changes are observed is 150 (Fig. 5a):

$$\mathbf{c}_Y\left(\boldsymbol{\omega}_{X_1, Y}(150)X_1(150), \dots, \boldsymbol{\omega}_{X_k, Y}(150)X_k(150)\right) = Y(150)$$

Calculation of the left hand side provides:

$$(1 * 0.2753483 + 1 * 0.2776616 + 1 * 0.2792384)/3 = 0.2774161$$

This state Y corresponds to a value of 0.2781 at time 150 time, so the equation holds with accuracy $<10^{-3}$. Similar values can be observed in other calculations. This analysis provides evidence that the network model is correct and corresponds to a real situation.

Moreover, it has been analysed which equilibrium values are theoretically possible for the connection weights. The equilibrium equation for connection weight ω_{ijk} is

$$d\omega_{ijk}(t)/dt = \mu_{ij}\omega_{ijk}(t)(1 - \omega_{ijk}(t))(\tau - \sqrt{\sum_{k=1}^{m}\left(X_{ik}(t) - X_{jk}(t)\right)^2}) = 0$$

Assuming $\mu_{ij} > 0$, this equation has three solutions:

$$\omega_{ijk}(t) = 0 \text{ or } \omega_{ijk}(t) = 1 \text{ or } \sqrt{\sum_{k=1}^{m}\left(X_{ik}(t) - X_{jk}(t)\right)^2} = \tau \text{ and } \omega_{ijk}(t) \text{ any value}$$

It turns out that the third option is not attracting, it does not occur naturally; in the simulations it turns out that always each connection weight ω_{ijk} converges to either 0 or 1, thus generating emerging clusters with connection weights 1. This also provides evidence that the implemented model does what is expected.

8   Discussion

In this work we studied the opinion dynamics in social group in combination with adaptation of the connections based a multicriteria homophily principle. Although a number of models for adaptive networks for the homophily principle exist (e.g., [8, 9]), an approach for modeling adaptive networks based on multicriteria homophily is new, as far as we know.

We applied the obtained network model to the dataset that we obtained from a popular social media platform – Instagram, using the official Instagram API. We believe that Instagram reflects interests and opinion of people. Bloggers on Instagram post about different topics and users can be subscribed to bloggers accounts and leave likes under posts that represent user's interests regarding those topics.

In our model we used data about three popular Russian bloggers that post about finance, education and photography. We obtained a list of people who subscribed to all three bloggers and each other, and calculated the number of likes those people leave under bloggers posts and each other's posts. We studied users who subscribed to each other to show how their relationships influence their opinion. The number of those likes in our model represents weights of connections between users and correspond to one's interest in the particular topic. The described model shows how the dynamics of one's opinion evolves over time. We compared the modeling results to the real dataset and implemented parameter tuning using the exhaustive search. Overall, we can conclude that the described model works well for describing the opinion dynamics in Instagram for active users, in other words, those users who leave a lot of likes under posts on Instagram.

Note that, as holds for many approaches based on social networks, the approach presented here only zooms in on the effects that can be observed within the considered social network. All effects from the context outside this social network (third-party effects) are neglected. This may not cause a problem when these are random effects for each individual. But global events outside the network affecting all members systematically in a direct manner will not be addressed, which can be considered a disclaimer that holds for many applications based on social networks.

For future research the introduced model can be extended in several ways. First, connections between states representing opinions of the same person can be added. This improvement is needed, for example, if some topics are in some way related or similar and so the opinion on one topic influences the opinion of the same person on another topic. Topology and weights of such connections should be the same for all people. Weights of these connections do not change over time. Second, the homophily threshold τ can depend on pair of persons i and j. Then, for some pair of persons it will be easier to become strongly connected than for other people in the network. For example, the threshold can relate to close geographical location or age. Note that in the scope of this model it cannot depend on topic otherwise $\omega_{ijk}(t) = \omega_{ijl}(t)$ will not hold anymore. Finally, other functions can be used to calculate similarity between two persons. For example, one can use sum of absolute differences:

$$\sum_{k=1}^{m} \left| X_{ik}(t) - X_{jk}(t) \right|$$

or a logistic sum function.

References

1. Treur, J.: Network-Oriented Modeling: Addressing Complexity of Cognitive, Affective and Social Interactions. Springer Publishers, Cham (2016). https://doi.org/10.1007/978-3-319-45213-5
2. van der Lubbe, L.M., Treur, J., van Vught, W.: Modeling internalizing and externalizing behaviour in autism spectrum disorders. In: Nguyen, N.-T., Manolopoulos, Y., Iliadis, L., Trawiński, B. (eds.) ICCCI 2016. LNCS, vol. 9875, pp. 13–26. Springer, Cham (2016). https://doi.org/10.1007/978-3-319-45243-2_2
3. Jonker, C.M., Treur, J.: A temporal-interactivist perspective on the dynamics of mental states. Cogn. Syst. Res. **4**(2), 137–155 (2003). https://doi.org/10.1016/S1389-0417(02)00103-1
4. Treur, J.: An integrative dynamical systems perspective on emotions. Biol. Inspired Cogn. Arch. **4**, 27–40 (2013). https://doi.org/10.1016/j.bica.2012.07.005
5. Treur, J.: Dynamic modeling based on a temporal-causal network modeling approach. Biol. Inspired Cogn. Arch. **16**, 131–168 (2016). https://doi.org/10.1016/j.bica.2016.02.002
6. Commu, C., Theelen, M., Treur, J.: An adaptive temporal-causal network model for enabling learning of social interaction. In: Bajo, J., et al. (eds.) PAAMS 2017. CCIS, vol. 722, pp. 257–270. Springer, Cham (2017). https://doi.org/10.1007/978-3-319-60285-1_22
7. Goedschalk, L., Treur, J., Verwolf, R.: A network-oriented modeling approach to voting behavior during the 2016 US presidential election. In: De la Prieta, F., et al. (eds.) PAAMS 2017. Advances in Intelligent Systems and Computing, vol. 619, pp. 3–15. Springer, Cham (2017). https://doi.org/10.1007/978-3-319-61578-3_1
8. Roller, R., Blommestijn, S.Q., Treur, J.: An adaptive computational network model for multi-emotional social interaction. In: Cherifi, C., Cherifi, H., Karsai, M., Musolesi, M. (eds.) COMPLEX NETWORKS 2017. Studies in Computational Intelligence, vol. 689, pp. 784–796. Springer, Cham (2018). https://doi.org/10.1007/978-3-319-72150-7_63
9. Blankendaal, R., Parinussa, S., Treur, J.: A temporal-causal modelling approach to integrated contagion and network change in social networks. In: Proceedings of the 22th European Conference on AI, ECAI 2016. Frontiers in Artificial Intelligence and Applications, vol. 285, pp. 1388–1396. IOS Press (2016). https://doi.org/10.3233/978-1-61499-672-9-1388
10. McPherson, M., Smith-Lovin, L., Cook, J.M.: Birds of a feather: homophily in social networks. Ann. Rev. Sociol. **27**, 415–444 (2001)
11. Aral, S., Muchnik, L., Sundararajan, A.: Distinguishing influence-based contagion from homophily-driven diffusion in dynamic networks. Proc. Natl. Acad. Sci. **106**(51), 21544 (2009)
12. Shalizi, C.R., Thomas, A.C.: Homophily and contagion are generically confounded in observational social network studies. Sociol. Methods Res. **27**, 211–239 (2011)
13. Rogers, E.M.: Diffusion of Innovations, 4th edn. Free Press, New York (1995)
14. Bessi, A., et al.: Homophily and polarization in the age of misinformation. Eur. Phys. J. Spec. Top. **225**(10), 2047–2059 (2016)

Restoring the Succession of Magistrates in Ancient Greek Poleis: How to Reduce It to Travelling Salesman Problem Using Heuristic Approach

Michael Levshunov, Sergei V. Mironov, Alexey R. Faizliev,
and Sergei P. Sidorov$^{(\boxtimes)}$

Saratov State University, Saratov, Russian Federation
sidorovsp@info.sgu.ru

Abstract. In 2–6 centuries BC many ancient Greek polies had an elective post of the magistrate of the polis (or astinom) who was engaged in the quality control of ceramic amphoras production. Historians suppose that an elected magistrate could hold this position for a fixed term (usually one year) and only once in his lifetime. One of the tasks of historical science is the problem of restoring the chronological sequence of the elected magistrates. This research uses a database with the information about amphoras and their stamps found by archaeologists in Sinop, one of such polies. We also take into account the facts discovered by historians describing the organization of amphora production in ancient Greek polies in 2–6 centuries BC. The paper proposes an algorithm for solving the problem of restoring the succession of magistrates in ancient Greek poleis on the basis of archaeological excavation data. We will show that this problem can be reduced to the travelling salesman problem with some additional restrictions and can be solved using dynamic programming approach.

Keywords: Traveling salesman problem · Dynamic programming
Weighted graph · Social graphs · Event order

1 Introduction

In the ancient world, magistrates (astinoms) were government officials whose activities were related to the economic life of the polis. The functions of astinoms were described in many works by historians [1,2,11]. In particular, astinoms participated in the quality control of ceramic production. In historical science, it is commonly believed that amphora stamping was associated with production quality standards. An amphora stamp contains the name of the astinom, i.e. a person responsible for quality control of amphora production at the time of making the amphora. The exact dates of the beginning and end of the stamping in the ancient Greek settlements have not yet been established. However,

The work was supported by RFBR (grant 18-37-00060).

approximate dates for many poleis are known. For example, the college of astinoms in Chersonesos existed from 325 to 180 years BC [10]. It is believed that
the magistrate was elected for a period of one year [6]. On this assumption, a
chronology of amphora stamping in ancient Greek poleis is built. One of the
tasks of historical science is the problem of restoring the chronological sequence
of the elected magistrates [6,8]. We will show that this problem can be reduced
to the travelling salesman problem with some additional restrictions. Another
approach to the solution of this problem was considered in the paper [4].

There were more that five hundred Greek poleis at the ancient time scattered
across the Black sea cost, and these communities were actively trading with each
other [6]. In these poleis, ceramic amphoras were used to transport wines and
olive oil by ships. Most of the amphoras were disposable and, therefore, they
were produced in huge quantities.

During the excavations on the Black Sea coast by archeologists, a significant
amount of the remains of such amphoras was found [7,10,12]. In addition, many
amphoras were marked with one or two stamps usually containing

- the name of the magistrate who was occupying the position of astinom at the
  time of the amphora production,
- the name of the manufacturer who owned the pottery workshop in which the
  amphora was produced by potters.

More details on the topic can be found in the books and papers of S. Yu. Monakhov, N. F. Fedoseyev and B. I. Katz [7,10,12], among many others.

In this paper we examine the task of restoring the chronological sequence
of the names of magistrates in the order of their election. Based on ancient
manuscripts, we know that some of them held the position before some of the
others. Historians suppose that one magistrate might be elected for only one
term and could not be re-elected. We also assume that all excavated amphoras
provide complete information in the sense that if some manufacturer produced
an amphorae in the period of some magistrate's term, at least one such amphora
with the stamp mentioning both of them was found by archaeologists and was
reflected in the database.

2   Heuristic Approach

2.1   Graph Representation Model

To represent information on the amphoras found by archaeologists, we use a
matrix

$$A = (a_{pm})_{p,m=1}^{P,M}, \tag{1}$$

where P is the number of manufacturer (producer) identifiers and M is the
number of magistrate identifiers. Columns of this matrix characterize the magistrates, and the lines correspond to manufacturers.

We set $a_{pm} = 1$ if there is an amphorae with the stamp containing both the name of manufacturer p and the name of the magistrate m. We let $a_{pm} = 0$ otherwise.

In addition, historians provided the list of pairs (magistrate u_k, magistrate u_s), which characterizes the already known relationships over the over the time of duties between some of magistrates. The list consists of the pair (u_k, u_p) if the magistrate with the identifier u_k held the post before the magistrate with the identifier u_p. The list was formed using ancient chronicles and manuscripts.

Denote the list with s such pairs by $\{(u_{k_1}, u_{p_1}), (u_{k_2}, u_{p_2}), \ldots, (u_{k_s}, u_{p_s})\}$. The list reflects the partial order on the set of u_k, $k = 1, \ldots, M$:

$$u_{k_1} \prec u_{p_1}, \; u_{k_2} \prec u_{p_2}, \ldots, u_{k_s} \prec u_{p_s}. \tag{2}$$

It is necessary to rearrange the columns of the matrix in the order corresponding to an unknown chronological order of elected magistrates using the matrix A and the known order (2).

To solve this problem, we assume that each pottery owner worked in some continuous period of time which could cover the terms of several magistrates. Thus, in the matrix, it is necessary to ensure that in each row all the units form one continuous segment, and the columns satisfy additional conditions.

To address the problem, we will use the following heuristics: two magistrates should be neighbors (i.e. one of them was elected right after another, so they served on two adjacent time intervals) when the number of manufacturers who worked with the both magistrates is maximized.

We denote by $f(u, v)$ the number of manufacturers who worked with magistrates u and v, $u, v = 1, \ldots, M$. We assume that $f(u, u) = 0$ for any magistrate u, $u = 1, \ldots, M$.

Then the optimal sequence of magistrates' names should maximize the sum of the quantities $f(u, v)$ over all possible paths through magistrates. In other words, we would like to maximize the following objective function:

$$\sum_{m=1}^{M-1} f(u_m, u_{m+1}) \to \max \tag{3}$$

over all possible chronological sequences of magistrates $u_1, u_2, \ldots, u_M$ satisfying the partial order relations (2).

Note that the data can be represented as a complete weighted graph [9] with M vertices, in which vertices correspond to magistrates, and the weight of the edge between the vertices u and v is equal to $f(u, v)$. Loops with zero weight are not added to this graph; since $f(u, u) = 0$ for all u, they do not affect the solution anyway.

In such graph, the optimal path will be the path that passes through each vertex of the graph exactly once and the sum of the edges weights in this path is maximal.

In graph theory, the path that passes through all vertices of the graph exactly once is called the Hamiltonian path [13]. The problem of maximizing the sum of the weights of edges in such paths is a special case of the traveling salesman problem.

2.2   Algorithm

In the theory of computation, the traveling salesman problem belongs to NP-complete class [5], and therefore its exact solution can not be obtained in polynomial time. In this paper we give an algorithm that allows finding the exact solution to this problem using a technique called dynamic programming [3].

We have to take into account that for some pairs of magistrates the order of election is already known. It is obvious that (2) must specify a strict partial order on the set of magistrates. Consequently, there should be irreflexivity, anti-symmetry and transitivity. If any of these conditions are not met, there is no solution for the given input data.

The proposed algorithm is based on the Bellman–Held–Karp algorithm [3] and consists of eight steps.

1. Consider all vertices of the graph obtained above.
2. Denote the vertex at the current iteration as s. Assume that it is the initial vertex in the desired path.
3. Before running the main algorithm, we check that in the given partial order there are no pairs in which the vertex s is in second place, i.e. there is not one vertex that must go in the path exactly before s. If this condition is not met, we immediately go to the next vertex.
4. Construct a two-dimensional array of states over the graph. Each state is determined by a number of a vertex u and a subset $mask$. It encodes a subproblem: construct the required path, provided from the vertex u, by visiting all the vertices that do not enter the subset $mask$. In this case, the state contains the answer to this task. This set of subtasks can be solved by induction on the number of vertices not contained in $mask$:
   (a) If the subset $mask$ already contains all the vertices of the graph, then the path can not be extended anymore and the answer is 0.
   (b) If there is exactly one vertex that does not belong to the subset $mask$, then it is necessary to go along the edge to it and finish the path. Since the constructed graph is complete, this is always possible. The answer in this case is the weight of this edge.
   (c) Let the answer for all subtasks, in which $mask$ does not contain $k-1$ and less vertices, is already calculated. Then for any subtask that does not contain exactly k vertices in $mask$, you can go through all the remaining vertices and select the best vertex by maximizing the sum of the edge weight over which the transition and the response to the subtask for this vertex will be made. Each transition we will add one vertex to $mask$, therefore, the answer for all such subtasks is already known.

   In addition, it is necessary to take into account the presence of a given partial order. To do this, with each transition to the vertex v, it is necessary to verify that there is no pair in which the vertex not belonging to the subset $mask$ is in the first place, and the vertex v in the second place. This will prevent the possibility that, in one of the following transitions, the vertex v will be in the path earlier than one of the vertices, which must meet in the path strictly before v.

5. Let us solve all this set of subtasks. Then, in the state corresponding to the vertex s and the subset mask containing only the vertex s, the answer to the required problem will be stored for the case when the path started at the vertex s. Remember it and go to step 2 and the next vertex.

6. Since the starting vertex in the task is not defined, the answer to it will be the maximum of the answers for each of the starting vertices.

7. To restore the sequence itself, in the recounting of states it is necessary to store transitions for which the best answers were received.

8. In addition, to speed up the work, $mask$ is best represented as a bitmask, in which only those bits that correspond to the vertices belonging to the subset are loaded.

At each step of the algorithm it is necessary to solve a set of $M \cdot 2^M$ subproblems, each of which requires a time proportional to $O(M + k)$, where k is the number of initial conditions. The number of such step is also equal to M, so the time execution of the algorithm is equal $O(M^2(M + k)2^M)$ asymptotically. However, due to the partial order conditions, a very large number of algorithm steps are cut off and the algorithm works much faster on real data.

In addition, the algorithm requires $O(M^2)$ additional memory to store the graph and another $O(M2^M)$ to preserve the state arrays. This leads to the fact that even for $M = 22$, the solution of the problem requires more than one gigabyte of PC memory. Note that this amount increases exponentially with the increase of M.

3 Empirical Results

3.1 Solution for Real Historical Data

We applied the described algorithm to the data of archaeological excavations in Sinop described in [6]. Seaport Sinop (historically Sinope) was one of ancient Greek poleis located on the southern coast of the Black Sea, now Turkey. The data contains information on 164 magistrates from the time interval from 375 to 203 BC. The scope of this paper does not allow us to present the results of work on the entire database, besides this is not the main purpose of the article. Therefore, we give only a small fragment of the database containing information on 15 astinoms.

Extracts of database consist of information on the stamps of 15 different magistrates and 27 manufacturers (Table 1). Table 1 presents the known data in the form of a binary matrix in which zeros are omitted for simplicity. The initial restrictions were $\{(5, 15), (9, 10), (4, 8)\}$, i.e. it is known that the magistrate 5 was elected earlier than the magistrate 15, the magistrate 9 was earlier than 10, and the magistrate 4 was earlier than 8. The algorithm produces a sequence

Table 1. Input data is the matrix A with stamp information

	1	2	3	4	5	6	7	8	9	10	11	12	13	14	15
250		1	1	1		1		1						1	
46		1	1	1	1						1				
56		1	1	1	1	1					1	1			
74	1	1	1	1	1	1	1	1	1		1	1	1	1	1
86		1	1	1	1						1				
128		1			1		1								
153		1	1	1	1										
186			1		1										
189	1	1	1	1	1			1		1	1				
194					1										
203	1	1	1	1	1	1	1	1	1		1	1	1	1	1
238		1	1	1	1						1				
33	1	1	1	1			1	1			1	1	1		
182	1	1		1		1	1	1	1		1		1	1	
195		1													
36				1							1				
124			1	1											
83			1					1			1			1	
125			1												
162	1						1	1	1	1	1	1	1		1
197											1				
233								1			1				
149						1							1		1
60												1			
221						1				1					
234								1							
126															1

of names of magistrates in chronological order. Table 2 presents the rearranged columns of the Table 1 according to the found chronological sequence. For clarity, we rearranged the rows of the matrix so that the manufacturers also are in the chronological order.

3.2   Stability/Robustness Analysis on Real Data

The graph-based approach described above is based on the assumption that we have complete stamps data which connect magistrates and manufacturers, i.e. if some manufacturer produced an amphorae in the period of some magistrate's

Table 2. Chronological order of magistrate succession

	6	14	9	11	4	3	5	2	1	8	13	7	12	15	10
250	1	1	1		1	1		1							
182	1	1	1	1	1			1	1	1	1	1			
56	1			1	1	1	1	1					1		
74	1	1	1	1	1	1	1	1	1	1	1	1	1	1	
203	1	1	1	1	1	1	1	1	1	1	1	1	1	1	
83		1	1	1		1									
233			1	1											
162			1	1					1	1	1	1	1	1	1
197			1												
36				1	1										
46				1	1	1	1	1							
86				1	1	1	1	1							
238				1	1	1	1	1							
33				1	1	1		1	1	1	1	1	1		
189				1	1	1	1	1	1	1					1
124				1	1										
153				1	1	1	1								
125					1										
186					1	1									
194						1									
128						1	1					1			
195							1								
60											1				
149												1	1	1	
221												1			1
126														1	
234															1

term, at least one such amphora with the stamp mentioning both of them was found by archaeologists and was reflected in the database. Unfortunately, it can not be absolutely asserted that all such stamps had been found during archaeological excavations and therefore not all links between magistrates and manufacturers have been reflected in matrix A.

This and the next subsections examines the stability of the algorithm's work and the reliability of its resulting sequence. In this subsection we conducted three different series of experiments on real data.

(1) The first series of experiments assesses how the shuffling of the initial order of the magistrates (i.e. the input matrix columns) affects the solution

Table 3. Mean and standard deviation values of output chronological sequences obtained by the algorithm on real data. The first line of the table specifies the sequential number of the magistrate in the "true" chronological order. Mean and St.Dev. represent average values and the variance of the sequential number of the corresponding magistrate according to the test results in 1st, 2nd and 3rd series of simulations

		1	2	3	4	5	6	7	8	9	10	11	12	13	14	15
1st series	Mean	2.3	1.7	2.0	6.7	6.3	6.0	5.7	5.3	9.5	9.5	11.0	12.0	13.0	14.0	15.0
	St.Dev.	0.9	0.2	0.7	3.6	0.9	0.0	0.9	3.6	0.3	0.3	0.0	0.0	0.0	0.0	0.0
2nd series	Mean	3.5	3.2	3.6	6.0	5.5	5.3	4.9	5.1	10.6	10.7	10.7	11.7	11.7	12.6	15.0
	St.Dev.	7.8	7.2	7.0	4.0	2.4	2.5	4.7	3.5	4.6	3.8	5.4	2.2	5.0	3.7	0.0
3rd series	Mean	3.0	2.4	2.7	6.4	5.9	5.6	5.2	5.2	10.2	10.2	10.9	11.9	12.3	13.2	15.0
	St.Dev.	4.7	3.8	3.4	3.7	1.9	1.5	3.3	3.5	2.7	2.5	3.0	0.5	2.6	2.7	0.0

obtained by the algorithm. We assume that data on the magistrate–manufacturer connections are complete and that the chronological order that was obtained by the algorithm is the real order. There were generated 10,000 input matrices in which columns of the input matrix A were randomly re-ordered. For each of the obtained input matrices, the output sequence was found by the algorithm. The results of the comparison of the obtained sequences and the "true" order are presented in Table 3.

It should be noted that only six different solutions with the same value of the objective function were found for the 10,000 different input matrices. However, the mean values given in Table 3 show that the "true" order is not equal to the most probable one.

(2) The second series of experiments examines how the loss of some magistrate–manufacturer links in the input data affects the solution. We assess the difference between the "true" order and the chronological order obtained by the algorithm in the case of the dispossession of some links in the input graph, i.e. some of magistrate–manufacturer connections are not confirmed by stamps. For each of $10,000$ runs of our algorithm, the input matrix A' was generated in the following way:

$$a'_{pm} = \begin{cases} 0, & (a_{pm} = 0) \vee (a_{pm} = 1) \wedge (\xi_{pm} \leq 2) \\ 1, & (a_{pm} = 1) \wedge (\xi_{pm} > 2), \end{cases} \tag{4}$$

where ξ_{pm} is a random integer uniformly distributed between 1 and 100. After that we randomly shuffled the order of columns in matrix A'. To compare the obtained solutions with the "true" order, we calculated the correlation between these vectors. The results are shown in Fig. 1 and Table 3.

Despite the considerable loss of links in the input matrix, the proposed method reproduces the chronological order of the magistrates rather well. In more than 89% of cases, the Spearman correlation coefficient was more than 0.7. However, the variance increased significantly.

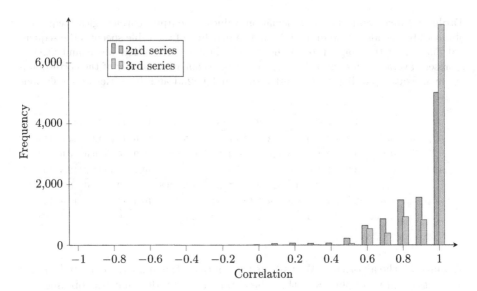

Fig. 1. Frequency plots for Spearman's correlation coefficient values in 2nd and 3rd series of experiments

(3) The next series of computational experiments employed the bootstrap method. Each time we excluded exactly two random observations from our input matrix (i.e. two links between magistrates and manufacturers) and again randomly rearranged the columns of the matrix. Then we applied the algorithm to obtain the corresponding solution. This process was repeated 10,000 times. The results are shown in Fig. 1 and Table 3.

The results show that the difference between the "true" and the average order is quite similar to the case without the loss of links. These solutions exhibit reduced variance in comparison with the previous test. Moreover, the proportion of solutions having at least 0.7 value of the Spearman correlation coefficient has increased to 94%. This can be explained by the fact that in this test the number of lost links is less than in the previous test.

3.3   Stability/Robustness Testing on Artificially Generated Data

In the subsequent experiments we used an artificially generated set of input data with a known chronological order.

In fourth series of experiments we modeled situations in which the likelihood of finding a stamp confirming the connection between magistrate m and manufacturer p depends on the volume of production of the manufacturer p in the corresponding year m. To do so, we generated the matrix $B = (b_{pm})_{p,m=1}^{P,M}$, where b_{pm} denotes the amount of amphoraes produced by the manufacturer p during the period of magistrate m. On the basis of this matrix, 10,000 matrices of the form (1) were constructed according to the following rule: $a_{pm} = 0$, if the event

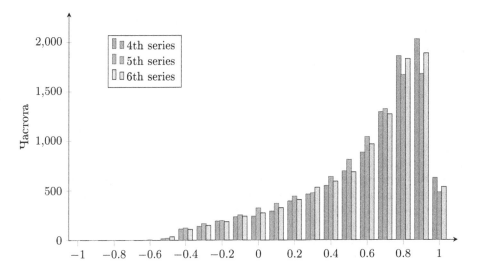

Fig. 2. Frequency plots for Spearman's correlation coefficient values in 4th, 5th and 6th series of experiments

did not appear at least once during b_{pm} Bernoulli trials with probability of success 0.02, otherwise we let $a_{pm} = 1$. For each matrix, its columns were randomly re-ordered. Then we applied the algorithm to obtain the corresponding solution. Figure 2 and Table 4 present the results of these simulations.

The obtained chronological order is on average close to the given true order, although the variances of the obtained solutions are quite big.

Table 4. Mean and standard deviation values of output chronological sequences obtained by the algorithm on artificially generated data. The first line of the table specifies the sequential number of the magistrate in the "true" chronological order. Mean and St.Dev. represent average values and the variance of the sequential number of the corresponding magistrate according to the test results in 1st, 2nd and 3rd series of simulations

		1	2	3	4	5	6	7	8	9	10	11	12	13	14	15
4th series	Mean	3.9	5.0	5.3	5.7	6.5	6.8	7.1	7.9	7.8	10.0	11.6	8.6	10.4	12.2	11.4
	St.Dev.	7.1	13.7	13.8	12.1	15.0	14.1	14.1	15.1	14.1	14.6	9.3	12.9	13.1	8.4	7.5
5th series	Mean	4.0	5.4	5.6	6.0	6.7	6.9	7.1	7.9	7.6	9.8	11.4	8.3	10.1	12.1	11.3
	St.Dev.	7.4	15.7	15.2	13.8	15.9	14.9	14.8	15.5	14.2	15.3	9.7	13.3	13.9	8.8	8.0
6th series	Mean	3.9	5.2	5.4	5.8	6.6	6.9	7.2	7.8	7.7	9.9	11.4	8.5	10.3	12.2	11.4
	St.Dev.	7.4	15.0	14.1	13.2	15.2	14.8	14.6	15.0	13.8	15.2	9.6	13.0	13.4	8.3	7.9

In the fifth series of experiments, we assumed that the probability of finding a stamp linking a magistrate and a manufacturer does not depend on the production volume of the manufacturer. For each of the 10,000 runs of our algorithm, the input matrix A was generated by the following rule:

$$a_{pm} = \begin{cases} 0, & (b_{pm} = 0) \vee (b_{pm} > 0) \wedge (\xi_{pm} \leq 2) \\ 1, & (b_{pm} > 0) \wedge (\xi_{pm} > 2), \end{cases} \tag{5}$$

where ξ_{pm} is a random integer uniformly distributed from 1 to 100. Results are shown in Fig. 2 and Table 4.

In the sixth series of experiments we again applied the bootstrap method with the exclusion of two links magistrate–manufacturer from our input matrix in each simulation. This process was repeated 10,000 times. Results are shown in Fig. 2 and Table 4.

The last three series of experiments on artificially generated data demonstrated almost identical results.

4   Conclusion

In this paper we propose an approach for solving the problem of restoring the succession of magistrates in ancient Greek poleis on the basis of archaeological excavations data. We used heuristics to reduce the task to the travelling salesman problem with some additional restrictions. The proposed algorithm is based on the dynamic programming approach. The CPU time and the required additional memory depend primarily on the number of magistrates.

Note that the number of initial conditions also affects the CPU time. Each additional condition allows us to cut off a large number of possible variants in search space. The number of manufacturers does not affect the final working time. We use it only when reading data and converting it to the graph.

Based on the results of simulations it can be concluded that the proposed method is robust. In more than half the cases, the correlation coefficients between the obtained and "true" solutions were more than 0.7.

We also note that the solution of the problem (3) exists, but it is not always unique. However, our algorithm finds only one of the possible solutions. As shown by the experiments, the chronological order obtained as a result of the algorithm can significantly differ from the true one even in the case without link losses. It is not possible to verify which of the solutions is closer to the true chronology. Therefore, the application of the method should use additional historical information.

The developed algorithm allows us to solve not only analogous problems (e.g., with the stamps of Heracleia, Phasos, Rhodes, etc.), but also to solve different problems from areas where chronologization is needed.

References

1. Badoud, N.: The contribution of inscriptions to the chronology of Rhodian amphora eponyms. In: Lawall, M., Guldager Bilde, P. (eds.) Pottery, Peoples and Places: The Late Hellenistic Period, c. 200–50 BC Between the Mediterranean and the Black Sea, Aarhus, pp. 17–28 (2014)
2. Badoud, N.: Deciphering greek amphora stamps. CHS Res. Bull. **5**(2) (2017). http://nrs.harvard.edu/urn-3:hlnc.essay:BadoudN.Deciphering_Greek_Amphora_Stamps.2017
3. Bellman, R.: Dynamic programming treatment of the travelling salesman problem. J. ACM **9**(1), 61–63 (1962)
4. Bobylev, A.B., Fedoseev, N.F.: The expert system astinom. Methods Syst. Tech. Diagn. **12**, 112–115 (1989)
5. Cormen, T.H., Leiserson, C.E., Rivest, R.L., Stein, C.: Introduction to Algorithms. MIT Press (2009)
6. Fedoseev, N.F.: Classification des timbres astynomiques de Sinope. In: Production et Commerce des Amphores anciennes en Mer Noire, pp. 27–48. l'Université de Provence, Provence (1999)
7. Fedoseev, N.F.: From the history of Sinope. Ceramic aspect. Tauride studios. Hist. Sci. (6), 90–97 (2014)
8. Fedoseev, N.F.: About the chronology of ceramic stamps of Sinope. Ancient World Archaeol. **17**, 352–364 (2015)
9. Harary, F.: Graph Theory. Addison-Wesley, Reading (1991)
10. Kac, V.I.: Ceramic Stamps of Chersonesus Taurica. Saratov State University, Saratov (1994)
11. Lawall, M.L.. Amphoras and hellenistic economies: addressing the (over) emphasis on stamped amphora handles. In: Archibald, Z.H., Davies, J.K., Gabrielsen, V. (eds.) In Making, Moving, and Managing: The New World of Ancient Economies, 323–31 BC, pp. 188–232. Oxbow books, Oxford (2005)
12. Monakhov, S.Y.: Greek amphoras in the black sea: complexes of ceramic containers of 7th-2nd centuries B.C. Saratov State University, Saratov (1999)
13. Sedgewick, R.: Algorithms in C - Part 5: Graph Algorithms. Addison-Wesley-Longman, Boston (2002)

Keeping up on Current Events! A Case Study of Newcomers to Wikipedia

Ang Li and Rosta Farzan[✉]

University of Pittsburgh, Pittsburgh, PA 15213, USA
rfarzan@pitt.edu

Abstract. Online production communities such as Wikipedia and OpenStreetMap play an important role in connecting the public with major events in society. The popularity of a major event, together with the popularity of online communities brings the general public to collaborate on and co-create knowledge about the event. The high level of interest in capturing what draws the attention of society can particularly help online production communities meet one of the essential challenges they face: attracting and retaining newcomers. In this work, we explore how newcomers in such communities respond to knowledge production around major societal events. Analysis of the participation of 506 newcomers to Wikipedia articles related to three highly popular events shows that the popularity of the events attracts a new wave of users to the online community. These newcomers provide valuable contributions to the community, however, at a differing level depending on their initial motivation and experiences. Those participants who joined the online community solely to contribute to one topic or event are more likely to face challenges in contribution and leave Wikipedia after limited contribution. We discuss factors and patterns of newcomers' early and longer-term participation in Wikipedia in relation to three popular events.

Keywords: Online production community · Wikipedia · Newcomers Current events

1 Introduction

Online production communities play an essential role in connecting the general population with popular events happening in society. They serve as places for the public to seek and share information, learn about responses, collectively make sense, and build memories of the events that attract attention from the whole society. For example, researchers have found that online production communities, such as Wikipedia and OpenStreetMap, serve as a source for the latest information about humanitarian aid and in response unexpected and traumatic events such as natural disasters, disease outbreaks or mass shootings [10,25]. Studies on Wikipedia coverage of the Black Lives Matter social movement found

© Springer Nature Switzerland AG 2018
S. Staab et al. (Eds.): SocInfo 2018, LNCS 11185, pp. 348–369, 2018.
https://doi.org/10.1007/978-3-030-01129-1_22

that such prominent events drive periods of high online participation. The peak levels of activities in the Wikipedia page views, revisions, and the number of active editors closely correspond to the breaking events offline [26,45].

These studies reveal a strong connection between what happens in the real world and users' participation in online communities, and how the popularity of online communities and major current events feed off each other. What remains as an open question, however, is who are the individuals who participate in knowledge production specific to the current events. Of particular interest to online production communities is to discover whether the popularity of major current events can drive new audiences to online communities; as one of the major challenges for online production communities such as Wikipedia has been to attract and sustain newcomers [31] as well as to ensure high quality contributions by the newcomers. 60% of registered Wikipedia editors never make another edit after the first 24 hours [36]. Similarly, a study of open source development projects found that over half of developers did not return after making their first contribution [12]. New members are the source of new information, new ideas, and innovations; they assume the role of providing the diversity of opinions and perspectives needed to support the goals of online production communities [1,9,36].

The impact of societal affairs on the new workforce, as well as their subsequent experiences and performance in online production communities, can play an important role in the success of these communities. Understanding the dynamics of participation around current events can help the online communities to (1) best support identifying and documenting important social events and building collective memories about such events; (2) capitalize on the power of these events to support the goals of the online community. The present study seeks to determine if and how the strong connection between the offline current events and online participation relates to newcomers' behavior in the online production community. We aim to explore the role of newcomers in cdocumenting the major events in Wikipedia, in terms of the quality and quantity of their initial participation as well as their subsequent behavior in the community. We analyze the behavior of newcomers in English Wikipedia across the topics of politics, health, and sports in relation to three major events in 2014. Specifically, we focus on the following three research questions:

- RQ1: At what level the popularity of current events are associated with newcomers participation in Wikipedia?
- RQ2: What are the entry paths for newcomers editing current event articles? How does the entry path explain the subsequent behavior of newcomers?
- RQ3: What factors play a role in continued participation of newcomers editing current event articles?

Our research contributes to studies of the challenges in dealing with newcomers in online communities. We present an approach that employs mixed quantitative and qualitative methods to explore the connections between popular offline events and newcomers' behavior in online production communities. We propose an approach to classify newcomers based on their initial behavior and highlight how each group exhibits different subsequent behavior. We provide insights on the challenges and opportunities associated with online participation as a result of the attention paid to an important offline event.

2   Related Work

Our work relates to and extends, the existing literature from two major research areas: (1) the research on the challenges of engaging newcomers in the online production communities; (2) the studies of how current events affect the peer-production community. Below we highlight the key research from each of these areas and discuss how our work is informed by, and situated within, the current body of research.

2.1   Challenges of On-Boarding Newcomers in Online Production Communities

Online production communities have been successful in many areas, from creating best-known and most-used open source software such as Linux and Apache, to building Wikipedia, the largest free online encyclopedia; however, those success stories have been also accompanied by major challenges. One critical challenge that has been identified within a range of online production communities is the high turnover rate [30] due to low leaving cost [9,36]. Therefore, to survive, online production communities must retain successive generations of new members to replace those who leave.

However, recruiting and sustaining newcomers to an existing community can be particularly challenging. Newcomers have not yet developed the commitment to the community, are less motivated than old-timers, and are sensitive to their initial experiences in the community. As a result, they may leave soon after they join [31]. In addition, since they have insufficient knowledge or experience about the community norms and guidance [42], they may behave in ways that can be harmful to the group. For example, new editors in Wikipedia may fail to follow the policy of writing from a neutral point of view, or new participants may be more likely to introduce bugs to an open-source development project.

Prior studies have found that newcomers' motivation is one of the most important drivers to their sustained participation [31]. The Self-Determination Theory [3,40] has distinguished between the intrinsic motivations, where individuals are driven by their inherent interests, and the extrinsic motivations, where individuals are encouraged by external factors. In the context of online communities, researchers have identified both intrinsic motivations, (such as altruism [46], enjoyment [34], and a sense of obligation) to contribute [4], and extrinsic motivation, (such as peer recognition, career concerns, personal value, and rewards [39]), to be crucial to the member's continuing contribution. Prior research has claimed that the initial motivation and the resultant early-on behavior can be a strong predictor of future commitment and level of contribution. While the claim of "Wikipedians are born, not made" proposed by Panciera et al. has been debated, [36,37], it has not been refuted. Research on other production communities such as OpenStreetMap has also revealed a similar trend. Prolific contributors began contributing at a high level and maintain this trend for the majority of their lifespan, resulting in distinctive profile of behavior and contribution among different classes of users [44].

Subsequent studies thus identified a set of factors from newcomers early-on experiences within the community that can be particularly associated with their future performance. In a study of newcomers editing Wikipedia articles, Farzan and Kraut [13] showed that cohort support resulted in a higher level of production and helped newcomers deal with the often negative feedback they received from established members of the community. Lampe et al. [32] found that newcomers' subsequent performance in the online community can be influenced by both their observation of others and the feedback they received from the community. Choi et al. [8] found that the more interactions newcomers had with existing members, the more productive they subsequently were. Similarly, Arguello et al. demonstrated that newcomers to Usenet groups were more likely to return when they received responses from older members of the group [2]. Burke et al. found that newcomers are more likely to continue posting pictures on Facebook if their pictures received comments from their network of friends [5]. However, the content of such interactions can moderate how they influence newcomers' subsequent behavior. Constructive feedback and more inclusive language, such as the use of first person plural pronouns rather than second-person pronouns have been associated with greater subsequent participation by newcomers [6,32]. Negative criticism may discourage longer-term participation [47], even when it results in newcomers fixing problems pointed out to them. In Wikipedia, where old-timers frequently send newcomers critical messages and delete work that does not comply with Wikipedia's standards [18], interactions with old-timers frequently drive newcomers away [19].

In addition to newcomers' online experiences, a recent study of the OpenStreetMap community posits that newcomers' real-world interactions with the community members, such as regular opportunities for social encounters and peer learning, are associated with a significant increase in newcomer retention [11].

We aim to extend the previous work by exploring the impact of exogenous offline events on newcomers' motivation to join the community and how their early-on experiences in conjunction with exogenous motivations can influence their subsequent contribution and commitment.

2.2   How Current Events Affect the Peer-Production Community

Current events play an important role for peer-production communities such as Wikipedia and OpenStreetMap. For example, Wikipedia, which defines itself as an online encyclopedia, includes a large number of highly visited and edited articles reflecting the most up-to-date information about current events, which is different from the traditional publication methods that prevent Encyclopedias from updating their articles to reflect the most current information. OpenStreetMap (OSM) – the Wikipedia of Maps – is created to serve as a global community that creates a common open digital map of the world [17]. Starting in 2009, several natural disasters such as the Haiti earthquake and Tropical Storm Ondoy in the Philippines catalyzed the OpenStreetMap community to provide humanitarian aid [41]. From then on, the Humanitarian OpenStreetMap Team has formed and coordinated thousands of volunteers in the creation of maps for humanitarian purposes [10].

Studies examining the volunteers' collaboration and coordination practices for current events within online production communities demonstrate that the contribution activities and participation around current affairs and natural disasters display unique patterns. For example, Wikipedia editors are able to respond to and commemorate current events by creating event related articles within minutes of the disasters and catastrophes occuring [22], to adjust collaboration strategies to support high-tempo interactions [23], and to adopt different emergent social roles [27]. In response to disaster events, OSM has shaped the orientation of experienced mappers in new ways and created the need to make mapping simple for new contributors who know little about OSM otherwise [35].

More specifically, studies that examined the participation and attention paid to Wikipedia articles connected with the Black Lives Matter movement show that prominent offline breaking events drive periods of higher levels of online activities: the peak periods in Wikipedia page views, revisions as well as active editing correspond closely breaking offline events [45]. However, it remains unclear whether these current affairs shift the editors' work within the production community from one set of artifacts to another, or if they bring new workforces into the production communities. More importantly, it is unclear how an exogenous motivation such as an important event in society influences newcomers' subsequent behavior in the production community as compared to those motivated by factors more internal to the production community.

3   Research Platform

Wikipedia is history's largest encyclopedia, created and maintained by volunteer editors. New editors can join Wikipedia and start editing almost any article without much training. Once the edit is done, it is immediately reflected on the article page. Wikipedia provides detailed documentation on how editors should behave and has developed institutions such as the Teahouse, which is introduced as "a friendly place to help new editors become accustomed to Wikipedia" [16]. Despite these accommodations, as in many other online communities, Wikipedia still identifies high turnover among newcomers as a major problem [15]. Wikipedia is also a place where editors collaboratively cover breaking news [24, 26] as well as a place where public collectively build memories and construct knowledge around historical events [14, 33, 38]. Wikipedia offers supplementary pages to the content pages to facilitate social interaction and coordination necessary for content production, including article talk pages for coordination around specific article and user talk pages for communication among Wikipedia editors. All the revisions to any Wikipedia page are stored in revisions history and are publicly available. Therefore, Wikipedia provides an intriguing platform to study the relationships between current societal affairs and newcomers' participation in online production communities.

4   Method

To explore the behavior of newcomers in relation to major events, we employed a mixed-methods approach. We used the Wikipedia public API[1] to collect articles' and users' performance data. We conducted statistical analyses to model the relationships between newcomers' early-on experiences and their subsequent performance in terms of effort, contribution quality, and commitment. We then complemented the quantitative analyses with content analysis of comments associated with newcomers' contributions to gain a deeper understanding of the value of their participation and challenges they faced.

4.1   Data Collection

To collect data on the activities of the newcomers who edited the events articles, we leveraged the current event portal in Wikipedia[2]. We selected three major current events in the year 2014 across the topics of politics, health and sports: The "Black Lives Matter" shootings and protests, the "West African Ebola outbreaks", and the "2014 FIFA World Cup". These three events are all important events that attracted high levels of attention globally at the time they happened. We purposefully selected historical events in order to study the long-term retention of newcomers.

The three major events included a series of related events. We utilized the Wikipedia categories[3] to build a list of all articles associated with each of the events: "Black Lives Matter"[4] (BLM), "2014 FIFA World Cup"[5] (FIFA), and "West African Ebola outbreaks"[6] (Ebola). As the events had different timelines, to create a comparable dataset across the three different events, we limited data collection to any related events during the time period of Jan 1, 2014 until Dec 31, 2015. This resulted in a total of 133 event related articles. In the remainder of this paper, we refer to these articles as **event articles**.

We defined the list of newcomers editing these event articles as those who (1) edited any of the 133 event articles; (2) registered and edited at least one of the event articles within two weeks after the event happened[7]. Our dataset includes a total of 506 newcomers, including 174 related to Black Lives Matter events, 197 related to Ebola events, and 135 related to the FIFA events. We then collected all the Wikipedia edits of these newcomers, including their edits to article pages,

---

[1] https://www.mediawiki.org/wiki/API:Main_page.
[2] https://en.wikipedia.org/wiki/Portal:Current_events.
[3] https://en.wikipedia.org/wiki/Help:Category.
[4] https://en.wikipedia.org/wiki/Category:Black_Lives_Matter.
[5] https://en.wikipedia.org/wiki/Category:2014_FIFA_World_Cup.
[6] https://en.wikipedia.org/wiki/Category:West_African_Ebola_virus_epidemic.
[7] We excluded any editors who had been blocked from Wikipedia.

article talk pages, user talk pages, and user pages. In order to understand their entire social interactions with the Wikipedia community and their integration into the community, we also collected all the messages exchanged on the newcomers' user talk pages with other newcomers or any members of Wikipedia. Our data includes all the edits until October 15, 2017.

In addition, to understand the popularity of each event outside Wikipedia, we utilized Google Trend[8] to estimate global interest in each event by collecting data on pertinent search terms. We used the search terms "2014 FIFA World Cup" and "2014 ebola outbreak" to retrieve the trend data related to the 2014 FIFA, and Ebola events accordingly. We used the search terms of "Black Lives Matter", "Ferguson unrest", "2015 Baltimore protests", "Death of Eric Garner", "Death of Freddie Gray", "Shooting of John Crawford III", "Shooting of Jordan Davis", "Shooting of Michael Brown", and "Shooting of Tamir Rice" to retrieve the trend data about attention related to the series of protests and violent deaths related to Black Lives Matter during 2014–2015.

4.2 Constructing an Interaction Network

To understand the interaction of newcomers within the Wikipedia community, we constructed a network of their interactions with other newcomers and members of the Wikipedia community. The network included newcomers' interactions on the user talk pages. The nodes in the network represent the newcomers as well as other Wikipedians who have ever communicated with any of the newcomers through posting on their user talk pages. The links are defined by *edit* in user talk page, and the links are weighted by *number of edits*. For the purpose of analysis, we calculated network measures including *in-degree centrality*, *out-degree centrality*, and *eigenvector centrality* to distinguish the source, direction, and importance of each node embedded within the network. The degree centrality provides us with a measure of the amount of social interactions among newcomers and other users, while eigenvector centrality provides the degree of communication among newcomers and key well-connected individuals in the Wikipedia community.

4.3 Defining Early-On Experiences

Factors such as whether the newcomers had been reverted; i.e. their edits undone by other Wikipedia editors, and newcomers' overall level of effort and ambition when joining the community further contribute to newcomers' early-on experiences. To account for such factors, we included the following variables in our statistical models:

- Number of reverted edits: refers to the number of edits that was reverted by another Wikipedia editor.

---

[8] https://trends.google.com/trends/.

- Number of edits on article talk pages: The total number of edits a focal newcomer had made on any Wikipedia article talk pages during their first week on Wikipedia.
- Number of edits on user pages: The total number of edits a focal newcomer had made on any Wikipedia user page during their first week on Wikipedia.
- Number of unique articles: The total number of unique articles a focal newcomer edited during their first week on Wikipedia.

The threshold of one weeks was chosen based on the general survival rate of the editors to ensure the largest possible number of editors to be included in our study. We have also confirmed that our results are not sensitive to this threshold and start consistent even if we change this to two weeks but it decreases the population size of our study.

4.4 Defining Dependent Variables

We assessed the level of contribution and commitment of newcomers in terms of the **amount of production, quality** of their edits and **retention** as defined below. We operationalized production using *the number of edits* and *the size of edits*. To assess the *edit quality*, we adopted two widely used measures: Wikipedia ORES edit quality measure – *goodfaith*[9] and the number of *revert revision*.

- *Average size of content* added to article by a focal newcomer after the first week.
- *Total Number of article edits* made by a focal newcomer after the first week.
- The *Good-faith* edit quality measure is an automatic assessment of whether an edit was done with a good vs. vandalism intention. It generates a probability score of good-faith edit for each revision to an article: the higher the score the better the edit quality. It is available through the Wikipedia ORES API[10]. We calculated the good-faith score for every edit made by newcomers within four months after their registration[11]. As our unit of analysis is an editor, we aggregated the data as the average good-faith score for each newcomer.
- The *Revert revision* refers to when an edit was reverted by another Wikipedia editor. Revert is a behavioral evidence that the edit did not satisfy the requirements and norms of Wikipedia. It has been widely used in many studies to measure the edit quality [13,20,43]. Common reasons for reverting an edit include failure to include proper citations, using copyrighted materials, failure to follow a neutral point of view, poor writing, or potential vandalism. We extracted all reverts of edits made by newcomers within four months after their registration using MediaWiki Revert library[12]. We calculated the revert

---

[9] https://www.mediawiki.org/wiki/ORES.

[10] https://ores.wikimedia.org/.

[11] Due to computing limitation, we only collected the good-faith quality and reverts within four months after registration. As newcomers' editing quality has already converged at a relatively stable level within even first couple weeks, the four months data is a reasonable time period to evaluate the contribution quality.

[12] http://pythonhosted.org/mwreverts/.

ratio for each newcomer as the proportion of the number of reverted edits over the total number of the article edits.

- To assess newcomers' commitment, we analyzed their *retention* as the number of days they continued editing Wikipedia. If their last edit was within one month of the end of our data collection period, i.e. Oct 15, 2017, we considered the participant censored with an unknown end date. Our results are robust to censoring thresholds of 30 days vs. 60 days. For simplicity, we report our results using the one month threshold, which is a common industry practice [21,29].

4.5   Statistical Model

We conducted time lagged regression analyses in which we collected explanatory variables about newcomers from their first week on Wikipedia and then conducted regression analyses to model their subsequent commitment and performance. Our statistical models included (1) linear regression models to assess the association between the newcomers early-on experiences and their subsequent production; (2) Survival analysis to examine how variations in the newcomers early-on experiences predicted their time to withdraw from Wikipedia. Survival analysis is a regression technique to measure time to an event, e.g. new editors stop editing [28]. The results of the survival analysis are presented in terms of the hazard ratio (HR), the instantaneous likelihood of an undesirable event (i.e. leaving Wikipedia) happening. If HR is larger than one, the predictor is associated with an increased risk of dropout (a decrease in retention); if HR is smaller than one, the predictor is associated with decreased risk of dropout (an increase in retention). Both survival analyses and regression analyses were multilevel models, to account for the non-independence of observations among same editors participating in the same event.

5   Results

5.1   RQ1: The Popularity of Offline Events is Associated with Increased Newcomers' Contribution to the Event Articles

We first explored whether the popularity of the current offline events relates to newcomers' contribution to events' articles. We utilized Google Trend index as a representation of the overall popularity of the topic in the society. We then compared the timeline under which newcomers edited the event articles and the total number of edits to the event articles, against the Google trend. Figure 1 represents newcomers activity and Google trend for the Ebola-related events. The left y-axis shows the number of edits, the right y-axis represents the Google Trend aggregated over monthly data.

As presented in the graph, we observed that peaks in the newcomers' editing activity (orange line) closely corresponds to the Google search trend (Blue dotted line) and the timeline of the offline events. During the Ebola outbreak, the

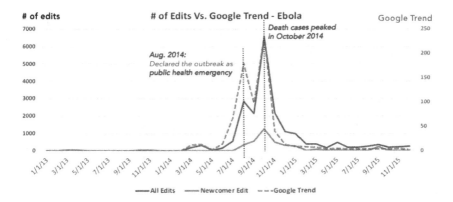

Fig. 1. Current events related articles: # of edits from newcomers (monthly) correspond closely to the Google Trend and current events happened offline (Color figure online)

newcomers editing activities started to increase from August when the WHO declared a public health emergency[13], their activities then reached the peak during October when the number of infection cases also increased to the peak level and was the major concern by the whole society – the Google search trend also increased to the peak around the same time. The same pattern can be observed for Black Lives Matter and FIFA events[14]. The results thus suggest that newcomers' participation pattern closely relates to the popularity of the events and the general public attention.

5.2 RQ2: Newcomers Editing Event Articles Exhibit Distinctive Entry Paths and Their Path Leads to Different Subsequent Level of Contribution and Commitment

We posit that the first action of the newcomers in Wikipedia can serve as a proxy for understanding their initial motivation to join Wikipedia. Therefore, we distinguished two groups of newcomers based on their initial actions: (1) **Event-Driven Newcomers:** newcomers who edit one of the event articles or their associated article talk pages as their first action after joining Wikipedia; (2) **Contrast Group** as newcomers who edited one of the event articles within two weeks of joining Wikipedia but not as their first action. Their first action included editing other Wikipedia articles pages, User pages, or User talk pages. We hypothesize that as compared to "event-driven newcomers", this group of newcomers is less directly motivated by the events to join Wikipedia and possibly

---

[13] http://www.who.int/mediacentre/news/statements/2014/ebola-20140808/en/.

[14] Represented graphs are included in Appendix Fig. 5. Figure 6 visualized the editors' registration activities which are also corresponding to the major current events.

Table 1. First week behavior of newcomers editing event articles on Wikipedia

	Unique article	Edits in article talk pages	Edits in user talk pages	Edits in user pages
Event-driven group	1.37	0.09	0.15	0.21
Contrast group	10.94	1.69	1.96	2.83

Table 2. Modeling Newcomers' long term behavior based on their first week

	Production				Quality				Retention	
	# of edits		Size of edits		Quality score		Revert ratio		Survival	
	β	P	β	P	β	P	β	P	HR	P
Event-driven (vs Contrast)	-4.63	< .001	-.20	< .1	-.35	<.05		NS	2.5	<.001
In-degree					Not significant					
Out-degree	9.12	< .05		NS	2.25	<.05		NS	.0001	<.001
Eigen					Not Significant				1.43	<.001
# of reverts	-.25	< .001		NS	-0.03	.2	.09	<.001	1.08	<.001
# of article talk page edits	.29	<.01			Not Significant				.91	<.001
# of user page edits	.21	<.05	.06	<.05	Not Significant				.95	<.001
# of unique articles edited		NS	.05	<.1	.05	<.1	-.13	<.001		NS

they were motivated in editing Wikipedia intrinsically and the popularity of the events article draw their attention into those specific articles. Out of our sample of 506 newcomers, 296 belong to "event-driven newcomers" group and 210 to the "Contrast" group.

Table 1 presents data of the first week editing behavior of newcomers in terms of the number of unique articles edited, number of edits on user pages, user talk pages, and article talk pages. As presented in Table 1, we found that *event-driven newcomers* whose entry path is through event articles continue their activities majorly on a few event articles in their first week. In contrast, the other group demonstrates a broader range of activities and interests by editing a larger number of different articles and connecting to the Wikipedia community by posting on user pages and talk pages.

To assess the success of each group of newcomers after they join the Wikipedia community, we measured their production effort and quality of contribution, and their retention. Table 2 summarized the results of our statistical analyses.

As presented in the table, compared with the Contrast group, *event-driven newcomers* contributed a lower number of edits ($\beta = -4.63, p < .001$) and the size of edits ($\beta = -.20, p < 0.1$) with significantly lower good-faith edit quality ($\beta = -.35, p < .05$). Additionally, the *event-driven newcomers* were 2.5 times less likely to continue editing as compared to the Contrast group (HR = 2.5, p < .001). As demonstrated in Fig. 2, the *event-driven newcomers* exhibit

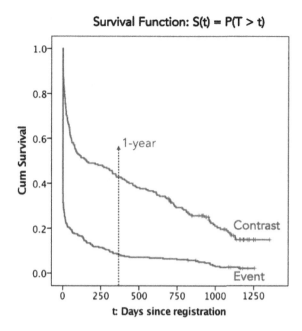

Fig. 2. Survival curves for event-driven newcomers. The x-axis indicates days after the registration.

significantly lower retention rate: only 8.0% of the *event driven newcomers* continued editing Wikipedia after one year while 42.9% of the Contrast group continued to edit in Wikipedia one year after the registration. We should highlight the 42.9% is a much higher survival rate compare the general around 10% survival rate of Wikipedia editors which further confirms the popularity of editing current events in Wikipedia.

Furthermore, we observed significant differences between the two groups of newcomers in terms of their integration within the Wikipedia community. Figure 3 presents the network of the first week of social interactions of newcomers. The blue nodes in the network represent the event-driven newcomers and the green nodes represent the Contrast group. The grey nodes represent the rest of Wikipedians who had exchanged any messages with the newcomers through the user talk pages. As illustrated in the Fig. 3 the Contrast group are in the more central network positions than the *event-driven newcomers*, as they have significantly higher in-degree (Event-driven = .66 vs. Contrast = 4.52) and out-degree (Event-driven = .10 vs. Contrast = 1.54).

Event
Contrast
Other Wikipedians

Fig. 3. Newcomers' interaction network

5.3   RQ3: Early-On Social Interactions, Community Feedback, and Diversity of Contribution Play an Important Role in Newcomers' On-Boarding

We evaluated the effect of amount and direction of social interaction on newcomers' effort, quality of contribution, and commitment. As presented in Table 2, newcomers with higher out-degree centrality (i.e. higher level of reaching out to others), are more likely to contribute more edits in Wikipedia subsequently ($\beta = 9.12, p < .05$). They also contribute higher quality content ($\beta = 2.25, p < .05$), and are more likely to stay on Wikipedia longer (HR = .0001, p < .001)[15]. However, communication with well-connected Wikipedians, as measured by Eigen centrality, was associated with 42.6% less likelihood to continue editing Wikipedia (HR = 1.426, p < .001). Our observation of such communication indicates that messages exchanged with highly connected Wikipedians often involve criticism of newcomers' edits which in return can be interpreted as a negative feedback by the newcomers and demotivate their further contribution.

Table 2 demonstrated that a higher number of reverts in the first week is associated with a decreased subsequent number of article edits ($\beta = -.25, p < .001$) as well as a lower retention rate (HR = 1.076, p < .001), while it has no significant effect on the quality of subsequent edits. A higher degree of participation in the discussions in the article talk pages was also associated with an increased

---

[15] Hazard Ratio can be interpreted as: one degree increase in out-degree reduces the hazard by a factor of 0.0001, or 99.99%.

number of article edits ($\beta = .29, p < .01$), but a lower retention rate (HR $= .91$, p $< .001$). Newcomers who edit their user profile page more in the first week also go on to contribute a higher number of edits ($\beta = .27, p < .05$), a larger size of contribution ($\beta = 0.06, p < 0.05$), and are more likely to stay longer (HR $= 0.949$, p < 0.001). Newcomers who demonstrate a broader interests and edit more unique number of articles are less likely to be reverted ($\beta = -0.13, p < 0.001$).

5.4 A Closer Look into the Contribution of Newcomers

Overall, our results indicate that both groups of newcomers contributed content to Wikipedia which is similarly likely to be accepted by the Wikipedia community and not be reverted. However, we also observed that the content contributed by the *event-driven newcomers* received lower quality score as indicate by good-faith score. To gain a deeper understanding of what has contributed to their lower quality score, we conducted content analyses of the comments associated with deleted content added by newcomers since those comments often include editors' explanation of why they have deleted some content. These comments often include specific templates associated with Wikipedia policies that have been violated in the reverted revision. The Wikipedia short policy templates provide a systematic way for Wikipedia editors to justify their revert actions. Therefore, to make sense of the comments, we collected and analyzed the Wikipedia short policy templates included in the comments in our dataset. Following core content policies of Wikipedia, we categorized those comments based on their associated short policy templates into the three revert reasons: *Neutral point of view*, *Verifiability*, and *No original research*. Additionally, we reviewed the content of the free text associated with those comments for a random subset of 200 reverts. Highlighting the keywords in this sample of comments, we observed that many of the keywords represent the same core policies of *Neutral point of view*, *Verifiability*, and *No original research*. Therefore, we classified all the comments based on appearance of keywords representing each of the three aforementioned policies; presence of keywords such as 'pov', 'neutral' were associated with *Neutral point of view* policy; 'notable', 'source', 'citation', 'link', and 'reliable' were associated with *Verifiability*; and the keyword 'original' was associated with *No original research*. We also observed many of comments including the phrase "vandalism type editing" which we classified as the fourth category of reverts, *Vandalism*.

Fig. 4. Example of a "vandalism" edit of event-driven newcomers

In our dataset, 506 event-driven newcomers contributed a total of 81,908 revisions within four months after their registrations. 345 of newcomers were at least once reverted and a total of 4,920 reverted revisions. We collected the comments for all of those reverted revisions, which included comments associated with 4,280 reverted revisions. While Wikipedia encouraged editors to always include informative comments along with reverting revisions, very small percentage of them actually include such comments. In our data, a total of 925 reverts out of a total of 4,925 were associated with any comments that we were able to classify into one of our aforementioned four categories. 129 of these reverts were associated with edits contributed by the *event-driven newcomers*. In general, the most frequently mentioned two reasons for reverts were the lack of verification (587 times) and Vandalism (223 times), following by violations of neutral point of view (68 times). Assessment of the frequency of revert reasons among our two groups of newcomers showed that the revisions made by the *event-driven newcomers* were more likely to be reverted due to *Vandalism* ($\beta = 1.029, p < 0.05$). We did not find significant differences for other types of revert reasons.

An example of vandalism cases by event-driven newcomers is presented in Fig. 4[16]. As shown in the figure, the newcomer has deleted a full paragraph of informative information about Ebola virus and replaced with an emotional statement. Such edits are typical of what is known as Vandalism in Wikipedia and can be reflective of newcomers' stronger attachment to the exogenous event than Wikipedia community.

6   Discussion and Conclusion

Prior research has highlighted how popular events draw attention to knowledge production online about those events. In this work, we extended the prior work by exploring the value of popular events in attracting newcomers to online production communities and the impact on quantity and quality of their contribution. We analyzed the newcomers' contribution to 133 Wikipedia articles related to three major events in 2014. We studied how the newcomers' activity in Wikipedia connect to the unfolding of the events in the society, what paths

---

[16] Another example can be found at https://en.wikipedia.org/w/index.php?title=Charlestonchurchshooting&type=revision&diff=667541754.

those newcomers take in Wikipedia, and how their initial path leads to their subsequent behavior on Wikipedia. Our results demonstrate that the popular offline events attract a large number of newcomers and promote a significant contribution of reasonable quality. Our results also highlight two major paths into editing event articles: direct focus on articles versus a broader participation in Wikipedia. While overall these newcomers benefit the Wikipedia community significantly, our results suggest that a narrow event-related focus can lead into less desirable subsequent behavior in the online production community, in terms of the amount of work, quality of work and likelihood of continued participation. This result is aligned with prior work that highlights that the goal-specific users are likely to act in the short-term, and that they are less likely to return soon after they achieve their goal [7]. Event-focused newcomers might feel the sense of achievement shortly after they have contributed the immediate information about their event of interest. Their higher level of focus on the events rather than Wikipedia also can hinder their adherence of Wikipedia rules and norms.

These challenges, however, provide opportunities for the Wikipedia community as well as other similar online production communities to develop strategies to best capitalize on the potential these newcomers can bring to the community. While the nature of our study, which does not involve a randomized control experiment, prevent us to draw strong causal conclusions, our results provide evidence in support of close monitoring of early-on behaviors of newcomers and adjusting strategies accordingly to best support newcomers as well as the community. By providing targeted guidance and socialization procedures, Wikipedia community can aim to benefit from encouraging a higher level quality contribution among those who might be only interested in short term communication and encouraging a higher level of commitment among those demonstrating signs of longer term interests. For example, our analyses indicate that encouraging newcomers to communicate with others and spend effort on broader contributions can lead into both a higher quality of contribution as well as a higher level of commitment. We believe our research inspires future research to carefully consider the connection between exogenous processes that can connect online communities into individuals' daily experiences and we provide insights into methodologies to conduct such studies.

Appendix

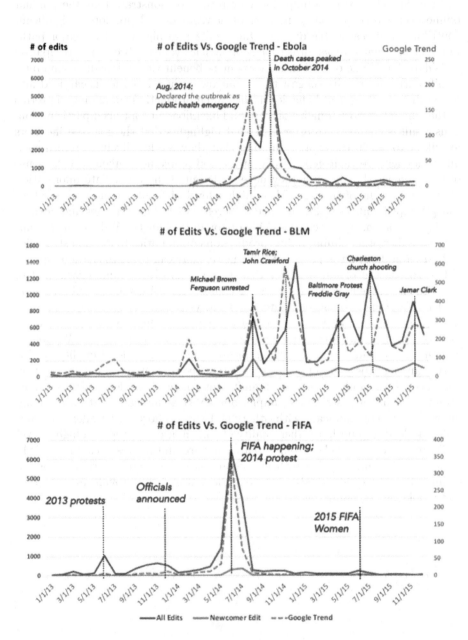

Fig. 5. Newcomer editing activity timeline correspond closely with the Google trend as well as the offline current event timeline

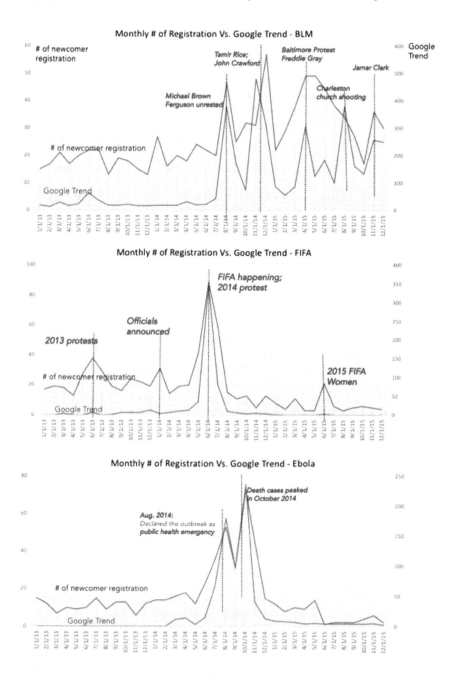

Fig. 6. Newcomer registration timeline correspond closely with the Google trend as well as the offline current event timeline: This figure visualizes the monthly registration activity of the event-driven newcomers. As presented in the graph, we observed that peaks in the event-driven newcomers' registration activity closely corresponds to the offline events for all three cases.

References

1. Allen, N., Meyer, J.: The measurement and antecedents of affective, continuance and normative commitment to the organization. J. Occup. Psychol. **63**(1), 1–18 (1990)
2. Arguello, J., et al.: Talk to me: foundations for successful individual-group interactions in online communities. In: Proceedings of the SIGCHI Conference on Human Factors in Computing Systems, CHI 2006, pp. 959–968. ACM, New York (2006). https://doi.org/10.1145/1124772.1124916. http://doi.acm.org/10.1145/1124772.1124916
3. Beauvois, J., et al.: Intrinsic motivation and self determination in human behavior (1985)
4. Bryant, S.L., Forte, A., Bruckman, A.: Becoming wikipedian: transformation of participation in a collaborative online encyclopedia. In: Proceedings of the 2005 International ACM SIGGROUP Conference on Supporting Group Work, pp. 1–10. ACM (2005)
5. Burke, M., Marlow, C., Lento, T.: Feed me: motivating newcomer contribution in social network sites. In: Proceedings of the SIGCHI Conference on Human Factors in Computing Systems, CHI 2009, pp. 945–954. ACM, New York (2009). https://doi.org/10.1145/1518701.1518847. http://doi.acm.org/10.1145/1518701.1518847
6. Burke, M., Settles, B.: Plugged in to the community: social motivators in online goal-setting groups. In: Proceedings of the 5th International Conference on Communities and Technologies, C&T 2011, pp. 1–10. ACM, New York (2011). https://doi.org/10.1145/2103354.2103356. http://doi.acm.org/10.1145/2103354.2103356
7. Cheng, J., Lo, C., Leskovec, J.: Predicting intent using activity logs: how goal specificity and temporal range affect user behavior. In: Proceedings of the 26th International Conference on World Wide Web Companion, International World Wide Web Conferences Steering Committee, pp. 593–601 (2017)
8. Choi, B., Alexander, K., Kraut, R.E., Levine, J.M.: Socialization tactics in Wikipedia and their effects. In: Proceedings of the 2010 ACM Conference on Computer Supported Cooperative Work, CSCW 2010, pp. 107–116. ACM, New York (2010). https://doi.org/10.1145/1718918.1718940. http://doi.acm.org/10.1145/1718918.1718940
9. Dabbish, L., Farzan, R., Kraut, R., Postmes, T.: Fresh faces in the crowd: turnover, identity, and commitment in online groups. In: Proceedings of the ACM 2012 Conference on Computer Supported Cooperative Work, pp. 245–248. ACM (2012)
10. Dittus, M., Quattrone, G., Capra, L.: Analysing volunteer engagement in humanitarian mapping: building contributor communities at large scale. In: Proceedings of the 19th ACM Conference on Computer-Supported Cooperative Work and Social Computing, pp. 108–118. ACM (2016)
11. Dittus, M., Quattrone, G., Capra, L.: Social contribution settings and newcomer retention in humanitarian crowd mapping. In: Spiro, E., Ahn, Y.-Y. (eds.) SocInfo 2016. LNCS, vol. 10047, pp. 179–193. Springer, Cham (2016). https://doi.org/10.1007/978-3-319-47874-6_13
12. Ducheneaut, N.: Socialization in an open source software community: a sociotechnical analysis. Comput. Support. Coop. Work **14**(4), 323–368 (2005). https://doi.org/10.1007/s10606-005-9000-1
13. Farzan, R., Kraut, R.E.: Wikipedia classroom experiment: bidirectional benefits of students' engagement in online production communities. In: Proceedings of the SIGCHI Conference on Human Factors in Computing Systems, pp. 783–792. ACM (2013)

14. Ferron, M., Massa, P.: Collective memory building in Wikipedia: the case of north African uprisings. In: Proceedings of the 7th International Symposium on Wikis and Open Collaboration, pp. 114–123. ACM (2011)
15. Foundation, W.: Wikimedia strategic plan: a collaborative vision for the movement through 2015. Technical report, Wikimedia Foundation (2011)
16. Foundation, W.: Wikipedia, Teahouse (2017)
17. Haklay, M., Weber, P.: Openstreetmap: user-generated street maps. IEEE Pervasive Comput. **7**(4), 12–18 (2008)
18. Halfaker, A., Geiger, R.S., Morgan, J.T., Riedl, J.: The rise and decline of an open collaboration system: how wikipedia's reaction to popularity is causing its decline. Am. Behav. Sci. **57**(5), 664–688 (2013)
19. Halfaker, A., Kittur, A., Riedl, J.: Don't bite the newbies: how reverts affect the quantity and quality of Wikipedia work. In: Proceedings of the 7th International Symposium on Wikis and Open Collaboration, WikiSym 2011, pp. 163–172. ACM, New York (2011). https://doi.org/10.1145/2038558.2038585
20. Halfaker, A., Kittur, A., Riedl, J.: Don't bite the newbies: how reverts affect the quantity and quality of Wikipedia work. In: Proceedings of the 7th International Symposium on Wikis and Open Collaboration, pp. 163–172. ACM (2011)
21. Java, A., Song, X., Finin, T., Tseng, B.: Why we Twitter: understanding microblogging usage and communities. In: Proceedings of the 9th WebKDD and 1st SNA-KDD 2007 Workshop on Web Mining and Social Network Analysis, pp. 56–65. ACM (2007)
22. Keegan, B., Gergle, D., Contractor, N.: Hot off the wiki: dynamics, practices, and structures in Wikipedia's coverage of the tōhoku catastrophes. In: Proceedings of the 7th International Symposium on Wikis and Open Collaboration, pp. 105–113. ACM (2011)
23. Keegan, B., Gergle, D., Contractor, N.: Staying in the loop: structure and dynamics of Wikipedia's breaking news collaborations. In: Proceedings of the Eighth Annual International Symposium on Wikis and Open Collaboration, WikiSym 2012, pp. 1:1–1:10. ACM, New York (2012). https://doi.org/10.1145/2462932.2462934. http://doi.acm.org/10.1145/2462932.2462934
24. Keegan, B., Gergle, D., Contractor, N.: Hot off the wiki: structures and dynamics of Wikipedia's coverage of breaking news events. Am. Behav. Sci. **57**(5), 595–622 (2013)
25. Keegan, B.C.: A history of newswork on Wikipedia. In: Proceedings of the 9th International Symposium on Open Collaboration, WikiSym 2013, pp. 7:1–7:10. ACM, New York (2013). https://doi.org/10.1145/2491055.2491062. http://doi.acm.org/10.1145/2491055.2491062
26. Keegan, B.C.: A history of newswork on Wikipedia. In: Proceedings of the 9th International Symposium on Open Collaboration, p. 7. ACM (2013)
27. Keegan, B.C.: Emergent social roles in wikipedia's breaking news collaborations. In: Bertino, E., Matei, S.A. (eds.) Roles, Trust, and Reputation in Social Media Knowledge Markets. CSS, pp. 57–79. Springer, Cham (2015). https://doi.org/10.1007/978-3-319-05467-4_4
28. Klein, J.P., Moeschberger, M.L.: Survival Analysis: Techniques for Censored and Truncated Data. Springer, New York (2005)
29. Kloumann, I., Adamic, L., Kleinberg, J., Wu, S.: The lifecycles of apps in a social ecosystem. In: Proceedings of the 24th International Conference on World Wide Web, International World Wide Web Conferences Steering Committee, pp. 581–591 (2015)

30. Kraut, R., Wang, X., Butler, B., Joyce, E., Burke, M.: Beyond information: developing the relationship between the individual and the group in online communities. Inf. Syst. Res. **10** (2010)

31. Kraut, R.E., et al.: Building Successful Online Communities: Evidence-Based Social Design. MIT Press (2012)

32. Lampe, C., Johnston, E.: Follow the (slash) dot: effects of feedback on new members in an online community. In: Proceedings of the 2005 International ACM SIGGROUP Conference on Supporting Group Work, GROUP 2005, pp. 11–20. ACM, New York (2005). https://doi.org/10.1145/1099203.1099206. http://doi.acm.org/10.1145/1099203.1099206

33. Luyt, B.: Wikipedia, collective memory, and the vietnam war. J. Assoc. Inf. Sci. Technol. **67**(8), 1956–1961 (2016)

34. Nov, O.: What motivates Wikipedians? Commun. ACM **50**(11), 60–64 (2007)

35. Palen, L., Soden, R., Anderson, T.J., Barrenechea, M.: Success and scale in a data-producing organization: the socio-technical evolution of openstreetmap in response to humanitarian events. In: Proceedings of the 33rd Annual ACM Conference on Human Factors in Computing Systems, pp. 4113–4122. ACM (2015)

36. Panciera, K., Halfaker, A., Terveen, L.: Wikipedians are born, not made: a study of power editors on Wikipedia. In: Proceedings of the ACM 2009 International Conference on Supporting Group Work, pp. 51–60. ACM (2009)

37. Panciera, K., Priedhorsky, R., Erickson, T., Terveen, L.: Lurking? cyclopaths?: a quantitative lifecycle analysis of user behavior in a geowiki. In: Proceedings of the SIGCHI Conference on Human Factors in Computing Systems, pp. 1917–1926. ACM (2010)

38. Pentzold, C.: Fixing the floating gap: the online encyclopaedia wikipedia as a global memory place. Mem. Stud. **2**(2), 255–272 (2009)

39. Roberts, J.A., Hann, I.H., Slaughter, S.A.: Understanding the motivations, participation, and performance of open source software developers: a longitudinal study of the apache projects. Manag. Sci. **52**(7), 984–999 (2006)

40. Ryan, R.M., Deci, E.L.: Intrinsic and extrinsic motivations: classic definitions and new directions. Contemp. Educ. Psychol. **25**(1), 54–67 (2000)

41. Soden, R., Palen, L.: From crowdsourced mapping to community mapping: the post-earthquake work of openStreetMap Haiti. In: Rossitto, C., Ciolfi, L., Martin, D., Conein, B. (eds.) COOP 2014 - Proceedings of the 11th International Conference on the Design of Cooperative Systems, 27-30 May 2014, Nice (France), pp. 311–326. Springer, Cham (2014). https://doi.org/10.1007/978-3-319-06498-7_19

42. Steinmacher, I., Silva, M.A.G., Gerosa, M.A., Redmiles, D.F.: A systematic literature review on the barriers faced by newcomers to open source software projects. Inf. Softw. Technol. **59**, 67–85 (2015)

43. Tausczik, Y., Farzan, R., Levine, J.M., Kraut, R.: Consequences of socializing newcomers collectively in online communities. INGroup: Interdisciplinary Network for Group Research (2014)

44. Thebault-Spieker, J., Hecht, B., Terveen, L.: Geographic biases are 'born, not made': exploring contributors' spatiotemporal behavior in openstreetmap. In: Proceedings of the 2018 ACM Conference on Supporting Groupwork, GROUP 2018, pp. 71–82. ACM, New York (2018). https://doi.org/10.1145/3148330.3148350. http://doi.acm.org/10.1145/3148330.3148350

45. Twyman, M., Keegan, B.C., Shaw, A.: Black lives matter in Wikipedia: collective memory and collaboration around online social movements. In: Proceedings of the 2017 ACM Conference on Computer Supported Cooperative Work and Social

Computing, CSCW 2017, pp. 1400–1412. ACM, New York (2017). https://doi.org/10.1145/2998181.2998232. http://doi.acm.org/10.1145/2998181.2998232

46. Zeitlyn, D.: Gift economies in the development of open source software: anthropological reflections. Res. Policy **32**(7), 1287–1291 (2003)

47. Zhu, H., Zhang, A., He, J., Kraut, R.E., Kittur, A.: Effects of peer feedback on contribution: a field experiment in Wikipedia. In: Proceedings of the SIGCHI Conference on Human Factors in Computing Systems, CHI 2013, pp. 2253–2262. ACM, New York (2013). https://doi.org/10.1145/2470654.2481311

Who Gets the Lion's Share in the Sharing Economy: A Case Study of Social Inequality in AirBnB

Afra Mashhadi[1]($\boxtimes$) and Clovis Chapman[2]

[1] University of Washington, Seattle, WA 98195, USA
mashhadi@uw.edu
[2] University College London, Gower Street, London WC1E 6EA, UK
c.chapman@cs.ucl.ac.uk

Abstract. Sharing economy platforms have rapidly disrupted and transformed many traditional markets. Companies such as AirBnB, in the housing market, and Uber, in the ride-sharing space, have thrived by creating opportunities for so-called "micro-entrepreneurs", allowing them to leverage existing personal assets, such as a spare room or car, to generate additional income. While often heralded as an opportunity to reduce income inequality, opening opportunities through technology to a much larger segment of the population, there is however a latent concern that these platforms are in practice not as inclusive as advertised. In this paper we study the AirBnB listings in Chicago and examine a number of different dimensions regarding the hosts, their property and the environment within which they operate. Specifically we examine who the hosts are by detecting hosts' ethnicity, gender and age using images posted publicly on the site. Leveraging this information and socioeconomic metrics from the Census, we examine the properties different hosts offer and what is received in return. Finally we study how these hosts present their properties by measuring the aesthetic score of the main listing photographs using a deep learning algorithm. Our results suggest an ethnical discrepancy that affects minorities from lower socioeconomic backgrounds, even when taking into account location and other attributes such as price of AirBnB listings. The findings also suggest that a wider range of factors, such as poorer pictures of listings, maybe affecting the inclusion and that could be corrected with internal policies and assistance of the platform owners.

1 Introduction

Sharing Economy platforms provide services and connections between individuals with under-utilized tangible assets such as a car or a house, and other individuals or businesses in need of those assets [8,25]. In the past years, these platforms have become extremely popular as they offer to increase consumer welfare by opening up competition in an increasingly large variety of domains [24]. Indeed some speculators including Milbourn [16] and Nunberg [19] widely believe

© Springer Nature Switzerland AG 2018
S. Staab et al. (Eds.): SocInfo 2018, LNCS 11185, pp. 370–385, 2018.
https://doi.org/10.1007/978-3-030-01129-1_23

that the sharing economy will substantially displace traditional equivalents in the future.

Despite this promise, the sharing economy raises important concerns regarding socio-economic inequality, manifested as age and racial discrimination. A recent study of Uber, the ride sharing platform, showed that African-american passengers were subject to longer waits [9]. Similarly, a field study of AirBnB has shown that guests with African-american names were more likely to be turned down [5], criticizing AirBnB for not being an inclusive platform. In fact, this widespread critic manifested itself on social media where users shared their discriminatory experiences using the hash tag #Airbnbwhileblack and led to AirBnB's new anti-discrimination policy and internal report to build inclusion [17].

However due to lack of data, independent studies of social inequality in sharing economy platforms are still limited and we are yet to understand how race, gender and age affect the users of these platforms. As a result, it can be difficult for effective policies to be derived or to determine the potential effectiveness of such policies. Cue et al. have argued for example that AirBnB suffers from the *statistical* discrimination rather than *taste-based* discrimination [4]. Through a field experiment with 1,000 Airbnb hosts, they found that when guests have even one positive review on their profiles, it statistically eliminates racial discrimination against them. They hence suggest that closer examination of the reviewing process should be an important aspect of any policy in this domain. In short, a better understanding of the user population, the behaviors of the hosts and their customers, the socio-economic environment can yield to better and more effective solutions to problems of inequality and discrimination.

In this paper, we are interested in understanding (i) who are the hosts on AirBnB, how are they distributed across age, race and gender; (ii) what they offer in terms of property (shared, vs entire place) and where these listings are geographically; (iii) how they visually present their property on the platform; (iv) and finally what ratings and number of reviews they receive. To answer these questions we investigate AirBnB listings of Chicago, and detect the ethnicity, age and gender of 2700 hosts. We match the information found on the Airbnb platform to the US Census data on the census-tract levels in which listings are located. This allows us to study the impact of income on the economic activity of the platform and measure racial disparity. Finally, leveraging advances in machine learning we quantify the aesthetic score of the main photo of the property and study how hosts from different socio-economic and racial backgrounds present their property on AirBnB platform.

Our findings show that listings are typically geographically located in richer and denser areas with respect to median household income. We also identify that minorities are under-represented even in minority-majority areas. This discrepancy is further confirmed with respect to the visual presentation of properties and listing prices, where potential earnings of African-Americans appear to be 12% less than that of other hosts. We aim for our methodology to help organizations both explore issues of inequality and discrimination on sharing economy platforms and discuss various ways in which policies can be put in place to assist.

2   Related Work

The issue of social inequality in the broader geospatial socio-technical space has been examined extensively in the past. For instance, in the field of Volunteered Geographical Information (VGI), which includes projects such as OpenStreetMap, Haklay et al. reported that areas with higher deprivation levels were also more likely to suffer from lack of mapping coverage [10]. Mashhadi et al. [15] found that both socio-economic factors (e.g., income deprivation) and physical distance from the city centre are negatively correlated with OpenStreetMap coverage in London, UK. Hecht et al. [11] showed that there is a geographical bias (towards urban areas) in adoption rates, quantity and quality of information in VGI. Quattrone et al. showed that there is a strong culture bias in editing behavior in VGI and that countries with lower Power Distance are more likely to contribute to such platforms [20,21].

Examining social inequality in the geospatial socio-technical literature with specific focus on *tangible* assets, Quattrone et al. [22] found that Airbnb listings of London have increased over time to cover poorer and less educated neighborhoods but these offerings did not attract as many guests. Similarly, Thebault-Spieker et al. [26] compared the relative effectiveness of two sharing economy platforms, UberX and TaskRabbit from a geographical perspective. They showed that because of the correlation between low social-economic neighborhoods and ethnical minority, these neighborhoods suffer from identical lower sharing economy effectiveness.

In contrast to these works, Fraiberger et al. argued that sharing economy platforms (in particular ride-sharing) benefit mostly poorer populations [7]. Although their work has been criticized because of its reliance on simulation, the economic modeling of their data makes it a valuable paper that cannot be dismissed. Kooti et al. studied the UberX ride-sharing platform by collecting source and destination of the rides from Uber receipts that are sent at the end of each trip to 4.1 million riders and 222 thousand drivers who have Yahoo Mail account [13]. They argued that Uber is not an *all-serve-all* market, rather the riders have higher income than drivers and differ along racial and gender groups.

Other works have taken a qualitative approach to examine the impact of the sharing economy on inequality, but often limitations in scale. Schor et al. [23] has claimed an increasing inequality within the bottom 80% of users of sharing economy platforms. Their study is based on qualitative interviews of 43 earners of three platforms (Airbnb, RelayRides and TaskRabbit) from which they conclude the following two reasons for this disparity: first the well-off and highly educated providers are using the platforms to increase their earnings. Second this group is doing work that is traditionally done by people of low educational status. Similarly, Edelman et al. showed the impact of race as a factor of inequality by showing that users with stereotypically African American names in Airbnb are less likely to be accepted as guests compared to identical profiles with stereotypically white names [5].

Unlike previous works, we aim here to build a more complete picture of service providers on sharing economy platforms, by leveraging a more diverse range of data points: in particular, census data, demographic data, and aesthetic analysis. By leveraging deep learning technology, we can also achieve this at a much larger scale allowing us to draw additional insights into the cost and benefits of these platforms.

3   Datasets and Methodology

In order to answer the research questions posited above, we require to overlap two dataset of AirBnB and census together. In studying any correlations based on each of these datasets we need to account for spatial autocorrelation. Spatial autocorrelation describes the tendency for measurements nearby each other in space to be correlated and thus violates the assumption of the independence of observations that approaches such Pearson and Spearman's require. In our analysis we leverage the technique that was introduced by Clifford et al. [3] and applied to geo-referenced data by [11] to account for spatial autocorrelation. The significance of the correlation coefficients reported in the rest of the paper is based on calculating a (reduced) effective sample size to address the redundant, or duplicated, information contained in spatial autocorrelation. We describe each of the datasets in detail next.

3.1   AirBnB Dataset

AirBnB does does not provide an API to access their dataset, therefore for our study we relied on external sources that collected listings. More specifically we used the listings of Chicago that were last scraped in May 2017 by InsideAirbnb[1]; an independent, non-commercial website that provides set of tools and data that allows everyone to explore how Airbnb is really being used in cities around the world.

This dataset includes the all the listed properties in the Chicago region along with the following information about the hosts and property. Specifically in our study we consider the following attributes:

- Host: name, photo URL, the date the host joined AirBnB, the number of listings they have, whether they are a super-host[2] or not and finally information on the number of reviews and a user generated scores broken down by communication, interaction and location.

---

[1] http://insideairbnb.com/ last retrieved on Jan 2018.
[2] Super-hosts in the AirBnB platform are those who hosted at least 10 trips, maintaining at least a 90% response rate and received a 5-star for at least 80% of the time they have been reviewed.

– Property: photo URL, price, type of the property (Private/Shared room or Entire Place) as well as latitude and longitude.

The dataset includes 5200 listings of which 60% are for renting the entire home. Moreover, these listings are offered by 3500 uniques hosts. Indeed, the dataset in hand presents that 48% of the listings are by hosts who offer more than one property, with some of the hosts offering up to one hundred different rooms and houses. These hosts often present lodging business or state agents who use AirBnB platform to rent their various properties. In this paper as we are interested to uncover social inequality on the individual scale, we filter out all those hosts (and their listings) that have more than one property presented in Chicago during the same time period that the dataset was scrapped. The resulting dataset includes 2700 listings by same number of hosts. Figure 1 presents the placements of all AirBnB listings. As it is expected most of listings are placed in the downtown area. Furthermore, we observe that there are more listings in the richer northern suburbs of Chicago as opposed to the poorer and more racially diverse southern suburbs.

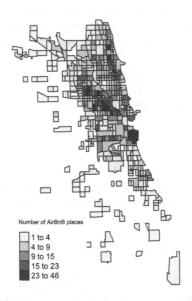

Fig. 1. Geographical distribution of AirBnB listings

3.2 American Community Survey

In addition to the AirBnB dataset we also required information about the socio-economic status of the hosts. We gathered median household income data (Fig. 2) from the 2016 American Community Survey (ACS). This metric is known as an indicator of socioeconomic status [14]. It is also been shown to be highly correlated with education and unemployment. We also collected the number of household units and the population of African-American, White and Asian households per tract from the ACS (Fig. 2). Throughout our analysis, we chose the level of the census tracts[3] in terms of granularity as it provides us with a relatively small geographical unit. Furthermore it allows us to keep consistent and thus making our findings comparable with other geographical studies [26] on the sharing economy. By combining this dataset with the host demographics identified through photo identification, we calculate an ethnical discrepancy metric for each census tracts as we will describe in the next section.

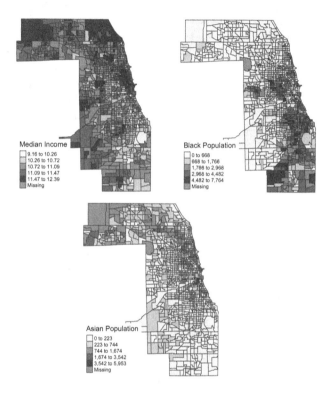

Fig. 2. Median household income (in log scale), geographical distribution of African-American population, and geographical distribution of Asian population in the greater Chicago area based on the 2016 American Community Survey Data.

4   Primary Analysis

4.1   Aesthetic Analysis

In order to measure the representation difference of properties in AirBnB we web-scrapped the main photos of the listed properties in our dataset. We then

---

[3] Census tracts are geographic areas defined by the U.S. census and generally have a population size between 1,200 and 8,000 people, with an optimum size of 4,000 people.

leveraged state of the art neural network techniques to assign an aesthetic score to each photo. More precisely, we used advances in deep convolutional neural network (DCNN) that capture both global and local features. Local characteristics include noise, blur and contrast while global characteristics include composition features such as rule of thirds, foreground/background separation, depth of field etc. In particular we used ILGNet [12] a DCNN based algorithm which introduces the inception module that connects intermediate local layers to the last layer which extracts the global features for the output. The network is 13 layers deep when counting only layers with parameters or 17 layers if we also count pooling. Three inception layers and one pre-treatment layer are involved. The output layer is 1 dimension which directly gives the classification result of low or high aesthetic quality. Furthermore this algorithm is based on a pre-trained image classification CNN called GoogLeNet on the ImageNet dataset and fine tuned on the Aesthetic Visual Analysis (AVA), a large dataset formed by more than 250 thousands of images [18]. The classification accuracy of ILGNet is 85.5% far higher than non-fully connected deep networks [12].

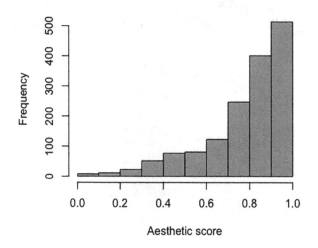

Fig. 3. The frequency distribution of the aesthetic scores of the main property photos.

Figure 3 presents the frequency distribution of the aesthetic scores of all the images. As it can be seen the distribution is skewed toward higher scores, demonstrating that most of the images in our dataset are both of good quality (local features), and well composed (global features). Indeed, we manually checked the images that had a very low aesthetic score (falling below the first interquartile range – IQR) and found that most of those images suffer from low local properties and in many cases are blurred. Figure 4 shows an example of the photos that were classified with a high and low aesthetic score.

a) Low Aesthetic Score

b) High Aesthetic Score

Fig. 4. Example of images with low and high aesthetic score calculated based on ILGNet [12].

4.2 Demographic Analysis

As our data does not include any demographic information about the hosts, we required a technique to automatically detect gender, age and ethnicity. According to [2] there are currently two main possible techniques to do so: one is to process the textual content such as name and the description of the host, to detect the demographics. However this method is known to be error prone as hosts can present themselves with nicknames or arbitrary usernames, and the language used in providing the description of themselves is likely to follow a formal template, making it hard to detect age and the language skill of the writer. An alternative method is to extract demographic data using the host profile picture. Relying on the latter choice we crawled the host profile photos from the AirBnB website and used the Face++[4] API to process them. Face++ provides a set of powerful, and cross-platform vision services which enable us to detect age, gender and race through facial recognition techniques. The API does not provide an estimation of accuracy, however studies that used this API for the similar identification purpose such as [1] have reported of 97% accuracy when validated against crowd-sourced Mechanical Turk platforms. It is worth noting that racial and ethnic identity is complex and evaluations by others may not match an individual's self-identification. In this paper however we are interested in the *perceived* ethnicity of the AirBnB hosts and how the race is commonly evaluated by the users of this platform (as opposed to self-reported).

Table 1 provides an overview of the demographic makeup of AirBnB hosts. Our analysis identified that 30% of the photos showed more than one person. As we are unable to guarantee the host identity in these cases (listings may represent friends, companies, etc.), we eliminate these listings from our analysis. The analysis reported in the rest of this paper is based on the remaining 1700 hosts and their listings. The remaining hosts are 47% female 53% male, 13% Asian, 11% African-American and 76% White[5]. Table 1 reports the demographic properties of the hosts.

5   Results

In this section, we report the results of our work based on three complimentary sets of analyses: racial discrepancy, aesthetic presentation and potential earnings of the hosts.

5.1   Racial Discrepancy

In order to study the racial inclusion in AirBnB platform we calculate a residual metric which measures the discrepancy between the actual ratio of African-American/asian hosts in AirBnB and the expected ratio based on the census population of these communities. We measure the actual ratio by dividing the

---

[4] Face++. http://en.faceplusplus.com/, 2013.

[5] Note that Face++ does not identify hispanic as a separate ethnic classification.

Table 1. Demographic properties of AirBnB Chicago hosts based on the analysis of their profile picture.

Race	Percentage	Age Distribution	Female - Male	Superhost-ratio
Asian	13%		53%-47%	17%
African-American	11%		43%-57%	20%
White	76%		48%-52%	24%

Table 2. Regression analysis of the discrepancy value for African-American and asian communities in relation to the income and population data.

	African American		Asian	
	β	p-value	β	p-value
Median income	−0.29	***	0.00	
No. household	−0.07	**	0.03	.
Adjusted R-squared	0.224		0.001	

number of African-American/Asian hosts by the total number of AirBnB hosts in each census tract. We then calculate the residual by subtracting this measure from the ratio of the census. The higher the value of the ethnicity residual the bigger is the discrepancy between the ethnical background of the residents and the AirBnB hosts.

Figure 5 presents area cartograms of the ethnicity gap for African-American and Asian population in the greater Chicago area. In this figure, the tracts are colored according to the level of over- or under-representation, with a green color representing the tract with extreme under-representation of the African-American (or Asian) hosts compared to the residential population. To put these discrepancy values into context, we calculated two linear regression models with the dependent variable as the discrepancy value and census variables as independent variables. Table 2 presents the details of these models. As it can be seen we observe a significant negative correlation with the median household income for the African-American discrepancy. That is the poorer areas (those concentrated in southern part of Chicago) also exhibit higher under-representation in AirBnB. This result indicates that those who could perhaps most benefit from the opportunities of micro-entrepreneurship are those who are not sufficiently represented in the system.

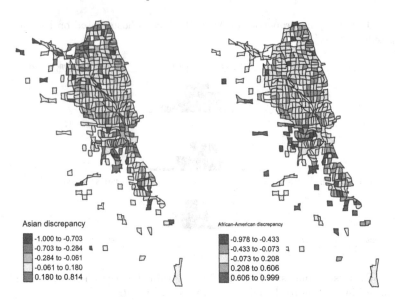

Fig. 5. An area cartograms based on the ethnicity gap where the green color (higher values) present areas in which there is the highest discrepancy between the ethnical background of the residents and the AirBnB hosts.

5.2 Aesthetic Presentation

We now turn our attention to how the hosts present their properties on the AirBnB platform. Figure 6 presents the choropleth map of the median aesthetic scores for each tract. We observe a weak positive correlation (r = 0.14, p-value = 0.005) between the median household income and the median aesthetic scores of the images, suggesting that hosts in the poorer neighborhoods do not present listings as well as others, perhaps due to socio-technical challenges.

We then incorporate demographic of the hosts and conduct a series of Welch Two Sample t-tests to compare the aesthetic scores between different (i) female vs male (ii) African-American vs white (iii) asian vs white (iv) super-hosts vs non super-hosts. We find no significant difference between the aesthetic scores of different genders. However, we find a significant difference in the aesthetic scores for the African-American (mean = 0.75, sd = 0.18) and White(mean = 0.79, sd = 0.18) hosts, with t(242) = −1.85 and p-value = 0.03. This gap widens even more (t(124) = −2.31, p-value = 0.01) when we compare the aesthetic scores for the African-American(mean = 0.74, sd = 0.18) and White (mean = 0.8, sd = 0.18) hosts in the neighborhoods where the median household income is in the first IQ (i.e., the poorest) and diminishes for the richer neighborhoods (with median income larger than the third IQ). Similar results were observed in comparing the aesthetic score of the Asian and White hosts. Finally we find a significant difference (t(622) = 2.09, p-value = 0.01) between the aesthetic scores of super-hosts(mean = 0.8, sd = 0.17) compared to non super-hosts(mean = 0.77, sd = 0.19). We do not observe any correlation between the aesthetic

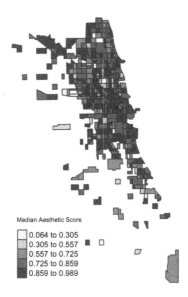

Fig. 6. The choropleth map of the median aesthetic scores. The lower shades present the areas with lower median aesthetic score.

score of the images and the age of the host or the price of the property. In summary, and complementing the prior section, it is primarily minorities from poorer neighborhoods that suffer from missteps in presenting their offerings.

Finally, we are interested in examining whether the aesthetic score actually has any impact on the host's success on the platform. We use for this purpose the number of reviews per month as a proxy for demand and so an indicator of how successful a host is in renting out their property. We used reviews instead of ratings as an indicator of success because previous research has shown that ratings are generally inflated and not very accurate [27]. Furthermore Fradkin et al. have shown that more than 70% of the times people leave reviews after staying at a place [6]. As the popularity of a rental place is first and foremost dictated by its location, we calculate the median aesthetic scores and the median reviews per month for each census tract. We find a positive correlation of $r = 0.16$ ($p < 0.001$) between these two variables, indicating that the better the quality of the images, the higher the likelihood of the place being rented.

A possible interpretation of these results is that hosts from a minority group and a lower socioeconomic background are those who require internal policies from AirBnB to assist them in presenting and offering their property on the platform. We discuss this implication in details in the next section.

5.3   Potential Earnings

Finally, we investigate whether there is any indication of social inequality when it comes to how the hosts of different background are treated, and how they price their listings. More specifically, we analyze social inequality in two ways: (i) what price do hosts from different gender and ethnical backgrounds ask for; (ii) whether the demographics of the host or their super-host status play a part in the ratings they receive from their guests.

Logically, both price and ratings are highly influenced by the type of property (number of rooms) and experience (e.g., amenities that are available on the site such as Wi-Fi or a hot tub) that is offered to the guests. To control for this dimension we conduct our analysis only for single private room places in AirBnB.

Starting with pricing, for each tract we compute the average price based on all the private room properties that fall within that tract. We then compute a metric referred to as the *price residual* by dividing the price of each listing by the average private room price for that tract. A value of less that one for this metric would indicate that the host is under-selling their property compared to the average room in the same area. We then compute a multiple linear regression model with the price residual as the dependent variable and age, gender, race and the super-host status as the independent variables. The model suggests a negative association between the African-American ethnicity and the price residual. A one-unit increase on the listings by African-Americanhosts predicts a decrease of 0.12 in the price residual (se = 0.05); this decrease is significant, $t(643) = -2.141$, $p < 0.01$. This result suggests that African-American AirBnB users earn 12% less rent than other hosts for the same type of house in the same type of location. We do not find any associations between the rest of the independent variables, which also suggests that the super-hosts do not over/under-sell their property.

To understand whether there is a racial bias in how the hosts are rated, we use the location rating of the hosts as it corresponds to the satisfaction of the guests with the location of the property and is meant to be independent of other factors such as amenities available at the property. Similar to the previous metric we calculate the *location rating residual* which corresponds to the location rating of a listing divided by the average location rating of the tract. A value of less that one for this metric indicates that the hosts are unfairly scored down. We then compute a multiple linear regression model with the location rating residual as the dependent variable and age, gender, race and the super-host status as the independent variables. The model suggests a positive association between the super-host status and the location rating residual. That is a one-unit in the number of super-hosts predicts a slight increase of 0.01 in the location rating residual (se = 0.003); this increase is significant, $t(643) = -2.755$, $p < 0.01$. We do not find any associations between the rest of the independent variables, which also suggests that based on our dataset we do not observe that hosts of different demographic and racial background get scored down systematically. However, our result suggests that the super-hosts have a slight advantage and they are scored higher in terms of location rating compared to others hosting the same neighborhood.

6   Discussion

In this paper we studied the demographics of AirBnB hosts who listed their properties in the greater Chicago area during March 2017, to understand the impact of social inequality in the sharing economy platform. Our results show that listings are typically geographically located in richer and denser areas with respect to median household income, and that minorities are under-represented even in minority-majority areas. Furthermore, we showed that social inequality manifests itself not only in the lack of participation of the minorities but also in the way they present their listings visually and the price they ask for. We showed that the potential earnings of African-Americans hosts appear to be 12% less than that of other hosts for the same type of property in the same location. However, in our study we did not observe any unequal treatment of female or elderly hosts.

6.1   Implication

Documenting and providing information on social inequality in the sharing economy is only a first step. As a second step, it is important to know how these results can be used to prevent social inequality. Many critics of the sharing economy argue that external regulations posed by authorities is the way forward to prevent social inequality and discrimination. However, we believe there are big opportunities for the sharing economy platforms to assist the under-represented users through *internal policies*. In a recent report[6], AirBnB has suggested withholding information regarding the users as a means to tackle discrimination against the users from different ethnical backgrounds. We argue that while this may change usage patterns, a potentially more efficient approach would be to introduce internal policies that could assist hosts by enabling them to present their property in more aesthetically pleasing ways and for a fairer price. AirBnB as a frontier example of sharing economy platforms should aim to bring to the fore means of leveling the playing field that help under-represented communities increase their visibility on the platform.

6.2   Limitation

Our data and so in turn our analysis has some inherent limitations as we only study hosts and their listings based on the property type, price, location and images, and not based on other factors that could impact the success of a host such as house rules and cancellation policy. Furthermore, we did not look into the linguistics and how the hosts present themselves in terms of both summary and description of their place as well as their exchanges and interactions with the guests. Nonetheless believe that our findings are a significant contribution to the debate of social inequality in the sharing economy. As part of future direction

---

[6] https://blog.atairbnb.com/wp-content/uploads/2016/09/REPORT_Airbnbs-Work-to-Fight-Discrimination-and-Build-Inclusion.pdf.

we believe it is essential to conduct a temporal study of social inequality in AirBnB to understand how hosts of different background behave and adapt to the platform overtime.

References

1. Bakhshi, S., Shamma, D.A., Gilbert, E.: Faces engage us: photos with faces attract more likes and comments on instagram. In: Proceedings of the 32nd Annual ACM Conference on Human Factors in Computing Systems, pp. 965–974. ACM (2014)
2. Cesare, N., Grant, C., Nsoesie, E.O.: Detection of user demographics on social media: a review of methods and recommendations for best practices. arXiv preprint arXiv:1702.01807 (2017)
3. Clifford, P., Richardson, S., Hémon, D.: Assessing the significance of the correlation between two spatial processes. Biometrics **45**, 123–134 (1989)
4. Cui, R., Li, J., Zhang, D.J.: Discrimination with incomplete information in the sharing economy: field evidence from Airbnb (2016)
5. Edelman, B., Luca, M., Svirsky, D.: Racial discrimination in the sharing economy: evidence from a field experiment. Am. Econ. J. Appl. Econ. **9**(2), 1–22 (2017)
6. Fradkin, A., Grewal, E., Holtz, D., Pearson, M.: Bias and reciprocity in online reviews: evidence from field experiments on Airbnb. In: Proceedings of the Sixteenth ACM Conference on Economics and Computation, pp. 641–641. ACM (2015)
7. Fraiberger, S.P., Sundararajan, A.: Peer-to-peer rental markets in the sharing economy (2015)
8. Frenken, K., Schor, J.: Putting the sharing economy into perspective. Environ. Innov. Societal Transitions **23**, 3–10 (2017). https://doi.org/10.1016/j.eist.2017.01.003. http://www.sciencedirect.com/science/article/pii/S2210422417300114. Sustainability Perspectives on the Sharing Economy
9. Ge, Y., Knittel, C.R., MacKenzie, D., Zoepf, S.: Racial and gender discrimination in transportation network companies. Technical report, National Bureau of Economic Research (2016)
10. Haklay, M.: How good is volunteered geographical information? a comparative study of openstreetmap and ordnance survey datasets. Environ. Plann. B Plann. Des. **37**(4), 682–703 (2010)
11. Hecht, B.J., Stephens, M.: A tale of cities: urban biases in volunteered geographic information. ICWSM **14**, 197–205 (2014)
12. Jin, X., Chi, J., Peng, S., Tian, Y., Xiaodong Li, C.Y.: Deep image aesthetics classification using inception modules and fine-tuning connected layer. In: 8th International Conference on Wireless Communications and Signal Processing, WCSP 2016, Yangzhou, China, 13–15 October 2016, pp. 1–6 (2016)
13. Kooti, F., Grbovic, M., Aiello, L.M., Djuric, N., Radosavljevic, V., Lerman, K.: Analyzing uber's ride-sharing economy. In: Proceedings of the 26th International Conference on World Wide Web Companion, International World Wide Web Conferences Steering Committee, pp. 574–582 (2017)
14. Li, L., Goodchild, M.F., Xu, B.: Spatial, temporal, and socioeconomic patterns in the use of Twitter and Flickr. Cartography Geogr. Inf. Sci. **40**(2), 61–77 (2013)
15. Mashhadi, A., Quattrone, G., Capra, L.: Putting ubiquitous crowd-sourcing into context. In: Proceedings of the 2013 Conference on Computer Supported Cooperative Work, pp. 611–622. ACM (2013)

16. Milbourn, T.: In the future, employees won't exist. Tech Crunch (2015)
17. Murphy, L.W.: Airbnb's work to fight discrimination and build inclusion. Report submitted to Airbnb 8 (2016)
18. Murray, N., Marchesotti, L., Perronnin, F.: AVA: a large-scale database for aesthetic visual analysis. In: 2012 IEEE Conference on Computer Vision and Pattern Recognition (CVPR), pp. 2408–2415. IEEE (2012)
19. Nunberg, G.: Goodbye jobs, hello 'gigs': how one word sums up a new economic reality. In: NPR, January 2016
20. Quattrone, G., Capra, L., De Meo, P.: There's no such thing as the perfect map: quantifying bias in spatial crowd-sourcing datasets. In: Proceedings of the 18th ACM Conference on Computer Supported Cooperative Work and Social Computing, pp. 1021–1032. ACM (2015)
21. Quattrone, G., Mashhadi, A., Capra, L.: Mind the map: the impact of culture and economic affluence on crowd-mapping behaviours. In: Proceedings of the 17th ACM Conference on Computer Supported Cooperative Work and Social Computing, pp. 934–944. ACM (2014)
22. Quattrone, G., Proserpio, D., Quercia, D., Capra, L., Musolesi, M.: Who benefits from the sharing economy of Airbnb? In: Proceedings of the 25th International Conference on World Wide Web, International World Wide Web Conferences Steering Committee, pp. 1385–1394 (2016)
23. Schor, J.B.: Does the sharing economy increase inequality within the eighty percent?: findings from a qualitative study of platform providers. Cambridge J. Reg. Econ. Soc. **10**(2), 263–279 (2017)
24. Smith, A.: Shared, collaborative and on demand: the new digital economy. Pew Internet & American Life Project, Washington, DC (2016). Accessed 21 May 2016
25. Sprague, R.: Worker (mis) classification in the sharing economy: trying to fit square pegs into round holes. ABA J. Labor Employ. Law **31**(1), 53 (2015)
26. Thebault-Spieker, J., Terveen, L., Hecht, B.: Toward a geographic understanding of the sharing economy: systemic biases in UberX and TaskRabbit. ACM Trans. Comput.-Hum. Interact. (TOCHI) **24**(3), 21 (2017)
27. Zervas, G., Proserpio, D., Byers, J.: A first look at online reputation on Airbnb, where every stay is above average (2015)

Offline Versus Online: A Meaningful Categorization of Ties for Retweets

Felicia Natali[(✉)] and Feida Zhu

Singapore Management University, Singapore, Singapore
{felician.2013,fdzhu}@smu.edu.sg

Abstract. With the recent proliferation of news being shared through online social networks, it is crucial to determine how news is spread and what drives people to share certain stories. In this paper, we focus on the social networking site Twitter and analyse user's retweets. We study retweeting patterns between offline and online friends, particularly, how tweet novelty and tweet topic differ between tweets retweeted by offline friends and those retweeted by online friends.

Keywords: Twitter · Retweet · Offline ties · Online ties

1 Introduction: Retweet and its Drivers

Retweets have long been an important research topic in the social media sphere. With the emergence over the last decade of online social network platforms like Facebook and Twitter, online interactions have produced large volumes of data, offering researchers the opportunity to examine the information users have shared. As a result, information dissemination has become a prominent area of study in the field of social media analysis.

Retweeting is one of the most popular ways of disseminating information on Twitter, a social media and microblogging site that is widely used to circulate news [8]. A retweet is a re-posting of a tweet on your feed, and so the feature allows you and others to share selected tweets with your followers. You can retweet your own tweets or tweets from someone else[1].

Understanding retweets is important since they are used for various practical purposes such as sharing news, promoting political views, marketing products, and tracking real time events. Java et al. attributed the high volume of tweets mostly to daily chatter, although tweets still usually contained a fair amount of news items [6]. Enli and Skogerbø explored Twitter and Facebook as arenas for political communication [3]. Thomases, meanwhile, wrote a guide book about how to create a successful Twitter marketing campaign [15].

Therefore, if the drivers of retweets were understood properly, then harnessing them would bring immense benefits to marketing campaigns and public

---

[1] Retweet FAQs https://help.twitter.com/en/using-twitter/retweet-faqs.

© Springer Nature Switzerland AG 2018
S. Staab et al. (Eds.): SocInfo 2018, LNCS 11185, pp. 386–402, 2018.
https://doi.org/10.1007/978-3-030-01129-1_24

policy interventions. Boyd et al. compiled a comprehensive list of the motivations behind retweets. It included making new audiences aware of certain tweets and increasing a listener's visibility [2]. In addition to these internal motivations listed by Boyd et al., a number of external attributes also influence retweets, such as URLs and hashtags, and also Twitter accounts' age and follower count [14]. The study by Kupavskii et al. determined that influential users with high scores on PageRank – a measure of a website page's importance applied to Twitter follow networks – received more retweets [7].

In this study, we aim to find how offline versus online ties can be harnessed to drive retweets. Our study is the first to reveal the retweet patterns of offline friends compared to online friends, and offer another promising way for Twitter users to increase the amount of retweets their tweets receive. In this way, based on the results, marketing and political campaigns can target a specific type of user (offline/online) to increase influence. Our study also highlights the importance of the offline-online categories when discussing retweets, and demonstrate that these categories cannot be replaced by other categories, such as the reciprocated-unreciprocated categories.

2   Literature Study

Types of ties have been known to drive retweets. Past research has looked into how different ties bring about retweets. Most determined that strong ties drove retweets [12,17], although some concluded that weak ties did [13]. Meanwhile, Natali et al. analysed how different ties resulted in different topics getting retweeted [10]. In an extended study of this study[2] that utilized a more extensive data, they discovered that Twitter users did not consider ties when retweeting any topic half of the time – though when they did pay attention to them, the results were largely similar to the previous study. Personal tweets were more likely to be disseminated through strong ties, whereas entertainment and news tweets were more likely to be disseminated through weak ties. These past studies, however, defined strong ties differently. Zhao et al. used the overlap of neighbours as the indicator of strong ties [17], while Peng et al. used mutual mentions, mutual retweets, mutual followers and mutual followees as the indicators of strong ties [12]. Natali et al. and Shi et al., meanwhile, used reciprocity of follow ties to define strong ties [10,13].

In this study, we focus on different categories of ties, namely offline versus online. We aim to find out if offline and online ties can be used in place of other tie categories that were previously utilised in studies that analysed retweets. These categories of ties are reciprocated and unreciprocated. We discover that offline versus online are indeed better tie categories because they can be distinguished more easily by their retweet patterns.

---

[2] This study is currently unpublished and is a part of a thesis. Please contact authors if you want to know more.

3   Tie Categories

Strong Ties. Granovetter first introduced the concept of strong ties in his seminal work *The Strength of Weak Ties* [5]. In the study, Granovetter described interpersonal ties as "a (probably) linear combination of the amount of time, the emotional intensity, the intimacy (or mutual confiding), and the reciprocal services which characterize each tie". In addition to this formula, Granovetter emphasized the uniqueness of strong ties. Strong ties had more overlapping friends compared to two individuals selected arbitrarily. Therefore, Granovetter concluded that information that circulated among close friends is usually stale and old.

Measuring Strong Ties on Offline and Online Social Network. There are several ways to measure a tie's strength. The first study to do so is the study by Marsden and Campbell [9]. They discovered that the question of how close a person to another was the best indicator of closeness. Their study applied to the offline setting.

In the online setting, Gilbert and Karahalios authored the most extensive study on the measurement of strong ties on Facebook [4]. They made use of 74 Facebook variables in order to predict strength of ties. Their method achieved a good accuracy. Meanwhile, Backstrom et al. revealed that mutual friends of very intimate friends were rarely unconnected [1]. Their study offered the distance of mutual friends as a potential measure of how intimate two friends are.

Reciprocated versus Unreciprocated. Reciprocated ties have often been used as an easy gauge of strong ties when studying retweets [10,13]. On Twitter, a reciprocated tie appears in a situation where a user follows another user, and he or she is also followed back. On the other hand, an unreciprocated tie appears in a situation where a user follows another user, but he or she is not followed back. When someone follows another person on Twitter, he subscribes to the updates published by that person's account. In this study, the analysis of how reciprocated versus unreciprocated ties retweet will be the baseline for assessing how different the tweet novelty and topic of offline and online ties are.

Offline versus Online. Offline ties are not exactly the same as reciprocated ties, although reciprocated ties can predict offline ties with 73% precision and 65% recall. No one has previously studied how offline versus online friends retweet. In this study, we define *offline friends* as connections on Twitter who have met outside of the internet. The connections include both reciprocated and unreciprocated connections. Meanwhile, *online friends* are connections on Twitter who have never met outside of the internet.

4   Dataset: Two-Hop Retweet Data

Determining whether each tie involved in a full retweet chain is offline or online is impossible; however we can find out if the ties in a retweet chain in an ego network are offline or online.

Therefore, in this study we use a dataset gathered by Xie et al. [16]. It contains the data of 98 Twitter users, including his ego network in 2011 and the list of his Twitter connections (followers or followees) whom he knows in real life. Overall, the dataset has 20030 Twitter users (ego users and their followers/followees) and 23225 edges labeled as an offline or an online friend. Additionally, we conducted another survey in 2015. We included the new survey data in our dataset. It consists of 41 Twitter users who filled out a survey asking them to label who their offline friends are among a random sample of at most one hundred of their connections (followers/followees) on Twitter.

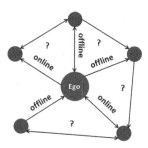

Fig. 1. Ground truth ego networks.

The illustration of the ground truth ego networks can be seen on Fig. 1. From the illustration, the definition of an ego network can be understood clearly. An ego network includes a Twitter user   called *ego user,* depicted by the red circle – and his followers and followees on Twitter. The edges among all of these users are crawled, producing a two-hop follow-networks that are bounded by the ego user and his followers/followees. In the ground truth data, we have the labels of who the offline friends among an ego user's followers or followees are. We procure these labels from the survey answers. However, there is a limitation to our ground truth data. The categories (offline or online) of the edges between the followers or followees of the ego users, are missing. These edges are marked by '?' in Fig. 1. Our experiment and analysis will take into account this limitation.

We crawl the tweets of all the users in our dataset on March 2018. Additionally, we also crawl the latest follow-edges among these users. Temporal changes in offline and online relationships from the year 2011 and 2015 to 2018 can happen. Although those who are offline friends cannot become online by our definition, those who are online friends can become offline. Therefore, the interpretation of the results may downplay the importance of offline friends and exaggerate the importance of online friends.

5   Methodology: Calculating Retweets Depth and Quantifying Retweets Topic

Before proceeding to the methodology, we will recap the issues our research focuses on. In this study, we want to reveal the retweet patterns of offline and online friends on Twitter. Specifically, we want to know the difference in the tweet novelty and retweet topic of offline and online friends. We also want to know whether this difference is greater than the difference between the retweet patterns of reciprocal and unreciprocal friend categories.

However, due to the limitation of the dataset explained in Sect. 4, we cannot analyse the whole retweet chain. Therefore the analyses performed will have the following limitations:

1. We can only analyse retweet patterns that happen among Twitter users in an ego network.
2. We can only analyse retweet patterns that go through public accounts, since their edges cannot be crawled otherwise.
3. Only when a retweet passes from or to an ego user, can we know whether a retweet passes through an edge that represents an offline or an online friendship. If the retweet does not come from or go to an ego user, we will only know whether the retweet passes from an ego user's offline or online friend, to another offline or online friend (See Fig. 1).

Given these limitations, there are seven categories of ties that we analyse in this study.

1. *Offline ties* that represent connections on Twitter who know one another offline.
2. *Online ties* that represent connections on Twitter who do not know one another offline.
3. *Offline-to-offline ties* that represent connections on Twitter between an ego user's offline friend and another offline friend.
4. *Online-to-offline ties* that represent connections on Twitter between an ego user's offline friend and an ego user's online friend.
5. *Online-to-online ties* that represent connections on Twitter between an ego user's online friend and another online friend.
6. *Reciprocated ties* that represent connections on Twitter between two users in which the users follow one another.
7. *Unreciprocated ties* that represent connections on Twitter between two users in which only one user follows another.

As Twitter only reveals the original source of a tweet, and not from whom a retweeter retweets, we must make several assumptions to construct a retweet chain. We use these two:

1. *Latest timing.* Twitter generally arranges feed based on chronological order. Although in the past few years, Twitter shows what it considers as the best tweets for you first, more current material will appear afterwards. The tweet of a user who tweets last will be likely to appear on top. Therefore, it makes sense to assume that the followee of a user who retweets something just before the user retweets, is the source of a retweet. If there are no retweeters in the ego network who retweet before the user retweets, the original source of the retweeted tweet is considered. If the original source is a followee, he is

considered as the source of retweet. Otherwise, the source of the retweet is unknown.

2. *Most popular.* Popular people have a lot of followers. They are also most influential. Therefore, it makes sense to assume that a user's followee who tweets or retweets before the user retweets a tweet, and has the most followers is the source of a retweet. When there are no followees who tweet or retweet before the user does, then the source of the retweet is unknown.

Figure 2 is used to illustrate these two assumptions. In the figure, each level represents the time a tweet is retweeted, with t_0 representing the time when the tweet first originates. Therefore, User B is the original source of tweet. The edges are the follow edges that exist among the nodes. Assuming that there are no other follow edges among the nodes outside the system, User C is the most popular. Based on this configuration, the source of retweet for User D is User A based on the latest timing assumption, and User C based on the most popular assumption.

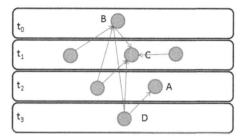

Fig. 2. Illustration of different assumptions for constructing a retweet chain.

In our analysis, we are concerned only with the retweet chain in an ego network. Therefore, all the analyses are based on the assumption that **a retweeter's source of a retweet can only come from the ego network being analysed.** We make such an assumption because we do not know the category of friendship that exists between the source of a retweet outside an ego network and the retweeter, that is, whether it is offline or online. By applying this assumption, we may not get the user who is the true source of a retweet, but we will get the user in an ego network who has the highest likelihood of being the source of a retweet.

In this study, we need to measure tweet novelty and quantify tweet topics. There are two ways to measure tweet novelty. The first is, how far in time the retweeted tweet is from the original tweet. The second is, the depth of the retweet chain. Now, we will explain these measurements sequentially.

5.1 Tweet Novelty by Duration

In measuring tweet novelty by duration, we measure how far in time the retweeted tweet is from the time when the original tweet is published.

5.2   Calculating the Depth of Retweet Chains

The depth of a retweet chain refers to the deepest level of a retweet chain. Each level represents not the time of a retweet, but the sequence of one. The value can change depending on the assumption that we make. If we stack nodes in Fig. 2 by depth level and, not by the time of a retweet, we will come up with Fig. 3. Figure 3 shows the depth level of different assumptions. The depth of the retweet chain is four if we use the latest timing assumption, and three if use the most popular assumption.

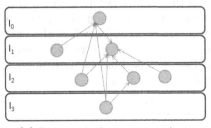

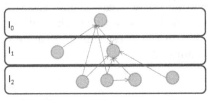

(a) Latest timing assumption.   (b) Most popular assumption.

Fig. 3. Levels of depth given different assumptions.

The depth of a retweet chain represents the greatest degree of separation that can be reached by the source of a tweet. When a retweet chain is made by employing the latest timing assumption, the depth of the retweet chain represents tweet novelty, not in terms of duration, but in terms of the length of the chain of direct or indirect friends among whom the tweet has circulated. The deeper the level at which a user retweets, the longer the tweet has circulated among friends who are directly or indirectly connected to the user.

In this study, we calculate the frequency of different tie categories at each level of depth for each assumption. We symbolize this frequency as f_l^c, where l represents the level of depth, a value that can range from one to infinity and c represents the frequency of ties that belong to the category c.

To ensure that the difference in the frequency of ties used for retweets is not due to the difference in the frequency of ties in the networks, we will normalize the frequency by N_c – the frequency of ties that belong to the category c in the networks. We symbolize the normalized f_l^c as $\hat{f}_l^c$ (See Eq. 1). f_l^c represents the proportion of ties in those networks that belong to category c and are used for retweets.

$$\hat{f}_l^c = \frac{f_l^c}{N_c} \tag{1}$$

5.3   Quantifying Retweet Topics

In this study, we also want to find out how well different tie categories can be distinguished by topics. Therefore, we apply Twitter-LDA [18] to extract topics

Table 1. Extracted topics from tweets.

Code	Topic	Sample words
P0	Sexually explicit words	girl, love, baby, hot, fuck
P1	Shows and videos	live, tonight, youtube, video
P2	Global news	new york, trump, people, news
P3	Singapore politics	singapore, lee, pm, pap
P4	Sports	team, great, chicago, race
P5	Singapore news	people, police, singapore, man
P6	Education and Jobs	students, education, school, work
P7	Global politics	trump, president, obama, india
P8	Stocks	latest, price, bitcoin, usd
P9	Traffic and weather	singapore, time, weather, rain
P10	Fun and socialize	song, tonight, happy, guys
P11	Technology	apple, iphone, app, google
P12	Friends and daily life	people, happy, life, day
P13	Social media	tech, social, google, online
P14	Family and finance	money, day, food, children

from the tweets that are retweeted by various tie categories. From implementing Twitter-LDA to process the tweets, we get out 15 topics that are listed in Table 1.

In addition to churning these 15 topics out, Twitter LDA also produces the distribution of these tweet topics that are retweeted by different tie categories.

6   Results: Categorizing Ties for Retweet

In this Section, we will discuss the results of calculating the depth of the retweet chains and quantifying retweet topics of tweets that belong to different tie categories.

6.1   "Offline Versus Online" as the Category of Ties by Tweet Novelty

Table 2 calculates the normalized frequency of ties that belong to category c at depth level l ($\hat{f}_l^c$) expressed in percentage. c can be offline, online, offline-to-offline, online-to-offline, or online-to-online. Therefore, the value 28.33 in the first cell means that 28.33% of offline ties are used to retweet at depth level 1. A user who retweets at depth level one is the start of a retweet chain.

The results show that there are more depth levels produced when the latest timing assumption is used. The results also demonstrates that a greater percentage of offline ties are used to retweet compared to online ties. Meanwhile, the greatest percentage of ties that are used to retweet are the online-to-online

Table 2. Normalized frequency of ties that belong to the offline-online categories at depth level l ($\hat{f}_l^c$) expressed in percentage.

Depth level	Latest timing assumption				
	Off	On	Off-to-off	On-to-off	On-to-on
1	28.33	17.57	22.93	28.19	58.29
2	2.17	0.55	0.94	0.63	1.98
3	0.09	0.02	0.16	0.06	0.31
4	0.02	0.01	0.06	0.01	0.06
5	0.00	0.00	0.03	0.00	0.01
6	0.00	0.00	0.02	0.00	0.00
7	0.00	0.00	0.01	0.00	0.00
8	0.00	0.00	0.01	0.00	0.00
9	0.00	0.00	0.00	0.00	0.00
10	0.00	0.00	0.00	0.00	0.00
>= 11	0.00	0.00	0.01	0.00	0.00
	Most popular assumption				
1	28.37	17.82	23.27	28.66	59.41
2	1.53	0.32	0.47	0.35	1.18
3	0.02	0.02	0.03	0.01	0.09
4	0.00	0.00	0.01	0.00	0.01
5	0.00	0.00	0.00	0.00	0.00
6	0.00	0.00	0.00	0.00	0.00

ties. However, when the latest timing assumption is used, offline-to-offline ties have the greatest percentage of retweeting ties compared to other ties at the lower depth levels (depth level ≥ 5). Such results indicate that offline-to-offline ties are more likely to retweet older news that has been retweeted by their direct or indirect Twitter friends at earlier times.

A previous study by Natali et al. discovered that a user's offline friends were more highly connected on Twitter than a user's online friends [11]. Therefore, we can conclude that friends who are likely to be offline (offline-to-offline ties) are more likely to retweet older news. Meanwhile, although a Twitter user's online friends are not as connected as their offline friends [11], they are the best circulator of information on Twitter networks at higher depth levels (depth level ≤ 4). These results support Granovetter's theory that strong ties confine information circulation within local clusters [5]. As such, novel news typically comes from weak ties.

However, when we measure the tweet novelty by duration (in weeks), we discover that online ties and online-to-online ties dominate the distribution of tweets across different number of weeks except for the first week when offline ties dominate. The results (See Table 4) show that tweet novelty matters to offline and online friends not so much in terms of duration but in terms of the number of direct and indirect friends among whom the tweet has circulated.

6.2 "Offline Versus Online" as the Category of Ties by Topic

We plot the topic distribution of tweets retweeted by ties that belong to the offline-online categories on Fig. 4. Twitter-LDA gives us f_t^c, the frequency of tweets of topic t retweeted by ties belonging to category c. We normalize the frequency by f_t, the total frequency of tweets of topic t.

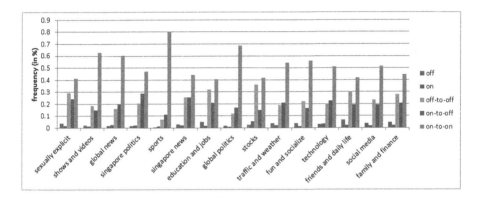

Fig. 4. Frequency of tweets by offline-online categories.

Across all topics, online-to-online ties dominate retweets, confirming the results in Sect. 6.1 that show these types of ties prompt the most retweets. The results also demonstrate that a high frequency of offline ties usually indicates a high frequency of offline-to-offline ties. This phenomenon appears in many topics, including "sexually explicit", "shows and videos", "education and jobs", "fun and socialize", "friends and daily life", "social media", and "family and finance". We conclude that these topics are more likely retweeted by offline ties, or the friends a user engages with outside of the internet.

Additionally, "global news", "Singapore politics", "sports", and "technology" are topics that are likely to be retweeted by online-to-offline ties or online ties. Meanwhile, other topics point to mixed results. Although the topics of "Singapore news", "global politics", and "traffic and weather" are more likely to be retweeted by offline ties than online ties, they are more likely to be retweeted by online-to-offline ties than offline-to-offline ties. Meanwhile, although the topic "stocks" is more likely to be retweeted by online ties than offline ties, it is more likely to be retweeted by offline-to-offline ties than online-to-offline ties.

When we compare these results to the research work conducted by Natali et al. [10], we can see some similarities as well as discrepancies. Natali et al. discovered that personal tweets were more likely to be disseminated through the stronger ties (reciprocated ties). In our study, personal topics such as "fun and socialize", "friends and daily life", and "family and finance", are also more likely to be disseminated through stronger ties (offline ties). However, while Natali et al. showed that entertainment tweets were more likely to be circulated through weaker ties (unreciprocated ties), our study demonstrates that entertainment-focused topics ("shows and videos") are more likely to be circulated by stronger ties (offline ties). Yet, a different entertainment topic, "sports" is more likely to be disseminated by weaker ties (online ties).

6.3 "Reciprocated Versus Unreciprocated" as the Category of Ties by Tweet Novelty

In order to discover how the different retweet patterns of "offline versus online" ties compare to those observed in "reciprocated versus unreciprocated" ties, we must analyse the retweet patterns of reciprocated and unreciprocated ties using the same dataset. Table 3 calculates the normalized frequency of ties that belong to category c at depth level l ($\hat{f}_l^c$) expressed in percentage. c can be reciprocated or unreciprocated.

The results (See Table 3) show that at all depth levels a higher percentage of reciprocated ties are used to retweet when compared to unreciprocated ties. At level one, the percentage is even greater than one hundred, meaning that on average, each tie is used more than one time to retweet. It is also important to remember that the information that flows through reciprocated ties can go two ways, naturally increasing the likelihood of any information passing through. However, even if we increase the frequency of unreciprocated ties in Table 3 by a factor of two, the frequency of reciprocated ties that is used to retweet is still higher at all depth levels.

Similarly, when duration of tweet (in weeks) is used to measure novelty, reciprocated tie dominates the distribution of tweets (See Table 5 in the Appendix).

Therefore, we cannot distinguish reciprocated-unreciprocated ties by tweet novelty, unlike how we can distinguish offline-online ties.

6.4 "Reciprocated Versus Unreciprocated" as the Category of Ties by Topic

We plot the topic distribution of tweets retweeted by ties that belong to the reciprocated-unreciprocated categories on Fig. 5. Twitter-LDA gives us f_t^c, that is the frequency of tweets of topic t retweeted by ties that belong to category c. We normalize the frequency by f_t, the total frequency of tweets of topic t.

Across all topics, reciprocated ties are used more than unreciprocated ties to retweet. Although these results contradict the results of the research by Natali et al. [10], they are not necessarily invalidated because the dataset used in this study is different than the one used by Natali et al. The contexts of the two studies are also different. In this study we examine the retweets in ego networks, whereas Natali et al. analysed the retweets that span beyond an ego network within a time period.

Table 3. Normalized frequency of ties that belong to the reciprocated-unreciprocated categories at depth level l ($\hat{f}_l^c$) expressed in percentage.

Depth level	Latest timing assumption	
	Reciprocated	Unreciprocated
1	137.25	24.88
2	6.89	0.57
3	1.12	0.11
4	0.28	0.03
5	0.12	0.01
6	0.06	0.00
7	0.03	0.00
8	0.02	0.00
9	0.01	0.00
10	0.01	0.00
>= 11	0.02	0.00
	Most popular assumption	
1	141.41	25.23
2	4.13	0.31
3	0.25	0.04
4	0.03	0.00
5	0.01	0.00
6	0.00	0.00

In conclusion, reciprocated-unreciprocated ties also cannot be distinguished by topics just as how they cannot be distinguished by tweet novelty. Meanwhile, offline-online ties can be distinguished by both criteria.

6.5 Putting It All Together: "Offline or Not and Reciprocated or Not" as Categories of Ties

We also want to know whether combinations of the above tie categories will improve the categorization of ties by making each category more distinguishable from one another.

Table 6 in the Appendix calculates the normalized frequency of ties that belong to category c at depth level l ($\hat{f}_l^c$) expressed in percentage. c can be any of the 10 categories made by combining the offline-online categories and the reciprocated-unreciprocated categories.

The results show that reciprocated-unreciprocated categories can help to explain the behaviours of ties in retweeting. At depth level one, a higher percentage of unreciprocated ties is used to retweet compared to reciprocated ties, regardless of which offline-online categories the ties belong to. Meanwhile, at the

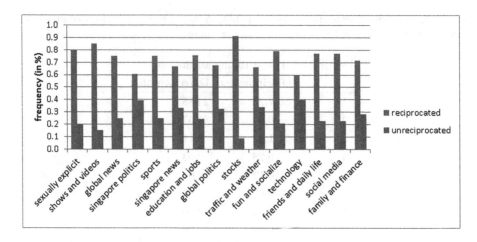

Fig. 5. Frequency of tweets by reciprocated-unreciprocated categories.

depth level two, a higher percentage of reciprocated ties is used to retweet. The results for level three and four are mixed. For some categories a higher percentage of reciprocated ties retweets more, while for other categories a higher percentage of unreciprocated ties retweet more. At the level beyond five, reciprocated offline-to-offline ties are the ones mostly used for retweet.

The results can be explained by the theory of weak ties [5]. At depth level one most tweets are novel, and therefore, the weaker (unreciprocated) ties of each offline-online category are used to retweet. Meanwhile, at depth level five and above, the tweets are old, and therefore, reciprocal offline-to-offline, the strongest category of ties is used to retweet. Although offline-online categories alone cannot distinguish retweet behaviour at depth level one, combinations of offline-online and reciprocal-unreciprocal categories can do so.

Meanwhile, when we look at the tweet novelty in terms of duration (in weeks), a different pattern emerges. Although tweets at week one are also circulated mainly by unreciprocated ties, offline-to-offline ties do not dominate the circulation of old tweets. Therefore, duration of tweets in weeks is again shown not to be as good as the depth of retweet chains to influence the types of ties used.

We also plot the topic distribution of tweets retweeted by ties that belong to the combined categories. We do not show the figure on this paper due to the page limit. Moreover, the results are also inconsequential. In the combined categories, offline-reciprocated and online-unreciprocated ties are more likely to be retweeted across all topics. We can conclude that combined categories cannot be distinguished by topics as well as the offline-online categories can be.

6.6   The Effect of Temporal Changes in Offline/Online Relationships

As we have explained on Section Dataset, temporal changes in offline and online relationships from the year 2011 and 2015 to 2018 can happen. Therefore, the interpretation of the results may downplay the importance of offline friends and exaggerate the importance of online friends. In summary, offline friends are proven to be more important than what the results show in circulating older news and personal tweets. Meanwhile, the huge importance of online-to-online ties in circulating news may be exaggerated.

7 Conclusion

Overall, we have analysed the retweet patterns, specifically tweet novelty and tweet topics, of offline and online ties on Twitter ego networks. We compare our results with the analysis of retweet patterns of reciprocal and unreciprocal ties. We have shown that offline ties and friends who are likely to be offline (offline-to-offline ties) are the ones who tweet old news. The age of tweets should be measured by how many times they have been circulated among direct and indirect friends on Twitter, not by duration. However, in general, online-to-online ties play the most important role in circulating information on Twitter.

Offline ties are also more likely to retweet about family and friends, while online ties are more likely to retweet news. On the other hand, reciprocated and unreciprocated ties show similar retweet patterns. Hence, offline versus online is a more reliable tie category with regard to retweets than reciprocated versus unreciprocated. In terms of practical application, someone who wants to increase a tweet's shelf life and popularise personal tweets should focus more effort on targeting offline friends. On the other hand, online ties should be harnessed for any new marketing compaigns. Our study highlights the importance of the offline-online network paradigm for retweets that cannot be replaced easily, such as by the reciprocated-unreciprocated network paradigm.

A Appendix: Supplementary Results

Table 4. Normalized frequency of ties that belong to the offline-online categories at week w expressed in percentage.

Week	Latest timing assumption				
	Off	On	Off-to-off	On-to-off	On-to-on
1	32.21	28.00	27.33	41.96	83.39
2	0.28	0.37	0.20	0.39	0.68
3	0.08	0.14	0.08	0.13	0.30
4	0.06	0.12	0.05	0.08	0.16
5	0.04	0.08	0.04	0.05	0.14
6	0.02	0.03	0.02	0.05	0.10
>=7	0.33	0.78	0.30	0.79	2.40
	Most popular assumption				
1	31.50	28.03	26.89	42.14	83.45
2	0.26	0.37	0.19	0.39	0.69
3	0.07	0.14	0.07	0.12	0.31
4	0.05	0.12	0.05	0.08	0.16
5	0.04	0.08	0.04	0.05	0.14
6	0.02	0.03	0.02	0.04	0.10
>=7	0.32	0.77	0.30	0.79	2.40

Table 5. Normalized frequency of ties that belong to the reciprocated-unreciprocated categories at week w expressed in percentage.

Week	Latest timing assumption	
	Reciprocated	Unreciprocated
1	140.02	24.99
2	1.25	0.14
3	0.47	0.06
4	0.24	0.04
5	0.20	0.02
6	0.14	0.01
>= 7	2.79	0.33
	Most popular assumption	
1	140.74	24.96
2	1.27	0.14
3	0.48	0.05
4	0.24	0.04
5	0.20	0.02
6	0.14	0.01
>= 7	2.72	0.37

Table 6. Normalized frequency of ties that belong to the combined categories at depth level l ($\hat{f}_l^c$) expressed in percentage.

Depth level	Latest timing assumption									
	Reciprocated					Unreciprocated				
	Off	On	Off-to-off	Off-to-on	On-to-on	Off	On	Off-to-off	Off-to-on	On-to-on
1	26.96	8.03	23.05	19.97	53.06	45.85	32.80	22.17	44.54	70.24
2	2.29	0.49	1.00	0.67	2.27	0.62	0.64	0.59	0.55	1.31
3	0.09	0.01	0.17	0.07	0.34	0.21	0.05	0.06	0.05	0.23
4	0.02	0.01	0.06	0.01	0.07	0.07	0.01	0.03	0.01	0.05
5	0.00	0.00	0.04	0.00	0.01	0.00	0.00	0.00	0.00	0.01
6	0.01	0.00	0.02	0.00	0.00	0.00	0.01	0.01	0.00	0.00
7	0.00	0.00	0.01	0.00	0.00	0.00	0.00	0.00	0.00	0.00
8	0.00	0.00	0.01	0.00	0.00	0.00	0.00	0.00	0.00	0.00
9	0.01	0.00	0.00	0.00	0.00	0.00	0.00	0.00	0.00	0.00
10	0.00	0.00	0.00	0.00	0.00	0.00	0.00	0.00	0.00	0.00
>= 11	0.00	0.00	0.01	0.00	0.00	0.00	0.00	0.00	0.00	0.00
	Most popular assumption									
1	27.07	8.01	23.41	20.39	53.99	45.02	33.50	22.34	45.11	71.81
2	1.63	0.37	0.50	0.37	1.31	0.34	0.25	0.32	0.29	0.89
3	0.03	0.02	0.04	0.01	0.08	0.00	0.03	0.02	0.00	0.13
4	0.00	0.01	0.01	0.00	0.01	0.00	0.00	0.00	0.00	0.02
5	0.00	0.00	0.00	0.00	0.00	0.00	0.00	0.00	0.00	0.00
6	0.00	0.00	0.00	0.00	0.00	0.00	0.00	0.00	0.00	0.00

References

1. Backstrom, L., Kleinberg, J.: Romantic partnerships and the dispersion of social ties: a network analysis of relationship status on Facebook. In: Proceedings of the 17th ACM Conference on Computer Supported Cooperative Work and Social Computing (CSCW 2014), pp. 831–841. ACM (2014)
2. Boyd, D., Golder, S., Lotan, G.: Tweet, tweet, retweet: conversational aspects of retweeting on Twitter. In: The 43th Hawaii International Conference on System Sciences (HICSS 2010), pp. 1–10. IEEE Publishing (2010)
3. Enli, G.S., Skogerbø, E.: Personalized campaigns in party-centred politics. Inf. Commun. Soc. **16**(5), 757–774 (2013)
4. Gilbert, E., Karah, K.: Predicting tie strength with social media. In: Proceedings of the SIGCHI Conference on Human Factors in Computing Systems (CHI 2009), pp. 211–220. ACM (2009)
5. Granovetter, M.S.: The strength of weak ties. Am. J. Sociol. **78**(6), 1360–1380 (1973)
6. Java, A., Song, X., Finin, T., Tseng, B.: Why we Twitter: understanding microblogging usage and communities. In: Proceedings of the 9th WebKDD and 1st SNA-KDD 2007 Workshop on Web Mining and Social Network Analysis (KDD 2007), pp. 59–65. ACM (2007)
7. Kupavskii, A., et al.: Prediction of retweet cascade size over time. In: Proceedings of the 21st ACM International Conference on Information and Knowledge Management, pp. 2335–2338. ACM Press (2012)
8. Kwak, H., Lee, C., Park, H., Moon, S.: What is Twitter, a social network or a news media? In: Proceedings of the 19th International Conference on World wide web (WWW 2010), pp. 591–600. ACM Press (2010)

9. Marsden, P.V., Campbell, K.E.: Measuring tie strength. Soc. Forces **63**(2), 482–501 (1984)

10. Natali, F., Carley, K.M., Zhu, F., Huang, B.: The role of different tie strength in disseminating different topics on a microblog. In: Proceedings of the 2017 IEEE/ACM International Conference on Advances in Social Networks Analysis and Mining (ASONAM 2017), pp. 203–207. ACM (2017)

11. Natali, F., Zhu, F.: A comparison of fundamental network formation principles between offline and online friends on Twitter. In: Wierzbicki, A., Brandes, U., Schweitzer, F., Pedreschi, D. (eds.) NetSci-X 2016. LNCS, vol. 9564, pp. 169–177. Springer, Cham (2016). https://doi.org/10.1007/978-3-319-28361-6_14

12. Peng, H.k., Zhu, J., Piao, D., Yan, R., Zhang, Y.: Retweet modeling using conditional random fields. In: IEEE 11th International Conference conference on Data Mining Workshops (ICDMW 2011), pp. 336–343. IEEE Computer Society (2011)

13. Shi, G., Shi, Y., Chan, A.K., Wang, Y.: Relationship strength in service industries. Int. J. Market Res. **51**(5), 659–685 (2009)

14. Suh, B., Hong, L., Pirolli, P., Chi, E.H.: Want to be retweeted? large scale analytics on factors impacting retweet in twitter network. In: Proceedings of the 2010 IEEE Second International Conference on Social Computing, pp. 177–184. IEEE Publishing (2010)

15. Thomases, H.: Twitter Marketing: An Hour a Day. Wiley, New Jersey (2009)

16. Xie, W., Li, C., Zhu, F., Lim, E.P., Gong, X.: When a friend in Twitter is a friend in life. In: The 4th ACM Web Science Conference (WebSci 2012), pp. 344–347. ACM (2012)

17. Zhao, J., Wu, J., Feng, X., Xiong, H., Xu, K.: Information propagation in online social networks: a tie-strength perspective. Knowl. Inf. Syst. **32**(3), 589–608 (2012)

18. Zhao, W.X., et al.: Comparing Twitter and traditional media using topic models. In: Clough, P., et al. (eds.) ECIR 2011. LNCS, vol. 6611, pp. 338–349. Springer, Heidelberg (2011). https://doi.org/10.1007/978-3-642-20161-5_34

Network Analysis of Anti-Muslim Groups on Facebook

Megan Squire[✉] [iD]

Elon University, Elon, NC 27244, USA
msquire@elon.edu

Abstract. Islamophobic attitudes and overt acts of hostility toward Muslims in the United States are increasingly commonplace. The goal of this research is to begin to understand how anti-Muslim political groups use the Facebook social network to build their own online communities, and to investigate crossover with other far-right political ideologies, such as anti-immigrant or white nationalist groups. We used the public Facebook Graph API to create a large dataset of 700,204 members of 1,870 Facebook groups spanning 10 different far-right ideologies during the time period June 2017–March 2018. We then applied social network analysis techniques to discover which groups and ideologies shared members with anti-Muslim groups during this period. Our results show that anti-Muslim groups serve as an "ideological center" for several other categories of far-right extremism.

Keywords: Data mining · Social media · Online communities
Social network analysis · Facebook · Ideological extremism · Islamophobia
Anti-Muslim · Anti-immigrant · Nativism

1 Introduction

In 2016, data provided by the United States Federal Bureau of Investigation (FBI) shows that the number of hate crimes committed against Muslims in the United States increased 40% over the prior year, surpassing 2001 levels for the first time [1]. Surveys by Pew Research indicate that Islamophobia and anti-Muslim bias is on the rise generally in the population as well, with 69% of US adults - and 75% of Muslims - reporting that there is "a lot" of discrimination against Muslims in America [2]. Also in 2016, businessman and television celebrity Donald J. Trump ran for US President on an explicitly anti-immigrant, anti-Muslim platform, and took action almost immediately after his inauguration to bring his nativist policies into effect. Within days of being elected, his administration issued a travel ban against Muslim-majority countries, and signed executive orders taking a hard line on immigration generally, and deportations of undocumented immigrants in particular [3].

© Springer Nature Switzerland AG 2018
S. Staab et al. (Eds.): SocInfo 2018, LNCS 11185, pp. 403–419, 2018.
https://doi.org/10.1007/978-3-030-01129-1_25

Riding this wave of perceived popular support for nativist ideas, in June of 2017, groups such as Act for America [4] and Proud Boys [5] started holding anti-Muslim rallies in cities across the United States. Billed as "anti-sharia law" rallies, the organizers claimed that they were simply speaking out against a fear that Islamic religious law could possibly "creep" into the country and supplant the established American legal code [6]. By December 2017 anti-Muslim groups had introduced 23 new "creeping sharia" or "anti-sharia law" bills into 18 state legislatures [7] and two of these laws were passed, in Arkansas and Texas.

The goal of this research is to understand both the ideological construction of the anti-Muslim political movement in the US during this volatile period, as well as its crossover and coordination with sympathetic nativist groups and ideologies. To investigate the overlap in ideologies and group membership in the nativist far-right, we decided to look at a popular place for coordinating extremist social activity: Facebook. We began in June 2017 by collecting data from a wide variety of extremist groups and events, including the membership rosters of 1,870 groups from 10 different far-right political ideologies. We then used network analysis techniques to understand these groups better. The main contribution of this work is the analysis of this data as a social network, showing the crossover between ideologies, and between groups within those ideologies, with particular attention to anti-Muslim groups.

Section 2 introduces the data set, including the process used to collect and store it, and the classification of groups and events into ideologically distinct divisions. Section 3 presents the method and results for social network analysis of group-level and ideological co-membership. A discussion of how these results extend prior scholarship follows in Sect. 4. Section 5 reviews some of the limitations of this approach and suggests avenues for future work with this data. Section 6 reviews the findings and conclusions.

2   Data Set

This project is based on a large data set of far-right extremist groups using the Facebook social network during the period June 2017–March 2018. The data set is comprised of 1,843 Facebook groups and 27 events from 10 different far-right ideologies. Descriptions of each far-right ideology came from two US-based not-for-profit extremist monitoring groups: The Southern Poverty Law Center (SPLC) [8] and The Anti-Defamation League (ADL) [9]. The data set includes the ten extremist ideologies that were the most prevalent in both real-world organizing and on Facebook itself during the 2017–2018 time period. To give a sense of the differences between ideologies, a few example keywords and concepts are listed in Table 1 below, along with references to the SPLC and ADL descriptions of each ideology.

Table 1. Five target ideologies and descriptions.

Ideology	Description/Concepts
Anti-Muslim	Anti-Muslim groups oppose the religion of Islam and are hostile to its adherents. Key groups and concepts include: ACT 4 America/ACT!, American Infidels, Bikers Against Radical Islam, creeping Sharia, Stop Islamization of America, Brigitte Gabriel [11, 12]
Neo-confederate	Neo-Confederate groups advocate secession from the United States, the creation of a separate state based in the American South, reverence for and valorization of Southern historical revisionism and symbols from the Civil War era such as the Confederate Flag [13, 14]
Anti-government/ "Patriot"/Militia	Militias are non-professional armies. Anti-Government groups promote conspiracy theories involving perceived government overreach. Concepts include: New World Order, Agenda 21, FEMA concentration camps, The Turner Diaries, militias, extreme traditional constitutionalism. Examples of groups include: Oath Keepers, Patriot Militias, Three Percent/3%/III% [15–17]
Anti-immigrant	These groups oppose immigration into the United States as well as the immigrants themselves. Some believe there exists a government conspiracy to unify Mexico and the United States in a "North American Union". Key groups, concepts, and personalities include: Center for Immigration Studies, ALIPAC, Federation for American Immigration Reform (FAIR), The Remembrance Project, nativism, border patrols, border guards, Plan de Aztlan, North American Union, David Horowitz, Glen Spencer [18, 19]
White nationalist	White Nationalist groups promote white supremacist, white separatist, or racist ideologies. Key concepts include white European ethno-nationalism, race realism, white pride, RaHoWa (racial holy war), racist Asatru/folkish beliefs, racist skinhead culture, racist prison gangs, Ku Klux Klan [20–22]

For space reasons, Table 1 only shows the five ideologies that are the subject of this particular study: anti-Muslim, neo-Confederate, white nationalist, anti-government/ militia, and anti-immigrant. (Other ideologies in the overall data set include: neo-Nazi, anti-Semitic, Proud Boys/Alt-Knights, alt-right, and misogynist/manosphere, which have been discussed in prior work [10]).

For this paper, we chose to focus a subset of ideologies for two reasons. First, these five ideologies were the largest in our data set in terms of either the number of people adhering to them or due to the number of groups in them. Table 2 will explore this in more detail. Second, these five ideologies were the ones that most exemplified the nativist and isolationist attitudes that rose to prominence during the 2016 election and afterward, and thus were the most likely to be associated with anti-Muslim viewpoints as well. We describe this finding in more detail in Table 3.

2.1 Ideological Classification

The primary ideology for each group or event was determined by visually inspecting its name, its description, its cover photo, its content (for Public groups only), its linked

Pages (for linked groups only), and its stated affiliation with extremist groups. Two expert panels were convened to check both the validity of these ideological categories and the soundness of our classification of the groups and events into the categories. One expert panel was comprised of subject matter experts from a non-profit extremist monitoring organization. The other panel was comprised of subject matter experts from a community-based watchdog group. Each panel independently reviewed the classification of the groups and events using the descriptions shown in Table 1.

2.2 Finding Groups and Events

Finding Groups. Finding groups matching these ideologies was accomplished by:

(1) Keyword searching using the browser-based Facebook "search box" feature,
(2) Automated keyword searching using the Facebook Search API,
(3) Using the "Suggested Groups" feature within Facebook,
(4) Accessing the visible group lists attached to the timelines of heavy users within each ideology,
(5) Using the "Linked Groups" feature provided by some Facebook Pages.

Groups and events were only collected if the name or description were in the English language, and groups that were clearly designed to represent users from non-US countries or regions were ignored. On Facebook, groups can be set up as one of three types [23]:

(1) Public, where the content and membership lists are viewable by anyone,
(2) Closed, where the group descriptions and (at least until June 2018) the membership lists were viewable by anyone, but content (such as posts and photos) is viewable by group members only,
(3) Secret, where the group information, content, and membership list are only viewable by members of the group.

For this project, group names, descriptions, and membership lists were collected from both Public and Closed groups.

Finding Events. Facebook events can be one of two types [24]:

(1) Public, where anyone can search for the event and the guest list may or may not be visible, or
(2) Private, where only invited guests can see the event.

Events have three classifications of guests:

(1) Going, indicating a positive response,
(2) Interested, indicating a maybe response, or
(3) Invited, indicating that the person has been issued an invitation but has not responded.

For this project, information was collected from Public events with visible guest lists, and only for respondents who had proactively indicated they were either Going or Interested. No lists of Invited participants were collected.

2.3   Group and Event Membership Roster Collection

Once the groups and events were selected and assigned to a primary ideology, the Facebook Graph API version 2.10 was used to collect group and event membership rosters. Until June 2018, the membership rosters for both Public and Closed groups and Public events were publicly viewable in any browser or via the Facebook app, and until April 4, 2018 these were also available via the Facebook developer API to anyone with a valid authentication token [25]. The API required only the unique group or event identification number and a valid developer token, and in return, the API yielded the list of current members for that group or event, including the user's display name and a unique user identification number called the *app_scoped_user_id*. Because users have the same *app_scoped_user_id* for each group or event that they are in, it is possible to connect users across multiple groups.

It is also possible to keep track of the changes to the group or event roster over time. Each time a roster of a group or event was collected, that activity was assigned a new collection number. The first collection activity was performed on June 20, 2017 and the final collection activity was performed on March 31, 2018. Over the course of this phase of the project, there were 5,059 different collection activities. Most groups and events were collected at least twice.

Sometimes it was not possible to collect the roster from a group or event more than once. There are multiple possible reasons for this. First, extremist groups and events are sometimes removed from Facebook for violating its community standards [26]. (It is important to note that when a group disappears, that has no effect on the data already collected, but it does preclude the collection of additional data for that group or event). Second, a group which was initially Closed could be made Secret, thus making it impossible to collect the membership roster using this method.

In constructing this data set, we followed Facebook's data collection policy, including using the Developer API and otherwise abiding by its Terms of Service and Platform Policy for data use [27]. Additionally, our app did not request or receive any private information from users themselves; we only asked Facebook itself via its API for the membership rosters of groups and events for which those rosters were already publicly viewable.

Table 2 (next page) shows the relative sizes for all ten ideologies in the master data set. The five target ideologies used in this study are highlighted with asterisks. The table provides the count of groups or events in each ideology, as well as the total number of people who were in one or more groups within that ideology. The last column shows the average number of groups joined by each adherent to that ideology. Neo-Confederate adherents tend to join the most Neo-Confederate groups, with an average of 1.7 groups per person. Neo-Nazi adherents tend to join the smallest number of other neo-Nazi groups (1.1 groups per person).

In the next section we begin to analyze the data by building a social network to show ideological crossover between these five ideologies, with a focus on the anti-Muslim groups in particular.

Table 2. Ideologies and counts, five target ideologies shown with *.

Ideology	Count of groups	Count of group members	Largest group size	Mean group size	Avg. count of groups
* Neo-Confederate	453	182,621	19,447	662	1.7
* White nationalist	379	73,582	14,712	233	1.3
* Anti-Gov/ Militia	273	101,211	11,509	473	1.3
* Anti-Muslim	136	128,467	17,824	1,270	1.4
* Anti-immigrant	51	115,511	51,117	2,823	1.2
Alt-Right	246	99,996	36,666	587	1.5
Proud Boys/ Alt-Knights	157	7,920	1,348	72	1.5
Manosphere	82	36,435	8,658	643	1.6
Neo-Nazi	48	6,218	1,251	139	1.1
Anti-semitic	45	16,498	9,310	400	1.2

3   Network Analysis and Visualization

In order to begin to understand ideological crossover between extremist groups, and how that relates specifically to an anti-Muslim context, we will first examine the degree to which members of the groups participate in other ideologies, then we will visualize this crossover using social network analysis.

3.1   Quantifying Ideological Crossover

Table 3 shows the rate at which the adherents of our ten ideologies participate in other ideologies. The table again highlights our five target ideologies with asterisks.

Table 3 reveals that the neo-Confederates are some of the *least* likely to participate in other ideologies (only 19% are multi-issue participants). Anti-government, anti-Muslim, and anti-immigrant ideological adherents participate in other ideologies at a rate of between 26% and 33%, while white nationalists cross ideological boundaries at a rate of 39%.

When a user cross ideological boundaries to participate in another ideology, which one do they choose? And at what rate? Table 4 shows the ideological crossover that occurs in this data set.

Table 3. Counts and percentages of multi-issue and single-issue users, by ideology.

Ideology	Count of people	Count of multi-issue	Count of single-issue	Percent of multi-issue	Percent of single-issue
* Neo-confederate	182,621	34,404	148,217	19%	81%
* White nationalist	73,582	28,449	45,133	39%	61%
* Anti-Gov/ Militia	101,211	32,921	68,290	33%	67%
* Anti-Muslim	128,467	38,051	90,416	30%	70%
* Anti-immigrant	115,511	29,665	85,846	26%	74%
Alt-Right	99,996	20,937	79.059	21%	79%
Proud Boys/ Alt-Knights	7,920	2,950	4,970	37%	63%
Manosphere	36,435	5,711	30,724	16%	84%
Neo-Nazi	6,218	3,555	2,663	57%	43%
Anti-semitic	16,498	3,988	12,510	24%	76%

Table 4. Ideological crossover among multi-issue users, top five ideologies only.

Smaller ideology (by people count)	Larger ideology	Count of shared members	Shared members as % of smaller ideology
Anti-immigrant	Anti-Muslim	17,959	61%
Anti-government	Neo-confederate	17,002	52%
Anti-government	Anti-Muslim	14,375	44%
Neo-confederate	Anti-Muslim	12,139	35%
White nationalist	Neo-confederate	10,664	37%
White nationalist	Anti-Muslim	10,600	37%
Anti-immigration	Anti-government	10,477	35%
Anti-immigration	Neo-confederate	10,168	34%
White nationalist	Anti-immigration	7,937	28%
White nationalist	Anti-government	7,521	26%

To clarify Table 4, we should again stress that the "smaller" and "larger" designations are based on the total number of multi-issue users in each ideology shown in Table 3. For example, even though Neo-Confederate groups have more total members (182,621), only 34,404 (19%) of these are multi-issue. Anti-Muslim groups have only 128,467 members, but because 38,051 of those are multi-issue, this makes the anti-Muslim multi-issue users a larger set than the neo-Confederate multi-issue users.

When considering membership crossover taken on a percentage basis, consider what percentage of the smaller ideology's multi-issue users is found in the larger ideology's multi-issue users. The range will be between a minimum of 0% (no crossover) and a maximum of 100% (the smaller ideology is a subset of the larger ideology).

We find the largest percentage crossover between anti-immigrant and anti-Muslim groups: 61% of the anti-immigrant multi-issue users will choose an anti-Muslim group in which to participate. In fact, three of the next five highest crossover percentages are for the anti-Muslim ideology. Both white nationalist (yellow) and anti-government (blue) are much closer to anti-Muslim (green) on the graph than they are to each other. Again, this is a confirmation of the figures in Table 4: white nationalists and anti-government crossover is only 26%, but their crossover rates with anti-Muslim are 44% and 37%.

3.2   Visualizing Ideological Crossover

In this section, social network analysis techniques are used to further understand anti-Muslim ideological co-membership.

3.2.1   Ideological Co-membership Within the Social Network

Figure 1 shows a network graph built using the five target ideologies: anti-Muslim, anti-immigrant, white nationalist, neo-Confedcrate, and anti-government.

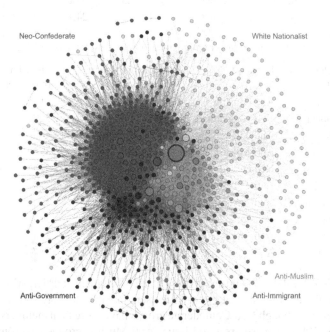

Fig. 1. Social network of Facebook groups with 10 or more members in common, colorized by ideology. Top five largest ideologies shown.

In the figure, each Facebook group or event is shown as a node on the graph, and the edges between the nodes indicate that there are individual members in common between the groups. In order to be included in the network as a node, a group or event must meet two criteria: first, the group must have been classified into one of the five target ideologies, and the group must share at least 10 members in common with at least one other node from those same five ideologies. Given these parameters, we were able to include 839 nodes and 25,853 edges in our social network. Each node in Fig. 1 is colorized by ideology and scaled to reflect its membership size (larger circles mean more users are in the group). Groups are placed in proximity to one another based on how many shared members the groups have in common using the Gephi network analysis software [28] and its implementation [29] of the force directed Fruchterman-Reingold algorithm [30]. For display reasons, edge weights and node labels are not shown in Fig. 1.

The center of the network diagram holds the groups and events with the highest rates of co-membership. It stands to reason that the groups at the center are also some of the larger groups in the collection: having more members means a higher likelihood that a subset of members will have diverse interests.

Nonetheless, this network graph confirms that even when we consider crossover as a percentage of the smaller ideology, as we did in Table 4, there are certain ideologies that are more (or less) natural "fits" with each other. Anti-Muslim (green) and anti-immigrant (pink) groups occupy much of the same space on the network graph, owing to the 61% crossover rate we saw earlier in Table 4. Neo-Confederate groups are numerous and tightly clustered, whereas white nationalist groups are diffused throughout the graph and are less tightly clustered.

3.2.2   Social Network Metrics

In this section we show how standard social network metrics can uncover the structural features of this network.

Node Degree.   First, we examine the connections between nodes, or node *degree*: to how many other nodes is each node in the network connected? Figure 2 shows a histogram of the degrees of all the nodes in the network.

Histogram of Node Degrees

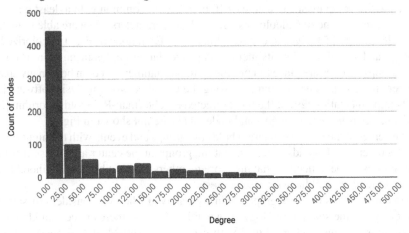

Fig. 2. Histogram of nodes in each degree bin, across all ideologies in the network.

Figure 2 shows that the minimum degree of nodes in this network is 1, the maximum degree is 485, and the mean node degree in this network is 49 (median = 19). The 50th percentile for degree is 20, meaning that half of the nodes in the network connect to 20 or fewer other nodes.

There are five anti-Muslim groups with a degree of 250 or higher, putting them in the 95th percentile for degree. Table 5 shows the ideologies for the other high-degree (95th percentile or higher) nodes. Only the neo-Confederate category stands out for having a large number of the high-degree nodes.

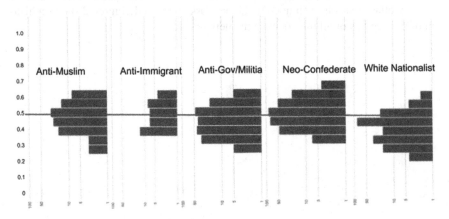

Fig. 3. Histograms of closeness centralities by ideology. Red line shows the 50% mark. Y-axis is log scale for better visibility. (Color figure online)

The reason for this large discrepancy between node degrees is related to the number of groups and mean group sizes presented earlier in Table 2. In short, because there are more neo-Confederate groups to join, and the average number of neo-Confederate groups joined by an adherent to that ideology is higher than the others, its number of interconnected nodes is correspondingly high.

Table 5. Count of nodes with degree higher than the 95th percentile, by ideology.

Ideology	Count of nodes at 95th percentile or higher
Neo-confederate	26
Anti-Muslim	5
Anti-immigrant	5
Anti-government	5
White nationalist	3

Closeness Centrality. Here we attempt to discern the influence of nodes in the network by measuring each node's shortest path to all other nodes in the network. A shortest path is the smallest number of steps to get from node A to node B. *Closeness centrality* as an influence metric asserts that well-connected nodes are more important than remote nodes. Figure 3 shows five different histograms of node closeness centrality – one graph per ideology. Closeness centrality is calculated for each group in the ideology, between 0 (no paths go through this node) and 1 (every path goes through the node). The red line shows the 50% marker. The y-axis is shown using a log scale in order to facilitate comparisons between ideologies of different sizes, and the histograms are shown horizontally in order to minimize space on the page.

The histograms help to confirm an observation made earlier: white nationalist groups are less well-connected compared to the other ideologies. White nationalism had the second highest count of groups in the data set, but these groups tend to have a lower closeness centrality number than the other ideologies.

For closeness centrality, the two top-scoring anti-Muslim groups are highlighted in Fig. 4 (left). One is *Infidel Brotherhood International*, which describes itself as "a group concerned with the islamification [sic] of Western countries and the decline of their values, cultures and identities." The second is called *Stop islamization of America*, or *SIOA*. This group is noteworthy not only because it is fairly large, with 22,000 members as of this writing, but also because its administrator is Pamela Geller, a vocal anti-Muslim activist and author [31, 32]. The Facebook group mirrors an offline version of a group by the same name, created by Geller in 2010 in opposition to the construction of the Park51 Islamic center in Lower Manhattan [33].

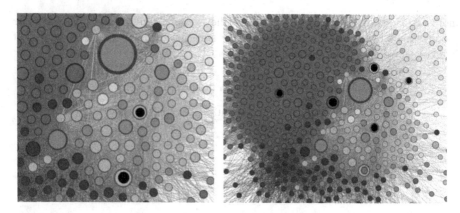

Fig. 4. (Left) Top two highest-scoring anti-Muslim groups for *closeness* centrality, shown in black; (Right) Top five *betweenness* nodes shown in black, and 13th highest node *"Stop islamization of America"*, shown in dark gray.

Betweenness Centrality. Another way to measure influence of a node is its *betweenness centrality*, or the number of the shortest network paths that pass through the node. In other words, how many shortest paths pass through Node A, and is that more or fewer paths than pass through Node B? The more shortest paths pass through Node A, the higher its betweenness measure is. Betweenness is a useful metric because it reveals not just the most popular or largest nodes, but which nodes may be able to tie together far-flung parts of the network.

Of the top five highest-scoring betweenness measures, two are classified as white nationalist, two are neo-Confederate, and one is anti-Muslim. These five nodes are shown with black circles in Fig. 4 (right). The anti-Muslim group we have seen before: *Infidel Brotherhood International*. Recall that this group was also the highest-scoring on centrality measures as well. Further down the betweenness list, the second-highest anti-Muslim scorer (13th overall) is once again the *Stop islamization of America* group. *SIOA* is shown in dark grey on Fig. 4 (right).

It is interesting to note that two of the highest-scoring groups on betweenness measures are classified as white nationalist. One of those is a standard white power group advertising itself as "THE LARGEST WHITE RACE GROUP IN THE WORLD ON SOCIAL MEDIA." (As of November 2017, this group is no longer on Facebook. It is unclear whether it was removed for a violation of Community Standards). The other is a *Sons of Odin* group, whose description states in part that the purpose of their group is explicitly nativist: to defend against "invasion of hostile foreign peoples to our lands." The *Sons of Odin* yellow node has relatively low centrality scores, but high betweenness scores. This means that it could serve as bridge between smaller, fringe white nationalist groups and the rest of this network.

We see a similar "bridge" opportunity with the two anti-Muslim groups that scored the highest on betweenness. Figure 5 shows both the *SIOA* and *Infidel Brotherhood International* (IBI) groups, and which groups they are connected to. *IBI* connects to more white nationalist (yellow) nodes and a slightly larger set of neo-Confederate nodes.

SIOA connects to a different set of militias (blue) and slightly more anti-immigrant (pink) groups.

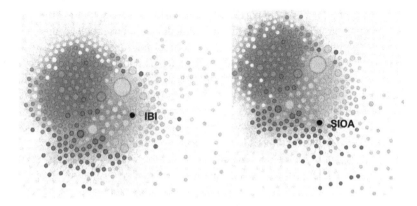

Fig. 5. Comparison of connected groups for two highest-scoring anti-Muslim groups on "betweenness", *SIOA* and *IBI*. (Color figure online)

As future work – discussed more in Sect. 5 – we would like to delve deeper into the groups that serve as bridges between subsets of the network: between white nationalism and anti-Muslim beliefs, or between anti-Muslim and anti-Government ideologies. First, we provide more detail about how our work confirms prior scholarship around anti-Muslim bias.

4   Relationship to Prior Work

Our findings confirm prior qualitative scholarship around how anti-Muslim bias serves as a common denominator among hate groups around the world, and in the United States in particular. For example, Farid Hafez's work explains that Islamophobia is a "common ground" for building unity among far-right groups in Europe, and that anti-Muslim bias and hostility has replaced anti-Semitism as a form of "accepted racism" found in the right-wing and increasingly in centrist politics [34, 35]. Deepa Kumar shows that there exists in the United States a network of anti-Muslim actors – including right-wing politicians, media, think tanks, academics, and security apparatus – that profit from manufactured controversies, such as that perpetrated by *SIOA* regarding the Park51 Islamic Center (a.k.a "the Gound Zero mosque") [36]. Nathan Lean's work on charting the "Islamophobia industry" also bears this out. He reflects on the role of online anti-Muslim activism bluntly: "The role of the Internet in fomenting hatred and prejudice cannot be overstated" [33]. Our work here confirms that there is indeed a network of hate groups operating on social media, and anti-Muslim groups are at its center.

This should not be surprising, given past research on extremism in online spaces. Hale [37] reviewed research on extremist groups using online platforms and concluded that the number of groups using internet communities for recruitment and propaganda has increased over time. De Koster and Houtman [38] determined that extremist groups rely on online communities because stigmatization of their beliefs makes offline organizing impossible. Adams and Roscigno [39] studied how Ku Klux Klan and Neo-Nazi groups use online communities to promote and hone their ideologies, and to recruit new members. Regarding Facebook in particular, Marichal [40] studied politically-oriented Facebook groups and why users create them, concluding that Facebook groups can help users express "political performances that are a form of micro–activism."

Our decision to use social network analysis to understand ideological co-membership in these online spaces is also not without precedent. Kitts [41] described how to use social networks to study actors in offline political movements. His work suggests that co-membership analysis can predict whether participation by one person will positively influence another person towards a movement. Burris, Smith, and Strahm [42] applied social network analysis to a collection of links between white supremacist web sites in order to reveal the latent ideological structure between Neo-Nazis, Holocaust revisionists, Skinheads, and other groups prevalent at the time. Their analysis shows that sharing of links is common between white supremacist web sites from different ideologies, although their work does not attempt to examine shared memberships between these organizations. Similarly, Zhou, et al. [43] and Gerstenfeld, Grant, and Chang [44] use network analysis to study links between extremist web sites to try to discern their ideological structure. Chau and Xu [45] also studied the relationship between 28 hate group blogs on Xanga, revealing a stratified community substructure.

Thus, this application of network analysis to Facebook groups rests on substantial foundation of research in trying to understand how political extremism persists in online communities. The quantitative application to anti-Muslim groups on Facebook is a unique contribution, and one that is particularly relevant in the current political climate.

5   Limitations and Future Work

The goal of this work is to quantify participation in groups from five large far-right extremist ideologies on the Facebook social media platform for ten months using basic summary statistics and network analysis techniques. One important limitation of this study is the potential for errors in the ideological classification of groups. Classification was straightforward for most of the groups, but we are very aware that groups may claim more than one ideology, or that the ideological focus of the group may change over time. Engaging closely with two expert panels helped with this issue a great deal, but it is true that a reclassification of groups could affect our results.

Another limitation of this work is in reproducibility and extension. Facebook blocked access to group or event membership rosters via the API as of April 4, 2018, and no longer allows access to Closed group membership rosters at all as of June 2018. Thus, this data set is now frozen in time, and cannot be expanded.

Nonetheless, there are many avenues for future work on this frozen data set. One interesting possibility is to extend this research by studying the text of the group descriptions and images, such as cover photos, used to promote the groups on Facebook. Embedded in these descriptions and images are some combination of the following: the beliefs of the group, its social norms and expected rules of behavior, its leadership structure, and an indication of what content is expected in the group. We are very interested in studying these aspects of extremist groups, within and across ideologies.

It is also important to take a much closer look at the individual groups responsible for cross-ideological "bridging". Detailed analysis of this network data will uncover even more relationships between ideologies, and the groups responsible for unifying disparate corners of the graph.

6 Conclusion

In reflecting on anti-Semitism in 1946 post-War France, Jean-Paul Sartre wrote that "[t]he Jew only serves [the anti-Semite] as a pretext; elsewhere his counterpart will make use of the Negro or the man of yellow skin…. [I]t is not the Jewish character that provokes anti-Semitism but, rather, that it is the anti-Semite who creates the Jew" [46]. Right-wing extremists in the United States demonize Muslims for similar reasons today: Muslims are the scapegoat *du jour*. If the image of a violent, terrorist Muslim horde did not exist in the United States, a racist and xenophobic far-right would need to create one – perhaps on Facebook.

To understand this phenomenon, and how it extends prior scholarship on far-right political activity on the Internet and social media, we have collected and visualized a large data set of online communities on Facebook. We classified these groups by right-wing extremist ideological subtype and used network analysis techniques to reveal that groups with nativist bias, in particular anti-Muslim groups, are front and center in far-right politics. Our analysis also shows that anti-Muslim groups attract the same audiences as other extremist ideologies, including secessionist neo-Confederates, militant anti-government conspiracy theorists, and racist white nationalists. We show that some of the anti-Muslim groups even serve as a convenient *lingua franca*; their brand of hate is a common denominator that ties people of disparate ideologies together.

Acknowledgements. We want to thank our contacts at the Southern Poverty Law Center and our two panels of experts for their kindness and leadership in answering many questions about the history and ideologies of far-right extremist groups in the United States of America.

References

1. United States Federal Bureau of Investigation: 2016 Hate Crime Statistics. https://ucr.fbi.gov/hate-crime/2016/hate-crime. Accessed 01 May 2018
2. Pew Research Center: U.S. Muslims Concerned About Their Place in Society, but Continue to Believe in the American Dream, 26 July 2017. http://assets.pewresearch.org/wp-content/uploads/sites/11/2017/07/09105631/U.S.-MUSLIMS-FULL-REPORT-with-population-update-v2.pdf
3. Kopan, T.: On immigration, Trump has plenty to show in 100 days. CNN, 27 April 2017. https://cnn.com/2017/04/27/politics/trump-100-days-immigration/index.html. Accessed 01 May 2018

4. Ali, S.S., Gostanian, A., Silva, D.: ACT for America rally. NBC, 10 June 2017. https://nbcnews.com/news/us-news/anti-muslim-act-america-stage-marches-against-sharia-law-nationwide-n767386. Accessed 01 May 2018
5. Proud Boys Magazine: June 10th March Against Sharia. http://officialproudboys.com/news/june-10th-march-against-sharia/. Accessed 08 May 2018
6. Hauslohner, A., Moyer, J.W.: Anti-sharia demonstrators hold rallies in cities across the country. Washington Post, 10 June 2017. https://washingtonpost.com/national/anti-sharia-marches-planned-for-numerous-cities-across-the-country-saturday/2017/06/10/40faf61e-4d6f-11e7-a186-60c031eab644_story.html. Accessed 01 May 2018
7. Pilkington, E.: Anti-sharia laws proliferate as Trump strikes hostile tone toward Muslims. The Guardian, 30 December 2017. https://theguardian.com/us-news/2017/dec/30/anti-sharia-laws-trump-muslims. Accessed 05 May 2018
8. Southern Poverty Law Center: Ideologies. https://splcenter.org/fighting-hate/extremist-files/ideology. Accessed 24 Apr 2018
9. The Anti-Defamation League: Alt Right: A Primer about the New White Supremacy. https://adl.org/education/resources/backgrounders/alt-right-a-primer-about-the-new-white-supremacy. Accessed 24 Apr 2018
10. Squire, M.: Analyzing Far-right extremist Facebook group co-membership during the "Summer of Hate". In: 4th International Conference on Computational Social Science (IC2S2), Evanston, IL, USA, 14 July 2018 (2018)
11. Southern Poverty Law Center: Anti-Muslim. https://splcenter.org/fighting-hate/extremist-files/ideology/anti-muslim. Accessed 24 Apr 2018
12. The Anti-Defamation League: Anti-Muslim Bigotry. https://adl.org/education/resources/backgrounders/anti-muslim-bigotry. Accessed 24 Apr 2018
13. Southern Poverty Law Center: Neo-Confederate. https://splcenter.org/fighting-hate/extremist-files/ideology/neo-confederate. Accessed 24 Apr 2018
14. Hague, E., Beirich, H., Sebesta, E.H.: Neo-Confederacy: A Critical Introduction. University of Texas Press, Austin (2009)
15. Southern Poverty Law Center: Active Patriot Groups in the US in 2016. https://splcenter.org/fighting-hate/intelligence-report/2017/active-patriot-groups-us-2016. Accessed 24 Apr 2018
16. The Anti-Defamation League: The "Patriot" movement. https://adl.org/education/resources/glossary-terms/patriot-movement. Accessed 24 Apr 2018
17. The Anti-Defamation League: Defining Extremism: A Glossary of Anti-Government Extremist Terms, Movements and Philosophies. https://adl.org/education/resources/glossary-terms/defining-extremism-anti-government. Accessed 24 Apr 2018
18. Southern Poverty Law Center: Anti-Immigrant. https://splcenter.org/fighting-hate/extremist-files/ideology/anti-immigrant. Accessed 24 Apr 2018
19. The Anti-Defamation League. Education resources on immigration, immigrants and anti-immigrant bias. https://adl.org/education/resources/tools-and-strategies/education-resources-on-immigration-immigrants-and-anti. Accessed 24 Apr 2018
20. Southern Poverty Law Center: White Nationalist. https://splcenter.org/fighting-hate/extremist-files/ideology/white-nationalist. Accessed 24 Apr 2018
21. Southern Poverty Law Center: Ku Klux Klan. https://splcenter.org/fighting-hate/extremist-files/ideology/ku-klux-klan. Accessed 24 Apr 2018
22. Southern Poverty Law Center: Neo-Volkisch. https://splcenter.org/fighting-hate/extremist-files/ideology/neo-volkisch. Accessed 24 Apr 2018
23. Facebook: What are the privacy settings for groups? https://facebook.com/help/220336891328465. Accessed 05 May 2018

24. Facebook: How do I control who sees or joins my event? https://facebook.com/help/208747122499067. Accessed 05 May 2018
25. Facebook: An update on our plans to restrict data access, 4 April 2018. https://newsroom.fb.com/news/2018/04/restricting-data-access/. Accessed 05 May 2018
26. Facebook: Community Standards. https://facebook.com/communitystandards. Accessed 08 May 2018
27. Facebook: Platform Policy. https://developers.facebook.com/policy. Accessed 08 May 2018
28. Gephi. https://gephi.org
29. Fruchterman   Reingold.   https://github.com/gephi/gephi/wiki/Fruchterman-Reingold. Accessed 28 Apr 2018
30. Fruchterman, T.M., Reingold, E.M.: Graph drawing by force-directed placement. Softw. Pract. Exp. **21**(11), 1129–1164 (1991)
31. Southern Poverty Law Center: Pamela Geller. https://splcenter.org/fighting-hate/extremist-files/individual/pamela-geller. Accessed 05 May 2018
32. Hammer, J.: Center stage: gendered Islamophobia and Muslim women. In: Ernst, C.W. (ed.) Islamophobia in America: The Anatomy of Intolerance, pp. 107–144. Palgrave Macmillan, New York, NY, USA (2013)
33. Lean, N.: The Islamophobia Industry. Pluto Press, London (2012)
34. Hafez, F.: Shifting borders: Islamophobia as common ground for building pan-European right-wing unity. Patt. Prejudice **48**(5), 479–499 (2014)
35. Hafez, F.: Comparing anti-semitism and Islamophobia: the state of the field. Islamophobia Stud. J. **3**(2), 16–34 (2016)
36. Kumar, D.: Islamophobia and the Politics of Empire. Haymarket Books, Chicago (2012)
37. Hale, W.C.: Extremism on the World Wide Web: a research review. Crim. Justice Stud. **25**(4), 343–356 (2012)
38. De Koster, W., Houtman, D.: 'Stormfront is like a second home to me': on virtual community formation by right-wing extremists. Inf. Commun. Soc. **11**(8), 1155–1176 (2008)
39. Adams, J., Roscigno, V.J.: White supremacists, oppositional culture and the World Wide Web. Soc. Forces **85**(2), 759–778 (2005)
40. Marichal, J.: Political Facebook groups: micro-activism and the digital front stage. First Monday (2013). http://firstmonday.org/article/view/4653/3800
41. Kitts, J.: Mobilizing in black boxes: social networks and participation in social movement organizations. Mobilization Int. J. **5**(2), 241–257 (2000)
42. Burris, V., Smith, E., Strahm, A.: White supremacist networks on the Internet. Sociol. Focus **33**(2), 215–235 (2000)
43. Zhou, Y., Reid, E., Qin, J., Chen, H., Lai, G.: U.S. domestic extremist groups on the Web: link and content analysis. IEEE Intell. Syst. **20**(5), 44–51 (2005)
44. Gerstenfeld, P., Grant, D.R., Chang, C.-P.: Hate online: a content analysis of extremist Internet sites. Anal. Soc. Issues Pub. Policy **3**(1), 29–44 (2003)
45. Chau, M., Xu, J.: Mining communities and their relationships in blogs: a study of online hate groups. Int. J. Hum. Comput. Stud. **65**(1), 57–70 (2007)
46. Sartre, J.P.: Anti-Semite and Jew. Schocken Books, New York (1946)

The Evolution of Developer Work Rhythms
An Analysis Using Signal Processing Techniques

Benjamin Traullé[1,2(✉)] and Jean-Michel Dalle[3,4]

[1] École Normale Supérieure de Rennes, Rennes, France
`benjamin.traulle@ens-rennes.fr`
[2] Télécom ParisTech, Paris, France
[3] Sorbonne Université, Paris, France
`jean-michel.dalle@sorbonne-universite.fr`
[4] Oxford Internet Institute, Oxford, OX1 3JS, UK

Abstract. We study the evolution of the work rhythms of software developers. We gather datasets and controls from GitHub, a prominent site among developers, and, with the help of signal processing techniques, we observe two temporal phenomena in the daily patterns (waveforms) related to daily work rhythms: regularization and precession. More regular daily work patterns, and earlier-in-the-day work patterns both appear in parallel to developers spending time in GitHub.

Keywords: Work rhythms · Software developers · GitHub
Signal processing

1 Introduction

Digital environments have contributed to change our attitudes towards work and leisure, which has fostered an active debate about the positive and negative consequences of these evolutions [3,10]. In this relatively heated context, a few recent studies have started to inquire more in-depth about the changes that the new digital environments have induced on our lives, and particularly on our work rhythms, by addressing these issues with empirical datasets. They have observed variable daily and weekly patterns (see below) and gathered interesting preliminary evidences. However, as far as we know, they have not dealt with the *persistence over time* of the new "digital" rhythms. To put it differently, are these changes transient – do they tend to disappear after a few years? For life has its own rhythms, associated with age, experience and varying family contexts, that might also bear heavily of our work rhythms and that could render digital changes non-stationary.

In this paper, we precisely focus on the evolution of the work rhythms of software developers, a population known to be specially affected by the digital revolution [5,9]. We use datasets and controls from GitHub, a well-known site

© Springer Nature Switzerland AG 2018
S. Staab et al. (Eds.): SocInfo 2018, LNCS 11185, pp. 420–438, 2018.
https://doi.org/10.1007/978-3-030-01129-1_26

among developers, and signal processing techniques. We observe both regularization and precession in the daily patterns (waveforms) related to daily work rhythms: over time, GitHub developers tend to adopt more regular and earlier-in-the-day work patterns. More precisely, Sect. 2 surveys the literature related to developer work patterns and to circadian cycles. Section 3 presents datasets and methods, while Sect. 4 shows results from longitudinal studies and on controls before Sect. 5 concludes.

2   Literature Review

2.1   Developer Work Rhythms

Developers work rhythms have recently attracted an increased attention in the context of the digital revolution. The idea according to which developers would work abnormal hours, and often during the night, has notably been of interest not only to the community of developers [16,19] but has also started to motivate research works, for instance in relation to the varying nature of the languages used for programming at day or at night [14]. In a similar vein, Claes et al. [6] have performed the first large-scale study of developer working hours by investigating the timestamps of commits activities of 86 open-source projects, observing that two thirds of software engineers followed typical office hours, though in the context of large variations between projects and individuals.

In an earlier work, Dalle, Daudet and den Besten [8] had also studied work patterns in open-source developer communities, observing for instance a stronger weekend effect in Mozilla compared to gcc. They had done so through an analysis making use of a Fourier transform applied to CVS signals from open-source projects (Mozilla and GCC), i.e. to the series of timestamps of contributions to the code base made by developers. This frequency analysis highlighted in most cases a fundamental peak at *7 commits per week* (1 commit per day) with rays and harmonics associated with regularity in contributions and to weekend effects (Fig. 1).

2.2   Circadian Rhythms

More in general, the analysis of daily activities has provided strong and consistent evidence for the existence of so-called circadian cycles [12]. Aledavood et al. [1], by analyzing the use of smartphones by students of the Technical University of Denmark, have for instance highlighted daily cycles independent of contextual changes for the individuals studied: they observe a double daily peak, and a drop in activity over the weekend. ten Thij et al. [20] have observed similar patterns on Twitter, that are further distinguished by region and language. Begole et al. [4] have also developed a graphical tool derived from physiology and called an "actogram", which basically represents the activity timeline of an individual and allows to more finely study work patterns and variability across individuals.

The existence of regular circadian cycles has further opened the way to studying whether there would exits "chronotypes", i.e. temporal patterns associated

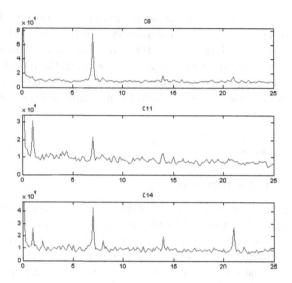

Fig. 1. Frequency analysis of contributors (Mozilla) - Dalle et al. [8].

with different types of individual behavior. Aledavood et al. [2] provided evidence for the existence of two such chronotypes called *owls* and *larks* that were found to be linked to a person's social network, in terms of size, relationships, communications and spatially. Similar to [8], a weekend effect was also observed for scientists [22]; in Twitter [20], where it was observed that the amplitude of the number of tweets decreases at the end of the week before going back up on Sunday, where an exception to this phenomenon was observed among Hebrew-speaking people, where the increase in activity occurs from Saturday and appears to be associated with Shabbat; and on Wikipedia [23].

2.3   Limitations

Most of these studies however, with the exception of [8], rely on temporal analysis and are therefore limited notably with respect to investigating changes over time. Typically, although Claes et al. [6] start to address this issue, they appear to be limited by their methodology as it imposes very strong hypothesis and benchmarks, such as setting 8-hour working day, and since it does not easily allow for the identification of sub-populations between large and more limited contributors, while the work patterns of the latter might typically be affected by other occupations.

Such a limitation is in a sense surprising considering the large array of available signal processing techniques, and specially spectral analysis, which in their very nature stand as potentially powerful tools that could make it possible to quickly extract from social signals aggregate information about frequencies and intensities, and to interpret it both in terms of redundancies or singularities.

In this paper, we try to move in this direction and to provide evidence for the potential of signal processing techniques when applied to social signals, by analyzing the longitudinal evolutions over time of the work rhythms of software developers in GitHub.

3 Datasets and Methods

We retrieved our datasets from GitHub. GitHub is a web-based hosting service launched in 2008 dedicated to the version control of software projects and that uses git, a solution developed by Linus Torvalds, the creator of Linux. It is extremely popular among developers and most notably among open-source software developers. It works through repositories and notably through "commits", the word used to characterize actual actions on the code base, such as additions, deletions or modifications. As a consequence, GitHub and notably commits have already been used to understand how developers work and work together. Dabbish et al. [7] have typically highlighted the social interactions that appear between developers and Tsay et al. [21] have provided further evidence that contributions and management within a project are related to social and technical information available among peers and therefore in the social network. In a different vein, Guzman et al. [11] have for instance analyzed empirically the commentaries to the commits, in order to point out the emotions of the developers depend on the day the commit is made and on the programming language.

3.1 Datasets

The first of our datasets (Case 1) is composed of all the commits by 100 large developers from France and the United Kingdom (respectively), observed longitudinally from 2012 to 2017, aggregating all the projects that they are working on. The second dataset (Case 2) will focus on 100 developers selected randomly each year from the sub-population of large developers, again both in France and the United Kingdom. In both cases, large developers are developers with contributions to more than 50 different GitHub projects (code repositories), in order to methodologically ensure that development in GitHub is their main focus, and therefore that we are not missing part of their activity that would take place elsewhere and bias our analysis. We studied both French and English developers in order to enhance the validity of our study beyond cultural differences (see also Sect. 4.3). More precisely:

– Longitudinal developer study in France and the UK (Case 1). This dataset is composed of data on 100 French developers and 100 English developers, each contributing to more than 50 repositories in 2017. These 2×100 developers were selected as those who had made the most numerous contributions in 2017. The timestamps of commits by each of the developers from January

1, 2012 to end of 2017 (GitHub returns local time) were retrieved through GitHub API[1].

- Randomly chosen French and UK developers (Case 2). This dataset is composed of the commits from developers who contributed to at least 50 repositories the same year each year from 2012 to 2017. Each calendar year, we retrieved developer names with more than 50 repositories. Then, the 300 largest French contributors (175 for English developers) were selected, out of which 100 were randomly drawn. This dataset is used as a control.

3.2 Methods

Commits timestamps are measured with a precision of a second, and we can therefore define a discrete function C^p for developer p, with $T_0 = 1\,\mathrm{s}$:

$$\forall n \in \mathbb{N}, C^p(nT_0) = \begin{cases} 1 \text{ if commit at time } nT_0; \\ 0 \text{ otherwise.} \end{cases} \tag{1}$$

Date $n = 0$ corresponds to January 2, 2012 and was selected because it was a Monday. In order to analyze temporally and in frequency commit data, a sampling T_e of 10 min was chosen: the number of commits during a period of 10 min was counted, in order to obtain a distribution of commit density.

It is then possible to define two time sequences of commits (S_n^p) and (M_n^p) for each developer p such that:

$$\forall n \in \mathbb{N}, S_n^p = \sum_{k=nT_e}^{(n+1)T_e - T_0} C^p(k) \tag{2}$$

$$\forall n \in \mathbb{N}, M_n^p = \begin{cases} 1 \text{ if } S_n^p > 0; \\ 0 \text{ otherwise.} \end{cases} \tag{3}$$

The sequence (S_n^p) represents the number of commits of the developer p during periods of 10 min. The sequence (M_n^p) represents the actogram of the activity of the developer p.

Frequency Analysis. The frequency analysis of the commit data is carried out from the sequence (M_n^p) because the objective is to get information on the activity cycles only, without any quantitative perspective on the level of this activity. For each sample, commit data is aggregated to observe the global evolution in the population. The analysis therefore focuses on the following sequence (M_n^Q), where Q represents a group of developers p[2]:

$$\forall n \in \mathbb{N}, M_n^Q = \bigvee_{p \in Q} M_n^p \tag{4}$$

---

[1] https://developer.github.com/v3/.
[2] For each time step n, a logical OR between sequences $(M_n^p)_{p \in Q}$ is applied.

This sequence (M_n^Q) is finally composed of 1 where there is at least one commit, and 0 otherwise. The spectrogram of this sequence is analyzed to see the evolution of the fundamental and the harmonics of the signal over time, the arithmetic mean of the terms of the sequence being subtracted from each term before frequency analysis in order to get rid of a 0 Hz spectral line. Here, fundamentals and harmonics are the elements that characterize a signal in the frequency domain, as is typical when using a Fourier transform that allows to switch from the time domain to the frequency domain [18]. The Fourier transform is the generalization of the Fourier series to non periodic functions. With a discrete signal (M_n^Q) with $n < N$, its Fourier transform (DFT_n^Q) is computed as this:

$$\forall n < N, DFT_n^Q = \sum_{k=0}^{N-1} M_k^Q \cdot e^{-\frac{2ik\pi}{N} \cdot n} \tag{5}$$

Then, for each n, we get a complex number DFT_n^Q, and its modulus $|DFT_n^Q|$ or "amplitude" gives a quantitative information of the presence of this frequency in the original signal. The transformation provides N amplitudes at frequencies which are equal to (in Hz):

$$\frac{n}{N} \cdot f_e \text{ with } n \in [\![0 \; ; \; N-1]\!] \text{ and } f_e = \frac{1}{T_e} \tag{6}$$

In our case, we changed the scale of the frequency from Hz to number of cycles per week. This transformation is given by the following:

$$f_{\text{cycles per week}} = f_{Hz} \cdot 3600 \cdot 24 \cdot 7 \tag{7}$$

The frequency with the highest value of its associated amplitude is defined as the "fundamental" and we call it f_0. The fundamental was at "seven cycles per week" for all the analyzed sequences. We then define harmonics of the sequence which are the frequencies f_n such as:

$$\forall n < \frac{f_e}{2 \cdot f_0}, \; f_n = n \cdot f_0 \tag{8}$$

In other words, harmonics are at 14 cycles per week, 21, 28 ... and so on. The number of harmonics is limited by the phenomena of aliasing[3] and is set to $\frac{f_e}{2 \cdot f_0}$ to prevent it.

Spectrogram. The first technique used is called a spectrogram. It is mainly a time-frequency (time as X-axis, frequency as Y-axis) representation of the signal [15][4]. To put it differently, a sliding time-window is defined and a Fourier transform (Eq. 5) is computed for each move of the window. To avoid continuity problem and edge effects of the windowing [13], the spectrogram is set by a

---

[3] http://pilot.cnxproject.org/content/collection/col10064/latest/module/m34847/latest.

[4] https://ccrma.stanford.edu/~jos/mdft/Spectrograms.html.

sliding Hamming window [15][5]. We choose a width of 15 days and an overlap of one week for the computation. Then, for each time step (weeks by weeks), amplitudes of the sequence (DFT_n^Q) are represented by a color scale (see Fig. 3 for example). This spectrogram therefore shows the different cycles in the signal and their evolutions over time in terms of intensity. For example, a high intensity of the harmonic at 14 cycles by weeks indicates that the corresponding weeks can be divided in 14 equal marked sub-parts, or equivalently that the corresponding days can be divided in 2 equal sub-parts.

Total Harmonic Distortion. Fundamental and harmonics can also be highlighted by evaluating the Total Harmonic Distortion (THD) [17] over time. The THD reflects the distortion of the signal compared to the same signal if it was a perfect one, i.e. without harmonics. Mathematically, it represents the ratio of the sum of the harmonic coefficients (in the Fourier transform) to the fundamental coefficient. We use here the definition of the THD_F in [17]:

$$THD = 10 \cdot log_{10}\left(\frac{\sum_{k>0}|DFT_{f_k}^Q|^2}{|DFT_{f_0}^Q|^2}\right) \tag{9}$$

The value of the THD gives an indication of the signal purity and thus notably of its regularity. The lower the THD, the more the fundamental predominates over the harmonics. It can be interpreted as a marker of regularization where large cycles predominate over multiple intra-day cycles.

Temporal Analysis

Commit Density. The temporal analysis of commit data is processed from the sequence (S_n^p). Commits are first aggregated by periods of a week to give a *typical day*, and then aggregated between developers of the same sample Q. Let w be the w-th weeks since January 2, 2012, we define the sequence $(\Gamma_{w,n}^p)_{(w,n)\in\mathbb{N}\times[\![0;143]\!]}^6$ by:

$$\forall w \in \mathbb{N}, \forall n \in [\![0;143]\!],$$

$$\Gamma_{w,n}^p = \sum_{k=0}^{6} S_{n+144\cdot k+1008\cdot(w-1)}^p \tag{10}$$

Aggregation of data for all developers p of sample Q is then defined: $\forall w \in \mathbb{N}, \forall n \in [\![0;143]\!]$,

$$\Gamma_{w,n}^Q = \sum_{p\in Q} \Gamma_{w,n}^p \tag{11}$$

In order to be able to compare days from 2012 to 2017 in terms of work rhythms, the density of commits was chosen to represent the *typical day* of week w.

---

[5] https://ccrma.stanford.edu/~jos/sasp/Hamming_Window.html.
[6] There are 144 periods of 10 min in one day and 1008 in one week.

We finally define the sequence $(D^Q_{w,n})_{(w,n)\in\mathbb{N}\times[\![0;143]\!]}$ i.e. the density of commits during the typical day of week w:

$\forall w \in \mathbb{N}, \forall n \in [\![0; 143]\!]$,

$$D^Q_{w,n} = \frac{\Gamma^Q_{w,n}}{\sum\limits_{n=0}^{143} \Gamma^Q_{w,n}} \tag{12}$$

Filtering and Correlation. The sequence $(D^Q_{w,n})$ is further filtered with a moving average window of 6 hours (width) with a step of T_e (10 min). To avoid edge effects, the signal was periodized. The result of the filtering for two random weeks w and for a window width of 1 h to 6 h is presented in Fig. 2.

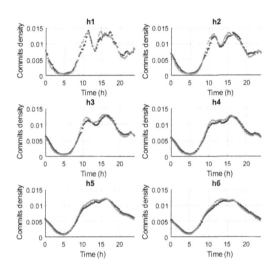

Fig. 2. Density of commits for two random weeks and 6 different window widths (French developers).

A width of 6 hours allows not to focus on lunch breaks and on the variability in the activity in the evening. For the sake of clarity, the filtered sequence will also be called $(D^Q_{w,n})$.

To observe the evolution of work habits, cross correlation is calculated between the density of commits of the typical day of week w and the density of commits of the typical day of all weeks. In other word, we compare each week to the average week of our 6 years samples (2012 to 2017). The density of commits of the typical day of all weeks is built according to, with Z the number of studied weeks:

$\forall n \in [\![0; 143]\!]$,

$$D_{Z,n}^{Q} = \frac{1}{Z} \sum_{w=0}^{Z-1} D_{w,n}^{Q} \tag{13}$$

For each week w, the result of the cross correlation provides us with two relevant measures:

- the phase shift ϕ_w^Q, given by the maximum of the cross correlation;
- the value of this maximum V_w^Q.

Analyzing the sequence (ϕ_w^Q) makes it possible to evaluate the evolution of work rhythms over time in terms of activity during the day: a negative value indicates a phase advance i.e. a precession: developers working earlier. By opposition, a positive value would indicate a phase delay. Analyzing the sequence (V_w^Q) informs us about the regularity of the *typical day*, by comparing it to the maximum of the autocorrelation in the sequence $(D_{Z,n}^{Q})^7$, in particular by observing the relative difference (or distance) from the autocorrelation:

$$(E_w^Q)_{w<Z} = \left(\frac{|V_w^Q - \frac{1}{144} \sum_{n=0}^{143} (D_{Z,n}^{Q})^2|}{\frac{1}{144} \sum_{n=0}^{143} (D_{Z,n}^{Q})^2} \right)_{w<Z} \tag{14}$$

4   Results

4.1   Case 1: Longitudinal Analysis

Frequency Analysis. The spectrograms of sequences (M_n^{fr}) for French developers and (M_n^{en}) for English developers are represented in Figs. 3 and 4, respectively.

These spectrograms exhibit a high power line in each case at 7 cycles per week and the presence of certain harmonics, in line with Dalle et al. [8]. The absence of the 21-cycle harmonic among English developers could be related to the fact that English developers have a day which mainly comprises 2 cycles (day and night), whereas French developers make a more pronounced break at noon, characterized by a spectral line at 21 cycles. In terms of spectral power, an increase over time of the intensity of the spectral line at 7 is observed. The evolution of the THD, as well as its denoising, are presented in Figs. 5 and 6. In both cases, they show a decrease in the trend of the THD, which confirms the increase in power of the spectral line at 7 and corresponds to a regularization in work patterns over time.

---

[7] Given by: $\frac{1}{144} \sum_{n=0}^{143} (D_{Z,n}^{Q})^2$.

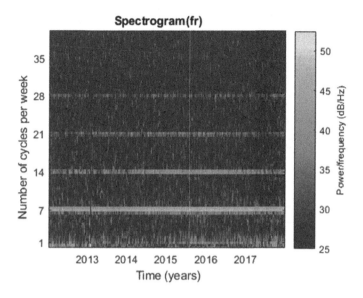

Fig. 3. Spectrogram for French developers.

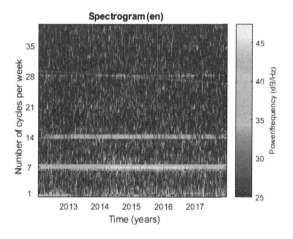

Fig. 4. Spectrogram for English developers.

Temporal Analysis. We focus on the observation of the evolution of the density of commits of the typical day of week w, thanks to the sequence $(\phi_w^Q)_{w<Z}$, and on the relative difference to the autocorrelation $(E_w^Q)_{w<Z}$ (Eq. 14). Figure 7 displays both of these metrics for French developers, while Fig. 8 presents a linear regression of the phase shift ϕ_w^{fr} using a bisquare robustness method. Regression coefficients are shown in Table 1.

These results, and specially the significantly negative values of the slope, signal a trend towards a work day that would have shifted towards an "earlier" schedule:

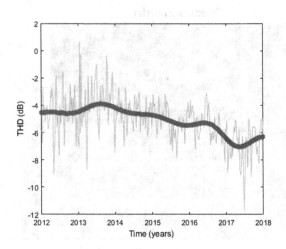

Fig. 5. THD from 2012 to 2017 (blue: THD; orange: filtered THD) - French developers. (Color figure online)

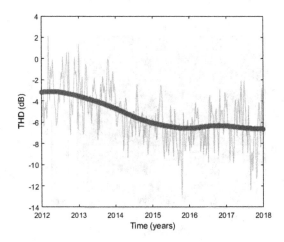

Fig. 6. THD from 2012 to 2017 (blue: THD; orange: filtered THD) - English developers. (Color figure online)

a precession over time in the work rhythms for French developers, who would work between 20 to 50 min earlier in late 2017 compared to 2012. It should be noted however that in 2017, developers nevertheless worked on average later than in 2016 (Fig. 7).

This phenomenon can visually be observed in Fig. 9 that plots the density of commits of the typical day of the year Y using a running average (width of 6 hours for the running window).

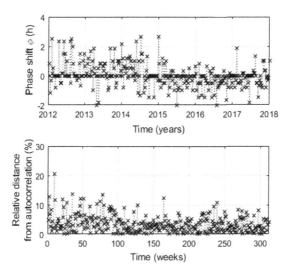

Fig. 7. Phase shift ϕ_w^{fr} (top) and relative distance E_w^{fr} in % (bottom) - French developers.

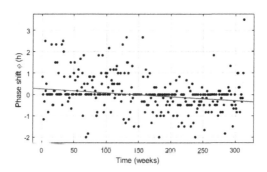

Fig. 8. Linear regression of phase shift (ϕ_w^{fr}) - French developers.

Table 1. Linear regression - French developers.

Linear model: $\phi_w^{fr} = a \cdot w + b$	
	Coefficients (with 95% confidence bounds)
a	-0.001834 $(-0.002618, -0.001051)^{***}$
b	0.2595 $(0.1175, 0.4014)^{***}$
a $p - value$	5.9928e−06
b $p - value$	0.00037464
R^2	0.4192

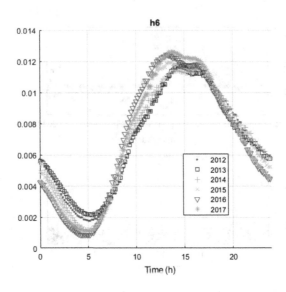

Fig. 9. Density of commits of the typical day of the year - French developers.

Similar results are presented for English developers, in Fig. 10, Table 2 and Fig. 11, respectively. As for French developers, we observe a trend towards an increasingly early work day. It should be noted that since the relative distance from autocorrelation is much larger in this population, especially since mid-2016, phase shifts corresponding to a relative distance of more than 15% were excluded from the linear regression.

Table 2. Linear regression - English developers.

Linear model : $\phi_w^{en} = a \cdot w + b$	
	Coefficients (with 95% confidence bounds)
a	-0.002392 $(-0.003317,\ -0.001466)$***
b	0.4364 $(0.2686,\ 0.6041)$***
$a\ p-value$	6.4383e$-$07
$b\ p-value$	5.3824e$-$07
R^2	0.4357

4.2   Case 2: Random Sample

Frequency Analysis. Spectrograms (not shown here) of sequences ($M_n^{fr,rand}$) for French developers and ($M_n^{en,rand}$) for English developers are very similar to

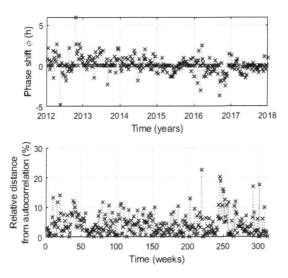

Fig. 10. Phase shift ϕ_w^{en} (top) and relative distance E_w^{en} in % (bottom) - English developers.

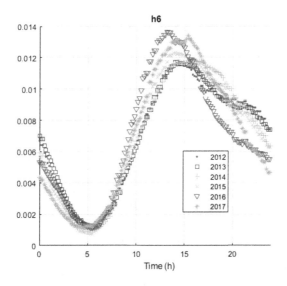

Fig. 11. Density of commits of the typical day of the year - English developers.

Figs. 3 and 4, with a high power line at 7 cycles per week. As expected, there is no power line at 21 for English developers. Differences show up in terms of THD (Fig. 12): there is no significant decline for French developers (orange line) i.e. no regularization effect, which suggests that the regularization in work rhythms observed for French developers in Case 1 was related to longitudinal effects i.e. to the evolution of work habits of individual developers over time. However, such a decline can still be observed for English developers (blue line in the Fig. 12): in this respect, we wonder whether our control might not be sufficient or whether there would be a cultural element that would more generally induces such a regularization phenomena in the UK developer population as a whole.

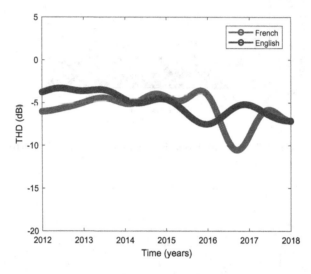

Fig. 12. Filtered THD from 2012 to 2018 (orange: French developers; blue: English developers). (Color figure online)

Temporal Analysis. Results similar to those presented above in the longitudinal case (Case 1) also hold for the random population, which could be related to the fact that the population of large GitHub developers remains mainly similar over time, with a limited number of newcomers. However, when we further control for the "GitHub age" age of developers (the time since their GitHub account was created), these patterns disappear, as evidenced in Figs. 13 and 14, where for each year Y only the "random" developers registered less 3 years before year Y were selected. Precession effects (working earlier during the day) disappear, suggesting that these effects were indeed related to longitudinal effects i.e. to the "GitHub-aging" of the population studied.

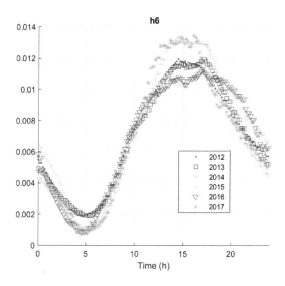

Fig. 13. Density of commits of the typical day of the year - "young" French developers (less than 3 years in GitHub).

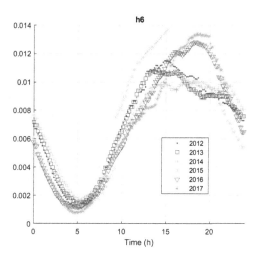

Fig. 14. Density of commits of the typical day of the year - "young" English developers (less than 3 years in GitHub).

4.3   Threats to Validity

As Claes et al. [6] mention, the time where a commit is made does not inform about the time spent by the developer that eventually resulted in that commit. However, we expect the reconstructed signals at the level of sufficiently large developer population to mitigate this phenomenon since we eventually observe quasi-continuous commit densities.

More significantly, we believe that further studies are needed in order to determine whether the results presented in this paper would hold in more countries and with more pronounced cultural differences.

5   Conclusion

By applying signal processing techniques to GitHub commit activity signals, we were able to highlight two dynamic phenomena with respect to developer work rhythms: regularization (working according to more regular daily cycles) and precession (working earlier during the day as observed through phase shifts). Studying longitudinally the same population for 6 years, and controlling with a sample based on a random population each year, we suggested that these phenomena could be related to either a learning effect with respect to the use of GitHub or to the aging the population studied. More in general, these results suggest that the effect of the digitalization of work environments might evolve over time for individuals, not necessarily in the direction of less regularity or less structured work rhythms but rather towards more traditional activity patterns. These results hold for both French and English developers, although regularization seems to hold for English developers irrespective of longitudinal effects.

Our aim in this study was first and foremost to try to shed further light on the potential of signal processing techniques when applied to analyzing activity and more generally social signals. In this respect, the results presented above suggest that the effect of digitalization might be partly transient in some contexts at least, i.e. might not last over the years, typically when developers gain experience and/or age. To put it simply, even open-source developers might gradually stop working at night and in unstructured ways, and fall back onto some more traditional daily rhythms. Needless to say, future studies should attempt to confirm or infirm these results by studying larger populations and more geographies. They should also try to control explicitly, perhaps through field work and interviews, for the basic characteristics of developers lives, notably in terms of age or of changing family structures.

References

1. Aledavood, T., Lehmann, S., Saramäki, J.: Digital daily cycles of individuals. Front. Phys. **3**, 73 (2015). https://doi.org/10.3389/fphy.2015.00073
2. Aledavood, T., Lehmann, S., Saramäki, J.: Social network differences of chronotypes identified from mobile phone data. ArXiv e-prints, September 2017. http://adsabs.harvard.edu/abs/2017arXiv170906690A

3. Bannai, A., Tamakoshi, A.: The association between long working hours and health: a systematic review of epidemiological evidence. Scand. J. Work Environ. Health **1**, 5–18 (2014). https://doi.org/10.5271/sjweh.3388. http://www.sjweh.fi/show_abstract.php?abstract_id=3388

4. Begole, J.B., Tang, J.C., Smith, R.B., Yankelovich, N.: Work rhythms: analyzing visualizations of awareness histories of distributed groups. In: Proceedings of the 2002 ACM Conference on Computer Supported Cooperative Work, CSCW 2002, pp. 334–343. ACM, New York (2002). https://doi.org/10.1145/587078.587125

5. Claes, M., Mäntylä, M., Kuutila, M., Adams, B.: Abnormal working hours: effect of rapid releases and implications to work content. CoRR abs/1704.03652 (2017). http://arxiv.org/abs/1704.03652

6. Claes, M., Mäntylä, M.V., Kuutila, M., Adams, B.: Do programmers work at night or during the weekend? In: Proceedings of the 40th International Conference on Software Engineering, ICSE 2018, pp. 705–715. ACM, New York (2018). https://doi.org/10.1145/3180155.3180193

7. Dabbish, L., Stuart, C., Tsay, J., Herbsleb, J.: Social coding in GitHub: transparency and collaboration in an open software repository. In: Proceedings of the ACM 2012 Conference on Computer Supported Cooperative Work, CSCW 2012, pp. 1277–1286. ACM, New York (2012). https://doi.org/10.1145/2145204.2145396

8. Dalle, J.M., Daudet, L., Besten, M.: Mining CVS Signals. In: Workshop on Public Data About Software Development. Como in Italy, July 2006

9. Eyolfson, J., Tan, L., Lam, P.: Do time of day and developer experience affect commit bugginess? In: Proceedings of the 8th Working Conference on Mining Software Repositories, MSR 2011, pp. 153–162. ACM, New York (2011). https://doi.org/10.1145/1985441.1985464

10. Greubel, J., Arlinghaus, A., Nachreiner, F., Lombardi, D.A.: Higher risks when working unusual times? a cross-validation of the effects on safety, health, and work–life balance. Int. Arch. Occup. Environ. Health **89**(8), 1205–1214 (2016). https://doi.org/10.1007/s00420-016-1157-z

11. Guzman, E., Azócar, D., Li, Y.: Sentiment analysis of commit comments in GitHub: an empirical study. In: Proceedings of the 11th Working Conference on Mining Software Repositories, MSR 2014, pp. 352–355. ACM, New York (2014). https://doi.org/10.1145/2597073.2597118

12. Hall, J.C., Rosbash, M., Young, M.W.: The 2017 nobel prize in physiology or medicine. https://www.nobelprize.org/nobel_prizes/medicine/laureates/2017/press.html

13. Harris, F.J.: On the use of windows for harmonic analysis with the discrete Fourier transform. Proc. IEEE **66**(1), 51–83 (1978). https://doi.org/10.1109/PROC.1978.10837

14. Markovtsev, V.: Daily commit activity on GitHub (2017). https://blog.sourced.tech/post/activity_hours/

15. O., S.J.: Mathematics of the Discrete Fourier Transform (DFT). W3K Publishing (2007). http://www.w3k.org/books/

16. Robinson, D.: What programming languages are used late at night? (2017). https://stackoverflow.blog/2017/04/19/programming-languages-used-late-night/

17. Shmilovitz, D.: On the definition of total harmonic distortion and its effect on measurement interpretation. IEEE Trans. Power Deliv. **20**(1), 526–528 (2005). https://doi.org/10.1109/TPWRD.2004.839744

18. Chapter I: The time-frequency approach: essence and terminology[0]. In: Boashash, B. (ed.) Time-Frequency Signal Analysis and Processing (Second Edition), 2nd edn., pp. 3–29. Academic Press, Oxford (2016). https://doi.org/10.1016/B978-0-12-398499-9.09991-X, https://www.sciencedirect.com/science/article/pii/B978012398499909991X

19. Teller, S.: Why programmers work at night? (2014). https://leanpub.com/nightowls/read

20. ten Thij, M., Kampstra, P., Bhulai, S.: Circadian patterns in Twitter. In: Laux, F., Pardalos, P., Crolotte, A. (eds.) 3rd International Conference, IARIA Data Analytics 2014, Rome, Italy, 24–28 August 2014, Proceedings, pp. 12–17. IARIA (2014)

21. Tsay, J., Dabbish, L., Herbsleb, J.: Influence of social and technical factors for evaluating contribution in GitHub. In: Proceedings of the 36th International Conference on Software Engineering, ICSE 2014, pp. 356–366. ACM, New York (2014). https://doi.org/10.1145/2568225.2568315

22. Wang, X., et al.: Exploring scientists' working timetable: Do scientists often work overtime? CoRR abs/1208.2686 (2012). http://arxiv.org/abs/1208.2686

23. Yasseri, T., Sumi, R., Kertsz, J.: Circadian patterns of wikipedia editorial activity: a demographic analysis. PLOS ONE 7(1), 1–8 (2012). https://doi.org/10.1371/journal.pone.0030091

Forecasting Purchase Categories with Transition Graphs Using Financial and Social Data

Danila Vaganov[(✉)], Anastasia Funkner, Sergey Kovalchuk,
Valentina Guleva, and Klavdiya Bochenina

ITMO University, Saint Petersburg 197101, Russia
{vaganov, funkner.anastasia, kovalchuk, guleva,
kbochenina}@corp.ifmo.ru

Abstract. Studies of debit market clearly show the existence of different stages of debit card user experience. These stages are related not only to a frequency of transactions but also to a range of adopted purchase categories. Given the history of transactions, one can identify for a user to which cluster (in terms of similar purchase interests) he or she belongs, and, thus, to refine probabilities of purchases in different categories. Moreover, possible trajectories of a user in a state space may be additionally tuned using the information about his or her socioeconomic strata. In this study, we consider a problem of purchase categories prediction from the perspective of state-transition modeling. Being defined by fixed amount of transactions (n-grams) or fixed time period (vectors of frequencies), states of customers are represented as weighted directed graph with clusters corresponding to different patterns of spending behavior. The procedure of forecasting assigns the user to one of the identified clusters and simulates the continuation of spending as evolutionary process. The experimental study of proposed approach was performed on the anonymized dataset of expenses of clients of large regional Russian bank.

Keywords: Socio-economic networks · State-transition modeling
Purchase forecasting · Financial behavior

1 Introduction

Digital traces of individuals are collected by enterprises allowing to provide personalized services and offers. Moreover, these data may be used in predictive analytics aimed at anticipating to predict future purchase intentions of customers. For example, transactions of clients attributed to different categories (e.g. Personal transport, Food, Tourism) may be used to predict their future purchase. This problem may be stated in different formulations, including short-term forecasts (e.g. which category has the highest chances to be the next for a given chain of transactions) or prediction of long-term patterns of payment behavior.

According to the recent studies [1], during the usage of a debit cards customers have different stages of adoption of this financial product. Thus, the chain of payments may consist of sub-chains having the types of expenses specific for adoption stage.

© Springer Nature Switzerland AG 2018
S. Staab et al. (Eds.): SocInfo 2018, LNCS 11185, pp. 439–454, 2018.
https://doi.org/10.1007/978-3-030-01129-1_27

The situation becomes even more challenging when one considers the existence of different payment behaviors between individuals as well as between different groups of them, and seasonal irregularities of spending patterns.

Here, we attempt to tackle the problem of purchase category prediction (Sect. 3) from several perspectives, including: (i) finding regularities in preferable categories of expenses for different socio-demographical strata (Sect. 5.1), (ii) uncovering regularities in chains of transactions from frequencies of transitions between adjacent elements (Sect. 5.2), (iii) distinguishing long-term patterns of debit card usage using monthly spending (Sect. 5.3). By doing so, we are aimed at covering repeated patterns of different lengths and sources, from short-term individual payment preferences to financial behavior of sectors of society. The investigation is performed on a massive transactional dataset provided by a large regional Russian bank (Sect. 4).

In this study, we use state-transition graphs with parameters estimated from transactional data, as a tool to extract the patterns of client behavior. As similar expenses may be used to create links between individuals (and then to group them in clusters), in fact, state-transition graphs for spending patterns may be viewed as a socio-economical networks. In such a case, the available socio-demographical information may be used to interpret the clusters (representing different types of payment behavior) or to make preliminary division of clients in order to extract spending patterns for strata independently. For a clustered state-transition graphs, possible chain continuations as well as transitions of users between clusters may be obtained by maximum likelihood estimation.

2 Related Work

The development of methods for purchasing patterns modeling and prediction is one of the steps to high-quality products recommendations, efficient contribution to the development of useful products, and to the increase in customer loyalty and satisfaction [2].

Customer behavior tends to evolve over time under current market trends, their personal interests and preferences, and their experience. In this way, one can observe a purchase trajectory as a combination of popular purchasing patterns, personal categories of interest rising from social status, friendship, and hobbies, and previous purchasing experience based on trust and loyalty. In addition, several consumption habits may be a priori affected by psychological and educational user properties (e.g., they are social influence, knowledge, emotions, altruistic motifs, ethical value, etc. for green purchase behavior [3] and posteriori emotionally affected, positively or negatively, by the level of satisfaction [4]. In terms of purchasing categories that means that for each person we can observe the evolution of category sets modified with increase of consumption experience and innovations adoption [1].

Learning the consumer behavior and preferences is now of great interest, especially after increase in data being available for analysis. On the one hand, relations between some innovations and customer attitude are studied [5], namely, the factors and personal characteristics, which will affect customer satisfaction [6]. On the other one, firms are interested in what will be the next and how they should satisfy customers' interests.

To disclose this question, the problems of consumption patterns discovery and purchasing behavior prediction are learned.

Goals of purchase prediction are varied from real-time advertising, campaign targeting, and missing category prediction, to the building purchase prediction profiles and discovering correlations between customer consumption habits and their socio-demographical characteristics. In was shown that purchasing behavior is correlated with socio-economic and demographic status, and the multi-dimensional interrelation between trade categories and purchase habits was discovered [7]. Building predictive profiles and shopping list predictions often use machine learning techniques, like perceptron, C4.5, winnow, and hybrid methods [8], mixture models and approximate Bayesian techniques [9], or nature language processing techniques for the building client2vec profile analogously to word2vec model [10]. Probability graphical models are used to reflect spatial, temporal, and categorial information presented in data [11]. Authors [11] also use a fast Fourier transform, autocorrelation, and segment probabilistic cut for the periodical component detection and Markov chains for discovering interconnected events and further probabilities evaluation based on recent activity. Memory incorporation can also be implemented by Hawkes processes allowing for modeling purchasing as a time-varying process [12].

Despite the advantages of these methods, they do not allow for the modeling or prediction of purchasing experience evolution and the customer adoption of innovations, and only a few of them [11, 12] provide mechanisms for reflecting dynamic time-evolving nature of customer preferences.

3 Problem Overview

The problem of purchase category prediction is, having the knowledge about payments of a user x in a period $[t_1(x), t_{N_x}(x)]$, and payments of set of users U, $x \notin U$, in a period $[t_b, t_e]$, $t_1(x) \geq t_b, t_{N_x}(x) \leq t_e$, to conclude about which categories will be met in transactions of user u in a period $\left[t_1^f(x), t_2^f(x) \right], t_1^f(x) \geq t_{N_x}(x)$. Here we use the following notations: $t_i(x), i = 1, .., N_x$ – time of i-th transaction of user x, N_x – a number of observed transactions of user x, $t_b = \min_{u \in U} t_i(u)$, $t_e = \min_{u \in U} t_i(u)$, $t_1^f(x)$ and $t_2^f(x)$ – the borders of forecasting period.

For a considered problem, the set of transactions of user x is represented as an ordered set of time-stamped categorized payments $S(x) = \{(t_i(x), c_i(x), v_i(x)\}$ where $c_i(x) \in C$ is a category of i-th transaction of user x, and $v_i(x)$ is the amount of this payment [1]. Timestamps in a dataset can be provided with arbitrary granularities, so we assume that there can be several transactions with the same timestamp; in such a case they are ordered by appearance. The forecasting period may be chosen by number of transactions which categories we are aimed at prediction or by fixed time window providing two different problem statements.

---

[1] In frames of this study, we use amounts of payments only for dividing the users to groups with different levels of average monthly turnover.

Problem Statement 1. Given a set $S(x)$ of N_x transactions, predict the categories of next k transactions (with indexes $N_{x+1}, .., N_{x+k}$) of user x.

Problem Statement 2. Given a set $S(x)$ of N_x transactions, predict the frequencies of different categories of transactions for a time period $\left[t_1^f(x), t_2^f(x)\right]$ for user x.

Additionally, to improve the quality of predictions and verification, data about the membership of users to some groups (e.g. socio-demographic) may be provided or extracted from transactional data, in the following way: for a given set of features $K_1, .., K_M$, for a given feature-dependent groups $\{k_{ij}\}, i = 1, .., M, j = 1, .., N_{K_i}$, we know if a user x belongs to group k_{ij} or not. For example, set of features may include gender and average monthly turnover. In such a case, groups k_{1j} are 'male' and 'female', and groups k_{2j} are turnover categories. When these memberships are given, they also serve as an input data in Statements 1 and 2.

4 Data and Preprocessing

The dataset used in this study is an anonymized set of transactions of 192,000 customers of large Russian regional bank collected for a period from January 2012 to February 2014. This set consists of payments made by debit cards with time granularity up to one day (31,691,000 transactions in total). The additional information about age and gender is also provided.

Firstly, debit cards with restricted list of supported categories[2] and corporate cards were filtered out from the dataset. For each user x, a chain of purchase events $S(x)$ was created. As we are interested in sequences of purchase events, we assume that each user has one chain of purchases, probably including transactions from different cards. For the further analysis, only the users with $t_{N_x}(x) - t_1(x) > 60$ days and $N_x > 5$ were selected (141,000 users in total). In this dataset, length of chain varies from 5 to 5928 with the median value equal to 83, and chain period varies from 60 to 785 days with median value equal to 593.

In this initial chain, the category of transactions is provided by Merchant Category Code (MCC) – a four-digit number which denotes a type of organization where the payment was made. Figure 1a depicts the average number of MCC contained in chains of different lengths. One can see that the number of adopted MCCs tends to increase with a number of transactions made. This means that either further adoption of a debit card leads to an extension of a list of MCC or transaction frequency has positive correlation with MCC count.

Although MCCs already denote the categories of transactions, their count (583) is too large to be used in the analysis. Also, between them there is a lot of MCC which are very poorly (e.g. by dozens of transactions) presented in a dataset. Following [13], we made a re-grouping of MCC codes to get meaningful and not excessive categorization. In total, 22 purchase categories were distinguished. Table 1 presents description of 18 categories with >0.5% of transactions per category.

---

[2] For example, there exist special-purpose cards for spending on children's needs.

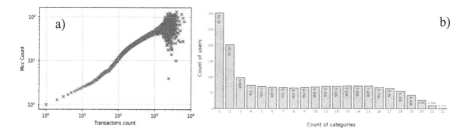

Fig. 1. (a) Average number of MCC for different chain lengths, log-log scale, (b) Count of users by number of categories

Table 1. Description of purchase categories (other are W – Celebrations and flowers, T – Tourism and traveling, E – Electronics and O – Education)

Abbreviation	Category name	Transactions	Clients
F	Financial operations	18.7%	96.8%
P	Food and meal delivery	40.4%	95.4%
G	Bars and restaurants	10.7%	70.9%
M	Health and medicine	4.01%	65.9%
L	Professional services	2.43%	59.2%
N	Special shops	1.92%	58.4%
H	Clothes, shoes and accessories	2.43%	58.1%
Q	Parenthood	3.43%	56.9%
J	Home and furniture	1.37%	48.4%
A	Cars and maintenance	4.91%	46.2%
Y	Self-care	1.14%	40.2%
K	Goods for construction and renovation	0.97%	38.1%
S	Communication services	2.14%	38.0%
X	Hobby	0.81%	34.8%
C	Sport	0.52%	33.7%
Z	Bookstores and stationary	0.53%	32.9%
B	Transport	1.96%	31.8%
D	Leisure	0.50%	29.7%

Finally, MCC in user chains were substituted with categories from Table 1. The example of a resulting chain is given in Fig. 2 (for the length of forecasting period equal to one month, Statement 2). The distribution of count of categories is presented in Fig. 1b, here we can see that the significant part of the users (up to 40%) has very restricted set of categories (three and less). For the remaining users, a distribution is almost uniform up to 15 categories with a gradual decrease after this point. This suggests that we have a large group of 'basic' debit card users with expenses only in very frequent categories, and a group (more likely several groups) of 'advanced' users having broader range of interests for which they pay with debit cards.

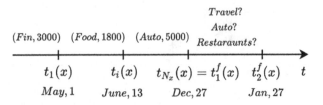

Fig. 2. An example of chain of transactions for user x

5 Modeling Purchase Behavior

5.1 Purchase Patterns for Different Socioeconomic Groups

In Sect. 3, there was introduced a categorical variable characterizing a user which is aimed at separating the users according to different purchase interests. Later, in Sects. 5.2 and 5.3, we will show how to derive the groups of users with similar payment behavior from the data. This section considers basic features which assumed to be known ab initio, namely, K_1 – age, K_2 – gender (with groups 'male', 'female') and K_3 – level - of monthly spending. For age, based on pseudonymized data about clients, six groups were distinguished. For the level of monthly spending, which users were divided into nine groups according to quantiles of distribution of average monthly purchases (total amount spent divided by number of months with at least one transaction).

Figures 3 and 4 show how different is the distribution of purchase categories between socioeconomic strata. For each case, we created two different heat maps for frequent (>5% of expenses) and non-frequent payments. Even this simple analysis allows for uncovering interesting patterns in data. Figure 3 gives a glimpse about how the payment interests vary over age. Older people are more conservative, and thus prefer cash in larger number of cases, which is illustrated by growth of F category[3] after age of 38 for both men and women. The 'weight' of food category (P) as well as health and medicine (M) is constantly growing with the growth of age while bars and restaurants (G) and public transport (T) decrease for people after 38. The peak of parenthood expenses (Q) occurs in 28–37, especially for women, while men of productive age have increased expenses for personal transport (A).

As for non-frequent categories, women have higher expenses for clothes (H) and self-care (Y). Older people, both men and women, frequently spend for communication services (S). Expenses to leisure (D) and hobby (X) decrease with an increase of age (men are much more attracted to hobby than women especially the youngest groups). Finally, men after 38 tend to increase the expenditures in goods for home, construction and renovation.

---

[3] 94% of transactions of this category are cash withdrawal operations.

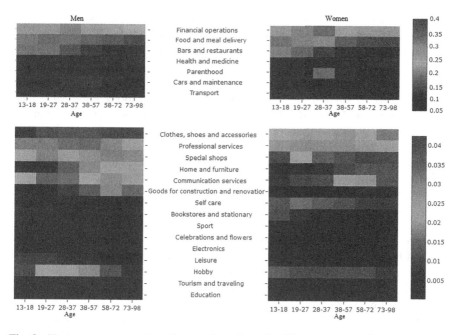

Fig. 3. Heat-map representation of parts of purchases in different categories (age and gender)

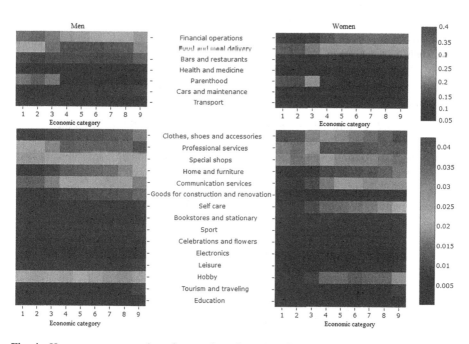

Fig. 4. Heat-map representation of parts of purchases in different categories (gender and groups of consumption power)

There is also a significant difference in preferable categories for people with different levels of income (Fig. 4). Significant part of income of groups with low consumption power (1–3) is allocated to parenthood. With the increase of average monthly turnover, there is also an increase in weight for professional services, home, communication, hobby, sport and tourism. Additionally, richer women demonstrate the increase in parts of purchases in 'clothes' and 'self-care' categories while richer men spend more on cars. Almost in all categories (except parenthood) the increase in the average monthly purchases leads to the increase in range of adopted categories.

The results presented in Sect. 5.1 suggest that the features $K_1 - K_3$ are meaningful for separation of groups with different purchase habits, and, thus, they have a predictive power for the considered problem of forecasting categories of purchases.

5.2   Short-Term Modelling of Purchase Categories

Short term modeling is aimed at predicting of the one next possible category of purchase and based on N-grams analysis [14] N-grams approach is commonly used for voice recognition, document categorization and DNA clustering [15–17]. An N-gram is an n-sized portion of information. For example, for text recognition N-gram can be a combination of N words, for DNA analysis – the one of N nucleotides. In our research, to find the next, most probable category, for each client we predict a cluster of certain behavioral pattern. To build N-grams, we collect all sorted binary grams (bigrams) for client purchase categories. Where each bigram represented as a state of Markov chain. Next steps were done to cluster all bigram sequences:

1. calculate frequencies of bigrams for each client;
2. normalize frequency vectors;
3. apply K-means method to cluster bigrams sequences;
4. define the best number of cluster using intraclustering and interclustering metrics [18];
5. visualize clusters with an order graph for further interpretation.

For Sect. 5.2, a restricted subset of 4,000 clients randomly chosen from the overall population was used. After that, steps 1–5 were applied, and 6 clusters were distinguished (clusters' sizes are shown in Table 2). Figure 5 shows the order graphs of two of the clusters. The graphs depict the most common bigrams of purchase categories and the order in which these bigrams occur in the clusters. Cluster 4 has the smallest number of purchases categories: food (P), financial operations (F) and communication services (S). Cluster 0 includes 393 clients with wider range of purchase categories compared to the very basic Cluster 4. Using the estimated clusters, it is possible to classify new clients to one of the existing clusters.

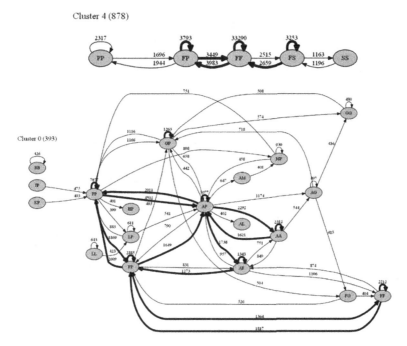

Fig. 5. Order graphs for cluster 4 and cluster 0 (edge weights are a number of transitions)

Bayes' theorem allows to define the probability of an event using prior knowledge of conditions that might be related to the event. In our case, we use the information about previous purchase categories to predict the cluster of a client. When a new purchase category is assimilated, the prediction is specified using the probabilities of previous clusters' predictions $P_{i-1}(C)$ and a new event b that follows an event a:

$$\bar{P}(C|a \rightarrow b) = \frac{P_{i-1}(C)P(a \rightarrow b|c)}{P(a \rightarrow b)}. \tag{1}$$

The accuracy of a prediction is 81.36% for the considered set of client purchases. Table 2 represent scores for precision, recall and f1-score of each cluster. For 76% of clients an appropriate cluster is defined in first 20 purchases, although the average length of sequences is 355.

Table 2. Metrics of clusters' predictions

	Cl #0	Cl #1	Cl #2	Cl #3	Cl #4	Cl #5	Average
Cluster size	393	314	1192	313	878	911	–
Precision	0.65	0.73	0.94	0.63	0.93	0.78	0.78
Recall	0.92	0.75	0.74	0.92	0.84	0.83	0.83
F1-score	0.76	0.74	0.83	0.75	0.88	0.80	0.79

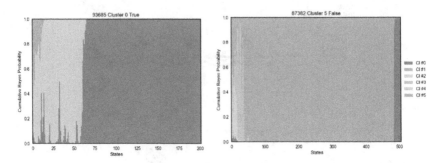

Fig. 6. Clusters' predictions for the client #93685 and the client #87382

Figure 6 shows personal predictions for two clients. With each new purchase the probabilities are recalculated, and some clusters become more probable than others (clusters are depicted with different colors in Fig. 6). For the first client the cluster was predicted correctly (cluster 0). Though, at first, cluster 4 was the most probable. For the second client the cluster was predicted incorrectly, although the correct cluster 5 was the most probable most of the time.

5.3 Forecasting of Next Period Purchases

To investigate long-term evolution of payment habits (frequencies of transactions for a certain time period, as stated in problem 2), we decided to consider aggregated states of clients in the form of purchase interest vectors for certain period. Here and further we use a month as an aggregation period. That is, a single state of a client is represented as a vector of relative numbers of transactions in 22 different categories per month (so we are aimed at studying the evolution of comparative frequencies of different categories, and not the absolute values of expenditures in them). To reduce a number of possible states for aggregating of behavioral patterns, we divided the possible number of transactions on the following groups: 0 – there was no transactions of this category in a considered month, 1 – a single occurrence, 2 – from two to four transactions, and 3 – more than five transactions. These borders were obtained after analysis of quantiles of distributions of number of transactions for different categories. Therefore, a single state of a client is represented as $[cat_1 nc_1, \ldots, cat_N nc_N]$ where $cat_1, \ldots, cat_N - N$ distinct categories observed for this client in a current month, $nc_1, \ldots, nc_N$ – numbers (0, 1, 2 or 3) which denote a group for each category according to a number of transactions in this month. For example, F2P3Q1 will match a user with three cash withdrawals, ten food purchases and one expenditure in a baby store.

Monthly states of a given user form a chain of states where a transition between subsequent states means change of monthly vectors of purchase. Accumulating the data from a set of users, we can create a state-transition graph where a node represents one of the observed monthly states, and the edge represents transition between two states in two subsequent months. The weight of an edge is equal to a number of such transitions observed in the data. The resulting state-transition graph may be clustered by methods for optimizing modularity for weighted networks.

Figure 7 shows the visualization of a state-transition graph for most frequent transitions (here we use three groups for number of transactions – 0, 1, and 2 for the remaining counts). One can observe that two most frequent categories, F and P, may be found in every node of this graph. It has clearly distinguishable core-periphery structure, with combinations of F (cash withdrawing) and P (food) (like F1P1, F2P2) in the core as a basic behavior of clients, and addition of less frequent categories while moving to the periphery. Despite the prevalence of core categories which hamper the interpretation, some interesting patterns may be observed.

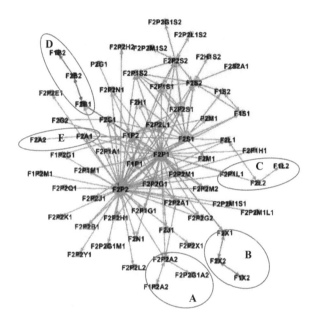

Fig. 7. State transition graph for the most frequent transitions (threshold for edge weight is equal to 80, different colors correspond to different clusters)

Firstly, some of the categories serve as a bridge to the adoption of another categories. This may be observed in a green cluster (here S (communications) lays between $\{F, P\}$ and other categories: health, restaurants, clothes and cars) as well as in zone A. While adopted, a periphery category tends to increase its frequency while in several cases this also leads to a decrease of core category (zones A–E).

Considering that core categories, F and P, are present in a majority of popular states, to observe interdependence of the more complex and less frequent states, we decided to transform state-transition graph into a bilayer network where layer 1 includes states having only F, P and their combinations (e.g. F1P3, P1, F3P3), and layer 2 is a state-transition graph created for 20 remaining categories. At layer 2, information about changes in F and P categories is neglected until all other categories diminish (i.e. F1P2M1S3 and F3P3M1S3 will be considered as the same state of layer 2, and transition F1P2M1S3 → F1P2 is a transition from layer 2 to layer 1).

Figure 8 shows a visualization of a structure of the second layer. The clusters of states are clearly distinguishable (Table 3 provides properties of clusters).

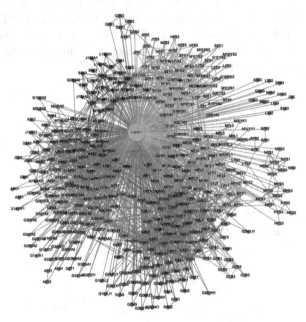

Fig. 8. State transition graph for layer 2 (threshold for edge weight is equal to 6)

Table 3. Socioeconomical groups for different clusters

Cluster	Clients, %	M:W, %	19-27	28-37	38-57	58-72	Top 3 AMP	Avg. trans. count
Layer1	**83.16**	53:47	20.1	33.6	37.8	7.4	Equal	**217**
0	**69.14**	53:47	19.1	35.3	38.3	6.7	Equal	341
1	**32.58**	51:49	**29.2**	34.0	30.0	5.1	5,7,6	315
2	4.05	36:64	**37.8**	33.7	25.0	2.8	Equal	346
3	3.07	33:67	5.3	**64.2**	30.0	0.4	2,3,1	**86**
4	**16.76**	**77:23**	11.8	**43.6**	40.6	3.7	9,8,7	375
5	3.08	23:76	4.2	**52.8**	38.5	4.3	5,3,4	263
6	**16.96**	**71:29**	4.8	35.3	**50.0**	9.2	9,8,7	333
7	**16.76**	32:68	12.3	30.8	**44.2**	**11.9**	7,6,8	310
8	**13.38**	51:49	15.0	29.5	**45.7**	9.0	8,9,7	345
9	0.90	32:67	4.8	**43.2**	**46.7**	5.2	8,5,6	289
10	1.46	**61:39**	10.1	38.3	**43.1**	7.9	7,5,6	**403**

Basically, clusters of layer 2 also have one or several core categories (e.g. restaurants (G) for cluster 1, health (M) and personal transport (A) for cluster 4). One can observe that some clusters are connected to some other clusters (e.g. cluster 4 and cluster 6, cluster 4 and cluster 1) while some (usually small) are isolated (like cluster 5 or 3).

We attributed a client to a cluster if he or she has at least single state of this cluster in a chain (then, client can be attributed to several clusters). Layer 1 (F&P) and cluster 0 do not have any difference in observed socioeconomic criteria suggesting that they represent purchase patterns that are common for different social groups (frequent categories in this clusters are F, P, A and S). Layer 1 has sufficiently smaller average number of transactions compared to most of the other clusters (this agrees with Fig. 1a).

Cluster 1 corresponds to young people with middle level of average monthly purchase and includes sufficiently wide range of categories with G as core category (notably, it does not include A and S). The remaining four largest clusters (4, 6, 7 and 8) include people with AMP from middle to high. That is, people with low and middle AMP usually do not go beyond the basic range of categories (we've seen the same in Figs. 3 and 4). Clusters 4&6 are associated with male population of adult age. Cluster 4 has core categories G and A (with 14 periphery categories including rare ones as T (tourism) and W (celebrations and flowers)). Cluster 6 contains older people compared to cluster 4 and has 'health' and 'personal transport' as core categories. Cluster 8 mostly contains people over 38 with frequent Y (self-care), M (health) and S (communications). Finally, cluster 7 (mostly woman) contains M, Y, H (clothes) and L (professional services). In general, the results are well agreed with basic analysis in 5.1.

To make a forecast of vector of purchase interests for the next month, we use the following procedure which is aimed at capturing the 'inertia' of being inside a cluster of interests. It is based on two main ideas: (i) both the previous states of a user and typical patterns of state changing (encoded in a state-transition graph) should influence the transition probabilities, (ii) the recent states should have larger influence than distant ones. To account for (i), we suggest, for any target state z, calculate the probability for z to be the next state of a client x, proportional to the sum of weights of edges connecting existing states of client x, to z. To account for (ii), we suggest multiplying each term of this sum to a coefficient increasing for more recent states. Hence, the resulting expression for calculating the probability of transition from chain $a_0, \ldots, a_t$ to state z is:

$$P(z|a_0, \ldots, a_t) = \frac{\sum_i f(L - (t - i)) \cdot P(a_i \to z)}{\sum_z \sum_i f(L - (t - i)) \cdot P(a_i \to z)}, \tag{2}$$

where the denominator is a normalizing constant, function f is a monotonically increasing function having non-negative values in range $[0; L]$, $L + 1$ is a maximum length of chain among the clients. As a weighting function f, here we use sigmoid $f(x) = \frac{1}{1 + e^{-x+y}}$, y is a constant to be tailored for a specific L (here we use $y = 5$).

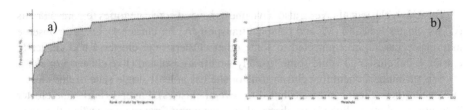

Fig. 9. (a) Distribution of correctly predicted states for top 100 most frequent states (without layer 1), (b) Accuracy of prediction for different thresholds

We applied the procedure to a set of 140 K clients with one last month excluded from their chains. Of 140 K, 35% correct answers were within top 5 with the highest probabilities estimated by (2). This result cannot be considered as good as 95% of these 60 K states belong to layer 1. Figure 9a shows that approximately 100 states have estimated probability of transitions among top 5. Figure 9b shows how the percentage of correctly predicted values increases with an increase of threshold and reaches over 40% for states with top 100 estimated probabilities.

6   Conclusion

The forecasting abilities of data-driven models of irregular event sequences significantly depend on the separability of chains to different classes representing different patterns of occurrences of events. As we have shown in this study, in socio-economic networks the situation is additionally complicated with the existence of several levels of core patterns which are frequent among all the classes. However, even for core-periphery structure of a transition network (that we have found both in short-term and long-term transition graphs) one is able to distinguish the clusters which are well-separated, interpretable by external criteria such as age, gender and the average level of monthly spending, and have a good agreement with observable purchase interests of different strata.

In this paper, we apply basic data analysis and different clustering methods to prepare the groups of purchase patterns with estimated probabilities of transitions between them for chains of transactions, and for chains of monthly payments. For the first case, we test the possibility of recovery of a correct group for a user with incomplete chain (that is, to predict a cluster from the several first initial states). The results can be considered as promising as we were able to predict a correct cluster for 76% of all the users in less than 20 steps of the chain (that is, using less than 6% of average length of a chain). This means that, having just few initial steps of user expenses, we are able to forecast his or her most probable future transitions. As for the second part, we scored the probabilities of transitions for the month next to the observed chain using the typical probabilities encoded in a general state-transition graph combined with states in a personal chain. The result of forecast should be improved further (most likely by creation of several multiplexes corresponding to different strata), although for more than 40% of the users an algorithm was able to place correct category among the 100 most probable. Further studies in this direction should include testing different machine learning and time series prediction methods as well as applying the point stochastic processes instead of simple frequency-based rule to include dependencies between time steps in a more sophisticated manner.

Acknowledgements. This research is financially supported by The Russian Science Foundation, Agreement #17-71-30029 with co-financing of Bank Saint Petersburg.

References

1. Bunn, M., Colvin, B., Pittier, C., Zanghi, A.: Understanding how consumers adopt a debit card payment preference (2012). https://www.mastercardadvisors.com
2. Oliver, R.L.: Whence consumer loyalty? J. Market. **63**, 33–44 (1999)
3. Joshi, Y., Rahman, Z.: Factors affecting green purchase behaviour and future research directions. Int. Strat. Manag. Rev. **3**(1–2), 128–143 (2015)
4. Westbrook, R.A., Oliver, R.L.: The dimensionality of consumption emotion patterns and consumer satisfaction. J. Consum. Res. **18**(1), 84–91 (1991)
5. Wang, G., Dou, W., Zhou, N.: Consumption attitudes and adoption of new consumer products: a contingency approach. Eur. J. Market. **42**(1/2), 238–254 (2008)
6. Lee, D., Park, J., Ahn, J.-H.: On the explanation of factors affecting e-commerce adoption. In: ICIS 2001 Proceedings, p. 14 (2001)
7. Leo, Y., Karsai, M., Sarraute, C., Fleury, E.: Correlations and dynamics of consumption patterns in social-economic networks. Soc. Netw. Anal. Min. **8**(1), 9 (2018)
8. Cumby, C., Fano, A., Ghani, R., Krema, M.: Predicting customer shopping lists from point-of-sale purchase data. In: Proceedings of the Tenth ACM SIGKDD International Conference on Knowledge Discovery and Data Mining, pp. 402–409 (2004)
9. Cadez, I.V., Smyth, P., Ip, E., Mannila, H.: Predictive profiles for transaction data using finite mixture models, Technical report. UCI-ICS 01–67 (2001)
10. Baldassini, L., Serrano, J.A.R.: client2vec: towards systematic baselines for banking applications, arXiv Preprint. arXiv:1802.04198 (2018)
11. Wen, Y.-T., Ych, P.-W., Tsai, T.-H., Peng, W.-C., Shuai, H.-H.: Customer purchase behavior prediction from payment datasets. In: Proceedings of the Eleventh ACM International Conference on Web Search and Data Mining, pp. 628–636 (2018)
12. Manzoor, E., Akoglu, L.: RUSH!: targeted time-limited coupons via purchase forecasts. In: Proceedings of the 23rd ACM SIGKDD International Conference on Knowledge Discovery and Data Mining, pp. 1923–1931 (2017)
13. Leo, Y., Karsai, M., Sarraute, C., Fleury, E.: Correlations of consumption patterns in social-economic networks. In: 2016 IEEE/ACM International Conference on Advances in Social Networks Analysis and Mining (ASONAM), pp. 493–500 (2016)
14. Milton, L., Robbins, B., Memon, A.: N-Gram-based user behavioral model for continuous user authentication, vol. c, pp. 43–49 (2014)
15. Volkovich, Z., Kirzhner, V., Bolshoy, A., Nevo, E., Korol, A.: The method of N-grams in large-scale clustering of DNA texts. Pattern Recognit **38**(11), 1902–1912 (2005)

16. Damavandi, B., Kumar, S., Shazeer, N., Bruguier, A.: NN-grams: unifying neural network and n-gram language models for speech recognition. In: Proceedings of the Annual Conference of the International Speech Communication Association, INTERSPEECH 2016, 08–12 September, pp. 3499–3503 (2016)

17. Miao, Y., Kešelj, V., Milios, E.: Document clustering using character N-grams: a comparative evaluation with term-based and word-based clustering. In: Proceedings of the 14th ACM International Conference on Information and Knowledge Management, pp. 357–358 (2005)

18. Ray, S., Turi, R.H.: Determination of number of clusters in k-means clustering and application in colour image segmentation. In: Proceedings of the 4th International Conference on Advances in Pattern Recognition and Digital Techniques, pp. 137–143 (1999)

Building and Validating Hierarchical Lexicons with a Case Study on Personal Values

Steven R. Wilson$^{(\boxtimes)}$, Yiting Shen, and Rada Mihalcea

University of Michigan, Ann Arbor, MI, USA
{steverw,yiting,mihalcea}@umich.edu

Abstract. We introduce a crowd-powered approach for the creation of a lexicon for any theme given a set of seed words that cover a variety of concepts within the theme. Terms are initially sorted by automatically clustering their embeddings and subsequently rearranged by crowd workers in order to create a tree structure. This type of organization captures hierarchical relationships between concepts and allows for a tunable level of specificity when using the lexicon to collect measurements from a piece of text. We use a lexicon expansion method to increase the overall coverage of the produced resource. Using our proposed approach, we create a hierarchical lexicon of personal values and evaluate its internal and external consistency. We release this novel resource to the community as a tool for measuring value content within text corpora.

Keywords: Lexicon induction · Crowd sourcing · Personal values

1 Introduction

Content analysis of large text corpora is often a useful first step in understanding, at a high level, what people are talking or writing about. Further, it can provide a means of quantifying a person or group's focus on emotional, political, or social themes which may be of interest to researchers in the social and information sciences. While unsupervised approaches such as topic modeling [1] can be useful in discovering potentially meaningful themes within corpus, researchers often turn to lexical resources that allow for the measurement of specific, pre-defined items such as those found in the Linguistic Inquiry and Word Count [13], the General Inquirer [15], or Wordnet Domains [8]. These domain- or concept-specific tools allow for greater control over the specific type of content being measured, and the manually crafted category names provide meaningful labels for the themes being measured. Additionally, these resources are easy to use and scale to huge amounts of text.

The manual construction of these lexical resources often requires expert linguistic or domain knowledge, and so a number of semi-supervised and crowd-sourced approaches to lexicon generation have been proposed [7,9,14,16,18].

© Springer Nature Switzerland AG 2018
S. Staab et al. (Eds.): SocInfo 2018, LNCS 11185, pp. 455–470, 2018.
https://doi.org/10.1007/978-3-030-01129-1_28

These approaches have been effective in the creation of lexical resources to measure sentiment, affect, and emotion where the categories to be measured are generally defined at the start of the process. Systems like Empath [5] allow users to quickly build new categories by providing sets of seed words that represent the desired concepts. However, it may also be useful to allow practitioners to define the set of categories to be measured later in the process for a number of reasons: the categories may not always be initially known, or researchers may decide to measure a concept at either a more general or specific granularity without creating an entirely new framework.

Rather than representing words belonging to a lexicon as a set of lists, we propose using a hierarchical tree structure in which any node can be represented by a combination of the nodes that are its descendents. This allows for explicit modeling of hierarchical relationships between concepts, and facilitates a configurable level of specificity when measuring concepts in the lexicon. For example, one researcher may want to measure positive emotions broadly, while another may want scores for more specific dimensions such as excitement, admiration, and contentment. A well-built hierarchical lexical resource can cater to either, and once formed, can be reused for different purposes depending on the research questions being asked.

In this paper, we introduce a crowd-powered approach for the creation of such a hierarchical lexicon for any theme given only a set of seed words that cover a variety of concepts within the theme. A theme could be anything from emotion to political discourse, and as an example of this approach, we create a resource that can be used to measure the expression of personal values in text.[1] Lastly, we demonstrate an evaluation framework that can be used to verify both the internal and external validity a lexical resource constructed using our method.

2   Methodology

First, we collect a set of seed terms that can be used to initialize the lexicon creation process. These seeds should provide good coverage of the core concepts that will end up in the final lexical resource, but various ways of expressing these concepts do not all need to be included. We embed the seed words into a vector space and cluster them hierarchically, and reorganize the initial structure using a human-powered tree sorting algorithm. Next, we automatically expand the set of concepts to increase their coverage. The resulting expanded hierarchy can be used to measure content within texts at a configurable level of specificity.

2.1   Hierarchy Initialization

Before beginning the crowd-powered sorting of the concepts, we create an initial hierarchy that represents a noisy sorting the seed terms. This will greatly reduce

---

[1] This new values lexicon, along with code that can be used to build an initial hierarchy, manage the human-powered sorting, and expand the sorted hierarchy can be found at: http://nlp.eecs.umich.edu/downloads.html.

the workload of the crowd, lowering the lexicon construction time and cost, by only tasking workers with correcting this noise rather than sorting the concepts from scratch. To create this initial hierarchical structure, we first embed each of the words or phrases from the seed set into a vector space using the Paragram model [17], which has been shown to perform competitively on a number of word- and phrase-level semantic similarity tasks. We represent phrases by averaging the vector representations of the individual words in each phrase. After obtaining the embeddings, we compute the distance between every pair of words and phrases using cosine distance, providing us with a distance matrix. Given these distances, we use the scikit-learn library [12] to perform hierarchical agglomerate clustering on the word and phrase vectors in order to generate an initial hierarchy in the form of a tree, where the leaves of the tree are the seed words and phrases. However, this organization still has room for improvement: the embedding model only loosely approximate the meanings of the seed terms and the clustering algorithm is just one step toward achieving the desired organization of the concepts. Further, the tree is binary at this stage, which may not be a flexible enough representation to capture the relationships between the seed terms.

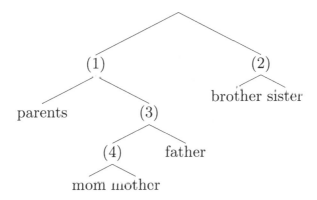

Fig. 1. Example semantic tree structure.

2.2   Crowd Powered Concept Sorting

Next, we turn to a human powered algorithm (Algorithm 1) to improve the initial sorting. Given an algorithmically pre-sorted, unordered tree $\mathcal{T}$, we want to find a *sorted* tree $\mathcal{T}'$ such that each branch follows an organization that would be selected by a majority of human annotators. We define a *direct subtree* of a tree, $\mathcal{T}$, as a subtree, $\mathcal{S}$, of $\mathcal{T}$ such that the root of $\mathcal{S}$ is a direct child of the root of $\mathcal{T}$. We employ a recursive traversal of the tree during which each direct subtree, $\mathcal{S}$, of the current tree is sorted before sorting the current tree itself. While sorting the current tree, it is possible that new subtrees are created, which are not guaranteed to be *sorted* themselves. Therefore, we must also traverse the set of

---

Algorithm 1: Crowd-powered Tree Sorting.

Data: T: Tree to be sorted, n: number of annotators, m: maximum HIT extensions

Result: T': Sorted Tree

Function traverseAndSortTree(T, n, m)

  if numChildren $(T) > 0$ **then**

    foreach $S \in$ DirectSubtrees (T) **do**

      $S \leftarrow$ traverseAndSortTree(S, n, m));

    $T' \leftarrow$ sortSubtree $(T$, n, $m)$;

    foreach $\mathcal{U} \in$ (DirectSubtrees (T') \ DirectSubtrees (T)) **do**

      $\mathcal{U} \leftarrow$ traverseAndSortTree $(\mathcal{U}$, n, $m)$;

  else

    $T' \leftarrow T$;

  return T';

Function sortSubtree $(T$, n, $m)$

  $G \leftarrow$ makeGroups (DirectSubtrees (T));

  $H \leftarrow$ createHIT (G);

  $n' \leftarrow n$;

  $s \leftarrow 0$;

  while $!s$ **do**

    $R \leftarrow$ checkHITResults (H);

    if $|R| \geq n'$ **then**

      if majorityAgree (R) or $n' \geq (m+1) \times n$ **then**

        $s \leftarrow 1$;

        $T' \leftarrow$ mostCommon (R);

      else

        $H \leftarrow$ extendHIT (H, n);

        $n' \leftarrow n' + n$;

  return T';

$T' \leftarrow$ traverseAndSortTree(T, n, m);

---

subtrees, $\mathcal{U}$, that did not originally exist in the unsorted tree T, and sort them (or verify that they are already *sorted*).

In order to actually sort a particular tree or subtree, we first identify the current set of *groups*, G, which are derived from the set of *direct subtrees* of the current tree's root. Each *group* consists of one or more *group-items*, which are in turn represented as one or more *terms*. For a given *group*, the *group-items* are comprised of the set of *terms* belonging to the leaf nodes of each *direct subtree* of the *group*'s root node. For example, in Fig. 1, the *groups* in G would be represented by subtrees with roots (1) and (2). The first *group* would consist of the *group-items* in node (1)'s direct subtrees, so the two items would be "parents" and "mother, mom, father". Regardless of the depth of a *direct subtree*, all words are combined into a single, flat list to abstract away the details of the subtree, making the sorting task less complicated for the annotators. Similarly, the second group would contain two items: "brother" and "sister".

To sort the *groups* in *G*, a Human Intelligence Task (HIT) is created in the AMT marketplace where it can be completed by crowd workers. In the sorting interface, (Fig. 2) each *group* is represented as a column of stacked *group-items*, followed by an empty space where new *group-items* can be placed. Crowd workers are asked to drag and drop the *group-items* (displayed as blue boxes) into to the configuration that they believe best represents a logical sorting of the *group-items* as semantic concepts. Within the cell representing each *group-item*, a list of up to ten randomly sampled *terms* that belong to the *group-item* are displayed so that the workers are able to glean the general concept that the *group-item* represents. Users are able to create new, empty *groups* with the click of a button, if desired. Because only one possible tree can be attained when sorting two leaf nodes (i.e., a single branch for each node), subtrees consisting of two (or fewer) leaf nodes are considered to be sorted *a priori* and do not require any human intervention.

After sorting, the users are asked to provide a label for each *group*, which can then be used as a label for the root node of the corresponding subtree. The label for a *group* could be identical to one of the *terms* belonging to the *group* if the workers feel that this *term* is particularly representative of the *group*. If a *group* only contains a single *group-item* which only contains a single *term*, that *term* will remain the label for the *group* instead of adopting the crowd assigned label.

It is likely that multiple, reasonable configurations are possible. Our goal is to find the organization that is preferred by a majority of annotators. At first, we create a fixed number (n) of identical tasks that are required to be completed by different crowd workers. If more than $n/2$ workers sort the *group − items* in the same way, this configuration is accepted as the majority view. However, if there is no majority view, we extend the HIT by creating n additional tasks that must be completed by a new set of workers, and then checking for a majority view once again. This will be repeated a maximum of m times. After m HIT extensions, when all $n + n \times m$ tasks have been completed, the most common configuration is accepted as the consensus view, regardless of whether or not a majority of the workers produced this result (this is done to avoid extending ambiguous HITs indefinitely). Then, from the set of results that match the consensus configuration, the most common label for each *group* is used to name the node that is the root of that *group*. All ties are broken randomly, and empty groups are ignored. When checking for consensus, the *group* labels, the order of the *groups* themselves, and the order of the *group-items* with the columns are not considered; only the unique sets of *group-items* that were assigned to each *group*. In order to encourage workers to select a reasonable arrangement of the concepts, we also advertise and provide a bonus reward for all workers who submit the configuration that eventually is chosen as the consensus.

We then translate the consensus group configuration, G', into the tree by rearranging the *direct subtrees* of the tree currently being sorted to reflect the set of *groups* selected by the crowd. Recall that each *group-item* corresponds to an entire subtree in $\mathcal{T}$. A tree representing each *group* is formed by making a link between the *group* tree's root and the root of each *group-item* tree. So, the branching factor will equal the number of *group-items* that were placed into the *group*. Similarly, the current tree's root will be connected to the root of each *group's* tree, with a branching factor of $|G'|$, the number of *groups* in the consensus configuration. Non-leaf nodes with a branching factor of one will be replaced with their children.

As an example, consider the HIT displayed in Fig. 2. Figure 3 shows the trees that would result from various user actions during the sorting task. It is possible that the concepts are already sorted in a desirable configuration. Workers are not forced to make changes and are allowed to simply "verify" that the current organization is suitable (they are still asked to provide labels for the

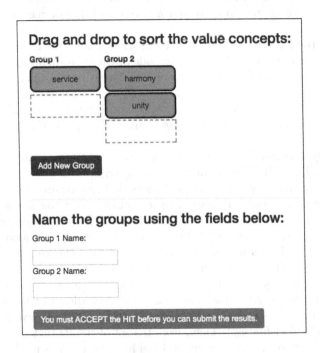

Fig. 2. Example sorting interface

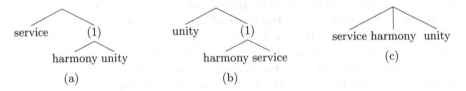

(a)   (b)   (c)

Fig. 3. Several possible tree configurations achieved by completing the same HIT in different ways.

groups). The tree that would result from taking no sorting action on the example HIT is displayed in Fig. 3a. On the other hand, a worker might decide that the concepts of "harmony" and "unity" do not belong together, and that "service" and "harmony" actually belong in the same grouping, separate from "unity". In this case, the worker can drag the box containing "harmony" into the empty cell below "service" so that these items are now members of the same *group*, resulting in tree displayed in Fig. 3b. Yet another option would be to place all three items in the same *group*, which gives tree shown in Fig. 3c. Note that this is equivalent to placing each *group-item* into a separate *group* of size one, since nodes with a branching factor of one will be replaced with their children. In the first two cases, the dummy label (1) in Fig. 3 would be replaced with the most common text-based label assigned to the subtree by crowd workers.

2.3   Lexicon Expansion

Next we seek to improve the coverage of this hierarchy by expanding the set of seeds that represent a given subtree to include other semantically related words. We achieve this goal using an iterative expansion process that leverages the structure of the sorted tree. First, we obtain a vector representation for node of the tree by averaging together the embeddings of all terms contained in leaf nodes that are descendents of that node. Then, a set of candidate terms is generated by searching a set of vectors learned from a very large background corpus. A good background corpus should include examples of the seed terms in contexts that exemplify the word senses and domain in which the lexicon is intended to be applied. For example, to successfully expand a lexicon of biological terms, a background corpus of scientific literature would be more appropriate than a news corpus. For a given node vector, the top k most similar word vectors to the node vector are selected as the expansion candidates (the node's expansion list).

If all candidates were accepted with a large enough k, it is very likely that siblings, or even distant nodes in the hierarchy, would shave intersecting sets of expanded terms. We would like to avoid accepting candidates that already belong to a sibling or another distant node, as this will lead to blurred boundaries across branches, and each node may no longer express a distinct, semantically coherent concept. This situation could be avoided by choosing a sufficiently small k, but this would also decrease the coverage of the lexicon. To remedy this, we examine each expansion candidate, one at a time, and determine which nodes it should belong to.

Iterating through the expansion candidates for a given node in order of their cosine similarity to the node vector (most similar first), we check if the current candidate is also a candidate for any other nodes. If it is not, then we accept the candidate as a new member of the list of words that can be used to represent the node. If all other nodes with the candidate in their expansion lists are either ancestors or descendents of the current node, we will also accept the node since it is reasonable that either more general or specific concepts will have some overlap with one another (e.g., a category about *animals* and a category about *mammals* might both contain the words "whale" and "cat", although the *mammals* category should not include "chameleon" even if this is a good word for the *animals* category). Otherwise, we only accept the candidate if it is closer to the current node than it is to any other node. If it is not, we say that the expansion for the current node has "collided" with that of another node, and we stop considering candidates for this node. The final set of words used to represent any node in the hierarchy then becomes the union of all expanded terms that belong the subtree of which the target node is the root. For an even cleaner final sets of words, human annotators can be tasked with manually removing noisy terms, as is done by the Empath system [5]. However, the authors of that work show that this filtering has a very small effect on the final scores procured when measuring the lexical categories in text.

2.4   Using a Hierarchical Lexicon

A category can be selected by choosing a target node that represents the category, and a score can be assigned to any piece of text for any category by computing the frequency of words and phrases in the text that belong to the category. As before, words the belong to a category are found by taking the union of all terms in leaf nodes that are descendents of the category's root node. To increase coverage even further (at the loss of syntactic form), words in both the lexicon and the target text can be lemmatized before frequencies are calculated. Due to the hierarchical structure of the lexicon, scores for more general or more specific versions of any category can be quickly obtained by selecting a higher or lower node in the hierarchy.

3   Evaluating Lexicons

We explore a series of evaluation methods to test the effectiveness of any newly created hierarchical lexicon. Each of these evaluations can be generally applied to any dictionary-like lexical resource. With these methods, we seek to answer the following three evaluation questions:

1. *Does the lexicon produce reasonable scores for documents that are known beforehand to be related to the theme of the lexicon?*
2. *Are the categories in the lexicon comprised of semantically coherent sets of words?*
3. *Do the categories in the lexicon actually measure meaningful concepts?*

A good hierarchical lexicon should lead to an answer of "yes" to each question. In the following sections, we describe approaches that can be used to quantitatively answer them.

3.1 Frequency Testing

As a simple yet informative first step, we measure the frequency of a set of pre-selected categories on documents that are known to be related to concepts in the lexicon. This will provide a preliminary understanding of the coverage and relative scores produced by the new resource, and it will help us to answer the first evaluation question. For example, a lexicon created to measure political language should certainly produce non-zero scores for many categories when applied to a corpus of political texts. Further, documents from left-wing media sources should achieve higher scores for categories intended to measure concepts such as liberalism than categories about conservative politics.

3.2 Word Intrusion Choose Two

Next, we employ a coherence method borrowed from the topic modeling literature: Word Intrusion Choose Two (WICT) [10], which is a modified version of the Word Intrusion task [3]. The premise of this approach is that for a set of semantically related words, it should be easy for humans to detect randomly inserted words that do not belong to the set. Coherence is determined by presenting some words from the same category to human judges along with an *intruder* word that does not belong to that category. The *intruder* should be a word that is semantically distant from the category being evaluated, but it should be a member of one of the other categories (otherwise, the *intruder* might be easy to detect simply because it is not related to the theme or the lexicon at all, or it may be a very uncommon word). If most, or all, of the human judges can correctly identify the *intruder*, then the set of true category words is said to be "coherent". This coherence is quantified for category c within model m using the Model Precision measure:

$$MP_c^m = p_{turk}(\mathbf{w}_{c,i}^m)$$

where $\mathbf{w}_c^m$ is the set of words chosen to represent category c by model m, $p_{turk}(\mathbf{w}_{c,k}^m)$ is the observed probability of a crowd worker selecting the kth word in $\mathbf{w}_c^m$ as an intruder word, and i is the index of the *intruder* word.

WICT adds a slight modification to this: for each category, judges are asked to identify *two intruders* even though only one actually exists. For a coherent category, two conditions must be met: First, all (or most) of the human judges should choose the true intruder as one of their guesses; second, the judges' other guesses should follow a uniform random distribution across all of the true category words. If any of the true category words is selected much more often than the others, then this word does not appear to semantically fit quite as well as the others. To quantify the coherence of a category, Model Precision Choose Two for category c within model m is computed as:

$$MPCT_c^m = H(p_{turk}(\mathbf{w}_{c,1}^m), \ldots, p_{turk}(\mathbf{w}_{c,n}^m))$$

where $H(\cdot)$ is the Shannon Entropy [4], and n is the total number of words displayed to the judges. Higher values indicate more even distributions, and therefore more coherent categories.

Concretely, each time that we test a category's coherence, we select five words from that category and an intruder word from another category (that is not also a member of the category being tested). These words are then presented to ten human judges on the AMT platform, and each judge is asked to label two intruders. As an attention check, we also randomly insert sets in which four highly related words are presented with two very unrelated words. We do not use scores provided by judges who fail these attention checks. Finally, we compute $MPCT_c^m$ for a set of pre-selected categories from the hierarchical lexicon in order to answer our second evaluation question.

3.3   Category-Text Matching

Lastly, we aim to answer the third evaluation question by determining how well the categories of our new lexicon actually capture meaningful concepts. To quantify this, we first select a set of interesting categories from the lexicon. Next, we obtain scores for each of these categories across text corpus in order to find the documents that have high, middle, and low scores for each category. To test a category, we select two documents: one that has a high score for that category and another than doesn't. These two documents are presented to a set of judges on AMT who are given the category label and asked to decide which document best expresses the concept described by the label. If the judges can select the correct document significantly more than half of the time, we know that the lexicon is able to identify text that expresses the category being evaluated. There are two settings for Category-Text Matching: *high-low* and *high-median*. In *high-low*, one of the top q scoring documents is paired with one of the bottom scoring q documents for the category, while high-median pairs this same high-scoring document with one of the q documents surrounding the median scoring document. The score for either version of the task is reported as the percentage of judges who correctly selected the high-scoring text. In each HIT, a crowd worker is shown seven pairs of texts, one of which is a randomly inserted checkpoint question based on a Wikipedia article title and contents: the title of the article is shown, and the first paragraph of the article is shown as one choice while the first paragraph of a *different* article is shown as an alternative. HIT are rejected when workers are unable to identify the correct article.

4   Case Study: A Lexicon for Values

Previous lexical resources have been created to measure moral values [6] and tools like the Linguistic Inquiry and Word Count [13] do measure some concepts that might be considered personal values, such as "family" and "work". However, no word-level lexical resource has previously been released that focuses on a wide range of personal values. Therefore, we consider personal values as the theme for our case study, exemplifying the hierarchical lexicon creation process. In this section, we describe the process of creating and evaluating this novel resource.

4.1   Collecting Seed Data

In order to collect sets of English words that are known to be related to values across multiple cultural groups, we turn to four sources:

Mobile Phone Surveys: Using the mSurvey platform, we distributed short surveys to 500 participants each in Kenya, the Phillipines, and Trinidad and Tobago. Respondents were paid a fee via their mobile phone to respond with text messages listing the values that are most important to them. Each respondent provided three values for a total of 1,500 value words or phrases. The phrases were manually examined and corrected for spelling mistakes. Examples of values collected include: *peace, harmony, patience, family*, and *money*.

Online Value Surveys: We use the text data from [2] in which participants recruited via Amazon Mechanical Turk (AMT) were asked to write about their personal values for 6 min. Respondents were from both the United States and India. We extract all unigrams and bigrams that appear at least 10 times in this corpus and add them to our set of seed words. Some of the seed words and phrases extracted from this data set are: *children, wisdom, nature, honesty*, and *dignity*.

Abridged Value Surveys: We also collected additional surveys from the United States and India in which AMT workers were asked to list their three most important values. We collected 500 such surveys from each country, for a total of 3,000 additional value words and phrases. Here, the respondents shared that things such as *hard work, love, kindness, belief in god*, and *integrity* were important to them.

Templeton Foundation Values: Sir John Templeton formulated a list of 50 terms thought to outline values that people hold. We add this list of terms to our seed set, as well. Some examples of these items are *optimism, spirituality, generosity, courage*, and *creativity*.

In the end, we remove duplicate value words and phrases and manually correct the items for spelling and grammatical errors. At the end of this process, we are left with 376 value words and phrases due to a high number of duplicate answers. Collecting these responses from a range of diverse populations means that the set of words represent concepts that are important to people in many cultures.

4.2   Organizing the Value Words

When sorting the concepts in the values hierarchy, we initially collect $n = 5$ results per HIT for a maximum of $m = 10$ results per HIT. The average proportion of workers that selected the consensus configuration was 0.530, and the consensus configuration was chosen as the result of breaking a tie with a frequency of 0.11. Many cases requiring a tie-breaker are somewhat ambiguous, such as the two alternatives depicted in Fig. 4 (an actual example of a tie that

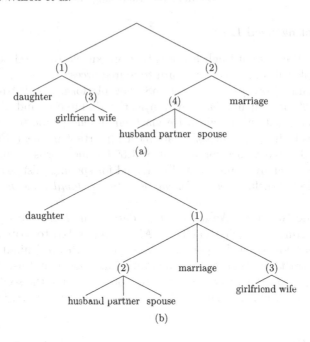

Fig. 4. Two equally common configurations submitted for the same set of nodes.

had to be broken while creating the values lexicon; each configuration was submitted by three workers). One configuration (Fig. 4a) appears to group the words by gender, while the other (Fig. 4b) groups the words by the type of relationship: romantic partner and child. Due to a high amount of noise in the mturk workers' node labels, we manually corrected or replaced a number of them to get cleaner category names. After viewing the hierarchy, we also manually moved a small number of subtrees to account for long-distance relationships that the mturk workers were not able to consider because of their narrow view of the overall tree structure. For the lexicon expansion, we find the counter-fitted paragram vector space [11] provided the cleanest and most coherent sets of expansion candidates. We set the number of expansion candidates at $k = 100$.

4.3   Evaluation

For the Frequency Testing evaluation, we collect a corpus of recent posts from a set of Reddit[2] online communities (subreddits) focused on topics that are expected to be related to personal values (e.g., /r/family, /r/christian) and apply the lexicon to these texts in order to verify that categories related to the community are expressed to a higher degree than other categories (Table 1). Many of the results are expected, such as high scores for the Religion category (includes words like *pray, jesus, divinity*) in the /r/christian category and high scores for

---

[2] reddit.com.

Table 1. Average category word frequency × 100 for selected value categories measured on content from various topical online communities.

	Cognition	Emotion	Family	Learning	Optimism	Relationships	Religion	Respect	Society	Wealth
/r/christian	1.96	0.68	0.92	0.56	0.19	1.82	**6.26**	1.51	3.74	0.48
/r/college	1.34	0.57	0.39	**3.73**	0.10	0.95	0.26	1.79	3.08	1.26
/r/finance	1.29	0.29	0.09	1.26	0.17	0.58	0.04	1.01	2.07	**3.20**
/r/family	1.54	0.60	5.58	0.60	0.10	**7.20**	0.10	2.04	3.55	0.89
/r/love	2.63	1.21	0.39	0.33	0.23	1.79	0.85	1.75	**4.72**	0.39
/r/mentalhealth	2.43	1.20	0.57	0.40	0.18	1.12	0.05	1.62	**3.77**	0.73
/r/mom	1.36	0.50	4.38	0.51	0.10	**5.08**	0.08	1.73	3.93	0.91
/r/money	1.58	0.16	0.42	0.61	0.06	0.91	0.00	1.13	2.94	**5.29**
/r/parenting	1.23	0.38	3.92	0.68	0.12	**5.08**	0.10	1.78	2.76	0.81
/r/positivity	2.35	1.05	0.36	0.46	2.74	1.13	0.48	1.40	**4.71**	0.64
/r/work	1.25	0.38	0.21	0.44	0.10	0.73	0.03	1.75	**2.98**	1.22

the Wealth category (includes *revenue*, *wage*, and *cash*) in the /r/money posts. Interestingly, the Relationships category, which is a supercategory of the Family category, actually has the highest score for the posts in /r/family. This is likely because the Relationships category contains words from the Family category in addition to others like *companion*, *buddy*, and *coworker*.

For the Word Intrusion Choose Two task, we evaluate each category five times, each time querying ten unique judges on AMT. The scores in Table 2 show the regular Model Precision (MP; frequency with which judges correctly identified the intruder) and the entropy-based Model Precision Choose Two (MPCT) score described in Sect. 3.2. The baseline for MP is random guessing, and for MPCT it is the lower bound achieved by repeatedly selecting the same term, causing the greatest imbalance in the distribution. Art and Family are some of the most semantically coherent categories, while Respect is the least coherent.

Finally, we evaluate using Category-Text Matching in both the *high-low* (CTMhl) and *high-median* (CTMhm) settings. For this, we use the same Reddit corpus as the Frequency Testing evaluation and set $q = 5$ (i.e., we select one of the top 5 scoring texts for the category and compare it with one of the middle/bottom 5 scoring texts). We evaluate the same set of categories as were used in the WICT experiments. We evaluate each category five times, using ten judges each time. The scores reported in Table 2 are the per-category averaged scores across all judges and trials. For both settings, the baseline is random guessing. The high-scoring Religion and Siblings texts were easiest for human judges to differentiate from other texts, while high scoring Work-ethic and Order texts were essentially indistinguishable from random texts, indicating that these categories are unreliable and may need to be removed from the final set of categories to be used.

Table 2. Word Intrusion and Category-Text Matching results for each value category.

Category	MP	MPCT	CTMhl	CTMhm	Category	MP	MPCT	CTMhl	CTMhm
Accepting-others	0.68	1.40	0.74	0.43	Achievement	0.82	1.16	0.93	0.75
Advice	0.72	1.16	0.63	0.44	Animals	0.96	0.59	0.86	0.93
Art	1.00	0.92	0.83	0.50	Autonomy	0.80	0.80	0.50	0.83
Career	0.90	1.13	1.00	0.96	Children	0.94	1.14	0.91	1.00
Cognition	0.94	1.32	0.76	0.44	Creativity	0.84	1.02	0.64	0.73
Dedication	0.92	1.39	0.85	0.50	Emotion	0.82	1.29	0.68	0.46
Family	0.95	0.87	0.85	1.00	Feeling-good	0.92	1.01	0.70	0.69
Forgiving	0.90	1.02	0.64	0.95	Friends	0.74	0.92	0.65	0.72
Future	0.62	1.29	0.58	0.65	Gratitude	0.94	0.93	0.42	0.64
Hard-work	0.90	1.01	0.71	0.52	Health	0.96	0.43	0.71	0.95
Helping-others	0.86	1.37	0.36	0.31	Honesty	0.94	1.07	0.67	0.78
Inner-peace	0.70	1.01	0.96	0.24	Justice	0.82	1.29	0.43	0.39
Learning	0.84	0.86	0.97	0.61	Life	0.74	1.27	0.89	0.26
Marriage	0.80	0.90	0.93	0.69	Moral	0.92	1.19	0.54	0.67
Optimism	0.84	0.93	0.96	0.91	Order	0.90	1.05	0.54	0.30
Parents	0.80	0.99	0.77	0.91	Perseverance	0.94	1.04	0.68	0.23
Purpose	0.64	0.83	0.38	0.30	Relationships	0.92	1.06	1.00	0.78
Religion	0.66	1.26	1.00	1.00	Respect	0.36	1.03	0.11	0.48
Responsible	0.60	1.06	0.77	0.65	Security	0.78	1.11	0.83	0.64
Self-confidence	0.78	0.91	0.85	0.75	Siblings	0.68	0.91	1.00	1.00
Significant-others	0.89	0.81	0.71	0.73	Social	0.63	1.11	0.84	0.75
Society	0.68	0.69	0.07	0.54	Spirituality	0.68	0.85	0.65	0.83
Thinking	0.90	1.37	1.00	0.92	Truth	0.68	1.11	0.63	0.81
Wealth	0.96	0.69	1.00	0.92	Work-ethic	0.86	1.15	0.45	0.50
					Baseline	*0.33*	*0.00*	*0.50*	*0.50*
					Average	**0.81**	**1.04**	**0.66**	**0.72**

5   Conclusions

We have proposed a methodology for the creation of hierarchical lexicons with any theme, including a crowd-powered sorting algorithm and tree-based lexicon expansion. Researchers only need to provide a set of seed terms that are related to the theme of the lexicon and provide some high-level oversight during the lexicon creation process. To show the utility of this approach, we create a lexical resource for the measurement of personal values in text data and release this resource to the community. The values lexicon achieves promising results across a series of evaluation methods designed to test both intrinsic and extrinsic validity.

Acknowledgements. This material is based in part upon work supported by the Michigan Institute for Data Science, by the National Science Foundation (grant #1344257), and by the John Templeton Foundation (grant #48503). Any opinions, findings, and conclusions or recommendations expressed in this material are those of the author and do not necessarily reflect the views of the Michigan Institute for Data Science, the National Science Foundation, or the John Templeton Foundation.

References

1. Blei, D.M., Ng, A.Y., Jordan, M.I.: Latent Dirichlet allocation. J. Mach. Learn. Res. **3**(Jan), 993–1022 (2003)
2. Boyd, R.L., Wilson, S.R., Pennebaker, J.W., Kosinski, M., Stillwell, D.J., Mihalcea, R.: Values in words: using language to evaluate and understand personal values. In: ICWSM, pp. 31–40 (2015)
3. Chang, J., Gerrish, S., Wang, C., Boyd-Graber, J.L., Blei, D.M.: Reading tea leaves: how humans interpret topic models. In: Advances in Neural Information Processing Systems, pp. 288–296 (2009)
4. Cover, T.M., Thomas, J.A.: Elements of Information Theory. Wiley, Hoboken (2012)
5. Fast, E., Chen, B., Bernstein, M.S.: Empath: understanding topic signals in large-scale text. In: Proceedings of the 2016 CHI Conference on Human Factors in Computing Systems, pp. 4647–4657. ACM (2016)
6. Graham, J., Haidt, J., Nosek, B.A.: Liberals and conservatives rely on different sets of moral foundations. J. Pers. Soc. Psychol. **96**(5), 1029 (2009)
7. Igo, S.P., Riloff, E.: Corpus-based semantic lexicon induction with web-based corroboration. In: Proceedings of the Workshop on Unsupervised and Minimally Supervised Learning of Lexical Semantics, pp. 18–26. Association for Computational Linguistics (2009)z
8. Magnini, B., Cavaglia, G.: Integrating subject field codes into wordnet. In: LREC, pp. 1413–1418 (2000)
9. Mohammad, S.M., Turney, P.D.: Crowdsourcing a word-emotion association lexicon. Comput. Intell. **29**(3), 436–465 (2013)
10. Morstatter, F., Liu, H.: A novel measure for coherence in statistical topic models. In: Proceedings of the 54th Annual Meeting of the Association for Computational Linguistics (Short Papers), vol. 2, pp. 543–548 (2016)
11. Mrkšić, N., Séaghdha, D.O., Thomson, B., Gašić, M., Rojas-Barahona, L., Su, P H , Vandyke, D., Wen, T.H., Young, S.: Counter-fitting word vectors to linguistic constraints. arXiv preprint arXiv:1603.00892 (2016)
12. Pedregosa, F., Varoquaux, G., Gramfort, A., Michel, V., Thirion, B., Grisel, O., Blondel, M., Prettenhofer, P., Weiss, R., Dubourg, V., Vanderplas, J., Passos, A., Cournapeau, D., Brucher, M., Perrot, M., Duchesnay, E.: Scikit-learn: machine learning in Python. J. Mach. Learn. Res. **12**, 2825–2830 (2011)
13. Pennebaker, J.W., Boyd, R.L., Jordan, K., Blackburn, K.: The development and psychometric properties of liwc2015. Technical report (2015)
14. Rao, D., Ravichandran, D.: Semi-supervised polarity lexicon induction. In: Proceedings of the 12th Conference of the European Chapter of the Association for Computational Linguistics, pp. 675–682. Association for Computational Linguistics (2009)
15. Stone, P.J., Bales, R.F., Namenwirth, J.Z., Ogilvie, D.M.: The general inquirer: a computer system for content analysis and retrieval based on the sentence as a unit of information. Syst. Res. Behav. Sci. **7**(4), 484–498 (1962)

16. Thelen, M., Riloff, E.: A bootstrapping method for learning semantic lexicons using extraction pattern contexts. In: Proceedings of the ACL-02 Conference on Empirical Methods in Natural Language Processing, vol. 10, pp. 214–221. Association for Computational Linguistics (2002)
17. Wieting, J., Bansal, M., Gimpel, K., Livescu, K.: Towards universal paraphrastic sentence embeddings. arXiv preprint arXiv:1511.08198 (2015)
18. Wilson, T., Wiebe, J., Hoffmann, P.: Recognizing contextual polarity in phrase-level sentiment analysis. In: Proceedings of the Conference on Human Language Technology and Empirical Methods in Natural Language Processing, pp. 347–354. Association for Computational Linguistics (2005)

Diversity of a User's Friend Circle in OSNs and Its Use for Profiling

Qiu Fang Ying[1]($\boxtimes$) (ID), Dah Ming Chiu[1] (ID), and Xiaopeng Zhang[2]

[1] Department of Information Engineering, The Chinese University of Hong Kong,
Hong Kong, Hong Kong
{qfying,dmchiu}@ie.cuhk.edu.hk
[2] Data Application Center, Tencent Inc., Shenzhen, China
xpzhang@tencent.com

Abstract. In past studies, Online Social Networks (OSNs) is commonly assumed to build on triadic closure, implying that alters in a user's ego network form either a single connected component, or a small number of connected components. In real-world OSNs, we find a significant number of users with a different ego network pattern consisting of a more diverse social circle with many friends not connected to each other. We conjecture this is caused by the increasing use of OSNs for functional (e.g. business or marketing) rather than traditional socializing activities. We refer to the resulting prototypical users as *functional* and *social* users respectively. In this paper, we use a manually tagged dataset (from Tencent social platform) to identify these two type of users and demonstrate their different friend circle patterns using examples. To help sort out functional users from social users, we develop metrics to measure diversity of a user's friend circle, borrowing concepts from classic works on structural holes and community detection. We show how the different measures of diversity perform in classifying the two types of users. Then we combine the structural diversity measures and behavioral measures to train machine leaning models. We further study ego network diversity in groups of users with different demographics (profession, gender and age). Our results bring new insights to the heterogeneous nature of today's OSNs and help better profile users. Our study also shed new light on structural hole theory and Dunbar's number in the OSN context.

Keywords: Online social network · Usage purpose · Diversity

1 Introduction

Traditional online social network (OSN) [13,29] builds on homophily: people alike tend to connect with each other, and mutual friends tend to connect with each other because of their common friends. But todays OSN platforms are increasingly used for multiple purposes. Users may often be connected for nonsocial reasons: for example, (a) User X tries to become a key opinion leader (KOL)

© Springer Nature Switzerland AG 2018
S. Staab et al. (Eds.): SocInfo 2018, LNCS 11185, pp. 471–486, 2018.
https://doi.org/10.1007/978-3-030-01129-1_29

through building an online community of fan club by attracting and connecting with many acquaintances, and feeds content regularly; or (b) User Y runs a small online business, and uses the OSN for posting product information and answering customer inquiries, or even receive orders. In these examples, users are connected not because they are social friends, but because of functional (or business) reasons. We observed a very different topology of friend circle: the functional user tends to have more friends than a typical social user, but these friends often sparsely connected with each other. Inspired by this observation, we study people with functional usage purpose of OSNS by comparing their topological structures with people with social purpose.

1.1 Previous Work

Most previous studies on OSN focus on detecting highly connected communities of users [1,2,14,25,30], or modeling how users get influenced by multiple friends via information cascades or viral marketing [5,9,20,22]. One particular interest is the study of [6]. In [24,31], the authors explored using user attributes to more reliably discover communities. The attributes they use are usually static (e.g. the college you graduate from, the company you work for etc.) metadata associated with users. The hypothesis is that users belonging to the same community are more likely share the same attribute values. They showed that such additional information help improve the result of community detection. But their objective and underlying assumptions about the network graph and activities are the same as in the community detection formulation. One past work [4] went notably beyond the study of typical social relationships in OSNs, which is very inspirational to us. The problem is how to automatically determine a pair of users who have a romantic relationship. It is rather the differences in the two users' friend circles that help identify the romantic relationship. Thus the authors define a function called dispersion that measures how many different friends that two users help connect, and demonstrated how the dispersion metric helps identify romantic relationships, validated by real world data from Facebook.

Before the advent of OSNs, when sociologists study social networks they have recognized the importance of both strong ties (friendships) and weak ties (acquaintances) [13,17,18]. A well-known social scientist Robin Dunbar [12], based on both biological arguments as well as observations of real world social networks, claimed that human capacity to keep close friends is limited to about 150, though there can be many more acquaintances (weak ties). Yet weak ties were observed to serve an important role of keeping a loose tie between communities. In the OSN context, several studies of weak ties gave statistics of observed number of strong ties and weak ties in OSNs.

The motivation of individuals who maintain lots of weak ties in social and organizational structures was formulated and studied as a theory known as *structural holes* [7]. This study considered an individual and all the persons connected to this individual, and all the mutual connections, i.e. an ego network. Structural holes refer to the lack of connection between mutual friends, which is also a non-social property. The main insight of the structural holes study is to point out the advantages for structural holes from the ego's point of view. For example, the ego may gather more information because of the diverse sources she enjoys and her friends cannot match with; the ego also has more control and influence on the alters, since they cannot reach each other without going through the ego. This implication of structural holes has been validated and applied in the real-world situations, including economic, political as well as social aspects. More recently, Kleinberg et al. [19] tried to characterize the structure of a social network in which everyone tried to benefit from structural holes.

Recently, many papers studied the role of social media for informations spreading and business advertising [27, 28]. The study in [21] showed the power of Twitter as a medium of information sharing. [3, 10] studied the viral advertising in Facebook groups. But there are still not too much work focusing on the usage purpose to run personal business.

The main objective of our paper is to find easy and reliable ways to tell whether a user is more likely a social user or functional user by just looking at the structural information, i.e. a user friend circle. Our study is based on a large set of sampled users from a real world OSN, with a subset of these manually tagged as functional users. The main idea is to design a good diversity metric to capture the ego network structural patterns observed from our data, and demonstrate its use for user profiling and classification.

1.2 Paper Contribution and Organization

Our paper is organized as follows. In Sect. 2, we first describe our datasets, and briefly explain the Tencent social network platforms. We also describe how we manually tag a subset of users as functional users. We then pick a few example users from our data to illustrate the ego networks of typical social users and functional users, or users with mixed purpose, to help illustrate intuitive ideas we will use in our methodology later. In Sect. 3, we define, discuss and evaluate various diversity measures, and discuss the physical meanings of these metrics. In the process, we point out the relationship of these diversity metrics to metrics in the literature. In Sect. 4, we evaluate the use of our diversity metrics for distinguishing users as social or functional users. For one of our datasets that we have some manually tagged ground truth, we do a standard comparison between different diversity metrics using accuracy, recall and precision as comparison criteria, and show the superiority of our proposed diversity metric. For the other dataset where we have tagged users by their demographic attributes, we show the correlation of diversity to different attributes, such as profession, age and gender of the users. Finally, conclusions and discussion of future work are given in Sect. 5.

2 Data

2.1 Tencent OSN Platforms

Tencent's original online social network is known as QQ. It provides messaging and blogging service to more than 840 million users. But in 2011, a new social network application called WeChat was introduced, and it has become the most popular OSN platform provided by Tencent, with more than 980 million active users (statistics from the latest Wikipedia page of "Tencent"). WeChat has become a platform for many different functions, including messaging, voice calls, groups, and payment. Users can also post a variety of content (links, photos, videos or text) to share with all their friends. A user can see all the postings from friends in chronological order on a page called *Moment*. When a user comments (or likes) an entry in that user's *Moment*, it can only be seen by the author of the content and the mutual friends with that author. Clearly, a user can use such a platform for a wide variety of purposes and activities, including regular social sharing with friends and relatives, as well as business and other functional type of activities mentioned in the introduction.

2.2　Two Datasets

Two separately sampled datasets from Tencent social platforms are used in this paper. The real identities of all samples are anonymized.

Dataset 1 contains a randomly sampled set of 10K users and each user's ego network, from the WeChat platform. Since these users are randomly sampled from a much larger pool, their ego networks can be considered to be disjoint from each other. We refer to each sampled user as *ego*, and the neighbors of the ego as *alters*. Totally we have $1,107,782$ nodes (egos plus alters) and $4,221,199$ edges between them.

Tagging the real usage purpose of users is a big challenge. We use a method to manually tag users by their public profile information: alias name and description. This is more likely the case for functional users, who tend to indicate their functional purpose (e.g. a personal business, professional affiliation etc.) using keywords or explicit phrases in their public profile. For example, a user who runs a bakery shop and registers an OSN account to publish the shop's information and receive online orders. The user can adopt the shops name, such as "Little Tiger Cake Shop as the alias name. Another example can be a user who includes keywords "xxx company", "car loan", "life insurance", to indicate the user's functional purpose of using a particular OSN account. In both examples, keywords in their proiles give strong evidence of their functional (business) intentions to operate the OSN accounts. The 10K sample users alias and description texts are collected and used to tag userss as either a functional user or a social users. Obviously, this manual process, without additional features used, cannot be completely accurate.

Especially, some functional users might be tagged as social users if they do not include specific keywords in profiles. In this sense, our data can be considered to only have partial ground truth.

Dataset 2 is a smaller one with 1662 users (egos) sampled from the QQ platform. On the QQ platform, many users provide their demographic information with their account, so our sampled users all come with selected demographic information, including profession, age and gender. For this dataset, we have a total of $445,907$ nodes(egos plus alters) and $5,057,603$ edges.

Table 1. Statistics of the three example ego networks. The last two columns correspond to percentage of single alters and alters in the largest component

User	#nodes	#edges	Density	%alters Single	%alters in largest comp
S	135	665	0.073	0.059	0.904
M	140	345	0.035	0.178	0.807
F	212	126	0.007	0.509	0.401

2.3 Typical Ego Networks

In order to illustrate the difference between the ego network of typical functional and social users, we pick out three examples (from the first dataset): a social user denoted S, a functional user denoted F, and a mixed user who is tagged as social user but has some characteristics of a functional purpose, denoted M.

The ego network in our paper refers to the one with all edges from the ego to alters removed. Some basic properties of these ego networks are summarized in Table 1. Conforming to our expectation, the social user's ego network size is relatively smaller, but the number of edges (hence density) is relatively larger; also, the social user has fewer alters as single (unconnected) nodes, and a bigger largest component. In comparison, the functional users takes the opposite extreme, and the mixed user is in-between.

To help visualize the structural differences between the ego networks of these three users, we define *degree ratio* r_i for alter i as: $r_i = \frac{d_i}{N}$ where d_i is the degree of the alter, and N is the size of the ego network. For each example user, we plot the distribution of *degree ratio* (from highest to lowest), and show the ego network in a circular layout in an inset, in Figs. 1, 2 and 3. We discuss each case in more detail below.

Social User: The degree ratio of user S distributes smoothly across all values, indicating that S has a rich set of friends of both high, medium and low degree ratios. This ego has a very large giant component connecting over 90% of the friends of the ego. Besides, S's giant component contains more closely connected small communities (resulting likely from triadic closure). Only around 6% of the friends are *single nodes* (with no mutual friend with the ego). We expect S to be a very typical social user.

Functional User: In contrast to user S and user M, the degree ratio distribution of user F is visibly much more skewed. For F, over 50% of friends are single nodes, i.e. without mutual friends with the ego. There is still a moderate sized giant component, connecting about 40% of friends. But there seems to be hardly any *community* (namely highly connected small circle of friends) in this giant component. The giant component is connected together almost by a tree.

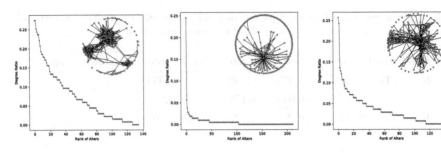

Fig. 1. Social user S   **Fig. 2.** Functional user F   **Fig. 3.** Mixed user M

Mixed User: User M has a rather large giant component as in the case for user S, but there are also quite a few weak tie connections. This is reflected by a more steep degree ratio distribution, especially at the low degree ratio end. Though M is tagged as a social user, we expect M to be quite likely a mixture of functional and social user because of the much larger number of weak ties.

3   Diversity

From the example users discussed in the previous section, we built up an expectation that users with social purpose tend to have the following patterns: (a) comparatively smaller ego networks, (b) relatively fewer weak tie friends, (c) one giant component connecting most of friends, and (d) friends in the giant components are mostly connected into communities. Users with functional purpose are assumed to have just the opposite traits.

3.1   Actual Size

As a baseline, we firstly use the ego network size to differentiate functional and social users. The empirical distributions of the two tagged groups of users from dataset 1 are shown in Fig. 4. Obviously, the two groups of users show distinctive peaks clearly separated apart - the functional users peak at more than 200 friends, whereas the social users peak at small values less than 50 friends. The much smaller peak in the curve of social users, is due to the impurity of user tags that we discussed in Sect. 2.2: some proportion of users with functional purposes have not been detected and then tagged as social.

As mentioned in the introduction, an interesting benchmark for number of friends is the *Dunbar's Number* [12] of 150. It is of interest to study how this limit might be different in the digital age, in OSNs. While our relatively small sample cannot give a definitive conclusion to this end, it is entirely reasonable for us to find overall comparable number of users in the ego networks of our OSN users compared to the Dunbar number. From the very beginning, we expected the ego network size for functional users to be larger than that for social users. The significant gap found from our data implies the ego network size by itself a decent metric for separating the two kind of users.

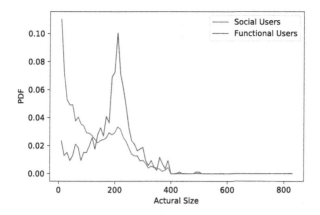

Fig. 4. Probability distribution of ego network size for social and functional users

3.2 Effective Size

To be better able to separate functional users from social users, we want to dig deeper into what functional users and social users care about their ego networks besides pure size. In this regard, we find the work on *weak ties* [13,18] and Burt's theory of *structural holes* [7] quite helpful.

Based on our empirical study, we find that functional users look for more *diversity* of its friend circle. Suppose we have ego X, alter Y and Z. If Y and Z are not connected by a link, then X plays as an agency between them. X gain benefit of information control with as many structural holes as possible. On the other hand, suppose G is a connected graph consisting of alters of X; then the diversity each alter of G brings to X is reduced because of the information redundancy among the connected alters. This is straightly inspired from the classic weak tie and structural holes theory.

To quantify the extent of the structural hole, which is quite similar to our notion of diversity, Burt defined a metric called *Effective Size*, defined as follows. Let N be the size of an unweighted and undirected ego network, and d_i be the degree of alter i (excluding the link between the alter and the ego), then

$$E = N - \sum_i \frac{d_i}{N}$$

Essentially, the original ego network size N is reduced by the cumulated *redundancy*. We consider Effective Size E as a candidate for our definition of diversity. Based on our preliminary study, unfortunately, *Effective Size* only gains a little improvement of separating the two groups of users.

3.3 Generalized Definition of Diversity

Inspired from the idea of structural holes and weak tie, we give a more general definition of ego network diversity as follows. Let there be K connected components among alters in an ego network, denoted $G_j, j = 1, 2, \ldots, K$. The diversity

D of the ego network can be generally expressed as

$$D = \sum_j w(j)s(j) \tag{1}$$

where $s(j)$ is some measure of *size* of the jth component; and $w(j)$ is some weighting factor for the jth component.

The actual size of the ego network can be seen as a special case of this general definition of D by setting

$$w_a(j) = 1$$
$$s_a(j) = |G_j|$$

where the subscript a refers to *actual size*.

Similarly, effective size is also a special case, by setting

$$w_e(j) = 1$$
$$s_e(j) = \sum_{i=1}^{|G_j|}(1 - \frac{d_i}{N})$$

It is now possible to consider a whole family of diversity metrics by designing different functions for $w(j)$ and $s(j)$. For this paper, we explain only two other variations among many we tried: (1) Density-dependent size (DDS), and (2) Expected number of communities (ENC). Both these metrics are defined by new functions of $s(j)$, while keeping $w(j) = 1$ for all j. But it is flexible to extend the definition by new $w(j)$. They are the main contribution of this work. We use the metrics of actual size and effective size as baselines when evaluating the new metrics.

3.4 Density-Dependent Size

As observed from our example users (in particular F and M), although functional users may have sizable giant components, they tend to be much less dense, often barely connected by a tree, as shown in Fig. 2. So we would like this factor to be reflected in computing the value of a component. In particular, we would like the value of an arbitrary component j to be a function of both the number of nodes n_j and number of links m_j. When $m_j = n_j - 1$, the component is connected by a tree, and we would like to set the value of component to n_j, as if the nodes in the component are not connected. When $m_j \geq n_j$, we want the value of component $s(j)$ to drop exponentially until it reaches 1 (and stay at 1). We use a logistic function for this purpose:

$$s(m_j, n_j) = 1 + \frac{2(n_j - 1)}{1 + e^{a(m_j - n_j + 1)}}$$

which satisfies our requirements above. The parameter a controls how fast the function drops as the number of links m increases. We will discuss the performance of this metric later, together with all other variations of diversity metric for comparison in the next section.

3.5   Expected Number of Communities

The density-dependent size (DDS) is a simple measure of diversity with low computation complexity. But DDS only captures the overall characteristics of the network structure (density), and fails to include the detailed pattern of a component's graph. There are two directions to include more structural information in the component graph: following the ideas of (a) structure holes, and (b) community detection.

If we follow the structural holes theory, what matters is the extent the ego provides a bridging function connecting otherwise unconnected (or sparsely connected) friends. In [19], the authors defined an objective function for egos who want to maximize their role in bridging structural holes. For each pair of friends in an ego network, a score is given depending on the number of ways these pair of friends are already connected by paths of 2-hops or less; since the ego is providing one 2-hop connection for the pair of friends, the ego's value of connecting the pair is just a fraction of the sum of ways to connect them. In particular, if the ego is the only way to connect the pair, the ego's bridging function for these pair has the maximum value of 1. The ego's objective is then to maximize its total bridging function for all pairs of alters. While this method of scoring is promising, it requires more information from full graph. Since the ego network is a subgraph of the full graph, we can't apply this method to score the ego directly. Instead, we will follow the idea of community detection.

Instead of measuring the ego's contribution to each pair of friends, we measure the ego's bridging function in terms of how many communities it is helping to bridge together. The concept of community in an OSN is usually well recognized but only vaguely defined, even in the community detection literature. One key challenge in community detection algorithms, as an unsupervised learning problem, is determining the number of communities in the graph. For our purposes, we want to consider all possible partitions of communities and give a probabilistic score of community count as diversity. We approach this in two steps.

A. Modified Girvan Newman Algorithm

First, we use the well-known Girvan-Newman (GN) clustering algorithm [16] to have a hierarchical partition of each component and a dendrogram as well (a hierarchical representation of the community structure). Note, alters in different components of the ego network are assumed to belong to different communities, so we run the GN algorithm in each component separately. The GN algorithm prioritizes where in a given graph the nodes are mostly likely partitioned to become two subgraphs (using betweenness of links) to recursively derive the dendrogram tree. For the GN algorithm, each node of the component becomes a leaf of the dendrogram. Since we assume that a fully connected subgraph (clique) will not be broken down to sub-communities, we modify the original GN algorithm by stopping further partitioning when a subtree of the dendrogram is fully connected (e.g., triangle). Our modified algorithm will stop when all leaves of the dendrogram are either a node or a fully connected subgraph. In Fig. 5, we show an example component and the resulting dendrogram from running our modified GN algorithm.

Let us denote the dendrogram (tree) derived from component G_j as T_j. We also assign a probability q_k to each internal node k of the dendrogram, as illustrated in Fig. 5. At each internal node denoted by k, the original subtree partitions into two subtrees, referred to as L_k and R_k. Let the number of cutting edges crossing L_k and R_k in G_j be denoted as e_k. Then the probability at internal node k indicates the possibility of the two subtrees to be merged as one community, and is defined as:

$$q_k = \frac{e_k}{|L_k||R_k|}$$

The resulting dendrogram $(T_j, \{q_k^j\})$ is referred to as a *hierarchical random graph* representation of the original component G_j, according to [11]. In [11], authors derive such hierarchical random graphs as a more robust representation of the original graphs, with many potential applications. In our case, we use the hierarchical random graph to derive the expected number of communities in G_j, as explained in Step B.

B. Expected Number of Communities

By our definition of a dendrogram, the original graph can be partitioned starting at the root node of the dendrogram, with the probably q_1 associated with the root. If the a partition occurs at the parent node, then the child components can be partitioned, again with probability q_k associated with the corresponding child nodes. If partitioning does not occur at the parent node, however, the partitioning at the child nodes can no longer happen, as such partitions are not well defined any more. If we consider a particular ordering of internal nodes for possible partitioning following the above definition, and represent the ordering by $(1, 2, ..., h-1)$, assuming a total of h leaves for the dendrogram, then the probability of resulting with i partitions is given by

$$p_j(i) = q_i \prod_{k=0}^{i-1} (1 - q_k)$$

For ease of notation, every dendrogram is augmented by auxiliary $q_0 = 0$. Since the final partition of the modified GN algorithm is with all leafs as fully

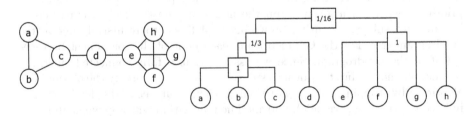

Fig. 5. An example of component and resulting dendrogram

connected graphs, the largest number of partitions C_j satisfies: $1 \leq C_j \leq n_j$, and $1 \leq i \leq C_j$. We assume that the number of partitions is actually interpreted as the number of communities, with the given probability above. In other words, the number of communities in a given hierarchical random graph (dendrogram) is random, and our algorithm above gives the probabilities of different number of communities. Based on this, we can compute the expected number of communities as the value of the component $s(j)$:

$$s(j) = \sum_i i p_j(i)$$

And the diversity, based on the ENC definition is as follows (c refers to the diversity definition based on ENC):

$$D_c = \sum_j 1 * s(j)$$

4   Experiments and Results

4.1   Performance of Diversity Measures

We use a simple binary classification to evaluate the performance of each measure for separating functional and social users. For a measure X, and given a threshold parameter T, an instance is classified as *functional* if $X > T$, and as *social* otherwise. For the standard measures of performance, the best T is used to derive Accuracy, Precision and F1-score, and different Ts are used to derive the Area Under the ROC Curve (AUC). We summarize the performance of different definitions of Diversity in Table 2. Note, since we use the T that gives the best F1-score, the value of Recall is just derived from the F1-score and Precision for reference. In the experimental result of The Density-Dependent Size(DDS), we used $a = 0.01$ which produced the best performance. From the table, we can find that the Expected Number of Community (ENC) has the best overall performance among the four diversity definitions.

The performance of Effective Size (ES) as a measure improves only slightly over Actual Size (AS). This is expected since the values of Effective Sizes are very close to Actual Sizes for our data, based on its definition. The DDS we designed gains higher Accuracy and AUC than AS and ES, but it has lower F1-score due to the lower Recall. The value of DDS drops quickly with the increase of a component's density, therefore it cannot discriminate between structural differences in large components with relatively dense connectivity. As we expected, by accounting for number of communities in a component, ENC works best, with improvements of 8% in Accuracy, 16% in Precision and 11% in AUC compared to the baseline AS. The superiority of ENC is also illustrated by the ROC curves of the four classifiers in Fig. 6.

Table 2. Comparison of different diversity measures for user purpose prediction

Scheme	Accuracy	Precision	Recall	F1-score	AUC
Actual Size	0.6871	0.6341	0.8444	0.7243	0.7106
Effective Size	0.6880	0.6367	0.8445	0.7260	0.7152
Density-Dependent Size	0.6974	0.6909	0.7088	0.7000	0.7499
Expected Num of Community	0.7397	0.7364	0.84279	0.7860	0.7869

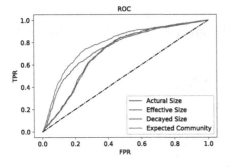

Fig. 6. Roc curves of different diversity metrics for functional user prediction

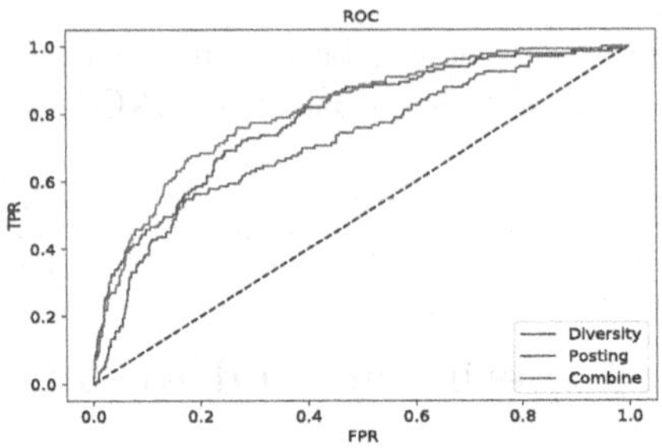

Fig. 7. Roc curves of Logistic Regression classifier by combined features

The performance still falls short from the best accuracy. After analyzing the wrong predictions, we conclude two reasons: (1) The manual process of tagging users only identified a subset of functional users, and missed some functional user who do not include relevant keywords in their public profile. Thus the group tagged as *social* tagged users is noisy; (2) In reality, a user can be a mixture of *functional* and *social*, as shown by the example of the Mixed User M. The ego networks of mixed users include both densely connected components and loosely connected structure holes. We will tackle these problems in our future work.

4.2   Combining Diversity and Behavioral Measures

Beside using ego network structure as a feature, other features can be derived from a variety of user behaviors, to learn a user's purpose in joining an OSN [8,26,32]. In [32], authors used users' posting behavior to determine their type using a T-LDA algorithm. We implement similar LDA based algorithm to generate the hidden features of users' temporal posting series, which reflect users' habit to publish content over 24 h. We also use the posting frequency as another behavioral feature. Combining the features of structural diversity and posting behavior patterns, we predict users' purpose by machine learning models.

Three prevalent classification models are chosen for this analysis:

1. Logistic Regression (LR)
2. Random Forest (RF) [23]
3. Gradient Boosting Decision Tree (GBDT) [15]

We train and test the classifiers using cross validation. The performance comparison of using the diversity feature and behavior features are shown in Table 3. For simplicity, we only use AUC for comparison, but other evaluation metrics show similar results. In the first column, we use the four diversity definitions, and in the second column we use features derived from LDA (setting the number of topics to 6) and posting frequency. We find that classifiers using diversity as feature have better performance than that using posting features, suggesting that the network structure tells more about usage purpose than posting behavior. Furthermore, the combination of both kinds of features gives best performance. Figure 7 also shows the ROC curves of the LR classifiers.

4.3 Diversity vs. Demographics

While diversity of ego network composition helps identify functional users, it is interesting to ask who are more likely to be functional users? To have a qualitative study of this question, we collect a smaller group of users with self stated demographics (gender, age and professions), which is dataset 2 as described in Sect. 2. Then we compute the diversity (ENC) for different groups of users.

Table 3. Performance (AUC) of combined features

	Diversity measures	Posting features	Combined
Logistic Regression	0.7725	0.7335	0.8103
Random Forest	0.7706	0.7422	0.8045
Gradient Boosting Tree	0.7647	0.7637	0.8121

First, We separate users into 25 groups by their profession, and remove groups with insufficient number of users. The average Expected Number of Communities for the top 14 groups are shown in Fig. 8. We find that users from the domain of Human Resource and Administration (HA) have significantly higher diversity scores, nearly two times of the second highest group Sales. Furthermore, users from Sales, Sports and Law have around 100 expected number of communities in their friends circle. Users working in government office, education, state-company and medical jobs have lowest diversity (less than 50). Though our definition of diversity is different than Dunbar's number, they are consistent: except for the group of HA, users maintain relations to fewer than 150 different communities. Thus, ENC can be used to develop some other bound similar to Dunbar's number: when maintaining social relationships, people are not only limited by the

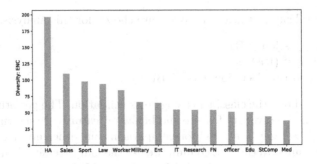

Fig. 8. Diversity of users with different professions

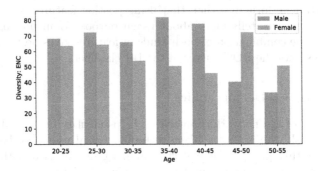

Fig. 9. Diversity of users with different ages and gender

number of close friends, but also the number of communities (as defined in ENC), and the reasons for that can make another interesting study.

Secondly, we measure the average diversity of different gender and age. As shown in Fig. 9, females and males show different trends of diversity change with increasing age. The diversity of females first decreases after age of 30 but then increases sharply after 45. Males show the opposite trend: the highest diversity of males occurs for age from 35 to 45, and drops after 45. Though this result needs further validation with larger sampled data, it gives a glimpse of potentially different social strategies of female and male.

From the above analysis, we believe our study of diversity of users in OSN may have broad applications for many interesting questions in social science.

5   Discussion and Conclusions

In this paper, we start from real-world data, and observe a phenomenon in today's OSNs, that is there are two types of users, one type have mostly friends of strong ties, and the other with lots of friends of weak ties. We call the former social users and the latter functional users. We give explanations for how these different users may have different intentions in their use of the OSN. We develop a type of metric called diversity to distinguish these users. There are different variations of the diversity metric, making use of different amount of structural information from the user's ego network. We use the size of the ego network, and the effective size of the ego network (defined in the literature for structural holes) as baselines, and develop two new diversity metrics called Density-dependent Size (DDS) and Expected Number of Communities (ENC). We then give a performance analysis of these metrics for classifying users into the two types. As expected, both DDS and ENC out-perform the baseline metrics, and ENC performs the best as it uses the most amount of information of the ego networks. Furthermore, we show that when these diversity metrics are used together with other behavioral (posting) features, the diversity metrics help improved classification performance. Besides classification, we also study how diversity of ego network is different for different group of users, based on other demographic information, and discuss our observations.

References

1. Ahn, Y.Y., Bagrow, J.P., Lehmann, S.: Link communities reveal multiscale complexity in networks. Nature **466**(7307), 761–764 (2010)
2. Airoldi, E.M., Blei, D.M., Fienberg, S.E., Xing, E.P.: Mixed membership stochastic blockmodels. J. Mach. Learn. Res. **9**(Sep), 1981–2014 (2008)
3. Alhabash, S., Mundel, J., Hussain, S.A.: Social media advertising. In: Digital Advertising: Theory and Research, vol. 285 (2017)
4. Backstrom, L., Kleinberg, J.: Romantic partnerships and the dispersion of social ties: a network analysis of relationship status on facebook. In: Proceedings of the 17th ACM Conference on Computer Supported Cooperative Work & Social Computing, pp. 831–841. ACM (2014)
5. Bakshy, E., Rosenn, I., Marlow, C., Adamic, L.: The role of social networks in information diffusion. In: Proceedings of the 21st International Conference on World Wide Web, pp. 519–528. ACM (2012)
6. Barbieri, N., Bonchi, F., Manco, G.: Influence-based network-oblivious community detection. In: 2013 IEEE 13th International Conference on Data Mining (ICDM), pp. 955–960. IEEE (2013)
7. Burt, R.S.: Structural Holes: The Social Structure of Competition. Harvard University Press, Cambridge (1992)
8. Cadez, I., Heckerman, D., Meek, C., Smyth, P., White, S.: Visualization of navigation patterns on a web site using model-based clustering. In: Proceedings of the Sixth ACM SIGKDD International Conference on Knowledge Discovery and Data Mining, pp. 280–284. ACM (2000)
9. Centola, D.: The spread of behavior in an online social network experiment. Science **329**(5996), 1194–1197 (2010)
10. Chu, S.C.: Viral advertising in social media: participation in Facebook groups and responses among college-aged users. J. Interact. Advertising **12**(1), 30–43 (2011)
11. Clauset, A., Moore, C., Newman, M.: Hierarchical structure and the prediction of missing links in networks. Nature **453**, 98–101 (2008)
12. Dunbar, R.I.: Neocortex size as a constraint on group size in primates. J. Hum. Evol. **22**(6), 469–493 (1992)
13. Easley, D., Kleinberg, J.: Networks, Crowds, and Markets: Reasoning About a Highly Connected World. Cambridge University Press, Cambridge (2010)

14. Fortunato, S., Hric, D.: Community detection in networks: a user guide. Phys. Rep. **659**, 1–44 (2016)
15. Friedman, J.H.: Greedy function approximation: a gradient boosting machine. Ann. Stat. **29**(5), 1189–1232 (2001)
16. Girvan, M., Newman, M.: Community structure in social and biological networks. Proc. Nat. Acad. Sci. **99**(12), 7821–7826 (2002)
17. Granovetter, M.: Problems of explanation in economic sociology. Netw. Org. Struct. Form Action **25**, 56 (1992)
18. Granovetter, M.S.: The strength of weak ties. Am. J. Sociol. **78**(6), 1360–1380 (1973)
19. Kleinberg, J., Suri, S., Tardos, E., Wexler, T.: Strategic network formation with structural holes. In: Proceedings of the 9th ACM Conference on Electronic Commerce, EC 2008, pp. 284–293. ACM, New York (2008). https://doi.org/10.1145/1386790.1386835
20. Kramer, A.D., Guillory, J.E., Hancock, J.T.: Experimental evidence of massive-scale emotional contagion through social networks. Proc. Nat. Acad. Sci. **111**(24), 8788–8790 (2014)
21. Kwak, H., Lee, C., Park, H., Moon, S.: What is Twitter, a social network or a news media? In: Proceedings of the 19th International Conference on World Wide Web, pp. 591–600. ACM (2010)
22. Lerman, K., Ghosh, R.: Information contagion: an empirical study of the spread of news on digg and Twitter social networks. ICWSM **10**, 90–97 (2010)
23. Liaw, A., Wiener, M.: Classification and regression by randomforest. R News **2**(3), 18–22 (2002)
24. Mcauley, J., Leskovec, J.: Discovering social circles in ego networks. ACM Trans. Knowl. Discov. Data (TKDD) **8**(1), 4 (2014)
25. Palla, G., Derényi, I., Farkas, I., Vicsek, T.: Uncovering the overlapping community structure of complex networks in nature and society. Nature **435**(7043), 814–818 (2005)
26. Reubold, J., Boubekki, A., Strufe, T., Brefeld, U.: Bayesian user behavior models (2018)
27. Richardson, M., Domingos, P.: Mining knowledge-sharing sites for viral marketing. In: Proceedings of the Eighth ACM SIGKDD International Conference on Knowledge Discovery and Data Mining, pp. 61–70. ACM (2002)
28. Romero, D.M., Meeder, B., Kleinberg, J.: Differences in the mechanics of information diffusion across topics: idioms, political hashtags, and complex contagion on twitter. In: Proceedings of the 20th International Conference on World wide web, pp. 695–704. ACM (2011)
29. Wasserman, S., Faust, K.: Social Network Analysis: Methods and Analysis. Cambridge University Press, Cambridge (1994)
30. Yang, J., Leskovec, J.: Community-affiliation graph model for overlapping network community detection. In: 2012 IEEE 12th International Conference on Data Mining (ICDM), pp. 1170–1175. IEEE (2012)
31. Yang, J., McAuley, J., Leskovec, J.: Community detection in networks with node attributes. In: 2013 IEEE 13th international conference on Data Mining (ICDM), pp. 1151–1156. IEEE (2013)
32. Ying, Q., Venkatramanan, S., Chiu, D.M.: Profiling OSN users based on posting patterns. In: OSNED 2018 (2018)

Vitriol on Social Media: Curation and Investigation

Xing Zhao$^{(\boxtimes)}$ ⓘ and James Caverlee ⓘ

Texas A&M University, College Station, TX 77840, USA
{xingzhao,caverlee}@tamu.edu

Abstract. Our online discourse is too often characterized by vitriol. Distinct from hate speech and bullying, vitriol corresponds to a persistent coarsening of the discourse that leads to a cumulative corrosive effect. And yet, vitriol itself is challenging to formally define and study in a rigorous way. Toward bridging this gap, we present in this paper the design of a vitriol curation framework that serves as an initial step toward extracting vitriolic posts from social media with high confidence. We investigate a large collection of vitriolic posts sampled from Twitter, where we examine both user-level and post-level characteristics of vitriol. We find key characteristics of vitriol that can distinguish it from non-vitriol, including aspects of popularity, network, sentiment, language structure, and content.

Keywords: Vitriol · Social media · Personal attacks
Abusive language · Text classification

1 Introduction

The widespread adoption of social media has led to positive developments like community formation, information discovery, image and video sharing, and access to allies and audiences for traditionally disenfranchised groups. Alas, social media platforms have also become rife with undesired effects, including bullying [18,20], personal attacks [22,27], hate speech [2,4,5,11,21,25,26], arguments [3,13], and trolling [7,8,15].

Indeed, we can view many of these examples as parts of a broad class of online discourse that is *vitriolic*. Vitriol corresponds to a persistent coarsening of the discourse that leads to a caustic, corrosive, and negative experience in our online interactions. For example, consider the following two tweets:

- *So my damn property and school taxes go up to pay for the damn illegals. Your doing crap for middle class*
- *Then if you want to switch back to produce the soil ruined. Nice going, moron*

We argue that these tweets are vitriolic: they are caustic and corrosive. However, this vitriol does not meet the requirements of hate speech, bullying, trolling,

S. Staab et al. (Eds.): SocInfo 2018, LNCS 11185, pp. 487–504, 2018.
https://doi.org/10.1007/978-3-030-01129-1_30

or other anti-social activities. For example, hate speech typically is an attack on a target's race, religion, ethnic origin, sexual orientation, and so on. Angry and resentful posts such as these two examples need not contain such attacks to be vitriolic. Similarly, bullying corresponds to a person using strength or influence to harm or intimidate those who are weaker, often including persistent and targeted behaviors to induce harm in another. Vitriol need not rise to the level of bullying, and vitriol is often initiated by ordinary people (weaker) and targeted at well-known users (stronger). While considerable previous work has focused on uncovering evidence of bullying, hate speech, and trolling, there is a research gap in curating and investigating such vitriol that creates an unwelcoming, corrosive online experience.

Hence in this paper, our goal is to begin an investigation into vitriol on social media, including: How can we define vitriol? How can we operationalize such a definition for extracting evidence of vitriol? Can we detect vitriol at scale? And how does vitriol differ from posts that just happen to include profanity? Many previous methods for extracting abusive language have focused on content-based features, and yet, some profanity can be well-meant or just joking. For example, Table 1 shows examples of what we consider to be vitriol versus profanity-laden non-vitriol posts sampled from Twitter. We find that these false positive samples are often meant as banter between friends. This observation illustrates that the detection of vitriol is challenging if we just use profanity filters or topical analysis, which are widely used in previous works.

Table 1. Example vitriolic tweets vs. non-vitriolic tweets

Vitriol	Non-Vitriol
@HouseGOP So my damn property and school taxes go up to pay for the damn illegals. Your doing crap for middle class	@josel767 @rosariolopezn And remember kids, you'll always be shit, but you wanna be the best shit to have ever been created [emoji]
@WolfForPA Then if you want to switch back to produce the soil ruined. Nice going, moron	@essjaxin bitch if you wasn't my mfn friend
@RCorbettMEP Your peddling fear mongering bull shit. You don't mention Fracki that's a serious ecological risk. You arrogantly assume the ..	@Applied_press Weak as hell. Can you believe I'm ready to come back to Charleston
@DMVBlackLives You idiots are responsible for this shit	@Stonekettle Is this fucking fuck fucking serious?
@WayneDupreeShow Can you spell traitor	@EthanDolan @BryantEslava Your so cute wtf
	@Rival_Laxno @HypeWicked @VillainGoofys Holy shit theirs been hella beef today

In the rest of the paper, (i) we design a curation framework for identifying vitriol from ordinary profanity-laden language online and build a vitriolic dataset; (ii) we analyze vitriolic users and their language, comparing with other users and tweets on Twitter; and (iii) we propose a suite of features to build classifiers to distinguish vitriolic tweets from other tweets, distinguish vitriolic users from random users, and ultimately detect vitriol from the wider social media space. We find that vitriolic posts vary in both user-level and post-level features compared with other tweets, with key differences in popularity, network, sentiment, language structure, and content characteristics that could provide a basis for continued exploration of vitriol in social media.

2   Related Work

Many existing studies focus on hate speech. For example, Banks examined the complexities of regulating hate speech on the Internet through legal and technological frameworks [2]. Warner et al. further presented an approach to detecting hate speech in online text, and contributed a mechanism for detecting some commonly used methods of evading common "dirty word" filters [26]. Burnap et al. developed a supervised machine learning classifier for hateful and antagonistic content on social media, which can assist policy and decision makers in monitoring the public reaction to large-scale events [4]. To detect hate speech incorporating context information, Gao et al. presented a logistic regression model with context feature, and a neural network model with learning components for context [11]. Chandrasekharan el ul. studied the 2015 ban of two hate communities on Reddit in terms of its effect on both participating users and affected subreddits [5]. Clarke et al. used a new categorical form of multidimensional register analysis to identify the main dimensions of functional linguistic variation in a corpus of abusive language, specifically consisting of racist and sexist Tweets [9]. While certainly hate speech is a kind of online vitriol, we seek to find corrosive vitriolic posts even in the absence of specific targeting of race, religion, and other features of hate speech.

Trolling is another antisocial behavior on social media. Hardaker et al. defined "troll" as a person that engages in negative online behavior [15]. Cheng et al. characterized trolling behavior in three large online discussion communities – CNN, IGN, and Breitbart – by analyzing their suspended users [8]. In their latest study, they analyzed the causes of trolling behavior on discussions, and their predictive model indicates trolling can be better explained by incorporating mood and discussion context [7]. Many of these anti-social phenomena – and specifically vitriolic posts in news comments – have been attributed to granting *"someone anonymity and he or she is apt to behave poorly, namely with malevolence in their comments"* [24].

In a related, but potentially less harmful direction, sarcasm is a form of speech act in which the speakers convey their message in an implicit way [10]. Davidov et al. experimented with semi-supervised sarcasm identification on Twitter and Amazon dataset [10], and Bamman improved the detection performance by including extra-linguistic information from the context of an utterance [1]. González-Ibánez *et al.* provided a method for constructing a corpus of sarcastic Twitter messages in which determination of the sarcasm of each message has been made by its author, and investigated the impact of lexical and pragmatic factors on machine learning effectiveness for identifying sarcastic utterances [13].

3   Curating Vitriol

In this section, we propose a vitriol curation framework for sampling vitriol from social media, before turning in the following section to an investigation of the factors impacting what is and is not considered vitriol. Since vitriol may come in many forms, our key intuition is to focus on posts that demonstrate three observable characteristics:

- *Personal:* the post should target another user, rather than just "shouting to the wind";
- *Context-free:* the post should ignore the substance of what the target user cares about (the context); and
- *Unilateral:* the post should be one-way from a vitriolic user to a target user, and not a back-and-forth argument.

While not representative of all forms of online vitriol, these three characteristics do allow us to operationalize our definition of vitriol for sampling evidence at scale from social media. And while vitriol exists on every social media and content-based platform – including Facebook, Twitter, Reddit, and commenting systems on news websites – we focus on Twitter since Twitter collects many user-level features, such as the popularity and social relationships, and we can track a specific user using the *user_id* to analyze the user's history of posts.

3.1   Raw Data Collection

First, to collect a sample of *potentially* vitriolic posts (English language only) from Twitter, we begin by sampling based on a keyword list derived from Liu *el al.* 's Negative Opinion Word List [19], augmented with a set of frequently used abusive words on Twitter and their synonyms.[1] Some of these keywords are shown in Table 2.

Table 2. Vitriolic wordbag

bullshit	lie	fake	fuck	shit	ass	stupid	spew
idiot	liar	crap	asshole	moron	damn	hell	corrupt
fool	shutup	horseshit	bastard	bitch	traitor	fraud	$\cdots$

---

[1] All data, annotated samples, code, and experiments are available at https://github.com/xing-zhao/Vitriol-on-Social-Media.

In total, we sampled more than 3 million *potential vitriolic tweets* (denoted P_{VT}) sent by 1.7 million *potential vitriolic users* (denoted P_{VU}) over the period June 30th 2017 to September 14th 2017. We additionally sampled the target of these posts (recall that our definition requires a post to be sent in response to another post). We call these original targeted posts the set P_{ST} and the users of these original targeted posts as P_{SU}. This raw dataset is summarized in Table 3.

3.2 Refining the Sample

Of course, using these keywords alone to select vitriolic tweets is insufficient – for example, many of these selected keywords can be used as jokes or banter between friends. For reducing such false positives, we further refine the sample down to a curated

Table 3. Raw dataset statistics

Set	Size	Set	Size
P_{VU}	1,720,281	P_{VT}	3,336,477
P_{SU}	1,374,420	P_{ST}	2,883,092

set of vitriolic tweets V_T sent by vitriolic users V_U. Our goal here is to focus on precision (identifying only real vitriol) rather than on recall (finding all possible vitriol, but at the risk of many false positives). We adopt the following curation strategies:

Direct Replies Only. *The vitriolic tweets must be the first layer replies of an originally generated post.* We aim to find those vitriolic users that directly targeted the person being replied to. However, on Twitter, there are many formats of tweets, such as retweets and replies. This diversity can bring noise into our curation method. For instance, user A could reply to user B's tweet which is retweeted from user C. In such a case, it is hard to identify if A's target is B or C. To maximize the likelihood that the attack target from a reply tweet is the person who is replied to, we restrict the format of the replied tweet to be the original tweet, and restrict the format of reply tweets to be at the first layer, which means it directly replies to the original poster rather than other repliers or re-tweeters.

Avoid Copy-Paste Tweets. *The replies posted by a vitriolic user cannot be identical to each other.* Through our manual investigation, we found that some users repeatedly send reply tweets with identical content to different users, in essence spamming out the same (or similar) content to a wide audience. We assume such behaviors can be dealt with using traditional spam detection methods and do not reflect vitriol sent by real users.

Focus on "Real" Active Users. *Users must have sent at least some minimum number of tweets, but not too many repeated tweets.* There is wide evidence of paid posters and bots that frequently post similar comments or articles on different online communities and Websites for hidden purposes, e.g., to influence the opinion of other people towards certain social events or particular markets [6]. Since our focus is on the behavior of real users and not bots or other spam-like accounts, we set an upper bound of to avoid these accounts. We additionally set a lower bound of tweeting frequency to capture users who are actually active and not isolated users with only a few tweets. We do experiments for maximumly avoiding pre-annotated isolated or spam-like accounts using different settings of the lower and upper bound (please refer to the project website for further details: https://github.com/xing-zhao/Vitriol-on-Social-Media). In practice, we ultimately consider users with a statuses count $>= 200$, and a total number of tweets during our collection time of between 25 and 200.

Unilateral Relationship. *The relationship between the original poster and vitriolic replier should be unilateral.* To avoid bullying-specific tweets (which have been studied in previous works) and to focus on vitriol originating from a power imbalance

Table 4. Vitriol dataset statistics

	Tweets	Users
Vitriolic	14,001	926
Targeted	11,938	3,188

(from "weaker" to "stronger" users), we consider the relative popularity of both a vitriolic user and the targeted user. We use both *# of followers* of the user and *# of retweet times* of a tweet to represent a person's popularity. We do experiments for maximizing the number of unilateral relationship using pre-annotated dataset (see https://github.com/xing-zhao/Vitriol-on-Social-Media). Ultimately, we keep only users who have # of followers < 500 but who target users with # of followers > 5000.

3.3   The Curated Vitriol Dataset

With these selection strategies, we refine our raw dataset to arrive at the curated vitriol dataset shown in Table 4. We identify 14,001 Vitriolic Tweets (V_T) sent by 926 Vitriolic Users (V_U). Furthermore, we collect all the users who are targeted by these vitriolic users during our observation, denoted as S_U, and their targeted tweets set S_T.

3.4   Validation

To validate the quality of our curation framework, we solicited three annotators to manually label a set of 500 randomly selected tweets from the sample of vitriolic tweets V_T. We took the majority vote as the ground truth for each tweet (see https://github.com/xing-zhao/Vitriol-on-Social-Media for details). After annotation, we find that 477 of the 500 tweets are considered vitriol, indicating a

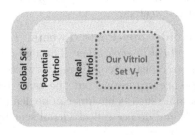

Fig. 1. The scope of our investigation.

precision of 95.4%. Hence, while our curation strategies are aggressive in terms of focusing on particular kinds of vitriol (meaning that there are certainly many forms of vitriol that this initial framework misses), we see that the output is of fairly high quality. See Fig. 1 for a summary of the scope of this investigation. In our continuing work, we are interested to vary these curation strategies to better explore the trade-offs between precision and recall.

4 Exploratory Analysis

In this section, we explore both tweet-centric and user-centric differences between vitriol and others. For comparison, we consider an equally-sized sample of general English tweets not contained in P_{VT}, defined as *Non-Vitriolic Tweets*; and define their posters as *Non-Vitriolic Users*. Last but not least, we present exploratory analysis of the people who were most targeted by vitriolic users.

4.1 Mood-Based Features

We begin by exploring the mood-based features of the tweets themselves. Since vitriol is fundamentally caustic, corrosive, and negative, we explore here the *emotional* attributes of the tweets as well as the underlying *social tendencies* of the users through an application of the IBM Watson Tone Analyzer [16] to the content of each tweet.

Emotional Attributes. We begin by considering five kinds of emotional attributes – anger, disgust, fear, joy, and sadness. Figure 2 shows the score for all vitriolic tweets versus a random sample of non-vitriolic tweets. The y-axis captures a likelihood score for each emotion; higher scores indicate higher degrees of each emotion. Overall, we see that vitriolic tweets score is high in anger, disgust, and sadness relative to non-vitriolic tweets, while scoring lower in joy. The original keywords that powered our curation method (see Table 2) overwhelmingly drive the *anger* score, but have little or no impact on the other scores. This suggests that even for vitriol not containing one of these original keywords, there may be clear patterns of disgust and sadness that can be used to identify additional vitriolic tweets.

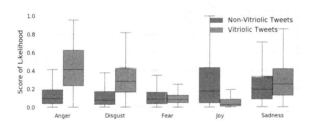

Fig. 2. Emotions of vitriolic and non-vitriolic tweets

Social Tendencies. We pair the emotional attributes of the tweets with five additional features that capture the social tendencies of the underlying user based on their language use – openness, conscientiousness, extroversion, agreeableness, and emotional range.

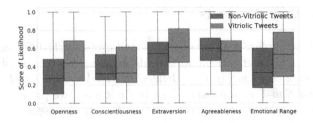

Fig. 3. Social tendencies of vitriolic and non-vitriolic tweets

Figure 3 shows the score for all vitriolic tweets versus a random sample of non-vitriolic tweets. The y-axis captures a likelihood score for each social tendency; higher scores indicate higher degrees of each tendency. Overall, we see obvious differences. Vitriolic tweets are more likely to demonstrate openness, extroversion and emotional range, and they are less likely to display agreeableness in comparison with non-vitriolic tweets.

4.2   User-Based Features

In addition to these content-based properties of vitriol, we also consider the popularity and activity properties of the users themselves.

Popularity. We measure a user's popularity from two aspects – their followers count and friends count. Both counts indicate whether a user has a certain level of being paid attention to by other users. Figure 4 shows the comparison between vitriolic users' and non-vitriolic users' popularities. In summary, both counts of vitriolic users are lower than non-vitriolic users, especially in term of follower count. This shows that vitriolic users are much less popular than average; that is, vitriolic users are recognized and accepted by a group of a smaller size.

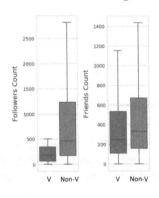

Fig. 4. Followers and friends count of each set of users.

Activities. To analyze a user's degree of activity, we examine their statuses count and social age. The statuses count in Twitter is the number of tweets (including retweets) issued by a user, which can be intuitively regarded as an indicator of user's degree of activity. Instead of using a user's actual age, which is not publicly accessed to in Twitter, we choose another determinant, social age, for indicating a user's activity durations on social media. This determinant is the lifespan of the account (from creation onward), calculated by subtracting the creation date of a user's account from the creation date of the latest tweet in our dataset. Social age could become an indicator of activity degree since on average, longer social age means the one have had more experiences on a certain social media platform, furthermore, the user was more active on this platform. Both activity features, statuses count and social age, are used in the comparison of user's degree of activity.

Through comparing the activity of vitriolic users and non-vitriolic users, we find that although the average of statuses count of vitriolic users (average about 7464) is slightly lower than non-vitriolic users (average about 9231), however, it is obvious that the social age of vitriolic users (average about 497 days) is much lower than non-vitriolic users (average about 1472 days). These observations indicate that vitriolic users are less active in social media than others.

4.3 Who Is Most Targeted by Vitriol?

But who are these users that are most targeted with vitriol? Recall that our operational definition of vitriol focuses on users who ignore the substance of a target user's post (that is, they do not engage on the merits, but rather rely on caustic or corrosive language). Here, we consider the users who have been targeted in dataset S_U where we see that vitriolic users, while often ignoring the substance of a post, do care about the social identity of target users.

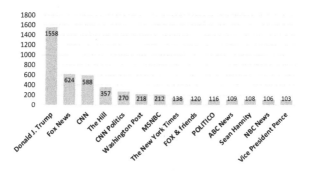

Fig. 5. The most targeted users

Figure 5 shows the top users who have been targeted by vitriolic users more than 100 times in our dataset. We find that (perhaps, unsurprisingly) most of these users are composed of politicians and news media accounts. To further study the categories of the users who were targeted the most, we manually labeled the categories of the top-100 most targeted users. The percentage of each category is presented in Fig. 6, which shows the largest slice is "politician" (31%), followed by "news media" (26%) and "journalist" (12%). This makes sense considering the divisiveness of politics, news and opinions among many people.

496   X. Zhao and J. Caverlee

4.4 Summary

In this section, we present several data-driven analysis from user-centric and tweet-centric perspectives. We found that there are obvious differences between vitriolic users and non-vitriolic users in terms of user popularity and the degree of activity, as well as the obvious differences between their

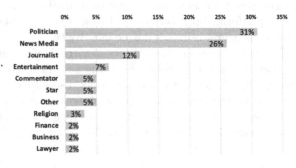

Fig. 6. Categories of the Top-100 most targeted users.

tweets in terms of emotions and social tendencies. Finally, our exploratory analysis of people who were targeted by vitriolic users shows clear patterns in their composition.

5 Vitriol Detection

In this section, we explore the potential of using features of vitriol – including from the perspectives of language patterns, communication sentiment, content relevance and latent topics – to distinguish vitriolic tweets from non-vitriolic tweets, and further distinguish vitriolic users from other users. Such models could power vitriol detection beyond our curated collection.

5.1 Features

To build our classifier to distinguish vitriolic tweets from others, we adopt four categories of features which can help us to characterize vitriol:

Language Patterns (LP). Through our manual annotation, we observed that vitriolic users use fewer at-mention markers (@), hashtags (#) and emoticons (i.e. ":-)", ":b"), but more adjectives and strong punctuations (i.e. "?!") than other tweets. Thus, we hypothesize that vitriolic users have certain patterns in their writing habits. To rigorously verify this hypothesis, we use Part-of-Speech Tagging [12] to analyze the language patterns of vitriolic tweets.

Communication Sentiment (CS). Unlike normal tweets, we have seen that vitriolic tweets include a certain set of emotions to fully express and vent writers' feelings. To fully analyze the sentiment of language style, we apply the IBM Watson Tone Analyzer [16] and Google Sentiment Analyzer [14]. *Emotion*, a subset of these features, shows the likelihood of a writer being perceived as angry, disgust, fear, joy and sadness. Another subset of features, *Language Style*, shows the writer's reasoning and analytical attitude about things, degree of certainty and inhibition. And the feature set *Social tendency* will help us to prove our hypotheses that this kind of people have specific social properties in terms of openness, conscientiousness, and do on. The Google Sentiment Analysis inspects the given text and identifies the prevailing emotional opinion within the text, especially to determine a writer's attitude as positive, negative, or neutral.

Content Relevance (CR). Our earlier feature category for language patterns focused on the part-of-speech patterns used on vitriol, such as nouns, adjectives, determiners, and so on. Here we consider the actual content of the tweets themselves; perhaps vitriolic tweets re-use certain phrases. Specifically, we adopt Doc2Vec [23] for learning a distributed representation [17] using hierarchical softmax. We consider each tweet as a document; Doc2Vec outputs a vector (of size 100) for each tweet such that "similar" tweets should be nearby in the dense Doc2Vec vector, where similarity here captures word order and deeper semantic similarity than in traditional bag-of-words models.

Latent Topics (LT). As we observed in Sect. 4, most of the people who are targeted by vitriolic users belong to categories such as famous politicians and news media accounts. We hypothesize that these vitriolic tweets are also topic-related. To fully analyze the latent topic of vitriolic tweets, we apply the LDA model [23], which allows both LDA model estimation from a training corpus and inference of topic distribution on new, unseen documents. We set the hyperparameter $\#topics = 10$ so that the model can return a vector of likelihoods of each topic a tweet belongs to.

Table 5 shows the details of top visible features listed above, and the Fisher score of every specific feature used in different classifiers. Since features on Content Relevance and Latent Topics sets are not directly interpretable, they are not shown on Table 5. In term of language patterns, the results fit our expectation and verify our hypothesis that common nouns, adjectives, and punctuations are used in vitriolic tweets more than other tweets. This result suggests that vitriolic users do have certain patterns compared with other tweets. On the other hand, in terms of communication sentiment, anger gets the highest fisher score, which is unsurprising since our selection strategy focuses on anger words. However, we also see that disgust and joy play an important rule to classify vitriol and non-vitriol.

5.2   Classification: Vitriol vs. Non-Vitriol

To train the classification model for vitriol vs. non-vitriol, we use all tweets in our vitriolic tweets set V_T ($size = 14001$) as the positive samples, and equal-size of non-vitriolic tweets in R_T as the negative samples. We build the classifier with four different categories of features: Language Patterns (LP), Communication Sentiment (CS), Content Relevance (CR), and Latent Topics (LT), to test which features work better. We create four more feature sets by combining these four basic categories in different ways: Language Patterns + Communication Sentiment (LP-CS), Language Patterns + Content Relevance + Latent Topics (LP-CR-LT), and all features together (ALL). Note that we exclude Communication Sentiment in LP-CR-LT since our strategy of selecting the potential

Table 5. Part of Selected features for classification

Feature Set	Source	Top Features (Fisher Score on V vs Non-V)
Language Patterns (# = 25)	Part-of-Speech Tagging from CMU	N-common noun (0.0863)
		A-adjective (0.0682)
		P-pre- or postposition (0.0501)
		,-punctuation (0.0465)
		D-determiner (0.0351)
		V-verb (0.0204)
		U-URL or email address (0.0169)
		$-numeral (0.0152)
		O-pronoun (0.0111)
		...
Communication Sentiment (# = 14)	IBM Watson & Google Tone Analyzers	Anger (0.4027)
		Google Sentiment (0.3721)
		Disgust (0.2928)
		Joy (0.1696)
		Openness (0.0756)
		Emotional_Range (0.0577)
		Extroversion (0.0366)
		Sadness (0.0180)
		Agreeableness (0.0142)
		...

vitriolic tweets relies on some profanity words as seed keywords. Hence, we want to evaluate the classifier when we leave out the influence of these profanity words.

We experiment with four classification algorithms: Logistic Regression, Support Vector Machine, Random Forest, and Multi-Layer Perceptron, and consider various settings of each classification algorithm. To evaluate, we perform five-fold cross validation and measure both the F1 score and AUC scores. We report the best result among all tested settings in Table 6 (F1 Score) and Table 7 (AUC Scores) for each feature set and classification algorithm.

There are many observations from Tables 6 and 7. Horizontally, Multi-Layer Perceptron outperforms the other three algorithms, and reaches the best $F1 = 0.9200$ and $AUC = 0.9749$, when we use all features at the same time. Vertically, the performance tends to increase as more features are combined together. These results show the great potential of our classifier serving as a preliminary vitriol auto-filter on social media.

It is important to emphasize that since we used the Vitriolic Wordbag (See Table 2) as the keywords for crawling the potential vitriolic tweets, and most of the words in this bag have strongly emotional factors, the sentiment features of such tweets would be affected by our sampling method. Thus, we also highlighted

Table 6. F1 score for vitriol vs non-vitriol

	Log-Reg	SVM	RF	MLP
CS	0.8290	0.8323	0.8424	0.8384
LP	0.7636	0.8053	0.8028	0.8061
CR	0.8486	0.8386	0.8492	0.8597
LT	0.5761	0.5861	0.7265	0.6642
LP-CS	0.8564	0.8832	0.8886	0.8865
LP-CR-LT	0.8780	0.8810	0.8832	**0.8978**
all	0.8983	0.9007	0.9050	**0.9200**

the performance of our classifier only using LP+CR+LT (without sentiment) features in Tables 6 and 7. In this way, we can evaluate the performance of our classifier when we avoid bias introduced by the curation strategies we used. As a result, excluding the sentiment features, the performance of the classifier is still reasonably good ($F1 = 0.8978$ and $AUC = 0.9650$) when we use the Multi-Layer Perceptron algorithm. These results indicate that the models built over our curation strategy may be able to generalize to other domains (as we will test in more detail in a following experiment).

Table 7. AUC score for vitriol vs non-vitriol

	Log-Reg	SVM	RF	MLP
CS	0.8899	0.8992	0.8424	0.8384
LP	0.8289	0.8837	0.8912	0.8960
CR	0.9241	0.9154	0.9243	0.9342
LT	0.6095	0.6237	0.8101	0.7293
LP-CS	0.9263	0.9506	0.9541	0.9567
LP-CR-LT	0.9460	0.9504	0.9496	**0.9650**
all	0.9614	0.9628	0.9636	**0.9749**

5.3   Uncovering Vitriol In-the-wild

Since our curation framework is designed with many constraints to identify vitriol with high confidence, an open question is how well the trained models can perform over a collection of social media posts in-the-wild. That is, can we uncover evidence of vitriol even in cases where our original requirements are not observed (e.g., such as the relationship between replier and poster)? Toward answering this question, we evaluate the quality of distinguishing vitriol from all tweets containing profanity in the original set of potential vitriolic tweets P_{VT}. That is, can our models trained over a set of highly-curated vitriolic tweets still apply to the wider space of tweets?

Concretely, we randomly select 100,000 tweets from P_{VT} and apply the Multi-Layer Perceptron classifier – which has the best performance in our previous experiments – to predict whether a tweet is vitriolic or not. In total, we uncover 55,650 tweets that are predicted to be vitriolic out of 100,000 (55.65%). We further manually annotated a random 100 of these positive tweets and find that 77 meet our definition of vitriol[1]. This suggests that: (i) the phenomenon of vitriol on social media seriously exceeds our expectation, and our vitriolic tweets set V_T is an accurate but small dataset out of all vitriol online; (ii) we still need to make greater efforts to design more sophisticated methods or features to capture the subtleties of vitriol, for distinguishing vitriolic tweets, because of the similarities between vitriol and posts that include profanity; and (iii) we may be able to relax our strategy of vitriol curation to identify even more vitriol for building more robust models.

5.4   Vitriol in Other Domains

Complementing this tweet-based validation, we further evaluate the design of our vitriol classifier over Wikipedia comments [27], where the format and intent of the comments is quite different from our original tweet scenario. We adopt the annotated Personal Attacking comments on Wikipedia dataset [27] as an alternative dataset which has similar characteristics as vitriol. This dataset collects over 100 k annotated discussion comments from Wikipedia in English. These comments from ordinary readers are similar to the replies on Twitter domain in terms of their unilateralism (there is no back-and-forth). In this data, every comment has been labeled by around 10 annotators on whether it is a personal attack or not. In summary, there are around 13,590 comments annotated as personal attacks out of 115,864 comments in total [27]. Note that this comment-based dataset does not contain any features of the repliers, so that we only use the linguistic features for analyzing and classifying. Also, the comment history of a single user in this dataset is not trackable, therefore, we can only recognize the attacking languages, not users.

First, we tested different classifiers and different feature sets over the Wikipedia personal attacks data as shown in Table 8. In this case, we train and test over the Wikipedia data, but use the features we identified from our tweet-based classifier presented earlier. We see that the MLP algorithm performs the best when we use all linguistic features, achieving an $AUC = 0.9356$. Not surprisingly, this result is below the result ($AUC = 0.9719$) published in [27] over a classifier designed specially for Wikipedia comments. However, the good performance of our tweets-informed approach suggest that vitriol has common properties across domains that could be leveraged for high-quality vitriol detection.

We further construct a Wikipedia-specific classifier following the approach presented in Wulczyn et al. in [27]. Using this approach, we apply it to our set of vitriolic tweets where we see in Table 9 that the Wikipedia-based model

Table 8. AUC scores of attacks vs non-attacks on wikipedia dataset

	Log-Reg	SVM	RF	MLP
CS	0.8859	0.8752	0.8851	0.8953
LP	0.7120	0.6022	0.7178	0.7514
CR	0.9052	0.8982	0.8895	0.8875
LT	0.6277	0.6031	0.7997	0.6494
LP-CS	0.8389	0.8465	0.8943	0.8989
LP-CR-LT	0.8034	0.8207	0.8799	0.8942
all	0.8646	0.9063	0.9244	**0.9356**

results in an $AUC = 0.8830$, which is around 9.2% lower than our classifier's performance on the same dataset.

Table 9. Comparing AUC scores for models across domains

	Tweets	Wiki comments
Our approach	0.9749	0.9356
Wulczyn approach	0.8830	0.9719

This suggests that while there are some commonalities across domains, that care should be taken in transferring models from domain to the other. In particular, since vitriol is an accumulated behavior that relies on a user's history, approaches that consider user history may be more appropriate than those that rely on only a single post (be it tweet or comment).

6   Conclusion and Future Work

Vitriol has become a prominent societal issue, especially in social media. Distinct from hate speech and bullying, vitriol corresponds to a persistent coarsening of the discourse that leads to a more cumulative corrosive effect. Vitriol is challenging to define and study. Hence, in this paper, we have designed a vitriol curation framework as an initial step in our ongoing effort to extract vitriolic posts from social media with high confidence. We investigated a large collection of vitriolic posts sampled from Twitter, and examined both user-level and post-level characteristics of vitriol. We found key characteristics of vitriol that can distinguish it from non-vitriol, including popularity, network, sentiment, language structure, and content characteristics.

This is an initial attempt at formally studying vitriol on social media. While we have focused on one type of vitriol, our framework leaves open many questions about the size and composition of the larger space of all vitriol. What if we relax our (admittedly) strict requirements in Sect. 3? What if we change our initial tweet sampling strategy? What changes do we observe over time as vitriol evolves and transforms? While we have seen good success in distinguishing vitriol from non-vitriol posts over our sample, do these results hold over other varieties of vitriol?

In our ongoing work, we aim to continue this line of research through several avenues. First, since our curation framework of extracting vitriol on social media is primarily precision-focused, we will aim to expand our vitriol dataset by using well-designed statistical methods to relax our requirements. Second, we will relax our requirement that vitriol be unilateral to consider back and forth vitriol discourse as well. Third, we will temporally track the behaviors of our vitriolic users, e.g., to explore how many of them have been ultimately suspended. Fourth, we will incorporate more indicators to help us better characterize vitriol, such as the social networks around each user. Finally, we are interested in studying vitriol from the perspective of the users who are the targets of vitriol; are there strategies to incite or minimize the number of vitriolic attacks?

References

1. Bamman, D., Smith, N.A.: Contextualized sarcasm detection on twitter. In: ICWSM, pp. 574–577 (2015)
2. Banks, J.: Regulating hate speech online. Int. Rev. Law Comput. Technol. **24**(3), 233–239 (2010)
3. Bosc, T., Cabrio, E., Villata, S.: Dart: a dataset of arguments and their relations on twitter. In: Proceedings of the 10th edition of the Language Resources and Evaluation Conference (2016)
4. Burnap, P., Williams, M.L.: Cyber hate speech on twitter: an application of machine classification and statistical modeling for policy and decision making. Policy Internet **7**(2), 223–242 (2015)
5. Chandrasekharan, E., Pavalanathan, U., Srinvasan, A., Glynn, A., Eisenstein, J., Gilbert, E.: You can't stay here: the efficacy of reddit's 2015 ban examined through hate speech (2017)
6. Chen, C., Wu, K., Srinivasan, V., Zhang, X.: Battling the internet water army: Detection of hidden paid posters. In: 2013 IEEE/ACM International Conference on Advances in Social Networks Analysis and Mining (ASONAM), pp. 116–120. IEEE (2013)
7. Cheng, J., Bernstein, M., Danescu-Niculescu-Mizil, C., Leskovec, J.: Anyone can become a troll: causes of trolling behavior in online discussions. arXiv preprint arXiv:1702.01119 (2017)

8. Cheng, J., Danescu-Niculescu-Mizil, C., Leskovec, J.: Antisocial behavior in online discussion communities. In: ICWSM, pp. 61–70 (2015)
9. Clarke, I., Grieve, J.: Dimensions of abusive language on twitter. In: Proceedings of the First Workshop on Abusive Language Online, pp. 1–10 (2017)
10. Davidov, D., Tsur, O., Rappoport, A.: Semi-supervised recognition of sarcastic sentences in twitter and amazon. In: Proceedings of the Fourteenth Conference on Computational Natural Language Learning, pp. 107–116. Association for Computational Linguistics (2010)
11. Gao, L., Huang, R.: Detecting online hate speech using context aware models. arXiv preprint arXiv:1710.07395 (2017)
12. Gimpel, K., et al.: Part-of-speech tagging for twitter: Annotation, features, and experiments. In: Proceedings of the 49th Annual Meeting of the Association for Computational Linguistics: Human Language Technologies: short papers, vol. 2, pp. 42–47. Association for Computational Linguistics (2011)
13. González-Ibáñez, R., Muresan, S., Wacholder, N.: Identifying sarcasm in twitter: a closer look. In: Proceedings of the 49th Annual Meeting of the Association for Computational Linguistics: Human Language Technologies: Short Papers, vol. 2, pp. 581–586. Association for Computational Linguistics (2011)
14. Google: Cloud natural language API (2017). https://cloud.google.com/natural-language. Accessed 12 Oct 2017
15. Hardaker, C.: Trolling in asynchronous computer-mediated communication: from user discussions to academic definitions (2010). https://www.degruyter.com/view/j/jplr.2010.6.issue-2/jplr.2010.011/jplr.2010.011.xml
16. IBM: Watson tone analyzer (2016). https://www.ibm.com/watson/services/tone-analyzer. Accessed 10 Oct 2017
17. Le, Q., Mikolov, T.: Distributed representations of sentences and documents. In: Proceedings of the 31st International Conference on Machine Learning (ICML-2014), pp. 1188–1196 (2014)
18. Lieberman, H., Dinakar, K., Jones, B.: Let's gang up on cyberbullying. Computer 44(9), 93–96 (2011)
19. Liu, B., Hu, M., Cheng, J.: Opinion observer: analyzing and comparing opinions on the web. In: Proceedings of the 14th International Conference on World Wide Web, pp. 342–351. ACM (2005)
20. Macbeth, J., Adeyema, H., Lieberman, H., Fry, C.: Script-based story matching for cyberbullying prevention. In: CHI 2013 Extended Abstracts on Human Factors in Computing Systems, pp. 901–906. ACM (2013)
21. Nobata, C., Tetreault, J., Thomas, A., Mehdad, Y., Chang, Y.: Abusive language detection in online user content. In: Proceedings of the 25th International Conference on World Wide Web, pp. 145–153. International World Wide Web Conferences Steering Committee (2016)
22. Pavlopoulos, J., Malakasiotis, P., Androutsopoulos, I.: Deep learning for user comment moderation. arXiv preprint arXiv:1705.09993 (2017)
23. Rehurek, R., Sojka, P.: Software framework for topic modelling with large corpora. In: Proceedings of the LREC 2010 Workshop on New Challenges for NLP Frameworks. Citeseer (2010)
24. Santana, A.D.: Virtuous or vitriolic: the effect of anonymity on civility in online newspaper reader comment boards. Journalism Pract. 8(1), 18–33 (2014)
25. Serra, J., Leontiadis, I., Spathis, D., Stringhini, G., Blackburn, J., Vakali, A.: Class-based prediction errors to detect hate speech with out-of-vocabulary words. In: Proceedings of the First Workshop on Abusive Language Online, pp. 36–40 (2017)

26. Warner, W., Hirschberg, J.: Detecting hate speech on the world wide web. In: Proceedings of the Second Workshop on Language in Social Media, pp. 19–26. Association for Computational Linguistics (2012)
27. Wulczyn, E., Thain, N., Dixon, L.: Ex machina: personal attacks seen at scale. In: Proceedings of the 26th International Conference on World Wide Web, pp. 1391–1399. International World Wide Web Conferences Steering Committee (2017)

Author Index

Printed in the United States
By Bookmasters